ONE WEEK LOAN

OPTIONS
AND
FUTURES

OPTIONS
AND
FUTURES

CONCEPTS, STRATEGIES, AND APPLICATIONS

by

R. Stafford Johnson
Xavier University

Carmelo Giaccotto
University of Connecticut

West Publishing Company
Minneapolis/St. Paul • New York • Los Angeles • San Francisco

PRODUCTION CREDITS

Production Management: Michael Bass & Associates
Copyediting: Elliot Simon
Text and Cover Design: Richard Kharibian
Composition: Publication Services of Boston
Interior Artwork: American Composition & Graphics, Inc.
Index: Melanie Belkin Associates

WEST'S COMMITMENT TO THE ENVIRONMENT

In 1906, West Publishing Company began recycling materials left over from the production of books. This began a tradition of efficient and responsible use of resources. Today, up to 95 percent of our legal books and 70 percent of our college and school texts are printed on recycled, acid-free stock. West also recycles nearly 22 million pounds of scrap paper annually—the equivalent of 181,717 trees. Since the 1960s, West has devised ways to capture and recycle waste inks, solvents, oils, and vapors created in the printing process. We also recycle plastics of all kinds, wood, glass, corrugated cardboard, and batteries, and have eliminated the use of Styrofoam book packaging. We at West are proud of the longevity and the scope of our commitment to the environment.

Prepress, printing, and binding by West Publishing Company.

British Library Cataloguing-in-Publication Data. A catalogue record for this book is available from the British Library.

COPYRIGHT © 1995   By WEST PUBLISHING COMPANY
                      610 Opperman Drive
                      P.O. Box 64526
                      St. Paul, MN 55164-0526

LIBRARY OF CONGRESS CATALOGING-IN-PUBLICATION DATA

Johnson, Stafford.
    Options and futures: concepts, strategies, and applications /
  Stafford Johnson, Carmelo Giaccotto.
      p.   cm.
    Includes index.
    ISBN 0-314-04353-5
    1. Options (Finance) 2. Futures. I. Giaccotto, Carmelo.
  II. Title.
  HG6024.A3J64 1995
  332.63'228—dc20   94-34052
                                                            CIP

To Jan

R. S. J.

To:

Carolyn Alex

John Meyer

Joshua Alex

and

Leah Rose

C. G.

BRIEF CONTENTS

CONTENTS

PART **II**

Option Pricing *101*

CHAPTER **4**

PREFACE

Courses in options and futures have grown enormously in recent years and are often the most popular undergraduate and graduate electives offered by finance departments. The academic interest in the field of derivative securities in part mirrors the surge in the trading of such securities. In 1990, for example, over 220 million option contracts, valued at over $75 billion, were traded on five major U.S. securities exchanges; from the early 1970s to the mid-1980s, the U.S. futures market grew from an annual trading volume of 20 million contracts to over 300 million. The increased popularity of options and futures courses also reflects a growing appreciation among finance professors of the educational value such courses can provide their students. The study of derivative securities is inherently challenging because it incorporates theory, mathematics, and statistics; mastery of it can deepen a student's knowledge of finance.

Options and Futures: Concepts, Strategies, and Applicaitons is an introductory textbook for advanced undergraduate finance students and MBA students. It is intended to provide students with a foundation in the study of options, futures, and other derivative securities. The book is designed for a one-semester course. Undergraduate students should previously have had an introductory course in investments, and MBA students are assumed to have had an introductory corporate finance course. Some basic statistics and calculus is used; sections using calculus are noted and can be omitted without losing continuity. At the back of the text will be found appendices on short sales, margins, and other topics, as well as a statistical appendix to help students who have not had statistics or who need a review. A Glossary of Terms and a Glossary of Symbols are also included.

ORGANIZATION

The book is divided into five parts: Part I deals with the markets and strategies associated with options on stock; Part II examines the pricing of stock options; Part III focuses on nonstock options; Part IV discusses futures; Part V examines futures options, swaps, and other derivative securities.

Chapter 1 begins the analysis of options by first examining fundamental strategies associated with calls and puts. With this foundation, we next discuss the funtions and characteristics of the Chicago Board Option Exchange and other exchanges. Chapter 3 expands the analysis of options by reviewing the fundamental strategies in more detail and by defining and describing other option strategies.

Part II consists of five chapters. Chapter 4 delineates the fundamental option pricing relationships. Chapters 5 and 6 derive and examine the properties and applications of the binomial option pricing model; Chapter 7 describes the Black-Scholes pricing model. Chapter 8 concludes the analysis of option pricing by showing how the models can be estimated, their validity, and their applications.

In Part III nonstock options are analyzed. Chapter 9 focuses on stock index and debt options; Chapter 10 analyzes foreign currency options. Each of these instruments is examined in terms of each option's underlying security or instrument, the market in which it is traded, the uses and strategies that can be made of each, and the pricing of each option. Chapter 11 examines the option features of corporate securities: callable and putable bonds, warrants, convertible securities, and equity and debt as option positions.

Part IV covers futures and forward contracts. Chapter 12 provides an overview of futures trading. Chapters 13, 14, and 15 deal with the markets, uses, and pricing of index, interest rate, and foreign currency futures contracts.

Part V deals with other derivative securities. Chapter 16 examines the relationship between options and futures and describes options on futures contracts. In Chapter 17, interest rate and currency swaps are discussed along with other derivative securities.

The text stresses concepts, model derivations, and numerical examples, enabling the reader to understand the tools used to find answers. For example, Chapters 5 and 6 present a detailed derivation of the binomial option pricing model, including mathematical derivations and examples. The derivation is given not for the sake of engendering a formula for pricing options, but rather to emphasize the thought process and tools used in the study of options.

TEXT SUPPLEMENTS

An Instructor's Manual with test bank is available to instructors. The Instructor's Manual contains instructor's teaching notes, key concepts, and answers to end-of-chapter problems and questions. At the end of each chapter in the Instructor's Manual are test questions that make up a test bank of approximately 700 multiple choice and true/false questions.

A student diskette is included in the Instructor's Manual, which can be used on a network or copied individually for student use. The diskette contains spreadsheet software programs for option pricing models, strategies, and implied variances. Detailed instructions on the use of these programs is also provided in the Instructor's Manual.

ACKNOWLEDGMENTS

Many people have contributed to this book. First, we wish to thank our colleagues at Xavier University and the University of Connecticut, who have helped us in many different ways. Special thanks go to Professor James Pawlukiewicz. We also wish to thank the following reviewers for their thoughtful critiques:

Kent G. Becker
Temple University

Paul Bolster
Northeastern University

Francis Boabang
St. Mary's University, Canada

Charles Corrado
University of Missouri

Donald Fehrs
University of Notre Dame

Dorothy E. Koehl
University of Puget Sound

Hung-Gay Fung
University of Baltimore

Jeong W. Lee
University of North Dakota

John G. Gallo
University of Texas—Arlington

Thomas W. Miller, Jr.
University of Missouri

John M. Geppert
University of Nebraska

Joseph P. Ogden
SUNY—Buffalo

Anthony Herbst
University of Texas—El Paso

William Pugh
Auburn University

Joan C. Junkus
DePaul University

Steve Swidler
University of Texas—Arlington

Peppi M. Kenny
Western Illinois University

John Wingender
Oklahoma State University

Our appreciation is extended to the staff at West Publishing Company, particularly Arnis Burvikovs (our original editor) and Al Bruckner (our current editor). We especially wish to thank Susanna Smart, development editor at West, who oversaw the book's development and was a continual source of encouragement. Thanks as well to Michael Bass & Associates (production coordination) and to Elliot Simon (copy editor). Our appreciation is extended to Shirlee James, who typed the manuscript and whose expertise, encouragement, and patience were invaluable to this project. We also are indebted to: Judy George, whose reading and editing of the manuscript added value to this book; Paul Laux, Case Western Reserve University, for his insight and advice; Lyle Fiore, for his developing the computer software accompanying the book; Mohamed Dahi, Barbara Fenning, and Murray Wilson, for their assistance; and the O'Connor family, who helped support this effort through endowing the O'Connor Chair in Business Administration at Xavier University.

We also wish to thank our families for their support and understanding, and to acknowledge two special people for their inspiration—James McDonald and Jo Ann Erhart. Finally, we wish to recognize the pioneers in the development of options and futures theories and strategies: Fisher Black, Myron Scholes, John Cox, Stephen Ross, Mark Rubinstein, Richard Rendlemann, Brit Bartter, Robert Merton, Giovanni Barone-Adesi, William Sharpe, Robert Whaley, Peter Ritchken, Hans Stoll, and others cited in the pages that follow. Without their contributions, this text could not have been written.

We encourage you to send your comments and suggestions to the authors.

R. S. J.
C. G.

OPTIONS
AND
FUTURES

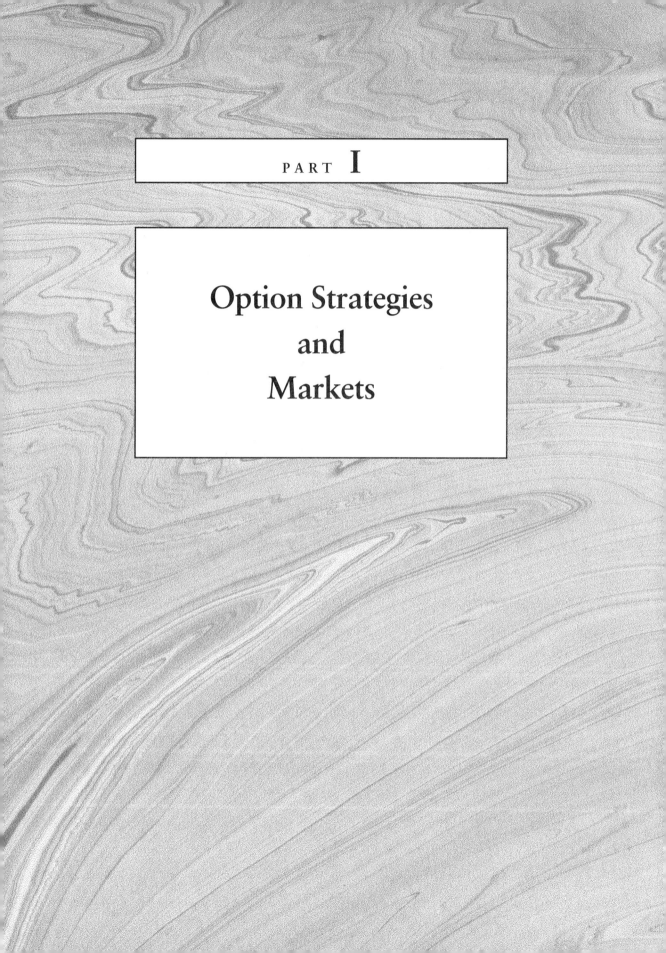

PART **I**

Option Strategies
and
Markets

CHAPTER 1

Option Concepts and Fundamental Strategies

Options and futures are known as *derivative securities*. A derivative security is one whose value depends on the values of another asset. Derivatives are important as a risk management tool. Farmers, portfolio managers, multinational businesses, and financial institutions often buy and sell derivatives to hedge positions they have in the derivative's underlying asset against adverse price changes. Derivatives also are used for speculation. Many investors find buying or selling options or futures an attractive alternative to buying or selling the derivative's underlying security. Finally, many investors and portfolio managers use derivatives for *financial engineering*, buying and selling different derivatives and the underlying security to create a portfolio that has certain desired features.

Because of their speculative, hedging, and financial engineering uses, derivatives are an important part of our financial system. Today there are a number of organized futures and option exchanges operating in the United States and other countries. These exchanges make it easy for speculators and hedgers to buy or sell derivative contracts. There also are a number of dealer markets in which larger institutions and businesses take positions in derivative contracts written by financial institutions and dealers. The objective of this book is to describe the markets in which derivatives are traded, how they are used for speculating, hedging, and financial engineering, and how their prices are determined. We begin by examining options.

1.1 OPTION MARKET

The option market in the United States can be traced back to the 1840s, when options on corn meal, flour, and other agriculture commodities were traded in New York. These option contracts gave the holders the right, but not the obligation, to purchase or to sell a commodity at a specific price on or possibly before a specified date. The early market for commodity option trading, though, was relatively thin. The market did grow marginally in the early 1900s when a group of investment firms formed the Put and Call Brokers and Dealers Association to trade options on stocks on the over-the-counter (OTC) market. An investor who wanted to buy an option could do so through a member of the association, who either would find a seller through other members or would sell (write) the option himself.

The OTC option market was functional, but suffered because it failed to provide an adequate secondary market. In 1973, the Chicago Board of Trade (a futures exchange) formed the Chicago Board Option Exchange (CBOE). The CBOE was the first organized exchange for option trading, and helped to increase the trading of options by standardizing contracts, establishing margin requirements to ensure delivery, and setting up trading rules. From 1973 to the early 1990s, option contracts traded on the CBOE grew from just over 1 million to approximately 127 million.

Since the creation of the CBOE, organized stock exchanges such as the New York Stock Exchange (NYSE), the American Stock Exchange (AMEX), the Philadelphia Stock Exchange (PHLX), and the Pacific Stock Exchange (PSE), most of the organized futures exchanges, and many security exchanges outside the United States have begun offering markets for the trading of options. As the number of exchanges offering options has increased, so has the number of securities and instruments with options written on them (see Table 1.1-1). Today, option contracts exist not only on stock but also on foreign currencies, bonds, and security indices.

In this chapter we begin our analysis of options by defining common option terms, discussing the fundamental stock option strategies, and identifying some of the important factors that determine the price of an option. This chapter will provide a foundation for the more detailed analysis of the markets, strategies, and pricing of stock options that will be examined in Parts I and II of this book, as well as the analysis of the nonstock options, which will be examined in Part III.

TABLE 1.1-1

U.S Stock Option Exchanges			
EXCHANGE		TYPES OF OPTION CONTRACTS LISTED	PERCENTAGE OF OPTION VOLUME
Chicago Board Option Exchange	CBOE	Stocks, security indices, treasury bonds, foreign currency	56%
Philadelphia Stock Exchange	PHLX	Stock, stock indices, gold, silver, foreign currency, security indices	12
American Stock Exchange	AMEX	Stock, stock indices, treasury bills, treasury notes, oil and gas index, oil index, transportation index, computer technology index, institutional index	22
New York Stock Exchange	NYSE	Stock market indices, beta index	2
Pacific Stock Exchange	PSE	Stock, technology index	8

1.2 OPTION TERMINOLOGY

By definition, an option is a security that gives the holder the right to buy or sell a particular asset at a specified price on, or possibly before, a specific date. A call option would be created, for example, if on February 1, Ms. B paid $1000 to Mr. A for a contract that gives Ms. B the right, but not the obligation, to buy ABC Properties from Mr. A for $20,000 on or before July 1. Similarly, a put option also would be created if Mr. A sold Ms. B a contract for the right, but not the obligation, to sell ABC Properties to Mr. A at a specific price on or before a certain date.

Depending on the parties and types of assets involved, options can take on many different forms. Certain features, however, are common to all options. First, with every option contract there is a right, but not the obligation, either to buy or to sell. Specifically, by definition a *call* is the right to buy a specific asset or security, whereas a *put* is the right to sell. Second, every option contract has a buyer and a seller. The option buyer is referred to as the *holder*, and as having a *long position* in the option. The holder buys the right to *exercise*, or evoke the terms of the option claim. The seller, often referred to as the option *writer*, has a *short position* and is responsible for fulfilling the obligations of the option if the holder exercises. Third, every option has an option price, an exercise price, and an exercise date. The price paid by the buyer to the writer for the option is referred to as the *option premium* (call premium and put premium). The *exercise price* or *strike price* is the price specified in the option contract at which the underlying asset can be purchased (call) or sold (put). Finally, the *exercise date* is the last day the holder can exercise. Associated with the exercise date are the definitions of European and American options. A *European option* is one that can be exercised only on the exercise date, while an *American option* can be exercised at any time on or before the exercise date. Thus, in our previous example, Mr. A is the writer, Ms. B is the holder, $1000 is the option premium, $20,000 is the exercise or strike price, July 1 is the exercise date, and the option is American.

1.3 FUNDAMENTAL OPTION STRATEGIES

Many types of option strategies exist, with esoteric names such as *straddles, strips, spreads*, and *combinations*. All these strategies can be understood easily once you grasp the features of six fundamental option strategies: call and put purchases, call and put writes, and call and put writes in which the seller covers her position. The features of these strategies can be seen by examining the relationship between the price of the underlying security and the possible profits or losses that would result if the option either is exercised or expires worthless.*

---

*As we will see later, most options are not exercised, but instead are closed by holders selling their contracts and writers buying their contracts. As a starting point in developing a fundamental understanding of options, though, it is helpful first to examine what happens if the option is exercised.

1.3.1 Call Purchase

To see the major characteristics of a *call purchase*, let us examine an example. Suppose an investor buys a call option on ABC stock with an exercise price (X) of $50 at a call premium (C) of $3. If the stock price reaches $60 and the holder exercises, a profit of $7 will be realized as the holder acquires the stock for $50 by exercising, then sells the stock in the market for $60: a $10 capital gain minus the $3 premium. If the holder exercises when the stock is trading at $53, he will break even: The $3 premium will be offset exactly by the $3 gain realized by acquiring the stock from the option at $50 and selling it in the market at $53. Finally, if the price of the stock is at $50 or below, the holder will not find it profitable to exercise, and, as a result, will let the option expire, realizing a loss equal to the call premium of $3. Thus, the maximum loss from the call purchase is $3.

The investor's possible profit or loss and stock price combinations can be seen graphically in Figure 1.3-1 and the accompanying table. In the graph, the profits and losses are shown on the vertical axis and the market prices of the stock (at the

FIGURE 1.3-1

Call Purchase Profit Graph and Value Graph

$X = \$50, C_0 = \$3$

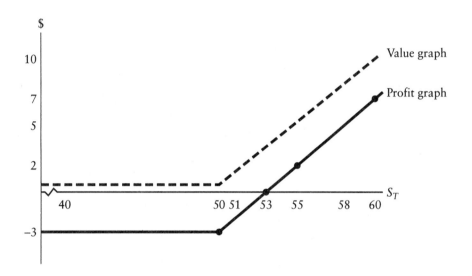

Call Purchase		
S_T	PROFIT/LOSS (SOLID LINE)	CALL VALUE (DASHED LINE)
$40	− $3	$ 0
45	− 3	0
50	− 3	0
53	0	3
55	2	5
60	7	10

NOTE: *Profit* is defined as the capital gain on the call, minus the cost of the call. For example, if the stock price is $60, the profit is $7: $10 gain ($60 − $50) minus the $3 initial cost. The call value is the cash flow from the call at expiration. For example, if the stock price is $40, the call is worthless and the cash flow is zero; if the stock price is $55, the call value is $5 ($55 − $50).

time of the exercise and/or expiration, signified as T: S_T) are shown along the horizontal axis. This graph is known as a ***profit graph***. The line from the coordinate $(50, -3)$ to the $(60, 7)$ coordinate and beyond shows all the profit and losses per call associated with each stock price. That is, the $(60, 7)$ coordinate shows the $7 call profit realized when the stock is at $60, and the $(55, 2)$ coordinate shows a profit of $2 when the stock is at $55. The horizontal segment shows a loss of $3, equal to the premium paid when the option was purchased. Finally, the horizontal intercept shows the break-even price at $53. The break-even price can be found algebraically by solving for the stock price at the exercise date (S_T) in which the profit (π) from the position is zero. The profit from the call purchase position is:

$$\pi = (S_T - X) - C_0,$$

where C_0 is the initial $(t = 0)$ cost of the call. Setting π equal to zero and solving for S_T yields the break-even price of S_T^*:

$$S_T^* = X + C_0 = \$50 + \$3 = \$53.$$

The profit graph in Figure 1.3-1 highlights two important features of call purchases. First, the position provides an investor with unlimited profit potential; second, losses are limited to an amount equal to the call premium. These two features help explain why some ***speculators*** prefer buying a call rather than the underlying stock itself. Speculators are those who accept greater risk in return for greater expected returns. In our example, suppose that the price of ABC stock could range from $30 to $70 at expiration. If a speculator purchased the stock for $50, the profit from the stock would range from $-\$20$ to $+\$20$, or, in percentage terms, from -40% to $+40\%$ (see Table 1.3-1). On the other hand, the return on the call option would range from $+567\%$ to -100%! Thus, the potential reward to the speculator from buying a call instead of the stock can be substantial—in this example, 566% compared to 40% for the stock; but the potential for loss also is large, -100% for the call versus -40% for the stock.

In addition to the profit graph, option positions also can be described graphically by ***value graphs***. A value graph shows the option's value or cash flow at expiration, associated with each level of the stock price. The dashed line in Figure 1.3-1 displays the value graph for the call purchase. The graph shows that if

TABLE 1.3-1					
	Rates of Return from Call and Stock Positions				
STOCK PRICE AT EXPIRATION	PROFIT FROM STOCK PURCHASED AT $50	RATE OF RETURN FROM STOCK	PROFIT FROM CALL PURCHASED AT $3	RATE OF RETURN FROM CALL	
$70	$ 20	40%	$17	567%	
60	10	20	7	233	
50	0	0	-3	-100	
40	-10	-20	-3	-100	
30	-20	-40	-3	-100	

$S_T \leq X(S_T \leq \$50)$, then the call will have no value ($C_T = 0$), whereas if $S_T > X(S_T > \$50)$, the call will have a value of $C_T = S_T - X$.

1.3.2   Naked Call Write

The second fundamental option strategy involves the sale of a call in which the seller does not own the underlying stock. Such a position is known as a *naked call write*. To see the characteristics of this position, again assume the exercise price on the call option on ABC stock is $50 and the call premium is $3. The profits or losses associated with each stock price from selling the call are depicted in Figure 1.3-2 and its accompanying table. As shown, when the price of the stock is at $60, the seller suffers a $7 loss if the holder exercises the right to buy the stock from the writer at $50. Since the writer does not own the stock, she would have to buy it in the market at its market price of $60, then turn it over to the holder at $50. Thus, the call writer would realize a $10 capital loss, minus the $3 premium

FIGURE 1.3-2

Naked Call Write Profit Graph and Value Graph

$X = \$50, C_0 = \$3$

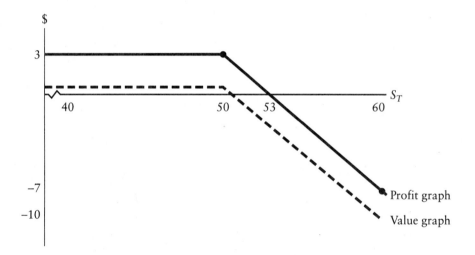

Naked Call Write		
S_T	PROFIT/LOSS (SOLID LINE)	CALL VALUE (DASHED LINE)
$40	$3	$ 0
45	3	0
50	3	0
53	0	− 3
55	− 2	− 5
60	− 7	− 10

NOTE: *Profit* is defined as the capital gain on the call, plus the call premium. At $S_T = \$40$, the call will not be exercised and the profit to the writer will be the initial premium of $3. At $S_T = \$55$, the call writer will have to buy the stock for $55 and sell it (to the call holder) for $50. The net loss is $2. The call value is 0 for $S_T \leq \$50$, and is $-(S_T - \$50)$ for $S_T > \$50$.

received for selling the call, for a net loss of $7. When the stock is at $53, the writer will realize a $3 loss if the holder exercises. This loss will offset the $3 premium received. Thus, the break-even price for the writer is $53, the same as the holder's break-even price. This price also can be found algebraically by solving for the stock price S_T^* in which the profit from the naked call write position is zero. That is:

$$\pi = -(S_T^* - X) + C_0 = 0$$

$$S_T^* = X + C_0 = \$50 + \$3 = \$53.$$

Finally, at a stock price of $50 or less, the holder will not exercise, and the writer will profit by the amount of the premium, $3.

As highlighted in the graph, the payoffs to a call write are just the opposite of those to the call purchase; that is, gains/losses for the buyer of a call are exactly equal to the losses/gains of the seller. Thus, in contrast to the call purchase, the naked call write position provides the investor with only a limited profit opportunity, equal to the value of the premium, with unlimited loss possibilities. While this limited profit and unlimited loss feature of a naked call write may seem unattractive, the motivation for an investor to write a call is the cash or credit received and the expectation that the option will not be exercised. As we will discuss in Chapter 2, though, there are margin requirements on an option write position in which the writer is required to deposit cash or risk-free securities to secure the position.

The dashed line in Figure 1.3-2 shows the value graph for the naked call write. As shown in this graph, if the stock price is below the exercise price, the call value is $C_T = 0$. If $S_T = \$60$, the call writer will have to buy the stock for $60 and sell it (when the call is exercised) for $50. Thus, the cash flow is a $10 loss: $C_T = -(\$60 - \$50) = -\$10$.

1.3.3   Covered Call Write

One of the most popular option strategies is to write a call on a stock already owned. This strategy is known as a *covered call write*. For example, an investor who bought ABC stock at $50 some time ago and who did not expect its price to appreciate in the near future, might sell a call on ABC stock with an exercise price of $50. As shown in Figure 1.3-3 and its accompanying table, if ABC stock is $50 or more, the covered call writer loses the stock when the holder exercises, leaving the writer with a profit of only $3. The benefit of the covered call write occurs when the stock price declines. For example, if ABC stock declined to $40, then the writer would suffer an actual loss of $10 (if the stock is sold) or a paper loss of $10. The $3 premium received from selling the call, though, would reduce this loss to just $7. Similarly, if the stock is at $47, a $3 loss will be offset by the $3 premium received from the call sale.

1.3.4   Put Purchase

Since a put gives the holder the right to sell the stock, profit is realized when the stock price declines. With a decline, the put holder can buy the stock at a low price in the stock market, then sell it at the higher exercise price on the contract. To see

FIGURE 1.3-3

Covered Call Write Profit Graph

$X = \$50$, $C_0 = \$3$, $S_0 = \$50$

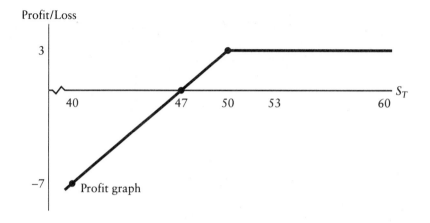

Covered Call Write			
(1) S_T	(2) PROFIT ON UNCOVERED CALL SOLD AT \$3	(3) PROFIT ON STOCK PURCHASED AT \$50	(4) PROFIT ON COVERED CALL WRITE (2) + (3)
\$40	\$3	− \$10	− \$7
45	3	− 5	− 2
47	3	− 3	0
50	3	0	3
55	− 2	5	3
60	− 7	10	3

the features related to the ***put purchase*** position, assume the exercise price on an ABC put is again \$50 and the put premium (*P*) is \$3. If the stock price declines to \$40, the put holder could purchase the stock at \$40, then use the put contract to sell the stock at the exercise price of \$50. Thus, as shown by the profit graph in Figure 1.3-4 and its accompanying table, at \$40 the put holder would realize a \$7 profit (the \$10 gain from buying the stock and exercising, minus the \$3 premium). The break-even price in this case would be \$47:

$$\pi = (X - S_T) - P_0 = 0$$

$$S_T^* = X - P_0$$

$$S_T^* = \$50 - \$3 = \$47.$$

Finally, if the stock is \$50 or higher at expiration, it will not be rational for the put holder to exercise. As a result, a maximum loss equal to the \$3 premium will occur when the stock is trading at \$50 or more.

FIGURE 1.3-4

Put Purchase Profit Graph and Value Graph

$X = \$50, P_0 = \$3$

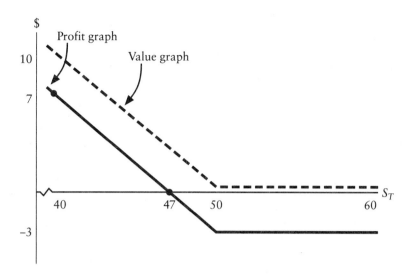

Put Purchase		
S_T	Profit/Loss (solid line)	Put Value (dashed line)
$40	$7	$10
45	2	5
47	0	3
50	− 3	0
55	− 3	0
60	− 3	0

NOTE: At T, if $S_T \geq \$50$, then the put is worthless; that is, $P_T = 0$, and there is a loss of $3. If $S_T < 50$, the put will be exercised. The put value is $P_T = \$50 − S_T$ ($50 received from the put writer minus S_T needed to buy the stock) and the profit is ($50 − S_T$) less the cost of the put ($3).

The put purchase position is also described in Figure 1.3-4 by its value graph (dashed line). As shown, if S_T is below the exercise price, the value of the put is $P_T = X − S_T$, and if $S_T \geq \$50$, the put is worthless.

Thus, similar to a call purchase, a long put position provides the buyer with potentially large profit opportunities (not unlimited, since the price of the stock cannot be less than zero), while limiting the losses to the amount of the premium. Unlike the call purchase strategy, the put purchase position requires the stock price to decline before profit is realized.

1.3.5 Naked Put Write

The exact opposite position to a put purchase (in terms of profit or loss and stock price relations) is the sale of a put, known as the **naked put write**. This position's profit and value graphs are shown in Figure 1.3-5. Here, if the stock price is at $50 or more, the holder will not exercise and the writer will profit by the amount of

FIGURE 1.3-5

Naked Put Write Profit
Graph and Value Graph

$X = \$50, P_0 = \$3$

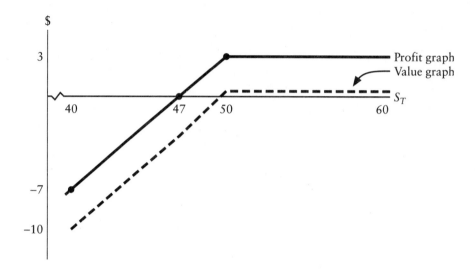

	Naked Put Write	
S_T	PROFIT/LOSS (SOLID LINE)	PUT VALUE (DASHED LINE)
$40	− $7	− $10
45	− 2	− 5
47	0	− 3
50	3	0
55	3	0
60	3	0

NOTE: At $S_T = \$40$ the put writer has the obligation to buy the stock for $50, even though the stock is only worth $40. The − $10 net cash flow is the value of the put. The actual loss is − $10 + $3 = − $7. At $S_T = \$60$, the put is worthless, and the profit is $3 (cash received when the put was sold).

the premium, $3. In contrast, if the stock decreases, a loss is incurred. For example, if the holder exercises at $40, the put writer must buy the stock at $50. An actual $10 loss will occur if the writer elects to sell the stock and a paper loss if he holds on to it. This loss, minus the $3 premium, yields a loss of $7 when the market price is $50. As indicated in the graph, the break-even price in which the profit from the position is zero is $S_T^* = \$47$, the same as the put holder's. That is:

$$\pi = -(X - S_T) + P_0$$

$$S_T^* = X - P_0 = \$50 - \$3 = \$47.$$

1.3.6   Covered Put Write

The last fundamental option strategy is the ***covered put write.*** This strategy requires the seller of a put to cover her position. Because a put writer is required to buy the stock at the exercise price if the holder exercises, the only way she can cover the obligation is by selling the underlying stock short. (Short sale trading is explained in Appendix A at the end of the book.) Using our same numbers, suppose a writer of the ABC 50 put shorts ABC stock: borrows a share of ABC stock and then sells it in the market at $50. At expiration, if the stock price is less than the exercise price and the put holder exercises, the covered put writer would buy the stock with the $50 proceeds obtained from the short sale, then return the share that was borrowed to cover the short sale obligation. The put writer's obligation is thus covered, and the writer profits by an amount equal to the premium, as shown in Figure 1.3-6 and its accompanying table. In contrast, losses from covered put writes occur when the stock price rises above $53. When the stock price rises above $50, the put is worthless, since the holder would not exercise, but losses would occur from covering the short sale. For example, if the writer had to cover the short sale when the stock was at $60, she would incur a $10 loss. This loss, minus the $3 premium the writer received, would equate to a net loss of $7. Finally, the break-even price for the covered put write in which profit is zero occurs at $53.

FIGURE 1.3-6

Covered Put Write Profit Graph

$X = \$50, P_0 = \$3,$
$S_0 = \$50$

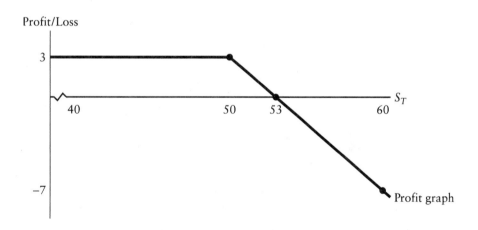

Covered Put Write			
(1)	(2)	(3)	(4)
			PROFIT ON
	PROFIT ON	PROFIT ON	COVERED
	NAKED PUT	STOCK SOLD	PUT WRITE
S_T	SOLD AT $3	SHORT AT $50	(2) + (3)
$40	− $7	$10	$3
45	− 2	5	3
50	3	0	3
53	3	− 3	0
55	3	− 5	− 2
60	3	− 10	− 7

1.4   OTHER OPTION STRATEGIES

One of the important features of an option is that it can be combined with stock and other options to generate a number of different investment strategies. In this section, we introduce two well-known strategies: straddles and spreads. In Chapter 3, we will examine these and other strategies in more detail.

1.4.1   Straddle

A *straddle* purchase is formed by buying both a call and a put with the same terms—same underlying stock, exercise price, and expiration date. A straddle write, in contrast, is constructed by selling a call and a put with the same terms.

In Figure 1.4-1 and its accompanying table, the profit graphs are shown for a call, a put, and straddle purchases in which both the call and the put have exercise prices of $50 and premiums of $3.* The straddle purchase shown in Figure 1.4-1(c) is generated geometrically by vertically summing the profits on the call purchase position [Figure 1.4-1(a)] and the put purchase position [Figure 1.4-1(b)] at each stock price. The resulting straddle purchase position is characterized by a V-shaped profit and stock price relation. Thus, the motivation for buying a straddle comes from the expectation of a large stock price movement in either direction. For example, at the stock price of $40, a $4 profit is earned: $7 profit on the put, minus a $3 loss on the call; similarly, at $60, a $4 profit is attained: $7 profit on the call, minus a $3 loss on the put. Losses on the straddle occur if the price of the underlying stock remains stable, with the maximum loss equaling the costs of the straddle ($6) and occurring when the stock price is equal to the exercise price. Finally, the straddle is characterized by two break-even prices ($44 and $56).

In contrast to the straddle purchase, a straddle write yields an inverted V-shaped profit graph. The seller of a straddle is betting against large price movements. A maximum profit equal to the sum of the call and put premiums occurs when the stock price is equal to the exercise price; losses occur if the stock price moves significantly in either direction. (A straddle write problem is included at the end of this chapter.)

1.4.2   Spread

A *spread* is the purchase of one option and the sale of another on the same underlying stock, but with different terms: different exercise prices, different expirations, or both. Two of the most popular spread positions are the bull spread and the bear spread. A bull call spread is formed by buying a call with a certain exercise price and selling another call with a higher exercise price, but with the

---

*In many of our examples we assume calls and puts with the same terms are priced the same. We do this for simplicity. In reality, though, calls and puts with the same terms are seldom priced equally. The relation between call and put prices is discussed briefly in Section 1.6 and examined in detail in Chapter 4.

same expiration date. A bear call spread is the reversal of the bull spread: It consists of buying a call with a certain exercise price and selling another with a lower exercise price. (The same spreads also can be formed with puts.)

In Figure 1.4-2 and its accompanying table, the profit graph for a bull call spread strategy is shown. The spread is formed with the purchase of a 50 call for $3 and the sale of a 55 call for $1 (same underlying stock and expirations). Geometrically, the profit and stock price relation for the spread shown in Figure 1.4-2(c) is obtained by vertically summing the profits from the long 50 call position

FIGURE 1.4-1

Straddle Purchase

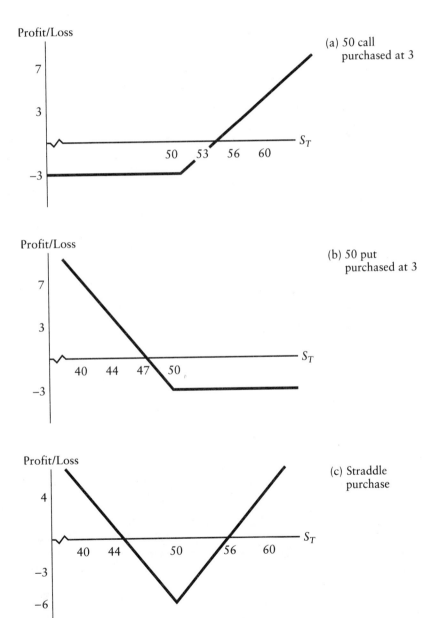

FIGURE 1.4-1

(*continued*)

(1) S_T	(2) PROFIT FROM 50 CALL BOUGHT AT $3	(3) PROFIT FROM 50 PUT BOUGHT AT $3	(4) TOTAL PROFIT (2) + (3)
		Straddle Purchase	
$40	− $3	$7	$4
44	− 3	3	0
47	− 3	0	− 3
50	− 3	− 3	− 6
53	0	− 3	− 3
56	3	− 3	0
60	7	− 3	4

and the short 55 call position at each stock price. The bull spread is characterized by losses limited to $2 when the stock price is $50 or less, limited profits of $3 starting when the stock price hits $55, and a break-even price of $52.

A bear call spread results in the opposite profit and stock price relation from the bull spread: Limited profits occur when the stock price is equal to or less than the lower exercise price, and limited losses occur when the stock price is equal to or greater than the higher exercise price.

1.5   OPTION PRICE RELATIONSHIPS

In our discussion of the fundamental option strategies, we treated the option premium as a given. The price of an option, though, is determined in the market and is a function of the time to expiration, the strike price, the price and the volatility of the underlying security, and the rate of return on a riskless bond. The pricing of option contracts is explained in Part II of this book. However, at this point we can identify some of the factors that determine the price of an option.

1.5.1   Call Price Relationships

The relationship between the price of a call and its expiration time, exercise price, and stock price can be seen by defining the call's intrinsic value and time value premium. By definition, the **intrinsic value** (IV) of a call at a time prior to expiration (let *t* signify any time *prior* to expiration) or at expiration (*T* again signifies expiration date) is the maximum (Max) of the difference between the price of the stock (S_t) and the exercise price or zero (since the option cannot have a negative value). That is:

$$IV = Max[S_t - X, 0]. \tag{1.5-1}$$

Thus, if a call has an exercise price of $50 and the stock is trading at $60, then the intrinsic value of the call would be $10; if it is trading at $48, the IV would be zero. The intrinsic value can be used as a reference to define *in-the-money, on-the-money,* and *out-of-the-money calls.* Specifically, an in-the-money call is one in which the price of the underlying stock exceeds the exercise price; as a result, its IV is positive. When the price of the stock is equal to the exercise price, the call's IV is zero, and the call is said to be on the money (or at the money). Finally, if the

FIGURE 1.4-2

Bull Call Spread

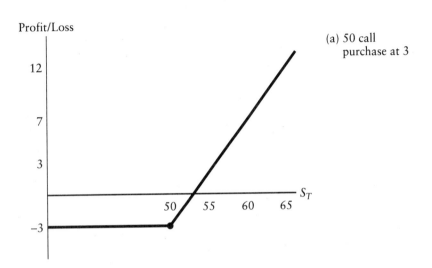

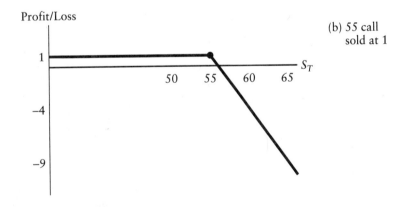

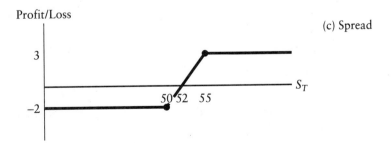

FIGURE 1.4-2

(*continued*)

		Bull Call Spread	
(1)	(2)	(3)	(4)
S_T	PROFIT FROM 50 CALL BOUGHT AT $3	PROFIT FROM 55 CALL SOLD AT $1	TOTAL PROFIT (2) + (3)
$40	− $3	$1	− $2
45	− 3	1	− 2
50	− 3	1	− 2
52	− 1	1	0
55	2	1	3
60	7	− 4	3
65	12	− 9	3

exercise price exceeds the stock price, the call would be out of the money, and the IV would be zero. In summary:

In-the-money call: $S_t > X \Rightarrow IV > 0$
$$\$60 > \$50 \Rightarrow IV = \$10$$

On-the-money call: $S_t = X \Rightarrow IV = 0$
$$\$50 = \$50 \Rightarrow IV = 0$$

Out-of-the-money call: $S_t < X \Rightarrow IV = 0$
$$\$40 < \$50 \Rightarrow IV = 0$$

The other component of the value of an option is the *time value premium* (TVP). By definition, the TVP of a call is the difference between the price of the call and its IV. That is:

$$TVP = C_t - IV. \qquad (1.5\text{-}2)$$

If the call premium is $12 when the price of the underlying stock on a 50 call is $60, the TVP would be $2. The TVP decreases as the time remaining to expiration decreases. Specifically, if the call is near expiration, we should expect the call to trade at close to its IV; if, however, six months remain to expiration, then the price of the call should be greater and the TVP positive; if nine months remain, then the TVP should be even greater. In addition to the intuitive reasoning, an arbitrage argument also can be used to establish that the price of the call is greater with a greater time to expiration (this argument is presented in Chapter 4).

Combined, the IV and the TVP show that two factors influencing the price of a call are the underlying stock's price and the time to expiration. Specifically, by expressing Equation (1.5-2) in terms of C_t,

$$C_t = TVP + IV, \qquad (1.5\text{-}3)$$

we can see that the greater the time to expiration, the higher the TVP and thus the higher the call price; the higher the stock price, the greater the IV of an in-the-money call and thus the higher its price.

Graphically, the relationship between C_t and the TVP and IV, as defined in Equation (1.5-3), can be seen in Figure 1.5-1. In the figure, graphs plotting the call price and the IV (on the vertical axis) against the stock price (on the horizontal axis) are shown for a 50 call option. The IV line shows the linear relationship between the IV and the stock price. The line emanates from a horizontal intercept equal to the exercise price. When the price of the stock is equal to or less than the exercise price of \$50, the IV is equal to zero; when the stock is at \$55, the IV is \$5; when $S_t = \$60$, the IV = \$10, and so on.

The IV line, in turn, serves as a reference for the call price curves (CC). Arbitrage opportunities (discussed in the next section) dictate that the price of the call cannot trade (for long) at a value below its IV if the call is American. Graphically, this means that the call price curve cannot go below the IV line. Furthermore, the IV line would be the call price curve if we are at expiration, since the TVP = 0 and thus C_T = IV. The call price curves (CC) in Figure 1.5-1 show the positive relationship between C_t and S_t. The vertical distance between a CC curve and the IV line, in turn, measures the TVP. Thus, the CC curve shown with 3 months to expiration has a call price of \$1 when the stock is below its exercise price at $S_t = \$40$: Its IV = 0, and TVP = \$1. When the stock is trading at its exercise price, the call is priced at \$5, the IV = 0, and the TVP = \$5; and when the stock is at \$60, the call is at \$12, the IV = \$10, and the TVP = \$2. The CC curve for the 9-month option is above the 3-month CC curve, reflecting the fact that the call premium increases as the time to expiration increases.

In summary, the graphs in Figure 1.5-1 show: (1) A direct relationship exists between the price of the call and the stock price, as reflected by the positively sloped CC curves; (2) the call will be priced above its IV, as shown by the CC curves being above the IV line; and (3) the price of the call will be greater the longer the time to expiration, as reflected by the distance between CC curves with different expiration periods. Finally, it should be noted that the slopes of the CC curves approach the slope of the IV line when the stock price is relatively high (known as a ***deep in-the-money-call***), and the slope approaches zero (flat) when the price of

FIGURE 1.5-1

**Call and Stock
Price Relationship**

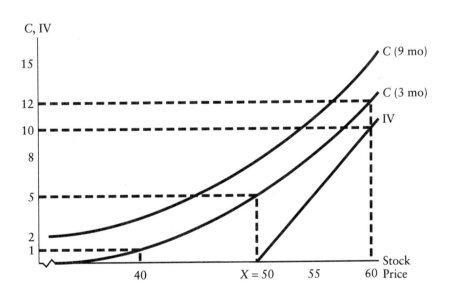

the stock is relatively low (a ***deep out-of-the-money call***). These relationships, as well as how arbitrage ensures the other three relationships and similar ones for European options, are discussed in Chapter 4.

1.5.2   Put Price Relationships

Analogous to calls, the price of a put at a given point in time prior to expiration (P_t) also can be explained by reference to its IV and TVP. In the case of puts, the IV is defined as the maximum of the difference between the exercise price and the stock price or zero:

$$IV = Max[X - S_t, 0]. \qquad (1.5\text{-}4)$$

In-the-money, on-the-money, and ***out-of-the-money puts*** are defined in a way similar to calls:

In-the-money put: $X > S_t \Rightarrow IV > 0$
                         $\$50 > \$40 \Rightarrow IV = \$10$

On-the-money put: $X = S_t \Rightarrow IV = 0$
                         $\$50 = \$50 \Rightarrow IV = 0$

Out-of-the-money put: $X < S_t \Rightarrow IV = 0$
                         $\$50 < \$60 \Rightarrow IV = 0$

Similarly, the TVP for the put is defined as:

$$TVP = P_t - IV. \qquad (1.5\text{-}5)$$

Thus, the price of the put can be explained by the time to expiration and the stock price in terms of the put's TVP and IV:

$$P_t = TVP + IV. \qquad (1.5\text{-}6)$$

Graphically, the put and stock price relationships are shown in Figure 1.5-2, which shows negatively sloped put price curves (PP) for different exercise periods, and a negatively sloped IV line going from the horizontal intercept (where $S_t = X$) to the vertical intercept, where the IV is equal to the exercise price when the stock is trading at zero (i.e., $IV = X$, when $S_t = 0$). The graphs show: (1) The price of the put increases as the price of the underlying stock decreases, since the put's IV is greater the lower the stock price; (2) the price of the put is above its IV with time remaining to expiration (if the put is American), else arbitrage opportunities (discussed in the next section) would ultimately push the price up to equal the IV; (3) the greater the time to expiration, the higher the TVP and thus the greater the put price; and (4) the slope of the PP curve approaches the slope of the IV line for relatively low stock prices (***deep in-the-money puts***) and approaches zero for relatively large stock prices (***deep out-of-the money puts***).

FIGURE 1.5-2

Put and Stock
Price Relationship

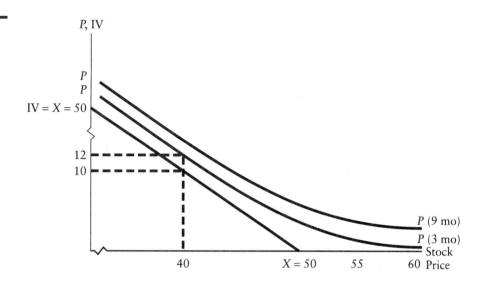

1.6   PUT-CALL PARITY

1.6.1   Law of One Price and Arbitrage

Suppose an American call option on ABC stock with an exercise price of $50 was trading at $9 when the stock was trading at $60 [IV = Max($60 − $50, 0) = $10]. In this situation we have an asset (the stock) selling at two different prices: One is $60, offered in the stock market; the other is $59 ($9 call premium plus $50 exercise price), available in the option market. Given this situation, an arbitrage opportunity exists. An **_arbitrage_** is any risk-free profit or "free-lunch" situation. In this case, an arbitrageur could realize a riskless profit of $1 (excluding commissions) per call by: (1) buying the call at $9, (2) immediately exercising it (buying ABC stock at $50), and (3) selling the stock in the market for $60. However, arbitrageurs seeking to profit from this opportunity would increase the demand for the ABC call, causing its price to go up until the call premium was at least $10 and the arbitrage opportunity disappeared.* Thus, in equilibrium, the American call would have to trade at a price at least equal to its IV.

Similar to the arbitrage arguments for calls, an arbitrage case also can be made for the prices that American puts must command. Specifically, if an American put is trading at a price less than its IV, then an arbitrage profit can be earned by following a strategy of (1) purchasing the underlying stock, (2) purchasing the put, and (3) exercising the put. For example, if an ABC 50 put was trading at $9 when the stock was at $40, then a $1 profit per put would be earned by buying the stock at $40 and the put at $9, then using the put option to sell the stock at $50. As in

---

*Except in the rare case when a large disparity exists between the stock and exercise prices, most investors cannot profit on an after-commission cost basis from executing this arbitrage strategy. Thus, it is the market makers, dealers, and other members of the exchange who do not pay commissions who profit by employing such a strategy.

the case of calls, arbitrageurs pursuing this strategy would increase the demand for puts until the put price was equal to at least the $10 difference between the exercise and stock prices. Thus, in the absence of arbitrage, an American put would have to trade at a price at least equal to its IV.

These examples, in turn, show the meaning of the *Law of One Price*: An asset can have only one price. Any price discrepancy between two different markets should quickly disappear due to the actions of arbitrageurs.

1.6.2   Put-Call Parity Relation

We earlier defined option strategies in terms of their profit and stock price relationship at expiration. We also observed that an alternative way to define option positions is in terms of their values (or cash flows) at expiration. A similar approach exists for positions in stocks and (risk-free, pure discount) bonds. For example, Figure 1.6-1 shows the values of long and short stock positions. The positively sloped 45° line emanating from the origin shows the long position, and the negatively sloped 45° line shows the short position. Thus, if the stock price at time T is $20, then the value of the long stock position is also +$20, and the value of the short stock position is −$20.

Similarly, in Figure 1.6-2 we see the value graph (at maturity) of a long, riskless discount bond (i.e., lent money) and of a short bond (borrowed money) with a face value equal to the exercise price of the option and a maturity the same as the option's expiration date (T). The current price (B_0) or present value, PV(X), of the bond is $B_0 = $ PV(X) $= X/(1 + R_f)$, in which R_f is the risk-free rate of interest for the period. The value of the bond at maturity is $X = B_0(1 + R_f)$ for a long position and $-X = B_0(1 + R_f)$ for a short one, regardless of the stock price. Hence, the value graph, as shown in Figure 1.6-2, is a horizontal line.

Now consider a strategy of buying a share of stock for $50 and a put on the stock with an exercise price of $50. The total cash flow from this portfolio at expiration is shown in Table 1.6-1 and graphed in Figure 1.6-3. As shown in column 7 and in Figure 1.6-3, this stock-and-put portfolio has a minimum value

FIGURE 1.6-1

Value of Long and Short Stock Positions

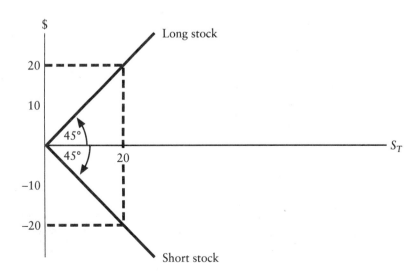

FIGURE 1.6-2

Value of Long
and Short Bonds

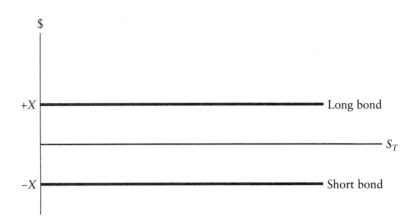

TABLE 1.6-1

Cash Flows on Call, Put, Stock, and Bond Positions at Expiration						
	CASH FLOWS AT EXPIRATION					
(1)	(2)	(3)	(4)	(5)	(6)	(7)
	LONG CALL		{+ BOND, +CALL}	LONG PUT		{+STOCK, +PUT}
S_T	$(X = 50)$	BOND	(3) + (4)	$X = 50$	STOCK	(5) + (6)
$30	$ 0	$50	$50	$20	$30	$50
40	0	50	50	10	40	50
50	0	50	50	0	50	50
60	10	50	60	0	60	60
70	20	50	70	0	70	70

FIGURE 1.6-3

Stock and Put
Value Graphs

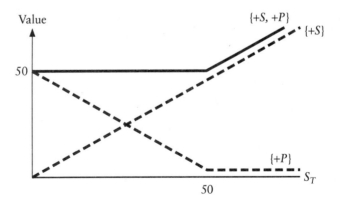

of $50 (the exercise price) for $S_T < \$50$, and a value equal to the stock for $S_T \geq$ $50. Thus, an investor who purchased the stock some time ago could eliminate the downside risk of the stock by buying a put. In this case, the stock value has been "insured" not to fall below $50, the exercise price on the put. A combined stock-and-put position such as this is known as a ***portfolio insurance*** strategy. Portfolio insurance represents an example of how options can be used by hedgers. By

FIGURE 1.6-4

Bond and Call Value Graphs

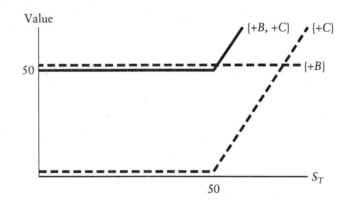

definition, **hedgers** are investors who take a position in certain securities (e.g., a long put position) to reduce or possibly eliminate the risk germane to another position (e.g., a stock position).

Next consider a portfolio consisting of a bond with a face value of $50 and a 50 call. As shown in column (4) of Table 1.6-1 and by the value graphs in Figure 1.6-4, the values of this portfolio at time T are identical to the stock-and-put portfolio's values at each stock price. If the stock appreciates, the call becomes more valuable, and the return on the bond is enhanced by the appreciation in the call price. On the other hand, if the stock falls below the exercise price, the call is worthless, and the portfolio simply is equal to the face value of the bond ($50). A bond-and-call portfolio such as this is referred to as a **fiduciary call**, and it can be used as a substitute for buying the stock and put.

The equality between the stock-put portfolio and the bond-call portfolio may be expressed algebraically as:*

$$S_0 + P_0 = C_0 + B_0, \qquad (1.6-1)$$

or as

$$\{+S, +P\} = \{+C, +B\},$$

where the plus sign indicates a long position.

This expression is commonly referred to as **put-call parity**. Since the two portfolios have exactly the same cash flows at expiration, their aggregate prices at any time t must be identical, else arbitrage opportunities will exist. For example, if the bond-call combination is cheaper than the stock-put portfolio, an arbitrageur can earn a profit without taking risk and without investing any of her own money. To expedite the strategy, the arbitrageur would have to buy the cheap portfolio (bond and call) and sell the expensive one (stock and put).

Finally, note that if we move $+P$ (long put) from the left to the right of the equals sign and change plus to minus, we obtain a new identity:

*We are assuming the options are European and the stock pays no dividends.

TABLE 1.6-2

	Synthetic Stock Values				
$\{+C, -P, +B\}$ at Expiration					
	CASH FLOWS AT EXPIRATION				
(1)	(2)	(3)	(4)	(5) $\{+C, -P, +B\}$	(6)
S_T	LONG 50 CALL	SHORT 50 PUT	LONG BOND	(2) + (3) + (4)	$\{+S\}$
$30	$ 0	−$20	$50	$30	$30
40	0	− 10	50	40	40
50	0	0	50	50	50
60	10	0	50	60	60
70	20	0	50	70	70

$$S_0 = C_0 + P_0 - B_0 \qquad (1.6\text{-}2)$$

$$\{+S\} = \{+C, -P, +B\}.$$

where the minus sign indicates a short position.

This expression suggests that a portfolio consisting of long call, short put, and long bond should yield exactly the same cash flows at expiration as a long stock position. The cash flows displayed in Table 1.6-2 verify this statement. Similarly, we may create a synthetic short stock position by reversing the signs in Equation (1.6-2).

$$-S_0 = -C_0 + P_0 - B_0 \qquad (1.6\text{-}3)$$

$$\{-S\} = \{-C, +P, -B\}.$$

Several variations of the put-call parity equations may be used to create a synthetic long or short call, put, or bond. Put-call parity will be discussed in more detail in Chapter 4.

1.7 CONCLUSION

In this chapter, we have provided an overview of options by defining option terms, examining fundamental option strategies, and defining some of the basic determinants of the price of an option. The discussion, however, was general in nature. When investors speak of options, most of them refer specifically to options that can be purchased or sold on the option exchanges. In the next chapter, we examine those exchanges and the institutional aspects associated with trading options on them.

KEY TERMS

call	profit graph	time value premium
put	speculator	deep in-the-money call
holder	value graph	deep out-of-the-money call
long position	naked call write	in-the-money put
exercise	covered call write	on-the-money put
writer	put purchase	out-of-the-money put
short position	naked put write	deep in-the-money put
option premium	covered put write	deep out-of-the-money put
exercise price	straddle	arbitrage
strike price	spread	Law of One Price
exercise date	intrinsic value	portfolio insurance
European option	in-the-money call	hedger
American option	on-the-money call	fiduciary call
call purchase	out-of-the-money call	put-call parity

SELECTED REFERENCES

Bookstaber, R. *Option Pricing and Strategies in Investing*. Reading, Mass.: Addison-Wesley, 1981.

Cox, J. C., and Rubinstein, M. *Option Markets*. Englewood Cliffs, N.J.: Prentice-Hall, 1985.

Gastineau, G. *The Stock Options Manual*. New York: McGraw-Hill, 1979.

Khoury, S. *Speculative Markets*. New York: Macmillan, 1984.

Williams, J. C. "The Origin of Futures Markets." *Agriculture History* 56 (1982): 306–316.

PROBLEMS AND QUESTIONS

1. Show graphically the profit and stock price relationships at expiration for the following option positions. In each case, show the profit graph for each position at various stock prices, then aggregate at each stock price to generate the profit graph for the position.

    a. A straddle purchase formed with ABC call and put options, each with exercise prices of $60 and premiums of $5.

    b. A straddle write formed with ABC call and put options, each with exercise prices of $40 and premiums of $2.

    c. A covered call write formed by purchasing ABC stock at $48 and selling an ABC 50 call at $3.

    d. A synthetic long stock position formed by buying an ABC 50 call at $3 and selling an ABC 50 put at $3.

    e. A synthetic short stock position formed by selling an ABC 50 call at $3 and buying an ABC 50 put at $3.

    f. A put spread formed by buying an ABC 50 put at $1 and selling an ABC 55 put at $2.

    g. A stock insurance strategy formed by purchasing ABC stock at $50 and buying an ABC 50 put at $3.

2. Construct a value graph for the stock insurance position in Problem 1g.

3. Determine the break-even prices at expiration for the following:

    a. A covered call write formed by purchasing ABC stock at $45 and selling an ABC 50 call at $4.

    b. A covered put write formed by selling ABC stock short at $45 and selling an ABC 50 put at $6.

    c. A stock insurance strategy formed by purchasing ABC stock at $48 and buying an ABC 50 put at $4.

4. Suppose you bought a six-month call option on ABC stock for $1.50. Suppose also that the call option has an exercise price of $10 and that the price of ABC stock is $11. At what price would ABC stock have to sell at the call's expiration for you to break even? At what price would the stock have to trade at expiration for you to earn a 10% rate of return for the six-month period?

5. Suppose you are bearish about ABC stock and buy a six-month ABC 30 put option on the stock for $3 when ABC stock is trading at $29. At what price would ABC stock have to sell at the put's expiration for you to break even? At what price would the stock have to trade at expiration for you to earn a 10% rate of return for the six-month period?

6. Construct a profit graph for a bull call spread formed with an ABC 50 call trading at $2 and an ABC 55 call trading at $6 (include stock prices at expiration of $40, $50, $55, $60, and $70). What do you find significant about the position? How would the market react to this situation? What impact would its reactions have on the prices of the ABC 50 call and the ABC 55 call?

7. Explain what arbitrageurs would do if the price of an American call was below its intrinsic value. What impact would their actions have on the call's price in the option market? Would arbitrageurs follow the same strategy if the call option was European? If not, why?

8. Explain what investors would do if the price of an American put was below its intrinsic value. What impact would their actions have on the put's price in the option market?

9. Compare and contrast buying stock with a call purchase strategy.

10. Compare and contrast selling stock short with a put purchase strategy.

11. If the premium on an option increases, does that mean there is a greater demand for the option? Comment.

12. Let the exercise price X be 40 for both the put and the call, and assume there is a risk-free discount bond with face value of $X = \$40$, the same maturity as the options, and trading at price of B.

    a. Construct a table of expiration values (or cash flows) of the portfolio $\{+S, +P\}$. Does it look like the cash flow for another position? Construct a table for that position. Comment on put-call parity.

    b. Construct a table of expiration values that shows that a $\{+B, +C, -S\}$ portfolio is equivalent to the put.

    c. Construct a table of expiration values that shows that a $\{+S, +P, -B\}$ portfolio is equivalent to the call.

CHAPTER 2

The Option Market

2.1 INTRODUCTION

The buying and selling of most securities in the United States and other countries with major financial markets is done through a network of brokers and dealers who operate through security exchanges. By definition, brokers are agents who, for a commission, bring security buyers and sellers together. Dealers, in turn, provide markets for investors to buy and sell securities by taking temporary positions in securities; they buy from investors who want to sell, and sell to investors who want to buy. In contrast to brokers, dealers receive compensation, which is the spread between the bid price at which they buy securities and the ask price at which they sell.

While brokers and dealers serve the function of bringing buyers and sellers together, the exchanges, in turn, serve the function of linking brokers and dealers. The members of the exchanges consist almost exclusively of brokers and dealers, who, as members, are the only ones who can trade securities on the exchange. In general, the primary objective of an exchange is to provide marketability to securities. An asset's *marketability* refers to the ease or speed with which it can be traded. The exchanges provide this not only by linking brokers and dealers, but by standardizing the security contracts and establishing trading rules and procedures.

The option exchanges such as the CBOE, Philadelphia, Pacific, and others operate similarly to the U.S. security exchanges in linking brokers and dealers and standardizing contracts. Different from the stock and bond exchanges (but similar to the futures exchanges), the option exchanges use clearing corporations that guarantee and break up contracts after trades have been completed. In this chapter, the institutional aspects associated with trading options are examined: the structure of the option exchange, the standardization of options contracts and trading rules as established by the exchanges, and the functions and operations of option clearing corporations. In addition, this chapter will also examine the transaction costs incurred by investors in buying and selling options.

2.2 OPTION EXCHANGES

2.2.1 Structure

The option exchanges can be described in a number of ways. For one, an exchange such as the CBOE, Philadelphia, Pacific, New York, or the like is a physical exchange, a building where brokers and dealers go to buy and sell securities on behalf of their investor/clients. On the trading floor of the CBOE are trading posts where exchange members and other brokers trade one of the options listed. Encircling the floor of the CBOE are telephone and communication areas where brokers receive calls on orders from their retail brokerage firms across the country. With those orders the brokers go to the trading post where the particular option is traded and execute the order (either buy or sell) by means of an auction with **open outcry**, meaning the transaction is conducted orally.

The option exchanges also can be described as a corporate association consisting of member brokers. By exchange rules, only members can trade on the exchange. To obtain a membership, also referred to as a *seat on the exchange*, a company or individual must purchase it from an existing member who wants to sell.*

Members of the exchange can be classified in terms of their functions. Most brokerage firms with seats on the option exchanges function as floor brokers. *Floor brokers* execute buy and sell orders on behalf of their clients. Thus, an investor interested in buying or selling an option would set up an account with the member's investment brokerage firm and buy or sell the option for a commission through the firm's floor broker. A second type of member is the floor trader. *Floor traders* buy and sell securities only for themselves and not for others. They often consist of wealthy individuals who own seats in order to avoid commission costs. A third type of member, depending on the exchange, is a specialist or a market maker. Both *specialists* and *market makers* can be described as dealers who specialize in the trading of a specific option. Finally, the Philadelphia and American exchanges have **Registered Option Traders** (ROTs) as part of their membership, while the CBOE and Pacific do not. ROTs are members who can buy and sell options for themselves and also act as brokers, but who cannot act as market makers or specialists.

2.2.2 Market Makers and Specialists

Security markets can be described as being either a "call market" or a "continuous market." A call market, such as the Tokyo Exchange System or the Paris Bourse (security exchange), is designed so that investors who wish to trade in a particular security can do so only at that time when the exchange "calls" the security for trading. Once the security is called, market clearing is accomplished via an auction: Prices are quoted until a price is found in which the amount demanded is equal to the amount supplied. In contrast, a continuous market attempts to have constant trading in a security. To do so, time discrepancies caused by different times when

---

*An alternative to purchasing is to rent a seat on the exchange from an existing member.

some investors want to sell and others want to buy must be eliminated or at least minimized. Continuous markets, like the NYSE, AMEX, and the American option exchanges, accomplish this by requiring specialists or market makers to take temporary positions in a security whenever there is a demand.

Trading on the American and Philadelphia exchanges centers around specialists. Under the specialist system, the exchange's board assigns the options on a specific security to a specialist to deal. In this role, specialists, like dealers, act by buying options from sellers at low bid prices, hoping to sell to buyers at higher ask prices. Specialists quote a *bid* price (the maximum price they would be willing to pay) to investors interested in selling options and an *ask* price (the maximum price at which they would sell) to investors interested in buying. They hope to profit by the difference in the bid and ask prices, that is, the bid-ask spread. In addition to their dealing, the exchange also requires specialists to maintain the limit-order book on the option they are assigned and to execute the orders.* A *limit order* is an investor's request to a floor broker to buy or sell a security at a given price or better. On the option exchange such orders are taken by floor brokers and left with the assigned specialist for execution. The specialist records the order in his limits book, then acts either as a broker, by trying to trade the option at the client's specified price, or as a dealer, by buying (selling) the option for (from) his inventory.

The CBOE and the Pacific Exchange do not use specialists. Instead, they use market makers who act as dealers and Order Book Officials who keep the limit-order book. Like specialists, market makers are required by the exchange to trade in an assigned option if an investor cannot find someone with whom to trade. Market makers who buy options at the bid price and then sell them at the ask price within a very short period of time (e.g., a minute)—hoping to sell before the market receives information that would change the price of the option—are referred to as *scalpers*. In contrast, market makers who hold their position for a longer period of time are referred to as *position traders*.

The **Order Book Official** (OBO) is an employee of the exchange who keeps the limit-order book.† The OBO stands at the trading post of the option that has been assigned to her and, unlike the specialist, shows the order book to other members, who are allowed to execute the order. The OBO is not allowed, though, to engage in any trading. Market makers, in turn, use the limit orders in the OBO's book to help them determine their own spreads. It should be noted that some of the past work of the OBO is gradually being done on the CBOE by its computerized Retail Automatic Execution System (RAES). This system is designed to fill public orders by matching buyers and sellers via computer.

In terms of the rules of the exchange, both the CBOE and the Pacific Exchange assign more than one market maker to the options on a given stock. This contrasts to the specialist system, in which typically only one specialist is assigned to a security. This rule serves to ensure a more competitive price. Also, the rules of the CBOE prohibit market makers from handling public (nonmember) orders in their assigned option, although a market maker can handle public orders in other options. Finally, exchange rules allow the exchange board to impose limits on the

---

*This latter responsibility often is used by the specialist to determine his bid and ask prices.

†In addition, there is also a board broker, who is responsible for recording transactions. This is a specialist responsibility on the other exchanges.

bid-ask spread. For example, the CBOE as of 1990 imposed limits of ¼ of a point for options trading less than $0.50; ½ of a point for options trading between $0.50 and $10; ¾ of a point for options trading between $10 and $20; and 1 point for options trading over $20.

In summary, the CBOE and the Pacific Exchange use market makers to ensure a continuous market for the options they list, employ Order Book Officials to record limit orders, and assign more than one market maker to one option to stimulate competition. In contrast, the American and Philadelphia exchanges use specialists who, like the market makers, maintain positions in a specific option to ensure a continuous market. Unlike the market maker system, the American and Philadelphia exchanges assign only one specialist to an option, with that specialist being responsible for handling the limit book on the specific option.

2.2.3   Standardization

One of the important contributions provided by a security exchange is the standardization of security contracts. An exchange does this by establishing rules and procedures with respect to the securities that can be listed and the way in which they can be traded. By establishing such rules, the exchange enhances the marketability of an option by making it possible for investors to know exactly what is being offered and the terms of the transaction.

Listing

A corporation that wants an option on its stock listed on the CBOE or some other exchange offering option trading must meet the exchange's initial listing requirements. Once the stock option is listed, the corporation also must adhere to the exchange's continuous listing requirements. As described in Table 2.2-1, the initial requirements of the CBOE relate to the company's ability to satisfy sufficient size and ownership distribution standards. The listing requirements of nonstock options, such as bond and stock indices, foreign currency, and futures, include satisfying an approved proposal that specifies conditions such as the terms of the

TABLE 2.2-1

CBOE Initial Listing Requirements for Stock
1. The company's profit before extraordinary items must be at least $1 million over the last eight quarters.
2. The company must not have defaulted on any obligation in the last 12 months.
3. The trading volume of the company's stock must be at least 2.4 million shares over the last year.
4. The company must have at least 6000 shareholders.
5. The company must have at least 7 million shares owned by noninside traders.
6. The stock of the company must have traded for at least $10 per share for the preceding six months.

contract and, if it's an index, how it is to be constructed. The proposal must have been approved by both the option exchange and the Securities and Exchange Commission (SEC), the federal regulatory authority for stocks and options.*

2.2.4   Trading Procedures

Exercise Dates

The expiration dates on options are set by the exchanges. The dates, in turn, are defined in terms of an expiration cycle. Until 1984, the cycles on most exchanges were the January cycle, with expiration months of January, April, July, and October; the February cycle, with February, May, August, and November expiration months; and the March cycle, with expiration months of March, June, September, and December. On the CBOE and many other U.S. option exchanges, the exercise time is 10:59 AM central time on the Saturday after the third Friday of the expiration month. The last day on which the expiring option trades, though, is Friday (Saturday is used so investors can settle by transferring cash or stock resulting from exercising or paying or receiving premiums from closing their positions). In a three-month option cycle, only the options with the three nearest expiration months trade at any time. Thus, as an option expires, the exchange introduces a new option that, at its introduction, would have nine months remaining before expiration; the remaining two options would accordingly have three and six months left to expiration. For example, in late March, as the March option in the March cycle expires, December options are introduced, giving investors options with three expiration months: June, September, and December.

Because of a high demand for short-term options in the early 1980s, the CBOE and other option exchanges introduced new exercise cycles in 1984. These cycles have options with expirations in the current month, the next month, and then the next two months in either the original January, February, or March cycle. For example, on June 1 a stock with a January cycle has options with expirations of June, July, October, and January (of the next year). As the June option expires, the April option is introduced. This includes both stock and nonstock options.† In 1990, in addition to the short-term option cycles, the CBOE and AMEX began offering options with expirations of up to two years on a limited number of securities.

Exercise Price

The exchange chooses the exercise prices for each option. Usually, at least three strike prices (sometimes as many as five) are associated with each option, when an option cycle begins. For stock options, the exercise prices usually are set 2.5 points

---

*In discussing listing requirements, it should be noted that the SEC does allow some multiple listings (that is, the listing of the option on more than one exchange). This SEC policy reflects a compromise position. It is aimed at appeasing both the CBOE, which has argued against multiple listings, maintaining that exchanges should specialize, and other option exchanges, which argue for the benefits from competition that multiple listing provides.

†An exception, however, is some stock index options having a cycle that includes the current month, the next month, and the next one or two months in one of the original January, February, or March cycles.

apart for stocks trading at less than $25 per share, 5 points apart for stocks trading at between $25 and $200, and 10 points apart for stocks trading at over $200.

Once an option with a specific exercise price has been introduced, it will remain listed until its expiration date. The exchange can, however, introduce new options with different exercise prices at any time. For example, if one month after introducing a January 50 option, the stock price increases dramatically from $45 to $60, the exchange could introduce a new January option with an exercise price of $65. Also, while an option, once listed, must remain so until expiration, the exchange can restrict trading on it. The exchange defines a *restricted* option as one in which holders or writers are not allowed to enter an order if the order represents an initial transaction. Usually, options are restricted when they are selling at a very low price, with little or no demand.

It should be noted that when a company declares a cash dividend, the exchange does not adjust the exercise price. This policy contrasts to the dividend adjustment policies used when options traded on the over-the-counter (OTC) market. Under the old OTC policy, if a company paid a cash dividend, the exercise price on the option was reduced by the amount of the dividend.

Option Contract Size

The standard size for a stock option contract is 100 calls. Thus, a per-share quote of an ABC July 50 call at $3 means that a call buyer actually would be purchasing 100 calls at $3 per call ($300 investment), giving him the right to buy 100 shares of stock at $50 per share (total exercise value of $5000) on or before (if American) the third Friday of July.

In discussing the size of a stock option contract, one should note that the CBOE and other option exchanges automatically adjust options for stock splits and stock dividends. For example, if ABC stock is trading at $50, and there is a put option on it with an exercise price of $60, then a two-for-one stock split would result in an automatic adjustment in which the number of contracts doubles and the exercise price is halved. Thus, the owner of one ABC 60 put contract (100 puts) would now have two ABC 30 puts (200 puts). Options also are adjusted automatically for stock dividends by changing the number of shares and the exercise price. For example, if the ABC Company declares a 2.5% stock dividend, then the 100 shares underlying an ABC 60 call option contract would be adjusted up to equal 102.5 shares, and the exercise price would be adjusted down by 2.5%. The exercise price then would equal $1/1.025 = .9756$ of its initial value: $(.9756)(\$60) = \$58.536$.

Contract sizes for nonstock options also are specified as multiples. For example, an investor who buys one S & P 100 index option contract is actually buying 100 options, and an investor buying one option on the Canadian dollar is by contract actually purchasing 50,000 options, the standard contract size on this foreign currency option.

Limits

The CBOE and other option exchanges impose two limits on option trading: exercise limits and position limits. These limits are intended to prevent an investor or groups of investors from having a dominant impact on a particular option.

An *exercise limit* specifies the maximum number of option contracts that can be exercised on any five consecutive business days by any investor or investor group. An exercise limit is determined by the exchange for each stock and nonstock option.

A *position limit* sets the maximum number of options an investor can buy and sell on one side of the market; the limit for each stock and nonstock option is the same as the exercise limit. A side of the market is either a bullish or a bearish position. An investor who is bullish could profit by buying calls or selling puts, while an investor with a bearish position would hope to profit by buying puts and selling calls. A position limit of 3000 contracts on ABC stock, for example, would limit a bullish investor to no more than 3000 contracts involving the purchase of the ABC call and the sale of the ABC put. The exchange sets the limits for each stock at either 3000, 5000, or 8000 contracts. The limit assigned each stock, in turn, depends on the option's trading volume and the number of shares of stock outstanding.

Option Quotation

Exhibit 2.2-1 shows part of the daily quotations for options on individual stocks from the *Wall Street Journal* (WSJ) for January 13, 1994. In the exhibit, the first column gives the names of the companies and below it the closing price of their stock. The second column shows the exercise prices. The next four columns show the expiration months, volume, and premiums for both call and put options. For example, in Exhibit 2.2-1, AT&T stock closed on January 14, 1994, at 54⅝. The AT&T call options with an exercise price of $50 that expired in January had a premium of $4, and the AT&T 50 put option with an expiration in January closed at 1/16.

Two new option terms, option *class* and option *series*, can be noted in examining option price quotations. The term *option class* refers to all options on a given stock or security that are of a particular type, either call or put. Thus, all AT&T calls in Exhibit 2.2-1 are one option class, and all the AT&T puts represent another option class. The term *option series* means all of the options of a given class with the same exercise price and expiration. Thus, the AT&T January 50 call is one series, and the AT&T January 50 put is another.

2.2.5   Option Clearing Corporation

The **Option Clearing Corporation** (OCC) is a corporation whose primary function is to facilitate the marketability of option contracts. The OCC does this by acting as a clearinghouse; it acts as an intermediary for each option transaction that takes place on the exchange, and guarantees that all option writers fulfill the terms of their options if holders exercise.

As an intermediary, the OCC functions by breaking up each option trade. After a buyer and seller complete an option trade, the OCC steps in to become the effective buyer to the option seller and the effective seller to the option buyer. At that point, there is no longer any relationship between the original buyer and seller. If the buyer of the option decides to exercise, she does so by notifying the OCC (through her broker on the exchange). The OCC (who is the holder's effective option seller) will randomly select one of the option sellers who is short on the exercised security and assign that writer the obligation of fulfilling the terms of the exercise request.

By breaking up each option contract, the OCC makes it possible for option investors to close their positions before expiration. If a seller (buyer) of an option later becomes a buyer (seller) of the same option, the OCC computer will note the

EXHIBIT 2.2-1

Stock Option Quotes

Option/Strike	Exp.	—Call— Vol.	Last	—Put— Vol.	Last
AFLAC 35	Aug	20	5/8	...	...
A M R 55	Nov	...	...	21	1 3/4
57 7/8 60	Aug	45	7/8	50	2 3/4
57 7/8 65	Nov	23	1 3/8	...	...
A S A 40	Aug	2	6 7/8	50	1/16
46 7/8 45	Aug	88	2 1/16	180	1/2
46 7/8 45	Sep	36	2 3/8	200	3/4
46 7/8 45	Nov	72	3 5/8	5	1 7/8
46 7/8 50	Aug	30	5/16	...	...
46 7/8 50	Nov	43	1 7/16	6	4 1/4
46 7/8 50	Feb	53	2 3/8	...	...
AST Rs 12 1/2	Aug	76	1/2	48	3/16
13 3/4 12 1/2	Sep	110	1 7/8	487	3/8
13 3/4 12 1/2	Nov	10	2 5/8	43	1
13 3/4 12 1/2	Feb	36	3 1/2	10	1 5/8
13 3/4 15	Aug	204	3/8	186	1 1/2
13 3/4 15	Sep	147	13/16	106	1 13/16
13 3/4 15	Nov	114	1 9/16	33	2 1/4
13 3/4 15	Feb	66	2 1/4	10	2 3/4
13 3/4 17 1/2	Feb	70	1 3/8	10	4 3/4
AT&T 50	Aug	806	4 1/2	60	1/16
54 5/8 50	Sep	245	4 7/8	...	...
54 5/8 50	Oct	56	5 1/8	...	...
54 5/8 50	Jan	15	6	913	1
54 5/8 55	Aug	2997	5/8	...	...
54 5/8 55	Sep	198	1 1/8	...	...
54 5/8 55	Oct	66	1 5/8	...	...
54 5/8 55	Jan	60	2 5/8	80	2 9/16
54 5/8 60	Jan	48	3/4	...	...
Abbt L 30	Aug	75	1/8	10	2
Aclaim 15	Sep	...	...	35	1
Actava 10	Dec	20	1	...	...
AdobeS 25	Sep	400	6 3/8	...	...
29 7/8 30	Aug	176	1 1/4	5	1 3/8
29 7/8 30	Oct	27	3 1/8	...	...
A M D 25	Aug	61	1 3/8	10	1/2
25 3/4 25	Sep	50	2 1/4	5	1 1/8
25 3/4 25	Oct	25	2 7/8	11	1 3/4
25 3/4 30	Jan	170	1 7/8	...	...
Aetna 60	Jan	124	2	...	...
Agnico 12 1/2	Sep	30	13/16	...	...
Ahman 20	Aug	20	3/4	...	...
19 5/8 20	Oct	30	1 1/8	...	...
19 5/8 20	Jan	...	...	20	1 1/2
AirPd 45	Sep	30	3	...	...
AirbFr 30	Aug	5	3/8	40	3
Airtch 20	Oct	...	...	60	3/16
26 25	Aug	7	1 3/4	150	7/16
26 30	Sep	39	1/4	...	...
26 30	Oct	46	5/8	...	...
26 30	Jan	31	1 3/8	...	...

SOURCE: *Wall Street Journal*, January 15, 1994

offsetting position in the option investor's account and will therefore cancel both entries. For example, suppose in January an investor sells an ABC March 50 call for $3. When the OCC breaks up the contract, it records the investor's short position in its computer, indicating the writer is subject to possible assignment if any holder of an ABC March 50 call decided to exercise. If this did occur, the writer then actually would have to buy the ABC stock in the market and sell it to the exercising holder at the $50 exercise price. If the writer at a later date wanted to close his position (either to avoid assignment, to take advantage of a profit opportunity, or to minimize losses), he could do so by simply buying the ABC March 50 call at the prevailing call price. The OCC would step in after the new transaction and enter the investor's position on its records. The OCC's records then would show an entry with the investor's long position, giving him the right to buy ABC stock at $50, and the investor's previous short position, giving the OCC the right to assign the investor the responsibility to sell ABC stock for $50 if there is an exercise. The offsetting positions (the right to buy and the obligation to sell) cancel each other, and the OCC computer system thus simply erases both entries. Since the second transaction serves to close out the position, it is referred to as a *closing purchase* or an *offsetting order* or simply an *offset*. Similar closing positions exist for an option buyer. Instead of exercising, a call buyer can close her position by later selling the option. In this case, the OCC record showing the investor with the right to buy would be canceled by the new entry showing the investor with the responsibility to sell the security if another holder exercises. This offset is referred to as a *closing sale*. To recapitulate: By breaking up each transaction, the OCC provides marketability to options by making it easier for investors to close their position.

The OCC also enhances the marketability of option contracts by guaranteeing that the terms of a contract will be fulfilled if a holder exercises. To provide this insurance, the OCC has a claim on the securities and deposits that the option writer is required to maintain in an account with her brokerage firm as security or collateral. All covered option writers are required by the option exchanges to place their stock (for calls) or the cash or cash equivalents (for puts) in an escrow account of their brokerage firm, and all naked option writers are required to maintain cash or a cash equivalent in a deposit account with the brokerage firm equal to a certain percentage of the contract value. (Margin requirements will be discussed further in Section 2.4 of this chapter.) If an option writer defaults on an assignment, the OCC can use its claim on the writer's security held in escrow or the margin deposit to obtain the cash or the security needed to honor the writer's responsibility. In addition to this claim, the OCC also maintains a special fund generated by its members to ensure sufficient capital to protect option buyers against assignment default. The OCC, by assuming the responsibility of guaranteeing the option writer's performance, eliminates the uncertainty option buyers might have concerning default and their need to examine the writer's credit worthiness. The elimination of such risk also helps to make options more marketable.

Operationally, the OCC functions through its members. Referred to as *clearing firms*, these members typically are brokerage firms that are members of the exchange. Each one maintains an account with the OCC, records and keeps track of the positions for each option buyer and seller the OCC places with it, maintains all margin positions, and contributes to the special fund used to guarantee assignment.

2.2.6   Summary

Brokers and dealers, combined with the option exchanges and the Option Clearing Corporation, create a network whereby investors in almost any part of the world can be linked to buy and sell options. It is a sophisticated system. However, for most investors the procedures for buying and selling options, as with most securities, is quite simple. It usually takes a phone call to a local broker or a local division of a national brokerage firm. In many cases the investor is then assigned an account executive who usually sets up an account (like a checking account) in which the investor can deposit cash when options and other securities are purchased or receive credits or proceeds when options are sold. Once the account is set up, all an investor needs to do to buy or sell an option or any security is to call his account executive.

2.3   TYPES OF TRADES AND ORDERS

Investors can make four types of trades on the option market: opening, expiring, exercising, and closing transactions.

2.3.1   Opening Transactions

The *opening transaction* occurs when investors initially buy or sell an option. An investor would buy or sell an option through her broker, who, if he is a member of the exchange, would execute the order, or if not a member, would use one of his correspondent brokerage firms that is a member.

In making an opening transaction, the investor can instruct her broker to execute either: (1) a *market order* to buy or sell the option at the best price as soon as the order reaches the market; (2) a *market nonheld* or *not-held order*, which gives the broker the right to use his own discretion in executing the order; (3) a *limit order*, which specifies the maximum price the broker can pay when buying an option or the minimum he can accept when selling an option (a limit order, in turn, can be either a *good-till-canceled order*, which is a limit order that stays in effect until either the investor cancels it or the option expires, or a *day order*, which is only in effect for the duration of the day); (4) a *stop-loss order*, which requires that the broker execute a market order once the option hits a specific price; (5) a *stop-limit order*, which instructs the broker to execute a limit order when the option hits a specific price; or (6) a *market-on-close order*, which requires that the order be executed at or near the close of trading for the day.

In addition to instructing the broker as to the type of order, the investor also needs to tell her broker the number of options she wants to trade. For large orders in which the option investor wants multiple contracts (e.g., a market order to buy 20 option contracts), it is possible the market maker or specialist would fill only part of the order at a market price, or perhaps fill the entire order but at a lower price. Given this possibility, an investor also can instruct her broker to make the order either an *all-or-none order*, which tells the broker to execute the order in its entirety or not at all but allows for different prices; an *all-or-none, same-price order*, which instructs the broker to fill the entire order at the same price or not all; or an *all-or-none order* with a stipulation that the order be canceled if the entire order cannot be executed when it is initially introduced to the market.

2.3.2   Expiring Transactions

A second type of option trade (the *expiring transaction*) involves allowing the option to expire, that is, doing nothing when the expiration date arrives. A holder of an option has the right to buy or sell the stock, but has no obligation to do so. Thus, if an investor buys an "ABC 50 call," he would lose money if the option were exercised when the price of ABC stock was at $50 or below: Hence, the investor would allow the option to expire. Moreover, the value of the call would be zero when its exercise price is above the market value of the stock at expiration. In contrast, a put holder would not exercise when the stock price exceeds the exercise price. The put's value in this case would be zero at expiration, and the holder would allow the put to expire.

2.3.3   Exercising Transactions

The third type of trade available to the option holder is the exercise, or *exercising transaction*. Most options on the CBOE and other exchanges offering options can be exercised at any time during the exercise period. To exercise, a holder of a stock option first notifies his broker, who, in turn, gives the investor's instructions to the clearing firm of the OCC where the initial trade was cleared. The clearing firm then notifies the OCC who, after examining its records, randomly selects a clearing firm that has a short position in the option being exercised. Upon notification from the OCC, the assigned clearing firm then randomly selects one of the brokerage firms on its account with a short position in the option. Finally, the assigned brokerage firm selects one of its customers who is short in the stock option (either on a first-in/first-out basis or randomly). The assigned writer must then fulfill the terms of the option: selling the called stock at the exercise price, or, in the case of a put, buying the stock at the strike price. The holder who exercises a call then can keep the stock or notify his broker to sell it in the stock market; the holder who exercises a put would instruct his broker to purchase the stock in the market and then give an exercise order on the put.

It should be noted that option holders who exercise and writers who are assigned are charged a stock commission cost, since their trades involve the purchase and sale of stock in terms of the option contract and possibly later in the stock market (commission costs are discussed in Section 2.4). Such costs can be relatively high. It also should be noted that most brokerage firms stipulate in their contracts with option investors that if the investor is remiss in exercising or closing a profitable option by expiration, they will exercise (not close) the option for her. If the brokerage contract is silent on this point, however, and if at expiration the holder forgets or fails to exercise, the OCC automatically will exercise the option if it is profitable for it to do so. In fact, one of the reasons for choosing Saturday as the expiration date is that it gives the OCC an opportunity to review its records to determine which contracts to exercise automatically and to whom they should be assigned.*

2.3.4   Closing Transactions

The fourth type of trade available is a *closing transaction*, or offsetting order. Instead of exercising, an option holder could close his position by selling the option in the market, and an option writer, instead of being assigned, could close by buying the option. In each case, the holder or writer would instruct his broker to execute one of the six types of orders already noted in discussing opening transactions. If Mr. A bought an ABC July 50 call at $3 when ABC stock was

---

*As a matter of policy, the OCC exercises stock options owned by individuals in which the price of the stock exceeds the exercise price by at least ¾ point and for options owned by institutions in which the difference is ¼ point.

trading at $48 and wanted to close his transaction near expiration when the stock hit $60, he could do so by selling the call. If he sold, it should trade at a price at least equal to the difference between the underlying stock price and the exercise price ($60 − $50). Thus, he should be able to sell it for at least $10 per call and realize a profit of at least $700 [($10 − $3)100], or $7 per call. If there is some time to expiration, the holder will be able to sell the call with a time value premium (TVP).

Similarly, if Ms. B sold an ABC 50 call at $10 when the stock was trading at $58, and near expiration the stock went to $53, then she could close by buying the call at a price at least equal to $3 per call. If she does close her transaction by buying the call back at $3, then she will realize a profit of $700. Again, if there is some time to expiration, then the cost of buying back the call will be higher, since the call will include a TVP. As we noted previously in discussing the function of the OCC, the writer, by buying the contract, technically is closing, since the OCC record of the writer's assignment obligation is erased as a result of the creation of his exercise right resulting from the purchase. To close put positions would, of course, be similar to calls, except that the holder would hope to sell when the stock price moved down, and the writer would hope to buy back his put when the stock traded up.

In discussing closing transactions, it should be emphasized that it is usually advantageous for an option holder to sell the option instead of exercising, since the selling price includes a TVP, whereas exercising does not. Also, exercising incurs higher commission costs than closing. For these reasons most options that are traded in the market are closed rather than exercised.

Since many options are closed, the amount of trading, and thus the marketability of a particular option, can be determined by ascertaining the number of option contracts that are outstanding at a given point in time. The number of option contracts outstanding is referred to as *open interest*. Thus, in terms of closing transactions, open interest represents the number of closing transactions on an option that could be made before it expires. The exchange, in turn, keeps track of the amount of opening and closing transactions that occur. For example, an opening order to buy five calls would increase open interest by 5, and a closing order to sell five calls would lower open interest by 5. By following the open interest presented in several financial papers, investors can determine the amount of activity on an option.

2.4 MARGINS, TRANSACTION COSTS, AND TAXES

2.4.1 Margins on Option Positions

With the right to buy or sell securities, call and put holders need some assurance that if they decide to exercise, the writer will be able to deliver the stock (if it's a call) or cash (if it's a put). As noted in Section 2.2.5, the OCC provides this guarantee. Like option holders, the OCC also needs to know that any writer they assign to an exercised option can deliver. Accordingly, to provide assurance to the OCC, the option exchanges set margin requirements on short option positions, requirements that brokerage firms are allowed to increase. The requirements specify an initial amount of cash or risk-free securities a writer must deposit in an account with the broker (***initial margin***) and the value of the account that must be maintained (***maintenance margin***). The cash or risk-free securities deposited is used to secure the position; it does not represent borrowing. This is different than purchasing stock on margin. A stock margin purchase means that part of the purchase is financed by borrowing (see Appendix B for a discussion on margins on stock position). In fact, all option purchases, whether they involve calls or puts, must be paid for in full; margin purchases are not allowed in option buying. The reason for this rule is that the risk associated with call or put purchases is equivalent to the risk of buying securities on margin.

Naked Short Positions

For a naked call write, the initial margin requirement is the maximum of either: (1) the call premium plus 20% of the market value of the stock, less an amount equal to the difference in the exercise value and the stock value if the call is out of the money, or (2) the call premium plus 10% of the market value of the stock. Mathematically, for a written call on a stock, the initial margin requirement (M_0) is:

$$M_0 = (\text{Max}\{[C_0 + .20S_0 - \text{Max}(X - S_0, 0)], [C_0 + .10S_0]\})N,$$

where:

N = number of calls.

If a writer sells an ABC 50 call contract for $3 when ABC is selling for $48, then the initial margin requirement would be $1060. That is:

$$M_0 = (\text{Max}\{[\$3 + .20(\$48) - \text{Max}(\$50 - \$48, 0)],$$
$$[\$3 + .10(\$48)]\})100$$

$$M_0 = [\text{Max}(\$10.60, \$7.80)]100 = \$1060.$$

The writer would therefore have to have $1060 in cash in his margin account with the brokerage firm. Since part of the cash comes from the $300 premium received from the option sale, the writer needs to deposit only $760 cash in his margin account.

The margin requirements for a naked put are similar to that for the call. The only difference is that in calculating the first value, the exercise price is subtracted from the stock price, if the put is out of the money. Thus, for a naked put on a stock, the initial margin requirement is:

$$M_0 = (\text{Max}\{[P_0 + .20S_0 - \text{Max}(S_0 - X, 0)], [P_0 + .10S_0]\})N.$$

If a writer sells an ABC 50 put contract for $4 when the stock is trading for $49, then the initial margin would be $1380:

$$M_0 = (\text{Max}\{[\$4 + .20(\$49) - 0], [\$4 + .10(\$49)]\})100$$

$$M_0 = [\text{Max}(\$13.80, \$8.90)]100 = \$1380.$$

With the premium proceeds of $400, the writer would need to deposit $980 to satisfy the initial margin requirement.

The maintenance margin requirement on naked option write positions are the same as the initial margin requirements. In the preceding naked call example, if the closing price on ABC stock later increased from $48 to $50 while the call price stayed at $3, the investor's margin at the new price would increase from $1060 to $1300:

$$M_0 = (\text{Max}\{[\$3 + .20(\$50) - 0], [\$3 + .10(\$50)]\})100$$

$$M_0 = [\text{Max}([\$13, \$8)]100 = \$1300.$$

The writer would therefore have to deposit an additional $240 in his margin account or close the option position by buying the ABC 50 call. In contrast, if the price decreased, the call writer's margin requirement would decrease, and the writer could withdraw some cash from his margin account. Similar situations would exist for the put writer: If the price of the underlying security decreased, additional cash would be needed to maintain the margin requirement; if the security increased in price, cash could be withdrawn.

Covered Short Positions

In a covered call write position, the writer does not need to maintain a margin account, since she owns the underlying stock. The writer is required, however, either to keep the stock in escrow at the brokerage firm or, if the stock is held at the writer's bank, to have the bank (for a fee) issue an *Escrow Receipt*, which is a letter of guarantee from the bank to the brokerage firm stating it will deliver the writer's stock should there be an assignment.* If the option expires or if the writer closes the position, she can have access to the stock.

In setting up a covered call write position, the writer can purchase the stock on margin (i.e., borrow to finance part of the purchase). In this case, the margin requirements on the leveraged security are the same as the requirements for any margin purchase, provided the call option the writer is selling has an exercise price below or equal to the security's price (i.e., the call is an out-of-the-money or on-the-money option). However, if the writer sells a call when the underlying stock price is above the exercise price (in-the-money call), she can borrow only an amount equal to 50% of the exercise price (not the stock's price) to finance the purchase of the stock. In both cases, the writer can include the proceeds from the option sale as part of her margin.

By way of example, suppose a writer sells an ABC 45 call for $7 when ABC stock is trading at $50 and then covers the position by purchasing the stock on margin. Since the stock price exceeds the exercise, the maximum amount of funds the writer can borrow would be (.5)($45) = $22.50. Since the call premium of $7 can be used to satisfy the margin requirement, the writer would need to deposit in her margin account only ($50.00 − $22.50) − $7 = $20.50.

---

*If the writer's stock is deposited at a bank that is a member of the Depository Trust Corporation, then the bank can guarantee the OCC directly that it will deliver the stock should there be an assignment notice.

For a covered put position in which the writer has sold a put and the underlying stock short, the brokerage house generally requires the covered writer to maintain the usual margin requirements on a short sale. However, analogous to the rule for a margined covered call, if the price of the stock is below the exercise price when the put is sold (i.e., the put is in the money), the writer then is required to deposit additional cash in her margin account for the short sale equal to the difference in the exercise and security price $(X - S)$.

Spreads

Recall from Chapter 1 that a spread is formed by buying a call (put) and selling another call (put) with different terms. With a spread, the short option position is considered covered by the long option. As a result, the margin requirements on the short position are not as large as a naked option write position. While spreads with different times to expiration and spreads with both different exercise prices and different expirations are treated differently, as a general rule, if the spread results in a debit, the spreader must deposit the net cost of the spread in his margin account; if the spread results in a credit, the spreader must deposit the difference between the exercise prices.

Summary

Given the number of margin rules that apply to both securities and options, as well as the number of possible strategies that exist from combining different security and option positions, the calculations of margins for option positions can become quite complex. The calculations we have discussed provide a general approach that can be applied to many of the other option positions. Investors considering more complex option position (spreads, straddles, combinations, and the like), though, should consult their brokers on what their possible margin requirements could be.

2.4.2   Cost of Trading

Through the option exchanges, brokers, dealers, market makers, specialists, and the OCC have created a network whereby an investor can buy and sell options in a matter of minutes simply by calling her broker. The cost of maintaining this complex system is paid for by investors through the commission costs they pay to their brokers, through the bid-ask spread investors pay to market makers or specialists when they set up and then later close their positions, and through the fees charged by the clearing firms of the OCC that are usually included in the brokerage commission and paid by their brokers.

Commissions

In accordance with the Security Act Amendment of 1975, commissions on all security transactions are negotiable between the investor and the broker. For stocks involving a medium-size trade, the commission costs range from approximately 1% of the total stock value for discount brokerage firms, which provide basically trade execution, to 2% for full brokerage firms, which provide current quotes, research reports, account executives, and other ancillary services. For institutional investors who trade in larger volumes, the percentages typically are lower.

The commission costs for trading options historically have been higher than those for stock trading. As an example, a hypothetical but representative stock option commission schedule applicable to an individual investor is shown in Table 2.4-1. If an investor buys or sells one ABC 50 call contract for $2.50, then from Table 2.4-1 his total premium, commission costs, and minimum commission cost would be:

$$\text{Premium} = (\$2.50)(100) = \$250.$$

$$\text{Commission cost} = (.015)(\$250) + \$21 = \$24.75.$$

$$\text{Minimum commission cost} = \$30.$$

Thus, in this case the investor would be charged the minimum commission of $30. If the investor bought ten ABC 50 contracts for $2.50 per contract then his premium, commission costs, and minimum and maximum charges would be:

$$\text{Premium} = (\$2.50)(100)(10) = \$2500.$$

$$\text{Commission cost} = (.01)(\$2500) + \$36 = \$61.$$

$$\text{Minimum commission cost} = (\$30)(1) + (\$1.50)(9) = \$43.50.$$

$$\text{Maximum commission cost} = (\$30)(5) + (\$20)(5) = \$250.$$

In this case he would pay the broker $61 in commission costs for executing the trade, unless they could negotiate a better rate.

In the first case the commission costs are equal to 12% of the option value, and in the second example the commissions are equal to 2.44%. To the extent that the schedule is representative of the fees charged by most brokerage firms, these commission costs are relatively high when compared to the 1%–2% commissions associated with stock trading.

The option buyer pays a commission when he buys the option and when he sells the option. In the first example, the total round-trip cost of buying and selling an option would therefore be $60. Similarly, the option writer pays a commission

TABLE 2.4-1

Sample Commission Cost Schedule	
TRANSACTION VALUE	COMMISSION RATE
Under $2500 $2500–$9999 $10,000 and over	$21 + .015 (transaction value) $36 + .01 (transaction value) $84 + .0025 (transaction value)
Minimum charge Maximum charge	$30 for the first contract, plus $1.50 per contract thereafter $30 per contract on the first five contracts, plus $20 per contract thereafter

when he sells and again later if he closes by buying the option. Usually, no brokerage fee is charged if the option expires.

If the option holder exercises, he is charged a commission for buying (calling) or selling (putting) the stock. Since the call (put) holder in exercising would eventually (initially) sell (buy) the stock, the total commission costs to exercise an option instead of closing it are relatively high. For example, suppose an investor bought an ABC 50 call contract for $3 when the stock was trading at $49, then, near the expiration date, exercised the call when the stock was at $60, subsequently selling the stock in the market. The investor's before-commission cost profit would be ($10 − $3)100 = $700. If the broker charges the same commission rate of 1% for exercising as he does for stock trading, and if the broker charges the rates specified in Table 2.4-1 for trading options, then the investor's total commission costs would be $140. That is:

Commissions for:	
Option Purchase	$ 30
Exercise ($50)(100)(.01)	50
Stock Sale ($60)(100)(.01)	60
Total	$140

On the other hand, if near expiration the call holder sells the ABC 50 call for $10, the before-commission costs profit still would be $700, but the commission costs would be only $66 instead of $140: $30 for the purchase, plus (.015)($10)(100) + $21 = $36 for the sale. Thus, as we emphasized earlier, because of the commission costs associated with exercising (as well as the time value premium), it usually is preferable to close an option instead of exercising.

For the same reason, an option writer always should want to avoid being assigned. Like an exercise, a call or put writer who is assigned must buy or sell the stock, and as a result is charged a stock commission cost. Since the writer does not control this situation, it is important that he be cognizant of those circumstances when a call holder would exercise. Such circumstances will be noted in subsequent chapters.

Fees

Part of the commission fees investors pay their brokers goes to cover the fees charged by the clearing firms of the OCC for handling, recording, and intermediating option transactions. These fees range from $0.50 to $1.00 per contract. The OCC also imposes fees on market makers or specialists and other members for clearing their transactions. The fees are lower than those charged commission brokers handling the public's transactions.

Bid-Ask Spread

The market maker's and specialist's primary function is to ensure a continuous market. To do this, they stand ready to buy and sell securities at their bid and ask prices. The bid-ask spread thus represents their compensation for providing liquidity. To the investor, though, the bid-ask spread represents another transaction cost involved in trading securities. For example, if a market maker's bid price is $4 and her ask price is $4.50, an option buyer who paid $4.50 for the option, then immediately sold it for $4.00, would be paying the market maker $0.50 for the services of providing a continuous market.

In summary, we reiterate that while the transaction costs of trading options may seem high, such costs are necessary to provide a continuous market that can link buyers and sellers across the world. Whether the trading costs are too high is difficult to determine. The fact that commissions are negotiable and brokers are competitive suggests that brokerage fees probably are priced efficiently.

2.4.3 Taxes

An investor's dollar return from an option position takes the form of a capital gain or loss. With the passage of the Tax Reform Act of 1986, an individual investor aggregates all her capital gains and losses from all assets (including options) that are liquidated for the year, to obtain a net capital gain or net capital loss figure. A net capital gain is taxed as ordinary income. A net capital loss less than or equal to $3000 is deducted from the investor's ordinary income; all net losses exceeding $3000 can be deducted from income in future years, with a $3000 cap per year. Based on the Tax Reform Act there are two different schedules of tax rates: one for single taxpayers and one for married taxpayers filing jointly.

Taxable gains and losses result for option buyers when they sell their options to close, when they sell stock from an exercised call, when they exercise a put, and when their options expire. For option writers, gains and losses occur when writers buy back their options to close, when they sell securities on an assigned call option, when they sell the securities obtained from an exercised put option that they have been assigned, and when the option expires.

For example, suppose an investor buys an ABC 50 call contract for $3 and then near expiration sells the call for $10 when the stock is trading for $60. The call buyer would therefore have a capital gain of $7, and if she were in the 28% income tax bracket, for that investment her tax per option would be $(.28)(\$7) = \$1.96$. Alternatively, if the call buyer exercised the ABC 50 call, then she would be considered as having bought the stock for a purchase price equal to the exercise price plus the call premium $(X + C)$. If the investor subsequently sells the stock in the market at $60, then a capital gain is realized, and the investor is subject to a tax. It should be noted that for exercised stock options, taxes apply to the gains or losses *when they are realized*. Thus, if the investor held onto the exercised stock for two years, then sold it for $40, she would have a capital loss of $\$40 - \$53 = \$13$ to apply to her tax calculations for the year in which the sale was realized. Finally, if the option expires at the end of the period, then the option holder would have a capital loss equal to the option premium, $3 in this example.

Similar tax considerations apply to a put holder. Capital gains or losses resulting from buying a put and then selling it and capital losses (equal to the premium) resulting if the put expires must be included with all asset gains and losses in determining the taxpayer's net capital gain or loss position. Unlike the long call position, if a put holder exercises, the gain or loss is realized at the time of the exercise, since the put holder is selling. In this case, the selling price of the stock is the exercise price minus the put premium $(X - P)$. For example, if a put holder bought an ABC 50 put for $3, then later bought the stock at $40 and exercised the put, her capital gain would be ($50 − $3) − $40 = $7; her tax on that investment, given a 28% tax bracket, would be (.28)($7) = $1.96.

For writers, if a call or put writer closes her position by buying back the option, then for tax purposes there is a capital gain or loss equal to the difference between the selling price when the option was sold and the purchase price when it is later closed (the order of transaction is not important). For example, if a put writer sells an ABC 50 put for $3 and then later closes the position by buying back the ABC 50 put for $10 when the stock is trading at $40, there would be a $7 gain the investor would need to include in her total capital gain and loss calculations.

Call and put writers also are subject to a tax on the option premium when the option expires. In the case of an assignment for a call writer, a capital loss is realized at the time of the exercise. To the assigned call writer, the loss is equal to the difference between the exercise price minus the call premium $(X − C)$ (the sale price) and the price the writer pays for the securities in the market. When a put writer is assigned, the exercise price she pays the option buyer who is exercising minus the put premium she receives from the put sale represents the purchase price on the security. A capital loss or possibly a gain, though, is not realized for most put options until the assigned writer sells the stock, which could be years later.

In discussing taxes on options, several additional points should be noted. First, commission costs are tax deductible. In computing the capital gains or losses, the commission paid when buying an option is added to the purchase price; when selling an option, the commission is subtracted from the selling price.

Second, while stock options, are subject to taxes or deductions only when the capital gain or loss is realized, the same treatment does not apply to index, debt, and foreign currency options. Specifically, in accordance with tax rules, all realized and unrealized capital gains resulting from many nonstock option positions must be included in the investor's calculations of her net capital gains or losses for the year in which they are initiated. Capital losses are deductible from nonstock option positions, though, in the year in which they are realized. For example, if an investor realized a profit of $1000 in 1993 from buying and selling a call option on the yen and also had a call option on the Canadian dollar that she had paid $1000 for during the year and that was worth $2000 at the end of the year, the investor would be subject to taxes on the $1000 realized gain on the yen option and also the $1000 unrealized gain on the Canadian dollar option.

Third, the tax laws disallow the deduction of capital losses in the case of a wash sale in which the security is sold at a loss at the end of the year but replaced shortly afterwards with basically the same security. Under the tax rules, the purchase of a call option 30 days before or after the option's underlying stock has been sold for tax purposes at a loss constitutes a wash sale, making the loss nondeductible.* While call purchases in conjunction with the underlying security's sale represent a wash sale, an investor can buy a put option to protect a capital gain in a given year while deferring tax payments until the subsequent year. For example, an investor who wanted to sell her stock in December to realize a gain but did not want to pay

---

*It should be noted that many brokerage firms provide a list of stocks that are similar so that investors can sell a stock and purchase a similar stock, thereby being able to realize a tax deduction while still having the same type of security in their portfolio.

taxes for that year could delay taxes a year and protect her position by buying an on-the-money January put option on the stock.

Finally, it should be noted that tax laws are quite detailed and always changing. As such, current regulations always should be checked. The material given in this section, in turn, should be considered only as an overview aimed at giving the reader a perspective, but not as providing instructions for tax preparation.

2.5   CONCLUSION

In this chapter we've examined the characteristics of the option exchange market, where the majority of puts and calls are traded, and we've discussed the margin requirements, transactions costs, and taxes involved in trading options. With this foundation we are now ready to expand our treatment of options by looking at the many sophisticated positions that can be created with these claims.

KEY TERMS

marketability	opening transaction
open outcry	expiring transaction
specialist	exercising transaction
market maker	closing transaction
Registered Option Traders	initial margin
Order Book Official	maintenance margin
Option Clearing Corporation	

SELECTED REFERENCES

Chance, Don M. *An Introduction to Options and Futures*. Fort Worth, Tex.: Dryden Press, 1991, ch. 1.

Chicago Board Options Exchange. *Reference Manual*. Chicago: Chicago Board Options Exchange, 1982.

———. *Market Statistics 1990*. Chicago: Chicago Board Options Exchange, 1990.

Chicago Board Options Exchange and Options Clearing Corporation. *Constitution and Rules*. Chicago: Commerce Clearing House, 1985.

Cox, John C., and Rubinstein, Mark. *Options Markets*. Englewood Cliffs, N.J.: Prentice-Hall, 1985, chs. 1, 3.

Gastineau, Gary. *The Stock Options Manual*. New York: McGraw-Hill, 1988.

Kramer, Andrea S. *Taxation of Securities, Commodities, and Options*. New York: Wiley, 1987.

Russo, T. *Regulation of the Commodities Futures and Options Markets*. New York: McGraw-Hill, 1983.

Strong, Robert A. *Speculative Markets*. New York: Harper-Collins, 1994, pp. 92–93.

Tucker, Alan L. *Financial Futures, Options, and Swaps*. St. Paul, Minn.: West, 1991, ch. 11.

PROBLEMS AND QUESTIONS

1. What are the purpose and functions of the market maker and the specialist on the option exchanges? What is the difference between them?

2. Describe the role and functions of the Option Clearing Corporation.

3. Suppose in February Ms. X sold a June ABC 100 call contract to Mr. Z for $5, then later closed her position by buying a June ABC 100 call contract for $7 from Mr. Y. How would the OCC handle these contracts?

4. Describe the various types of option transactions.

5. What adjustments in the option contracts would the option exchanges undertake for the following cases?

   a. An ABC 50 call contract with the ABC company declaring a three-for-two stock split.

   b. An ABC 50 put with the ABC company declaring a 5% stock dividend.

   c. An ABC 50 call with the ABC company declaring a $10 cash dividend.

6. How have the organized exchanges contributed to the growth of option trading?

7. Determine the initial margin requirements you would have if you were to sell a December ABC 60 call for $5 when ABC stock is trading at $58. How much cash would you have to deposit with your broker to satisfy your margin requirement? How much additional cash would you need to deposit if the maintenance margin requirement is the same as the initial requirement and the price of ABC stock increased to $62 and the price of the 60 call option rose to $6?

8. What would your initial margin be if you sold a June ABC 40 put for $4 when the price of ABC stock was trading at $38? How much cash would you have to deposit with your broker? How much additional cash would you need to deposit if the maintenance margin requirement is the same as the initial requirement and the price of ABC stock decreased to $36 and the price of the 40 put option increased to $6.50?

9. How much margin would an investor be required to deposit in order to secure a covered call write formed by selling an ABC 50 call contract at $2 and purchasing 100 shares of ABC stock at $48 per share on margin? Assume an initial margin requirement on the stock purchase of .6. How much margin would be required on the covered call write if the investor sells an ABC 45 call contract at $5 per call instead of the ABC 50? (Part of this problem is based on information about margins on stock positions that is presented in Appendix B.)

10. How much margin would an investor be required to deposit in order to secure a covered put write formed by selling an XYZ 100 put contract at $5 and selling 100 shares of XYZ stock short at $100 per share? Assume an initial

margin requirement on the short sale of .6. How much margin would be required on the covered put write if the investor sold an XYZ 110 put contract at $12 per put instead of the XYZ 100 put? (This problem is based on information about margins on stock positions that is presented in Appendix B.)

11. Using the commission schedule in Table 2.4-1, compute the commission costs on the following transactions:

   a. An ABC 80 call contract priced at $4 per call.
   b. Ten ABC 50 put contracts priced at $5 per put.
   c. Thirty XYZ 100 call contracts priced at $5 per call.

12. Using a personal tax rate of 28%, determine the capital gain or loss and the tax liability for the following cases:

   a. The sale of an ABC March 50 put contract for $3 per put, closed one month later at $2 per put.
   b. The purchase of an ABC December 50 call contract for $3 per call, exercised in December with the exercised stock sold six months later at $56 per share.
   c. The purchase of an ABC 50 call contract at $3 per call, later sold at $1 per call when the stock was trading at $49 per share.
   d. The purchase of an ABC June 50 put at $2 per put, exercised when the stock was trading at $45 per share.

CHAPTER 3

Option Strategies

In Chapter 1, we defined the six fundamental option strategies and the straddle and spread in terms of their profit and stock price relationships near expiration. In this chapter we extend that discussion to a more detailed analysis of those strategies and introduce some new strategies.

3.1 CALL PURCHASE

The call purchase is one of the more popular option strategies. It often is viewed by investors as a leveraged alternative to purchasing stock. As discussed in Chapter 1, compared to a long stock position, the purchase of a call yields higher expected returns, but like buying stock on margin, it also is more risky. For example, as shown in Figure 3.1-1, the stock purchased at $50 yields only a 20% rate of return (excluding any dividends) when its price reaches $60, while a 50 call option with a premium of $3 yields a rate of return of ($10 − $3)/$3 = 233% when exercised or sold at its intrinsic value of $10 at expiration. In contrast, if the stock decreased to $40 (near expiration), then the loss on the stock would be 20%, compared to a 100% loss on the call. Thus, like a leveraged stock purchase, a long call position yields a higher return-risk combination than a stock purchase.

In addition to providing investors with a short-run alternative to a long stock position, call purchases also can be used by investors as a way to purchase stock when they are temporarily illiquid. For example, suppose an investor has funds tied up in illiquid securities at a time when he wanted to buy the stock of a company that is expected to release unexpectedly good earnings information. The investor could acquire the stock first by buying a call option on it, then, after becoming liquid, exercising the option.

FIGURE 3.1-1

Call and Stock Purchase Profit Graphs

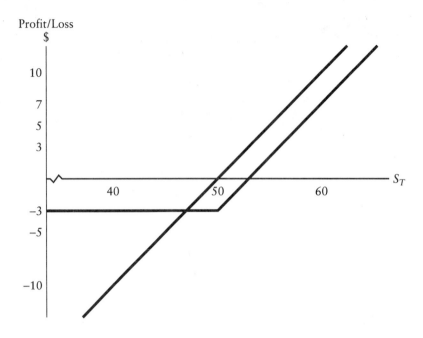

3.1.1 Follow-up Strategies*

A call purchase position is used when the price of the stock is expected to increase in the short run. Expected stock increases could be based on fundamental factors such as an anticipated increase in a company's earnings, technical factors related to stock price movements, or market factors such as an expectation of future national economic growth. Whatever the reason, once you have selected a call option, you must monitor the position and determine what to do with the option if the price of the stock changes differently than expected. Strategies used after setting up an initial option position are known as *follow-up strategies*. These strategies, in turn, can be classified as either aggressive follow-up strategies, used when the price of the stock moves to a profitable position, or defensive follow-up strategies, employed when the stock price moves to an actual or potentially unprofitable position.

Aggressive Follow-up Strategies

To see the types of aggressive strategies you can use, consider the case of an investor who, in October, buys an ABC December 60 call contract for $3 per call when the stock is trading at $58. Furthermore, suppose that shortly after buying the call, the price of ABC stock unexpectedly increases to $68, causing the 60 call to increase to $9. Faced with this positive development, the call investor has a number of alternatives open to her.

First, the investor could liquidate by selling the 60 call for $9, realizing a profit of $600. The advantage of liquidating is certainty: The investor knows that even

---

*The discussions of follow-up strategies in this chapter are based on Lawrence McMillan's (1986) presentation of option management. See Selected References.

if the price of ABC stock declines, she will still earn $600. The disadvantage of liquidating, of course, is the opportunity loss if the stock increases in price.

If the investor strongly feels that the stock will continue to rise, then a second follow-up strategy is simply to do nothing. As shown in column 3 in Table 3.1-1, if the stock reaches $80 at expiration ($T$) then the investor would realize a profit of $1700 by selling the call at a price equal to its intrinsic value of $20, $1100 more than if she had liquidated. Of course, if the price of the stock decreases after reaching $68 and moves to $60 or less, then the investor loses the premium of $300 and will regret not liquidating the call back when the stock was at $68.

If the call purchaser wants to gain more than just $600, in case the stock continues to rise, but does not want to lose if the stock declines, she could follow up the call purchase strategy by creating a spread. As discussed in Chapter 1, a call spread is formed by buying and selling a call option simultaneously on the same stock, but with different terms. In the case of aggressive follow-up strategies, a spread often is created by selling a call with a higher exercise price. In our example, suppose the investor sells an ABC December 70 call for $3 when the stock is at $68. As shown in column 4 of Table 3.1-1, at expiration the investor would realize a limited profit of $1000 if the price of ABC stock were $70 or above and would break even if the stock fell to $60 or less. Thus, the spread would yield more profit than the liquidating strategy if the stock price were to increase, and would lose less than the do-nothing strategy if the stock price were to fall.

If, after the price of the stock reaches $68, the expectation is that the price will continue to rise, then you might want to consider a roll-up follow-up

TABLE 3.1-1

				Aggressive Follow-up Actions: Profit at Expiration		

				Actions on a 60 call bought at $3 and now trading at $9 when the stock is at $68		

(1)	(2)	(3)	(4)	(5) ROLL-UP SELL 60 CALL AT $9, BUY THREE 70 CALLS AT $3 EACH	(6) ROLL-UP SELL 60 CALL AT $9, BUY TWO 70 CALLS AT $3 EACH	(7) COMBINATION KEEP 60 CALL, BUY 70 PUT AT $3
S_T	LIQUIDATE SELL 60 CALL AT $9	DO NOTHING	SPREAD SELL 70 CALL AT $3			
$50	$600	− $ 300	$ 0	− $ 300	$ 0	$1400
55	600	− 300	0	− 300	0	900
60	600	− 300	0	− 300	0	400
63	600	0	300	− 300	0	400
64	600	100	400	− 300	0	400
65	600	200	500	− 300	0	400
66	600	300	600	− 300	0	400
67	600	400	700	− 300	0	400
70	600	700	1000	− 300	0	400
71	600	800	1000	0	200	500
75	600	1200	1000	1200	1000	900
80	600	1700	1000	2700	2000	1400
85	600	2200	1000	4200	3000	1900

strategy. As the name implies, a roll-up strategy requires moving to a higher exercise price. This can be accomplished in several ways. For example, our investor could sell the 60 call and use all of the $900 proceeds to buy three December 70 calls at $3. As shown in column 5 of Table 3.1-1, this roll-up strategy would provide the investor with a relatively substantial gain near expiration if the stock were to increase in price, but also would engender losses if the stock were to decline. To minimize the range in potential profits and losses, the investor alternatively could implement a roll-up strategy by selling the 60 call and then using only $600 of the $900 profit to buy two 70 calls. The profit and stock price relation for the initial call purchase with this follow-up strategy is shown in column 6. As can be seen, the investor has the initial investment covered if the stock decreases and will gain if the price rises, but not by as much as the first roll-up strategy.

Finally, the call purchaser could set up a combination as a follow-up strategy. A combination purchase is defined as a long position in a call and a put on the same stock with different terms. For aggressive follow-up strategies, a combination could be formed by buying a put with a higher exercise price. The impact of this combination strategy is shown in column 7 for the case in which our investor buys an ABC December 70 put for $3.

Defensive Follow-up Strategies

If, after purchasing a call, the price of the stock decreases, the investor then needs to consider defensive follow-up strategies. With some modifications, defensive follow-up strategies are similar to aggressive ones. The investor could either: liquidate, hoping to minimize his losses by selling the call at a price reflecting a time value premium; do nothing, hoping that the price decrease is only temporary; or create a spread or roll-down to a lower exercise price, hoping to profit if the stock price changes moderately.

In our example, suppose that after the investor purchased the 60 call for $3, the stock decreased to $55, causing the premium on the 60 call to drop to $1.50. As shown in Table 3.1-2, if the holder liquidated, she would realize a loss of $150, compared to a $300 loss if she did nothing and the price of the stock stayed below the exercise price near expiration. In contrast to the do-nothing strategy, liquidating does eliminate potential profit if the stock price reverses itself. If the investor thinks, however, that the price decline is a signal of further price decreases, she could create a spread and possibly realize a profit (if the stock falls). As shown in column 4, if the holder combined the long position in the 60 call with a short position in a 50 call trading for $7, the investor would earn a limited profit of $400 if the stock reached $50 or less. However, if after hitting $55, the stock increases to $60 or higher, the investor would lose $600. Finally, if the holder felt that the stock would move back up but only modestly, she could create a roll-down spread by selling the 60 call plus another 60 call for $1.50 each, then using the $300 from the sale to buy a 55 call for $3. Thus, the investor would be long in a 55 call and short in a 60 call. As shown in column 5, the investor would realize a limited profit of $200 if the stock increased to $60 or higher near expiration with this spread, but would lose $300 if the stock stayed at $55 or decreased.

TABLE 3.1-2

		Defensive Follow-up Actions: Profit at Expiration		

Actions on a 60 call contract bought at $3 and now trading at $1.50 when the stock is at $55

(1)	(2)	(3)	(4)	(5)
	LIQUIDATE SELL 60		SPREAD KEEP 60 CALL AND SELL 50	ROLL-DOWN SPREAD SELL TWO 60 CALLS AT $1.50 EACH AND BUY
S_T	CALL AT $1.50	DO NOTHING	CALL AT $7	55 CALL AT $3
$40	− $150	− $ 300	$400	− $300
45	− 150	− 300	400	− 300
50	− 150	− 300	400	− 300
54	− 150	− 300	0	− 300
55	− 150	− 300	− 100	− 300
58	− 150	− 300	− 400	0
60	− 150	− 300	− 600	200
63	− 150	0	− 600	200
65	− 150	200	− 600	200
70	− 150	700	− 600	200
75	− 150	1200	− 600	200
80	− 150	1700	− 600	200
85	− 150	2200	− 600	200

The defensive strategies shown in Table 3.1-2, as well as the aggressive ones shown in Table 3.1-1, are just some of the follow-ups an investor can use. Spreads or combinations using different expiration dates and/or expiration prices, liquidating only part of the initial strategy, investing more equity in a different call, or selling more than one call are examples of follow-up strategies an investor can employ. Whatever the strategy, though, it is important to remember that there is no optimum; rather, the correct follow-up depends ultimately on where the investor thinks the stock eventually will close, and on how strongly she believes in that forecast.

3.1.2 Call Purchases in Conjunction with Other Positions

Simulated Put

Purchasing a call and selling the underlying stock short on a one-to-one basis yields the same type of profit and stock price relationship as does a put purchase. This strategy is known as a *simulated put*.

In Table 3.1-3, the profit and stock price relation at expiration is shown for an investor who sold 100 shares of ABC stock short at $50 per share and purchased an ABC June 50 call contract at $3. The total profit and stock price relations at expiration are plotted in the table's accompanying figure. As can be seen, the simulated put strategy yields the same relationship as the purchase of a 50 put at $3.

Two strategies with the same profit and stock price relationships are referred to as *equivalent strategies*. Note, however, that while the put purchase and the

TABLE 3.1-3

Simulated Put Formed with Long Call and Short Stock			
{+C, −S}			
S_T	PROFIT ON STOCK SOLD SHORT AT $50 (100 SHARES)	PROFIT ON 50 CALL CONTRACT PURCHASED AT $3	TOTAL PROFIT
$30	$2000	− $ 300	$1700
40	1000	− 300	700
47	300	− 300	0
50	0	− 300	− 300
60	− 1000	700	− 300
70	− 2000	1700	− 300

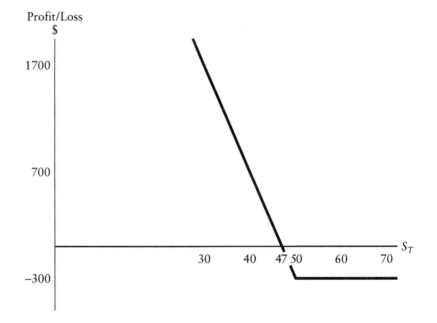

simulated put formed with a long call and short stock position are equivalent in terms of their profit and stock price relations, they are not identical. Given the put-call parity relation discussed in Chapter 1, the equilibrium price of the 50 put is not likely to be $3 when the 50 call is priced at $3. Thus, the short sale and call purchase strategy do not yield an identical long 50 put position. To form an identical long put position with a put price consistent with put-call parity, a synthetic put, requires not only buying the call and shorting the stock, but also buying a bond with a face value equal to the exercise price: $\{+P\} = \{+C, -S, +B\}$. See Table 3.1-4 for an example of the cash flows at expiration from this position.

For short-run investments, the put purchase is a better strategy than a simulated or synthetic put. The simulated put requires the investor to post collateral on the stock shorted, to pay dividends to the share lender if they are declared, and to pay

TABLE 3.1-4

Synthetic Long Put: Value (or Cash Flow) at Expiration				
$\{+P\} = \{+C, -S, +B\}$				
S_T	SHORT STOCK	LONG CALL	LONG BOND	TOTAL VALUE
$30	− $3000	0	$5000	$2000
40	− 4000	0	5000	1000
50	− 5000	0	5000	0
60	− 6000	1000	5000	0
70	− 7000	2000	5000	0

NOTE: If $S_T \geq \$50$, the cash flows from short stock, the call, and the bond add up to 0. If $S_T < \$50$, the maturity value of the bond is more than sufficient to cover the cash outflow on the short position. The total value represents the cash flow from a synthetic put: $Max(0, X - S_T)$.

the higher commission costs. The simulated put, though, is worth keeping in mind. For example, it may be that an investor wants to buy a put on a stock in conjunction with another position (e.g., a call purchase to construct a straddle), but there is no trading on the desired put, either because the exchange has restricted trading on it or the put on the stock is not listed.* In such a case, a simulated put would be a correct strategy.

A simulated put also could be used as a hedge or follow-up strategy for a short sale. For example, an investor who went short in a stock as a long-run strategy might purchase a call to offset potential losses if the price of the stock increased due to an unexpectedly good earnings announcement. Such a strategy would represent an insurance strategy on a short stock position.

Simulated Straddle

The purchase of two calls for each share of stock shorted $\{+2C, -S\}$ yields a strategy equivalent to a straddle purchase. This strategy is called a *simulated straddle*. To illustrate, suppose in our previous example that the investor bought two 50 calls after going short in 100 shares of the stock at $50. As shown in Table 3.1-5 and its accompanying figure, the investor would obtain a V-shaped profit and stock price relation. She would have a limited maximum loss equaled to $600 when the stock price equaled $50, two break-even prices at $44 and $56, and virtually unlimited profit potential if the stock price increased or decreased past the respective upper and lower break-even prices.

Similar to the simulated put, a simulated straddle is less attractive as a short-run investment than its equivalent straddle strategy because of the higher commission costs, required dividend coverage on the short sale, and collateral associated with the short sale. However, like the preceding comparison of the put and the simulated put, the simulated straddle is a strategy worth keeping in mind if a straddle were desired on a stock but a put did not exist, and as a possible follow-up strategy for a short sale.

---

*In the early days of the CBOE, many stocks had calls but no puts.

TABLE 3.1-5

	Simulated Straddle: Profit at Expiration		
$\{2C, -S\}$			
S_T	PROFIT ON SHORT SALE OF STOCK SOLD AT $50 (100 SHARES)	PROFIT ON TWO 50 CALL CONTRACTS PURCHASED AT $3	TOTAL PROFIT
$30	$2000	− $ 600	$1400
40	1000	− 600	400
44	600	− 600	0
50	0	− 600	− 600
56	− 600	600	0
60	− 1000	1400	400
70	− 2000	3400	1400

NOTE: If the stock price remains unchanged at $50, the investor will experience the maximum loss of $600. For a straddle to be profitable, the stock price must surge past $56 or fall below $44.

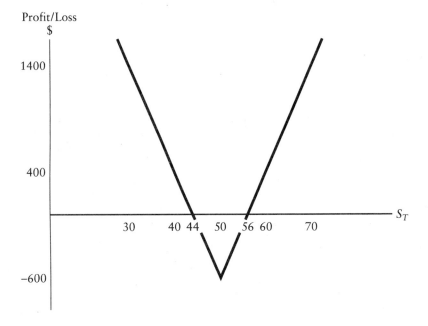

3.2 NAKED CALL WRITE

The second fundamental strategy examined in Chapter 1 was the naked call write. Because of its limited profit and unlimited loss characteristic, this strategy is not very popular among option investors. However, it does have some attractive features. One such feature is that the option loses its time value premium as time passes. For example, if a writer sold a call, he could profit some time later if the price of the stock did not change. That is, the writer would be able to buy back the call at a lower price because of the lower time value premium. Of course, if the stock increased in price, then the writer would lose if the increase in intrinsic value exceeded the decrease in the time value premium.

It should be remembered, however, that in order to establish a naked call write, an investor must post collateral in the form of cash and/or a risk-free instrument as security in the event the call is exercised and he is assigned.

3.2.1   Follow-up Strategies: Rolling Credit

While a naked call write is less attractive than other strategies because of its limited profit and unlimited loss characteristic, one interesting but risky tactical or defensive follow-up strategy that could be used with a naked call write is the ***rolling-credit*** strategy. Under this strategy, if the stock price increases, the naked call writer sells calls with a higher exercise price and then uses the proceeds (or credit) to close the initial short position by buying the call back. This strategy then is repeated every time the stock increases to a new, uncomfortable level. The hope, in turn, is that the stock eventually will stabilize or decrease, and the writer will realize a profit approximately equal to the proceeds from the initial call sale.

For the rolling-credit strategy to work, three conditions must hold: First, the stock price eventually must stop rising. If the stock does not stop, then, with continuous follow-ups, the writer will realize losses when the stock exceeds the break-even price on the option position with the highest possible exercise price. Second, even if the stock eventually stops rising, a rolling-credit writer must have sufficient collateral (the collateral requirements increase exponentially as the stock price increases). Finally, the success of the rolling-credit strategy requires that the writer not be assigned. Since the writer has no control over assignment, he needs to select options that have a small chance of being exercised. A case in which early exercise is advantageous will be discussed in Chapter 4.

In summary, the rolling-credit strategy, on the surface, appears to be a simple strategy, as well as an easy way of making money. However, for the strategy to work, the aforementioned conditions must hold. If they do not, then the rolling-credit writer can incur substantial losses, perhaps more than he initially had been prepared for.

3.2.2   Aggressive Follow-up Strategies

If the stock price stays below the exercise price or decreases, the naked call writer may want to pursue an aggressive follow-up action. Such actions could include: closing the present position and moving to a short position in a call with a lower exercise price; closing the short position and using the proceeds to buy a put if the investor is relatively more bearish; closing and buying a call with a low exercise price if he feels the stock has bottomed out, or simply liquidating the position.

As noted earlier, there is no optimum follow-up strategy but rather a number of strategies available that an investor can use, depending on what price he feels the stock eventually will reach.

3.3 COVERED CALL WRITE

The third fundamental option strategy examined in Chapter 1 was the covered call write, namely: long in the stock and short in the call, $\{+S, -C\}$. This strategy is quite popular among institutional investors, who see it as a way of enhancing the return on a particular stock.

To understand how this works, suppose an investor already owned a stock but that its price was not expected to appreciate in the near term. By writing a call, the investor may be able to increase the total return on the stock. The rate of return on this strategy [over the time interval from the present (0) to expiration (T)] is given by

$$\frac{S_T - S_0 + C_0 - \text{Max}(0, S_T - X)}{S_0},$$

in which C_0 is the call premium and $S_T - S_0$ is the stock price change. Obviously, if the initial expectation turns out to be true ($S_T \leq S_0 = X$), then the return is increased by C/S_0. But, if the expectation is erroneous, any capital gains in the stock will be offset by losses in the call.

As a short-run investment strategy, a covered call write has a lower return-risk tradeoff than a long stock position. This may be seen by comparing columns 2 and 4 in Table 3.3-1. Column 2 shows the profits for each stock price obtained from purchasing 100 shares of ABC stock at $50; column 4 shows the profits for a covered call position formed by purchasing 100 shares of ABC at $50 and selling an ABC 50 call contract at $5. As shown, if at expiration the stock had declined from $50 to $40, the investor would realize a profit of $500 from the call premium, which would offset the $1000 actual (if stock is sold) or paper loss from the stock. If the stock price stayed at $50 or increased beyond it, then the covered call writer would receive a profit of only $500. For example, if the stock were at $60 at expiration, the option would be trading at its intrinsic value of $10. To close the option position, the writer would have to pay $1000 to buy the calls, which would negate the $1000 actual or paper gain he would earn from the stock. Thus, the investor would be left with a profit equal to just the call premium of $500.

3.3.1 Types of Covered Call Writes

All covered writes require selling a call against the stock owned. This strategy, though, can be divided into two general types: an out-of-the-money covered call write and an in-the-money covered call write. The out-of-the-money write yields a higher return-risk tradeoff than the in-the-money write.

For example, suppose, after buying 100 shares of ABC stock for $45 per share, an investor considered forming a covered call write either by selling an in-the-money ABC June 40 call trading at $8 or selling an out-of-the-money ABC June 50 call trading at $1. As shown in Table 3.3-2, if the stock declined to $35 at expiration, then the investor would lose only $200 if she selected the in-the-money call, compared to losing $900 if she had selected the out-of-the-money call. Similarly, at $40 the investor would receive a profit of $300 from the covered call write strategy with the 40 call, compared to a loss of $400 from the 50 call. Thus,

TABLE 3.3-1

	Covered Call Write: Profit at Expiration		
(1)	(2)	(3)	(4)
	PROFIT FROM STOCK	PROFIT FROM THE	PROFIT FROM
	BOUGHT AT $50	SALE OF 50 CALL	COVERED CALL WRITE
S_T	(100 SHARES)	CONTRACT AT $5	(2) + (3)
$30	− $2000	$ 500	− $1500
40	− 1000	500	− 500
50	0	500	500
55	500	0	500
60	1000	− 500	500
70	2000	− 1500	500

NOTE: The maximum profit on the covered call write is $500, equal to the call premium. If the stock price falls below $50, losses on the stock are sweetened by the $500 call premium.

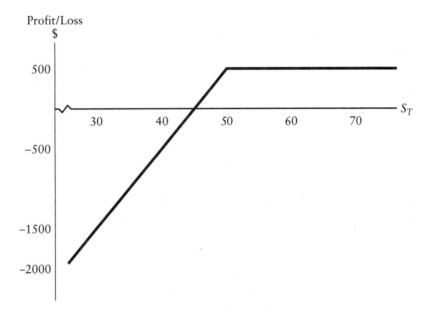

greater losses are associated with the out-of-the-money covered call write if the price of the underlying stock declines. In contrast, if ABC increased to $50 or higher, then the covered call write position formed with the out-of-the-money 50 call would yield the investor a profit of $600, while the in-the-money 40 call would yield a profit of only $300. The out-of-the-money call therefore provides a higher return if the price of the stock increases. Finally, the break-even price for the in-the-money covered call write is less than the price for the out-of-the-money covered call write; that is, the 40 covered call has a break-even price of $37, compared to the 50 covered call's break-even price of $44. To recapitulate, the out-of-the-money covered call write is a higher return-risk strategy than the in-the-money covered call write.

TABLE 3.3-2

	Types of Covered Call Write: Profit at Expiration		

In-the-money covered call write with a 40 call contract

(1) S_T	(2) PROFIT FROM STOCK BOUGHT AT $45 (100 SHARES)	(3) PROFIT FROM A 40 CALL CONTRACT SOLD AT $8	(4) PROFIT FROM IN-THE-MONEY CALL (2) + (3)
$35	− $1000	$ 800	− $200
37	− 800	800	0
40	− 500	800	300
45	0	300	300
50	500	− 200	300
55	1000	− 700	300
60	1500	− 1200	300

Out-of-the-money covered call write with a 50 call contract

(1) S_T	(2) PROFIT FROM STOCK BOUGHT AT $45 (100 SHARES)	(3) PROFIT FROM A 50 CALL CONTRACT SOLD AT $1	(4) PROFIT FROM OUT-OF-THE-MONEY COVERED CALL WRITE (2) + (3)
$35	− $1000	$100	− $900
40	− 500	100	− 400
44	− 100	100	0
45	0	100	100
50	500	100	600
55	1000	− 400	600
60	1500	− 900	600

Covered call write with fifty 40 calls and fifty 50 Calls

(1) S_T	(2) PROFIT FROM STOCK BOUGHT AT $45 (100 SHARES)	(3) PROFIT FROM FIFTY 40 CALLS SOLD AT $8	(4) PROFIT FROM FIFTY 50 CALLS SOLD AT $1	(5) TOTAL PROFIT (2) + (3) + (4)
$35	− $1000	$400	$ 50	− $550
40	− 500	400	50	− 50
45	0	150	50	200
50	500	− 100	50	450
55	1000	− 350	− 200	450
60	1500	− 600	− 450	450

TABLE 3.3-2
(*continued*)

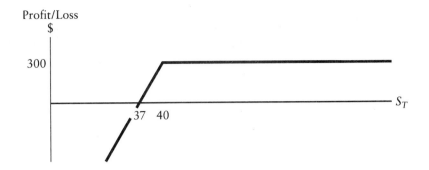

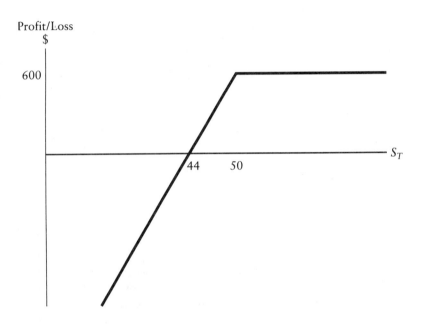

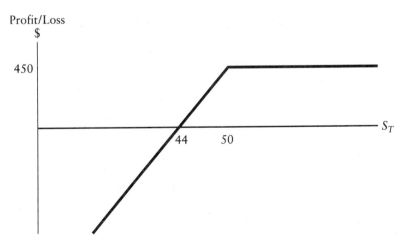

It should be noted that the investor is not limited to constructing covered call writes from the options available on the exchange. The investor could construct a covered call write using a portfolio of written calls with different exercise prices. For instance, in the preceding example, if a 45 call did not exist, then, as shown in Table 3.3-2, the investor could obtain the same profit-stock price relation as available from selling fifty 40 calls and fifty 50 calls (half the standard contract size). This strategy would provide a moderate return-risk combination between those obtained with the 40 and the 50 calls.

3.3.2   Follow-up Strategies

As with all option positions, if the price of the underlying stock changes unexpectedly, then an investor may want to pursue a follow-up strategy. From our previous discussions of follow-up strategies, you should know that there are a number of possible actions you can take (creating a spread, combination, etc.). The proper action to pursue ultimately depends on the price one expects the stock to reach.

3.4   RATIO CALL WRITE

A *ratio call write* is a combination of a naked call write and a covered call write. It is constructed by selling calls against more shares of stock than you own, for example, selling two calls for each share of stock purchased or owned $\{S_0, -2C_0\}$. Table 3.4-1 and its accompanying figure summarize the profit and stock price relations for a ratio call write formed by purchasing 100 shares of ABC stock for $60 per share and selling two June 60 calls at $5 per call. The ratio call write strategy generates an inverted V profit and stock price relation, with two break-even prices and a maximum profit occurring when the price of the stock equals the exercise price.

Moreover, different ratio call write strategies (differing by their ratios) generate the same types of characteristics, provided the ratio is greater than 1. As a result, an investor, by varying the ratio, can obtain a number of inverted V relations, with each ratio call write differing in terms of its maximum profit, the magnitude of its gains and losses at each stock price, and its break-even prices. For example, as shown in Table 3.4-2 and its accompanying figure, if the ratio is changed from two written calls per share to three written calls per share, the break-even prices go from $50 and $70 (Table 3.4-1) to $45 and $67.50 (column 4, Table 3.4-2), respectively. The maximum profit increases from $1000 to $1500, and it occurs at $60 for both ratio call write strategies. Different profits and losses at each stock price also are realized with three rather than with two written calls. In contrast, if the ratio is reduced from two to 1.5 written calls per share, then the range in break-even prices changes to $52.5 and $75 (column 6, Table 3.4-2), the maximum profit is less ($750), and the profits and losses at each stock price are different.

TABLE 3.4-1

	2-to-1 Ratio Call Write: Profit at Expiration		
(1) S_T	(2) PROFIT FROM STOCK BOUGHT AT $60 (100 SHARES)	(3) PROFIT FROM TWO 60 CALL CONTRACTS SOLD $5 PER CALL	(4) TOTAL PROFIT (2) + (3)
$40	− $2000	$1000	− $1000
45	− 1500	1000	− 500
50	− 1000	1000	0
55	− 500	1000	500
60	0	1000	1000
65	500	0	500
70	1000	− 1000	0
75	1500	− 2000	− 500
80	2000	− 3000	− 1000

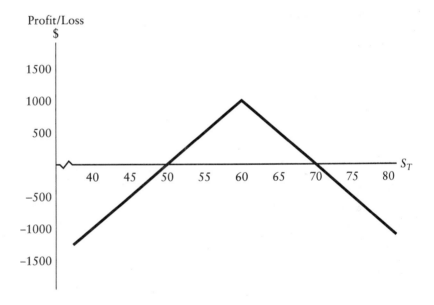

In summary, the ratio call write is a useful strategy for investors who believe a certain stock will stabilize near a certain price. Thus, in the examples, any of the ratio call write strategies would be ideal for an investor who felt the stock would be at $60 near expiration. In addition, by varying the ratio, an investor can use a ratio call write strategy to determine the return/risk he wants to assume.

TABLE 3.4-2

		Ratio Call Write, 3-to-1 and 1.5-to-1: Profit at Expiration			
(1)	(2)	(3)	(4)	(5)	(6)
S_T	PROFIT FROM STOCK BOUGHT AT $60 (100 SHARES)	PROFIT FROM THREE 60 CONTRACTS SOLD FOR $5 PER CALL	TOTAL PROFIT (2) + (3)	PROFIT FROM 1.5 60 CONTRACTS SOLD FOR $5 PER CALL	TOTAL PROFIT (2) + (5)
$35	− $2500	$1500	− $1000	$ 750	− $1750
40	− 2000	1500	− 500	750	− 1250
45	− 1500	1500	0	750	− 750
50	− 1000	1500	500	750	− 250
52.5	− 750	1500	750	750	0
55	− 500	1500	1000	750	250
57.5	− 250	1500	1250	750	500
60	0	1500	1500	750	750
62.5	250	750	1000	375	625
65	500	0	500	0	500
67.5	750	− 750	0	− 375	375
70	1000	− 1500	− 500	− 750	250
75	1500	− 3000	− 1500	− 1500	0
80	2000	− 4500	− 2500	− 2250	− 250
85	2500	− 6000	− 3500	− 3000	− 500
90	3000	− 7500	− 4500	− 3750	− 750

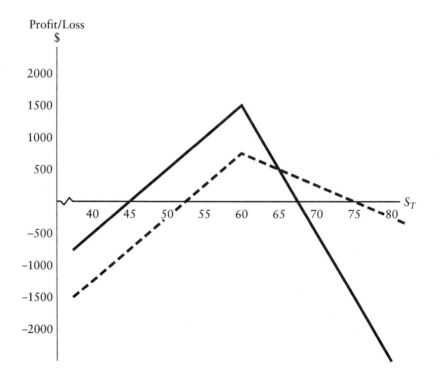

3.5 PUT PURCHASE

Just as the purchase of a call can be viewed as an alternative to a leveraged stock purchase, a put purchase can be thought of as a leveraged alternative to a short sale. As illustrated in Figure 3.5-1, a stock sold short at $50 will provide an investor with a $10 return and a rate, expressed as a proportion of a 50% margin, of 40% [$10/($50(.50)] when the stock declines to $40, and a 40% loss when it increases to $60. In contrast, the purchase of a 50 put at a premium of $5 yields a 100% rate of return [($10 − $5)/$5] when the stock is at $40, but a 100% loss if the stock is at $50 or higher. Thus, for short-run investments, investors who are bearish on a stock will find that the purchase of a put represents a higher return-risk alternative to the short sale. In addition, the short sale carries with it an obligation to cover dividends, which the put does not (although its price does increase at the stock's ex-dividend date), and total commission costs are higher for short sales than for put purchases.

3.5.1 Put Selection

Put purchases are used when the price of a stock is expected to decline in the short run. Such anticipated declines could be due to fundamental reasons governing the value of a stock, such as an expectation that a company's earnings will be lower than projected when next reported, or technical factors, such as a belief that speculators may be selling the stock in the near term for profit-taking motives, or, possibly, market factors, such as an expectation that the Federal Reserve will be pushing interest rates up.

FIGURE 3.5-1

Put Purchase and Short Sale Profit Graphs

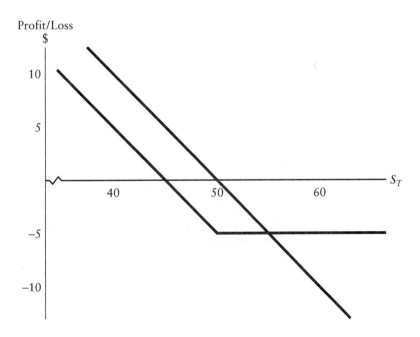

Whatever the reason, bearish investors should keep two points in mind in selecting puts: First, an out-of-the-money put provides a higher return-risk investment than an in-the-money put. For example, suppose that ABC stock is at $59, an out-of-the-money ABC June 55 put is trading at $1, and an in-the-money ABC June 60 put is at $3. If the price of ABC decreases to $50 near expiration, then the 55 put could be sold at its intrinsic value of $5, yielding a rate of return of 400% [($5 − $1)/$1], while the 60 put could be sold at its intrinsic value of $10 to yield a rate of 233% [($10 − $3)/$3]. In contrast, if ABC drops to only $55, then the out-of-the-money 55 put would be worthless, while the 60 put provides a profit of $2 (at $60 or higher, both puts yield 100% losses). Thus, an out-of-the-money put offers higher potential rewards but also higher risk than an in-the-money put.

Second, in-the-money puts tend to lose their value faster than out-of-the-money puts when the price of the stock increases. This is because, when the price of the underlying stock increases over time, the in-the-money put loses both its intrinsic value and its time value premium, while the out-of-the-money put loses just its time premium.

3.5.2   Follow-up Strategies

Once you have purchased a put, you need to be able to identify the possible follow-up actions you can pursue if the stock price changes are different from what you expect. Aggressive follow-up actions can be taken if the stock decreases, and defensive actions can be used if the stock increases in price.

Aggressive Follow-up Strategies

If the stock price unexpectedly declines after purchasing a put, a put holder can liquidate, do nothing, roll down, create a put spread, or create a combination. Suppose an investor, after buying an ABC June 60 put contract at $2 per put when the stock was at $62, sees the price of ABC decline to $55. Also, suppose at the stock price of $55 the ABC June 60 put contract is trading at $6, the ABC June 55 put contract is at $2, and the ABC June 55 call contract is trading at $3. The investor could: (1) liquidate the 60 put to realize a profit of $400; (2) do nothing, thereby keeping the chances of increased profit at expiration still open, but risking a loss if the stock price increases; (3) roll down by selling the 60 put for $600 and then using $400 to buy two 55 puts, thereby capturing his initial investment and keeping open the opportunity to profit if the stock declines further; (4) spread, by selling the June 55 put at $2 to match against the long position in the 60 put, thereby locking in a profit of $500 if the stock stays at $55 or decreases, ensuring a profit if the stock increases to just below $60, and providing a break-even position if the stock increases to $60 or higher; or (5) create a combination by buying the June 55 call at $3 to match with the long 60 put, thereby providing profit if stock moves dramatically up or down, or a break-even position if the stock stays within the $55–$60 range.

The aggressive follow-up strategies are evaluated in Table 3.5-1 in terms of their profit and stock price relations at expiration. As is always the case in follow-up strategies, the strategy to choose depends on the price you expect and how confident you are in your expectation.

TABLE 3.5-1

	**Aggressive Follow-up Actions: Profit at Expiration**

Actions for a 60 put contract purchased at $2 and now trading at $6 when the stock is at $55

(1)	(2)	(3)	(4)	(5)	(6)
			ROLL DOWN		
		LIQUIDATE	SELL 60 PUT	SPREAD	COMBINATION
		SELL 60 PUT	AND BUY TWO 55	SELL 55 PUT	BUY 55 CALL
S_T	DO NOTHING	AT $6	PUTS AT $2 EACH	AT $2	AT $3
$40	$1800	$400	$3000	$500	$1500
45	1300	400	2000	500	1000
51	700	400	800	500	400
52	600	400	600	500	300
53	500	400	400	500	200
55	300	400	0	500	0
56	200	400	0	400	0
58	0	400	0	200	0
60	− 200	400	0	0	0
64	− 200	400	0	0	400
70	− 200	400	0	0	1000

Defensive Follow-up Strategies

If the price of the stock increases unexpectedly after an investor purchases a put, the investor needs to consider defensive actions. In the preceding example, suppose ABC stock increased to $65, in turn causing the investor's ABC June 60 put to decrease to $1 and an ABC June 65 put to trade at $3. Under these circumstances, the investor could: (1) liquidate by selling the June 60 put for $1 (its time value premium), thereby losing only $100 instead of the initial $200 premium that would be lost if the stock equaled $60 or greater at expiration; (2) do nothing, hoping that the price increase is only temporary; or (3) create a spread by selling the 65 put for $3, thereby profiting by $100 if the stock continues to increase but losing if it declines. These defensive strategies are shown in Table 3.5-2.

3.5.3   Put Purchase in Conjunction with a Long Stock Position: Stock Insurance

Purchasing a put while owning the underlying stock on a one-to-one basis ({ $+P$, $+S$}) yields the same type of profit and stock price relation as does a call purchase. In column 4 of Table 3.5-3, the profits at expiration for various stock prices are shown for a long put and stock position consisting of 100 shares of ABC stock purchased at $50 per share and an ABC 50 put contract purchased at $3. As can be seen in the table and the accompanying figure, the combined put and stock position yields the same relation as does the purchase of a 50 call contract at $3. Remember, however, that more often than not, calls and puts with identical terms are not likely to be equally priced.

As discussed in Chapter 1, the combined stock and put position is known as a *portfolio insurance* or stock insurance strategy. The features of such a strategy are

TABLE 3.5-2

	Defensive Follow-up Actions: Profit at Expiration		
Actions on a 60 put contract purchased at $2 and now trading at $1 when the stock is at $65			
S_T	Do Nothing	LIQUIDATE SELL 60 PUT AT $1	SPREAD SELL 65 PUT AT $3
$50	$800	− $100	− $400
55	300	− 100	− 400
58	0	− 100	− 400
60	− 200	− 100	− 400
65	− 200	− 100	100
70	− 200	− 100	100
75	− 200	− 100	100

best seen by examining the position's cash flows and value graph, shown in column 7 of Table 3.5-3 and the accompanying figure. As shown, the 50 put provides downside protection against the portfolio's falling below $5000. Thus, for the cost of the put premium, an investor can obtain insurance against decreases in the stock's price.

3.6   NAKED PUT WRITE

The naked (or uncovered) put write strategy provides only limited profit potential if the stock price increases, with the chances of large losses if the stock price decreases. The position as defined in terms of its profit and stock price relationship near expiration is equivalent to that of the covered call write. Besides being equivalent to the covered call write, the naked put write strategy also is like the naked call write in that it provides an opportunity for investors to profit from the decrease over time in the option's time value premium. For example, an ABC June 60 put sold in March for $10 when ABC stock was trading at $55 would, with no change in the stock price, trade at $5 at expiration. Thus, a profit of $5 could be earned by the naked put writer from the decrease in the time value premium.

Also, similar to the naked call write, naked put writes with in-the-money puts provide higher return-risk combinations than those with out-of-the-money puts. For example, the June 60 put in the preceding example would provide profits of $1000, $500, or 0 to the writer if the stock closed at $60, $55, or $50 at expiration, and losses of $500, $1000, or $1500 if the stock decreased to $45, $40, or $35. In contrast, an out-of-the-money June 50 put sold for $3 when the stock was at 55 would provide only $300 profit if the stock traded at $50, $55, $60 or higher at expiration, and would incur losses of $200 or $700 if the stock traded at $45 or $40. Thus, the more the put is in the money, the greater return-risk possibilities (at expiration) available from a naked put write position.

TABLE 3.5-3

		Long Stock and Put Stock Insurance				
	PROFITS			CASH FLOWS		
(1)	(2)	(3)	(4)	(5)	(6)	(7)
S_T	PROFIT FROM 50 PUT CONTRACT PURCHASED AT $3	PROFIT FROM STOCK PURCHASED AT $50 (100 SHARES)	TOTAL PROFIT (2) + (3)	VALUE OF PUT (100 SHARES)	VALUE OF STOCK (100 SHARES)	COMBINED STOCK AND PUT VALUE (5) + (6)
$30	$1700	− $2000	− $300	$2000	$3000	$5000
40	700	− $1000	− 300	1000	4000	5000
50	− 300	0	− 300	0	5000	5000
53	− 300	300	0	0	5300	5300
55	− 300	500	200	0	5500	5500
60	− 300	1000	700	0	6000	6000

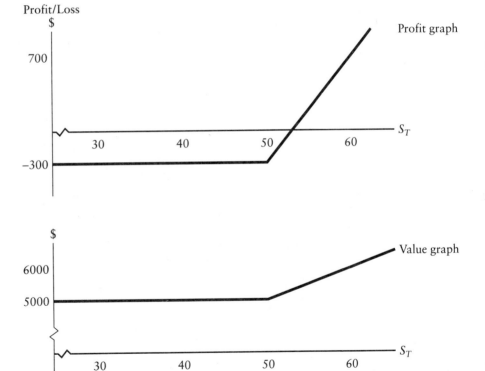

Finally, the defensive rolling-credit follow-up strategy defined for the naked call write position (Section 3.2.1) can be applied to the naked put write strategy for cases in which the stock decreases in price. For example, if ABC decreased from $55 to $50, causing the June 60 put to go from $10 to $15, the writer of the June 60 put could roll down by selling ABC June 55 puts, then using the proceeds (or credit) to close the June 60. Like the rolling-credit strategy for the uncovered call position, this strategy needs to be repeated each time the stock decreases to a new, uncomfortable level. In turn, the put writer will profit from this follow-up strategy provided the stock eventually stops decreasing, the option is not exercised, and the writer has sufficient collateral to cover each follow-up adjustment.

3.7   COVERED PUT WRITE

The covered put write strategy involves selling a put and the underlying stock short: $\{-P, -S\}$. It is equivalent to the naked call write, providing limited profit potential if the stock declines and unlimited loss possibilities if the price of the stock increases. The naked call write, though, has smaller commission costs and lower collateral requirements than the covered put write. As a short-run strategy, the covered put write is not as good as the naked call write and, as such, is seldom used as a strategy by option traders.

3.8   RATIO PUT WRITE

The *ratio put write* is a combination of a covered put write and a naked put write. It is formed by selling puts against shares of stock shorted at a ratio different than 1-to-1, for example, selling two puts for each share of stock shorted: $\{-2P, -S\}$. In terms of its profit and stock price relationship near expiration, the ratio put write is equivalent to the ratio call write. Like the ratio call write, the ratio put position is characterized by an inverted V-shaped profit and stock relation, two break-even prices, and a maximum profit occurring when the stock price is equal to the exercise price. Both strategies have relatively high commission costs, since they both involve stock positions, and both are affected by dividends. The major difference between these equivalent strategies is that the ratio call write requires an investment to purchase the stock, while the ratio put write requires posting collateral to cover the short sale.

The ratio put write position can be reversed; puts and shares of stock can be purchased in a ratio different than 1-to-1, for example: $\{+2P, +S\}$. This strategy is known as a *reverse hedge* with puts. The strategy yields a V-shaped profit and stock price relation and is equivalent to the straddle purchase defined in Chapter 1 and the simulated straddle described in Section 3.1.2.

3.9   CALL SPREADS

As first defined in Chapter 1, a call spread is a strategy in which you simultaneously buy one call option and sell another on the same stock but with different terms. Since options on a given stock differ only in terms of their exercise prices and expiration dates, only three types of spreads exist: (1) the *vertical* (or money or price) *spread*, in which the options have the same expiration dates but different exercise prices; (2) the *horizontal* (or time or calendar) *spread*, in which the options have the same exercise price but different expiration dates; and (3) the *diagonal spread*, which combines the vertical and horizontal spreads by having options with both different exercise prices and different expiration dates.

The terms *vertical, horizontal,* and *diagonal* derive from the way in which options are presented in financial papers. In the old *Wall Street Journal* format, for example, the exercise prices were read down (vertically), exercise months across (horizontally), and options with different exercise prices and months diagonally.

3.9.1   Vertical (Money) Spreads

The most popular vertical or money spreads are the bull, bear, ratio, and butterfly spreads.

Bull and Bear Call Spreads

The *bull* money *call spread* is suited for investors who are bullish about a stock. As discussed in Chapter 1, the strategy is to go long in a call with a given exercise price and to go short in another call on the same stock with a higher exercise price. For example, suppose that when ABC stock is trading at $42, there is an ABC June 40 call trading at $3 [C(40) = $3] and an ABC June 45 call trading at $1 [C(45) = $1]. To form a bull spread, a spreader would buy the June 40 call and sell the June 45 call: { + C(40), − C(45)}. As shown in Table 3.9-1 and its accompanying figure, this bull money spread is characterized by: (1) losses limited to $200 when the price of the stock hits $40 (the low exercise price) or less; (2) limited profits of $300, starting when the stock price reaches $45 (the high exercise price); and (3) a break-even price of $42. This strategy is, in turn, suited for spreaders whose expectation is that the stock price will appreciate from $42 but not increase much beyond $45.

The *bear* money *call spread* is the exact opposite of the bull call spread. It is formed by buying a call at a specific exercise price and selling a call on the same stock but with a lower strike price. In the previous example, if the spreader bought the ABC June 45 call at $1 and sold the ABC June 40 at $3—{ + C(45), − C(40)}— then as shown in Table 3.9-2 and its accompanying figure, her profit would be limited to $200 if the stock price were $40 or less, her loss would be $300 if the price of the stock were $45 or higher, and the break-even price would be $42, the same as for the bull spread. This bear spread would be suited for investors whose expectation is that the price of the stock would fall in a narrow range around $40.

Ratio Money Spread

The bull and bear spreads just described are balanced spreads, or one-to-one money spreads. A *ratio money spread*, in turn, is formed by taking long and short positions in options that have not only different exercise prices but ratios different than one-to-one. The ratio money spread can be formed, for example, either by taking a long position in the low exercise call and a short position in the high one in different ratios, or by going short in the low exercise call and long in the high one in different ratios. For a given ratio these two spreads yield exactly opposite results.

TABLE 3.9-1

Bull Money Call Spread: Profit at Expiration			
$\{+C(40), -C(45)\}$			
S_T	PROFIT FROM 40 CALL CONTRACT BOUGHT AT $3	PROFIT FROM 45 CALL CONTRACT SOLD AT $1	TOTAL PROFIT
$30	−$ 300	$100	− $200
35	− 300	100	− 200
40	− 300	100	− 200
42	− 100	100	0
45	200	100	300
50	700	− 400	300
55	1200	− 900	300

NOTE: The $100 premium on the 45 call reduces the cost of the spread to $200. All of the profit is obtained in a narrow stock price range: $42 to $45.

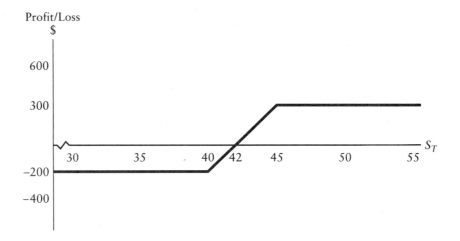

In the previous example, a ratio money spread could be formed by buying one ABC 40 call at $3 and selling two 45 calls at $1 each: $\{+C(40), -2C(45)\}$. As shown in Table 3.9-3, this 1-to-2 ratio money spread is characterized by two break-even prices at $41 and $49, a maximum profit of $400 when the stock price reaches the exercise price of $45, limited losses of $100 if the stock declines, and unlimited losses if the stock increases. Hence, the motivation for this strategy is that the investor expects the stock price to increase to $45 and then to stabilize around that value.

In general, the characteristics of the money spread can be varied by changing the spread's ratio. This can be seen by comparing the profit and stock price relations for the 1-to-1 bull spread (Table 3.9-1) with the 1-to-2 ratio spread (Table 3.9-3) and the 1-to-3 ratio spread, shown in Table 3.9-4. The three spreads are shown together in Figure 3.9-1.

TABLE 3.9-2

	Bear Money Spread: Profit at Expiration		
$\{-C(40), +C(45)\}$			
S_T	PROFIT FROM 45 CALL CONTRACT BOUGHT AT $1	PROFIT FROM 40 CALL CONTRACT SOLD AT $3	TOTAL PROFIT
$30	− $100	$ 300	$200
35	− 100	300	200
40	− 100	300	200
42	− 100	100	0
45	− 100	− 200	− 300
50	400	− 700	− 300
55	900	− 1200	− 300

NOTE: The 45 call protects the 40 call in case the stock price should surge beyond $45. The initial $300 profit is reduced by $100, but the potential loss is also reduced to a maximum of $300.

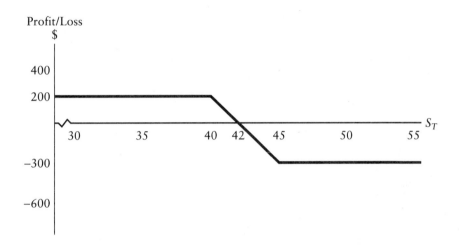

TABLE 3.9-3

	1-to-2 Ratio Money Spread: Profit at Expiration		
$\{+C(40), -2C(45)\}$			
S_T	PROFIT FROM 40 CALL CONTRACT BOUGHT AT $3	PROFIT FROM TWO 45 CALL CONTRACTS SOLD AT $1	TOTAL PROFIT
$30	− $ 300	$ 200	− $100
35	− 300	200	− 100
40	− 300	200	− 100
41	− 200	200	0
42	− 100	200	100
45	200	200	400
47	400	− 200	200
49	600	− 600	0
50	700	− 800	− 100
55	1200	− 1800	− 600

TABLE 3.9-4

		1-to-3 Ratio Money Spread: Profit at Expiration		
$\{+C(40), \ -3C(45)\}$				
S_T	PROFIT FROM 40 CALL CONTRACT BOUGHT AT $3		PROFIT FROM THREE 45 CALL CONTRACTS SOLD AT $1	TOTAL PROFIT
$30	− $ 300		$ 300	$ 0
35	− 300		300	0
40	− 300		300	0
41	− 200		300	100
42	− 100		300	200
45	200		300	500
47	400		− 300	100
47.5	450		− 450	0
48	500		− 600	− 100
49	600		− 900	− 300
50	700		− 1200	− 500
55	1200		− 2700	− 1500

FIGURE 3.9-1

Comparison of Ratio Money Spread Profit Graphs

1-to-1 (Table 3.9-1); 1-to-2 (Table 3.9-3); 1-to-3 (Table 3.9-4)

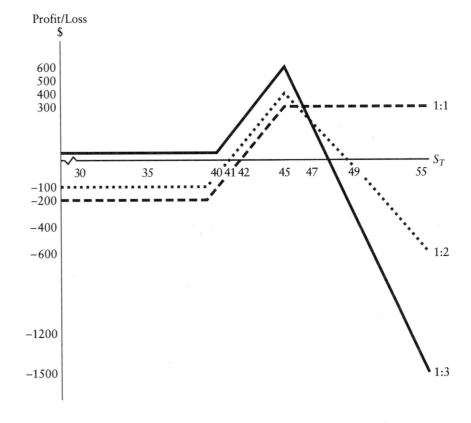

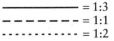

Butterfly Money Spread

A fourth type of horizontal spread is the **butterfly money spread** (also referred to as the *sandwich spread*). This is a combination of the bull and bear spreads. Specifically, a long butterfly money call spread is formed by buying one call at a low exercise price, selling two calls at a middle exercise price, and buying one call at a high exercise price. To see the profit and stock price relations that a long butterfly provides, suppose that when ABC's stock is selling for $50, the June 40 call on ABC is trading at $12, the June 50 is at $6, and the June 60 is at $3. As shown in Table 3.9-5 and its accompanying figure, buying one June 40, selling two June 50s, and buying one June 60 [{+C(40), -2C(50), +C(60)}] would generate an inverted-V profit and stock price relation, with limited losses at high and low stock prices. The maximum profit occurs when the stock price equals the middle exercise price, and the limited losses start when the stock price is equal to the high ($60) or low ($40)

TABLE 3.9-5

	Long Butterfly Call Money Spread: Profit at Expiration			
{+C(40), -2C(50), +C(60)}				
S_T	PROFIT FROM 40 CONTRACT BOUGHT AT $12	PROFIT FROM TWO 50 CONTRACTS SOLD AT $6 EACH	PROFIT FROM 60 CONTRACT BOUGHT AT $3	TOTAL PROFIT
$30	-$1200	$1200	-$300	-$300
40	- 1200	1200	- 300	- 300
43	- 900	1200	- 300	0
45	- 700	1200	- 300	200
50	- 200	1200	- 300	700
55	300	200	- 300	200
57	500	- 200	- 300	0
60	800	- 800	- 300	- 300
70	1800	- 2800	700	- 300

NOTE: If the stock price S_T finishes in a narrow range, $43 to $57, the butterfly spread will be profitable. A large increase in volatility may result in a (maximum) loss of $300.

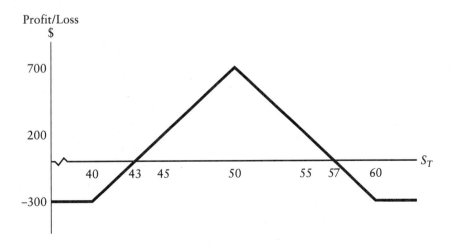

TABLE 3.9-6

Short Butterfly Call Money Spread: Profit at Expiration				
$\{-C(40),\ +2C(50),\ -C(60)\}$				
S_T	Profit from 40 Call Contract Sold at $12	Profit from Two 50 Call Contracts Bought at $6 Each	Profit from 60 Call Contract Sold at $3	Total Profit
$30	$1200	− $1200	$300	$300
40	1200	− 1200	300	300
43	900	− 1200	300	0
45	700	− 1200	300	− 200
50	200	− 1200	300	− 700
55	− 300	− 200	300	− 200
57	− 500	200	300	0
60	− 800	800	300	300
70	− 1800	2800	− 700	300

NOTE: The maximum profit of $300 is achieved only if the stock experiences a great deal of volatility (up or down). If the stock settles around $50, the maximum loss possible is $700.

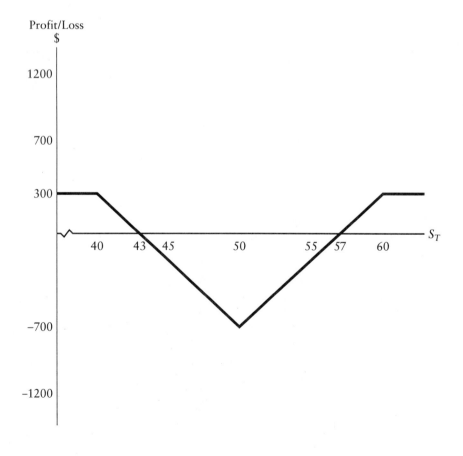

exercise price. The long butterfly money spread is, in turn, a strategy that can be used if one expects the stock to be near the middle exercise price near expiration.

A short butterfly money call spread is the exact opposite of the long butterfly. It is formed by selling a low exercise call, buying two middle exercise calls, and selling a high exercise call. Table 3.9-6 and its accompanying figure illustrate the profit and stock price relations for the short butterfly spread formed by selling the June 40 call, buying two June 50s, and selling the June 60: $\{-C(40), +2C(50), -C(60)\}$. As can be seen, the short butterfly yields a V-shaped profit and stock price relation, with limited profits at the high and low stock prices.

3.9.2   Horizontal (Time) Spreads

The horizontal (or time or calendar) spread is formed by simultaneously buying and selling options that are identical except for the time to expiration. For example, a horizontal spread could be formed by selling an ABC June 40 call at $5 and buying a September 40 call at $9.

A number of different types of time spreads exist. For example, a spreader may want to form a ratio time spread by going long in one long-term call and short in two short-term calls. An option investor also could form a butterfly time spread with three options with the same exercise prices but with different exercise dates.

Since horizontal as well as diagonal spreads have different exercise dates, it is impossible to know the value of the long-term option position at the expiration date of the short-term option position. As a result, time and diagonal spreads do not lend themselves to the same type of profit and stock price analysis associated with the strategies we have analyzed to this point. We can, however, estimate profit and stock price relations by using the option pricing model to estimate the price of the longer-term option for each possible stock price at the expiration of the shorter-term one. In Chapter 8 we will discuss time and diagonal spreads.

3.10   PUT SPREADS

Horizontal, vertical, and diagonal *put spreads* are formed the same way as their corresponding call spreads, and they produce the same profit and stock price relation as their corresponding call spreads. For example, a call bear spread is formed by selling a call with a lower exercise price and buying one with a higher, and a put bear spread is formed by going short in a low exercise put and long in a higher exercise one. Both strategies yield the same profit and stock price relation. Similarly, a calendar put spread is constructed like its corresponding call, by buying (or selling) a short-term put and selling (buying) a longer-term one.

In general, our preceding discussion on call spreads also applies to put spreads. It should be kept in mind that, even though the put and call spreads are equivalent in terms of profit and stock price relation, differences do exist. For instance, with a bear put spread, the higher-exercise-price put will sell for more than the lower-exercise one, leading to a debit position. The bear call spread, however, will have a higher premium associated with its lower-exercise-price option and a lower premium associated with its higher-exercise call, thus leading to an initial credit position. In contrast, the bull put spread will yield a net credit position, and the bull call a net debit one. Also, in comparing equivalent call and put spreads, it is important to note that the time value premium for puts may respond differently to stock price changes than do the time premiums for calls, thus leading to different uses of calendar put and calendar call spread strategies.

3.11 STRADDLE, STRIP, AND STRAP POSITIONS

The straddle is one of the more well-known option strategies. As defined earlier in Chapter 1, a straddle purchase is formed by buying both a put and a call with the same terms—same underlying stock, exercise price, and expiration date: $\{+C, +P\}$. A straddle write, in contrast, is formed by selling a call and a put with the same terms: $\{-C, -P\}$. For the straddle positions, the ratio of calls to put is 1-to-1. Changing the ratio, in turn, yields either a strip or a strap option strategy. Specifically, the *strip* is formed by having more puts than calls, and the *strap* is constructed with more calls than puts.

3.11.1   Straddle Purchase

The straddle purchase yields a V-shaped profit and stock price relation near expiration, with two break-even prices and the maximum loss equal to the sum of the call and put premium, which occurs when the stock is equal to the options' exercise price. In Table 3.11-1 and its accompanying figure, the profit and stock price relation is shown for a straddle purchase consisting of an ABC June 50 call purchased for $3 and an ABC June 50 put bought for $2.

The straddle purchase (or long straddle) is equivalent to the simulated straddle and the reverse hedge strategy. Since the simulated straddle and reverse hedge strategies involve stock positions, they have the disadvantage of higher commission cost compared to the straddle purchase. Thus, the straddle purchase is the preferable short-run strategy.

The straddle purchase, as with all strategies characterized by V-shaped profit and stock price relations, is well suited for cases in which an investor expects substantial change in the price of the stock but is not sure whether the change will be positive or negative. While all long straddles are characterized by V-shaped profit graphs, different straddles on the same stock—differing in terms of their maximum loss, their break-even prices, and the rate of change in profits per change in stock prices (i.e., slopes)—can be generated by purchasing either an out-of-the-money call and in-the-money put, an out/in (call/put) straddle, or an in/out straddle.

Since many straddle strategies are based on anticipated events that could occur before the options' expiration date, they lend themselves to follow-up actions. As an example, suppose that when XYZ Oil Company's stock was trading at $50, an investor bought an XYZ 50 straddle, anticipating an OPEC crude oil price announcement in the near term. Then suppose that after the straddle was purchased, but before the options expired, OPEC announced an increase in crude oil

TABLE 3.11-1

	Straddle Purchase: Profit at Expiration		
50 call purchased at $3 and 50 put purchased at $2			
S_T	PROFIT FROM 50 CALL CONTRACT BOUGHT AT $3	PROFIT FROM 50 PUT CONTRACT BOUGHT AT $2	TOTAL PROFIT
$30	− $ 300	$1800	$1500
35	− 300	1300	1000
40	− 300	800	500
45	− 300	300	0
50	− 300	− 200	− 500
55	200	− 200	0
60	700	− 200	500
65	1200	− 200	1000
70	1700	− 200	1500

NOTE: The maximum loss possible from a long straddle is $500, equal to the call plus put premiums. To achieve a profit, the stock price must increase beyond $55 or decrease below $45.

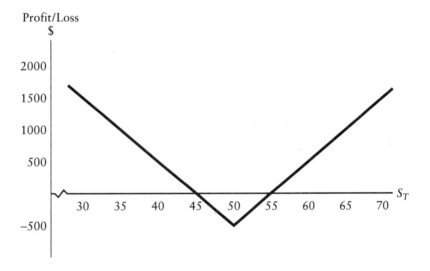

prices, causing an increase in the price of XYZ stock and in the prices on XYZ calls, and a decrease in the prices of XYZ puts. Given this new situation, the investor could: (1) liquidate, if he felt the stock was at a maximum and would stay there; (2) sell the call and keep the put, if he believed the market overreacted to the announcement and that the stock therefore would decline; (3) sell the put and hold the call, if he believed the stock would increase even further; or (4) roll up the call (put) by liquidating the straddle and using the profit to buy XYZ calls (puts) with higher exercise prices. If the anticipated event does not occur, or if it does but its impact on the stock's price is less than expected, then the investor may want to consider either liquidating, spreading one of the options (selling a put and/or a call with different exercise prices), or some other defensive action. As always, which follow-up strategy to choose depends on the investor's expectation after an event and on his confidence in that expectation.

3.11.2   Straddle Write

The straddle write (or short straddle) yields an inverted-V-shaped profit and stock price relation near expiration, with two break-even prices and a maximum profit equal to the sum of the call and put premiums occurring when the price of the stock is equal to the options' exercise price. The short straddle is equivalent to the ratio call write strategy, discussed in Section 3.4. In Table 3.11-2 and its accompanying figure, the profit and stock price relation is shown for a straddle sale consisting of an ABC June 50 call sold for $3 and an ABC June 50 put sold for $2.

The straddle write and other equivalent strategies yielding inverted-V-shaped profit graphs are ideal for cases in which you either expect little change to occur in the price of the stock, or, given the stock's variability, are confident the price of the stock will fall within the range of the break-even prices. Thus, in contrast to the straddle purchaser, the straddle writer does not anticipate an event in the near term that would affect the price of the underlying stock.

TABLE 3.11-2

S_T	Straddle Write: Profit at Expiration		
	50 call sold at $3 and 50 put sold at $2		
	PROFIT FROM 50 CALL CONTRACT SOLD AT $3	PROFIT FROM 50 PUT CONTRACT SOLD AT $2	TOTAL PROFIT
$30	$ 300	− $1800	− $1500
35	300	− 1300	− 1000
40	300	− 800	− 500
45	300	− 300	0
50	300	200	500
55	− 200	200	0
60	− 700	200	− 500
65	− 1200	200	− 1000
70	− 1700	200	− 1500

NOTE: The maximum profit is $500 at S_T = $50. Losses are incurred for S_T outside the $45–$55 range.

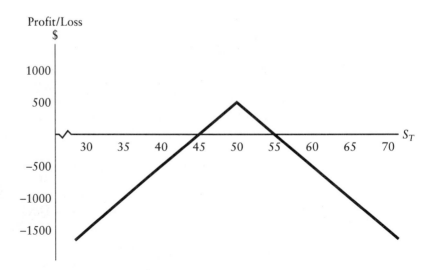

If an event does occur that increases or decreases the stock price, the writer may need to consider defensive follow-up action. For example, in our previous case, in which the price of oil unexpectedly went up, a straddle writer who sold the straddle expecting no crude oil price changes could consider liquidating the short straddle, thus limiting her losses, possibly closing the call by buying it back, or closing the put position. A number of strategies, both defensive and aggressive, can be employed, including positions with different exercise prices and exercise dates.

3.11.3 Strips and Straps

Strips and straps are variations of the straddle. They are formed by adding another call position (strap) or put position (strip) to a straddle. Specifically, the strip purchase (sale) consists of the long (short) straddle position plus the purchase (sale) of an extra put(s); the strap purchase (sale) consists of the long (short) straddle plus the additional purchase (sale) of a call(s). In Table 3.11-3 and its accompanying figure, the profit and stock price relations for long straddle, strip, and strap positions formed with an ABC 50 call trading at $3 and an ABC 50 put trading for $2 are shown. In Table 3.11-4 and its accompanying figure, the short positions for the strip, strap, and straddle formed with the same options are shown.

In comparing the three long positions, a number of differences should be noted. First, as we move from the straddle to the strip, the break-even prices move up from $45 and $55 to $46.5 and $57, and as we move from the straddle to the strap, the break-even prices move down to $42 and $54. Second, the range in break-even prices for the strip ($10.50) and the strap ($12) are greater than the range for the straddle position ($10). Third, the maximum losses are greater for the strip and the strap than for the straddle, by an amount equal to the cost of the additional option. Finally, compared to the symmetrical returns on the straddle, the strip and the strap positions provide asymmetrical payoffs. The strip's rate of increase in profit exceeds that of the straddle when the stock decreases from its maximum-loss price ($50) and equals the straddle's rate when the stock increases. Thus, a strip is particularly well suited for cases in which (like a straddle) an investor expects a stock either to increase or decrease in response to an event, but also expects that a stock decrease will be more likely than an increase. A strap, on the other hand, has a greater rate of increase in profit than the straddle when the stock increases, and the same rate when the stock decreases. Thus, this strap is better suited for those cases in which an investor thinks the probability of a stock increase is greater than the probability of a stock decrease.

Comparing the three short positions in Table 3.11-4 and its accompanying figure, we see that the writer obtains wider ranges in the break-even prices and a greater maximum profit from selling a strip and a strap than a straddle. A strip's losses, however, increase at a greater rate than a straddle write's when the stock price decreases from the maximum profit price, and at the same rate if the stock increases. The opposite results occur in the case of the strap write.

Finally, note that the characteristics of strips and straps can be changed by varying the ratios. This is illustrated in Table 3.11-5, in which the long strip position with a 2-to-1 call-to-put ratio is compared to a 3-to-1 strip.

TABLE 3.11-3
Straddle, Strip, and Strap
Purchases

50 Call at $3 and 50 Put
at $2

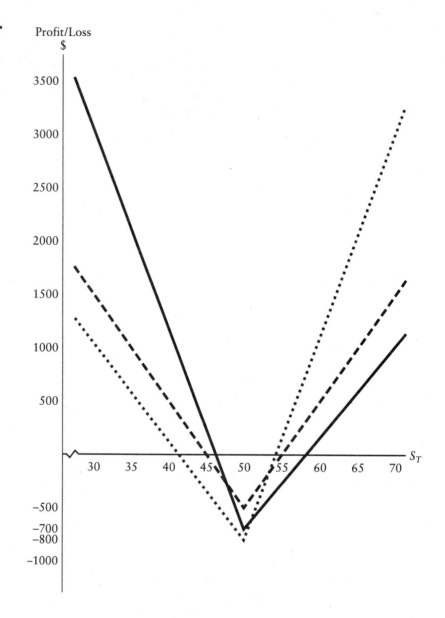

TABLE 3.11-3
(*continued*)

	Straddle, Strip, and Strap Purchases: Profit at Expiration		
	50 call purchased at $3 and 50 put purchased at $2		
S_T	STRADDLE 50 CALL AT $3, 50 PUT AT $2	STRIP 50 CALL AT $3, TWO 50 PUTS AT $2	STRAP TWO 50 CALLS AT $3 EACH, 50 PUT AT $2
$30	$1500	$3300	$1200
35	1000	2300	700
40	500	1300	200
42	300	900	0
45	0	300	− 300
46	− 100	100	− 400
46.5	− 150	0	− 450
47	− 200	− 100	− 500
48	− 300	− 300	− 600
50	− 500	− 700	− 800
54	− 100	− 300	0
55	0	− 200	200
57	200	0	600
60	500	300	1200
65	1000	800	2200
70	1500	1300	3200

TABLE 3.11-4

	Straddle, Strip, and Strap Writes: Profit at Expiration		
	50 call sold at $3 and 50 put sold at $2		
S_T	STRADDLE 50 CALL AT $3, 50 PUT AT $2	STRIP 50 CALL AT $3, TWO 50 PUTS AT $2	STRAP TWO 50 CALLS AT $3 EACH, 50 PUT AT $2
$30	− $1500	− $3300	− $1200
35	− 1000	− 2300	− 700
40	− 500	− 1300	− 200
42	− 300	− 900	0
45	0	− 300	300
46	100	− 100	400
46.5	150	0	450
47	200	100	500
48	300	300	600
50	500	700	800
54	100	300	0
55	0	200	− 200
57	− 200	0	− 600
59	− 400	− 200	− 1000
60	− 500	− 300	− 1200
65	− 1000	− 800	− 2200
70	− 1500	− 1300	− 3200

TABLE 3.11-4
(*continued*)
**Straddle, Strip, and
Strap Writes**

50 call at $3 and 50
put at $2

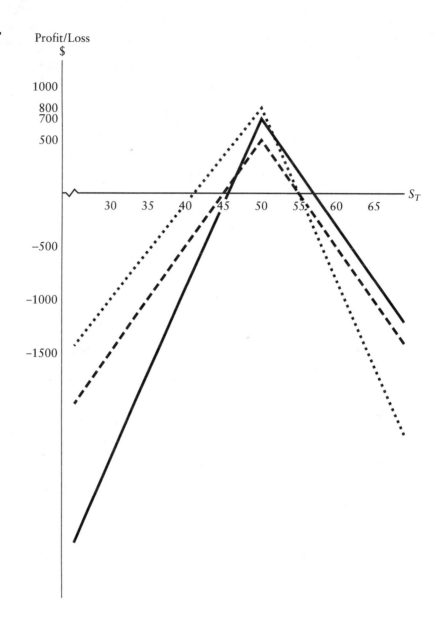

TABLE 3.11-5	Long Strips with Different Ratios: Profit at Expiration

50 call at $3 and 50 put at $2		
S_T	PROFIT FROM STRIP WITH TWO 50 PUTS AND ONE 50 CALL	PROFIT FROM STRIP WITH THREE 50 PUTS AND ONE 50 CALL
$30	$3300	$5100
35	2300	3600
40	1300	2100
42	900	1500
45	300	600
46.5	0	150
47	− 100	0
48	− 300	− 300
50	− 700	− 900
55	− 200	− 400
57	0	− 200
59	200	0
60	300	100
65	800	600
70	1300	1100

3.12 COMBINATIONS

A *combination* is a position formed with a call and a put on the same underlying stock but with different terms, that is, either different exercise prices (referred to as a *money* or *vertical* combination), exercise dates (called a *time, calendar,* or *horizontal* combination), or both (*diagonal* combination). The most common combinations are the ones formed with different exercise prices—money combinations, often called *strangles.*

In Table 3.12-1 and its accompanying figure, the profit and stock price relations are shown for a long money combination (a long strangle) constructed with a 45 call purchased at $6 and a 40 put purchased at $1. With the price of the stock assumed to be at $48, the long combination consists of an in-the-money call and an out-of-the-money put; that is, a 45/40 (call/put), in/out combination. As shown, the combination position is characterized by a limited loss [equal to the combination cost ($700)] over a range of stock prices, with the prices equal to the range in exercises prices ($40 and $45), and virtually unlimited profit potential if the stock increases or decreases. Short money combinations, of course, yield just the opposite—limited profit over a range of stock prices, and potential losses if the price of the stock changes substantially in either direction. Like straddles, different combinations on the same stock can be formed with in-the-money and out-of-the-money calls and puts: out/in (call/put), in/out, out/out, and in/in combinations.

TABLE 3.12-1

	Long Combination (or Strangle): Profit at Expiration		
S_T	PROFIT ON 40 PUT CONTRACT PURCHASED AT $1	PROFIT ON 45 CALL CONTRACT PURCHASED AT $6	PROFIT ON 45/40 COMBINATION
$25	$1400	− $ 600	$ 800
30	900	− 600	300
33	600	− 600	0
35	400	− 600	− 200
39	0	− 600	− 600
40	− 100	− 600	− 700
42	− 100	− 600	− 700
45	− 100	− 600	− 700
46	− 100	− 500	− 600
50	− 100	− 100	− 200
52	− 100	100	0
55	− 100	400	300
60	− 100	900	800
63	− 100	1200	1100

NOTE: The initial cost of the combination is $100 + $600 = $700. This amount is lost in its entirety if S_T ends up between $40 and $45. To realize a profit, the stock price must be greater than $52 or less than $33.

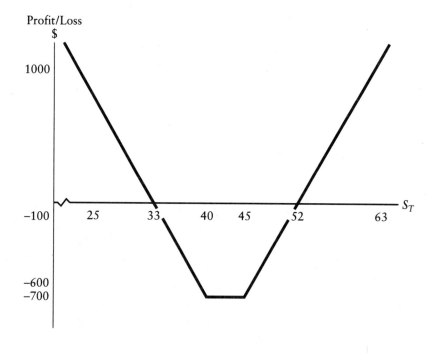

3.13 CONDORS

Condors are formed with four call and/or put options on the same stock but with different terms. They are a special type of butterfly spread involving bull and bear spreads with different exercise prices. Condors can be constructed in a number of ways. Table 3.13-1 shows several ways in which a long condor can be formed with call and put options at four exercise prices: $X_1, X_2, X_3,$ and X_4, in which $X_1 < X_2 < X_3 < X_4$, and Figure 3.13-1 shows the general shape of the long condor. As shown in the figure, the long condor is similar to a short money combination, providing limited profit over a range of stock prices and possible losses if the stock price changes in either direction. Different from the combination, the losses on the long condor are limited. This limited loss feature, in turn, makes the condor less risky than the combination.

A short condor position is formed by simply reversing the long condor's positions. As shown in Figure 3.13-2, the short condor has the opposite characteristics of the long position.

TABLE 3.13-1

Constructing a Long Condor	
Call and put exercise prices are X_1, X_2, X_3, X_4, where $X_1 < X_2 < X_3 < X_4$	
Calls	Long X_1 and X_4; short X_2 and X_3
Puts	Long X_1 and X_4; short X_2 and X_3
Calls and puts	Long X_1 call, short X_2 call, short X_3 put, long X_4 put
Calls and puts	Long X_1 put, short X_2 put, short X_3 call, long X_4 call

FIGURE 3.13-1

**Long Condor
Profit Graph**

$X_1 < X_2 < X_3 < X_4$

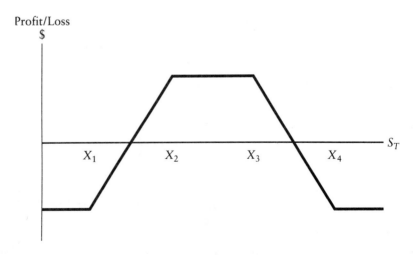

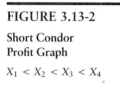

FIGURE 3.13-2

Short Condor Profit Graph

$X_1 < X_2 < X_3 < X_4$

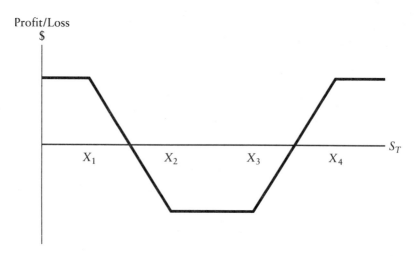

3.14 SIMULATED STOCK POSITIONS

From our discussions on option strategies in this chapter, it should be clear that options can be used in different combinations to obtain virtually any potential profit and stock price relation. Given this, it should not be too surprising to find that options can be used to form synthetic securities, such as long and short stock positions. A simulated long position may be formed by buying a call and selling a put with the same terms. Similarly, a simulated short position, constructed by selling a call and buying a put with the same terms, is equivalent to the profit and stock price relation associated with selling the underlying stock short.

3.14.1 Simulated Long Position

In Table 3.14-1 and its accompanying figure, the profit and stock price relations are shown for a long stock position established by buying 100 shares of ABC stock at $50 per share, and a *simulated long position* formed by buying an ABC June 50 call at $5 and selling an ABC June 50 put at $5. As can be seen, the relations in this example are exactly the same.

Several differences should be noted between the two equivalent positions shown in Table 3.14-1. First, the costs of the positions are different. In the example, it would cost $5000 to buy the stock, while the simulated long position would have a net cost equal to the difference in call premium, minus the put (zero in the example), plus a margin requirement. Second, the long stock position could provide dividends that the simulated position does not. However, on an ex-dividend date the price of the stock, call, and put all will change. Third, the option position has a fixed life that ends at expiration, while an investor can hold the stock indefinitely. Finally, the call and the put would more than likely not be equally priced. If they are not, then the simulated position would not be identical to the stock position. As we will discuss in Chapter 4, to attain an identical position (a synthetic position) requires that a long bond position be included with the long call and short put positions.

TABLE 3.14-1

(1) S_T	(2) PROFIT FROM 50 CALL CONTRACT BOUGHT AT $5	(3) PROFIT FROM 50 PUT CONTRACT SOLD AT $5	(4) PROFIT FROM SIMULATED LONG (2) + (3)	(5) PROFIT FROM STOCK BOUGHT AT $50
		Simulated Long Position: Profit at Expiration		
$40	− $500	− $500	− $1000	− $1000
45	− 500	0	− 500	− 500
50	− 500	500	0	0
55	0	500	500	500
60	500	500	1000	1000

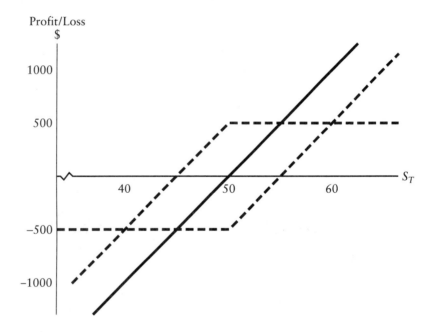

3.14.2 Simulated Short Position

In Table 3.14-2 and its accompanying figure, the profit and stock price relations are shown for a short stock position set up by selling 100 shares of ABC stock short at $50 and a *simulated short position* formed by selling an ABC June 50 call at $5 and buying an ABC June 50 put at $5. With the same premiums on the call and the put, the actual and simulated short positions are the same. If the premiums differ, a bond also would be needed to form an identical short stock position (synthetic short position).

The differences in the short and simulated short positions are similar to the differences in the corresponding long positions. The simulated short position has different margin requirements and commission costs than does the short stock position; the short stock position requires dividend coverage while the simulated position does not, and the simulated short position has an expiration date, while the short stock position does not (although the holder is subject to covering the borrowed shares any time a share lender requests).

TABLE 3.14-2

	(1) S_T	(2) PROFIT FROM 50 CALL CONTRACT SOLD AT $5	(3) PROFIT FROM 50 PUT CONTRACT BOUGHT AT $5	(4) PROFIT FROM SIMULATED SHORT (2) + (3)	(5) PROFIT FROM STOCK SHORTED AT $50
		Simulated Short Position: Profit at Expiration			
	$40	$500	$500	$1000	$1000
	45	500	0	500	500
	50	500	− 500	0	0
	55	0	− 500	− 500	− 500
	60	− 500	− 500	− 1000	− 1000

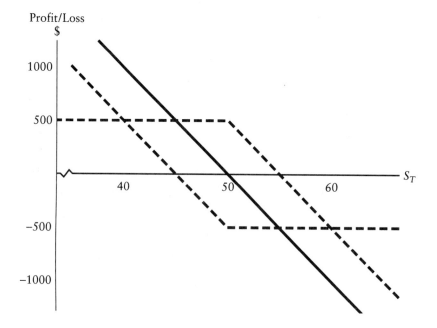

3.14.3   Splitting the Strikes

Simulated long and short positions can be altered by setting up strategies similar to the ones just described but with different terms—exercise prices, dates, or both. When the differing term is the exercise price, the strategy is referred to as *splitting the strikes*.

In splitting the strike, an investor would go long in a call with a high exercise price and short in a put with a lower exercise price (usually both out of the money) if she was bullish, and would do the opposite (write a call with a low exercise and buy a put with a high) if she was bearish. The profit and stock price relation for a bullish splitting-the-strikes position with ABC options is shown in Table 3.14-3 and its accompanying figure, and the bearish position is shown in Table 3.14-4, in which it is assumed that an out-of-the-money ABC June 60 put is trading at $2 and an ABC out-of-the-money June 70 call is at $1, when ABC stock is trading at $63.

TABLE 3.14-3

	Splitting the Strikes, Bullish Position: Profit at Expiration		
$\{+C(70), -P(60)\}$			
S_T	PROFIT FROM 60 PUT CONTRACT SOLD AT $2	PROFIT FROM 70 CALL CONTRACT BOUGHT AT $1	TOTAL PROFIT
$50	− $800	− $100	− $ 900
55	− 300	− 100	− 400
59	100	− 100	0
60	200	− 100	100
65	200	− 100	100
70	200	− 100	100
75	200	400	600
80	200	900	1100

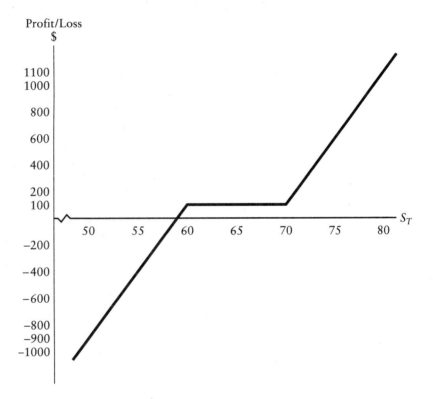

As shown, the bullish and bearish positions provide a range of stock prices in which profits or losses are fixed and also smaller losses and profits at each stock price than their respective long and short stock positions.

TABLE 3.14-4

	Splitting the Strikes, Bearish Position: Profit at Expiration		
$\{+P(60), \ -C(70)\}$			
S_T	Profit from 60 Put Contract Bought at $2	Profit from 70 Call Contract Sold at $1	Total Profit
$50	$800	$100	$ 900
55	300	100	400
59	− 100	100	0
60	− 200	100	− 100
65	− 200	100	− 100
70	− 200	100	− 100
75	− 200	− 400	− 600
80	− 200	− 900	− 1100

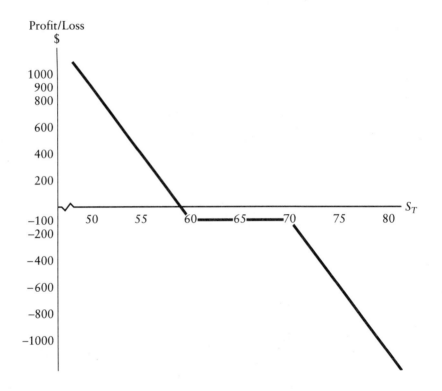

3.15   CONCLUSION

One important feature of an option is that it can be combined with other options and the underlying security to produce a myriad of profit and stock price relations. In this chapter, we've examined how many of these strategies are formed and their characteristics. Since the value of an option at expiration is equal to its intrinsic value, our analysis of option strategies was done in terms of the position's profit and stock price relation or value and stock price relation at expiration. Option strategies also can be evaluated in terms of their profit and stock price relation prior to expiration and in terms of how the position changes in value in response to changes in such parameters as time to expiration and the variability of the underlying stock. These descriptions of option strategies are based on option pricing models. In the next four chapters we will examine how call and put options are priced; in Chapter 8 we will return to our analysis of option strategies by evaluating the option strategies using the option pricing model.

KEY TERMS

follow-up strategies	reverse hedge	put spread
simulated put	vertical spread	strip
equivalent strategies	horizontal spread	strap
simulated straddle	diagonal spread	combination
rolling credit	bull call spread	condor
ratio call write	bear call spread	simulated long position
portfolio insurance	ratio money spread	simulated short position
ratio put write	butterfly money spread	splitting the strikes

SELECTED REFERENCES

Bookstaber, Richard M. *Option Pricing and Investment Strategies*. Chicago: Probus, 1987, chs. 4, 5.

Chance, Don M. *An Introduction to Options and Futures*. Forth Worth, Tex.: Dryden Press, 1991, chs. 5, 6.

Gombola, Michael J., Roenfeldt, Rodney L., and Cooley, Philip L. "Spreading Strategies in CBOE Options: Evidence on Market Performance." *Journal of Financial Research* 1 (Winter 1978): 35–44.

Grube, R. Corwin, Panton, Don B., and Terrell, J. Michael. "Risks and Rewards in Covered Call Positions." *Journal of Portfolio Management* 5 (Winter 1979): 64–68.

McMillan, Lawrence G. *Options as a Strategic Investment*, 2d ed. New York: New York Institute of Finance, 1986.

Mueller, P. "Covered Call Options: An Alternative Investment Strategy." *Financial Management* 10 (Winter 1981): 64–71.

Pozen, R. "The Purchase of Protective Puts by Financial Institutions." *Financial Analysts Journal* 34 (July–August 1978): 47–60.

Ritchken, Peter. *Options: Theory, Strategy, and Applications*. Glenview, Ill.: Scott, Foresman, 1987, ch. 3.

Slivka, Ron. "Call Option Spreading." *Journal of Portfolio Management* 7 (Spring 1981): 71–76.

Tucker, Alan L. *Financial Futures, Options, and Swaps*. St. Paul, Minn.: West, 1991, ch. 15.

EXERCISE

Evaluate the following strategies in terms of their profit and stock price relation at expiration. In your evaluation include a table that breaks down each strategy. Assume each stock position has 100 shares and each option contract has 100 options.

a. The short sale of ABC stock at $60 per share and the purchase of two ABC March 60 call contracts at $3 per call. Evaluate at expiration stock prices of 40, 45, 50, 54, 60, 66, 70, and 80.

b. The purchase of ABC stock at $75 per share and the sale of an ABC December 70 call contract at $8. Evaluate at expiration stock prices of 60, 65, 67, 70, 74, 75, 80, 85, and 90.

c. The purchase of 100 shares of ABC stock at $39 per share and the sale of two ABC October 40 call contracts at $6. Evaluate at expiration stock prices of 20, 27, 35, 40, 45, 53, and 60.

d. The purchase of an ABC September 50 call contract at $12 and the sale of an ABC September 60 call contract at $6. Evaluate at expiration stock prices of 40, 45, 50, 55, 56, 60, 65, and 70.

e. The purchase of one ABC July 50 call contract at $12, the sale of two July 60 call contracts at $6, and the purchase of one ABC July 70 call contract at $3. Evaluate at expiration stock prices of 40, 50, 53, 56, 60, 64, 67, 70, and 80.

f. The purchase of one ABC September 50 call contract at $12 and the sale of two ABC 60 September call contracts at $5. Evaluate at expiration stock prices of 40, 45, 50, 52, 55, 60, 65, 68, 70, and 75.

g. The purchase of ABC stock at $35 per share and the purchase of an ABC September 35 put contract for $3. Evaluate at expiration stock prices of 20, 25, 30, 35, 38, 40, 45, and 50.

h. The purchase of an ABC July 70 call contract at $3 and the purchase of an ABC July 70 put contract at $2. Evaluate at expiration stock prices of 50, 60, 65, 70, 75, 80, and 90.

i. The sale of an ABC June 65 call contract at $4 and the sale of an ABC June 65 put contract at $3. Evaluate at expiration stock prices of 50, 55, 58, 60, 65, 70, 72, 75, and 80.

j. The purchase of an ABC 40 call contract at $3 and the purchase of two ABC 40 put contracts at $2 each. Evaluate at expiration stock prices of 25, 30, 35, 36.5, 40, 45, 47, 50, and 55.

k. The sale of two 40 call contracts at $3 each and the sale of one 40 put contract at $2. Evaluate at expiration stock prices of 20, 25, 30, 32, 35, 40, 44, 45, and 50.

l. The purchase of an ABC 40 call contract at $3 and the purchase of an ABC 35 put contract at $3. Evaluate at expiration stock prices of 20, 25, 29, 30, 35, 40, 45, 46, 50, and 55.

m. The sale of an ABC 70 call contract at $4 and the sale of an ABC 60 put contract at $3. Evaluate at expiration stock prices of 40, 50, 53, 57, 60, 65, 70, 73, 77, 80, and 90.

n. The sale of an ABC 60 put contract at $2 and the purchase of an ABC 70 put contract at $7, when ABC stock is trading at 65. Evaluate at expiration stock prices of 50, 55, 60, 65, 70, 80, and 90.

o. The sale of an ABC 40 put contract at $3 and the purchase of an ABC 40 call contract at $3. Evaluate at expiration stock prices of 30, 35, 40, 45, and 50.

p. The purchase of an ABC 50 put contract at $2 and the sale of ABC 60 call contract at $1, when ABC stock is trading at 53. Evaluate at expiration stock prices of 40, 45, 49, 50, 55, 60, 65, and 70.

PROBLEMS AND QUESTIONS

1. Suppose shortly after Mr. Zapp purchased an IBL September 70 call contract at $3 per call, the price of IBL increased to $77, causing the price of his call to rise to $9 per call. Evaluate in terms of their profit and stock price relations the following follow-up actions Mr. Zapp could pursue:

   • Liquidate.
   • Do nothing.
   • Spread by selling an IBL 80 call trading at $3 per call.
   • Roll up by selling the 70 call and using the profit to buy two IBL 80 calls at $3 per call.

   Evaluate the strategies at expiration stock prices of 60, 65, 70, 73, 75, 80, 81, 85, and 90.

2. Suppose shortly after you purchased an ABC September 50 call for $3, the price of the stock decreased to $46 per share on speculation of a future announcement of low quarterly earnings for the ABC company. Suppose you believe the speculation is warranted and as a result believe the price of ABC stock will decline further. Explain how you could profit at expiration by changing your potentially unprofitable long call position to a profitable spread position. Assume there is an ABC September 40 call available at $8, and evaluate the spread at expiration stock prices of 35, 40, 45, 50, 55, and 60.

3. Suppose after selling an ABC June 50 call for $3 when the stock was at $50, the price of the stock increases to $55. Assume at the $55 stock price, the June 50 call is trading at $6 and there is an ABC June 55 call available that is trading at $2.50. Assuming that ABC stock will stay at $55 at least until expiration, show how you could change your current unprofitable position to a profitable one by implementing a rolling-credit strategy. How would your collateral requirements change? (Use margin formulas from Chapter 2.)

4. Compare and contrast the following strategies:

   a. Call purchase and leveraged stock purchase.
   b. Put purchase and simulated put.
   c. In-the-money covered call write and out-of-the-money covered call write.

    d. Ratio call writes with different ratios of short calls to shares of stock.

    e. Bull spread and bear spread.

5. Suppose after you purchased an ABC June 40 put at $2, the price of ABC stock dropped from $40 per share to $35 per share, causing the 40 put to increase to $6. Evaluate in terms of profit and stock price relations the following follow-up strategies:

- Liquidate.
- Do nothing.
- Spread by selling a 35 put contract at $2.
- Roll down by selling the 40 put and purchasing two 35 puts at $2.

Evaluate at expiration stock prices of 20, 25, 30, 35, 38, 40, 45 and 50.

6. Compare and contrast the following positions:

    a. Put purchase and short sale.

    b. Naked put write and covered call write.

    c. Covered put write and naked call write.

    d. Straddle, strip, and strap purchases.

7. List a number of strategies that will yield an inverted-V-shaped profit and stock price relation at expiration.

8. List a number of strategies that will yield a V-shaped profit and stock price relation at expiration.

9. Construct a value table for a simulated long straddle and graph it. Assume the stock sells for $50 and the calls for $3.

10. Construct a portfolio with 80 calls, 90 calls, and 100 calls that would yield an investor the following cash flows at expiration:

S_T	CF_T
$ 70	0
75	0
80	0
85	5
90	10
95	5
100	0
105	0
110	0

11. Set up a portfolio with calls with $X = \$40$, $\$50$, and $\$60$ that will yield the following cash flows:

S_T	CF_T
$30	0
40	0
45	5
50	10
55	5
60	0
70	0

COMPUTER PROBLEMS

Using information from the *Wall Street Journal* or other financial source, analyze the following strategies using the OPTIONS software program.

1. Bull call spread.

2. Bear call spread.

3. Long butterfly call spread.

4. Simulated put.

5. Simulated straddle.

6. Out-of-the-money covered call write.

7. In-the-money covered call write.

8. Ratio call write.

9. Bull put spread.

10. Bear put spread.

11. Long butterfly put spread.

12. Short butterfly put spread.

13. Straddle purchase.

14. Straddle sale.

15. In/out straddle purchase.

16. Out/in straddle purchase.

17. Strip purchase.

18. Strap purchase.

19. Strap write.

20. Combination purchase.

21. Combination sale.

22. In/in combination.

23. In/out combination.

24. Simulated long position.

25. Simulated short position.

PART II

Option Pricing

CHAPTER 4

Fundamental Option Price Relations

4.1 INTRODUCTION

In Chapter 1 we described how the price of an option is a function of both the underlying stock price and the time to expiration. An option's price also depends on other factors, such as the volatility of the underlying security and the risk-free return, whether the option is American or European, and, in the case of stock options, whether the stock is expected to pay a dividend during the period. In this chapter we begin our analysis of option price relationships by examining how these factors determine the minimum and maximum prices of options, the price relationships between options with different exercise prices and times to expiration, and how dividends, interest rates, and volatility influence the price of an option. In our analysis we will examine each relationship separately. In Chapter 5 we will integrate many of the relationships by deriving the binomial option pricing model.

To facilitate our discussion, the symbols for the call premium (C) and put premium (P) will be expressed (when it is helpful) in the following functional form: $C = C(S, X, T)$ or $P = P(S, X, T)$, where T is the time to expiration (which may be expressed as a proportion of the year (a three-month option would expire in $T = .25$ of a year). Thus, $C(S, X, T) = C(60, 50, .5) = \$15$ says that the price of a six-month option, with an exercise price of $50, is $15 when the stock is at $60. Also, since some relations are applicable for European options while others hold only for American, a superscript e or a (e.g., C^a or C^e) will be used when clarification is necessary. Similarly, when needed, the subscript 0 will be used to indicate the current period, the subscript T to indicate the option's expiration period or date, and the subscript t to signify any time period between the present ($t = 0$) and expiration ($t = T$). Finally, we will concentrate only on stock options, and to simplify our analysis we will examine option relationships without factoring in commission costs.

4.2   MINIMUM AND MAXIMUM CALL PRICES

4.2.1   Maximum American and European Call Prices

Since a call option gives an investor the right to buy a specific stock, it would be irrational for the investor to pay more for the call than for the underlying stock itself. Thus, whether the call is American or European, its maximum price, Max C, is the market price of the stock.

> RELATION: The maximum price an investor would pay for a call is the underlying stock's price:
>
> $$\text{Max } C_t = S_t.$$

The **maximum call price** defines the upper limit, or upper bound, of the call premium. The upper limit is depicted graphically in Figure 4.2-1 by the 45° line, which shows the one-to-one relation between Max C_t and S_t.

4.2.2   Minimum Price of an American Call

As noted in Chapter 1, if a call option is American, then the call cannot trade at a price below its intrinsic value (IV). If it did, arbitrageurs could realize riskless returns by buying the call, exercising it, and selling the stock (see Section 1.5). For example, suppose a 40 American call is trading at $5 when the stock is trading at $50. Given these prices, an investor could buy the stock in the open market at a cost of $50 or alternatively buy the call and exercise it immediately at a cost of only $5 + $40 = $45. Obviously, the investor would opt to acquire the stock indirectly through the option market. This would lead to an increase in the demand for the call, until the price of the call was equal to at least $10. In addition, with the call trading at $5 there also would be arbitrage opportunities from executing the aforementioned arbitrage strategy: Buy the call and exercise it immediately at a cost

---

FIGURE 4.2-1

Call Option Boundary Conditions (Non-Dividend-Paying Stock)

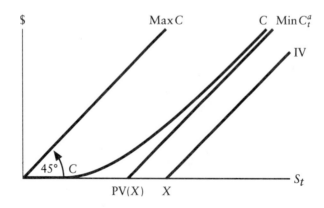

of $45, then sell the stock for $50. In implementing this strategy, arbitrageurs would push the call premium up until it was at least equal to the intrinsic value of $10 and the arbitrage profit was zero.

RELATION: To preclude arbitrage, an American call will trade at a price that is *at least equal* to its intrinsic value:

$$C_t^a \geq Max[S_t - X, 0].$$

If this condition does not hold, then an arbitrage opportunity exists by buying the call, exercising immediately, and selling the stock.

The intrinsic value defines a boundary or limit that governs the price of an American call. This boundary condition is shown graphically in Figure 4.2-1 by the IV line. The IV, though, is not the minimum price of an American call on a non-dividend-paying stock. That is, if an American call trades at a price above its intrinsic value, satisfying the aforementioned boundary condition, then riskless profit is still possible. For instance, suppose in the preceding example that the 40 call was trading at $11 when the stock was at $50, the call had an expiration of one year, and there was a riskless pure discount bond available in the market with a face value equal to the call's exercise price of $50 and trading at a discount rate of 6%. In this case, an arbitrageur could receive a cash inflow of $1.26 by buying the call at $11, buying the bond for PV(X) = PV(40) = $40/1.06 = $37.74, and selling the stock short at $50 (i.e., $50 − $11 − $40/1.06 = $1.26). At expiration, if the stock price is equal or greater than $40 ($S_T \geq X$), the arbitrageur could use the proceeds from the bond to exercise the call, then use the stock to cover the short position; the net cash flow in this case is zero. On the other hand, if the stock price is less than $40 ($S_T < X$), the call would be worthless. In this case the arbitrageur would only need to use a portion of the $40 from the bond to buy the stock and cover the short position, realizing a cash inflow of $40 − S_T$. Thus, if the call is trading at $11, an arbitrageur receives an initial cash inflow of $S_o - PV(X) - C_0^a$ = $50 − $37.74 − $11 = $1.26, and at expiration receives additional cash if $S_T < 40, and then is able to cover the short position so there are no losses if $S_T \geq 40. Given this riskless opportunity, arbitrageurs would try to buy the call, in turn pushing its price up until the initial cash flow (CF$_0$) is at least zero. This would occur when the price of the American call is equal to the difference between the stock price and the present value of the exercise price. That is:

$$CF_0 = S_0 - PV(X) - C_0^a$$

$$O = S_0 - PV(X) - C_0^a$$

$$C_0^a = S_0 - PV(X).$$

Thus, in our example, the arbitrageurs would push the price of the American call to at least $12.26:

$$C_0^a = S_0 - PV(X) = \$50 - \$37.74 = \$12.26.$$

The boundary condition $S_t - PV(X)$, in turn, defines the **minimum American call price** at any time t(Min C_t^a).

RELATION: In the absence of arbitrage the minimum price of an American call is:

$$\text{Min } C_t^a = \text{Max}[S_t - PV(X), 0].$$

If the price of the American call is below this minimum, then an arbitrage opportunity exists by taking long positions in the call and a bond with a face value equal to the exercise price and a short position in the underlying stock.

The minimum price boundary condition is shown graphically in Figure 4.2-1 where Min $C_t^a = S_t - PV(X)$ is plotted against S_t.

Formal Proof of the Boundary Condition

The preceding boundary condition was established by showing that if the condition is violated, then an arbitrage opportunity exists that provides an initial positive cash flow with no liabilities. As a rule, the arbitrage strategy underlying any boundary condition can be defined in terms of the violation of the condition, with the arbitrageur going long in the lower-valued position and short in the higher-valued one. Thus, in a case in which the minimum price condition for the American call is violated $\{C_0^a < [(S_0 - PV(X)]\}$, the arbitrage strategy, as we saw earlier, should consist of a long position in the call and a short position in $[(S_0 - PV(X)]$. That is:

BOUNDARY CONDITION	BOUNDARY CONDITION VIOLATION	ARBITRAGE STRATEGY		DETAILS
$C_0^a \geq S_0 - PV(X)$	$C_0^a < S_0 - PV(X)$	Long call Short $[S_0 - PV(X)]$	$\{+C_0^a\}$ $\{-[S_0 - PV(X)]\} = \{-S_0, +PV(X)\}$	Buy call Buy bond Short stock

This strategy would provide an initial positive cash flow of:

$$CF_0 = S_0 - PV(X) - C_0^a > 0,$$

and as shown in Table 4.2-1, there would be no liabilities when the position is closed at expiration. That is, at expiration if $S_T \geq X$, the total cash flow is $(S_T - X) + X - S_T = 0$ [$(S_T - X)$ is from the call, $+X$ from the bond, and $-S_T$ from the short position]; if $S_T < X$, the total cash flow is positive. Given this riskless opportunity, the price condition is then established by arguing that if the market is efficient, then arbitrageurs, in seeking the opportunity, would drive the price of the call to a level where the initial cash flow is zero. In our case, the price that satisfies that condition (i.e., $CF_0 = 0$) is $S_0 - PV(X)$. That is:

$$CF_0 = S_0 - PV(X) - C_0^a = 0$$

TABLE 4.2-1

		Cash Flows of a Long Call, Long Bond, and Short Stock Portfolio			
			CASH FLOW AT EXPIRATION		
STRATEGY	CURRENT CASH FLOW	$S_T < X$	$S_T = X$	$S_T > X$
Long call	$-C_0$	0	0	$S_T - X$
Long bond	$-PV(X)$	X	X	X
Short stock	S_0	$-S_T$	$-S_T$	$-S_T$
Total	$-C_0 - PV(X) + S_0$	$(X - S_T) > 0$	0	0

NOTE: To preclude arbitrage, the current cash flow, $-C_0 - PV(X) + S_0$, must be negative:
$$-C_0 - PV(X) + S_0 < 0 \qquad \text{or} \qquad C_0 > S_0 - PV(X).$$

$$C_0^a = S_0 - PV(X)$$

$$\text{Min } C_0^a = \text{Max}[S_0 - PV(X), 0].$$

(The methodology just described for establishing the boundary condition for an American call price is summarized in row 2 of Table 4.14-1 at the end of this chapter. That table describes the arbitrage strategies underlying all the boundary conditions delineated in this chapter.)

4.2.3   Minimum Price of a European Call

In the preceding case, the minimum price for the American option was established by an arbitrage portfolio that required closing the positions in the call, bond, and stock at the call's expiration date. Since the call is closed at expiration, the distinction between American and European is not important in defining the minimum price. Thus, the **minimum European call price** option on a stock not paying a dividend can be determined by the same arbitrage argument used for the American option.

RELATION:
$$\text{Min } C_t^e = \text{Max}[S_0 - PV(X), 0].$$

It should be noted that since both the American and European calls (on a stock not paying a dividend during the life of the call) have exactly the same lower bounds, the right to early exercise, implicit in an American call, is worth nothing. Thus, the American call option should not be exercised early; it is worth more "alive" than "dead."

4.3   MINIMUM PRICE CONDITIONS FOR CALLS ON DIVIDEND-PAYING STOCKS

4.3.1   Boundary Condition

In the earlier example, we established the minimum price of the call (whether American or European) to be $12.26. That is:

$$\text{Min } C_0 = \text{Max}[S_0 - PV(X), 0]$$

$$\text{Min } C_0 = \text{Max}[\$50 - \frac{\$40}{1.06}, 0] = \$12.26.$$

As discussed earlier, if the 40 call (American or European) in our example was trading below $12.26, then an arbitrage profit could be realized by going long in the call, long in the bond, and short in the stock. Suppose the 40 call, though, was trading below its minimum at $10 but that the stock was expected (with certainty) to pay a dividend of $3.00 in three months. In this case, the arbitrage strategy governing the minimum call price, if implemented, would earn an initial cash flow of $50 − ($40/1.06) − $10 = $2.26. At the end of three months, however, an arbitrageur would have to pay $3.00 to the share lender to cover the dividend payment on the short stock position. Since this dividend payment exceeds the initial excess cash of $2.26, the strategy is no longer a free lunch.

This example suggests that the boundary condition of $S_0 - PV(X)$ holds only for cases in which the underlying stock does not pay a dividend. A boundary condition (not the minimum price condition) for call options (American and European) on a dividend-paying stock can be established by simply adding to the arbitrage strategy a long position in a pure discount bond with a face value equal to the dividend (D) and a maturity equal to the time of the dividend payment date (t^*). At the dividend date, this bond would pay the arbitrageur $D, which he would use to cover the dividend obligation on the short stock position. As previously discussed, the stock, call, and other bond positions would yield either zero or positive cash flows at expiration. To preclude arbitrage in this dividend-paying case, the initial cash flow of the position must be negative. That is:

$$S_0 - PV(X, T) - PV(D, t^*) - C_0 < 0$$

where:

$PV(X, T)$ = price of bond with face value of X and maturity at T

$PV(D, t^*)$ = price of bond with face value of D and maturity at t^* (dividend payment date).

Thus, in this example the price of the call (American or European) on the dividend-paying stock must equal at least $9.31.

$$C_0 \geq \text{Max}[S_0 - PV(X, T) - PV(D, t^*), 0]$$

$$C_0 \geq \text{Max}\left[\$50 - \frac{\$40}{(1.06)} - \frac{\$3}{(1.06)^{.25}}, 0\right]$$

$$C_0 \geq \$9.31.$$

In summary:

RELATION: The price of an American or European call on a stock that is expected to pay a D dividend at time t^* (prior to the option's expiration) must be greater than $S_0 - PV(D, t^*) - PV(X, T)$. If this condition does not hold, an arbitrage profit may be obtained by shorting the stock and buying the call, a bond with D face value and t^* maturity, and another bond with X face value and T maturity.

4.3.2   Minimum Price on European Call

Since a European call cannot be exercised early, this boundary condition also defines the minimum price condition of a European call on a dividend-paying stock.

RELATION:
$$\text{Min } C_0^e = \text{Max}[S_0 - PV(X, T) - PV(D, t^*), 0].$$

4.3.3   Minimum Price on American Call

$3 Dividend Case
If the call in the preceding example is American and is priced at the minimum European value of $9.31, then an arbitrage profit of $0.69 can be attained by buying the call, exercising immediately, and selling the stock. In the absence of arbitrage, the price of the American call would therefore have to be at least equal to its IV of $10, a condition we established earlier. Thus, in this example the $3 dividend makes the American call, with its early exercise right, more valuable than the comparable European call. In this case, the early exercise feature makes it possible for arbitrageurs to close their arbitrage portfolios before they have to make dividend payments to their share lenders.

Suppose, though, the American call is trading at $10.25 (above its IV). At $10.25, an arbitrageur would still be able to realize another free lunch, this time by shorting the stock, buying the American call, and buying a three-month bond with a face value of $X = \$40$, then exercising the call just before the dividend-payment date. At the end of three months, if the call is in or on the money ($S_t \geq \$40$), the arbitrageur would be able to use the $40 from the bond to exercise the call, then use the stock received from the exercise to cover the short position, realizing a zero net cash flow. On the other hand, if the call is out of the money ($S_t < \$40$), exercising the call would be worthless. In this case, the arbitrageur would be able to use some of the $40 bond principal to cover the short position, realizing a cash flow of $40 - S_t$ (plus, the arbitrageur may be able to sell the out-of-the-money call with a time value premium). Thus, whether the call is in, on, or out of the money, this strategy has no liabilities at the dividend-payment date. To preclude arbitrage, the price on the American call would have to be equal to at least $10.58, the price at which the strategy's initial cash flow is zero. That is:

$$CF_0 = S_0 - PV(X, t^*) - C_0^a$$

$$0 = S_0 - PV(X, t^*) - C_0^a$$

$$C_0^a = S_0 - PV(X, t^*)$$

$$C_0^a = \$50 - \frac{\$40}{(1.06)^{.25}} = \$10.58.$$

The example suggests that for American calls on stocks with dividends, the time of the early exercise will ensure a specific minimum call value. In our example, immediate exercise ensures that C_0^a will be equal to or greater than $10, exercising just before the dividend is paid ensures that C_0^a will be equal to or greater than $10.58, and exercising at expiration ensures that C_0^a will be equal to or greater than $9.31. Since the second bound is the largest, it determines the American call's minimum price. Thus:

$$\text{Min } C_0^a = \text{Max}[S_0 - X, S_0 - PV(X, t^*), S_0 - PV(D, t^*) - PV(X, T), 0]$$

$$\text{Min } C_0^a = \text{Max}\left[\$50 - \$40, \$50 - \frac{\$40}{(1.06)^{.25}}, \$50 - \frac{\$3}{(1.06)^{.25}} - \frac{\$40}{1.06}, 0\right]$$

$$\text{Min } C_0^a = \text{Max}[\$10, \$10.58, \$9.31, 0] = \$10.58.$$

$1 Dividend Case

Now suppose that the stock paid only a $1 dividend, instead of $3. If the call is European, its minimum price would be $11.28:

$$\text{Min } C_0^e = \text{Max}[S_0 - PV(D, t^*) - PV(X, T), 0]$$

$$\text{Min } C_0^e = \text{Max}\left[\$50 - \frac{\$1}{(1.06)^{.25}} - \frac{\$40}{1.06}, 0\right]$$

$$\text{Min } C_0^e = \text{Max}[\$11.28, 0] = \$11.28.$$

For an American call, this $11.28 value is greater than the $10.58 value ensured from exercising just before the dividend is paid. As a result, if the dividend is only $1, the minimum price of the American call would be $11.28, the same as the European. That is:

$$\text{Min } C_0^a = \text{Max}[S_0 - X, S_0 - PV(X, t^*), S_0 - PV(D, t^*) - PV(X, T), 0]$$

$$\text{Min } C_0^a = \text{Max}\left[\$50 - \$40, \$50 - \frac{\$40}{(1.06)^{.25}}, \$50 - \frac{\$1}{(1.06)^{.25}} - \frac{\$40}{1.06}, 0\right]$$

$$\text{Min } C_0^a = \text{Max}[\$10, \$10.58, \$11.28, 0] = \$11.28.$$

In this case, the $1 dividend is not large enough to justify early exercise. As a result, the American and European calls have the same minimum values.

Threshold Dividend

The preceding examples show that just the payment of a dividend is not enough to justify early exercise; rather, the dividend must be greater than a specific level for the American call to be more valuable than the European. The *threshold dividend* for determining whether early exercise is advantageous or not for the arbitrageur can be found algebraically by solving for the dividend (D^*) that makes the minimum American call value from exercising just prior to the dividend date (t^*) equal to the minimum European value. As shown next, this dividend level is the one where $D^* = X - [X/(1 + R)^{T-t^*}]$:

$$S_0 - PV(X, t^*) = S_0 - PV(X, T) - PV(D, t^*)$$

$$S_0 - \frac{X}{(1 + R)^{t^*}} = S_0 - \frac{X}{(1 + R)^T} - \frac{D}{(1 + R)^{t^*}}$$

$$\frac{D}{(1 + R)^{t^*}} = \frac{X}{(1 + R)^{t^*}} - \frac{X}{(1 + R)^T}$$

$$D = X - \frac{X}{(1 + R)^T}(1 + R)^{t^*}$$

$$D^* = X - \frac{X}{(1 + R)^{T-t^*}}.$$

In our example, the threshold dividend would be $1.71:

$$D^* = \$40 - \frac{\$40}{(1.06)^{1-.25}} = \$1.71,$$

and the minimum American and European call prices when the dividend is $1.71 would be $10.58:

$$\text{Min } C_0^a = \text{Max}[S_0 - X, S_0 - PV(X, t^*), S_0 - PV(D, t^*) - PV(X, T), 0]$$

$$\text{Min } C_0^a = \text{Max}\left[\$50 - \$40, \$50 - \frac{\$40}{(1.06)^{.25}}, \$50 - \frac{\$1.71}{(1.06)^{.25}} - \frac{\$40}{1.06}, 0\right]$$

$$\text{Min } C_0^a = \text{Max}[\$10, \$10.58, \$10.58, 0] = \$10.58;$$

and

$$\text{Min } C_0^e = \text{Max}[S_0 - PV(D, t^*) - PV(X, T), 0]$$

$$\text{Min } C_0^e = \text{Max}\left[\$50 - \frac{\$1.71}{(1.06)^{.25}}, - \frac{\$40}{1.06}, 0\right]$$

$$\text{Min } C_0^e = \text{Max}[\$10.58, 0] = \$10.58.$$

Thus, if the dividend is greater than $1.71, then the minimum value of the American call would be greater than the European call; if the dividend is equal to or less than $1.71, then there would be no early exercise advantage to arbitrageurs and the minimum values for the American and European calls would be the same.

Finally, note that $X - [X/(1 + R)^{T-t*}] = \$40 - [\$40/(1.06)^{.75}] = \$1.71$ is the present value of the interest foregone on a bond held to T. Thus, if the dividend is greater than the present value of the interest foregone, then the American call would be more valuable; if it is not, then the American and European values are the same.

To summarize:

RELATION: The price of an American call on a stock that is expected to pay a $D dividend at time t^* is dependent upon the dividend and the value of the interest (I) earned on an amount equal to the exercise price from time t^* to T. If $D \leq I$, the minimum call value is the same as the European:

$$\text{Min } C_0^a = \text{Max}[S_0 - \text{PV}(D, t^*) - \text{PV}(X, T), 0].$$

On the other hand, if $D > I$, then

$$\text{Min } C_0^a = \text{Max}[S_0 - \text{PV}(X, t^*), 0].$$

4.3.4   Summary

The preceding examples with different dividends illustrate several points. First, as shown in Table 4.3-1, dividends have a negative impact on call values. In our examples, the minimum price for the European call decreased from $12.26 to $11.28 to $9.31 as we changed the dividend from zero to $1 to $3, and the price of the American call decreased from $12.26 to $11.28 to $10.58. Second, if the dividend is low, the early exercise advantage for arbitrageurs may not exist, and as a result, the American call would have the same minimum value as the European. In our example, this was the case when the dividend was $1.71 or less. Finally, if the dividend is high, the early exercise advantage for arbitrageurs may exist; if so, the minimum value of the American call would be greater than that of the European one. This was the case in our example when the dividend was greater than $1.71.

TABLE 4.3-1

Minimum Call Prices with Different Dividends				
$S_0 = \$50, X = \$40, T = 1$ year, $t^* = 3$ months (.25 per year)				
	No Dividend	$1 Dividend	$1.71 Dividend	$3 Dividend
Minimum European call price	$12.26	$11.28	$10.58	$ 9.31
Minimum American call price	$12.26	$11.28	$10.58	$10.58

4.4 OPTION PRICES WITH DIFFERENT EXERCISE PRICES

4.4.1 Price Relation of Calls with Different Exercise Prices

Suppose a July ABC 50 European call is trading at $3 while a July ABC 60 European call is at $4. Upon reflection, something is wrong. Intuitively, we expect the price of the call with the lower exercise price of $50 to be greater than the one with the higher exercise price of $60, since the former gives us the right to buy ABC stock at a lower price. To exploit this price imbalance, an arbitrageur could buy the 50 call and sell the 60 one (i.e., set up a bull spread). As shown in Table 4.4-1 and its accompanying figure, at expiration arbitrageurs/spreaders would earn a profit regardless of the price of ABC stock. By exploiting this opportunity, though, they would increase the price of the 50 call and lower the price of the 60 call until $C_0^e(50) > C_0^e(60)$ and the arbitrage opportunity disappears. Thus, arbitrageurs would ensure that the price of a lower-exercise-priced call is greater than a higher-priced one. That is:

TABLE 4.4-1

	Profit and Stock Price Relation for a Bull Spread		
$C^e(50) < C^e(60)$			
S_T	PROFIT ON 50 CALL CONTRACT PURCHASED AT $3	PROFIT FROM 60 CALL CONTRACT SOLD AT $4	TOTAL PROFIT
$40	− $300	$400	$ 100
45	− 300	400	100
50	− 300	400	100
55	200	400	600
60	700	400	1100
65	1200	− 100	1100
70	1700	− 600	1100

Bull Spread

ABC 50 call purchased at $3 and ABC 60 call sold at $4

ABC 50 call purchased at 3 and ABC 60 call sold at 4

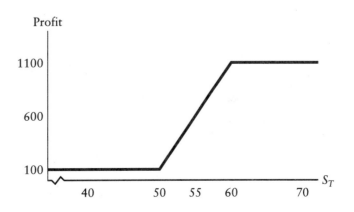

RELATION: $C_0^e(X_1) > C_0^e(X_2)$, for $X_2 > X_1$.

A more formal proof of the condition $C_0^e(X_1) > C_0^e(X_2)$ is presented in Table 4.4-2. In the table, the cash flows at expiration are shown for a bull spread formed with a long position in an X_1 call and a short position in an X_2 call. As shown, there are three possible cases at expiration: $S_T < X_1$; $X_1 \leq S_T \leq X_2$; and $S_T > X_2$. If $X_1 \leq S_T \leq X_2$ or $S_T > X_2$, then the cash flows from the bull spread will be positive; if $S_T < X_1$, then the spread's cash flows will be zero. An arbitrage opportunity would therefore exist if there was no cost incurred in setting up the bull spread. To preclude this free lunch, the initial cash flows of the bull spread must therefore be negative. That is:

$$CF_0 = -C_0^e(X_1) + C_0^e(X_2) < 0$$

or

$$C_0^e(X_1) > C_0^e(X_2).$$

In summary:

RELATION: Given two European call options identical except for their exercise prices, the one with the lower exercise price (X_1) will be priced higher than the one with the higher exercise price (X_2); if not, then an arbitrage opportunity exists by forming a bull money spread.

The condition that $C_0^e(X_1) > C_0^e(X_2)$ also holds for an American option in which early exercise is possible. If it did not, then an arbitrageur/spreader again could take a long position in the call with the lower exercise price and a short position in the call with the higher exercise price. If she could hold the positions to expiration, then the same arbitrage profit discussed earlier for the European calls could be earned.

TABLE 4.4-2

		Cash Flows at Expiration from Bull Spread		
			CASH FLOW AT EXPIRATION	
POSITION	CURRENT CASH FLOW	$S_T < X_1$	$X_1 \leq S_T \leq X_2$	$S_T > X_2$
Long X_1 call	$-C_0^e(X_1)$	0	$S_T - X_1$	$S_T - X_1$
Short X_2 call	$C_0^e(X_2)$	0	0	$-(S_T - X_2)$
Total	$-C_0^e(X_1) + C_0^e(X_2)$	0	$(S_T - X_1) > 0$	$(X_2 - X_1) - 0$

NOTE: To preclude arbitrage, the initial cash flow must be negative. Thus:

$$-C_0^e(X_1) + C_0^e(X_2) < 0 \quad \text{or} \quad C_0^e(X_1) > C_0^e(X_2)$$

However, it is possible for the spreader to be assigned on the short position. If this occurred, then the arbitrageur/spreader would have to buy the stock in the market at S_t and sell it to the option holder at X_2, for a loss on the short position of $X_2 - S_t$. Still, the spreader can more than offset this loss by simply selling her lower-exercise-price call at $C_t^a(X_1) = S_t - X_1 + \text{TVP}$. Since $X_2 > X_1$, the cash flow from closing would exceed the cost of the assignment. Thus, if there was an early exercise at time t, the arbitrageur/spreader would still be able to earn a positive cash flow of:

$$\text{CF}_t = C_t^a(X_1) - (S_t - X_2)$$

$$\text{CF}_t = (S_t - X_1 + \text{TVP}) - S_t + X_2$$

$$\text{CF}_t = X_2 - X_1 + \text{TVP} > 0.$$

Hence, an American option, like the European, is governed by the condition that $C_0^a(X_1) > C_0^a(X_2)$.[*]

4.4.2   Price Limits on Calls with Different Exercise Prices

In addition to the condition that $C(X_1) > C(X_2)$, we also can establish with an arbitrage argument that the difference in the call premiums cannot be greater than the present value of the difference in the calls' exercise prices for European calls,

$$C_0^e(X_1) - C_0^e(X_2) < \text{PV}(X_2 - X_1),$$

and greater than the difference in the calls' exercise prices for American calls,

$$C_0^a(X_1) - C_0^a(X_2) < X_2 - X_1.$$

In the case of the European calls, if the price-limit condition does not hold [i.e., $C^e(X_1) - C^e(X_2) > \text{PV}(X_2 - X_1)$], then an arbitrage opportunity would be available by going long in a bond with a face value of $X_2 - X_1$ and maturing at the option's expiration date, $\{+\text{PV}(X_2 - X_1)\}$, short in the X_1 call, $\{-C(X_1)\}$, and long in the X_2 call $\{+C(X_2)\}$. This strategy would yield an initial positive cash flow of $C_0^e(X_1) - C_0^e(X_2) - \text{PV}(X_2 - X_1)$; and as shown in Table 4.4-3, at expiration the cash flows would be either positive or zero, but not negative, when the position is closed. To preclude this free lunch, the initial cash flow must therefore be negative:

> RELATION: $C_0^e(X_1) - C_0^e(X_2) < \text{PV}(X_2 - X_1)$,   for $X_2 > X_1$.

---

[*]An exception to this rule can occur when there is a deep out-of-the-money option. With such options, it is quite possible for the premiums for options with different exercise prices to be the same.

TABLE 4.4-3

	Cash Flow from Bear Spread and Bond with Face Value of $X_2 - X_1$		
	CASH FLOW AT EXPIRATION		
POSITION	$S_T < X_1$	$X_1 \leq S_T \leq X_2$	$S_T > X_2$
Short in X_1 call	0	$-(S_T - X_1)$	$-(S_T - X_1)$
Long in X_2 call	0	0	$(S_T - X_2)$
Long in bond	$X_2 - X_1$	$X_2 - X_1$	$X_2 - X_1$
Total	$(X_2 - X_1) > 0$	$(X_2 - S_T) > 0$	0

For the example in the preceding section, if the options' expirations and the bond's maturity are one year and the risk-free rate of return is 6%, then the difference in the prices of the ABC 50 European call and the ABC 60 European call should not be greater than $9.43:

$$C_0^e(X_1) - C_0^e(X_2) < PV(\$60 - \$50) = \frac{\$10}{1.06} = \$9.43.$$

The preceding condition is applicable for European calls. Suppose an arbitrageur, though, is long in the bond and has a bear spread formed with American calls $[\{-C_0^a(X_1), +C_0^a(X_2)\}]$ and both calls are exercised early at time t. The arbitrageur, in turn, would incur a negative cash flow of $X_2 - X_1$ at time t, which he can finance by borrowing $X_2 - X_1$ dollars at a rate R for the remainder of the period $(T - t)$. At expiration, closing the loan would cost $(X_2 - X_1)(1 + R)^{T-t}$. Since $(X_2 - X_1)(1 + R)^{T-t}$ is greater than the bond's cash flow of $(X_2 - X_1)$, the arbitrageur's strategy is no longer riskless. Thus, the price limit condition for European calls needs to be adjusted for American calls. This can be done by defining the price limit in terms of an arbitrage portfolio consisting of the bear spread and a riskless bond purchased for $X_2 - X_1$, instead for $PV(X_2 - X_1)$. This bond investment would have a face value of $(X_2 - X_1)(1 + R)^T$ at expiration, which would exceed the maximum cost of covering the bear spread, regardless of when the spread is exercised. Thus, for American call options the price limits condition would be:

RELATION:　　$C_0^a(X_1) - C_0^a(X_2) < X_2 - X_1,$　　for $X_2 > X_1$.

If this condition does not hold, then an arbitrage opportunity would exist by purchasing a riskless bond for $X_2 - X_1$ and forming a bear spread by selling the X_1 American call and buying the X_2 American call.

4.5　CALL PRICE AND TIME-TO-EXPIRATION RELATIONS

In Chapter 1 we noted that the greater a call's time to expiration, the greater its time value premium. The positive relation between a call's time to expiration and its price suggests that, given two American call options on the same stock, with the same exercise prices but with different expirations, the call with the greater expiration time (T_2) will be priced higher than the one with the smaller time (T_1). That is:

$$C_0^a(T_2) > C_0^a(T_1), \qquad \text{for } T_2 > T_1.$$

While this relationship is intuitive, an arbitrage argument involving a time spread can be used to establish the condition. Specifically, suppose that an ABC 50 call that expires in six months $(T_2 = .5$ per year) is selling for $C_0^a(.5) = \$5$, while an ABC 50 call expiring in three months $(T_1 = .25)$ is selling at a higher price of $C_0^a(.25) = \$7$. An arbitrageur/spreader could realize a $2 cash flow immediately by forming a time spread: buy the longer-term call and sell the shorter-term one:

STRATEGY	CASH FLOW
Buy longer-term call: $C_0^a(.5)$	− $5
Sell shorter-term call: $C_0^a(.25)$	$7
Cash Flow	$2

If the short-term ABC 50 call is ever exercised, whether at expiration or before, the arbitrageur can simply exercise the longer-term option in order to meet the assignment; that is, she can buy the stock at $X = \$50$ on the longer-term option, then deliver it on the shorter-term call's assignment. Thus, once the arbitrage is set, there are no further liabilities. Given this riskless opportunity, arbitrageurs in the market would buy the longer-term call, increasing its demand and price, and sell the shorter-term call, depressing its price, until $C_0^a(.5) > C_0^a(.25)$ and the arbitrage opportunity disappears. Thus:

> RELATION: Given two American call options on the same stock, with the same exercise prices but with different expiration dates, the price of the longer-term call will be greater than the price of a shorter-term one. If this condition does not hold, then an arbitrage profit can be realized by forming a time spread: Buy the longer-term call and sell the shorter-term call. Such actions by arbitrageurs will ensure:
>
> $$C_0^a(T_2) > C_0^a(T_1), \qquad \text{for } T_2 > T_1.$$

This particular arbitrage strategy is not applicable to European options, since the spreader cannot exercise his longer-term call early to cover the expiring shorter-term call.

4.6 CALL PRICE RELATIONS WITH STOCK PRICES, VOLATILITY, AND INTEREST RATES

In the last four sections we've examined how arbitrageurs can ensure that certain price conditions are met. The actual price of the call will be within these price constraints. In this section we examine three factors that have determining impacts on the price of the call—the price of the underlying stock, the variability in the price of the underlying stock, and interest rates.

4.6.1 Call Price and Stock Price Relation

The arbitrage conditions delineated in Section 4.2 ensure that a positive relationship exists between C_t and S_t. This call and stock price relation, however, is not a linear one. Specifically, if the price of the stock is very high relative to the exercise price (a deep in-the-money call), then the costs of acquiring the option will be relatively expensive (large intrinsic value), resulting in a low demand. As a result, at relatively high stock prices, arbitrageurs would ensure that the call price is at least equal to $S_t - \text{PV}(X)$ [or $S_t - \text{PV}(X, T) - \text{PV}(D, t^*)$ or $S_t - \text{PV}(X, t^*)$ for calls on dividend-paying stocks], but the time value premiums would be very small.

In contrast, when the price of the stock is substantially below its exercise price (a deep out-of-the-money call), investors would most likely have very little confidence in the option being profitable. As a result, the demand and price of the call would be extremely low, and the price of the call would be equal or approximately equal to zero. Moreover, with a low or zero demand for a deep out-of-the-money call, any incremental change in the stock price would have a negligible impact on the price of the call.

The relationships between the call and stock prices when the stock price is either very low or very high is seen graphically in Figure 4.2-1. As shown, at the low stock prices, the call option curve CC approaches the horizontal axis, suggesting that the call is (or is almost) worthless, and that any marginal change in S_t has only a small impact on C_t. As the stock price increases, the call price curve begins to increase at an increasing rate, implying the TVP is increasing. This will continue until the stock is on or near the money; at that point, the TVP is at a maximum. Finally, as the stock price increases further, the TVP starts to decrease; at very high stock prices, the TVP is negligible, and the call option curve approaches the minimum boundary line.

4.6.2 Call Price and Volatility Relation

Most securities are governed by a negative relationship between the security's variability and its price. That is, assuming all other factors are constant, the greater a security's variability, the less demand for it and therefore the lower its price. The opposite relationship, however, exists for call options. Since a long call position is characterized by unlimited profits if the stock increases but limited losses if it decreases, a call holder would prefer more volatility rather than less. Specifically, greater variability suggests, on the one hand, a greater likelihood that the stock will increase substantially in price, causing the call to be more valuable. On the other hand, greater variability also suggests a greater chance of the stock price's decreasing substantially. However, given that a call's losses are limited to just the premium when the stock price is equal to the exercise price or less, the extent of the price decrease should be inconsequential to the call holder. Thus, the market will value a call option on a volatile stock more than a call on a stock with lower variability, all other factors being the same.

The positive relationship between a call's premium and its underlying security's volatility can be seen in terms of the example presented in Table 4.6-1. The table shows two call options: (1) an ABC 100 call, in which ABC stock is assumed to be trading at $100 and has a variability characterized by an equal chance of the stock price either increasing by 10% or decreasing by 10% by the end of the period (assume these are the only possibilities); (2) an XYZ 100 call, in which XYZ stock also is assumed to be trading at $100 but has a larger variability, characterized by an equal chance of XYZ price either increasing or decreasing by 20% by the end of the period. As can be seen in Table 4.6-1, given the characteristics of their underlying stocks, the XYZ call would be worth either $20 or 0 at the end of the period, compared to values of only $10 or 0 for the ABC call. Since the XYZ call cannot perform worse than the ABC call, and can do better, it follows that there would be a higher demand, and therefore a higher price, for the more volatile XYZ call than for the less volatile ABC option.

TABLE 4.6-1

Call Price and Variability Relation	
CURRENT	EXPIRATION
	ABC = $110 ABC 100 call: IV = $10
ABC stock = $100	
	ABC = $90 ABC 100 call: IV = 0
	XYZ = $120 XYZ 100 call: IV = $20
XYZ stock = $100	
	XYZ = $80 XYZ 100 call: IV = 0

In summary:

> RELATION: Given the limited loss characteristic of a call purchase position, a call option on a security with greater volatility (V_2) is more valuable than one with lower volatility (V_1), all other factors being equal:
>
> $$C(V_2) > C(V_1), \quad \text{for } V_2 > V_1.$$

4.6.3 Call Price and Interest Rate Relation

In general, a substitution effect exists among different securities that causes their prices to be inversely related to the rate of return on a risk-free security (also to be referred to as the interest rate). For example, if the rate on a risk-free treasury security increased, investors would want to substitute some of their other security holdings for the lower-priced treasury securities. As they made the substitution by selling their stocks and/or risky bonds, they would drive the price of those securities down. Thus, a priori, we should observe a negative relation between the rates on a risk-free security and the prices of other securities.

A call option, though, represents a deferred purchase of the underlying security. As a result, a direct, instead of an inverse, relationship between call prices and interest rates may exist. To see this, consider the case of investors interested in purchasing XYZ stock for $100 and holding it for one period. If there is also available in the market an XYZ 100 call option, expiring at the end of the period and trading at $14, investors could either buy the stock at $S_0 = \$100$ or, alternatively, buy the XYZ call at $14 and invest the remainder of $86 in a risk-free bond maturing at the end of the period. Each investor's selection of the stock or call and bond will depend on his risk-return preference. If rates on the bond were to increase, though, the call-and-bond portfolio would yield a relatively higher return per risk at the call price of $14. The relatively more attractive rates on the bond-and-call portfolio, in turn, would serve to increase the demand for this portfolio, causing the price of the call to increase until a new equilibrium is attained. Thus, an increase in interest rates can lead to an increase in the price of a call.[*] In summary:

> RELATION: An increase in interest rates makes a bond-and-call portfolio relatively more attractive than a stock portfolio, causing, in turn, the demand and price of the call to increase. Alternatively, an interest rate decrease makes a bond-and-call portfolio less attractive, causing the price of the call to decrease. Thus, with other factors constant, a direct relationship exists between interest rates and call prices.

---

[*]The direct relationship between the price of the call and the interest rates requires assuming that other factors are constant. If we relax the assumption, then the total impact of an interest rate change on call prices may be ambiguous.

4.7 EARLY EXERCISE OF AN AMERICAN CALL

In Chapter 2 we noted that in most cases a call holder should close her position by selling the call instead of exercising. That is, prior to expiration the call holder who sells receives the intrinsic value and the time value premium as part of the selling price, while the call holder who exercises receives just the call's intrinsic value. An exception to this rule occurs, though, in the case in which the call's underlying stock is expected to go "ex-dividend" during the period and the expected dividend exceeds the call's time value premium.

Most stock exchanges specify an "ex-dividend" date for a stock. Investors who purchase shares of the stock before the ex-dividend date are entitled to receive the dividend, "cum-dividend," while those who buy on or after the ex-dividend date are not. On the ex-dividend date the price of the stock should decrease by an amount approximately equal to the dividend, since those who buy the stock at such time do not receive the dividend.* Given the decrease in the price of the stock, a holder of an in-the-money call on that stock might find it profitable to exercise the call just before the stock goes ex-dividend.

The argument for early exercise can be seen by considering a call holder's alternative cash flow positions on the ex-dividend date: one position resulting from exercising the call just prior to the date, and the other position from not exercising. In the first case, if the holder exercises *just prior* to the ex-dividend date, then his cash flow *on* the ex-dividend date would equal the value of the stock on that date plus the value of the dividend (D) he is entitled to on the stock's date of record, minus the X used by the holder to buy the stock on the call just prior to the ex-dividend date. If the stock is worth S_t just prior to the ex-dividend date, and we assume that the stock will decrease by an amount equal to the value of the dividend on the ex-dividend date, then the price of the stock on the ex-dividend date (S_x) would be: $S_x = S_t - D$. Thus, the holder's cash flow on the ex-dividend date (W_{ex}) from exercising is:

$$W_{ex} = S_x + D - X$$

$$W_{ex} = (S_t - D) + D - X$$

$$W_{ex} = S_t - X.$$

---

*For example, suppose investors expected ABC stock to sell for $54 at the end of the period and to pay a $1 dividend. If investors, in turn, required a 10% expected rate of return for the period [$E(R)$] from buying the stock, then just prior to the ex-dividend date they would pay $50 for ABC stock:

$$E(R) = \frac{Div + [E(S) - S_0]}{S_0} = \frac{\$1 + (\$54 - \$50)}{\$50} = .10;$$

and at the ex-dividend date they would pay $49.09:

$$E(R) = \frac{Div + [E(S) - S_0]}{S_0} = \frac{0 + (\$54 - \$49.09)}{\$49.09} = .10.$$

Thus, on the ex-dividend date the price of the stock would have to fall by an amount approximately equal to the dividend to yield investors the same rate.

Alternatively, if the call holder does not exercise and $S_t - X > 0$, then his cash flow on the ex-dividend date would simply equal the price of the call on the date, C_{ex}, which would equal the call's intrinsic value plus its time value premium:

$$C_{ex} = IV + TVP$$

$$C_{ex} = (S_x - X) + TVP$$

$$C_{ex} = (S_t - D) - X + TVP.$$

In comparing the two positions, a call holder should exercise if $W_{ex} > C_{ex}$.[*] This early exercise condition is met when $D > TVP$, provided the call is in the money on the ex-dividend date. That is:

$$W_{ex} > C_{ex}$$

$$S_t - X > S_t - D - X + TVP$$

$$D > TVP.$$

In this case the early-exercise advantage exists because the dividend the holder is entitled to after exercising exceeds the TVP he is giving up.

If the size of the dividend is such that the call is out of the money on the ex-dividend date ($D > S_t - X$), then the holder should exercise early if $S_T - X > TVP$. That is, $W_{ex} > C_{ex}$ when $S_t - X > TVP$:

$$W_{ex} > C_{ex}$$

$$S_t - X > Max[S_t - D - X, 0] + TVP$$

$$S_t - X > TVP, \quad \text{for } D > S_t - X.$$

These conditions suggest that call options that would be likely candidates for early exercise are those with low TVP and/or high dividend payments.[†]

4.8 MINIMUM AND MAXIMUM PUT PRICES

In a similar fashion to call options, put premiums also are governed by arbitrage conditions. As we will see, many of the conditions and relationships germane to puts are similar to the ones just examined for calls.

---

[*]The TVP on the ex-dividend date may be slightly different than the TVP just prior to the expiration date.

[†]Our discussion here did not include commission costs, which are relatively high for exercising; such costs would necessarily need to be included before deciding whether early exercise is profitable.

4.8.1   Maximum American and European Put Prices

Since a put increases in value as the stock decreases, its maximum price occurs when the stock price is equal to zero. For an American put with the stock price at zero, a put holder could sell the worthless stock for the exercise price. Thus, the value of the put would have to be the exercise price. For a European put with the price of the stock at zero, the holder would be able to sell the stock at X, but not until expiration. Thus, the put would be worth the present value of the exercise price (assuming the stock price is zero and will remain there because the company is bankrupt). In summary, the *maximum American and European put prices are:*

RELATION: Max P_0^a = X.

RELATION: Max P_0^e = PV(X).

4.8.2   Minimum Price of an American Put

As discussed in Chapter 1, the *minimum American put price* (on a stock that pays no dividends) is the put's intrinsic value. This condition is governed by arbitrage. For example, suppose ABC 50 puts are trading for $3 while the stock is at $45. You could achieve a riskless profit by buying the stock and the put for $48, then selling the stock immediately at $50 by exercising the put. The net result of these transactions would be an arbitrage profit of $2. By executing this strategy, arbitrageurs would augment the demand for the put, causing its price to increase until the arbitrage profit disappears. The minimum put price where the arbitrage return is zero is the put's intrinsic value.

RELATION: The minimum price of an American put on a stock that pays no dividends is the put's intrinsic value:

Min P_0^a = IV = Max[$X - S_0$, 0].

If this condition does not hold, then an arbitrage opportunity exists and may be exploited by buying the put and the underlying stock and then exercising the put immediately.

4.8.3   Minimum Price of a European Put

The *minimum European put price* on a stock that pays no dividends can be established by comparing an investment in a bond with a face value of X to an investment in a portfolio of the stock and put. Table 4.8-1 presents the end-of-the-period cash flows for the stock-and-put investment and for an investment in a bond with a face value of X, maturing at the expiration date on the put. As shown, if $S_T \leq X$, then the stock and put portfolio would yield the same cash flow as the bond (X); on the other hand, if $S_T > X$, then the put would be worthless but the

TABLE 4.8-1

	CASH FLOWS AT EXPIRATION		
POSITION	$S_T < X$	$S_T = X$	$S_T > X$
Investment 1: Bond purchase	X	X	X
Investment 2: Put purchase + Stock purchase	$X - S_T$ S_T	0 S_T	0 S_T
Total	X	X	S_T
Investor preference	Indifferent	Indifferent	Investment 2

Comparison of Bond with Put-and-Stock Portfolio

NOTE: Investment 1 (long bond) provides the same cash flow ($X) at expiration whether the stock goes up or down. Investment 2: $\{+P, +S\}$ provides a cash flow of $X when $S_T \leq X$, and a greater flow of S_T if the stock price at expiration is greater than X. Hence, investment 2 dominates investment 1 and should have a higher value at $t = 0$.

stock would be worth more than the face value of the bond. Thus, since the put-and-stock portfolio yields the same cash flows at expiration as does the bond investment in some cases ($S_T \leq X$) and a greater cash flow in others ($S_T > X$), it should be valued higher by investors. That is:

$$P_0^e + S_0 > PV(X). \tag{4.8-1}$$

Solving inequality (4.8-1) for P_0^e, and expressing it with a constraint that P_0^e cannot be negative, defines the minimum price of a European put:

$$P_0^e > Max[PV(X) - S_0, 0]$$

$$Min\ P_0^e = Max[PV(X) - S_0, 0].$$

In addition to the intuitive reasoning, an arbitrage argument also can be used to establish the minimum price of a European put. Similar to the arbitrage strategy presented earlier for determining the minimum price of a call, if an in-the-money European put is below its minimum price ($P_0^e < PV(X) - S_0$), then arbitrageurs will be able to earn riskless profit by going long in the put, short in a risk-free bond with a face value of X and maturity of T, and long in the stock.

For example, suppose the price of an ABC 50 European put expiring in one year was $5 when the stock price was $45. If the risk-free rate is 6%, the minimum price of the European put would be $50/1.06 − $45 = $2.17. If the put's market premium were $1.17, then an arbitrageur could realize a $1 arbitrage profit at $t = 0$ by buying the stock-and-put portfolio for $45 + $1.17 = $46.17 and shorting the bond for $47.17. As shown in Table 4.8-2, at expiration, if $S_T \leq X$, the stock-and-put portfolio would yield a cash flow equal to $X, which would just

TABLE 4.8-2

	Cash Flow at Expiration from Long Stock and Put and Short Bond Positions		
	EXPIRATION CASH FLOW		
POSITION	$S_T < X$	$S_T = X$	$S_T > X$
Long stock	S_T	S_T	S_T
Long put	$X - S_T$	0	0
Short bond	$-X$	$-X$	$-X$
Total	0	0	$S_T - X > 0$

cover the short bond; and if $S_T > X$, the put would be worthless but the stock's cash flow would exceed the proceeds needed to cover the bond, yielding a net cash flow of $S_T - X > 0$. This arbitrage opportunity would, in turn, force the price of the put to increase until it is at least equal to \$2.17.

RELATION: The minimum price of European put (on a stock not paying dividends) is:

$$\text{Min } P_0^e = \text{Max}[PV(X) - S_0, 0].$$

If this price condition does not hold, then an arbitrage opportunity exists by going long in the stock and the put and short in a riskless pure discount bond with a face value of X and maturity of T.

Since $PV(X) < X$, the minimum price of a European put is less than that of an American put: $\text{Min } P_0^e < \text{Min } P_0^a$. In our examples, the American put was worth at least \$2.83 more than the European (\$5 − \$2.17). In contrast, for call options on stocks that pay no dividends during the options' lives, the minimum prices of American and European calls are the same.

4.8.4   Boundary Conditions

The minimum and maximum put prices define the boundary conditions for this option. Graphically, these conditions are depicted in Figure 4.8-1 for European and American puts on a non-dividend-paying stock. In the figure, the negatively sloped IV line with the vertical intercept of X defines the lower limit of an American put. Parallel to the IV line is the IV_e line with an intercept of PV(X). This line defines the lower price limit for a European put. Finally, the horizontal line at X and the one at PV(X) define the upper limits for the American and European puts, respectively. The actual price of an American or European put will fall somewhere between these respective boundary lines.

FIGURE 4.8-1

Put Option Boundary
Conditions (Non-
Dividend-Paying Stock)

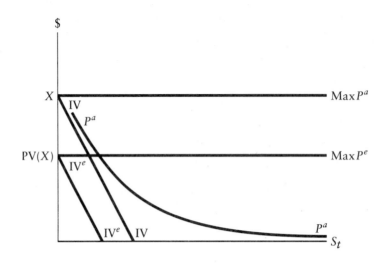

4.9   MINIMUM PRICE CONDITIONS FOR PUTS ON DIVIDEND-PAYING STOCKS

4.9.1   Minimum Price of a European Put

Suppose in the previous example that the stock paid a $3 dividend at the end of four months. Since the arbitrageur is long in the stock, she would receive an additional cash flow of $3.00. Since the present value of the dividend is $PV(D, t^*)$ = $\$3.00/(1.06)^{4/12}$ = $\$2.94$, the minimum price of the European put should be worth $2.94 more than the minimum price of the put without the dividend; thus, the minimum price should be $2.94 + $2.17 = $5.11. If the market price of the put were equal to its minimum European value without dividends of $2.17, an arbitrageur could realize a free lunch by buying the stock-and-put and by shorting (borrowing) both a bond with a face value of X = $50 and maturity of T and a bond with a face value of D = $3.00 and expiration of four months. This strategy would yield an initial cash flow of $2.94:

$$CF_0 = PV(X, T) + PV(D, t^*) - S_0 - P_0^e$$

$$CF_0 = \frac{\$50}{1.06} + \frac{\$3.00}{(1.06)^{4/12}} - \$45 - \$2.17 = \$2.94,$$

and there would be no liabilities when it is closed. That is, at the dividend-payment date the arbitrageur would finance the $3.00 debt with the $3.00 dividend receipt, and, as just stated, would close the stock, bond, and put positions at expiration, obtaining either a zero or positive cash flow. To preclude this arbitrage, the European put would have to trade for at least $5.11. That is:

$$CF_0 = PV(X, T) + PV(D, t^*) - S_0 - P_0^e$$

$$0 = PV(X, T) + PV(D, t^*) - S_0 - P_0^e$$

$$P_0^e = PV(X, T) + PV(D, t^*) - S_0$$

$$P_0^e = \frac{\$50}{1.06} + \frac{\$3.00}{(1.06)^{4/12}} - \$45 = \$5.11.$$

Thus, in the presence of dividends, the minimum European put price is governed by the following relation:

RELATION: If the stock pays a dividend of $D at time t^*, the minimum price of a European put is:

$$\text{Min } P_0^e = \text{Max}[PV(X, T) + PV(D, t^*) - S_0, 0].$$

If this condition does not hold, an arbitrage profit may be obtained by going long in the stock and the put and short in two discount bonds: the first with face value of $D and maturity date t^*, and the second with face value of $X and maturity date T.

4.9.2 Minimum Price of an American Put

If the put in the preceding example is American and priced at $5.11, an arbitrageur could obtain a riskless profit (even though the put is above its IV) by buying the put and the stock and shorting a bond with a face value equal in value to the exercise price and dividend and maturing at the dividend-payment date. Exploiting this, an arbitrageur would realize an initial cash flow of $1.87:

$$CF_0 = -S_0 - P_0^a + PV(X + D, t^*)$$

$$CF_0 = -\$45 - \$5.11 + \frac{\$50 + \$3}{(1.06)^{4/12}} = \$1.87.$$

At the dividend-payment date, the arbitrageur would finance the debt obligation of $53 with the receipt of the $3 dividend and the sale of the stock on the put for $50. To preclude this free lunch, the position's initial cash flow would therefore have to be negative. That is:

$$CF_0 = -S_0 - P_0^a + PV(X + D, t^*) < 0.$$

Thus, the put would have to sell for at least $6.98:

$$P_0^a = \text{Max}[PV(X + D, t^*) - S_0, 0]$$

$$P_0^a = \text{Max}\left[\frac{\$50 + \$3}{(1.06)^{4/12}} - \$45, 0\right]$$

$$P_0^a = \text{Max}[\$6.98, 0] = \$6.98.$$

As we saw earlier with the American call, the time of the early exercise ensures certain minimum put values. In this example, immediate exercise ensures that P_0^a will be equal to or greater than $5 (IV), exercising at the dividend-payment date ensures that P_0^a will be equal to or greater than $6.98, and exercising at expiration ensures that

P_0^a will be equal to or greater than $5.11 (the minimum European value). For American puts, the second bound is always greater than the third, and in this example it is also larger than the first. Thus, the minimum put price is the second bound:

$$\text{Min } P_0^a = \text{Max}[X - S_0, PV(X + D, t^*) - S_0, PV(X, T) + PV(D, t^*) - S_0, 0]$$

$$\text{Min } P_0^a = \text{Max}\left[\$50 - \$45, \frac{\$53}{(1.06)^{4/12}} - \$45, \frac{\$50}{1.06} + \frac{\$3}{(1.06)^{4/12}} - \$45, 0\right]$$

$$\text{Min } P_0^a = \text{Max}[\$5, \$6.98, \$5.11, 0] = \$6.98.$$

Note, if the dividend were $0.50, instead of $3.00, the minimum price with immediate exercise would be $5, the minimum price with exercising at the dividend-payment date would be $4.53:

$$P_0^a = PV(X + D, t^*) - S_0$$

$$P_0^a = \frac{\$50.50}{(1.06)^{4/12}} - \$45 = \$4.53,$$

and the minimum price with exercising at expiration would be $2.66:

$$P_0^a = PV(X, T) + PV(D, t^*) - S_0$$

$$P_0^a = \frac{\$50}{1.06} + \frac{\$0.50}{(1.06)^{4/12}} - \$45 = \$2.66.$$

Thus, the minimum price of the American put would be $5.00:

$$\text{Min } P_0^a = \text{Max}[X - S_0, PV(X + D, t^*) - S_0, PV(X, T) + PV(D, t^*) - S_0, 0]$$

$$\text{Min } P_0^a = \text{Max}[\$5, \$4.53, \$2.66, 0] = \$5.00.$$

In summary:

RELATION: In the absence of arbitrage, the minimum price of an American put on a dividend-paying stock is bound by the following condition:

$$\text{Min } P_0^a = \text{Max}[X - S_0, PV(X + D, t^*) - S_0, 0].$$

4.9.3   Summary

Table 4.9-1 summarizes the American and European minimum put prices we obtained for dividends of zero, $0.50, and $3.00. In examining the table, several points should be noted. First, the minimum price of the American put is greater than its European counterpart, regardless of whether the stock pays a low or a high dividend or no dividend at all. Second, since the American put's minimum price is always above the European's, the right to exercise is always positive. Finally, the price of the put options are a positive function of dividends: As dividends increase, both American and European minimum put prices increase.

TABLE 4.9-1	Minimum Put Prices with Different Dividends		
$S_0 = \$45, X = \$50, R = .06, T = 1$ year, $t^* = 4$ months			
OPTION PRICE	No DIVIDEND	$0.50 DIVIDEND	$3 DIVIDEND
Minimum European put price	$2.17	$2.66	$5.11
Minimum American put price	$5.00	$5.00	$6.98

4.10   PUT PRICES WITH DIFFERENT EXERCISE PRICES

4.10.1   Price Relation of Puts with Different Exercise Prices

In Section 4.4.1 we showed how an arbitrage strategy involving a bull call spread could be used to earn arbitrage returns if the price of the call with the lower exercise price exceeded the one with the higher exercise price. A similar arbitrage argument also can be used to establish the price relations between puts identical except for their exercise prices.

Intuitively, the put with the higher exercise price (X_2) should be priced higher than the one with the lower exercise price (X_1), since the former gives the put holder the right to sell the stock at a higher price. In addition, if the put with the higher exercise price is not priced higher, then in the case of European puts, arbitrageurs can earn riskless profit by forming a bear put spread—buying the higher-exercise-priced put for $P_0^e(X_2)$ and selling the lower-exercise-priced put for $P_0^e(X_1)$. For example, if an ABC July 50 European put is trading at $3 and an ABC July 60 European put is selling for $2 [$P_0^e(50) > P_0^e(60)$], then, as shown in Table 4.10-1 and its accompanying figure, an arbitrage return is earned at expiration by purchasing the 60 put and selling the 50 put. In turn, with this arbitrage opportunity arbitrageurs/spreaders will push up the price of the 60 put and push down the price of the 50 put until $P_0^e(60) > P_0^e(50)$ and the arbitrage profit disappears.

> RELATION: Given two European puts identical except for their exercise prices, the put with the higher exercise price will be priced higher than the one with the lower exercise price. If this condition does not hold, then an arbitrage opportunity will exist by executing a bear put spread. Thus:
>
> $$P_0^e(X_2) > P_0^e(X_1), \qquad \text{for } X_2 > X_1.$$

The condition that $P_0^e(X_2) > P_0^e(X_1)$ also holds for an American put. If the price on an American put with a lower exercise price exceeds a similar one with a higher strike price, then, as before, a riskless profit could be earned from the bear put spread at expiration. Prior to expiration, if the bear put spreader is assigned the lower-exercise-price put in which he is short, then the spreader could buy the stock on the assignment at X_1 and use his long put position to sell the stock for X_2 to earn

TABLE 4.10-1

			Arbitrage Bear Spread	
$P_0^e(50) > P_0^e(60)$				
S_T	Profit on 50 Put Contract Sold at $3	Profit on 60 Put Contract Bought at $2	Total Profit	
$40	− $700	$1800	$1100	
45	− 200	1300	1100	
50	300	800	1100	
55	300	300	600	
60	300	− 200	100	
65	300	− 200	100	
70	300	− 200	100	

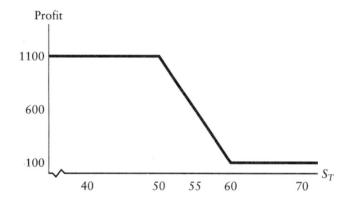

an arbitrage profit of $X_2 − X_1$. Thus, even with early exercise, an arbitrage profit still can be realized from a bear put spread when $P_0^a(X_1) > P_0^a(X_2)$.

RELATION: $P_0^a(X_2) > P_0^a(X_1)$,   for $X_2 > X_1$.

4.10.2   Price Limits on Puts with Different Exercise Prices

For European puts, the price difference between two puts identical except for their exercise prices must be less than the difference in the present values of the two puts' exercise prices. That is:

$$P_0^e(X_2) − P_0^e(X_1) < PV(X_2 − X_1).$$

If this condition does not hold $[P_0^e(X_2) − P_0^e(X_1) > PV(X_2 − X_1)]$, then an arbitrage opportunity exists by going long in a riskless bond with a face value of $X_2 − X_1$ and maturity of T and by going short in the X_2 put and long in the X_1 put (i.e., constructing a bull spread). This strategy would yield an initial positive cash flow of $P_0^e(X_2) − P_0^e(X_1) − PV(X_2 − X_1)$, and, as shown in Table 4.10-2,

TABLE 4.10-2

	Bull Put Spread and Bond with Face Value of $X_2 - X_1$		
	Cash Flows at Expiration		
Position	$S_T < X_1$	$X_1 \leq S_T \leq X_2$	$S_T > X_2$
Long X_1 put	$X_1 - S_T$	0	0
Short X_2 put	$-(X_2 - S_T)$	$-(X_2 - S_T)$	0
Long bond	$X_2 - X_1$	$X_2 - X_1$	$X_2 - X_1$
Total	0	$S_T - X_1 > 0$	$X_2 - X_1 > 0$

there would be no liabilities at expiration when the position is closed. To preclude this free lunch, the initial cash flow must be negative.

RELATION: $P_0^e(X_2) - P_0^e(X_1) < PV(X_2 - X_1)$, for $X_2 > X_1$.

Thus, if the annual rate on a risk-free security is 10%, then the price on an ABC 60 put expiring in one year should not be $9.09 greater than the price on an ABC 50 put expiring in one year:

$$P_0^e(60) - P_0^e(50) < PV(60 - 50) = \frac{\$10}{1.10} = \$9.09.$$

If the put bull spread in this arbitrage portfolio were formed with American puts that were exercised early at time t, the arbitrageur would lose $X_2 - X_1$. If we assume the arbitrageur finances this short fall by borrowing $X_2 - X_1$ dollars at rate R for the remainder of the period, then at expiration she would owe $(X_2 - X_1)(1 + R)^{T-t}$ on the debt, an amount that exceeds the face value of the bond. To ensure a free lunch, the arbitrageur would need to buy a bond that yields a cash flow at expiration at least equal to $(X_2 - X_1)(1 + R)^{T-t}$. This can be done by purchasing a riskless pure discount bond with a face value of $(X_2 - X_1)(1 + R)^T$ for the price of $X_2 - X_1$. Since $(X_2 - X_1)(1 + R)^T > (X_2 - X_1)(1 + R)^{T-t}$, the arbitrageur would thus have a bond that can generate a return at least as good as, and often better than, the put spread. To avoid arbitrage, the American puts would have to be priced such that:

RELATION: $P_0^e(X_2) - P_0^a(X_1) < X_2 - X_1$, for $X_2 > X_1$.

4.11 PUT PRICE AND TIME-TO-EXPIRATION RELATION

Similar to an American call, an American put with a greater time to expiration should be valued more than an identical put with a shorter time to expiration, since the former has a better chance of being in the money. Accordingly, given two puts on the same stock and with the same exercise price but with different times to expiration, the more distant put should be priced higher than the shorter-term one:

$$P_0^a(T_2) > P_0^a(T_1), \qquad \text{for } T_2 > T_1.$$

If the longer-term put is not priced higher, an arbitrage opportunity can be exploited by implementing a time spread. For example, suppose an ABC 50 put expiring in six months ($T_2 = .5$ per year) is trading at $5 while the ABC 50 put expiring in three months ($T_1 = .25$) is selling for $7: $P_0^a(50, .5) < P_0^a(50, .25)$. Given this situation, a $2 arbitrage opportunity can be realized by forming a time spread consisting of a short position in the higher-priced, short-term put and a long position in the lower-priced, long-term put. If the spreader is assigned on the short-term 50 put, whether at expiration or before, he can simply buy the ABC stock at $50 on the assignment and then sell the stock by exercising his longer-term 50 put. Thus, if the longer-term put is priced below the shorter-term one, a spreader is sure of earning a riskless return. As spreaders exploit this opportunity, though, they will push up the price of the longer-term put (as they try to buy it) and depress the price of the shorter-term one (as they try to sell) until $P_0^a(T_2) > P_0^a(T_1)$.

RELATION: Given two American put options on the same stock, with the same exercise prices but different expiration dates, the price of the longer-term put will be greater than that of the the shorter-term one. If this condition does not hold, then an arbitrage opportunity can be realized from a time spread formed by going short in the longer-term put and long in the shorter-term one. Thus:

$$P_0^a(T_2) > P_0^a(T_1), \qquad \text{for } T_2 > T_1.$$

Since a longer-term European put cannot be exercised when a shorter-term European put expires, this particular arbitrage/spread strategy cannot be applied to ensure the stated condition holds for European puts.

4.12   PUT PRICE RELATIONS WITH STOCK PRICES, VOLATILITY, AND INTEREST RATES

4.12.1   Put Price Relations with the Stock's Price and Volatility

The relationships described earlier between the price of a call and its underlying stock's price and variability apply similarly to puts. First, the negative relationship between a put premium and the price of the underlying stock is a nonlinear one: When a put is deep out of the money, its price changes very little in response to an incremental change in the price of the stock, and it will be equal (or almost equal) to zero; when a put is deep in the money, its price will have a very small TVP and will come closer to equaling the intrinsic value [or $PV(X) - S_t$ for European puts] as the stock price decreases. Second, since put losses are limited to the premium when the stock price is equal to or less than its exercise price at expiration, put holders will value puts on stocks with greater volatility more than those with lower volatility.

4.12.2   Put Price and Interest Rate Relation

In contrast to calls, put prices are inversely related to interest rates, assuming other factors are constant. The inverse relation can be seen by viewing a put as a security that defers the sale of a stock. That is, a stockholder has the alternative of either selling her stock now and investing the cash proceeds in a risk-free security or holding the stock and buying a put to provide protection against a decline in the price of the stock. If interest rates increase, the first alternative of selling the stock and investing in a risk-free security becomes relatively more attractive than the second of using a put as a hedging tool.

For example, suppose a holder of the XYZ stock described in Section 4.6.2 needs cash at the end of the year and is afraid that the price of XYZ could decrease. Her alternatives would be either to sell the stock for $100 and invest in a risk-free security for the remainder of the period or to hold the stock and hedge its value by buying an XYZ 100 put to ensure a minimum net cash flow of $100 (minus the cost of the put) from selling the stock and the put at expiration. The choice the stockholder makes depends on her risk-return preference. Whatever preference, more investors will opt for selling their stock and investing in a risk-free security than buying a put, if interest rates rise. Accordingly, the demand and the price of a put would decrease in light of an interest rate increase. Thus, the higher the interest rate, the lower the price of the put, all other factors being constant.*

4.13   PUT AND CALL RELATIONSHIPS

4.13.1   Put-Call Parity for Options on a Stock Paying No Dividends

Up to now we have examined separately how the limits on call and put prices are determined by arbitrage arguments involving positions in the underlying stock, bond, and option. As we might expect, since the prices of options on the same stock are derived from that stock's value, the put price and the call price are also related to each other.

Recall from Chapter 1 that the relationship governing put and call prices is known as put-call parity. This relation can be defined in terms of an arbitrage portfolio consisting of either a *conversion* [a long position in the stock, a short position in a European call, and a long position in a European put (a call and a put

---

*Keep in mind that this is a partial equilibrium analysis in which other factors are assumed constant. An interest rate increase may also cause the expected price of the stock to decrease, which would tend to increase the demand and the price of the put. Thus, just like the call and interest rate relationship described in Section 4.6.3, the total impact of an interest rate change on put prices may be ambiguous.

with the same exercise price and time to expiration): $\{+S, +P, -C\}$]; or a *reversal* [a short position in the stock, a long position in the European call, and a short position in a European put (a reversal is the negative of a conversion): $\{-S, -P, +C\}$].

A conversion yields a certain cash flow at expiration equal to the exercise price. This is shown in Table 4.13-1. To preclude arbitrage, the riskless conversion portfolio must be worth the same as a risk-free pure discount bond with a face value of X, maturing at the end of the option's expiration period. Thus, in equilibrium:

$$P_0^e - C_0^e + S_0 = PV(X). \tag{4.13-1}$$

Similarly, by reversing this strategy we create a reversal. As shown in Table 4.13-2, a reversal results in a required fixed payment equal to X at expiration. To preclude arbitrage, a reversal should be equal to a short position in a bond $[-PV(X)]$. Thus, the same equilibrium condition specified in Equation (4.13-1) holds for a reversal:

$$-P_0^e + C_0^e - S_0 = -PV(X)$$

$$P_0^e - C_0^e + S_0 = PV(X).$$

Equation (4.13-1) is referred to as the put-call parity model. If this equality does not hold, then an arbitrage opportunity will exist. For example, suppose an ABC 50 call and put expiring in one year were trading for $5 each, while the ABC

TABLE 4.13-1

Conversion $\{+S_0, +P_0^e, -C_0^e\}$			
	CASH FLOWS AT EXPIRATION		
POSITION	$S_T < X$	$S_T = X$	$S_T > X$
Long stock	S_T	S_T	S_T
Long put	$X - S_T$	0	0
Short call	0	0	$-(S_T - X)$
Total	X	X	X

TABLE 4.13-2

Reversal $\{-S_0, -P_0^e, +C_0^e\}$			
	EXPIRATION CASH FLOW		
POSITION	$S_T < X$	$S_T = X$	$S_T > X$
Short stock	$-S_T$	$-S_T$	$-S_T$
Short put	$-(X - S_T)$	0	0
Long call	0	0	$S_T - X$
Total	$-X$	$-X$	$-X$

stock was selling for $50. Furthermore, suppose the risk-free rate was 11.11%, so that a one-year pure discount bond with a face value of $X = \$50$ was worth $45. In this case, the put-call parity equilibrium condition is violated:

$$S_0 + P_0^e - C_0^e > PV(X)$$

$$\$50 + \$5 - \$5 > \$45.$$

The actual bond is cheap ($45) relative to the synthetic bond $\{+S, +P_0^e, -C_0^e\}$ ($50). Arbitragers, in turn, could exploit this price imbalance by buying the cheap real bond and selling the expensive synthetic one for an immediate profit of $5. At expiration, the $50 cash flow from the bond would exactly equal the cash flow needed to cover the short synthetic position. In implementing this strategy, though, arbitrageurs would alter the demands and supplies of calls and puts, causing their prices to change until the condition defined by Equation (4.13-1) is reached. A similar argument can be used if the actual bond is expensive relative to the synthetic one.

4.13.2   Price of a European Call and a European Put on a Stock Paying No Dividend

The put-call parity model can be used to determine the equilibrium price of a European put, given the equilibrium price of a European call and the interest rate, or the equilibrium price of a call, given the equilibrium price of the put and the interest rate. That is, from Equation (4.13-1):

$$C_0^e = P_0^e - PV(X) + S_0 \qquad (4.13\text{-}2)$$

$$P_0^e = C_0^e + PV(X) - S_0. \qquad (4.13\text{-}3)$$

The right-hand side of Equation (4.13-2) shows the value of a portfolio consisting of long positions in the put and the stock and a short position in the bond. This portfolio is referred to as a **synthetic call**, since it replicates the cash flows from a European call. Similarly, the right-hand side of Equation (4.13-3) represents a portfolio consisting of long positions in the call and the bond and a short position in the stock. Since this portfolio replicates the cash flows from a European put, it is referred to as a **synthetic put**. The proof of these relationships is straightforward and is left as end-of-chapter Problems 7 and 9.

4.13.3   Put-Call Parity for European Options on a Stock with a Dividend

If there are ex-dividend dates during the period the option positions are held, then, as shown in Table 4.13-3, the conversion will yield a riskless cash flow equal to the exercise price plus the value of dividends (D_T) (assumed to be known with certainty) at expiration. Since the conversion is riskless, its equilibrium value will equal the value of a risk-free bond with a face value equal to X, plus the value of the dividend at the options' expiration date. That is:

$$P_0^e - C_0^e + S_0 = PV(X + D_T). \qquad (4.13\text{-}4)$$

4.13.4   Price of an American Call and an American Put

The put-call parity model depends on the relationships among the values of options, the price of the underlying stock, and the rate of return on a risk-free bond. The model holds strictly for European options but not for American options.

4.13.5   Box Spread

In the put-call parity model, call and put premiums are related by real and synthetic stock positions. Another way of relating call and put prices is by a **box spread**.

A long box spread consists of a call bull money spread and a put bear money spread. As shown in Table 4.13-4, a long box spread with European options yields a certain return at expiration equal to the difference in the exercise prices. Since arbitrage ensures $C(X_1) > C(X_2)$ and $P(X_2) > P(X_1)$ for $X_2 > X_1$ (see Sections 4.4 and 4.10), a long box spread represents an investment expenditure, in which:

$$\text{Cost of box spread} = C_0^e(X_1) - C_0^e(X_2) + P_0^e(X_2) - P_0^e(X_1). \qquad (4.13\text{-}5)$$

In contrast, a short box spread (reverse box spread) is a combination of a call bear money spread and a put bull money spread. Since this spread is the opposite of the box spread, it generates a credit for the investor at the initiation of the strategy, and,

TABLE 4.13-3

Conversion with Dividend-Paying Stock			
	EXPIRATION CASH FLOW		
POSITION	$S_T < X$	$S_T = X$	$S_T > X$
Long put	$X - S_T$	0	0
Short call	0	0	$-(S_T - X)$
Long stock	S_T	S_T	S_T
Dividend	D_T	D_T	D_T
Total	$X + D_T$	$X + D_T$	$X + D_T$

TABLE 4.13-4

Long Box Spread			
$\{+C(X_1), \ -C(X_2), \ -P(X_1), \ +P(X_2)\}$			
	CASH FLOWS AT EXPIRATION		
POSITION	$S_T < X_1$	$X_1 \le S_T \le X_2$	$S_T > X_2$
Long X_1 call	0	$S_T - X_1$	$S_T - X_1$
Short X_2 call	0	0	$-(S_T - X_2)$
Short X_1 put	$-(X_1 - S_T)$	0	0
Long X_2 put	$X_2 - S_T$	$X_2 - S_T$	0
Total	$X_2 - X_1$	$X_2 - X_1$	$X_2 - X_1$

as shown in Table 4.13-5, requires a fixed payment at expiration equal to the difference in the exercise prices.

Since the return on a long box spread is riskless, in equilibrium we would expect the price of the spread to equal the price on a risk-free pure discount bond with a face value of $X_2 - X_1$ maturing at the same time as the options expire. That is:

$$C_0^e(X_1) - C_0^e(X_2) + P_0^e(X_2) - P_0^e(X_1) = PV(X_2 - X_1) \qquad (4.13\text{-}6)$$

$$C_0^e(X_1) - C_0^e(X_2) + P_0^e(X_2) - P_0^e(X_1) - PV(X_2 - X_1) = 0. \qquad (4.13\text{-}7)$$

Similarly, if we view a short box spread as a riskless loan, then with a fixed payment of $X_2 - X_1$ required on the short spread at expiration, the credit received from the spread should equal the proceeds from a loan requiring payment of $X_2 - X_1$ at maturity: $PV(X_2 - X_1)$. Thus:

$$-C_0^e(X_1) + C_0^e(X_2) - P_0^e(X_2) + P_0^e(X_1) = -PV(X_2 - X_1) \qquad (4.13\text{-}8)$$

If we assume borrowing and lending rates are the same, then equilibrium Equations (4.13-6) and (4.13-8) are equal.

If the preceding equations do not hold, then arbitrage opportunities will exist. For example, if Equation (4.13-7) is negative, an arbitrageur could borrow funds equal to $PV(X_2 - X_1)$ and buy the box spread, realizing a positive cash flow of $PV(X_2 - X_1) - [C_0^e(X_1) - C_0^e(X_2) + P_0^e(X_2) - P_0^e(X_1)]$. At expiration, the arbitrageur would then pay his debt of $X_2 - X_1$ with the proceeds of $X_2 - X_1$ from the box spread.

If Equation (4.13-7) is positive, then arbitrageurs could earn riskless profit of $PV(X_2 - X_1) - [C_0^e(X_1) - C_0^e(X_2) + P_0^e(X_2) - P_0^e(X_1)]$, by forming a short box spread and buying the bond. At expiration, the principal of $X_2 - X_1$ on the bond would then be used to cover the short box spread obligation of $X_2 - X_1$.

The actions of arbitrageurs when Equation (4.13-7) is not zero will serve to change the demand and the supply of the options until the combined spreads are priced equal to $PV(X_2 - X_1)$ and the arbitrage disappears. Thus, Equation (4.13-7) represents an equilibrium condition.

TABLE 4.13-5

Short Box Spread			
$\{-C(X_1),\ +C(X_2),\ +P(X_1),\ -P(X_2)\}$			
	EXPIRATION CASH FLOW		
POSITION	$S_T < X_1$	$X_1 \leq S_T \leq X_2$	$S_T > X_2$
Short X_1 call	0	$-(S_T - X_1)$	$-(S_T - X_1)$
Long X_2 call	0	0	$S_T - X_2$
Long X_1 put	$X_1 - S_T$	0	0
Short X_2 put	$-(X_2 - S_T)$	$-(X_2 - S_T)$	0
Total	$-(X_2 - X_1)$	$-(X_2 - X_1)$	$-(X_2 - X_1)$

As with the put-call parity model, Equation (4.13-7) can be solved in terms of any of the options' prices to define that option's equilibrium price. For example, solving for $C_0^e(X_1)$ we obtain:

$$C_0^e(X_1) = C_0^e(X_2) - P_0^e(X_2) + P_0^e(X_1) + PV(X_2 - X_1). \qquad (4.13\text{-}9)$$

This equation shows that the equilibrium price of the X_1 call depends on both the value of the bond $[PV(X_2 - X_1)]$, a synthetic stock position formed with the higher-exercise-priced call and put, $[C_0^e(X_2) - P_0^e(X_2)]$, and the price of the lower-exercise-priced put, $[P_0^e(X_1)]$. If the equilibrium price for this option does not hold, then an arbitrage opportunity exists.

As with the put-call parity relation, the box spread is defined in terms of the option values at expiration. As a result, the preceding equilibrium relations hold strictly for European options, not for American options.[*]

4.14 CONCLUSION

Arbitrage involves buying and selling equivalent positions that are not equally priced. The exploitation of such opportunities by arbitrageurs serves to change the relative supplies of and demands for the securities forming the positions until an equilibrium is attained in which the positions are equally valued. In this chapter we have explored how arbitrage strategies involving positions with options, underlying stocks, and bonds govern the minimum and maximum option prices, the relative values of options with different exercise prices and times to expiration, and the relative values of puts and calls. These relations are summarized in Table 4.14-1. In addition to examining arbitrage relationships, we have also analyzed the relationships between the price of the option and the underlying stock's price and volatility and the relationship between the option premium and interest rate. For the most part our analysis in this chapter has examined each relationship separately. We are now ready to develop a model that will integrate many of the relationships—the binomial option pricing model.

---

[*]For a long box spread, though, an early exercise of an in-the-money short call or an in-the-money short put could be handled by exercising the other call or put, respectively. The same profit of $X_2 - X_1$ would therefore be earned. For a short American box spread, early exercise would mean a loss of $X_2 - X_1$.

TABLE 4.14-1

Summary of Boundary Conditions and Arbitrage Strategies Governing the Conditions			
(1)	(2)	(3)	
		ARBITRAGE STRATEGY	
CONDITION	VIOLATION	STRATEGY	DETAILS
1. $C_t^a > \text{Max}[S_t - X, 0]$	$C_t^a < (S_t - X)$	Long C_t^a Short $(S_t - X)$	(1) Buy call (2) Buy stock at X (exercise) (3) Sell stock at S_t
2. $C_t > \text{Max}[S_t - PV(X), 0]$	$C_t < S_t - PV(X)$	Long C_t Short $[S_t - PV(X)]$	(1) Buy call (2) Buy bond at $PV(X)$ (3) Short stock at S_t
3a. *Dividend Case* $C_t^a > \text{Max}[S_t - PV(X, T) - PV(D, t^*), 0]$ if $D \leq X - \dfrac{X}{(1 + R)^{T-t*}}$	$C_t < S_t - PV(X, T) - PV(D, t^*)$	Long C_t Short $[S_t - PV(X, T) - PV(D, t^*)]$	(1) Buy call (2) Buy bond at $PV(X, T)$ (3) Buy bond at $PV(D, t^*)$ (4) Short stock at S_t (5) Exercise at T
b. $C_t^a > \text{Max}[S_t - PV(D, t^*), 0]$ if $D > X - \dfrac{X}{(1 + R)^{T-t*}}$	$C_t < S_t - PV(D, t^*)$	Long C_t Short $[S_t - PV(D, t^*)]$	(1) Buy call (2) Short stock at S_t (3) Buy bond at $PV(D, t^*)$ (4) Exercise at t^*
4. $C_t(X_1) > C_t(X_2)$	$C(X_1) < C(X_2)$	Long $C_t(X_1)$ Short $C_t(X_2)$	(1) Buy X_1 call (2) Sell X_2 call
5. $C_t^e(X_1) - C_t^e(X_2) < PV(X_2 - X_1)$	$C_t^e(X_1) - C_t^e(X_2) > PV(X_2 - X_1)$	Short $[C_t^e(X_1) - C_t^e(X_2)]$ Long $PV(X_2 - X_1)$	(1) Short X_1 call (2) Long X_2 call (3) Buy bond at $PV(X_2 - X_1)$
6. $C_t^a(X_1) - C_t^a(X_2) < (X_2 - X_1)$	$C_t^a(X_1) - C_t^a(X_2) > (X_2 - X_1)$	Short $[C_t^a(X_1) - C_t^a(X_2)]$ Long $(X_2 - X_1)$	(1) Short X_1 call (2) Long X_2 call (3) Buy bond at $(X_2 - X_1)$
7. $C_t^a(T_2) > C_t^a(T_1)$	$C_t^a(T_2) < C_t^a(T_1)$	Long $C_t^a(T_2)$ Short $C_t^a(T_1)$	(1) Long T_2 call (2) Short T_1 call
8. $P_t^e > \text{Max}[PV(X) - S_t, 0]$	$P_t^e < [PV(X) - S_t]$	Long P_t^e Short $[PV(X) - S_t]$	(1) Long put (2) Short bond at $PV(X)$ (3) Buy stock at S_t
9. $P_t^e > \text{Max}[PV(X, T) + PV(D, t^*) - S_t, 0]$	$P_t^e < [PV(X,T) + PV(D, t^*) - S_t]$	Long P_t^e Short $[PV(X, T) + PV(D, t^*) - S_t]$	(1) Long put (2) Sell bond at $PV(X, T)$ (3) Sell bond at $PV(D, t^*)$ (4) Buy stock at S_t
10. $P_t^a > \text{Max}[X - S_t, 0]$	$P_t^a < (X - S_t)$	Long P_t^a Short $(X - S_t)$	(1) Long put (2) Buy stock at S_t (3) Sell stock at X (exercise)
11. *Dividend Case* $P_t^a > \text{Max}[X - S_0, PV(X + D, t^*) - S_0, 0]$	a. $P_t^a < [PV(X + D) - S_t]$ b. $P_t^a < (X - S_0)$	a. Long P_t^a Short $[PV(X + D) - S_t]$ b. See 10.	a. (1) Long put (2) Short bond at $PV(X + D)$ (3) Buy stock at S_t b. See 10.

Summary of Boundary Conditions and Arbitrage Strategies Governing the Conditions

(1)	(2)	(3) ARBITRAGE STRATEGY	
CONDITION	VIOLATION	STRATEGY	DETAILS
12. $P_t^e(X_2) > P_t^e(X_1)$	$P_t^e(X_2) < P_t^e(X_1)$	Long $P_t^e(X_2)$ Short $P_t^e(X_1)$	(1) Long X_2 put (2) Short X_1 put
13. $P_t^e(X_2) - P^e(X_1) < PV(X_2 - X_1)$	$P_t^e(X_2) - P_t^e(X_1) > PV(X_2 - X_1)$	Long $[P_t^e(X_2) - P_t^e(X_1)]$ Short $PV(X_2 - X_1)$	(1) Long X_2 put (2) Short X_1 put (3) Short bond at $PV(X_2 - X_1)$
14. $P_t^a(X_2) - P_t^a(X_1) < (X_2 - X_1)$	$P_t^a(X_2) - P_t^a(X_1) > (X_2 - X_1)$	Long $[P_t^a(X_2) - P_t^a(X_1)]$ Short $(X_1 - X_2)$	(1) Long X_2 put (2) Short X_1 put (3) Short bond at $PV(X_2 - X_1)$
15. $P_t^a(T_2) > P_t^a(T_1)$	$P_t^a(T_2) < P_t^a(T_1)$	Long $[P_t^a(T_2)]$ Short $[P_t^a(T_1)]$	(1) Long T_2 put (2) Short T_1 put
16. $P_t^e + S_t = C_t^e + PV(X)$	$P_t^e + S_t > C_t^e + PV(X)$	Short $(P_t^e + S_t)$ Long $[C_t^e + PV(X)]$	(1) Short put (2) Short stock (3) Long call (4) Long bond at $PV(X)$
	$P_t^e + S_t < C_t^e + PV(X)$	Long $(P_t^e + S_t)$ Short $[C_t^e + PV(X)]$	(1) Long put (2) Long stock (3) Short call (4) Short bond at $PV(X)$
17. $C_t^e(X_1) - C_t^e(X_2) + P_t^e(X_2) - P_t^e(X_1)$ $- PV(X_2 - X_1) = 0$	$C_t^e(X_1) - C_t^e(X_2) + P_t^e(X_2)$ $- P_t^e(X_1) - PV(X_2 - X_1) < 0$	Long $[C_t^e(X_1) - C_t^e(X_2) + P_t^e(X_2)$ $- P_t^e(X_1) - PV(X_2 - X_1)]$	(1) Long X_1 call (2) Short X_2 call (3) Long X_2 put (4) Short X_1 put (5) Short bond at $PV(X_2 - X_1)$
	$C_t^e(X_1) - C_t^e(X_2) + P_t^e(X_2)$ $- P_t^e(X_1) - PV(X_2 - X_1) > 0$	Short $[C_t^e(X_1) - C_t^e(X_2) + P_t^e(X_2)$ $- C_t^e(X_1) - PV(X_2 - X_1)]$	(1) Short X_1 call (2) Long X_2 call (3) Short X_2 put (4) Long X_1 put (5) Long bond at $PV(X_2 - X_1)$

NOTES: (1) An option *without* an *a* or *e* superscript implies that the condition holds for either case.
(2) Maturity on bonds is the option's expiration.
(3) t^* = time to dividend payment date.
(4) $X_2 > X_1$.
(5) $T_2 > T_1$.

KEY TERMS

maximum call price

minimum American call price

minimum European call price

threshold dividend

maximum American put price

maximum European put price

minimum American put price

minimum European put price

conversion

reversal

synthetic call

synthetic put

box spread

SELECTED REFERENCES

Comprehensive analyses of option bounds can be found in Merton (1973), Jarrow and Rudd (1983), Chance (1991), and Cox and Rubinstein (1985). A number of studies have empirically examined option bounds: Klemkosky and Resnick (1980), Bhattacharya (1983), and Gould and Galai (1974). For a survey on empirical tests of option pricing, see Galai (1983).

Bhattacharya, M. "Transaction Data Tests of Efficiency of the Chicago Board Options Exchange." *Journal of Financial Economics* 12 (1983): 161–185.

Chance, Don M. *An Introduction to Options and Futures.* Fort Worth, Tex.: Dryden Press, 1991, ch. 3.

Cox, John C., and Rubinstein, M. *Option Markets.* Englewood Cliffs, N.J.: Prentice-Hall, 1985, pp. 127–163.

Galai, D. "Empirical Tests of Boundary Conditions for CBOE Options." *Journal of Financial Economics* 6 (June–Sept. 1978): 187–211.

———. "A Survey of Empirical Tests of Option Pricing Models." In *Option Pricing*, edited by M. Brenner. Lexington, Mass.: Lexington Books, 1983, pp. 45–80.

Gould, J., and Galai, D. "Transaction Costs and the Relationship Between Put and Call Prices." *Journal of Financial Economics.* 1 (June 1974): 105–129.

Jarrow, R., and Rudd, A. *Option Pricing.* Homewood, Ill.: Richard D. Irwin, 1983.

Klemkosky, R., and Resnick, B. "Put Call Parity and Market Efficiency." *Journal of Finance* 34 (Dec. 1979): 1141–1155.

Klemkosky, R., and Resnick, B. "An *Ex Ante* Analysis of Put-Call Parity." *Journal of Financial Economics* 8 (1980): 363–378.

Merton, R. "The Relationship Between Put and Call Option Prices: Comment." *Journal of Finance* 28 (March 1973): 183–184.

———. "Theory of Rational Option Pricing." *Bell Journal of Economics* 4 (Spring 1973): 141–183.

Ritchken, Peter. *Options: Theory, Strategy, and Applications*, Glenview, Ill.: Scott, Foresman, 1987, ch. 4.

Stoll, H. "The Relationship Between Put and Call Option Prices." *Journal of Finance* 24 (May 1969): 319–332.

EXERCISES

1. For each of the following equilibrium and boundary conditions, state when the condition is violated and the appropriate arbitrage strategy.

   a. $C_t^a > \text{Max}[S_t - X, 0]$

   b. $C_t^e > \text{Max}[S_t - \text{PV}(X), 0]$

   c. $P_t^a > \text{Max}[X - S_t, 0]$

   d. $P_t^e > \text{Max}[\text{PV}(X) - S_t, 0]$

   e. $C_t^e(X_1) > C_t^e(X_2)$

   f. $P_t^e(X_2) > P_t^e(X_1)$

   g. $C_t^e(X_1) - C_t^e(X_2) < \text{PV}(X_2 - X_1)$

   h. $P_t^e(X_2) - P_t^e(X_1) < \text{PV}(X_2 - X_1)$

   i. $C_t^a(T_2) > C_t^a(T_1)$

   j. $P_t^a(T_2) > P_t^a(T_1)$

   k. $P_t^e + S_t = C_t^e + \text{PV}(X)$

   l. $C_t^e(X_1) - C_t^e(X_2) + P_t^e(X_2) - P_t^e(X_1) = \text{PV}(X_2 - X_1)$

2. Prove the following conditions using an arbitrage argument. In your proof, show the initial positive cash flow when the condition is violated and prove there are no liabilities at expiration.

   a. $\text{Min } C_0 = \text{Max}[S_0 - \text{PV}(X), 0]$

   b. $\text{Min } P_0^a = \text{Max}[X - S_0, 0]$

   c. $\text{Min } P_0^e = \text{Max}[\text{PV}(X) - S_0, 0]$

   d. $C_0^e(X_1) - C_0^e(X_2) < \text{PV}(X_2 - X_1)$

3. Prove the following:

   a. End-of-period conversion value $= X$

   b. End-of-period reversal value $= -X$

   c. End-of-period long box spread value $= X_2 - X_1$

   d. End-of-period short box spread value $= -(X_2 - X_1)$

4. Assume the option's underlying stock pays a dividend of D at time t^*. Prove the following boundary conditions using an arbitrage argument.

   a. $C_0^e > \text{Max}[S_0 - \text{PV}(X, T) - \text{PV}(D, t^*), 0]$

   b. $P_0^e > \text{Max}[\text{PV}(X, T) + \text{PV}(D, t^*) - S_0, 0]$

5. Prove mathematically the following condition for the early exercise of a call by a call holder:

   $$D > \text{TVP}$$

PROBLEMS AND QUESTIONS

1. Explain what an arbitrageur would do in the following cases, and how her arbitrage strategy would have no liabilities at expiration.

   a. The price of an ABC 40 call, expiring at the end of six months, is trading at $1.05, ABC stock is at $40, and the annual rate on a risk-free security is 6%.

   b. The price of an ABC European 40 call expiring at the end of six months is trading at $0.75, ABC stock is trading at $40 and is expected to pay $0.25 dividend at the end of three months, and the annual risk-free rate is 6%.

   c. A September ABC 40 European call is trading at $3 and a September ABC 50 European call is trading at $4.

   d. A December ABC 40 European call is trading at $6 and a December ABC 45 European call is selling at $1, both options expire in one year, and the annual risk-free rate is 6%.

   e. A September ABC 40 American call is trading at $6 and an October ABC 40 American call is trading at $5.

   f. The price of an ABC 100 European put expiring at the end of one year is $1, ABC stock is trading at $92, and the annual risk-free rate is 6%.

   g. A March ABC 60 American put is trading at its intrinsic value, ABC stock is at $56 and is expected to pay $1 dividend at the end of three months (prior to the March expiration), and the annual risk-free rate is 5%.

   h. A December ABC 35 European put is selling at $1 and a December ABC 30 European put is selling for $3.

   i. A September ABC 45 European put is trading at $6 and a September ABC 40 European put is trading at $1, both puts expire in one year, and the annual risk-free rate is 6%.

   j. An ABC September 50 American put is trading at $6 and an ABC 50 October American put is trading at $5.

   k. ABC stock is selling at $50, an ABC October 50 European call is selling at $4, an ABC October 50 European put is selling at $5, and a pure discount bond with a face value of $50 and maturing at the options' expiration is trading at $49.

   l. ABC stock is selling at $60, an ABC October 60 European call is selling at $5, an ABC October 60 European put is selling at $3, and a pure discount bond with a face value of $60 and maturing at the options' expiration is trading at $59.

   m. An ABC September 50 European call is trading at $10, an ABC September 60 European call is at $8, an ABC September 50 European put is at $3, an ABC September 60 European put is at $1, and a pure discount bond with a face value of $10 is trading at $8.

2. Suppose that LM stock is expected to pay a dividend worth $2.50 on the ex-dividend date. What advice would you give to a holder of an in-the-money LM American call option trading with a TVP of $1?

3. Explain the condition and the likely circumstances in which an American call option might be exercised early.

4. Explain intuitively and with an example why call and put options are more valuable the greater their underlying stock's variability.

5. Explain the following option and stock price relations:

   a. Deep out-of-the-money call

   b. Deep in-the-money call

   c. Deep out-of-the-money put

   d. Deep in-the-money put

6. Suppose ABC stock is trading $30, an ABC 30 European call expiring in one year is trading at $3, and the annual risk-free rate is 6%. Using the put-call parity model, determine the equilibrium price of an ABC 30 European put expiring in one year.

7. Using the numbers in Question 6, show with profit graphs how the synthetic put is the same as the actual 30 put when it is trading at its equilibrium price.

8. Suppose ABC stock is trading at $50, an ABC 50 European put expiring in one year is trading at $2, and the annual risk-free rate is 5%. Using the put-call parity model, determine the equilibrium price of an ABC 50 European call expiring in one year.

9. Using the numbers in Question 8, show with profit graphs how the synthetic call is the same as the actual 50 call when it is trading at the equilibrium price.

10. Using the put-call parity model, establish the conditions at which a European put would be trading below its IV.

11. Suppose the current stock price of the ABC Corporation is $80 and the risk-free rate is 10% per year. Find the minimum price for an ABC 75 European call and an ABC 75 American call, both with expirations of one year, given the company is expected in three months to pay (a) no dividend, (b) a $4 dividend, and (c) a $10 dividend. Describe some of the relations you observed between the call prices and dividends.

12. Find the threshold dividend in Problem 11.

13. Suppose the current stock price of XAVR Corporation is $50 and the annual risk-free rate is 10%. Find the minimum prices for the 60 European and 60 American put options, expiring in one year, if in three months the company is expected to pay (a) no dividends, (b) a $4 dividend, and (c) a $10 dividend. Describe the relations you observed between the put prices and dividends.

14. Suppose a 40 American call with a one year life is trading at $5 when the stock is at $40, and the risk-free rate is 5%. Since $S_0 < C_0 + PV(X)$, it would seem

that writing a call, shorting a bond for $40/1.05 = \$38.09$, and buying the stock for \$40 would be an arbitrage portfolio because the net cash flow (at $t = 0$) is \$3.09. Is it?

15. Suppose you observe the following prices for European puts and calls (expiring in one year) on UConn Inc.:

	PRICES	
X	CALL	PUT
40	\$15	\$1.71
50	8.36	4.00

Suppose the current price of UConn is \$50 per share and the stock will pay a dividend (for sure) at the end of one year. Find the interest rate per year and the dividend implicit in these prices.

CHAPTER 5

Binomial Option Pricing Model

5.1 INTRODUCTION

In the traditional supply-and-demand models in economics, the equilibrium price of a good is defined as that price at which the quantity demanded of the good equals its quantity supplied. If this condition is not met, then a surplus or shortage of the good will result, causing the good's price to change until the condition is satisfied.

Like the supply-and-demand models of economics, the models for determining the equilibrium price of an option involve finding a unique value toward which the option price naturally tends. The two most widely used models for determining the equilibrium price are the Black and Scholes (B-S) Option Pricing Model (OPM) and the *binomial option pricing model* (BOPM). Black and Scholes derived their model in 1973 in a seminal paper in the *Journal of Political Economy*. The BOPM was derived by Cox, Ross, and Rubinstein (1979) and Rendleman and Bartter (1979).*

The B-S OPM and the BOPM are similar in a number of ways. First, both models explain the equilibrium price of an option in terms of the same parameters—stock price (S), exercise price (X), time to expiration (T), interest rate (R), and the underlying stock's variability (σ)—and both are capable of explaining the boundary conditions and behavioral relationships described in the last chapter. Second, each model is limited to cases involving European options and in which there are no dividend payments made on the underlying stock. Adjustments are therefore required in each model when the right for early exercise exists. Finally, each determines the equilibrium price of an option in terms of arbitrage forces. Such arbitrage models are based on the law of one price. As discussed in Chapter 1, this law states that two assets or portfolios with identical future cash flows must

---

*For a discussion of the early development of the option pricing model, see Smith (1976).

sell for the same price in order to avoid arbitrage opportunities. For example, if a call trades for $5 while a portfolio that exactly replicates the payoffs from a call trades for $10, we have an arbitrage opportunity. The price imbalance will create excess demand for the call and excess supply for the replicating portfolio, forcing their respective prices to converge to a single value. Both the B-S model and the BOPM are based on valuing options in terms of replicating a portfolio, thereby using the law of one price to establish the equilibrium price.

The major difference in the models emanates from the assumption each makes concerning the underlying stock price's fluctuations over time, statistically referred to as its stochastic (or random) stock process. In the BOPM, the time to expiration is partitioned into a discrete, or finite, number of periods, each with the same length. In each period the stock is assumed to follow a binomial process in which it either increases or decreases. The model then determines the equilibrium price of the option, in which the cash flows from an arbitrage strategy consisting of positions in the stock, the call, and a bond are zero for each discrete period. The B-S OPM, on the other hand, posits a continuous process in which the time intervals are partitioned into infinitely small periods or, equivalently, the number of periods to expiration is assumed to approach infinity. In this continuous model, the price of the option is determined by assuming that the same arbitrage strategy used in the BOPM is implemented and revised continuously. Thus, the BOPM should be viewed as a first approximation of the B-S OPM. As the lengths of the intervals in the BOPM are made smaller, the discrete process merges into the continuous one and the BOPM and the B-S OPM converge.

In this and the following three chapters we will examine the two option pricing models. In this chapter, we derive the binomial model for call options, and in Chapter 6 we will derive the binomial put model and explain how the binomial call and put models are adjusted when the underlying stock pays a dividend during the life of the option. In Chapter 7 we will examine the B-S model, and in Chapter 8 we will conclude our analysis of option pricing by discussing some of the empirical studies that have examined the validity of the models and by describing some new option strategies based on the option pricing models.

In examining the BOPM in this chapter we begin by first deriving the model for call options under the assumption that there is only one period to expiration. With this background, the single-period model will then be extended to the more realistic multiple-period case. Since the BOPM is based on arbitrage relations, we also will examine in this chapter the arbitrage strategies that market makers and other traders can pursue when the option's market price does not equal the BOPM value. Finally, we will conclude the chapter by explaining how the model can be estimated.

5.2 SINGLE-PERIOD BINOMIAL OPTION PRICING MODEL

5.2.1 Valuing Call Options Through a Replicating Portfolio

In the BOPM, the equilibrium price of an option is based on the law of one price. For calls this price is found by equating the price of the call to the value of a *replicating portfolio*, that is, a portfolio constructed so that its possible cash flows equal the call's possible payouts.

To construct a replicating portfolio, assume initially that options expire in one period and that at the end of the period there are only two possible states. In this one-period, two-state economy, assume that at the end of the period, a stock, currently priced at $S_0 = \$100$, will be worth either $S_u = \$110$ if the upstate occurs, or $S_d = \$95$ if the downstate occurs. Equivalently stated, assume that either the stock will increase to equal a proportion u times its initial price, where u is the relative stock price, S_u/S_0 ($u = 1.1$ in this case), or it will decrease to equal a proportion d times its initial value, S_d/S_0 ($d = .95$ in this case).

$$S_u = uS_0 = 1.1(\$100) = \$110$$

$$S_0 = \$100$$

$$S_d = dS_0 = .95(\$100) = \$95$$

Next, consider a one-period European call option on the stock with an exercise price of $100. If the upstate occurs, the call will be worth its intrinsic value of $C_u = \$10$; if the downstate occurs, the call will be worthless, that is, $C_d = 0$. Thus:

$$C_u = \text{IV} = \text{Max}[\$110 - \$100, 0] = \$10$$

$$C_0$$

$$C_d = \text{IV} = \text{Max}[\$95 - \$100, 0] = 0$$

Third, assume there is a risk-free security to which funds can be lent (invested) or borrowed (sold short) for the period at a rate of R_f. To preclude arbitrage opportunities, assume $d < r_f < u$, where $r_f = 1 + R_f$. That is, if $r_f > u$, there would be arbitrage profits by shorting the stock and buying the risk-free security; if $r_f < d$, there would be riskless profit by buying the stock and shorting bond. To satisfy this condition in our example, assume a period risk-free rate of 5% ($r_f = 1.05$).

Finally, for simplicity assume there are no taxes, margin requirements, commission costs, or dividends, and that the stock and the call are perfectly divisible.

With two securities (the stock and the risk-free security) and two states, a replicating portfolio whose outflows at the end of the period exactly match the call's outflows can be formed by buying H_0 shares of stock at a price of S_0 partially financed by borrowing B_0 dollars at the risk-free rate (i.e., selling the risk-free security short). The current value of this portfolio, V_{c0}, is:

$$V_{c0} = H_0 S_0 - B_0, \tag{5.2-1}$$

(where the negative sign signifies borrowing) and, contingent upon the future state, at the end of the period the portfolio will have one of the following two possible values:

$$V_{cu} = H_0 u S_0 - r_f B_0 \tag{5.2-2}$$

$$V_{cd} = H_0 d S_0 - r_f B_0. \tag{5.2-3}$$

Given these two possible values, the replicating portfolio can be formed by finding the unknowns, H_0 and B_0, that make the two possible portfolio values, V_{cu} and V_{cd}, equal to the two possible call values, C_u and C_d, in their respective states. Mathematically, this can be found by solving for H_0 and B_0,

where:

$$H_0 u S_0 - r_f B_0 = C_u$$
$$H_0 d S_0 - r_f B_0 = C_d.$$

The solutions are:

$$H_0^* = \frac{C_u - C_d}{u S_0 - d S_0} \tag{5.2-4}$$

$$B_0^* = \frac{C_u(d S_0) - C_d(u S_0)}{r_f(u S_0 - d S_0)}. \tag{5.2-5}$$

H_0^* in Equation (5.2-4) is the ratio of the range in possible call values to stock values, often referred to as the **hedge ratio** or *delta value*. In our example:

$$H_0^* = \frac{C_u - C_d}{u S_0 - d S_0} = \frac{\$10 - 0}{\$110 - \$95} = .6667$$

$$B_0^* = \frac{C_u(d S_0) - C_d(u S_0)}{(u S_0 - d S_0) r_f}$$

$$B_0^* = \frac{[(\$10)(\$95) - (0)(\$110)]}{[(\$110 - \$95)(1.05)]} = \$60.32.$$

Thus, to replicate the two possible call payouts you would need to purchase .6667 shares of the stock at $100 per share, partially financed by borrowing $60.32. At the end of the period this portfolio would replicate the two possible call payoffs of $10 or $0. That is:

$$V_{cu} = (.6667)(\$110) - (\$60.32)(1.05) = \$10$$

$$V_{cd} = (.6667)(\$95) - (\$60.32)(1.05) = 0.$$

Finally, by the law of one price you can determine the equilibrium price of the call, C_0^*, by setting the current call value equal to the current value of the replicating portfolio. That is:

$$C_0^* = H_0^* S_0 - B_0^*. \tag{5.2-6}$$

For our example, the equilibrium call price is therefore $6.35:

$$C_0^* = (.6667)(\$100) - \$60.32 = \$6.35.$$

5.2.2 Single-Period Arbitrage Call Strategy

In the economy we have just described, suppose the market price of the call, C_0^m, is not equal to C_0^*. Accordingly, an arbitrage portfolio consisting of a position in the call and an opposite position in the replicating portfolio can be formed to take advantage of this mispricing opportunity. For example, if the call price in our illustrative example was $5.35 instead of $6.35, arbitrageurs could buy the cheap call for $5.35 and short the replicating portfolio (sell .6667 shares of stock short at $100 and invest $60.32 in a risk-free security) to earn a positive cash flow (or credit) of $1. As shown in Table 5.2-1, at expiration the cash flows from the long call position and the short replicating portfolio position would cancel each other out at either stock price and the initial profit of $1 would be worth $1.05. Thus, arbitrageurs would earn $1.05 with no cash outflows. As arbitrageurs try to buy calls at $5.35, though, they will push the price of the call up until it is equal to $6.35. At that price the arbitrage opportunity is gone.

On the other hand, if the call is priced above $6.35, then the replicating portfolio is cheap relative to the call. In this case, arbitrage opportunities will exist by going short in the call and long in the replicating portfolio. For example, if C_0^m = $7.35, then, as shown in Table 5.2-2, arbitrageurs could sell the call and take a long position in the replicating portfolio to earn a riskless return at expiration of $1.05. These actions, by arbitrageurs, though, would serve to lower the price of the call until the market price is equal to $6.35 and the initial cash flow from the arbitrage portfolio is zero. Thus, in this binomial world, arbitrage forces ensure that the price of the call will equal the value of the replicating portfolio.

TABLE 5.2-1

Underpriced Call Arbitrage Strategy, Single-Period Case		
S_0 = $100, u = 1.1, d = .95, R_f = .05, X = $100, C_0^* = $6.35, C_0^m = $5.35		
INITIAL POSITION	CASH FLOW	
Long call	− $ 5.35	
Short H_0^* shares: (.6667)($100)	66.67	
Invest B_0^* dollars	− 60.32	
Cash Flow	$ 1.00	

	CASH FLOW AT EXPIRATION	
CLOSING POSITION	S_u = $110	S_d = $95
Call sale (C_T^m = IV)	$10.00	0
Stock purchase ($H_0^* S_T$)	− 73.34	− $63.34
Investment ($B_0 r_f$)	63.34	63.34
Value of initial cash flow ($C_0^* - C_0^m$)r_f	1.05	1.05
Cash Flow	$ 1.05	$ 1.05

TABLE 5.2-2

Overpriced Call Arbitrage Strategy, Single-Period Case	
$S_0 = \$100, u = 1.1, d = .95, R_f = .05, X = \$100, C_0^* = \$6.35, C_0^m = \$7.35$	
INITIAL POSITION	CASH FLOW
Short call	$ 7.35
Long H_0^* shares: $-(.6667)(\$100)$	$-$ 66.67
Borrow B_0^* dollars	60.32
Cash Flow	$ 1.00

	CASH FLOW AT EXPIRATION	
CLOSING POSITION	$S_u = \$110$	$S_d = \$95$
Call purchase ($C_T^m = $ IV)	$-\$10.00$	0
Stock sale ($H_0^* S_T$)	73.34	$63.34
Debt repayment ($B_0 r_f$)	$-$ 63.34	$-$ 63.34
Value of initial cash flow ($C_0^m - C_0^*)r_f$	1.05	1.05
Cash Flow	$ 1.05	$ 1.05

5.2.3 Rewriting the Equilibrium Call Price Equation

The equation (5.2-6) for the equilibrium price of the call can be rewritten by substituting the values of H_0^* and B_0^* into it, as follows, to obtain Equation (5.2-7):

$$C_0^* = H_0^* S_0 - B_0^*$$

$$C_0^* = \left[\frac{C_u - C_d}{(uS_o - dS_0)}\right]S_0 - \left[\frac{C_u(dS_0) - C_d(uS_0)}{r_f(uS_0 - dS_0)}\right]$$

$$C_0^* = \frac{r_f S_0[C_u - C_d] - [C_u(d) - C_d(u)]S_0}{r_f S_0(u - d)}$$

$$C_0^* = \frac{1}{r_f}\left[\left(\frac{r_f - d}{u - d}\right)C_u + \left(\frac{u - r_f}{u - d}\right)C_d\right]$$

$$C_0^* = \frac{1}{r_f}[pC_u + (1 - p)C_d], \tag{5.2-7}$$

where:

$$p = \frac{r_f - d}{u - d}$$

$$1 - p = \frac{u - d}{u - d} - \frac{r_f - d}{u - d} = \frac{u - r_f}{u - d}.$$

In terms of our illustrated example:

$$C_0^* = \frac{1}{1.05}[(.6667)(\$10) + (.333)(0)] = \$6.35,$$

where:

$$p = \frac{1.05 - .95}{1.1 - .95} = .6667.$$

5.3   MULTIPLE-PERIOD BINOMIAL OPTION PRICING MODEL FOR CALLS

The BOPM just defined is based on several simplifying assumptions. To obtain a more realistic model, we need to value options under the assumption that there are multiple periods to expiration. In constructing a multiple-period model, we divide the time to expiration into a number of subperiods of smaller length. As the length of the time period becomes smaller, the assumption that stock price changes follow a binomial process of either increasing or decreasing then becomes more plausible, and, as the number of periods increase, the number of possible states at expiration is greater, again adding more realism to the model.

5.3.1   Two-Period Binomial Option Pricing Model

In deriving the BOPM for multiple periods, let us begin with the case in which we divide the expiration period into just two subperiods ($n = 2$). As before, we will assume that the stock price at the end of each subperiod will equal a proportion u or d times its price at the beginning of the period. In addition, we also will assume that both u and d and the risk-free borrowing and lending rate R_f are the same for each period.

To illustrate option pricing in a two-period case, let us take our preceding one-period case in which $S_0 = \$100$, $R_f = .05$, $u = 1.1$, and $d = .95$ and break the expiration period into two periods in which $u = 1.0488$, $d = .9747$, and $R_f = .025$. The subperiod u and d values, in turn, reflect growth and decline rates in the stock price that are equal to approximately half of those reflected by u of 1.1 and d of .95 (how u and d can be estimated will be discussed in Section 5.4). With two periods, there are now three possible stock prices at expiration. As shown in Figure 5.3-1, the stock can either increase two consecutive periods to equal

FIGURE 5.3-1

Two-Period Binomial Stock Prices		
$u = 1.0488$, $d = .9747$		
		$S_{uu} = u^2 S_0 = 110$
	$S_u = u S_0 = \$104.88$	
$S_0 = \$100$		$S_{ud} = ud S_0 = \$102.23$
	$S_d = d S_0 = \$97.47$	
		$S_{dd} = d^2 S_0 = \$95$
t 0	1	2

$S_{uu} = u^2 S_0 = (1.0488)^2 \$100 = \$110$, decrease two periods to equal $S_{dd} = d^2 S_0 = (.9747)^2 (\$100) = \$95$, or increase one period and decrease another to equal $S_{ud} = ud S_0 = (1.0488)(.9747)(\$100) = \$102.23$.

The method for pricing a call option on a stock with two periods to expiration is to start at expiration, where we know the possible call values are equal to their intrinsic values, next move from expiration to period one and use the single-period BOPM to price the call at each possible stock price (S_u and S_d), and last, move to the present and price the call using again the single-period model.

As shown in Figure 5.3-2, the three possible call prices at expiration are: C_{uu} = Max[$\$110 - \$100, 0$] = $\$10$, C_{ud} = Max[$\$102.23 - \$100, 0$] = $\$2.23$, and C_{dd} = Max[$\$95 - \$100, 0$] = 0. Moving to period 1, the price of the call when the stock is $\$104.88$ is $\$7.32$, and the price when the stock is $\$97.47$ is $\$1.48$. That is, using the single-period BOPM, the call with one period to expiration would be priced at $C_u = \$7.32$ when the stock is at $S_u = \$104.88$:

$$C_u = \frac{p C_{uu} + (1 - p) C_{ud}}{r_f} \tag{5.3-1}$$

$$C_u = \frac{(.6788)(\$10) + (.3212)(\$2.23)}{1.025} = \$7.32,$$

FIGURE 5.3-2

Two-Period Binomial Call Prices

$u = 1.0488, d = .9747, S_0 = \$100, X = \$100, R_f = .025$

t	0	1	2
			$S_{uu} = \$110$ $C_{uu} = u^2 S_0 - X = \$110 - \$100 = \$10$
		$S_u = \$104.88$ $C_u = \$7.32$ $H_u = 1$ $B_u = \$97.56$	
	$S_0 = \$100$ $C_0^* = \$5.31$ $H_0^* = .7881$ $B_0^* = \$73.50$		$S_{ud} = \$102.23$ $C_{ud} = ud S_0 - X = \$102.23 - \$100 = \$2.23$
		$S_d = \$97.47$ $C_d = \$1.48$ $H_d = .3084$ $B_d = \$28.58$	
			$S_{dd} = \$95$ $C_{dd} = $ Max[$(d^2 S_0 - X), 0$] = Max[$(\$95 - \$100), 0$] = 0

where:

$$p = \frac{r_f - d}{u - d}$$

$$p = \frac{1.025 - .9747}{1.0488 - .9747} = .6788.$$

If the call is not priced at $7.32, an arbitrage portfolio could be formed with a position in the call (long if the call is underpriced and short if it is overpriced) and an opposite position in a replicating portfolio with $H_u = 1$ and $B_u = \$97.56$. That is:

$$H_u = \frac{C_{uu} - C_{ud}}{S_{uu} - S_{ud}}$$

$$H_u = \frac{\$10 - \$2.23}{\$110 - \$102.23} = 1.0$$

$$B_u = \frac{C_{uu}(udS_0) - C_{ud}(u^2S_0)}{(u^2S_0 - udS_0)r_f}$$

$$B_u = \frac{\$10(\$102.23) - \$2.23(\$110)}{(\$110 - \$102.23)1.025} = \$97.56.$$

When the stock is priced at $97.47, the call would have to be priced at $C_d = \$1.48$ or an arbitrage profit could be obtained by taking positions in the call and a replicating portfolio with $H_d = .3084$ and $B_d = \$28.58$:

$$C_d = \frac{pC_{ud} + (1 - p)C_{dd}}{r_f} \tag{5.3-2}$$

$$C_d = \frac{.6788(\$2.23) + .3212(0)}{1.025} = \$1.48.$$

$$H_d = \frac{C_{ud} - C_{dd}}{S_{ud} - S_{dd}}$$

$$H_d = \frac{\$2.23 - 0}{\$102.23 - \$95} = .3084.$$

$$B_d = \frac{C_{ud}(d^2S_0) - C_{dd}(udS_0)}{(udS_0 - d^2S_0)r_f}$$

$$B_d = \frac{\$2.23(\$95) - 0(\$102.23)}{(\$102.23 - \$95)1.025} = \$28.58.$$

Finally, given the possible stock prices S_u and S_d and call values C_u and C_d for period 1, we move to the present and again use the single-period BOPM to find the call's current value. In this example, the 100 call would be worth $C_0^* = \$5.31$. That is:

$$C_0^* = \frac{pC_u + (1 - p)C_d}{r_f} \tag{5.3-3}$$

$$C_0^* = \frac{.6788(\$7.32) + .3212(\$1.48)}{1.025} = \$5.31.$$

If the call is not priced at $5.31, an arbitrage profit could be earned from an arbitrage portfolio with $H_0^* = .7881$ and $B_0^* = \$73.50$:

$$H_0^* = \frac{C_u - C_d}{S_u - S_d}$$

$$H_0^* = \frac{\$7.32 - \$1.48}{\$104.88 - \$97.47} = .7881.$$

$$B_0^* = \frac{C_u(dS_0) - C_d(uS_0)}{(uS_0 - dS_0)r_f}$$

$$B_0^* = \frac{\$7.32(\$97.47) - \$1.48(\$104.88)}{(\$104.88 - \$97.47)1.025} = \$73.50.$$

5.3.2   Equation for the Two-Period Binomial Option Pricing Model

Mathematically, the model for pricing a European call with two periods consists of three equations, (5.3-1), (5.3-2), and (5.3-3). This model can be simplified to one equation by substituting (5.3-1) and (5.3-2) into (5.3-3) and rearranging:

$$C_0^* = \frac{1}{r_f}\left\{p\left[\frac{pC_{uu} + (1 - p)C_{ud}}{r_f}\right] + (1 - p)\left[\frac{pC_{ud} + (1 - p)C_{dd}}{r_f}\right]\right\}$$

$$C_0^* = \frac{1}{r_f^2}[p^2C_{uu} + 2p(1 - p)C_{ud} + (1 - p)^2C_{dd}]. \qquad (5.3\text{-}4)$$

5.3.3   *n*-Period Binomial Option Pricing Model

If the time interval to expiration (T) is subdivided into three subperiods ($n = 3$), then the terminal stock prices can take one of four possibilities: $S_{uuu} = u^3S_0$, $S_{uud} = u^2dS_0$, $S_{udd} = ud^2S_0$, and $S_{ddd} = d^3S_0$. Using the binomial approach to value a call option, we again would start at expiration, where we know the call's four possible intrinsic values, then we would move to each preceding period and use the single-period BOPM to price the call at each possible stock price. An example of pricing a call with three periods is presented in Figure 5.3-3. In the example, our earlier single-period case is broken into three periods, where $u = 1.03228$, $d = .98305$, and $R_f = .016667$.

In general, if the time interval is subdivided into n subperiods, the terminal stock prices can take on one of $n + 1$ possible values at expiration. Thus, for n periods the model consists of the equation for p and all the call expressions associated with each possible stock price in every period, with each expression being similar to Equations (5.3-1)–(5.3-3). To obtain a general n-period equation for the equilibrium call price that is similar to Equation (5.3-4), we again move from expiration to each preceding period, substituting the single-period OPM equations associated with each call value and stock price in each period. This process results in the following n-period BOPM equation:

$$C_0^* = \frac{1}{r_f^n}\left(\sum_{j=0}^{n}\frac{n!}{(n - j)!j!}p^j(1 - p)^{(n-j)}\{\text{Max}[u^jd^{(n-j)}S_0 - X, 0]\}\right). \qquad (5.3\text{-}5)$$

FIGURE 5.3-3

Three-Period Binomial Model

$u = 1.03228, d = .98305,$
$R_f = .016667, S_0 = \$100,$
$X = \$100$

t	0	1	2	3
				$S_{uuu} = u^3S_0 = \$110$ $C_{uuu} = \text{Max}[u^3S_0 - X, 0] = \$10$
			$S_{uu} = \$106.56$ $C_{uu} = \$8.20$ $H_{uu} = 1$ $B_{uu} = \$98.36$	
		$S_u = \$103.228$ $C_u = \$6.50$ $H_u = .9858$ $B_u = \$95.26$		$S_{uud} = u^2dS_0 = \$104.75$ $C_{uud} = \text{Max}[u^2dS_0 - X, 0] = \$4.75$
	$S_0 = \$100$ $C_0^* = \$5.03$ $H_0^* = .8856$ $B_0^* = \$83.53$		$S_{ud} = \$101.478$ $C_{ud} = \$3.19$ $H_{ud} = .9519$ $B_{ud} = \$93.405$	
		$S_d = \$98.305$ $C_d = \$2.14$ $H_d = .6594$ $B_d = \$62.68$		$S_{udd} = u^2dS_0 = \$99.76$ $C_{udd} = \text{Max}[ud^2S_0 - X, 0] = 0$
			$S_{dd} = \$96.64$ $C_{dd} = 0$ $H_{dd} = 0$ $B_{dd} = 0$	
				$S_{ddd} = d^3S_0 = \$95$ $C_{ddd} = \text{Max}[d^3S_0 - X] = 0$

In Equation (5.3-5), the index j can be defined as the number of upward moves in the stock price in n periods, the term $u^jd^{(n-j)}S_0$ defines the possible stock prices at expiration, and the expression $\text{Max}[u^jd^{(n-j)}S_0 - X, 0]$ defines the possible intrinsic values. The term $n!/(n - j)!j!$ calculates the number of ways in which the stock can increase (j) in n periods. The expression is referred to as the jth binomial coefficient and is often denoted by the simpler notation of $\binom{n}{j}$.* In our preceding two-period example ($n = 2$), three possible intrinsic values exist:

$$j = 2: \quad \text{Max}[u^2d^0S_0 - X, 0] = C_{uu}$$

$$j = 1: \quad \text{Max}[u^1d^1S_0 - X, 0] = C_{ud}$$

$$j = 0: \quad \text{Max}[u^0d^2S_0 - X, 0] = C_{dd}.$$

---

*In Equation (5.3-5), $n!$ (read as n factorial) is the product of all the numbers from n to 1; also, $0! = 1$.

We have $\binom{n}{j} = n!/(n-j)!j!$ for:

$$j = 0: \quad \binom{2}{0} = \frac{2!}{2!0!} = 1$$

$$j = 1: \quad \binom{2}{1} = \frac{2!}{1!\,1!} = 2$$

$$j = 2: \quad \binom{2}{2} = \frac{2!}{0!2!} = 1.$$

Thus, summing Equation (5.3-5) over $j = 0$ to $n = 2$ yields our two-period model Equation (5.3-4):

$$C_0^* = \frac{1}{r_f^2}\{1p^0(1-p)^2\text{Max}[(u^0d^2S_0 - X), 0] + 2p(1-p)$$
$$\text{Max}[(udS_0 - X), 0] + p^2(1-p)^0\text{Max}[(u^2d^0S_0 - X), 0]\}$$

$$C_0^* = \frac{1}{r_f^2}\{(1-p)^2C_{dd} + 2p(1-p)C_{ud} + p^2C_{uu}\}.$$

Extending Equation (5.3-5) to value the call options in the three-period example we obtain:

$$C_0^* = \frac{1}{r_f^3}((1)p^0(1-p)^3\{\text{Max}[u^0d^3S_0 - X, 0]\} + (3)p(1-p)^2\{\text{Max}[ud^2S_0 - X, 0]\}$$
$$+ (3)p^2(1-p)\{\text{Max}[u^2dS_0 - X, 0]\} + (1)p^3(1-p)^0\{\text{Max}[u^3d^0S_0 - X, 0]\})$$

$$C_0^* = \frac{1}{r_f^3}[(1-p)^3C_{ddd} + 3p(1-p)^2C_{udd} + 3p^2(1-p)C_{uud} + p^3C_{uuu}]$$

$$C_0^* = \frac{1}{1.016667^3}[(.317144)^3(0) + 3(.682856)(.317144)^2(0) + 3(.682856)^2(.317144)(\$4.75)$$
$$+ (.682856)^3(\$10)]$$

$$C_0^* = \$5.03,$$

where:
$$p = \frac{r_f - d}{u - d} = \frac{1.016667 - .98305}{1.03228 - .98305} = .682856.$$

To summarize, the n-period BOPM, like the single-period model, is based on the assumptions that arbitrageurs will form riskless hedging strategies if the option is not priced correctly in terms of the model, that in each period the stock will equal either a proportion u or d of its previous value, and that u, d, and R_f are the same for each period.

5.3.4   Multiple-Period Arbitrage Strategy

As in the single-period case, opportunities for arbitrage returns will exist if the initial market price, C_0^m, does not equal the BOPM value, C_0^*. Except for the last period (when the call's value equals its intrinsic value), no guarantees exist that the call option will be valued correctly at the end of each period. However, if the arbitrage portfolio is correctly adjusted each period, then the initial position eventually will be profitable. The mechanics required to adjust overpriced and underpriced arbitrage position are discussed next.

Overpriced Arbitrage Strategy

If the call is initially overpriced ($C_0^m > C_0^* = H_0^* S_0 - B_0^*$), then the overpriced arbitrage strategy can be set up by taking a short position in the call $\{-C_0^m\}$ and a long position in the replicating portfolio $\{+(H_0^* S_0 - B_0^*)\}$: buying H_0^* shares of stock at price S_0 and borrowing B_0^* dollars. Both to ensure that the initial profit of at least $C_0^m - C_0^*$ is kept and to avoid losses, this strategy must be adjusted at the end of each subsequent period t, if the option is overpriced for that period ($C_t^m > C_t^*$), by adjusting the replicating portfolio position for that period (H_t and B_t). This is done by buying or selling shares of stock necessary to obtain the hedge ratio (H_t) associated with that period and stock price (S_t). In adjusting, a self-financing requirement is needed to maintain the arbitrage position. This requirement prohibits any outside funds from being added or initial funds from being removed from the strategy. Thus, if additional shares are needed to obtain the new hedge (i.e., $H_t > H_{t-1}$), then to satisfy the self-financing requirement, funds equal to $(H_t - H_{t-1})S_t$ are borrowed at a rate R_f; if shares of stock need to be sold to move to the new hedge ($H_t < H_{t-1}$), then the proceeds from the sale [$(H_t - H_{t-1})S_t$] are used to pay off part of the debt. This adjustment of moving to a new hedge with a self-financing constraint will automatically move the debt level to its correct one: $B_t = (H_t - H_{t-1})S_t + r_f B_{t-1}$. Finally, readjustment needs to occur each period until that period is reached in which the option is underpriced or equal in value. Closing the position then will result in the optimal arbitrage return.

Three points should be noted with respect to implementing this multiple-period strategy. First, at expiration the option will have to equal its intrinsic value; thus, the option cannot be overpriced every period. Second, it is possible that arbitrageurs could realize a positive cash flow by closing the call at the end of a period when the call is overpriced. Such closing would be suboptimal, however, since cash flows equal to at least the compounded value of $C_0^m - C_0^*$ can be earned by readjusting until that period is reached when the option is underpriced or equal in value. Finally, if the option is closed at expiration, the arbitrage profit will be equal to the future value of the initial price difference: $(C_0^m - C_0^*)r_f^n$.

◆ **Example:** As an example of the adjustment process, consider the two-period case described in Section 5.3.1 (Figure 5.3-2) in which the market price of the call is initially $6 instead of the OPM price of $5.31. With the option overpriced, an arbitrageur would implement the overpriced arbitrage strategy by taking the following short position in the call and long position in the replicating portfolio:

$\{-C_0^m\}, \{+(H_0^* S_0 - B_0^*)\}$	
INITIAL POSITION	CASH FLOW
Short call Buy H_0^* shares: $\quad -.7881(\$100)$ Borrow B_0^*	$ 6.00 $-$ 78.81 73.50
Cash Flow	$ 0.69

This portfolio would net the arbitrageur $C_0^m - C_0^* = \$6 - \$5.31 = \$0.69$ at the initiation of this strategy, which we will assume the arbitrageur invests in a risk-free security. At the end of period 1, the call should trade at $7.32 if the stock is trading at $S_u = \$104.88$. As stated earlier, if the call is below this price (underpriced), the arbitrageur would earn an arbitrage return if he closes. For example, if the call is priced at $C_1^m = \$7$, the arbitrageur would earn $1.03 by closing the position.

$C_1^m < C_u \Rightarrow$ Close position	
CLOSING POSITION	CASH FLOWS
Call purchase	$- \$ \ 7.00$
Stock sale: (.7881)($104.88)	82.66
Debt repayment: $-(\$73.50)(1.025)$	$- \ 75.34$
Value of initial cash flow: ($0.69)(1.025)	0.71
Cash Flow	$\$ \ 1.03$

In contrast, if the call in period 1 is above $7.32, then closing the position would result in a loss or an arbitrage profit of less than the compounded value of $C_0^m - C_0^*$. For example, if the option is trading at $C_1^m = \$9$, closing the portfolio would result in a loss of $0.97. To avoid the loss, the arbitrageur would need to adjust the arbitrage portfolio. With the stock price at $104.88 and with one period to expiration, a portfolio of $H_u = 1$ share and a debt of $B_u = \$97.56$ is required to hedge the short call position. This adjustment, though, can be done by simply moving the hedge ratio from H_0 to H_u. In terms of the example, the arbitrageur would need to borrow $22.22 to buy $H_u - H_0 = 1 - .7881 = .2119$ shares at $104.88 per share. This adjustment would move both his hedge ratio to $H_u = 1$ and his debt to the required level of $B_u = \$73.50(1.025) + \$22.22 = \$97.56$. Next period, the arbitrageur would close the arbitrage portfolio at either stock price ($110 or $102.23) and call values ($10 or $2.23) to earn a profit equal to the future value of $C_0^m - C_0^*$: ($6.00 - $5.31)(1.025)^2 = \$0.72$.

	EXPIRATION CASH FLOW	
CLOSING POSITION	$S_{uu} = \$110$ $C_{uu} = \$10$	$S_{ud} = \$102.23$ $C_{ud} = \$2.23$
Call purchase: (C_T^m)	$- \$ \ 10.00$	$- \$ \ \ 2.23$
Stock sale: $(H_u S_T)$	110.00	102.23
Debt repayment: $[B_u r_f = \$97.56(1.025)]$	$- \ 100.00$	$- \ 100.00$
Value of initial cash flow: $[(C_0^m - C_0^*)r_f^2 = \$0.69(1.025^2)]$	$\$ \ \ 0.72$	0.72
Cash Flow	$\$ \ \ 0.72$	$\$ \ \ 0.72$

Thus, by readjusting when the option was overpriced in period 1, the arbitrageur is able to realize a profit of $0.72 instead of losing $0.97 if he had closed then.

If the stock price in period 1 was $97.47 and the call was underpriced, closing would result in a profit. For example, if the call was trading at $1.30 instead of $1.48, closing would yield a profit of $0.89.

$C_1^m < C_d \Rightarrow$ Close	
CLOSING POSITION	CASH FLOWS
Call purchase	− $ 1.30
Stock sale: (.7881)($97.47)	76.82
Debt repayment: − ($73.50)(1.025)	− 75.34
Value of initial cash flow: ($0.69)(1.025)	0.71
Cash Flow	$ 0.89

However, if the call was overpriced, closing would result in a loss or a less-than-optimal return. If $C_1^m = \$2.30$, for instance, closing would result in a loss of $0.11. To avert this, the arbitrageur would need to readjust by moving to the correct H_d and B_d values. With $C_1^m = \$2.30$, this can be done by selling $H_0^* - H_d$ = .7881 − .3084 = .4797 shares at $97.47 per share, then using the funds to repay $46.756 of the debt. This adjustment will give the arbitrageur the required replicating portfolio position with $H_d = .3084$ and $B_d = (\$73.50)(1.025) -$ $46.756 = \$28.581$. At expiration, closing this arbitrage position will yield an arbitrage profit of $0.72, regardless of whether the price is $102.23 or $95.00.

	EXPIRATION CASH FLOW	
CLOSING POSITION	$S_{ud} = \$102.23$ $C_{ud} = \$2.23$	$S_{dd} = \$95$ $C_{dd} = 0$
Call purchase: (C_T^m)	− $ 2.23	0
Stock sale: $(H_d S_T = .3084 S_T)$	31.53	$29.30
Debt repayment: $[B_d r_f = \$28.581(1.025)]$	− 29.30	− 29.30
Value of initial cash flow:	0.72	0.72
$[(C_0^m - C_0^*) r_f^2 = \$0.69(1.025)^2]$		
Cash Flow	$ 0.72	$ 0.72

◆

Underpriced Arbitrage Strategy
If the call option is initially underpriced, then the exact opposite strategy and adjustment rules to the overpriced strategy apply. Specifically, if $C_0^m < C_0^* = H_0^* S_0 - B_0^*$, then an underpriced arbitrage strategy should be formed by taking a long position in the call, $\{+C_0^m\}$, and a short position in the replicating portfolio, $\{-(H_0^* S_0 - B_0^*)\} = \{-H_0^* S_0 + B_0^*\}$: sell H_0^* shares short and invest B_0^* dollars in a risk-free security. To ensure a minimum arbitrage profit of $C_0^* - C_0^m$, this strategy must be adjusted each period t that the call is underpriced $(C_t^m < C_t^*)$ to obtain the correct replicating portfolio position with a hedge ratio of H_t and risk-free investment of B_t. If $H_t > H_{t-1}$, then to move to the new hedge, $(H_t - H_{t-1})$ shares of stock must be sold short at price S_t, with the proceeds invested in the

risk-free security at the rate R_f. On the other hand, if $H_t < H_{t-1}$, then $(H_t - H_{t-1})S_t$ funds must be borrowed at rate R_f and used to buy $(H_t - H_{t-1})$ shares of stock at price S_t to cover a portion of the short sale, with the investment being reduced by the amount of debt incurred. This readjustment must be done each period until a period is reached when the call is overpriced or equal in value. Closing the position then will yield an optimal arbitrage profit.

◆   **Example:**   Using the two-period example again, suppose the call is initially trading at a market price of $5 instead of the BOPM value of $5.31. Given this situation, an arbitrageur could: (1) buy one call at $C_0^m = \$5$, (2) borrow .7881 shares of stock and sell them in the market at $100 per share, and (3) invest $B_0^* = \$73.50$ in a risk-free security at 2.5% for the period. This portfolio would net the arbitrageur a positive cash flow of $C_0^m - C_0^* = \$0.31$, which she can invest in a risk-free security for the period.

$\{C_0^m\}, \{-(H_0^*S_0 - B_0^*)\}$	
INITIAL POSITION	CASH FLOW
Long call	$- \$ \ 5.00$
Short H_0^* shares: (.7881)($100)	78.81
Invest B_0^* dollars	$- \ 73.50$
Cash Flow	$\$ \ 0.31$

If the call in period 1 is $C_1^m = \$8$ when $S_u = \$104.88$ (overpriced), closing the position would yield a positive cash flow of $1.00:

$C_1^m > C_u \Rightarrow$ Close	
CLOSING POSITION	CASH FLOWS
Call sale	$\$ \ 8.00$
Stock purchase: $-(.7881)(\$104.88)$	$- \ 82.66$
Value of B_0^* investment: ($73.50)(1.025)	75.34
Value of initial cash flow: ($0.31)(1.025)	0.32
Cash Flow	$\$ \ 1.00$

On the other hand, if the call is trading at $C_1^m = \$6$ (underpriced), then closing the position would result in a loss of $1.00. To avoid this, the arbitrageur would need to readjust her portfolio by moving to a short position of $H_u = 1$ share of stock and a risk-free investment of $B_u = \$97.56$. The arbitrageur would accomplish this by selling $H_u - H_0 = 1 - .7881 = .2119$ shares short at $104.88 per share, then investing the proceeds of $22.22 in a risk-free security to obtain $B_u = \$73.50(1.025) + \$22.22 = \$97.56$. At expiration the arbitrageur would then receive $0.33, regardless of the stock's price.

CLOSING POSITION	EXPIRATION CASH FLOW	
	$S_{uu} = \$110$ $C_{uu} = \$10$	$S_{ud} = \$102.23$ $C_{ud} = \$2.23$
Call sale: (C_T^m)	$ 10.00	$ 2.23
Stock purchase: $(H_u S_T = 1 S_T)$	− 110.00	− 102.23
Value of B_u investment: $[B_u r_f = \$97.56(1.025)]$	100.00	100.00
Value of initial cash flow:		
$[(C_0^* - C_0^m) r_f^2 = (\$5.31 - 5.00)(1.025)^2]$	$ 0.33	0.33
Cash Flow	$ 0.33	$ 0.33

If the call is underpriced when the stock is at $S_d = \$97.47$ (for example, if $C_1^m = \$1$ instead of $C_d = \$1.48$), then readjustment would require being short $H_d = .3084$ shares and an investment of $B_d = \$28.581$. In this case an arbitrageur would need to borrow $46.756 to buy $.7881 - .3084 = .4797$ shares at $97.47 per share, returning the shares to the share lender; this would result in moving the arbitrageur's portfolio to one with $H_d = .3084$ shares short and a risk-free investment of $B_d = \$73.50(1.025) - \$46.756 = \$28.581$. By closing the next period (expiration), the arbitrageur would then earn $0.33 profit.

CLOSING POSITION	EXPIRATION CASH FLOW	
	$S_{ud} = \$102.23$ $C_{ud} = \$2.23$	$S_{dd} = \$95$ $C_{dd} = 0$
Call sale	$ 2.23	$ 0
Stock purchase: $(H_d S_t = .3084 S_T)$	− 31.53	− 29.30
Value of B_d investment: $(\$28.581)(1.025)$	29.30	29.30
Value of initial cash flow:		
$(\$5.31 - 5.00)(1.025)^2$	0.33	0.33
Cash Flow	$ 0.33	$ 0.33

Thus, as is the case of the initially overpriced option, an arbitrageur would find a riskless profit could be earned by readjusting her initially underpriced arbitrage portfolio each period until a period is reached where the option is over or equal in value and the arbitrage portfolio can be profitably closed.   ◆

5.3.5   Pricing American Call Options on Non-Dividend-Paying Stock

In using a multiple-period BOPM to price an American call option, we need to determine whether the right to exercise early adds value over and above the European value. The nodes in our two-period example where this may happen are at $t = 0$ and $t = 1$. At $S_u = \$104.88$ (Figure 5.3-2), if the call option was American and was exercised, the cash flow would only be $u S_0 - X = \$4.88$, whereas the BOPM price is $C_u = \$7.32$. Hence, early exercise is not optimal. At $S_d = \$97.47$, the call is out of the money; and at the current stock price ($S_0 = \$100$), the exercise value is also $0. The implication here is that for a non-dividend-paying stock, the American call is worth the same as the European call in the BOPM framework: $C_0^{*a} = C_0^{*e}$. Moreover, this implication would be consistent with our earlier point that American call options on stocks are worth more alive than dead, except for possible cases in which the underlying stock pays a dividend.

5.4   ESTIMATING THE BINOMIAL OPTION PRICING MODEL*

The BOPM is defined in terms of the stock price, the exercise price, the number of periods to expiration, the risk-free rate, and the upward and downward parameters u and d. The first four parameters are observable. The u and d parameters, though, need to be estimated. In this section we complete our delineation of the BOPM by defining the formulas for estimating u and d (the mathematical derivation of the u and d formulas is presented in Appendix 5A), and by showing how the model can be estimated.

5.4.1   Cox, Ross, and Rubinstein Formulas for Estimating u and d

In their derivation of the BOPM, Cox, Ross, and Rubinstein (CRR) derive the equations for estimating u and d. The estimating equations are obtained by mathematically solving for the u and d values that make the statistical characteristics of a binomial distribution of the stock's end-of-period logarithmic returns equal to the characteristic's estimated values. The resulting equations that satisfy this objective are:

$$u = e^{\sqrt{V_e/n} + \mu_e/n} \tag{5.4-1}$$

$$d = e^{-\sqrt{V_e/n} + \mu_e/n}, \tag{5.4-2}$$

where:

V_e	= estimated variance of the stock's logarithmic return
μ_e	= estimated mean of the stock's logarithmic return
logarithmic return = $r_n = \log_e(S_n/S_0)$	
S_n	= end-of-period stock price
$\log_e$	= natural logarithm
n	= number of periods to expiration.

In Equations (5.4-1) and (5.4-2), V_e and μ_e are estimates, respectively, of the variance and the mean of the underlying stock's end-of-period logarithmic return (r_n). A stock's logarithmic return is its continuously compounded rate of return.

*This section uses statistics and exponents. For a primer on these subjects see, Appendices C and D at the end of the book.

This rate can be found by taking the natural (Naperian) logarithm ($\log_e$) of the ratio of the end-of-period stock price (S_n) to its current value (S_0). For example, the logarithmic return on a stock with an end-of-period value of $S_n = \$110$ and current value of $S_0 = \$100$ is:

$$\log_e\left(\frac{S_n}{S_0}\right) = \log_e\left(\frac{\$110}{\$100}\right) = \log_e(1.1) = 0.0953;$$

the logarithmic return on a stock with $S_n = \$95$ and $S_0 = \$100$ is $\log_e(0.95) = -0.0513$.

To obtain u and d estimates using Equations (5.4-1) and (5.4-2) requires estimating the stock's logarithmic return for a period equal in length to the option's expiration. Given the two estimated parameter values, the u and d values for a period equal in length to the option's expiration are found by making $n = 1$ and, for a period of a different length, by using an appropriate n value.

For instance, in evaluating an option that expires in one quarter you could use quarterly stock price data to estimate the quarterly mean and variance of the stock's logarithmic return (μ_e^q and V_e^q). By setting $n = 1, 3,$ or 90, you then could obtain the u and d values for periods equal in length to a quarter ($n = 1$), month ($n = 3$), or day ($n = 90$). For example, if the estimated quarterly mean and variance are $\mu_e^q = .022$ and $V_e^q = .0054$, then the u and d values for a period equal in length to one quarter ($n = 1$) would be 1.1 and .95. That is:

$$u = e^{\sqrt{.0054/1} + .022/1} = 1.1$$

$$d = e^{-\sqrt{.0054/1} + .022/1} = 0.95.$$

For a period equal in length to one month ($n = 3$), u and d are:

$$u = e^{\sqrt{.0054/3} + .022/3} = 1.051$$

$$d = e^{-\sqrt{.0054/3} + .022/3} = 0.9655.$$

For a daily period ($n = 90$), u and d are:

$$u = e^{\sqrt{.0054/90} + .022/90} = 1.008$$

$$d = e^{-\sqrt{.0054/90} + .022/90} = 0.9925.$$

Thus, given estimates of the mean and variance, u and d values for periods with different lengths can be found simply by changing n.

5.4.2   Annualized Mean and Variance

To facilitate the process of estimating u and d when evaluating options with different expirations, it is helpful to use an **annualized mean** and **annualized variance** (μ_e^A and V_e^A), which are obtained by simply multiplying the estimated parameter values of a given length by the number of periods of that length that make up a year. Thus, if quarterly data is used to estimate the mean and variance

(μ_e^q and V_e^q), then you simply multiply those estimates by 4 to obtain the annualized parameters ($\mu_e^A = 4\mu_e^q$ and $V_e^A = 4V_e^q$); if weekly data is used, then the estimated parameters would need to be multiplied by 52. Thus, the annualized mean and variance for the stock in our earlier example would be $\mu_e^q = 4 \times .022 = 0.088$ and $V_e^A = 4 \times .0054 = .0216$.

If the annualized mean and variance are used in Equations (5.4-1) and (5.4-2) to calculate u and d, then those values must be multiplied by a proportion t, where t is the time to expiration, expressed as a proportion of the year [i.e., since μ_e and V_e in Equations (5.4-1) and (5.4-2) are defined for a period equal in length to the option's expiration]. That is:

$$u = e^{\sqrt{(V_e^A t)/n} + (\mu_e^A t)/n} \tag{5.4-3}$$

$$d = e^{-\sqrt{(V_e^A t)/n} + (\mu_e^A t)/n}. \tag{5.4-4}$$

Thus, if an option on the stock in our example expires in six months, then u and d for a period of length 6 months ($n = 1$) would be:

$$u = e^{\sqrt{(.0216 \times .5)/1} + (.088 \times .5)/1} = 1.159$$

$$d = e^{-\sqrt{(.0216 \times .5)/1} + (.088 \times .5)/1} = 0.9418,$$

and for a period of length 3 months ($n = 2$):

$$u = e^{\sqrt{(.0216 \times .5)/2} + (.088 \times .5)/2} = 1.1$$

$$d = e^{-\sqrt{(.0216 \times .5)/2} + (.088 \times .5)/2} = .95.$$

5.4.3 u and d Formulas for Large n

In Equations (5.4-1) and (5.4-2), as n becomes large or, equivalently, as the length of the period becomes smaller, the impact of the mean on u and d becomes smaller. This can be seen in Table 5.4-1, in which two sets of u and d values for various n values are shown for both the case in which $\mu_e = .022$ and $V_e = .0054$ and the case in which $\mu_e = 0$ and $V_e = .0054$. As shown in the table, as n increases the

TABLE 5.4-1

	u and d Values with Zero and Nonzero Means					
	$\mu_e = .022$ $V_e = .0054$		$\mu_e = 0$ $V_e = .0054$		DIFFERENCE	
n	u	d	u	d	u	d
1	1.1	.95	1.0762	.9291	.0238	.0209
3	1.051	.9655	1.0433	.9584	.0077	.0071
10	1.02576	.9792	1.0235	.9770	.0023	.0022
30	1.01425	.9874	1.0135	.9867	.00075	.0007
60	1.0099	.9909	1.0095	.9906	.0004	.0003

differences between the u and d values with the nonzero mean and those with the zero mean become smaller. Thus, for the cases of large n, u and d can be estimated by simply using the variance. That is:

$$u = e^{\sqrt{(V_e^A t)/n}} = e^{\sigma_e^A \sqrt{t/n}} \tag{5.4-5}$$

$$d = e^{-\sqrt{(V_e^A t)/n}} = e^{-\sigma_e^A \sqrt{t/n}} = \frac{1}{u}, \tag{5.4-6}$$

where σ_e^A = annualized standard deviation. Note that for cases where n is large or where $\mu_e = 0$, u and d are inversely proportional.*

5.4.4 Estimating μ_e and V_e Using Historical Data

The two most common ways to estimate μ_e and V_e are to calculate the stock's average mean and variance from a historical sample of stock prices or to determine the stock's implied parameter values. In Chapter 7 we will discuss the latter approach. In using averages, daily, weekly, or perhaps quarterly historical stock price data can be used to calculate the mean and variance of the stock's historical logarithmic return.

As an example, historical quarterly closing prices of a non-dividend-paying stock over 13 quarters are shown in Table 5.4-2. The 12 logarithmic returns (r_t) are calculated by taking the natural $\log_e$ of the stock price relatives (S_t/S_{t-1}). From this data, the historical quarterly logarithmic mean return ($\mu_e^q = \bar{r}_q$), variance (V_e^q), and standard deviation (σ_e^q) are found as follows:

$$\mu_e^q = \bar{r}_q = \sum_{t=1}^{12} \frac{r_t}{12} = \frac{0}{12} = 0$$

$$V_e^q = \sum_{t=1}^{12} \frac{(r_t - \bar{r}_q)^2}{11} = \frac{.046296}{11} = .004209$$

$$\sigma_e^q = \sigma_q = \sqrt{.004209} = .0649.$$

Multiplying the historical quarterly mean and variance by 4, we obtain an annualized mean (μ_e^A) and variance (V_e^A), respectively, of 0 and .016836:

$$\mu_e^A = 4\bar{r}_q = 4(0) = 0$$

$$V_e^A = 4V_e^q = 4(.004209) = .016836.$$

Taking the square root of V_e^A, we obtain the annualized standard deviation (σ_e^A) of .1298:†

$$\sigma_e^A = \sqrt{.016836} = .1298.$$

---

*The case of μ_e being insignificant for large n holds only if the underlying distribution of logarithmic returns is symmetrical.

†The annualized standard deviation cannot be obtained simply by multiplying the quarterly standard deviation by 4. Rather, we first must multiply the quarterly variance by 4 and then take the square root of the resulting annualized variance.

TABLE 5.4-2

		Estimating μ_e and V_e from Historical Sample of Quarterly Prices		
QUARTER	PRICE (S_t)	PRICE RELATIVES (S_t/S_{t-1})	LOGARITHMIC RETURN $(r_t = \log_e(S_t/S_{t-1}))$	$(r_t - \bar{r}_q)^2$
90.1	$106	—	—	—
90.2	100	100/106 = .9434	−.0583	.003399
90.3	94	94/100 = .9400	−.0619	.003832
90.4	88	88/94 = .9362	−.0659	.004343
91.1	94	94/88 = 1.0682	.0660	.004356
91.2	100	100/94 = 1.0638	.0618	.003819
91.3	106	106/100 = 1.0600	.0583	.003399
91.4	100	100/106 = .9434	−.0583	.003399
92.1	94	94/100 = .9400	−.0619	.003832
92.2	88	88/94 = .9362	−.0659	.004343
92.3	94	94/88 = 1.0682	.0660	.004356
92.4	100	100/94 = 1.0638	.0618	.003819
93.1	106	106/100 = 1.0600	.0583	.003399
			0	.046296
			$\bar{r}_q = \mu_e^q = 0$	$V_e^q = \dfrac{.046296}{11} = .004209$

$\mu_e^A = 4\mu_e^q = (4)(0) = 0$

$V_e^A = 4V_e^q = (4)(.004209) = .016836$

$\sigma_e^A = \sqrt{V_e^A} = \sqrt{.016836} = .1298$

Given the estimated mean and variance, u and d can be estimated using Equations (5.4–3) and (5.4–4), once we determine the number of periods to subdivide the expiration period (or equivalently once we have decided the length of the period we want for our binomial period). For example, for a three-month option, if we want to make the length of the period one month, then n would be 3, yielding $u = 1.0382$ and $d = .9632$. If we want a weekly period, then we set $n = 12$ to obtain $u \doteq 1.0189$ and $d = .9814$. Finally, if we want a daily period, then we make $n = 90$, and obtain u and d values of 1.00686 and .9932, respectively.

5.4.5   Note on the Risk-Free Rate

In the BOPM, the risk-free rate used is the rate for the period. In calculating the risk-free rate, the rate on a Treasury bill, commercial paper, or other money market security with a maturity equal to the option's expiration is usually selected. These rates often are quoted in terms of a simple annual rate (with no compounding). If a simple annual rate (R^A) is given, the period rate (R^P) needed for the BOPM is:

$$R^P = (1 + R^A)^{t/n} - 1, \tag{5.4-5}$$

where t is the time to expiration, expressed as a proportion of a year. Thus, given a three-month option ($t = .25$) and an annual risk-free rate of 9.27%, if the length of the period being evaluated when the stock can either increase or decrease is a day ($n = 90$), then the period (daily) risk-free rate would be .0246%:

$$R^P = (1 + .0927)^{.25/90} - 1 = .000246.$$

5.4.6 Binomial Option Pricing Model Computer Program

To use the BOPM to estimate the equilibrium value of a call first requires estimating V_e and μ_e, determining the risk-free rate, and specifying S_0, X, T, and n. Given these values, we can determine u, d, and r_f. Next, we need to determine the possible intrinsic values of the option. Finally, we use the recursive multiple-period model to obtain the option price. This procedure for determining the price of an option is rather cumbersome, especially when a number of subperiods to expiration are used. The recursive procedure of the BOPM, though, easily lends itself to computer analysis. An options program that values calls (and puts) is available as part of the software that accompanies this book. Several end-of-the-chapter problems are included that make use of this software.

◆ **Example:** The BOPM computer program was used to value a $100 call option expiring in one quarter on a non-dividend-paying stock with an estimated annualized mean of zero, annualized variance of 0.016836, and current stock price of $100, and where the annual risk-free rate is 9.27%. The BOPM call values are shown in Table 5.4-3 for different n values. As indicated in the table, if the number of subperiods to expiration is $n = 6$, then $u = 1.02684$, $d = .9739$, $r_f = 1.0037$, and the equilibrium call price is $C_0^* = \$3.25$. If the number of subperiods is divided into 30, then $u = 1.01192$, $d = .9882$, $r_f = 1.000739$, and the call price is $C_0^* = \$3.34$. Finally, if number of subperiods is 100, then $u = 1.00651$, $d = .9935$, $r_f = 1.00022$, and $C_0^* = \$3.35$ (note the small difference between call values at $n = 30$ and $n = 100$). ◆

TABLE 5.4-3					
			BOPM Values		
	$\mu_e^A = 0$, $V_e^A = .016836$, $R_f^A = .0927$, $t = .25$ per year, $S_0 = \$100$				
	n	u	d	r_f	C_0^*
	6	1.02684	.9739	1.0037	$3.25
	30	1.01192	.9882	1.000739	3.34
	100	1.00651	.9935	1.00022	3.35

5.5 CONCLUSION

The BOPM is based on the law of one price, in which the equilibrium price of an option is equal to the value of a replicating portfolio constructed so it has the same cash flows as the option. In this chapter we have derived that model for the cases of single and multiple periods to expiration, and we have investigated the arbitrage arguments by examining the strategies you can use if the option is not priced in the market to equal its BOPM value.

KEY TERMS

binomial option pricing model   annualized mean
replicating portfolio   annualized variance
hedge ratio

SELECTED REFERENCES

Cox, Ross, and Rubinstein (1979) and Rendleman and Bartter (1979) derived the BOPM. Cox and Rubinstein (1985) also provide a derivation of the model, as do several option and futures textbooks [Chance (1991), Ritchken (1987), Hull (1989), Jarrow and Rudd (1983)], and several investment textbooks [Sharpe and Alexander (1991), Francis (1991), and Elton and Gruber (1987)].

Black, Fischer, and Scholes, Myron. "The Pricing of Options and Corporate Liabilities." *Journal of Political Economy* 81 (May–June 1973): 637–659.

Boyle, P. "A Lattice Framework for Option Pricing with Two State Variables." *Journal of Financial and Quantitative Analysis* 23 (Mar. 1988): 1–12.

Breenan, M. "The Pricing of Contingent Claims in Discrete Time Models." *Journal of Finance* 34 (Mar. 1979): 53–68.

Chance, Don M. *An Introduction to Options and Futures*. Forth Worth, Tex.: Dryden Press, 1991, ch. 5, 6.

Cox, John C., and Ross, S. "The Valuation of Options for Alternative Stochastic Processes." *Journal of Financial Economics* 3 (Jan.–Mar. 1976): 145–166.

Cox, John C., Ross, S., and Rubinstein, M. "Option Pricing: A Simplified Approach." *Journal of Financial Economics* 7 (Sept. 1979): 229–263.

Cox, John C., and Rubinstein, M. *Option Markets*. Englewood Cliffs, N.J.: Prentice-Hall, 1985, ch. 5.

Elton, E., and Gruber, M. *Modern Portfolio Theory and Investment Analysis*, 2nd ed. New York: Wiley, 1987, ch. 20.

Francis, J. C. *Investments: Analysis and Management*. New York: McGraw-Hill, 1991, ch. 22.

Hsia, Chi-Cheng. "On Binomial Option Pricing." *Journal of Financial Research* 6 (Spring 1983): 41–50.

Hull, John. *Options, Futures, and Other Derivative Securities*. Englewood Cliffs, N.J.: Prentice-Hall, 1989: ch. 4, 8.

Jarrow, Robert, and Rudd, Andrew. *Option Pricing*. Homewood, Ill.: Richard D. Irwin, 1983: ch. 7–13.

Rendleman, R., and Bartter, B. "Two-State Option Pricing." *Journal of Finance* 34 (Dec. 1979): 1093–1110.

Ritchken, Peter. "Options: Theory, Strategy, and Applications." Glenview, Ill.: Scott, Foresman, 1987, ch. 8–10.

Rubinstein, M. "The Valuation of Uncertain Income Streams and the Pricing of Options." *Bell Journal of Economics* 7 (Autumn 1976): 407–424.

Sharpe, W., and Alexander, G. J. *Investments*. Englewood Cliffs, N.J.: Prentice-Hall, 1991, ch. 18.

Smith, Clifford W., Jr. "Option Pricing: A Review." *Journal of Financial Economics* 3 (Jan.–Mar. 1976): 3–51.

Tucker, Alan L. *Financial Futures, Options, and Swaps*. St. Paul: West, 1991, ch. 15.

PROBLEMS AND QUESTIONS

1. Consider a one-period, two-state case in which XYZ stock is trading at $S_0 = \$35$, has u of 1.05 and d of $1/1.05$, and for which the period risk-free rate is 2%.

   a. Using the BOPM, determine the equilibrium price of an XYZ 35 European call option expiring at the end of the period.

   b. Explain what an arbitrageur would do if the XYZ 35 European call was priced at \$1.35. Show what the arbitrageur's cash flow would be at expiration when she closed.

   c. Explain what an arbitrageur would do if the XYZ 35 European call was priced at \$1.10. Show what the arbitrageur's cash flow would be at expiration when she closed.

2. Assume two periods to expiration, $u = 1.05$, $d = 1/1.05$, $r_f = 1.02$, $S_0 = \$50$, no dividends, and $X = \$50$ on a European call expiring at the end of the second period.

   a. Find: C_{uu}, C_{ud}, C_{dd}, C_d, C_u, C_0^*, H_u, H_d, H_0^*, B_u, B_d, and B_0^*.

   b. Overpriced case:

      (1) Define the arbitrage strategy you would employ if the current market price of the call was \$2.60. Assume any positive cash flow is invested in a risk-free security.

      (2) What would be your cash flow from your arbitrage in period 1 if you closed your initial strategy when the stock was priced at S_u and the call was selling at $C_t^m = \$3.75$? How would you readjust your initial strategy to avoid a loss? Show what your cash flow would be when you

closed at the end of the second period (assume the stock will follow the binomial process and will be either uuS_0 or udS_0).

(3) What would be your cash flow from your arbitrage investment in period 1 if you closed your initial strategy when the stock was priced at S_d and the call was selling at $C_t^m = \$0.50$? How would you readjust your initial strategy to avoid the loss? Show what your cash flow would be when you closed at the end of the second period (assume the stock will follow the binomial process and will be either udS_0 or ddS_0.)

c. Underpriced case:

(1) Define the arbitrage strategy you would employ if the current market price of the call was $2.20. Assume any positive cash flow is invested in a risk-free security.

(2) What would be your cash flow from your arbitrage investment in period 1 if you closed your initial position when the stock was priced at S_u and the call was selling at $C_t^m = \$3.25$? How would you readjust your initial strategy to avoid the loss? Show what your cash flow would be when you closed at the end of the second period (assume the stock will follow the binomial process and will be either uuS_0 or udS_0).

(3) What would be your cash flow from your arbitrage investment in period 1 if you closed your initial position when the stock was priced at S_d and the call was selling at $C_t^m = 0$? Would you readjust your initial strategy?

3. Suppose XYZ stock is trading at $S_0 = \$101$, $u = 1.02$, $d = 1/1.02$, the period risk-free rate is 1%, and the stock pays no dividends. Using the n-period BOPM, determine the equilibrium price of an XYZ 100 European call expiring at the end of the third period ($n = 3$).

4. Explain how subdividing the number of periods to expiration makes the BOPM more realistic.

5. Describe the methodology used to derive the formulas for estimating u and d.

6. Suppose a stock has the following probability distribution of future prices after four months:

S_T	PROBABILITY OF OCCURRENCE
$66.23	.0625
63.32	.2500
60.54	.3750
57.88	.2500
55.34	.0625

a. Calculate the stock's expected logarithmic return and variance. Assume it is currently priced at $60.

b. Calculate the stock's annualized variance and mean.

c. What are the stock's u and d values for a period of length one month ($n = 4$), one week ($n = 16$), and one day ($n = 120$)?

d. Suppose the stock's mean is equal to zero. What are the stock's u and d values for the periods of lengths one month, one week, and one day? Comment on the importance of the mean in calculating u and d when n is large.

7. Suppose a stock has the following prices over the past 13 quarters:

QUARTER	S_t
91.1	$55
91.2	50
91.3	47
91.4	44
92.1	47
92.2	50
92.3	54
92.4	50
93.1	47
93.2	44
93.3	47
93.4	50
94.1	55

a. Calculate the stock's average logarithmic return and variance.

b. What is the stock's annualized mean and variance?

c. Calculate the stock's up and down parameters (u and d) for periods with the following lengths:

(1) One quarter

(2) One month

(3) One week (assume 12 weeks in a quarter)

(4) One day (assume 90 days in a quarter)

(5) One-half day

(6) One-eighth day

COMPUTER PROBLEMS

1. Use the BOPM computer program (Binopm) to show the call and stock price relationship for a 50 European call option on the stock in Problem 7. Assume the call expires at the end of the quarter, the annual risk-free rate is 6%, and there is frequent trading such that the period to expiration can be divided into a large number of subperiods where $n = 180$. Show the call and stock price relationship in table and graphical forms for stock prices of 42, 44, 46, 48, 49, 50, 51, 52, 53, 54, 55, 56, 58, and 60. Comment on the ability of the BOPM to capture the features of the call and stock price relationships described in Chapter 4.

2. Suppose the stock in Problem 7 is currently priced at $50, the annual risk-free rate is 6%, and call options on the stock are frequently traded such that $n = 180$. Use the BOPM computer program (Binopm) to determine the equilibrium prices for the following call options:

   a. Call with an exercise price of 50, expiring at the end of the quarter

   b. Call with an exercise price of 52, expiring at the end of the quarter

   c. Call with an exercise price of 48, expiring at the end of the quarter

   d. Call with an exercise price of 50, expiring at the end of one month

   e. Call with an exercise price of 50, expiring at the end of six months

   Comment on the BOPM ability to satisfy the following boundary conditions: $C^e(X_1) > C^e(X_2)$ and $C^e(T_2) > C^e(T_1)$.

APPENDIX 5A

Derivation of the Equations for Estimating u and d

In Section 5.4 we defined the formulas for estimating u and d. The equations (5.4-1 and 5.4-2) are obtained by solving mathematically for the u and d values that make the statistical characteristics of a binomial distribution of the stock's logarithmic return equal to the characteristics estimated values. In this appendix, we will derive the estimating equations for u and d. As background, though, we first need to examine the probability distribution that characterizes a binomial process.

5.A.1   Probability Distribution Resulting from a Binomial Process

In the binomial model, the proportions u and d can be referred to as stock price relatives. For each period, this random variable takes the general form of:

$$\tilde{Z}_t = \frac{\tilde{S}_t}{S_{t-1}}. \tag{5.A-1}$$

After n periods, the stock price relative to the total period is $\tilde{Z}_n$:

$$\tilde{Z}_n = \frac{\tilde{S}_n}{S_0}. \tag{5.A-2}$$

Taking the natural logarithm ($\log_e$) of the stock price relatives gives us the stock's logarithmic return. The logarithmic return for each period ($\tilde{r}_t$) and for the total period ($\tilde{r}_n$) is:

Note: The methodology described in this appendix uses statistics, logarithms, and exponents that are explained in Appendices C and D at the end of the book.

$$\tilde{r}_t = \log_e \tilde{Z}_t = \log_e\left(\frac{\tilde{S}_t}{S_{t-1}}\right) \qquad (5.A\text{-}3)$$

$$\tilde{r}_n = \log_e \tilde{Z}_n = \log_e\left(\frac{\tilde{S}_n}{S_0}\right).$$

The binomial process described earlier in Chapter 5 was specified in terms of possible stock prices. This process also can be described in terms of logarithmic returns. Table 5.A-1 shows the possible rates for each period obtained assuming $u = 1.1$, $d = .95$, and $S_0 = \$100$. As shown, our assumption that the stock price either will increase such that $u = 1.1$ or decrease such that $d = .95$ implies that the two possible logarithmic returns at the end of the first period would be $.0953 = \log_e(1.1)$ or $-.0513 = \log_e(.95)$, and the three possible rates at the end of the second period would be $.1906$, $.044$, and $-.1026$.

If we know the probabilities for each possible rate, then the distributions of possible rates shown in Table 5.A-1 can be defined in terms of their probability distributions and described by the distributions' characteristics: expected value $[E(\tilde{r}_n)]$, variance $[V(\tilde{r}_n)]$, and skewness $[S_k(\tilde{r}_n)]$. The probability of the stock being

TABLE 5.A-1

Binomial Process of Logarithmic Returns				
$u = 1.1$, $d = .95$, $S_0 = \$100$				
PERIOD (t)	0	1	2	3
Possible logarithmic returns (and their probabilities)	r_0	$r_{11} = \log_e(1.1) = .095$; (.5) $r_{10} = \log_e(.95) = -.0513$; (.5)	$r_{22} = \log_e(1.21) = .1906$; (.25) $r_{21} = \log_e(1.045) = .0440$; (.5) $r_{20} = \log_e(.9025) = -.1026$; (.25)	$r_{33} = \log_e(1.331) = .2859$; (.125) $r_{32} = \log_e(1.1495) = .1393$; (.375) $r_{31} = \log_e(.99275) = -.0073$; (.375) $r_{30} = \log_e(.8574) = -.1539$; (.125)
$E(\tilde{r}_n)$		$E(r_1) = .022$	$E(r_2) = 2E(r_1) = .044$	$E(r_3) = 3E(r_1) = .066$
$V(\tilde{r}_n)$		$V(r_1) = .0054$	$V(r_2) = 2V(r_1) = .0108$	$V(r_3) = 3V(r_1) = .0162$
$S_k(\tilde{r}_n)$		$S_k(r_1) = 0$	$S_k(r_2) = 2S_k(r_1) = .0$	$S_k(r_3) = 3S_k(r_1) = .0$

$\tilde{S}_{nj}$ or, equivalently, the probability of its yielding a rate of $\tilde{r}_{nj}$ is equal to the probability of the stock's increasing j times in n periods, p_{nj}. In a binomial process this probability is:

$$p_{nj} = \frac{n!}{(n-j)!j!} q^j (1-q)^{(n-j)}, \tag{5.A-4}$$

in which q is the probability of stock's increasing in one period. In the example in Table 5.A-1 it is assumed that there is an equal likelihood of the stock's increasing or decreasing each period; that is, $q = .5$. Thus, after two periods, the probabilities of the logarithmic return's equaling $\tilde{r}_{nj} = \tilde{r}_{22} = .1906$ is $p_{nj} = p_{22} = .25$, $\tilde{r}_{21} = .044$ is $p_{21} = .5$, and $\tilde{r}_{20} = -.1026$ is $p_{20} = .25$. Given the probabilities of each possible outcome (shown in the parentheses next to the outcome), the first three moments (expected value, variance, and skewness) of each period's distribution are found, in which:

$$E(\tilde{r}_n) = \sum_{j=0}^{n} p_{nj}(\tilde{r}_{nj}) \tag{5.A-5}$$

$$V(\tilde{r}_n) = E[\tilde{r}_{nj} - E(\tilde{r}_n)]^2 = \sum_{j=0}^{n} p_{nj}[\tilde{r}_{nj} - E(\tilde{r}_n)]^2 \tag{5.A-6}$$

$$S_k(\tilde{r}_n) = E[\tilde{r}_n - E(\tilde{r}_n)]^3 = \sum_{j=0}^{n} p_{nj}[\tilde{r}_{nj} - E(\tilde{r}_n)]^3. \tag{5.A-7}$$

These characteristics are shown for each distribution ($n = 1, 2,$ and 3) at the bottom of Table 5.A-1.

In examining each distribution's moments in the table, several characteristics of the binomial process should be noted. First, as the number of periods increase, the expected value and the variance of the logarithmic return increase by a multiplicative factor, such that $E(r_n) = nE(\tilde{r}_1)$ and $V(\tilde{r}_n) = nV(\tilde{r}_1)$. That is, for $n = 1$, $E(\tilde{r}_1) = .022$ and $V(\tilde{r}_1) = .0054$; for $n = 2$, $E(\tilde{r}_2) = 2E(\tilde{r}_1) = .044$ and $V(\tilde{r}_2) = 2V(\tilde{r}_1) = .0108$; for $n = 3$, $E(\tilde{r}_3) = 3E(\tilde{r}_1) = .066$ and $V(\tilde{r}_3) = 3V(\tilde{r}_1) = .0162$. Thus, if changes in the price of a security follow a binomial process, then the expected value and variance, as well as the other moments of the distribution, will equal the parameters' values for one period, times the number of periods defining the total period.

Second, if u and d are inversely proportional ($d = 1/u$) and also $q = .5$, then the expected rate in period 1, as well as in other periods, would be zero. That is:

$$E(\tilde{r}_1) = [q \log_e u + (1-q)\log_e d]$$

$$E(\tilde{r}_1) = \left[q \log_e u + (1-q)\log_e\left(\frac{1}{u}\right)\right]$$

$$E(\tilde{r}_1) = [.5 \log_e u - .5 \log_e u] = 0.$$

Under these conditions, $E(\tilde{r}_n)$ is constant (stationary) in every period, although the variance increases. Finally, as shown in the table, the skewness for each period's distribution is zero. As a result, each period's distribution is symmetrical.* In this example the zero skewness is a result of assuming $q = .5$. Thus, a sufficient but not necessary condition for symmetry is that an equal probability of the stock's increasing or decreasing exists in each period.[†]

5.A.2   Methodology for Estimating u and d

If a stock's possible logarithmic returns in the future are characterized by a symmetrical distribution, with a variance (and possibly an expected value) that increases with the length of the differencing period, then the binomial model for logarithmic returns probably is a good first approximation of the way a stock's logarithmic return performs over time. If this is the case, then we can estimate u and d by finding the u and d values that make $E(\tilde{r}_n)$ and $V(\tilde{r}_n)$ for the distribution resulting from the binomial process equal to the distribution's estimated parameters. For example, if we had started our previous example not knowing u and d but instead knowing $E(\tilde{r}_n) = .044$, $V(\tilde{r}_n) = .0108$, and $S_k(\tilde{r}_n) = 0$ for a period with a length equivalent to $n = 2$, then given the assumptions that changes in the stock prices follow a binomial process and that $q = .5$, we could have solved mathematically for u and d to find $u = 1.1$ and $d = .95$.

As a first step in finding the u and d values for which $E(\tilde{r}_n)$ and $V(\tilde{r}_n)$ equal their estimated parameters, we need to rewrite the equations for $E(\tilde{r}_n)$ and $V(\tilde{r}_n)$.

5.A.3 $E(\tilde{r}_n)$ and $V(\tilde{r}_n)$

The parameters $E(\tilde{r}_n)$ and $V(\tilde{r}_n)$ describing the distribution resulting from a binomial process can be redefined in terms of u, d, and n by first rewriting the random variable $\tilde{r}_n$ as:

$$\tilde{r}_n = \log_e\left(\frac{\tilde{S}_n}{S_0}\right) = \log_e[u^j d^{(n-j)}], \qquad (5.A\text{-}8)$$

or by applying the rules of logarithms as

$$\tilde{r}_n = \tilde{j} \log_e u + (n - \tilde{j})\log_e d$$

$$\tilde{r}_n = \tilde{j} \log_e u + n \log_e d - \tilde{j} \log_e d$$

$$\tilde{r}_n = \tilde{j} \log_e\left(\frac{u}{d}\right) + n \log_e d. \qquad (5.A\text{-}9)$$

---

*One distribution that is not symmetrical is a *lognormal* one. Such a distribution is characterized by positive skewness. Since a stock's price cannot be negative, its distribution may be lognormal. Moreover, a random variable has a lognormal distribution when its logarithm has a normal distribution. Thus, stock prices and stock price relatives would be lognormally distributed given that the logarithm of the stock price relatives is normal.

[†]It is not a necessary condition since it is possible for q not to equal .5, and yet the relative values of u and d could be such that $S_k(\tilde{r}_n) = 0$. Also, it is possible that the distribution could be influenced by the fourth moment, peakedness. For simplicity, we will assume the distributions are not characterized by this parameter.

Note in Equation (5.A-9) that the only random variable is j, the number of upward moves in n periods (u and d are variables to be solved for, and n would be known or can be specified). Taking the expected value of Equation (5.A-9), we therefore obtain:

$$E(\tilde{r}_n) = E(\tilde{j})\log_e\left(\frac{u}{d}\right) + n\,\log_e d. \qquad (5.A\text{-}10)$$

Given that the probability of an upward move in one period is q, the expected number of upward moves in n periods therefore is $E(\tilde{j}) = nq$. For example, if the probability of an upward move in one period is $q = 0.5$, then the expected number of upward moves in six periods is $E(\tilde{j}) = nq = 6(.5) = 3$. Substituting nq for $E(\tilde{j})$ in Equation (5.A-10) and rearranging the resulting equation, the expected value of $\tilde{r}_n$ can be expressed alternatively as follows:

$$E(\tilde{r}_n) = nq\,\log_e\left(\frac{u}{d}\right) + n\,\log_e d$$

$$E(\tilde{r}_n) = n(q\,\log_e u - q\,\log_e d + \log_e d)$$

$$E(\tilde{r}_n) = n[q\,\log_e u + (1 - q)\log_e d]. \qquad (5.A\text{-}11)$$

The bracket expression on the right-hand side of Equation (5.A-11) is the expected logarithmic return for one period. Thus, consistent with our earlier observation, Equation (5.A-11) shows that $E(\tilde{r}_n)$ is equal to the expected logarithmic return for one period times n.

The mathematical expression for $V(\tilde{r}_n)$ is found first by substituting the expressions for $\tilde{r}_n$ and $E(\tilde{r}_n)$ into the general equation for $V(\tilde{r}_n)$, then rearranging as follows to obtain Equation (5.A-12):

$$V(\tilde{r}_n) = E[\tilde{r}_n - E(r_n)]^2$$

$$V(\tilde{r}_n) = E\left[\tilde{j}\,\log_e\left(\frac{u}{d}\right) + n\,\log_e d - E(\tilde{j})\log_e\left(\frac{u}{d}\right) - n\,\log_e d\right]^2$$

$$V(\tilde{r}_n) = E\left\{[\tilde{j} - E(\tilde{j})]\log_e\left(\frac{u}{d}\right)\right\}^2$$

$$V(\tilde{r}_n) = E\left\{[\tilde{j} - E(\tilde{j})]^2\left[\log_e\left(\frac{u}{d}\right)\right]\right\}^2$$

$$V(\tilde{r}_n) = V(\tilde{j})\left[\log_e\left(\frac{u}{d}\right)\right]^2. \qquad (5.A\text{-}12)$$

For one period the number of upward moves (j) is either 1 or 0, with the expected value of the upward moves, $E(\tilde{j}_1)$, equal to q. With the probability of $j = 1$ being q and the probability of $j = 0$ being $1 - q$, the variance of upward moves for one period, $V(\tilde{j}_1)$, is $q(1 - q)$. That is:

$$V(\tilde{j}_1) = q(1 - q)^2 + (1 - q)(0 - q)^2$$

$$V(\tilde{j}_1) = q(1 - q)(1 - q) + q^2 - q^3$$

$$V(\tilde{j}_1) = q - 2q^2 + q^3 + q^2 - q^3 = q - q^2 = q(1 - q).$$

In a binomial process, the variance of j for n periods, $V(\tilde{j})$, is equal to the variance of upward moves in one period $[V(\tilde{j}_1)]$ times n; thus:

$$V(\tilde{j}) = nV(\tilde{j}_1) = nq(1 - q).\qquad(5.A\text{-}13)$$

Substituting (5.A-13) into (5.A-12), we obtain the alternative expression for $V(\tilde{r}_n)$:

$$V(\tilde{r}_n) = nq(1 - q)\left[\log_e\left(\frac{u}{d}\right)\right]^2.\qquad(5.A\text{-}14)$$

Note that the expression $q(1 - q)[\log_e(u/d)]^2$ in Equation (5.A-14) can be shown to equal the variance of the logarithmic return for one period. Thus, like $E(\tilde{r}_n)$, $V(\tilde{r}_n)$ is equal to its parameter value for one period times n.

5.A.4   Solving for u and d

Given the equations for $E(\tilde{r}_n)$ and $V(\tilde{r}_n)$, we next set Equation (5.A-11) for the mean equal to its estimated value, μ_e, and Equation (5.A-14) for the variance equal to its estimated value, V_e, to obtain the following equation system:

$$n[q \log_e u + (1 - q)\log_e d] = \mu_e\qquad(5.A\text{-}15)$$

$$nq(1 - q)\left[\log_e\left(\frac{u}{d}\right)\right]^2 = V_e.\qquad(5.A\text{-}16)$$

The u and d formulas are found by solving Equations (5.A-15) and (5.A-16) simultaneously for the unknowns. This equation system, however, consists of two equations and three unknowns, u, d, and q, and cannot be solved without a third equation or information about one of the unknowns. If we assume, however, that the distribution of $\tilde{r}_n$ is symmetrical such that $S_k(\tilde{r}_n) = 0$, then we can set $q = .5$ in Equations (5.A-15) and (5.A-16). Doing this yields the following two-equation system with two unknowns (u and d):

$$n[.5 \log_e u + (1 - .5)\log_e d] = \mu_e\qquad(5.A\text{-}17)$$

$$n\left\{(.5)(1 - .5)\left[\log_e\left(\frac{u}{d}\right)\right]^2\right\} = V_e.\qquad(5.A\text{-}18)$$

To solve Equations (5.A-17) and (5.A-18) simultaneously for u and d, we first rewrite Equation (5.A-17) in terms of $\log_e d$:

$$n[.5 \log_e u + (1 - .5)\log_e d] = \mu_e$$

$$.5(\log_e u + \log_e d) = \frac{\mu_e}{n}$$

$$\log_e d = 2\left(\frac{\mu_e}{n}\right) - \log_e u.\qquad(5.A\text{-}19)$$

Next we rewrite Equation (5.A-18) in terms of $\log_e u$:

$$n\left\{.5(1 - .5)\left[\log_e\left(\frac{u}{d}\right)\right]^2\right\} = V_e$$

$$(.5)^2\left[\log_e\left(\frac{u}{d}\right)\right]^2 = \frac{V_e}{n}$$

$$\sqrt{(.5)^2\left[\log_e\left(\frac{u}{d}\right)\right]^2} = \sqrt{\frac{V_e}{n}}$$

$$.5 \log_e\left(\frac{u}{d}\right) = \sqrt{\frac{V_e}{n}}$$

$$\log_e u = 2\sqrt{\frac{V_e}{n}} + \log_e d. \qquad (5.A\text{-}20)$$

Substituting Equation (5.A-19) for $\log_e d$ in Equation (5.A-20), we obtain:

$$\log_e u = 2\sqrt{\frac{V_e}{n}} + 2\left(\frac{\mu_e}{n}\right) - \log_e u$$

$$2 \log_e u = 2\sqrt{\frac{V_e}{n}} + 2\left(\frac{\mu_e}{n}\right).$$

Thus:

$$\log_e u = \sqrt{\frac{V_e}{n}} + \frac{\mu_e}{n}. \qquad (5.A\text{-}21)$$

Similarly, substituting Equation (5.A-21) for $\log_e u$ in Equation (5.A-19), we obtain:

$$\log_e d = 2\frac{\mu_e}{n} - \sqrt{\frac{V_e}{n}} - \frac{\mu_e}{n}$$

$$\log_e d = -\sqrt{\frac{V_e}{n}} + \frac{\mu_e}{n}. \qquad (5.A\text{-}22)$$

Finally, expressing Equations (5.A-21) and (5.A-22) as exponents, we obtain the equations for the u and d values that simultaneously satisfy Equations (5.A-17) and (5.A-18):

$$u = e^{\sqrt{V_e/n} + (\mu_e/n)} \qquad (5.A\text{-}23)$$

and

$$d = e^{-\sqrt{V_e/n} + (\mu_e/n)}. \qquad (5.A\text{-}24)$$

Equations (5.A-23) and (5.A-24) determine the values for u and d given the estimated variance and the mean of the logarithmic return for the period and the assumption that stock price changes follow a binomial process. In terms of our earlier example, if the estimated expected value and variance of the logarithmic return were known to be .066 and .0162, respectively, for a period equal in length to $n = 3$, then using Equations (5.A-23) and (5.A-24), u would be 1.1 and d would be .95. That is:

$$u = e^{\sqrt{(.0162/3)} + (.066/3)} = 1.1$$

$$d = e^{-\sqrt{(.0162/3)} + (.066/3)} = .95.$$

EXERCISES

Assume ABC stock follows a binomial process, is currently priced at $50, and has a u of 1.02, d of 1/1.02, and probability of its price increasing in one period of .5 ($q = .5$).

1. Show with an event tree ABC's possible stock prices, logarithmic returns, and probabilities after one period, two periods, and three periods.

2. What are the stock's expected logarithmic return, variance, and skewness for each period?

3. What are the stock's expected logarithmic return, variance, and skewness for each period if the probability of the stock increasing in one period is .6 ($q = .6$)?

4. What is a sufficient condition for the distribution to be symmetrical?

5. List the properties of a binomial distribution.

CHAPTER 6

Binomial Put Model and the Dividend-Adjusted Binomial Option Pricing Model

6.1 INTRODUCTION

In this chapter we continue our analysis of the BOPM by deriving the binomial model for puts and by incorporating dividends into the model. The derivation of the binomial put model parallels that for call options. That is, the value of the put is found by determining the value of a replicating portfolio constructed such that it has the same cash flows as the put's. As we will see, though, the BOPM value of a put on a non-dividend-paying stock, unlike that of a call, can be priced below its intrinsic value. Thus, the **binomial option pricing model for puts** needs to be adjusted for the case of an American put option. After deriving the multiple-period BOPM for puts, we will then show how the model is adjusted to price American puts.

As discussed in Chapter 4, on the ex-dividend date a dividend can cause the price of a call to decrease and that of a put to increase. This, in turn, can make the early exercise feature of both American calls and American puts more valuable. In Section 6.4 we will show how to adjust the BOPM for European options on stocks paying dividends and for American calls and puts on dividend-paying stocks. Finally, in Appendices 6A and 6B, we will present two alternative derivations of the BOPM: the risk-neutral pricing approach, and the state-preference pricing approach.

6.2 SINGLE-PERIOD BINOMIAL OPTION PRICING MODEL FOR PUT OPTIONS

6.2.1 Valuing Put Options Through a Replicating Portfolio

In the last chapter we showed how a European call can be priced by replicating its payoffs at expiration. Similarly, the equilibrium value of a European put also can be found by determining the value of a *replicating portfolio for puts*. To see this, consider first the one-period, two-state economy, in which a stock can either increase to equal uS_0 or decrease to equal dS_0. A European put on the stock that expires at the end of the period would, therefore, be worth either P_u or P_d:

$$P_u = IV = Max[X - uS_0, 0]$$

$$P_0$$

$$P_d = IV = Max[X - dS_0, 0]$$

Given the two possible stock prices and put values, a replicating put portfolio can be formed by purchasing H_0^p shares of stock and investing I_0 dollars in a risk-free security (where I_0 is the negative of borrowing B_0 dollars). The current value of this portfolio, V_{p0}, is:

$$V_{p0} = H_0^p S_0 + I_0, \tag{6.2-1}$$

and the portfolio's two possible values at expiration are:

$$V_{pu} = H_0^p u S_0 + r_f I_0 \tag{6.2-2}$$

$$V_{pd} = H_0^p d S_0 + r_f I_0. \tag{6.2-3}$$

For this portfolio to have values at expiration that match those of the put, H_0^p and I_0 must be such that:

$$H_0^p u S_0 + r_f I_0 = P_u \tag{6.2-4}$$

$$H_0^p d S_0 + r_f I_0 = P_d.$$

Thus, solving (6.2-4) simultaneously for H_0^{p*} and I_0^* we obtain:

$$H_0^{p*} = \frac{P_u - P_d}{uS_0 - dS_0} \tag{6.2-5}$$

$$I_0^* = \frac{-[P_u(dS_0) - P_d(uS_0)]}{(uS_0 - dS_0)r_f}. \tag{6.2-6}$$

Note that since $P_d > P_u$, H_0^{p*} will be negative and I_0^* will be positive, except for the case in which $P_d = 0$. This implies that the replicating put portfolio is constructed with a short position in the stock (selling H_0^{p*} shares short) and a long position in the risk-free security (investing I_0^* dollars in a risk-free security). Thus, this strategy contrasts with the replicating call portfolio, which is formed with a long position in the stock and by borrowing funds.

As an example, suppose in our last chapter's single-period call example (Section 5.2), in which $u = 1.1$, $d = .95$, $S_0 = \$100$, and $r_f = 1.05$, that there is a European put option on the stock with an exercise price of $\$100$. In our one-period, two-state model, the possible put values at expiration would be:

$P_u = \text{IV} = \text{Max}[\$100 - \$110, 0] = 0$

P_0

$P_d = \text{IV} = \text{Max}[\$100 - \$95, 0] = \$5$

To replicate the possible values of the put, we would need to sell .33333 shares short ($H_0^{p*} = -.33333$) at \$100 per share and to invest \$34.9206 in the risk-free security. That is:

$$H_0^{p*} = \frac{0 - \$5}{\$110 - \$95} = -.33333$$

$$I_0^* = \frac{-[0(\$95) - (\$5)(\$110)]}{(\$110 - \$95)(1.05)} = \$34.9206.$$

At the end of the period this portfolio would have possible values that match exactly those of the put:

$$V_{pu} = -.33333(\$110) + \$34.9206(1.05) = 0$$

$$V_{pd} = -.33333(\$95) + \$34.9206(1.05) = \$5.$$

Thus, by the law of one price, the equilibrium price of the put, P_0^*, would have to equal the value of the replicating put portfolio, or arbitrage opportunities would exist. The equilibrium price of the put therefore is:

$$P_0^* = H_0^{p*} S_0 + I_0^*. \tag{6.2-7}$$

And in terms of our example:

$$P_0^* = -.33333(\$100) + \$34.9206 = \$1.59.$$

6.2.2 Single-Period Arbitrage Strategy

If a put is not equal to its equilibrium value, then riskless profit can be earned from an arbitrage portfolio consisting of a position in the put and an opposite position in the replicating put portfolio. If the market price of the put, P_0^m, is above P_0^*, then arbitrageurs would take a short position in the put and a long position in the replicating portfolio.

For example, if the market price of the put in our earlier example was $P_0^m = \$2.00$, then, as shown in Table 6.2-1, an initial cash flow of \$0.41 could be earned by selling the put, selling .33333 shares of the stock short, and buying \$34.9206 worth of a risk-free security. At expiration, the replicating portfolio would have possible values of either 0 or \$5, which would cover the possible put obligations, and the \$0.41 initial cash flow would be worth (\$0.41)(1.05) = \$0.43.

In contrast, if the put is below P_0^*, then an initial positive cash flow could be earned by going long in the put and short in the replicating put portfolio. For example, as shown in Table 6.2-2, at $P_0^m = \$1.18$, a \$0.43 profit is earned by implementing this underpriced arbitrage strategy.

TABLE 6.2-1

Overpriced Put Arbitrage Strategy: Single-Period Case	

$S_0 = \$100, u = 1.1, d = .95, R_f = .05, X = \$100, P_0^* = \$1.59,$
$H_0^{p*} = .33333, I_0^* = \$34.92, P_0^m = \$2.00$

INITIAL POSITION	CASH FLOW
Short put	$ 2.00
Short H_0^{p*} shares: (.33333)($100)	33.33
Invest I_0^* dollars	− 34.92
Cash Flow	$ 0.41

	CASH FLOW AT EXPIRATION	
CLOSING POSITION	$S_u = \$110$ $P_u = 0$	$S_d = \$95$ $P_d = 5$
Put purchase ($P_T^m = IV$)	$ 0.00	−$ 5.00
Stock purchase ($H_0^{p*}S_T$)	− 36.67	− 31.67
Investment ($I_0^* r_f$)	36.67	36.67
Value of initial cash flow ($P_0^m - P_0^*)r_f$	0.43	0.43
Cash Flow	$ 0.43	$ 0.43

TABLE 6.2-2

Underpriced Put Arbitrage Strategy: Single-Period Case	

$S_0 = \$100, u = 1.1, d = .95, R_f = .05, X = \$100, P_0^* = \$1.59,$
$H_0^{p*} = .33333, I_0^* = \$34.92, P_0^m = \$1.18$

INITIAL POSITION	CASH FLOW
Long put	− $1.18
Long H_0^{p*} shares: −(.33333)($100)	− 33.33
Borrow I_0^* dollars	34.92
Cash Flow	$ 0.41

	CASH FLOW AT EXPIRATION	
CLOSING POSITION	$S_u = \$110$ $P_u = 0$	$S_d = \$95$ $P_d = \$5$
Put purchase ($P_T^m = IV$)	$ 0.00	$ 5.00
Stock sale ($H_0^{p*}S_T$)	36.67	31.67
Debt repayment ($I_0^* r_f$)	− 36.67	− 36.67
Value of initial cash flow ($P_0^* - P_0^m)r_f$	0.43	0.43
Cash Flow	$ 0.43	$ 0.43

6.2.3   Rewriting the Equilibrium Put Equation

The equilibrium put value defined by Equation (6.2-7) can be defined alternatively in terms of upcoming Equation (6.2-8) by respectively substituting Equations (6.2-5) and (6.2-6) for H_0^{p*} and I_0^* in Equation (6.2-7) and rearranging as follows:

$$P_0^* = H_0^{p*}S_0 + I_0^*$$

$$P_0^* = \left(\frac{P_u - P_d}{uS_0 - dS_0}\right)S_0 - \frac{P_u(dS_0) - P_d(uS_0)}{(uS_0 - dS_0)r_f}$$

$$P_0^* = \frac{r_fS_0(P_u - P_d) - [P_u(d) - P_d(u)]S_0}{r_fS_0(u - d)}$$

$$P_0^* = \frac{1}{r_f}\left[\left(\frac{u - r_f}{u - d}\right)P_d + \left(\frac{r_f - d}{u - d}\right)P_u\right]$$

$$P_0^* = \frac{1}{r_f}[pP_u + (1 - p)P_d], \tag{6.2-8}$$

where:

$$p = \frac{r_f - d}{u - d}$$

$$1 - p = \frac{u - d}{u - d} - \frac{r_f - d}{u - d} = \frac{u - r_f}{u - d}.$$

In terms of the example:

$$P_0^* = \left(\frac{1}{1.05}\right)[.6667(0) + .33333(\$5)] = \$1.59,$$

where:

$$p = \frac{1.05 - .95}{1.1 - .95} = .6667$$

$$1 - p = \frac{1.1 - 1.05}{1.1 - .95} = .33333.$$

6.2.4   Put-Call Parity Model

In Chapter 4 we delineated the put-call parity model. Recall that this model specifies the equilibrium relationship between the prices of call and put options on the same stock. In terms of the model, the equilibrium price of a European put is determined by the current value of a portfolio consisting of long positions in the call and a riskless bond with face value equal to the exercise price and a short position in the stock:

$$P_0^* = C_0^* + PV(X) - S_0. \tag{6.2-9}$$

Using this model, we can determine the same equilibrium put price that we obtained using the binomial put model by substituting the equilibrium call price, as determined by the binomial call model. In terms of our examples, substituting the call value of $6.35 (Section 5.2) into Equation (6.2-9), we obtain the same put value of $1.59 that we did using the binomial put model. That is:

$$P_0^* = \$6.35 + \frac{\$100}{1.05} - \$100 = \$1.59.$$

6.3   MULTIPLE-PERIOD BINOMIAL OPTION PRICING MODEL FOR PUTS

6.3.1   Two-Period Case

The multiple-period put model is similar to the multiple-period call model delineated in Chapter 5. For a European put with two periods to expiration, we start at expiration, where the three possible put values are equal to their intrinsic value: $P_{uu} = \text{Max}[X - u^2 S_0, 0]$, $P_{ud} = [X - udS_0, 0]$, and $P_{dd} = \text{Max}[X - d^2 S_0, 0]$. We then move to period 1 and use the single-period binomial put model to determine the put values P_u and P_d when the stock is at uS_0 and dS_0, respectively. Finally, we move to the present to determine P_0^* given P_u and P_d.

For example, to price a 100 European put on the stock in our two-period example where $u = 1.0488$, $d = .9747$, $R_f = .025$, there are, as shown in Figure 6.3-1, three possible put values at expiration: $P_{uu} = 0$, $P_{ud} = 0$, and $P_{dd} = \$5$.

FIGURE 6.3-1

Two-Period Put Values

$u = 1.0488, d = .9747,$
$R_f = .025, S_0 = \$100,$
$X = \$100$

		$S_{uu} = \$110$ $P_{uu} = \text{Max}[\$100 - \$110, 0] = 0$
	$S_u = \$104.88$ $P_u = 0$ $H_u^p = 0$ $I_u = 0$	
$S_0 = \$100$ $P_0^* = \$0.49$ $H_0^{p*} = -.2105$ $I_0^* = \$21.54$		$S_{ud} = \$102.23$ $P_{ud} = \text{Max}[\$100 - \$102.23, 0] = 0$
	$S_d = \$97.47$ $P_d = \$1.56$ $H_d^p = -.6916$ $I_d = \$68.97$	
		$S_{dd} = \$95$ $P_{dd} = \text{Max}[\$100 - \$95, 0] = \$5$
t 0	1	2

Moving to period 1, the put value is $P_d = \$1.56$ when the price of the stock is $S_d = \$97.47$, and $P_u = 0$ when $S_u = \$104.88$. That is, using the single-period put model:

$$P_d = \left(\frac{1}{r_f}\right)[pP_{ud} + (1 - p)P_{dd}] = H_d^p(dS_0) + I_d \qquad (6.3\text{-}1)$$

$$P_d = \left(\frac{1}{1.025}\right)[(.6788)(0) + (.3212)(\$5)]$$

$$= -.6916(\$97.47) + \$68.97 = \$1.56,$$

where:

$$p = \frac{r_f - d}{u - d} = \frac{1.025 - .9747}{1.0488 - .9747} = .6788$$

$$H_d^p = \frac{P_{ud} - P_{dd}}{udS_0 - d^2S_0} = \frac{0 - \$5.00}{\$102.23 - \$95} = -.6916$$

$$I_d = -\frac{P_{ud}(d^2S_0) - P_{dd}(udS_0)}{r_f(udS_0 - d^2S_0)} = -\frac{(0)(\$95) - (\$5)(\$102.23)}{1.025(\$102.23 - \$95)} = \$68.97.$$

$$P_u = \left(\frac{1}{r_f}\right)[pP_{uu} + (1 - p)P_{ud}] = H_u^p(uS_0) + I_u \qquad (6.3\text{-}2)$$

$$P_u = \left(\frac{1}{1.025}\right)[(.6788)(0) + (.3212)(0)] = 0(\$104.88) + 0 = 0,$$

where:

$$H_u^p = \frac{P_{uu} - P_{ud}}{u^2S_0 - udS_0} = \frac{0 - 0}{\$110 - \$102.23} = 0$$

$$I_u = -\frac{P_{uu}(udS_0) - P_{ud}(u^2S_0)}{(u^2S_0 - udS_0)r_f} = -\frac{0(\$102.23) - 0(\$110)}{(\$110 - \$102.23)1.025} = 0.$$

Finally, given $P_d = \$1.56$ and $P_u = 0$, the equilibrium price of the put using the single-period put model is $P_0^* = \$0.49$:

$$P_0^* = \left(\frac{1}{r_f}\right)[pP_u + (1 - p)P_d] = H_0^{p*}S_0 + I_0^* \qquad (6.3\text{-}3)$$

$$P_0^* = \left(\frac{1}{1.025}\right)[(.6788)(0) + (.3212)(\$1.56)]$$

$$P_0^* = -.2105(\$100) + \$21.54 = \$0.49,$$

where:

$$H_0^{p*} = \frac{P_u - P_d}{uS_0 - dS_0} = \frac{0 - \$1.56}{\$104.88 - \$97.47} = -.2105$$

$$I_0^* = -\frac{P_u(dS_0) - P_d(uS_0)}{(uS_0 - dS_0)r_f} = -\frac{0(\$97.47) - (\$1.56)(\$104.88)}{(\$104.88 - \$97.47)(1.025)} = \$21.54.$$

6.3.2 Equation for the Multiple-Period Put Model

The two-period put model can be expressed in terms of one equation by substituting Equations (6.3-1) and (6.3-2) for P_u and P_d in Equation (6.3-3) and rearranging. Doing this yields:

$$P_0^* = \frac{1}{r_f}\left\{(1-p)\left[\frac{(1-p)P_{dd} + pP_{ud}}{r_f}\right] + p\left[\frac{(1-p)P_{ud} + pP_{uu}}{r_f}\right]\right\}$$

$$P_0^* = \left(\frac{1}{r_f^2}\right)[(1-p)^2 P_{dd} + 2p(1-p)P_{ud} + p^2 P_{uu}]. \tag{6.3-4}$$

Equation (6.3-4) takes on the same form as the binomial equation for calls. Like calls, for n periods the equilibrium put price can be found by using the following n-period binomial equation:

$$P_0^* = \frac{1}{r_f^n}\left[\sum_{j=0}^{n} \frac{n!}{(n-j)!j!}(1-p)^j p^{n-j} \text{ Max}[X - u^j d^{n-j} S_0, 0]\right]. \tag{6.3-5}$$

6.3.3 Multiple-Period Arbitrage Strategies for Puts

The same overpriced and underpriced arbitrage strategies defined earlier for the single-period case can be used to set up the multiple-period arbitrage strategies for puts. For multiple periods, though, the arbitrage position (like those for calls) must be adjusted each period until profitable conditions exist to close.

For example, for the case of an initially overpriced put ($P_0^m > P_0^* = H_0^{p*} S_0 + I_0^*$), the arbitrage portfolio consisting of a short position in the put ($\{-P_0^m\}$) and a long position in the replicating put portfolio ($\{+(H_0^{p*} S_0 + I_0^*)\}$) must be readjusted each subsequent period t if the put is overpriced by moving the position to the H_t^p required for that period and stock price. The overpriced strategy is then closed in the first period in which the put is underpriced or equal in value. Moreover, given a self-financing requirement, the adjustments needed to attain H_t^p will require either additional investments or borrowing, which will automatically result in the required I_t^* needed for the correct replicating portfolio for that period.

An example using the two-period put model for an overpriced arbitrage portfolio with adjustments made in period 1 is presented in Table 6.3-1. The arbitrage strategy and adjustments for an initially underpriced put are just the opposite of those for the overpriced case. A problem that involves adjusting an underpriced put strategy is included as one of the end-of-chapter problems.

6.3.4 Put-Call Parity Model: Multiple Period

The same equilibrium put price also can be determined using the put-call parity model. In terms of our illustrative two-period example, the two-period binomial model's put value on the 100 put of $0.49 is obtained using the put-call parity model by substituting into the model the two-period binomial call value of $5.31 (Section 5.3.1). Doing this yields:

$$P_0^* = C_0^* + \text{PV}(X) - S_0$$

$$P_0^* = \$5.31 + \frac{\$100}{1.025^2} - \$100 = \$0.49.$$

TABLE 6.3-1

<table>
<tr><th colspan="2">Arbitrage Strategy for an Overpriced Put: Two-Period Case
(Based on Put Example in Figure 6.3-1)</th></tr>
</table>

Current period
$S_0 = \$100$, $R_f = .025$, $H_0^{p*} = -.2105$, $I_0^* = \$21.54$, $P_0^* = \$0.49$, $P_0^m = \$0.60$
Strategy: $\{-P_0^m\}$ and $\{+(H_0^{p*}S_0 + I_0^*)\}$

POSITION	CASH FLOW
Put sale	$ 0.60
Short H_0^{p*} shares at S_0	21.05
Investment of I_0^* in riskless security	− 21.54
Initial Cash Flow	$ 0.11

Period 1: Closing initial position
$S_d = \$97.47$, $R_f = .025$, $H_d^p = -.6916$, $I_d = \$68.97$, $P_d = \$1.56$
Possible prices: $P_1^m = \$1.50$ and $P_1^m = \$1.70$

CLOSING POSITION	$P_1^m = \$1.50$	$P_1^m = \$1.70$
Put purchase	−$ 1.50	−$ 1.70
Stock purchase ($H_0^p S_d$)	− 20.52	− 20.52
Investment ($I_0^* r_f$)	22.08	22.08
Value of initial cash flow ($\$0.11 r_f$)	0.11275	0.11275
Cash Flow	$ 0.17	−$ 0.027

Period 1: Readjusting when $P_1^m = \$1.70$

Readjustment strategy:
1. Sell $(H_d^p - H_0^{p*})$ shares short at S_d: $(.6916 - .2105)(\$97.47) = \$46.89$.
2. Invest short sale proceeds of $46.89 in risk-free security.

New position:
$H_d^p = -.6916$
$I_d = \$21.54(1.025) + \$46.89 = \$68.97$

Period 2: Closing position readjusted in period 1
S_T: $S_{ud} = \$102.23$ or $S_{dd} = \$95$; P_T: $P_{ud} = 0$ or $P_{dd} = \$5$

CLOSING POSITION	$S_{ud} = \$102.23$	$S_{dd} = \$95$
Put purchase	$ 0	−$ 5.00
Stock purchase ($H_d^p S_T$)	− 70.70	− 65.70
Investment ($I_d r_f$)	70.70	70.70
Value of initial cash flow ($\$0.11 r_f^2$)	0.1156	0.1156
Cash Flow	$ 0.1156	$ 0.1156

6.3.5   Pricing American Put Options

In examining Figure 6.3-1, note that with one period to expiration, the value of the European put is $P_d = \$1.56$ when the stock is at $S_d = \$97.47$. If the put was American and priced at this European BOPM value, then a put holder would find it advantageous to exercise the put, since it would provide him with a gain in wealth of $X - dS_0 = \$100 - \$97.47 = \$2.53$, compared to the put value of $\$1.56$. Thus, the just-described multiple-period BOPM for puts is applicable only for European puts.

The BOPM can be adjusted to value American puts, P_0^{a*}, by simply specifying each put price at each node in terms of the following condition: $P^a = \text{Max}[P^e, X - S]$ where P^e is the value of the European put as determined by the binomial model (P_u or P_d). In Figure 6.3-2, the two-period BOPM for pricing an American put is shown for our illustrative case. With the advantage of early exercise, the price of an American put is $\$0.79$ in this example, which, as we should expect, is greater than the BOPM's European put price of $\$0.49$.

FIGURE 6.3-2

Two-Period BOPM for American Put (European Values Appear in Figure 6.3-1)

---

t	0	1	2
			$S_{uu} = \$110$ $P_{uu} = \text{Max}[X - u^2S_0, 0]$ $P_{uu} = \text{Max}[\$100 - \$110, 0] = 0$
		$S_u = \$104.88$ $P_u^a = \text{Max}[P_u^e, X - uS_0]$ $P_u^a = \text{Max}[0, \$100 - \$110] = 0$	
	$S_0 = \$100$ $P_0^{a*} = \$0.79$		$S_{ud} = \$102.23$ $P_{ud} = \text{Max}[X - udS_0, 0]$ $P_{ud} = \text{Max}[\$100 - \$102.23, 0] = 0$
		$S_d = \$97.47$ $P_d^a = \text{Max}[P_d^e, X - dS_0]$ $P_d^a = \text{Max}[\$1.56, \$100 - \$97.47] = \$2.53$	
			$S_{dd} = \$95$ $P_{dd} = \text{Max}[X - d^2S_0, 0]$ $P_{dd} = \text{Max}[\$100 - \$95, 0] = \$5$

$P_0^{*a} = (1/r_f)[pP_u^a + (1 - p)P_d^a] = H_0^{p*}S_0 + I_0^*$

$P_0^{*a} = (1/1.025)[(.6788)(0) + (.3212)(\$2.53)] = -(.34143)(\$100) + \$34.9358 = \$0.79$

where:

$H_0^{p*} = (P_u^a + P_d^a)/(uS_0 - dS_0) = (0 - \$2.53)/(\$104.88 - \$97.47) = -.34143$

$I_0^* = -[P_u^a(dS_0) - P_d^a(uS_0)]/[r_f(uS_0 - dS_0)] = -[0(\$97.47) - (\$2.53)(\$104.88)]/[1.025(\$104.88 - \$97.47)] = \$34.9358$

6.4   DIVIDEND ADJUSTMENTS

Dividend payments affect the value of an option in two ways. First, on the ex-dividend date the price of the stock usually falls by an amount approximately equal to the dividend. This, in turn, will lead to a decrease in the price of a call and an increase in the price of a put. Second, as discussed in Chapter 4, a dividend payment may lead to an early exercise of a call just prior to the ex-dividend date and possibly a put on the ex-dividend date. If early exercise is advantageous, then an American option would be more valuable than a European one. In this section we explain the *dividend-adjusted binomial option pricing model*.

6.4.1   Pricing European Calls on Dividend-Paying Stocks

Single-Period Case

To see the implications dividends have on the BOPM, consider first the case of a European call option on a dividend-paying stock with a single period to expiration. For this case, assume that the period starts on a non-ex-dividend date and expires on the stock's ex-dividend date. For simplicity, also assume that the stock falls by an amount equal to the dividend (D_1) on the ex-dividend date and that the dividend-payment date and the ex-dividend date are the same.

In adjusting the BOPM for this dividend case, first note that since the stock is assumed to fall by an amount equal to the dividend on the ex-dividend date, the dividends an arbitrageur with an arbitrage portfolio would earn (pay), $H_0 D_1$, from her long (short) position in the stock would be negated by the decrease in the price of the stock on the ex-dividend date. Thus, as shown in Figure 6.4-1, the arbitrageur's stock position in her portfolio is unaffected by dividend payments when the ex-dividend date and expiration date are the same. On the other hand, since exchange-traded call options are not dividend protected, the price of the call will be lower on an ex-dividend date (as compared to a non-ex-dividend date) if the

FIGURE 6.4-1

Value of Replicating Call Portfolio and European Call: Single-Period Case with Ex-Dividend Date the Same as the Expiration Date and with a Dividend Paid on the Ex-Dividend Date

$$V_{c0} = H_0^* S_0 - B_0^*$$
$$C_0^* = H_0^* S_0 - B_0^*$$

$$V_u = H_0^*(uS_0 - D_1) + H_0^* D_1 - B_0^* r_f$$
$$= H_0^* uS_0 - B_0^* r_f$$
$$C_u^x = IV^x = Max[(uS_0 - D_1) - X, 0]$$

$$V_d = H_0^*(dS_0 - D_1) + H_0^* D_1 - B_0^* r_f$$
$$= H_0^* dS_0 - B_0^* r_f$$
$$C_d^x = IV^x = Max[(dS_0 - D_1) - X, 0]$$

where:

x = ex-dividend date value
$H_0^* = [C_u^x - C_d^x]/[uS_0 - dS_0]$
$B_0^* = [C_u^x(dS_0) - C_d^x(uS_0)]/(uS_0 - dS_0)r_f$

call is in the money. This implies that for the single-period BOPM the only adjustment needed is to subtract dividends from the two non-dividend-adjusted stock prices (uS_0 and dS_0) in computing both the call's possible intrinsic values (IV^x), C_u^x, and C_d^x (where x indicates the ex-dividend date), and the H_0^* and B_0^* values for the replicating portfolio.

As an example, suppose the stock in our single-period call example in Section 5.2.1 paid a $1 dividend on the ex-dividend date. Given $u = 1.1$, $d = .95$ (with no dividend adjustments for each), $r_f = 1.05$, and $S_0 = \$100$, the H_0^* and B_0^* values needed to form a replicating portfolio to match the possible call values of $C_u^x =$ Max[($110 - $1) - $100, 0] = $9 and $C_d^x =$ Max[($95 - $1) - $100, 0] = 0 would be:

$$H_0^* = \frac{C_u^x - C_d^x}{uS_0 - dS_0}$$

$$H_0^* = \frac{\$9 - 0}{\$110 - \$95} = .6$$

$$B_0^* = \frac{C_u^x(dS_0) - C_d^x(uS_0)}{(uS_0 - dS_0)r_f}$$

$$B_0^* = \frac{\$9(\$95) - 0(\$110)}{(\$110 - \$95)(1.05)} = \$54.2857.$$

The equilibrium call price therefore would be:

$$C_0^* = H_0^*S_0 - B_0^* = .6(\$100) - \$54.2857 = \$5.71,$$

or

$$C_0^* = \frac{pC_u^x + (1 - p)C_d^x}{r_f}$$

$$C_0^* = \frac{(.6667)(\$9) + (.3333)(\$0)}{1.05} = \$5.71.$$

Thus, when the ex-dividend date coincides with expiration, the BOPM can be adjusted simply by subtracting the dividends from the possible stock prices in computing the intrinsic values of the call.

Multiple-Period Case

To adjust the multiple-period BOPM for dividends, we use IV^x at expiration instead of IV, if the ex-dividend date and expiration date are the same, and we price the call at each node using, as before, the single-period BOPM. However, in pricing the call at each period we do need to know if the stock at that time is expected to trade ex-dividend, and if it is, to use the ex-dividend stock price.

To see the multiple-period dividend adjustments, suppose in our two-period call example in Section 5.3 ($u = 1.0488$, $d = .9747$, $R_f = .025$) that dividends of $1 are expected to be paid at the ex-dividend date at the end of period 1 ($D_1 = \$1$) and at the ex-dividend date at expiration ($D_2 = \$1$) and that the call is being valued on a non-ex-dividend date. As summarized in Figure 6.4-2, the three possible intrinsic values at expiration are:

FIGURE 6.4-2

Two-Period European Call Values with Dividends

$u = 1.0488, d = .9747, r_f = 1.025, S_0 = \$100, X = \$100, D_1 = \$1, D_2 = \$1$

$$
\begin{array}{llll}
& & & \begin{array}{l} S_{uu}^x = \$110 - \$1 = \$109 \\ C_{uu}^x = \text{Max}[(\$110 - \$1) - \$100, 0] = \$9 \end{array} \\[2em]
& \begin{array}{l} S_u^x = \$104.88 - \$1 = 103.88 \\ C_u^x = \$5.34 \\ H_u = 1 \\ B_u = \$98.54 \end{array} & & \\[3em]
\begin{array}{l} S_0 = \$100 \\ C_0^* = \$3.74 \\ H_0^* = .6343 \\ B_0^* = \$59.69 \end{array} & & \begin{array}{l} S_{ud}^x = \$102.23 - \$1 = \$101.23 \\ C_{ud}^x = \text{Max}[(\$102.23 - \$1) - \$100, 0] = \$1.23 \end{array} & \\[3em]
& \begin{array}{l} S_d^* = \$97.47 - \$1 = \$96.47 \\ C_d^x = \$0.64 \\ H_d = .1701 \\ B_d = \$15.77 \end{array} & & \\[3em]
& & \begin{array}{l} S_{dd}^x = \$95 - \$1 = \$94 \\ C_{dd}^x = \text{Max}[(\$95 - \$1) - \$100, 0] = 0 \end{array} &
\end{array}
$$

t	0	1	2

$$
\begin{aligned}
C_{uu}^x &= \text{Max}[(u^2 S_0 - D_2) - X, 0] \\
&= \text{Max}[(\$110 - \$1) - \$100, 0] = \$9
\end{aligned}
$$

$$
\begin{aligned}
C_{ud}^x &= \text{Max}[(udS_0 - D_2) - X, 0] \\
&= \text{Max}[(\$102.23 - \$1) - \$100, 0] = \$1.23
\end{aligned}
$$

$$
\begin{aligned}
C_{dd}^x &= \text{Max}[(d^2 S_0 - D_2) - X, 0] \\
&= \text{Max}[(\$95 - \$1) - \$100, 0] = \$0.
\end{aligned}
$$

Moving to period 1, the call prices using the single period dividend-adjusted model are $C_u^x = \$5.34$ when the stock price is ex-dividend at $103.88, and $C_d^x = \$0.64$ when the stock is $96.47. That is:

$$
C_u^x = H_u(uS_0 - D_1) - B_u = 1(\$103.88) - \$98.54 = \$5.34,
$$

where:

$$
H_u = \frac{C_{uu}^x - C_{ud}^x}{u^2 S_0 - udS_0} = \frac{\$9 - \$1.23}{\$110 - \$102.23} = 1
$$

$$B_u = \frac{C_{uu}^x(udS_0) - C_{ud}^x(u^2S_0)}{(u^2S_0 - udS_0)r_f}$$

$$= \frac{\$9(102.23) - \$1.23(\$110)}{(\$110 - \$102.23)1.025} = \$98.54.$$

$$C_d^x = H_d(dS_0 - D_1) - B_d = (.1701)(\$96.47) - \$15.77 = \$0.64,$$

where:

$$H_d = \frac{C_{ud}^x - C_{dd}^x}{udS_0 - d^2S_0} = \frac{\$1.23 - 0}{\$102.23 - \$95} = .1701$$

$$B_d = \frac{C_{ud}^x(d^2S_0) - C_{dd}^x(udS_0)}{(udS_0 - d^2S_0)r_f} = \frac{\$1.23(\$95) - 0(\$102.23)}{(\$102.23 - \$95)1.025} = \$15.77.$$

Substituting period 1's call prices into the single-period BOPM for the current period we obtain the equilibrium call value of $C_0^* = \$3.74$:

$$C_0^* = H_0^*S_0 - B_0^* = .6343(\$100) - \$59.69 = \$3.74,$$

where:

$$H_0^* = \frac{C_u^x - C_d^x}{uS_0 - dS_0} = \frac{\$5.34 - \$0.64}{\$104.88 - 97.47} = .6343$$

$$B_0^* = \frac{C_u^x(dS_0) - C_d^x(uS_0)}{(uS_0 - dS_0)r_f} = \frac{\$5.34(\$97.47) - \$0.64(\$104.88)}{(\$104.88 - \$97.47)1.025} = \$59.69.$$

To summarize, adjusting the BOPM for dividends first requires estimating the future dividends and ex-dividend dates. Given this information, we then apply the same recursive procedure as used for the multiple-period case of starting at expiration and working backwards, valuing the call at each period and stock price.

6.4.2   American Call Pricing on Dividend-Paying Stocks

In Chapter 4 we discussed how it would be more profitable for a call holder to exercise a call just prior to the ex-dividend date if the value of the dividend exceeded the call's time value premium. For American call options on dividend-paying stocks, early exercise can be incorporated into the BOPM by constraining each possible call price during the period to be the maximum of either its European value, as determined by the BOPM, or the call's intrinsic value *just prior* to the ex-dividend date. This constrained model is shown in Figure 6.4-3 for the two-period case.

In our previous dividend example, the $1 dividend in period 1 would not make early exercise advantageous if the call was American. As a result, the value of the call as determined by the BOPM would be the same regardless of whether it is

FIGURE 6.4-3

American Call Price on
Dividend-Paying Stock

$$C_0^a = H_0^*(S_0 - D_0) - B_0^*$$

$$C_u^a = \text{Max}[C_u^x, uS_0 - X]$$

$$C_d^a = \text{Max}[C_d^x, dS_0 - X]$$

$$C_{uu}^x = \text{Max}[u^2S_0 - D_2 - X, 0]$$

$$C_{ud}^x = \text{Max}[udS_0 - D_2 - X, 0]$$

$$C_{dd}^x = \text{Max}[d^2S_0 - D_2 - X, 0]$$

t	0	1	2

$$H_0^* = \frac{C_u^a - C_d^a}{uS_0 - dS}$$

$$B_0^* = \frac{(C_u^a)(dS_0) - (C_u^a)(uS_0)}{r_f(uS_0 - dS_0)}$$

European or American. However, suppose that instead of $1, a $2 dividend was expected (with certainty) to be paid on the ex-dividend date at the end of period 1. (We will continue to assume a $1 dividend at expiration.) As shown in Figure 6.4-4, if the stock is at $104.88 (just prior to the period 1 ex-dividend date), then on the ex-dividend date the stock will be trading at $102.88 and the call, as determined by the BOPM, will be $4.34. If the call is American, though, a call holder could realize a greater gain in wealth on the ex-dividend date (W_{ex}) of $4.88 by exercising just prior to it (purchasing the stock on the exercise just prior to the ex-dividend date, then receiving the dividend of $2). That is:

$$W_{ex} = -X + (uS_0 - D_1) + D_1$$

$$W_{ex} = -\$100 + (\$104.88 - 2) + 2 = \$4.88.$$

Thus, a call holder would value the American call as being worth its IV just prior to the ex-dividend date of $4.88 when the stock is at $104.88:[*]

$$C_u^a = \text{Max}[C_u^x, uS_0 - X] = \text{Max}[\$4.34, \$104.88 - \$100] = \$4.88,$$

where:

$$C_u^x = H_u(uS_0 - D_1) - B_u = (1)(\$102.88) - \$98.54 = \$4.34.$$

If the stock is $95.47 on the ex-dividend date at the end of period 1, then the value of the equilibrium call would be $0.47:

$$C_d^a = \text{Max}[C_d^x, dS_0 - X] = \text{Max}[\$0.47, \$97.47 - \$100] = \$0.47.$$

---

[*]In this example, the implied TVP on the ex-dividend date would be: TVP = C_u^x − IV = $4.34 − ($102.88 − $100) = $1.46. Thus, the dividend of $2 exceeds the TVP, satisfying the early-exercise criterion set out in Chapter 4.

FIGURE 6.4-4

Two-Period American Call Values with Dividends

$u = 1.0488, d = .9747,$
$r_f = 1.025, S_0 = \$100,$
$D_1 = \$2, D_2 = \$1$

		$S_{uu}^x = \$110 - \$1 = \$109$ $C_{uu}^x = \$9$
	$S_u^x = \$104.88 - \$2 - 102.88$ $C_u^x = H_u S_u^x - B_u$ $C_u^x = (1)(\$102.88) - \$98.54 = \$4.34$ $C_u^a = \text{Max}[C_u^x, uS_0 - X]$ $C_u^a = \text{Max}[\$4.34, \$104.88 - \$100] = \$4.88$	
$S_0 = \$100$ $C_0^{a*} = H_0^* S_0 - B_0^*$ $C_0^a = (.5951)(\$100) - \$56.13 = \$3.38$		$S_{ud}^x = \$102.23 - \$1 = \$101.23$ $C_{ud}^x = \$1.23$
	$S_d^x = \$97.47 - \$2 = \$95.47$ $C_a^x = H_d S_d^x - B_d$ $C_d^x = (.1701)(\$95.47) - \$15.77 = \$0.47$ $C_d^a = \text{Max}[C_d^x, dS_0 - X]$ $C_d^a = \text{Max}[\$0.47, \$97.47 - \$100] = \$0.47$	
		$S_{dd}^x = \$95 - \$1 = \$94$ $C_{dd}^x = 0$
t 0	1	2

$$H_0^* = \frac{C_u^a - C_d^a}{uS_0 - dS_0} = \frac{\$4.88 - \$0.47}{\$104.88 - \$97.47} = .5951$$

$$B_0^* = \frac{(C_u^a)(dS_0) - (C_d^a)(uS_0)}{r_f(uS_0 - dS_0)} = \frac{(\$4.88)(\$97.47) - (\$.047)(\$104.88)}{1.025(\$104.88 - \$97.47} = \$56.13$$

where:

$$C_d^x = H_d(dS_0 - D_1) - B_d = (.1701)(\$95.47) - \$15.77 = \$0.47.$$

Thus, given the two American call values in period 1, the current equilibrium price of the American call is $3.38:

$$C_0^{a*} = H_0^* S_0 - B_0^* = (.5951)(\$100) - \$56.13 = \$3.38,$$

where:

$$H_0^* = \frac{C_u^a - C_d^a}{uS_0 - dS_0} = \frac{\$4.88 - \$0.47}{\$104.88 - \$97.47} = .5951$$

$$B_0^* = \frac{C_u^a(dS_0) - C_d^a(uS_0)}{(uS_0 - dS_0)r_f} = \frac{(\$4.88)(\$97.47) - (\$0.47)(\$104.88)}{(\$104.88 - \$97.47)1.025} = \$56.13.$$

In valuing American calls with the BOPM, if the call had been European, its value would have been \$3.02, less than the \$3.38 American value:

$$C_0^* = H_0^* S_0 - B_0^*$$

$$C_0^* = (.5223)(\$100) - \$49.21 = \$3.02,$$

where:

$$H_0^* = \frac{C_u^x - C_d^x}{uS_0 - dS_0} = \frac{\$4.34 - \$0.47}{\$104.88 - \$97.47} = .5223$$

$$B_0^* = \frac{C_u^x(dS_0) - C_d^x(uS_0)}{r_f(uS_0 - dS_0)} = \frac{(\$4.34)(\$97.47) - (\$0.47)(\$104.88)}{1.025(\$104.88 - \$97.47)} = \$49.21.$$

Thus, as we should expect, the American call with its early exercise feature is more valuable than the European when the dividend payments expected to be paid during the option's life are such that early exercise is profitable.

6.4.3 Pricing European Puts on Dividend-Paying Stocks

Single-Period Case

The dividend adjustments required for European put options are similar to those for European calls. In the single-period case, if expiration is on the stock's ex-dividend date (with dividends assumed to be paid then), the dividend is subtracted from the stock price in determining the put's intrinsic value, and no changes are necessary in the composition of the replicating put portfolio, as shown in Figure 6.4-5.

As an example, consider a 100 European put option on the stock used in our illustrative one-period example ($u = 1.10$, $d = .95$, $r_f = 1.05$, and $S_0 = \$100$).

FIGURE 6.4-5

Value of Replicating Put Portfolio and European Put: Single-Period Case with Ex-Dividend Date the Same as the Expiration Date and with the Dividends Paid on the Ex-Dividend Date

$$V_{pu} = H_0^{p*}(uS_0 - D_1) + H_0^{p*}D_1 + r_f I_0^*$$
$$= H_0^{p*}(uS_0) + r_f I_0^*$$
$$P_u^x = IV^x = \text{Max}[X - (uS_0 - D_1), 0]$$

$$V_{p0} = H_0^{p*}S_0 + I_0^*$$
$$P_0^* = H_0^{p*}S_0 + I_0^*$$

$$V_{pd} = H_0^{p*}(dS_0 - D_1) + H_0^{p*}D_1 + r_f I_0^*$$
$$V_{pd} = H_0^{p*}dS_0 + r_f I_0^*$$
$$P_d^x = IV^x = \text{Max}[X - (dS_0 - D_1), 0]$$

where:
$$x = \text{ex-dividend date value}$$
$$H_0^{p*} = (P_u^x - P_d^x)(uS_0 - dS_0)$$
$$I_0^* = -\frac{[P_u^x(dS_0) - P_d^x(uS_0)]}{(uS_0 - dS_0)r_f}$$

If the stock is expected to pay a dividend of $D_1 = \$1$ on the ex-dividend date at expiration, then the put's possible intrinsic values at expiration would be:

$$P_u^x = \text{Max}[\$100 - (\$110 - \$1), 0] = 0$$

$$P_d^x = \text{Max}[\$100 - (\$95 - \$1), 0] = \$6,$$

and the equilibrium put price would be:

$$P_0^* = H_0^{p*}(S_0) + I_0^*$$

$$P_0^* = -.4(\$100) + \$41.90 = \$1.90,$$

where:

$$H_0^{p*} = \frac{P_u^x - P_d^x}{uS_0 - dS_0} = \frac{0 - \$6}{\$110 - \$95} = -.4$$

$$I_0^* = \frac{[-P_u^x(dS_0) - P_d^x(uS_0)]}{(uS_0 - dS_0)r_f} = \frac{-0(\$95) - \$6(\$110)}{(\$110 - \$95)1.05} = \$41.90.$$

Note, if the put did not pay a dividend, the premium would be only $1.59. Thus, by lowering the price of the stock on the ex-dividend date, dividends increase the value of the put.

Multiple-Period Case

For multiple periods to expiration, the binomial put model (like the call) prices the option at each period and for each possible stock price using the single-period model. In Figure 6.4-6, an example of put pricing for two periods is presented in which dividends of $1 are assumed to be paid on ex-dividend dates occurring at expiration and at the end of period 1. As shown, the equilibrium price for the European put is $P_0^{e*} = \$0.85$.

6.4.4   Pricing American Puts on Dividend-Paying Stocks

In Figure 6.4-6 the value of an American put also is shown, along with its European value. In this case, in period 1 the European put value is $2.71 when the stock is at its ex-dividend value of $96.47, while the intrinsic value of the put, obtainable from exercising on the ex-dividend date, is $X - (dS_0 - D_1) = \$3.53$. Thus, to preclude arbitrage the value of an American put would have to be $3.53 when $S_d^x = \$96.47$ in period 1, and, as shown in Figure 6.4-6, the current equilibrium price of the American put would have to be $1.10, compared to the European value of $0.85.

Note that in valuing puts on a dividend-paying stock, the value of early exercise resulting from the dividend payment occurs on the ex-dividend date when the decrease in the stock price augments the put's intrinsic value. Thus, for American puts the maximum condition is defined in terms of the ex-dividend stock price, on or just after the ex-dividend date. This contrasts with American calls, in which the optimal condition for early exercise would occur just before the ex-dividend date.

FIGURE 6.4-6

**Two-Period American
and European Put Values
with Dividends**

$u = 1.0488, d = .9747,$
$r_f = 1.025, S_0 = \$100,$
$X = \$100, D_1 = \$1,$
$D_2 = \$1$

		$S^x_{uu} = \$110 - \$1 = \$109$ $P^x_{uu} = \text{Max}[\$100 - \$109, 0] = 0$
	$S^x_u = \$104.88 - \$1 = \$103.88$ $P^x_u = 0$ $P^a_u = \text{Max}[P^x_u, X - S^x_u]$ $\quad = \text{Max}[0, \$100 - \$103.88] = 0$	
$S_0 = \$100$ $P^{e*}_0 = (-.3657)(\$100) + \$37.42 = \$0.85$ $P^a_0 = H^{a*}_0 + I^{a*}_0$ $\quad = (-.4764)(\$100) + \$48.74 = \$1.10$		$S^x_{ud} = \$102.23 - \$1 = \$101.23$ $P^x_{ud} = \text{Max}[(\$100 - \$101.23, 0] = 0$
	$S^x_d = \$97.47 - \$1 = \$96.47$ $P^x_d = (-.8299)(\$96.47) + \$82.77 = \$2.71$ $P^a_d = \text{Max}[P^x_d, X - S^x_d]$ $\quad = \text{Max}[\$2.71, \$100 - \$96.47] = \$3.53$	
		$S^x_{dd} = \$95 - \$1 = \$94$ $P^x_{dd} = \text{Max}[\$100 - \$94, 0] = \$6$

t	0	1	2

$$H_d = \frac{P^x_{ud} - P^x_{dd}}{udS_0 - d^2S_0} = \frac{0 - \$6}{\$102.33 - \$95} = -.8299$$

$$I_d = -\frac{[P^x_{ud}(d^2S_0) - P^x_{dd}(udS_0)]}{r_f(udS_0 - d^2S_0)} = \frac{-[(0)(\$95) - (\$6)(\$102.23)]}{1.025(\$102.23 - \$95)} = \$82.77$$

$$H_u = \frac{P^x_{uu} - P^x_{ud}}{uuS_0 - udS_0} = \frac{0 - 0}{\$110 - \$102.23} = 0$$

$$I_u = -\frac{[P^x_{uu}(udS_0) - P^x_{ud}(u^2S_0)]}{r_f(u^2S_0 - udS_0)} = -\frac{[(0)(\$102.23) - (\$0)(\$110)]}{1.025(\$110 - \$102.23)} = 0$$

$$H^*_0 = \frac{P^x_u - P^x_d}{uS_0 - dS_0} = \frac{0 - \$2.71}{\$104.88 - \$97.47} = -.3657$$

$$I^*_0 = -\frac{[P^x_u(dS_0) - P^x_d(uS_0)]}{r_f(uS_0 - dS_0)} = -\frac{[(0)(\$97.47) - (\$2.71)(\$104.88)]}{1.025(\$104.88 - \$97.47)} = \$37.42$$

$$H^{a*}_0 = \frac{P^a_u - P^a_d}{uS_0 - dS_0} = \frac{0 - \$3.53}{\$104.88 - \$97.47} = -.4764$$

$$I^{a*}_0 = -\frac{[P^a_u(dS_0) - P^a_d(uS_0)]}{r_f(uS_0 - dS_0)} = -\frac{[(0)(\$97.47) - (\$3.53)(\$104.88)]}{1.025(\$104.88 - \$97.47)]} = \$48.74$$

Also, it should be reiterated that, while the advantage of early exercise for a call requires the stock to pay a dividend, such a condition, as examined in Section 6.3.5, is not needed for puts.

6.4.5   Put-Call Parity Model with Dividends

From Chapter 4, recall that when the underlying stock pays a dividend, the put-call parity model must be adjusted so that the value of a conversion ($\{+S_0, +P_0^e, -C_0^e\}$) will equal the present value of a portfolio consisting of a riskless pure discount bond with a face value equal to X, plus the dividends paid on the stock. That is:

$$P_0^e - C_0^e + S_0 = PV(X) + \sum_{t=1}^{T} PV(D_t).$$

In our single-period example in which a \$1 dividend was paid at expiration, the price of the European call was \$5.71 and the price of the European put was \$1.90, using the dividend-adjusted binomial option model. The same put (call) price can also be found using this dividend-adjusted put-call parity model with the call (put) value determined from the binomial model. That is:

$$P_0^e = C_0^e - S_0 + \frac{X + D_1}{r_f}$$

$$P_0^e = \$5.71 - \$100 + \frac{\$100 + \$1}{1.05} = \$1.90.$$

Similarly, for the two-period example, in which dividends of \$1 were paid both at expiration and at the end of period 1, and the equilibrium European call value is \$3.74, the value of the European put, using the put-call parity model, is:

$$P_0^e = C_0^e - S_0 + PV(X) + \sum_{t=1}^{T} PV(D_t)$$

$$P_0^e = \$3.74 - \$100 + \left[\frac{\$100}{(1.025)^2} + \frac{\$1}{(1.025)} + \frac{\$1}{(1.025)^2} \right] = \$0.85.$$

This, too, is the same price we obtained using the dividend-adjusted binomial put model.

6.5   CONCLUSION

In this chapter we have derived the BOPM for put options and shown how to adjust the BOPM to value call and put options on dividend-paying stocks and American options. In Chapter 7 we will turn our attention to the Black-Scholes OPM. As we will see, this model is simpler to use (though more complicated to derive) and under certain assumptions yields the same values as the BOPM.

KEY TERMS

binomial option pricing model
  for puts
replicating portfolio for puts
dividend-adjusted binomial option
  pricing model

risk-neutral pricing (Appendix 6A)
risk-neutral probabilities (Appendix 6A)
redundant security (Appendix 6A)
state-preference pricing (Appendix 6B)

SELECTED REFERENCES

Arditti, F., and John, K. "Spanning the State Space with Options." *Journal of Financial and Quantitative Analysis* 15 (Mar. 1980): 1–9.

Arrow, K. "The Role of Securities in the Optimal Allocation of Risks Bearing." *Review of Economic Studies* (1964): 91–96.

Boyle, P. "A Lattice Framework for Option Pricing with Two-State Variables." *Journal of Financial and Quantitative Analysis* 23 (Mar. 1988): 1–12.

Breeden, D., and Litzenberger, R. "Prices of State-Contingent Claims Implicit in Option Prices." *Journal of Business* 51 (Oct. 1978): 621–651.

Chance, Don M. *An Introduction to Options and Futures.* Fort Worth, Tex.: Dryden Press, 1991, ch. 5, 6.

Copeland, T. E., and Weston, J. F. *Financial Theory and Corporate Policy*, 2nd ed. Reading, Mass.: Addison-Wesley, 1983, ch. 5.

Cox, John C., and Ross, S. "The Valuation of Options for Alternative Stochastic Processes." *Journal of Financial Economics* 3 (Jan.–Mar. 1976): 145–166.

Cox, John C., Ross, S., and Rubinstein, M. "Option Pricing: A Simplified Approach." *Journal of Financial Economics* 7 (Sept. 1979): 229–263.

Cox, John C., and Rubinstein, M. *Option Markets.* Englewood Cliffs, N.J.: Prentice-Hall, 1985, ch. 5.

Debreu, G. *The Theory of Value.* New York: Wiley, 1959.

Elton, E., and Gruber, M. *Modern Portfolio Theory and Investment Analysis*, 2nd ed. New York: Wiley, 1987, ch. 20.

Hull, John. *Options, Futures, and Other Derivative Securities.* Englewood Cliffs, N.J.: Prentice-Hall, 1989, ch. 4, 8.

Jarrow, Robert, and Rudd, Andrew. *Option Pricing.* Homewood, Ill.: Richard D. Irwin, 1983, ch. 7–13.

John, K. "Efficient Funds in Financial Markets with Options: A New Irrelevance Proposition." *Journal of Finance* 37 (June 1981): 685–695.

―――. "Market Resolution and Valuation in Incomplete Markets." *Journal of Financial and Quantitative Analysis* 19 (Mar. 1984): 29–44.

Levy, H. "Upper and Lower Bounds of Put and Call Option Value: Stochastic Dominance Approach." *Journal of Finance* 40(4) (Sept. 1985): 1197–1217.

Perrakis, S., and Ryan, P. "Option Pricing Bounds in Discrete Time." *Journal of Finance* 39 (June 1984): 519–525.

Rendleman, R., and Bartter, B. "Two-State Option Pricing." *Journal of Finance* 34 (Dec. 1979): 1093–1110.

Ritchken, Peter. "On Option Pricing Bounds." *Journal of Finance* 40(4) (Sept. 1985): 1218–1229.

———. *Options: Theory, Strategy, and Applications.* Glenview, Ill.: Scott, Foresman, 1987, ch. 8–10.

Rubinstein, M. "The Valuation of Uncertain Income Streams and the Pricing of Options." *Bell Journal of Economics* 7 (Autumn 1976): 407–424.

PROBLEMS AND QUESTIONS

1. Consider a one-period, two-state case in which XYZ stock is trading at $S_0 = \$35$, has u of 1.05 and d of 1/1.05, and the period risk-free rate is 2%.

   a. Using the BOPM, determine the equilibrium price of an XYZ 35 European put option expiring at the end of the period.

   b. Explain what an arbitrageur would do if the XYZ 35 European put was priced at $0.75. Show what the arbitrageur's cash flow would be at expiration when she closed.

   c. Explain what an arbitrageur would do if the XYZ 35 European put was priced at $0.35. Show what the arbitrageur's cash flow would be at expiration when she closed.

2. Suppose the XYZ company in Problem 1 was expected to go ex-dividend at the end of the period, with the company expected to pay a dividend worth $0.50 at the ex-dividend date.

   a. Using the BOPM, determine the equilibrium price of the XYZ 35 European call option.

   b. Using the BOPM, determine the equilibrium price of the XYZ 35 European put option.

   c. Using the put-call parity model, show that the put price is equal to BOPM's put value.

   d. Explain what an arbitrageur would do if the market priced the XYZ 35 call equal to the BOPM's value, but failed to factor in the $0.50 dividend (i.e., priced the call at $1.19). Show what the arbitrageur's cash flow would be at expiration when he closed.

   e. Explain what an arbitrageur would do if the market priced the XYZ 35 put equal to the BOPM's value, but failed to factor in the $0.50 dividend (i.e., priced the put at $0.50). Show what the arbitrageur's cash flow would be at expiration when he closed.

3. Assume two periods to expiration, $u = 1.05$, $d = 1/1.05$, $r_f = 1.02$, $S_0 = \$50$, no dividends, and $X = \$50$ on a European put expiring at the end of the second period.

a. Find: P_{uu}, P_{ud}, P_{dd}, P_d, P_u, P_0^*, H_u^p, H_d^p, H_0^{p*}, I_u, I_d, and I_0^*.

b. Overpriced case:

   (1) Define the arbitrage strategy you would employ if the current market price of the put was $0.55. Assume any positive cash flow is invested in a risk-free security.

   (2) In period 1, what would be your cash flow from your arbitrage investment if you closed your initial position when the stock was priced at S_d and the put was selling at $P_1^m = \$1.65$? How would you readjust your initial strategy to avoid a loss? Show what your cash flow would be when you closed at the end of the second period (assume the stock will follow the binomial process and be either udS_0 or ddS_0).

c. Underpriced case:

   (1) Define the arbitrage strategy you would employ if the current market price of the put was $0.30. Assume any positive cash flow is invested in the risk-free strategy.

   (2) In period 1, what would be your cash flow from your arbitrage investment if you closed your initial position when the stock was priced at dS_0 and the put was selling at $P_1^m = \$1.25$? How would you readjust your initial strategy to avoid any loss? Show what your cash flow would be when you closed at the end of the second period (assume the stock will follow the binomial process and will be either u^2S_0 or udS_0).

4. Determine the equilibrium price of a comparable call on the stock in Problem 3 using the put-call parity model.

5. If the put described in Problem 3 is American, what would be its equilibrium price?

6. Suppose in the two-period case, the ABC stock described in Problem 3 was expected to go ex-dividend at the end of the first period, with the ABC company expected to pay a dividend worth $1.00 at that date.

   a. Determine the equilibrium price of the ABC 50 European call expiring at the end of the second period.

   b. What would be the equilibrium price of the ABC 50 call if it was American?

   c. Determine the equilibrium price of the ABC 50 European put expiring at the end of the second period.

   d. What would be the equilibrium price of the ABC 50 put if it was American?

   e. Using the put-call parity model, show that the price of the European put is equal to BOPM's European put value.

7. Explain what an arbitrageur would do if the market price of the ABC 50 European call in Problem 6 equaled the BOPM's value of $2.36, a value without the $1.00 dividend factored in (see Problem 2, Chapter 5). Show

what the arbitrageur's cash flow would be at the end of the first period if ABC stock was trading at its ex-dividend price of $51.50 and the call was trading at its equilibrium value of $2.48. What would the investor's cash flow be if the call was trading at $3.48? What adjustments would the arbitrageur have to make to avoid this loss? (Include dividends as part of any readjustment financing, and show the profit at expiration after the readjustment.)

8. Explain what an arbitrageur would do if the market priced the ABC 50 European put in Problem 6 equaled the BOPM's value of $0.42, but failed to factor in the $1.00 dividend (see Problem 3). Show what the investor's profit would be at the end of the first period if ABC stock was trading at its ex-dividend price $46.62 and the put was trading at its equilibrium value of $2.40.

9. Suppose XYZ stock is trading at $S_0 = \$101, u = 1.02, d = 1/1.02$, the period risk-free rate is 1%, and the stock is not expected to go ex-dividend. Using the n-period BOPM, determine the equilibrium price of an XYZ 100 European put expiring at the end of the third period ($n = 3$).

COMPUTER PROBLEMS

1. Use the BOPM computer program (Binopm) to show the put and stock price relationship for a 50 European put option on the stock in Problem 7, Chapter 5. Assume the put expires at the end of the quarter, the annual risk-free rate is 6%, and there is frequent trading such that the period to expiration can be divided into a large number of subperiods where $n = 180$. Show the put and stock price relationship in tabular and graphical forms for stock prices of 42, 44, 46, 48, 49, 50, 51, 52, 53, 54, 55, 56, 58, and 60. Comment on the ability of the BOPM to capture the features of the put and stock price relationships described in Chapter 4.

2. Suppose the stock in Problem 7, Chapter 5, is currently priced at $50, the annual risk-free rate is 6%, and put options on the stock are frequently traded such that $n = 180$. Use the BOPM computer program (Binopm) to determine the equilibrium prices for the following put options:

   a. Put with an exercise price of 50, expiring at the end of the quarter

   b. Put with an exercise price of 52, expiring at the end of the quarter

   c. Put with an exercise price of 48, expiring at the end of the quarter

   d. Put with an exercise price of 50, expiring at the end of one month

   e. Put with an exercise price of 50, expiring at the end of six months

   Comment on the Binopm ability to satisfy the following boundary conditions: $P^e(X_1) < P^e(X_2)$ and $P^e(T_2) > P^e(T_1)$.

Risk-Neutral Probability Pricing

6.A.1 Single-Period Case

The traditional finance approach to determining the value of a risky asset is to discount the asset's expected cash flows at a risk-adjusted rate (k). For this methodology to work, you need to know (or at least be able to assume) a probability distribution for the cash flow and to know the risk-return preferences of investors. In our one-period, two-state economy described in Chapter 5 and earlier in Chapter 6 ($u = 1.1, d = .95, S_0 = \$100, X = \$100$, and $r_f = 1.05$), the values of the call, put, and stock using this methodology would be:

$$S_0 = \frac{E(S_T)}{1 + k} = \frac{q(uS_0) + (1 - q)(dS_0)}{1 + k} = \frac{q(\$110) + (1 - q)(\$95)}{1 + k} \qquad (6.A\text{-}1)$$

$$C_0 = \frac{E(C_T)}{1 + k} = \frac{q(C_u) + (1 - q)(C_d)}{1 + k} = \frac{q(\$10) + (1 - q)(0)}{1 + k} \qquad (6.A\text{-}2)$$

$$P_0 = \frac{E(P_T)}{1 + k} = \frac{q(P_u) + (1 - q)(P_d)}{1 + k} = \frac{q(0) + (1 - q)(\$5)}{1 + k}, \qquad (6.A\text{-}3)$$

where q is the objective probability of the stock's increasing in one period, and $1 - q$ is the probability of its decreasing.

Unfortunately, determining the call and put values with this traditional approach is impossible given the number of unknowns (q and k). Suppose, though, we assume that we have a market in which investors will accept the same expected rate of return from a risky investment as they would from a risk-free one, that is,

---

Note: This section requires knowledge of elementary statistics. For a primer see Appendix C at the end of the book.

assume $k = R_f$. In finance terminology, such a market is described as risk-neutral.* In a risk-neutral market, the prices of all assets (risky and risk-free) are priced without regard to risk and determined by discounting the expected future payouts at the risk-free rate.

In our option pricing example, if we assume a risk-neutral market, then the price of our stock, call, and put would be:

$$S_0 = \frac{q(uS_0) + (1 - q)(dS_0)}{r_f} = \frac{q(\$110) + (1 - q)(\$95)}{1.05} \tag{6.A-4}$$

$$C_0 = \frac{q(C_u) + (1 - q)(C_d)}{r_f} = \frac{q(\$10) + (1 - q)(0)}{1.05} \tag{6.A-5}$$

$$P_0 = \frac{q(P_u) + (1 - q)(P_d)}{r_f} = \frac{q(0) + (1 - q)(\$5)}{1.05}. \tag{6.A-6}$$

Given the current price of the stock ($S_0 = \$100$) and the period rate on the risk-free security ($R_f = 5\%$), we can now solve mathematically for the probabilities: q and $1 - q$ (that is, in a risk-neutral market, the market price of the stock determines the market's estimates of the probabilities of the stock increasing and decreasing). Solving Equation (6.A-4) for q we obtain:

$$\$100 = \frac{q(\$110) + (1 - q)(\$95)}{1.05}$$

$$q = .6667.$$

Or in parameter terms:

$$S_0 = \frac{q(uS_0) + (1 - q)(dS_0)}{r_f}$$

$$q = \frac{r_f - d}{u - d}.$$

Note, q is the same as the p term in the BOPM call and put equations, q and $1 - q$ are, in turn, referred to as **risk-neutral probabilities**. Substituting the risk-neutral probabilities into the call and put equations (6.A-5) and (6.A-6) we obtain:

$$C_0^* = \frac{1}{r_f}[qC_u + (1 - q)C_u] = \frac{1}{1.05}[.6667(\$10) + (.333)(0)] = \$6.35$$

$$P_0^* = \frac{1}{r_f}[qP_u + (1 - q)P_d] = \frac{1}{1.05}[.6667(0) + (.333)(\$5)] = \$1.59.$$

These option values match exactly those obtained by our replicating approach. Thus, the equilibrium prices of options can be obtained by assuming that the option values are determined as though they and other securities are trading in a risk-neutral market.

---

*A priori, we would expect most investors to want a higher expected rate of return from the risky investment. Such a market is referred to as *risk-averse*.

The reason options can be valued as though they were trading in a risk-neutral market is that they are *redundant securities.*[*] In financial theory, a redundant security is one in which the security's possible outflows can be replicated by another security or portfolio. This implies that the redundant security can be valued by its arbitrage relation with the replicating asset, and not by investor preferences or the probabilities investors assign to possible future outcomes. As we saw in deriving the BOPM, since we can replicate an option's payouts with a portfolio of its stock and a bond, the option is a redundant security, and therefore can be valued as though it were trading in a risk-neutral market. The theory underlying the pricing of redundant securities is state-preference theory. Pricing options in terms of state-preference theory is examined in Appendix 6B.

6.A.2   Multiple-Period Case

The call and put values obtained using the multiple-period BOPM replicating approach also can be found using a risk-neutral pricing approach. This approach values an option as the present value of the expected terminal value of the option, with the probabilities being the risk-neutral probabilities and the discount rate being the risk-free rate.

In a multiple-period case, the expected terminal value of a call $[E(C_T)]$ or a put $[E(P_T)]$ after n periods can be obtained once we know the probabilities of the option's intrinsic values. In a binomial process the probabilities of an option's equaling one of its possible intrinsic values is given by the probability of j upward moves in n periods, p_{nj}. The risk-neutral probability, p_{nj}, in turn, can be found using the following equation:

$$p_{nj} = \frac{n!}{(n-j)!j!}p^j(1-p)^{(n-j)}, \qquad (6.A\text{-}7)$$

where p is the risk-neutral probability of the stock's increasing in *one period*, which, as we showed in the last section, is equal to $(r_f - d)/(u - d)$.

In our two-period example in Chapter 5 and earlier in Chapter 6 ($u = 1.0488$, $d = .9747$, $r_f = 1.025$, $S_0 = \$100$, and $X = \$100$), the risk-neutral probability of the stock's increasing in one period is $p = (1.025 - 0.9747)/(1.0488 - .9747) = .6788$. Thus, the probabilities of the number of upward moves in n periods being $j = 2$, 1, or 0 in our example are:

---

[*]In financial theory, redundant securities are explained in terms of complete markets. A *complete market* is one in which all the possible state-contingent payouts are available to investors from a set of securities. Since a redundant security cannot add anything to the market, its value is determined solely by an arbitrage portfolio consisting of the redundant security and a portfolio of nonredundant securities constructed to have the same possible cash flows. In the presence of options, if the market is not complete, then an economic justification for options would be that they serve to make the market complete. For a discussion of complete markets, see Copeland and Weston (1983), Ritchken (1987), Debreu (1959), and Arrow (1964).

$$j = 2: \quad p_{22} = \frac{2!}{0!2!}(.6788)^2 = .46077$$

$$j = 1: \quad p_{21} = \frac{2!}{1!1!}(.6788)(.3212) = .43606$$

$$j = 0: \quad p_{20} = \frac{2!}{2!0!}(.3212)^2 = .10317.$$

With the period risk-free rate of 2.5%, the values of the 100 European call and the 100 European put are therefore:

$$C_0^* = \frac{E(C_T)}{r_f^n} = \frac{p_{22}C_{uu} + p_{21}C_{ud} + p_{20}C_{dd}}{r_f^2}$$

$$C_0^* = \frac{(.46077)(\$10) + (.43606)(\$2.23) + (.10317)(0)}{(1.025)^2} = \$5.31.$$

$$P_0^* = \frac{E(P_T)}{r_f^n} = \frac{p_{22}P_{uu} + p_{21}P_{ud} + p_{20}P_{dd}}{r_f^2}$$

$$P_0^* = \frac{(.46077)(0) + (.43606)(0) + (.10317)(\$5)}{(1.025)^2} = \$0.49.$$

The call and put values are the same as those we obtained using the replicating approach. In general, the call and put values for n periods using risk-neutral pricing are:

$$C_0^* = \frac{E(C_T)}{r_f^n} = \frac{1}{r_f^n} \sum_{j=0}^{n} p_{nj} \{Max[u^j d^{(n-j)}S_0 - x, 0]\} \qquad (6.A\text{-}8)$$

$$C_0^* = \frac{1}{r_f^n} \sum_{j=0}^{n} \frac{n!}{(n-j)!j!} \{Max[u^j d^{(n-j)}S_0 - X, 0]\}.$$

$$P_0^* = \frac{E(P_T)}{r_f^n} = \frac{1}{r_f^n} \sum_{j=0}^{n} p_{nj} \{Max[X - u^j d^{(n-j)}S_0, 0]\} \qquad (6.A\text{-}9)$$

$$P_0^* = \frac{1}{r_f^n} \sum_{j=0}^{n} \frac{n!}{(n-j)!j!} \{Max[X - u^j d^{(n-j)}S_0, 0]\}.$$

Equations (6.A-8) and (6.A-9) are identical to the multiple-period binomial call price equation (5.3-5) and put equation (6.3-5) defined using the replicating approach.

PROBLEMS AND QUESTIONS

1. Assume a binomial, risk-neutral world where: $n = 1$, $S_0 = \$50$, $R_f = .02$, $u = 1.05$, and $d = .975$.

   a. What are the risk-neutral probabilities of the stock's increasing in one period and decreasing in one period? Solve for the probabilities using the equation: $S_0 = PV[E(S_T)]$.

b. Using risk-neutral pricing, determine the equilibrium price of a call on stock with an exercise price of $50 and expiration at the end of the period.

c. Using risk-neutral pricing, determine the equilibrium price of a put on the stock with an exercise price of $50 and expiration at the end of the period.

d. Show that your answers in parts (b) and (c) are consistent with the BOPM's replicating approach.

2. Explain what is meant by risk-neutral pricing. What is the reason for pricing options using a risk-neutral pricing approach?

Binomial Option Pricing Model Using State-Preference Pricing

6.B.1   Single-Period Case

Instead of valuing options by replicating their cash flows with a stock and a bond or discounting their expected binomial payoffs at the risk-free rate, suppose we replicate an option's payoffs with portfolios consisting of two hypothetical contracts. Assume the first contract pays $1 if the upstate occurs and $0 otherwise; the second pays $1 if the downstate occurs and $0 otherwise. We will refer to these contracts as State 1 and State 2 contracts.

Portfolios of State 1 and State 2 contracts can be formed to replicate the stock and risk-free bond in Chapter 5 and earlier in Chapter 6 ($u = 1.1, d = .95, r_f = 1.05, X = \$100$, and $S_0 = \$100$). Specifically, given that the stock in our illustrative single-period example has possible end-of-period values of $110 and $95, to replicate its cash flows we would need a portfolio with 110 State 1 contracts and 95 State 2 contracts. To avoid arbitrage, this portfolio would have to equal the current price of the stock: $S_0 = \$100$. Similarly, given the risk-free pure discount bond with face value of $1, a portfolio of one State 1 contract and one State 2 contract would be needed to replicate the bond. With $R_f = .05$, the price of the bond would be $\$1/1.05 = \$0.95238$. Thus, to avoid arbitrage the value of the portfolio of one State 1 contract and one State 2 contract would have to be $0.95238.

Given the current values of the two portfolios of $100 and $0.95238, next let the price of the first contract be λ_1 and the price of the second be λ_2. Accordingly, the stock currently priced at $100 can be defined as a portfolio of 110 State 1 contracts priced at λ_1 and 95 State 2 contracts priced at λ_2. That is:

$$\$100 = 110\lambda_1 + 95\lambda_2.$$

Note: This section draws from the finance literature on state-preference theory.

Similarly, the bond worth $0.95238 can be defined as a portfolio of one State 1 contract priced at λ_1 and one State 2 contract priced at λ_2:

$$\$0.95238 = 1\lambda_1 + 1\lambda_2.$$

Given the two equations and two unknowns, we can solve simultaneously to find the values of λ_1^* and λ_2^*. Doing this we obtain:

$$\lambda_1^* = \$0.635 \qquad \text{and} \qquad \lambda_2^* = \$0.3174.$$

λ_1 and λ_2 are defined as *state prices*. In a two-state, one-period economy, all other assets also can be priced in terms of the two-state prices. Thus, the 100 call option would be equivalent to 10 State 1 contracts and 0 State 2 contracts, and the 100 put option would be equivalent to 5 State 2 contracts and 0 State 1 contracts. Given our λ_1^* and λ_2^* values, the value of these options would therefore be:

$$C_0^* = 10(\$0.635) = \$6.35$$

and

$$P_0^* = 5(\$0.3174) = \$1.59,$$

which are exactly the same prices as the portfolio's replication prices.* Thus, in addition to risk-neutral and replicating, a third way to value options is in terms of state prices.

6.B.2   Multiple-Period Case

In a two-period binomial model, we have three possible states of the economy: $u^2 S_0$, udS_0, and $d^2 S_0$, which we will respectively refer to as states uu, ud, and dd. Similar to state pricing in the single-period case, each state can be associated with a contract that pays $1 in that state and $0 in all others. Thus, with two periods, the state uu contract would pay $1 in state uu and $0 in state ud and state dd, the state ud contract would pay $1 in state ud and $0 in the other two states, and the state dd contract would pay $1 in state dd and $0 otherwise.

To find the prices of these three state contracts, we need to find the three state prices for a two-period binomial case: λ_{uu}, λ_{ud}, and λ_{dd}. To this end, we start with the first period and determine the price for the upstate (λ_u) and the downstate (λ_d). Assuming $u = 1.0488$, $d = .9747$, $R_f = .025$, and $S_0 = \$100$ (numbers from our illustrative two-period example), λ_u and λ_d can be found by solving simultaneously the equations for the option's underlying stock and a risk-free bond defined in terms of state u and state d contracts for one period. Specifically:

Stock: $\$100 = 104.88\lambda_u + 97.47\lambda_d$

Bond: $\$0.9756 = \dfrac{\$1}{1.025} = 1\lambda_u + 1\lambda_d.$

---

*In general, the state prices, in terms of u, d and r_f, are:
$\lambda_1^* = \frac{1}{r_f}\left(\frac{r_f - d}{u - d}\right)$ and $\lambda_2^* = \frac{1}{r_f}\left(\frac{u - r_f}{u - d}\right).$

Solving these equations simultaneously for λ_u and λ_d, we obtain the following one-period state prices:

$$\lambda_u = \$0.66238 \quad \text{and} \quad \lambda_d = \$0.31322.$$

Since u, d, and r_f are assumed to be the same for each period, the prices of the three state contracts for two periods would be:

State uu: $\lambda_{uu} = \lambda_u^2 = (\$0.66238)^2 = \$0.43875$

State ud: $\lambda_{ud} = \lambda_u\lambda_d + \lambda_d\lambda_u = 2\lambda_u\lambda_d = 2(\$0.66238)(\$0.31322)$
                $= \$0.41494$

State dd: $\lambda_{dd} = \lambda_d^2 = (\$0.31322)^2 = \$0.09811.$

Finally, given λ_{uu}, λ_{ud}, and λ_{dd}, we can price the 100 call option and the 100 put option. The 100 call option is equivalent to 10 state uu contracts, 2.23 state ud contracts, and 0 state dd contracts. Thus, the call as a portfolio of these state contracts is:

$$C_0^* = 10(\$0.43875) + 2.23(\$0.41494) + 0(\$0.09811) = \$5.31.$$

Similarly, the 100 put is equivalent to a portfolio of 0 state uu contracts, 0 state ud contracts, and 5 state dd contracts. The value of this portfolio of state contracts is:

$$P_0^* = 0(\$0.43875) + 0(\$0.41494) + 5(\$0.09811) = \$0.49.$$

These call and put prices are identical to the prices obtained using risk-neutral pricing and the replicating approaches.

PROBLEMS AND QUESTIONS

1. Assume: $n = 1$, $S_0 = \$50$, $R_f = .02$, $u = 1.05$, and $d = .975$.

   a. Define the stock, a riskless pure discount bond with a face value of $1 maturing at the end of the period, and a call and a put with $X = 50$ and expirations at the end of the period as portfolios of state u and state d contracts.

   b. Using the stock and bond, determine state u and state d prices.

   c. Using the state u and state d prices, determine the price of call and put options on the stock, with each option having an exercise price of $50 and expiring at the end of the period.

2. Describe the XYZ stock, call, and put in Problem 9 and the riskless pure discount bond as portfolios of state uuu, uud, udd, and ddd contracts ($S_0 = \$101$, $u = 1.02$, $d = 1/1.02 = 0.9804$, $R_f = .01$, $X = \$100$, and $n = 3$). Determine the state-preference prices for the four states. Determine the equilibrium call and put prices in terms of state prices.

CHAPTER 7

Black-Scholes Option Pricing Model

7.1 INTRODUCTION

The realism of the binomial option pricing model is questionable when only a small number of periods to expiration exist. As we subdivide the expiration period, or, equivalently, make the length of each period smaller, the number of possible stock prices at expiration increases, and the assumption of only two states in one period becomes more plausible. Thus, for most options the binomial model for large n is more realistic. Moreover, as we noted in Chapter 5, as n approaches infinity, the BOPM becomes the equation for the Black-Scholes (B-S) OPM. Thus, for large n the equilibrium values of a call derived by the BOPM are approximately the same as those obtained by the OPM developed by Black and Scholes. In this chapter we will examine the B-S OPM.

7.2 BLACK-SCHOLES CALL OPTION MODEL

7.2.1 Nature of the Black-Scholes Option Pricing Model

The B-S OPM, not the binomial, was the first of the two OPMs. Like the binomial, the B-S model is applicable to both European options and cases in which the underlying stock does not pay dividends. Similarly, the B-S model is derived by assuming that no transaction costs or margin requirements are incurred, that securities are perfectly divisible, that funds can be borrowed or invested at a constant risk-free rate, and that the distribution of the stock's logarithmic return is normal. Last, the B-S OPM, like the binomial, determines the equilibrium value as the call price, which is equal to the value of a replicating portfolio. Unfortunately, unlike the BOPM, the mathematics used in deriving the B-S OPM (stochastic calculus and a heat exchange equation) are complex; in fact, part of the contribution of the BOPM is that it is simpler to derive yet still yields the same solution as the B-S OPM for the case of large n. The B-S model, though, is relatively easy to use (the mathematical foundation of the B-S OPM is presented in Appendix 7A).

7.2.2   Black-Sholes Option Pricing Model Formula

The B-S formula for determining the equilibrium call price is:

$$C_0^* = S_0 N(d_1) - \left(\frac{X}{e^{RT}}\right)N(d_2) \tag{7.2-1}$$

$$d_1 = \frac{\log_e(S_0/X) + (R + .5\sigma^2)T}{\sigma\sqrt{T}} \tag{7.2-2}$$

$$d_2 = d_1 - \sigma\sqrt{T}, \tag{7.2-3}$$

where:

$T =$ time to expiration, expressed as a proportion of the year.
$R =$ continuously compounded risk-free rate of return, expressed annually.
$\sigma =$ annualized standard deviation of the logarithmic return.
$N(d_1), N(d_2) =$ cumulative normal probabilities.
$\log_e =$ natural logarithm.

In Equation (7.2-1), X/e^{RT} is the present value of the exercise price [PV(X)] continuously compounded. R in the equation is therefore the continuously compounded, annual, risk-free rate. This rate can be found by taking the natural logarithm of 1 plus the simple annual rate on a riskless security, such as a Treasury bill, with a maturity equal to the call's expiration date. Thus, if .06 is the annual discrete rate, then the continuous compounded rate is $\log_e(1 + .06) = .0583$. In Equations (7.2-2) and (7.2-3), σ^2 is the annualized variance of the natural log of the ratio of the end of the period stock price to the initial stock price. It is the annualized variance of the logarithmic return we defined in Chapter 5. The cumulative normal probabilities, $N(d_1)$ and $N(d_2)$, are the probabilities that deviations of less than d_1 and d_2 will occur in a standard normal distribution with a 0 mean and a standard deviation of 1. Table 7.2-1 gives the probabilities for sample values. In pricing options with the B-S OPM, $N(d_1)$ and $N(d_2)$ should be carried to several decimal places. Since the probabilities in Table 7.2-1 are extrapolated, the following power function can be used instead of the table to obtain better estimations of $N(d_1)$ and $N(d_2)$:

$$n(d) = 1 - .5[1 + .196854(|d|) + .115194(|d|)^2 \tag{7.2-4}$$
$$+ .000344(|d|)^3 + .019527(|d|)^4]^{-4}.$$

TABLE 7.2-1

	Standard Normal Probabilities																			
	0.00	0.01	0.02	0.03	0.04	0.05	0.06	0.07	0.08	0.09		0.00	0.01	0.02	0.03	0.04	0.05	0.06	0.07	0.08	0.09
−3.00	0.0014	0.0013	0.0013	0.0012	0.0012	0.0011	0.0011	0.0011	0.0010	0.0010	+0.00	0.5000	0.5040	0.5080	0.5121	0.5159	0.5199	0.5239	0.5279	0.5319	0.5358
−2.90	0.0019	0.0018	0.0018	0.0017	0.0016	0.0016	0.0015	0.0015	0.0014	0.0014	0.10	0.5398	0.5438	0.5478	0.5517	0.5557	0.5596	0.5636	0.5675	0.5714	0.5753
−2.80	0.0026	0.0025	0.0024	0.0023	0.0023	0.0022	0.0021	0.0021	0.0020	0.0019	0.20	0.5793	0.5832	0.5871	0.5909	0.5948	0.5987	0.6026	0.6064	0.6103	0.6141
−2.70	0.0035	0.0034	0.0033	0.0032	0.0031	0.0030	0.0029	0.0028	0.0027	0.0026	0.30	0.6179	0.6217	0.6255	0.6293	0.6331	0.6368	0.6406	0.6443	0.6480	0.6517
−2.60	0.0047	0.0045	0.0044	0.0043	0.0041	0.0040	0.0039	0.0038	0.0037	0.0036	0.40	0.6554	0.6591	0.6628	0.6664	0.6700	0.6736	0.6772	0.6808	0.6844	0.6879
−2.50	0.0062	0.0060	0.0059	0.0057	0.0055	0.0054	0.0052	0.0051	0.0049	0.0048	0.50	0.6915	0.6950	0.6985	0.7019	0.7054	0.7088	0.7123	0.7157	0.7190	0.7224
−2.40	0.0082	0.0080	0.0078	0.0075	0.0073	0.0071	0.0069	0.0068	0.0066	0.0064	0.60	0.7257	0.7291	0.7324	0.7356	0.7389	0.7421	0.7454	0.7486	0.7517	0.7549
−2.30	0.0107	0.0104	0.0102	0.0099	0.0096	0.0094	0.0091	0.0089	0.0087	0.0084	0.70	0.7580	0.7611	0.7642	0.7673	0.7703	0.7734	0.7764	0.7793	0.7823	0.7852
−2.20	0.0139	0.0136	0.0132	0.0129	0.0125	0.0122	0.0119	0.0116	0.0113	0.0110	0.80	0.7881	0.7910	0.7939	0.7967	0.7995	0.8023	0.8051	0.8078	0.8106	0.8133
−2.10	0.0179	0.0174	0.0170	0.0166	0.0162	0.0158	0.0154	0.0150	0.0146	0.0143	0.90	0.8159	0.8186	0.8212	0.8238	0.8264	0.8289	0.8315	0.8340	0.8365	0.8389
−2.00	0.0228	0.0222	0.0217	0.0212	0.0207	0.0202	0.0197	0.0192	0.0188	0.0183	1.00	0.8413	0.8437	0.8461	0.8485	0.8508	0.8531	0.8554	0.8577	0.8599	0.8621
−1.90	0.0287	0.0281	0.0274	0.0268	0.0262	0.0256	0.0250	0.0244	0.0239	0.0233	1.10	0.8643	0.8665	0.8686	0.8708	0.8729	0.8749	0.8770	0.8790	0.8810	0.8830
−1.80	0.0359	0.0351	0.0344	0.0336	0.0329	0.0322	0.0314	0.0307	0.0301	0.0294	1.20	0.8849	0.8869	0.8888	0.8906	0.8925	0.8943	0.8962	0.8980	0.8997	0.9015
−1.70	0.0446	0.0436	0.0427	0.0418	0.0409	0.0401	0.0392	0.0384	0.0375	0.0367	1.30	0.9032	0.9049	0.9066	0.9082	0.9099	0.9115	0.9131	0.9147	0.9162	0.9177
−1.60	0.0548	0.0537	0.0526	0.0516	0.0505	0.0495	0.0485	0.0475	0.0465	0.0455	1.40	0.9192	0.9207	0.9222	0.9236	0.9251	0.9265	0.9279	0.9292	0.9306	0.9319
−1.50	0.0668	0.0655	0.0643	0.0630	0.0618	0.0606	0.0594	0.0582	0.0571	0.0559	1.50	0.9332	0.9345	0.9357	0.9370	0.9382	0.9394	0.9406	0.9418	0.9429	0.9441
−1.40	0.0808	0.0793	0.0778	0.0764	0.0749	0.0735	0.0721	0.0708	0.0694	0.0681	1.60	0.9452	0.9463	0.9474	0.9484	0.9495	0.9505	0.9515	0.9525	0.9535	0.9545
−1.30	0.0968	0.0951	0.0934	0.0918	0.0901	0.0885	0.0869	0.0853	0.0838	0.0823	1.70	0.9554	0.9564	0.9573	0.9582	0.9591	0.9599	0.9608	0.9616	0.9625	0.9633
−1.20	0.1151	0.1131	0.1112	0.1094	0.1075	0.1057	0.1038	0.1020	0.1003	0.0985	1.80	0.9641	0.9649	0.9656	0.9664	0.9671	0.9678	0.9686	0.9693	0.9699	0.9706
−1.10	0.1357	0.1335	0.1314	0.1292	0.1271	0.1251	0.1230	0.1210	0.1190	0.1170	1.90	0.9713	0.9719	0.9726	0.9732	0.9738	0.9744	0.9750	0.9756	0.9761	0.9767
−1.00	0.1587	0.1563	0.1539	0.1515	0.1492	0.1469	0.1446	0.1423	0.1401	0.1379	2.00	0.9772	0.9778	0.9783	0.9788	0.9793	0.9798	0.9803	0.9808	0.9812	0.9817
−0.90	0.1841	0.1814	0.1788	0.1762	0.1736	0.1711	0.1685	0.1660	0.1635	0.1611	2.10	0.9821	0.9826	0.9830	0.9834	0.9838	0.9842	0.9846	0.9850	0.9854	0.9857
−0.80	0.2119	0.2090	0.2061	0.2033	0.2005	0.1977	0.1949	0.1922	0.1894	0.1867	2.20	0.9861	0.9864	0.9868	0.9871	0.9875	0.9878	0.9881	0.9884	0.9887	0.9890
−0.70	0.2420	0.2389	0.2358	0.2327	0.2297	0.2266	0.2236	0.2207	0.2177	0.2148	2.30	0.9893	0.9896	0.9898	0.9901	0.9904	0.9906	0.9909	0.9911	0.9913	0.9916
−0.60	0.2743	0.2709	0.2676	0.2644	0.2611	0.2579	0.2546	0.2514	0.2483	0.2451	2.40	0.9918	0.9920	0.9922	0.9925	0.9927	0.9929	0.9931	0.9932	0.9934	0.9936
−0.50	0.3085	0.3050	0.3015	0.2981	0.2946	0.2912	0.2877	0.2843	0.2810	0.2776	2.50	0.9938	0.9940	0.9941	0.9943	0.9945	0.9946	0.9948	0.9949	0.9951	0.9952
−0.40	0.3446	0.3409	0.3372	0.3336	0.3300	0.3264	0.3228	0.3192	0.3156	0.3121	2.60	0.9953	0.9955	0.9956	0.9957	0.9959	0.9960	0.9961	0.9962	0.9963	0.9964
−0.30	0.3821	0.3783	0.3745	0.3707	0.3669	0.3632	0.3594	0.3557	0.3520	0.3483	2.70	0.9965	0.9966	0.9967	0.9968	0.9969	0.9970	0.9971	0.9972	0.9973	0.9974
−0.20	0.4207	0.4168	0.4129	0.4091	0.4052	0.4013	0.3974	0.3936	0.3897	0.3859	2.80	0.9974	0.9975	0.9976	0.9977	0.9977	0.9978	0.9979	0.9979	0.9980	0.9981
−0.10	0.4602	0.4562	0.4522	0.4483	0.4443	0.4404	0.4364	0.4325	0.4286	0.4247	2.90	0.9981	0.9982	0.9982	0.9983	0.9984	0.9984	0.9985	0.9985	0.9986	0.9986
−0.00	0.5000	0.4960	0.4920	0.4880	0.4841	0.4801	0.4761	0.4721	0.4681	0.4642	3.00	0.9986	0.9987	0.9987	0.9988	0.9988	0.9989	0.9989	0.9989	0.9990	0.9990

$$n(d) = 1 - .5[1 + .196854(|d|) + .115194(|d|)^2 + .000344(|d|)^3 + .019527(|d|)^4]^{-4}$$
$$N(d) = 1 - n(d), \quad \text{for } d < 0$$
$$N(d) = n(d), \quad \text{for } d > 0$$

where:

$$|d| = \text{absolute value of } d.$$

If d is negative, then the $n(d)$ value obtained from Equation (7.2-4) is subtracted from 1; if d is positive, then the $n(d)$ obtained from Equation (7.2-4) is used. That is:

$$N(d) = 1 - n(d), \quad \text{for } d < 0$$

$$N(d) = n(d), \quad \text{for } d > 0.$$

◆ **7.2.3** **Example**

To see how to use the B-S OPM formula, consider the case of an ABC 50 call that expires in three months ($T = .25$), in which ABC stock is trading at $45 and has an estimated annualized variance of 0.25 ($\sigma = .5$) and in which the continuously compounded, annual, risk-free rate is 6%. To determine the equilibrium price of the ABC call, we first use Equations (7.2-2) and (7.2-3) to obtain the values for d_1 and d_2:

$$d_1 = \frac{\log_e(\$45/\$50) + [.06 + .5(.5)^2](.25)}{.5\sqrt{.25}} = -.2364.$$

$$d_2 = -.2364 - .5\sqrt{.25} = -.4864.$$

Next, we use Table 7.2-1 [or Equation (7.2-4)] to find the corresponding values of $N(d_1)$ and $N(d_2)$:

$$N(d_1) = N(-.2364) = 1 - \{1 - .5[1 + .196854(.2364) \\ + .115194(.2364)^2 + .000344(.2364)^3 \\ + .019527(.2364)^4]^{-4}\} = .4066.$$

$$N(d_2) = N(-.4864) = 1 - \{1 - .5[1 + .196854(.4864) \\ + .115194(.4864)^2 + .000344(.4864)^3 \\ + .019527(.4864)^4]^{-4}\} = .3131.$$

Last, we use Equation (7.2-1) to obtain the equilibrium call price:

$$C_0^* = (\$45)(.4066) - \frac{\$50}{e^{(.06)(.25)}}(.3131) = \$2.88. \quad ◆$$

As we noted previously, the B-S price differs from the BOPM prices for small n, but is approximately the same for large n. This can be seen in Table 7.2-2, in which the B-S price of $2.88 is compared with the prices obtained using the binomial model for different values of n. As shown in the table, at $n = 2$ the

TABLE 7.2-2

BOPM Values for Different n	
$S_0 = \$45, X = \$50, T = .25, R = .06^*, \sigma = .5$ For BOPM: $u = e^{.5\sqrt{.25/n}}, d = 1/u$	
n	BOPM C^*
2	$3.16
10	$2.94
16	$2.86
32	$2.87
B-S OPM price = $2.88	

$^*R$ is the continuously compounded, annual rate used in the B-S model.

In the BOPM, the period rate obtained from the simple annual rate (R^A) is used: R^A = simple annual rate = $e^R - 1 = e^{.06} - 1 = .061836$.

BOPM's call value is $0.28 greater than the B-S's; at $n = 10$, the binomial price is $0.06 greater than the B-S price; at $n = 16$, the difference is only $0.02; and at $n = 32$, only rounding errors exist. Thus, the example illustrates our earlier point that as n increases, the BOPM yields equilibrium call values approximately equal to the B-S OPM.

7.2.4 Comparative Analysis

In the B-S model, the equilibrium call price depends on the underlying stock price, exercise price, time to expiration, risk-free rate, and the stock's volatility. Mathematically, the effects that changes in these variables have on the equilibrium call price can be found by taking the partial derivatives of Equation (7.2-1) with respect to S, X, T, R, and σ. The effects that changes in the parameters have on the B-S OPM price also can be seen in terms of the simulation presented in Table 7.2-3. In the table, combinations of the B-S OPM values and stock prices are shown for different parameter values. The first column shows the call values given the parameter values used in the preceding example: $X = 50$, $T = .25$, $R = .06$, and $\sigma = .5$. For purposes of comparison, the other columns show the call and stock price relations generated with the same parameter values used in column 1, except for one variable: in column 2, $X = 40$; in column 3, $T = .5$; in column 4, $\sigma = .75$; and in column 5, $R = .08$.

In examining Table 7.2-3 you should note several of the relationships that were explained either intuitively or with arbitrage arguments in Chapter 4. First, as shown in any of the columns, when the stock is relatively low and the call is deep out of the money, the B-S OPM yields a very low call price, but (as we should expect) one that is nonnegative. As the price of the stock increases by equal increments, the OPM call prices increase at increasing rates, up to a point, with the values never being below the difference between the stock price and the present value of the exercise price. Thus, over a range of stock prices, the B-S OPM yields a call and stock price relation that is nonlinear and satisfies the minimum and maximum boundary conditions.

The nonlinear relationship also can be seen in Figure 7.2-1, where the B-S option call values and stock prices from column 1 are plotted. As shown, the slope of this B-S option price curve increases as the stock price increases, the curve does not yield negative values, and it is above the minimum boundary line defined by $S - PV(X)$. The slope of the curve is referred to as the option's **delta**. Delta is equal to H^* in the BOPM and to $N(d_1)$ in the B-S model. For a call, the delta ranges from 0 for deep-out-of-the-money calls to approximately 1 for deep-in-the-money calls. This can be seen in Figure 7.2-1, which shows that the option curve is relatively flat for low stock prices and starts to become parallel to the minimum boundary line for high stock values.

The nonlinear call and stock price relation also can be seen by the change in the slope of the B-S option price curve as the stock price increases. In option literature, the change in slope (i.e., delta) per small change in the stock price defines the option's **gamma** (the second-order partial derivative of the call price with respect to changes in the stock price).

TABLE 7.2-3

	B-S OPM Call Price and Stock Price Relation for Different Parameter Values				
	(1) $X = 50$ $T = .25$ $\sigma = .5$ $R = .06$	(2) $X = 40$ $T = .25$ $\sigma = .5$ $R = .06$	(3) $X = 50$ $T = .5$ $\sigma = .5$ $R = .06$	(4) $X = 50$ $T = .25$ $\sigma = .75$ $R = .06$	(5) $X = 50$ $T = .25$ $\sigma = .5$ $R = .08$
STOCK PRICE	C_0^*	C_0^*	C_0^*	C_0^*	C_0^*
$30	$ 0.0841	$ 0.5967	$ 0.5453	$ 0.6292	$ 0.0890
35	0.4163	1.9065	1.3751	1.5028	0.4328
40	1.2408	4.2399	2.8365	2.9852	1.2826
45	2.8756	7.5682	4.9626	5.1006	2.9550
50	5.2999	11.5935	7.6637	7.7452	5.4210
55	8.5584	16.0952	10.9683	10.9782	8.7103
60	12.3857	20.8355	14.6539	14.5768	12.5702
65	16.6919	25.7002	18.7114	18.5269	16.8996
70	21.2865	30.6342	23.0555	22.7703	21.5083

FIGURE 7.2-1

B-S Call Price Curve

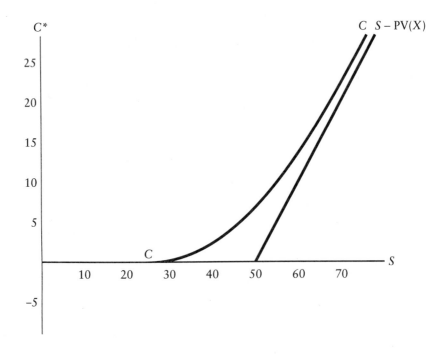

Second, by examining columns 1 and 2 in Table 7.2-3, you should observe that for each stock price, higher call prices are associated with the call with the lower exercise price. Thus, as the exercise price decreases, the B-S OPM call price increases.

Third, comparing column 3 with column 1 shows that the greater the time to expiration, the greater the B-S OPM call price. The changes in an option's prices with respect to a small change in the time to expiration (with other factors held constant) is defined as the option's *theta*. Fourth, a comparison of columns 4 and 1 shows that the greater the stock's variability, the greater the call price. The change in the call price given a small change in the stock's variability is referred to as the option's *vega* (also called kappa). Last, comparing columns 1 and 5 shows that the greater the interest rate, the greater the call price. The change in the call price given a small change in R is called the call's *rho*.

7.3 BLACK-SCHOLES ARBITRAGE PORTFOLIO

The B-S OPM's Equation (7.2-1) is equal to the value of the replicating call portfolio. That is:

$$C_0^* = H_0^* S_0 - B_0^*, \tag{7.3-1}$$

where, from the B-S model:

$$H_0^* = N(d_1)$$

$$B_0^* = \left(\frac{X}{e^{RT}}\right) N(d_2).$$

Thus, the OPM call value of $2.88 in our previous example is equal to the value of a replicating portfolio consisting of 0.4066 shares of stock, partially financed by borrowing $15.42:

$$C_0^* = H_0^* S_0 - B_0^* = .4066(\$45) - \$15.42 = \$2.88,$$

where:

$$H_0^* = N(d_1) = .4066$$
$$B_0^* = \frac{X}{e^{RT}} N(d_2)$$
$$B_0^* = \frac{\$50}{e^{(.06)(.25)}}(.3131)$$
$$B_0^* = \$15.42.$$

If the market price of the call does not equal the B-S value, then arbitrage opportunities will exist by taking a position in the call and an opposite position in the replicating portfolio. Like the multiple-period arbitrage strategies defined for the BOPM, arbitrageurs, after initiating the strategy, would need to close or readjust their arbitrage portfolios in each subsequent period using the same rules defined for overpriced and underpriced calls in Chapter 5.

In readjusting the arbitrage portfolio, two characteristics of the B-S model should be kept in mind. First, as we observed earlier, the slope of the option price curve changes as the stock price changes. In the B-S OPM, the slope of the curve is equal to $N(d_1)$. Thus, for arbitrageurs to maintain a riskless portfolio, they would need to readjust their hedge ratio by moving to the new $N(d_1)$ each time the stock price changes. Second, it should be noted that the hedge ratio also changes as the time to expiration changes. This characteristic suggests that even if the stock price does not change, arbitrageurs still need to readjust their hedge to keep the arbitrage portfolio riskless, since $N(d_1)$ is constantly changing in response to the continuous decrease in the call's time to expiration. Moreover, in the continuous-time B-S model, the hedge ratio is changing continuously with the passage of time as well as with stock price changes; thus, to keep the portfolio riskless, arbitrageurs would need to readjust frequently, and close as soon as profit opportunities appear.

As an example, if the call in our illustrative example is priced initially at $3.00 instead of $2.88, then arbitrageurs should go short in the overpriced call and long in the replicating portfolio, buying 0.4066 shares of stock at $45 per share and borrowing $15.42. As shown in Table 7.3-1, this would leave an initial cash flow of $0.12 ($C_0^m - C_0^* = \$3.00 - \$2.88$). As an approximation of continuous time, suppose that one hour after initiating the strategy, the price of ABC stock increased to $46 and the market price of the call increased to equal its B-S OPM value associated with $S_t = \$46$ of $C_t^* = \$3.30$. As shown in the table, closing the overpriced arbitrage portfolio would result in a cash flow of $0.10. If, however, the call was overpriced, then arbitrageurs would need to readjust their portfolio by moving to the new hedge. Like the BOPM's adjustments for the arbitrage portfolios, this move also would lead to the correct new debt level, given self-financing

TABLE 7.3-1

Arbitrage Strategy Using the Black-Scholes OPM*	
Initial Position: $C_0^m = \$3.00$, $C^* = \$2.88$, $T = .25$, $S_0 = \$48$	
INITIAL POSITION	CASH FLOW
Short Call	$ 3.00
Long $N(d_1)$ Shares of Stock: $-(.4066)(\$45)$	$-$ 18.30
Borrow $H_0^* = (X/e^{RT})N(d_2) = \$15.42$	15.42
Initial Cash Flow $(C^m - C^*) = \$3.00 - \$2.88$	$ 0.12

Closing Position when $C_t^m = C_t^*$ an hour later: $S_t = \$46$, $T = .25$ (approximately), $C_t^m = C_t^* = \$3.30$	
CLOSING POSITION	CASH FLOW
Call Purchase	$-\$ 3.30
Sell $N(d_1)$ Shares of Stock: $(.4066)(\$46)$	18.70
Debt Repayment: $-(\$15.42)(1.000026)^\dagger$	$-$ 15.42
Initial Profit: $(\$0.12)(1.000026)$	0.12
Cash Flow	$ 0.10

*Errors exist due to rounding.

†0.000026 is approximate hourly rate given a 6% annual rate.

constraints. For example, if the call price were $3.50, then a $0.10 loss would occur from closing. To avert this, arbitrageurs would need to move to the new hedge and debt level. At the stock price of $46 and with the time to expiration of approximately $T = .25$, $N(d_1) = .4412$ and $B_0^* = [\$50/e^{(.06)(.25)}]N(d_2) = \$17$. Thus, to readjust, arbitrageurs would have to borrow $1.59 to buy $.4412 - .4066$ additional shares at $46 per share. This adjustment would, in turn, leave them with the correct new debt level of $17 [$15.42(1.000026) + 1.59 = $17, where 0.000026 is the approximate hourly rate given a 6% annual rate]. With this readjustment, arbitrageurs would have an immunized portfolio for the next period (hour), hoping that the call then would be underpriced or equal to the OPM value.

When the call is underpriced initially, the arbitrage portfolio should consist of a long call position and a short position in the replicating portfolio. This portfolio would need to be readjusted frequently until the call becomes over or equal to the OPM value. The reader is encouraged to examine this strategy. Also, the same arbitrage return for mispriced calls can be earned by constructing an arbitrage portfolio consisting of the purchase of $N(d_1)$ shares of stock, financed by the sale of the call and borrowing. This portfolio is explained in Appendix 7B.

In summary, riskless arbitrage portfolios can be formed using the B-S OPM that are similar to the discrete strategies defined for the BOPM. By the nature of the B-S model, such portfolios theoretically should be adjusted continuously (very frequently) to keep the portfolio riskless. In fact, because of the frequent adjustments necessary to earn an arbitrage return, some traders refer to such a strategy as "picking up nickels and dimes in front of a steamroller."

7.4 DIVIDEND ADJUSTMENTS FOR THE BLACK-SCHOLES CALL MODEL

As we discussed in earlier chapters, dividends cause the price of a call to decrease on the ex-dividend date and can lead to an early exercise of the call if it is American. Since the B-S OPM values a European call without dividends, it needs to be adjusted for dividends and for American calls, given the early exercise possibility when dividends are expected. Two dividend adjustment models that use the B-S OPM are the pseudo-American call model, applicable to American calls when there are dividends, and the continuous dividend model.

7.4.1 Pseudo-American Call Model

In applying the *pseudo-American call model* to an American call option, we use a dividend-adjusted stock price in the OPM instead of the current stock price. When there is one dividend payment (D), the adjusted stock price is:

$$S_d = S_0 - \frac{D}{e^{Rt^*}}, \tag{7.4-1}$$

where:

t^* = time to ex-dividend date, expressed as a proportion of the year.

If more than one dividend payment is made during the option period, then the present value of each dividend is subtracted from the current stock price.

In the pseudo-American model, the call value computed with the dividend-adjusted stock price, $C^*(S_d, T, X)$, is compared to the estimated call value obtained by assuming the call is exercised just prior to the ex-dividend date. This early-exercise call price (C^{ex}) is found using the time to the ex-dividend date (t^*) instead of time to expiration (T), the dividend-adjusted stock price (S_d) instead of S_0, and a dividend-adjusted exercise price ($X - D$) instead of X; that is, $C^{ex}(S_d, t^*, X - D)$. The dividend-adjusted exercise price is used instead of X to account for the advantage of early exercise that occurs just before the ex-dividend date. Finally, given the two estimated call prices, the larger of the two is selected as the estimate for the equilibrium call price: $C_0^a = \text{Max}[C^*(S_d, T, X), C^{ex}(S_d, t^*, X - D)]$.

To illustrate the pseudo-American call model, consider again the B-S call pricing example in which the B-S price of the call was $2.88, given: $S_0 = \$45$, $X = \$50$, $T = .25$, $\sigma = .5$, and $R = .06$. In this example, also assume that ABC stock is expected to pay a dividend of $2 on the ex-dividend date, which is expected to occur two months from the present ($t^* = 2/12 = .16667$). Using the pseudo-American model to estimate the value of the ABC 50 call, we first compute the adjusted stock price:

$$S_d = \$45 - \frac{\$2}{e^{(.06)(.16667)}} = \$43.02.$$

Using $S_d = \$43.02$ in the B-S model instead of $S_0 = \$45$, we obtain a dividend-adjusted call price of $2.12, which is less than the B-S price of $2.88 obtained without the adjustment.

$$d_1 = \frac{\log_e(\$43.02/\$50) + [.06 + (.5)(.5^2)].25}{.5\sqrt{.25}} = -.41643$$

$$d_2 = -.41643 - .5\sqrt{.25} = -.66643$$

$$N(d_1) = N(-.41643) = .33834$$

$$N(d_2) = N(-.66643) = .25246$$

$$C_0^* = (\$43.02)(.33833) - \left(\frac{\$50}{e^{(.06)(.25)}}\right).25246 = \$2.12.$$

Next, we estimate the call price, assuming it will be exercised just prior to the ex-dividend date. In this example, the early-exercise call price is $1.85. This value is obtained by using $S_d = 43.02$, $X - D = \$50 - \$2 = \$48$, and $t^* = 2/12 = .16667$, for S_0, X, and T, respectively, in the B-S formula:

$$d_1 = \frac{\log_e(\$43.02/\$48) + [.06 + (.5)(.5^2)](.16667)}{.5\sqrt{.16667}} = -.38556$$

$$d_2 = -.38556 - .5\sqrt{.16667} = -.58969$$

$$N(d_1) = N(-.38556) = .34973$$

$$N(d_2) = N(-.58969) = .2775$$

$$C_0^{ex} = (\$43.02)(.34973) - \frac{\$48}{e^{(.06)(.16667)}}(.2775) = \$1.86.$$

Finally, given the two prices, we select the larger of the two. Thus, in this example the estimated call price is $2.12: $C_0^a = \text{Max}[\$2.12, \$1.85] = \$2.12$. Note, if the call option is European, then only the call values involving the time to expiration are used ($2.12).

7.4.2 Continuous Dividend Adjustment Model

The other dividend adjustment procedure is the ***continuous dividend adjustment model***. In this model, we substitute the following dividend-adjusted stock price for the current stock price in the B-S formula:

$$S_d = \frac{S_0}{e^{\Psi T}},$$

where:

Ψ = annual dividend yield = annual dividend/stock price.

In terms of the previous example, if the underlying stock is expected to generate an annual dividend yield of $\Psi = .0889$ (for example, a $4 annual dividend for a stock price of $45), then the dividend-adjusted stock price is $S_d = \$44.01$, and the continuous dividend-adjusted call price is $2.48:

$$S_d = \frac{\$45}{e^{(.0889)(.25)}} = \$44.01$$

$$d_1 = \frac{\log_e(\$44.01/\$50) + [.06 + (.5)(.5^2)].25}{.5\sqrt{.25}} = -.3254$$

$$d_2 = -.3254 - .5\sqrt{.25} = -.5754$$

$$N(d_1) = N(-.3254) = .3723$$

$$N(d_2) = N(-.5754) = .2823$$

$$C_0^* = (\$44.01)(.3723) - \frac{\$50}{e^{(.06)(.25)}}(.2823) = \$2.48.$$

Comparing the two models, we see that each approach yields a different call value. Which one to use depends on the circumstances. In the case of stock options, in which dividends may be paid only once or twice during the option's life, the pseudo-American call model may be more appropriate. However, in the case of a stock index option, in which the volume of stocks comprising the index causes a flow of dividends, the continuous dividend-adjusted model may be more appropriate.

7.5   BLACK-SCHOLES OPTION PRICING MODEL FOR PUTS

7.5.1   Black-Scholes Put Model

The B-S OPM model for puts can be derived via the same methodology used to determine the B-S call value. It also can be derived from the binomial model by letting n approach infinity. A simpler approach, though, is to make use of the put-call parity model. Specifically, assuming European options, the equilibrium put price in terms of the put-call parity model is:

$$P_0^* = C_0^* - S_0 + PV(X) \tag{7.5-1}$$

$$P_0^* = C_0^* - S_0 + \frac{X}{e^{RT}},$$

where:

$C_0^* =$ call price determined by the B-S OPM.

By substituting Equation (7.2-1) for C_0^*, the equilibrium put price can be specified alternatively as:

$$P_0^* = -S_0[1 - N(d_1)] + \frac{X}{e^{RT}}[1 - N(d_2)]. \tag{7.5-2}$$

Extending our illustrative example to determining the equilibrium price of a put, an ABC 50 put expiring in three months is $7.13 using Equation (7.5-2). That is:

$$P_0^* = -(.5934)\$45 + \frac{\$50}{e^{(.06)(.25)}}(.6869)$$

$$P_0^* = -(.5934)\$45 + \$33.83 = \$7.13,$$

where:

$$1 - N(d_1) = N(-d_1) = 1 - .4066 = .5934$$
$$1 - N(d_2) = N(-d_2) = 1 - .3131 = .6869.$$

7.5.2   Comparative Analysis

Like the B-S OPM for calls, most of the relationships between the equilibrium price of a put and S, T, σ, X, and R that were examined both intuitively and with arbitrage arguments in Chapter 4 are captured in the B-S put model. This can be seen by taking the partial derivatives of Equation (7.5-2) with respect to each of the explanatory variables and observing their sign. These relationships also can be seen in Table 7.5-1, in which combinations of the B-S put prices and stock prices are shown for different parameters: X (column 2), T (column 3), σ (column 4), and R (column 5). In examining any of the columns in the table, we first should observe

TABLE 7.5-1

	B-S OPM Put Price and Stock Price Relation for Different Parameter Values				
	(1) X = 50 T = .25 σ = .5 R = .06	(2) X = 40 T = .25 σ = .5 R = .06	(3) X = 50 T = .5 σ = .5 R = .06	(4) X = 50 T = .25 σ = .75 R = .06	(5) X = 50 T = .25 σ = .5 R = .08
STOCK PRICE	P_0^*	P_0^*	P_0^*	P_0^*	P_0^*
$30	$19.3397	$10.0012	$19.0675	$19.8848	$19.0990
35	14.6719	6.3110	14.8973	15.7584	14.4428
40	10.4964	3.6444	11.3588	12.2408	10.2926
45	7.1312	1.9727	8.4848	9.3562	6.9650
50	4.5555	0.9979	6.1860	7.0008	4.4309
55	2.8140	0.4996	4.4905	5.2338	2.7203
60	1.6413	0.2400	3.1761	3.8324	1.5801
65	0.9475	0.1046	2.2337	2.7825	0.9095
70	0.5421	0.0387	1.5778	2.0259	0.5182

FIGURE 7.5-1

B-S Put Price Curve

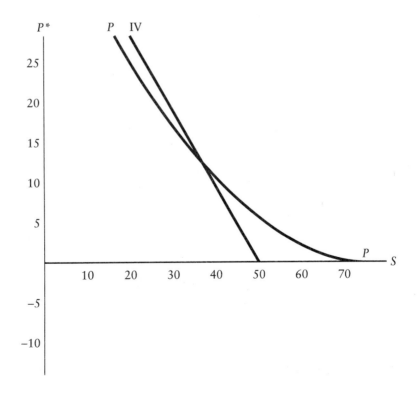

the negative, nonlinear relationship between the B-S put price and the stock price (i.e., the put has a negative delta and nonzero gamma). The negative relation is also shown in Figure 7.5-1, where the B-S put values and stock prices from column 1 are plotted. Next, comparing columns 2 and 5 with column 1, we can observe that for each stock price, the lower the exercise price or the lower the interest rate, the greater the B-S put price. Finally, comparing columns 3 and 4 with column 1, we can see that the greater the time to expiration or the greater the stock's variability, the greater the put price. Thus, the B-S put model captures many of the relationships described in Chapter 4.

It should be noted that the model is unconstrained. That is, the B-S put model does not constrain the put value to being equal to at least its intrinsic value. Thus, for an in-the-money put, the premium can be less than its IV, as shown in column 1 when the stock is at $30. The possibility that $P^* < IV$ reflects the fact that the B-S model is limited to determining the price of a European put, in which negative time-value premiums are possible.

7.5.3   Black-Scholes Arbitrage Put Portfolio

The B-S put Equation (7.5-2) is equal to the value of the replicating put portfolio. That is:

$$P_0^* = H_0^{p*} S_0 + I_0^*, \tag{7.5-3}$$

where, from the B-S model:

$$H_0^{p*} = -[1 - N(d_1)]$$

$$I_0^* = \frac{X}{e^{RT}}[1 - N(d_2)].$$

Thus, the put value of $7.13 in our previous example is equivalent to the value of a portfolio formed by selling .5934 shares of stock short at $45 per share and investing $33.83 in a risk-free security:

$$P_0^* = -.5934(\$45) + \$33.83 = \$7.13,$$

where:

$$H_0^{p*} = -[1 - N(d_1)] = -.5934$$
$$I_0^* = \frac{\$50}{e^{(.06)(.25)}}(.6869) = \$33.83.$$

If the market price of the put exceeds the B-S put value, then an arbitrage opportunity exists by taking a short position in the put and a long position in the replicating put portfolio; if the market price is below the equilibrium value, then a riskless arbitrage portfolio can be constructed by going long in the put and short in the replicating portfolio. The overpriced and underpriced arbitrage put portfolios would need to be readjusted continuously (very frequently) until it is profitable to close. The same readjustment rules defined for BOPM's multiple-period arbitrage strategies, though, apply to the continuous B-S arbitrage case.

7.5.4 Dividend Adjustments for the Black-Scholes Put Model

In the case of a put option, if a stock pays a dividend with the ex-dividend date occurring during the option period, then the price of the put would increase on the ex-dividend date as the price of the stock decreases, by an amount approximately equal to the dividend. The value of a European put when there is an ex-dividend date occurring during the period can be estimated by using either the continuous adjusted stock price model or the first equation in the dividend-adjusted pseudo-American model defined in Section 7.4. For example, if ABC stock paid a $2 dividend with an ex-dividend date expected in two months (assume dividends are paid at the ex-dividend date), then using Equation (7.4-1), the dividend-adjusted stock price for a discrete dividend payment is $43.02, and the dividend-adjusted put price is $8.356. That is:

$$P_0^* = -.66166(\$43.02) + \frac{\$50}{e^{(.06)(.25)}}(.74754) = \$8.356,$$

where:

$$1 - N(d_1) = 1 - .33834 = .66166$$
$$1 - N(d_2) = 1 - .25246 = .74754.$$

The dividend-adjusted put price of $8.356 also can be obtained using the put-call parity model and the dividend-adjusted call price:

$$P_0^* = C_0^* - S_d + \frac{X}{e^{RT}}$$

$$P_0^* = \$2.12 - \$43.02 + \frac{\$50}{e^{(.06)(.25)}}$$

$$P_0^* = \$8.356.$$

7.5.5 Value of an American Put with Dividends

When an ex-dividend date occurs during the option period, the pseudo-American option model defined for call options can be extended to estimate the value of an American put. Applied to puts, the *pseudo-American put model* selects the greater of either the European put value, as determined previously (with the dividend-adjusted stock price and time to expiration, T): $P^*(S_d, T, X)$, or the early-exercise put value obtained by assuming the put is exercised at or just after the ex-dividend date. As we did earlier for calls, in computing the early-exercise put price, the time to the ex-dividend date (t^*) is used instead of T, and the dividend-adjusted stock price (S_d) is used instead of S_0. For puts, however, the exercise price is used instead of the dividend-adjusted exercise price $(X - D)$ that was used for calls. This is done to account for the fact that the early-exercise advantage for puts occurs on or just after the ex-dividend date when the stock decreases, not just before as in the case of calls; thus, $P^{ex}(S_d, t^*, X)$. In terms of our previous example, if the put was American, then its value (P_0^a) would be the greater of either $8.356 or the early-exercise value, P_0^{ex}. In this case, P_0^{ex} is $7.84:

$$P_0^{ex} = -(\$43.02)(.72110) + \frac{\$50}{e^{(.06)(.16667)}}(.78510) = \$7.84,$$

where:

$$d_1 = \frac{\log_e(\$43.02/\$50) + [.06 + (.5)(.5)^2].16667}{.5\sqrt{.16667}} = -.58554$$

$$d_2 = -.58554 - .5\sqrt{.16667} = -.78967$$
$$N(d_1) = N(-.58554) = .27890$$
$$N(d_2) = N(-.78967) = .21490$$
$$1 - N(d_1) = .72110$$
$$1 - N(d_2) = .78510.$$

The American put price is therefore $8.356:

$$P_0^a = \text{Max}[P_0^*, P_0^{ex}] = \text{Max}[\$8.356, \$7.84] = \$8.356.$$

7.5.6   Value of an American Put Without Dividends

The pseudo-American model estimates the value of an American put given an ex-dividend date. When dividends are not paid, and as a result we do not have a specific reference date to apply the pseudo-American model, then determining the value of an American put becomes quite difficult. As we have pointed out before, this is not a problem with the B-S call model for stock options, since the advantage of early exercise occurs only when an ex-dividend date exists; in such a case, a reference point in time for early exercise is known, and therefore the pseudo-American call model can be applied to determine the value of an American call. In the B-S and the BOPM, if the price of the stock is such that the put is deep in the money, then it is possible for the price of the European put to be less than its intrinsic value. If the put were American, then at that stock price, it would have to be priced to equal at least its IV, or an arbitrage opportunity would exist by exercising the put early (buy the put, buy the stock, and exercise the put). Thus, the right of early exercise ensures that the minimum price of the put is the IV and makes the price of an American put greater than that of a European put, even if no dividends are to be paid during the life of the put. Also, as we will see in later chapters, early exercise may be advantageous on call options on some nonstock securities.

In the BOPM, the equilibrium price of an American put or call was determined by constraining, at each possible stock price, the put or call value to be the maximum of either its European value, as determined by the BOPM, or its IV. In the discrete BOPM, in which limits can be placed on the number of possible stock prices (which still can be quite large given that calculations are done by a computer), this approach is feasible. However, in the B-S model, in which time is continuous, the BOPM approach of constraining each possible put or call price cannot be applied. There are, though, several models that have been developed to estimate the price. One of these models—*Barone-Adesi and Whaley* (BAW) *model*—is explained in Appendix 7C.

7.6   ESTIMATING THE BLACK-SCHOLES OPTION PRICING MODEL

Like the BOPM, the B-S OPM is defined totally in terms of the stock price, exercise price, time to expiration, interest rate, and volatility. The first three variables are observable; the interest rate and the stock's volatility, though, need to be estimated.

7.6.1   Interest Rates

In estimating the risk-free rate for the B-S OPM, the rate on a Treasury bill (TB), commercial paper, or other money market security with a maturity equal to the option's expiration usually is selected. These rates sometimes are quoted in terms of a simple annual rate (with no compounding). The rate used in the B-S OPM, though, is the continuous, compounded annual rate. As we noted earlier in this chapter, the natural logarithm of 1 plus the simple annual rate, R^s, gives us the continuous compounded rate, R:

$$R = \log_e(1 + R^s). \tag{7.6-1}$$

Note that, in many financial papers, the rates reported for Treasury bills and other money market securities are the dealer's quoted bid discount rate (B) and ask rate (A), both quoted on an annual basis. To obtain the appropriate rate for the B-S model from the bid and ask quotes, we first need to find the price of the security. For a Treasury bill, the price, (P_{TB}), expressed as a proportion of the face value (F), can be found using the following formula:

$$P_{TB} = 1 - .01\left(\frac{B + A}{2}\right)\left(\frac{\text{Days to maturity}}{360}\right). \tag{7.6-2}$$

Given P_{TB}, the continuous, compounded annual rate then is found by solving Equation (7.6-2) for R:

$$P_{TB}e^{Rt} = 1. \tag{7.6-3}$$

$$R = \frac{\log_e(1/P_{TB})}{t}, \tag{7.6-4}$$

where:

t = time to maturity, expressed as a proportion of the year.

Thus, a T-bill expiring in one quarter ($t = .25$) and with a quoted bid yield of 8.8% and ask of 8.75% would have an estimated value equal to .97806 of its par value, and a continuous compounded rate of 8.87%.

$$P_{TB} = 1 - .01\left(\frac{8.8\% + 8.75\%}{2}\right)(.25) = .97806$$

$$R = \frac{\log_e(1/.97806)}{.25} = .0887.$$

In estimating the interest rate as an input for the B-S OPM, questions will arise concerning the appropriate money market rate to use, whether to use a borrowing or a lending rate, and whether adjustments should be made when the expected rates for the different periods occurring during the option's life are not the same. No definitive answers to these questions exist. Fortunately, the B-S OPM is not very sensitive to interest rate changes. Thus, obtaining an exact interest rate is not critical to estimating the equilibrium value of an option using the B-S OPM.

7.6.2   Volatility

The volatility of the underlying security is the only other input that needs to be estimated in the B-S OPM. Unlike interest rates, the price of the option as determined by the B-S OPM is quite sensitive to variability. As a result, the applicability of the model depends on obtaining a good estimate of this parameter.

As we noted in Chapter 5, two methods often are used to estimate the variance of the logarithmic return: (1) calculating the stock's historical variance, and (2) solving for the stock's implied variance. A stock's historical variability often is computed using a sample of historical daily stock prices obtained from a financial publication or computer database (see Section 5.4.4).*

The *implied variance* is the variance that equates the OPM's value to the market price. Unfortunately, we cannot merely set the option model's price equal to the option's market price, then solve algebraically to find a unique solution for the variance. The implied variance can be found, though, by trial and error: substituting different variance values into the B-S or binomial model until the variance that yields an OPM value equal to the market price is found. Using Taylor series expansion, the implied variance can also be approximated for an at-the-money option via the following formula:

$$\sigma = \frac{.5(C_0 + P_0)\sqrt{2\pi/T}}{X(1 + R)^T}.$$

For example, if the risk-free rate is 6% and an ABC 50 call and 50 put expiring in one quarter are trading at $2.86 and $2.12, respectively, when ABC stock is trading at $50, then the stock's implied variance would be approximately .25:

$$\sigma = \frac{.5(\$2.86 + \$2.12)\sqrt{2\pi/.25}}{\$50(1.06)^{.25}} = .25.$$

Conceptually, the implied variance can be thought of as the market's consensus on the stock's volatility. That is, if we assume that the OPM is specified correctly except for the variance, then differences in estimated option prices would be due to the different investors' estimates of the variance. The option price that ultimately

---

*While the calculation of the variance using daily prices is the most common approach to estimate a stock's historical volatility, other approaches have been proposed. For example, to keep the data recent and the sample size sufficiently large, daily high and low prices can be used instead of closing prices.

TABLE 7.6-1

Implied Variances on Coca-Cola	
OPTION	IMPLIED VARIANCE
November 40 Call	0.370
November 45 Call	0.365
February 40 Call	0.340
February 45 Call	0.311
Average	.0.3465

Call price data taken from the *Wall Street Journal*, October 19, 1990.

prevails in the market would then be the one associated with a variance that reflects the average of all investors' estimated variances.

Theoretically, we should expect the implied variance for different options on the same stock to be the same. In practice, this does not occur. For example, as shown in Table 7.6-1, the implied variances found for each option on Coca-Cola stock are different. For options with different expiration dates but the same exercise price, differences in implied variances might be explained by investors' believing that the stock's variance will change over time. For options that have different exercise prices only, the reasons for differences in implied variances are not as obvious. Whatever the reasons, though, when differences exist, we need to determine which implied variance to use.

One way to select an implied variance is to use the arithmetic average for the different implied variances on the stock. Thus, as shown in Table 7.6-1, given the four implied variances on Coke, their average of .3465 could be used as the stock's implied variance. With arithmetic averaging, though, equal weight is given to all the options. If the implied variance represents the market's consensus, then perhaps options with relatively low demands, such as for deep in- and out-of-the-money ones, should not be given the same weight as other options. A third approach is to select the one implied variance that has the minimum pricing error. In this approach, each option's implied variance is used to compute the OPM values for each option. The absolute deviations of the calculated OPM values from the market price, expressed as a proportion of the OPM price ($|C_0^m - C_0^*|/C_0^*$) are computed next for each implied variance. The implied variance that yields the smallest average proportional deviation is then selected. In Table 7.6.2, calculations using this approach are shown for the four options on Coca-Cola.

7.7   CONCLUSION

In this chapter, we've examined the nature of the B-S OPM for call and put options, the arbitrage strategies that underlie the models, the dividend adjustments required for both the call and put models, and how the OPM parameters can be estimated. In the next chapter, we will examine how well the OPM actually estimates option

TABLE 7.6-2

			Implied Variances and Error			

Implied Variances: November 40 call = 0.370; February 40 call = 0.340; November 45 call = 0.365; February 45 call = 0.311

VARIANCE		NOV 40	NOV 45	FEB 40	FEB 45	AVERAGE
0.37	C^*	$3.75	$1.08	$5.75	$3.25	
	C^m	3.75	1.06	5.50	2.62	
	Error	0	− 0.02	− 0.25	− 0.63	
	$\frac{\|C^m - C^*\|}{C^*}$	0	0.0185	0.0435	.1938	.0639
*0.365	C^*	$3.73	$1.06	$5.71	$3.15	
	C^m	3.75	1.06	5.50	2.62	
	Error	0.02	0	− 0.21	− 0.53	
	$\frac{\|C^m - C^*\|}{C^*}$	.0054	0	.0368	.1682	.0526
0.340	C^*	$3.64	$0.94	$5.50	$2.90	
	C^m	3.75	1.06	5.50	2.62	
	Error	0.11	0.12	0	− 0.28	
	$\frac{\|C^m - C^*\|}{C^*}$	.0302	.1277	0	.0965	.0636
0.311	C^*	$3.54	$0.81	$5.26	$2.62	
	C^m	3.75	1.06	5.50	2.62	
	Error	0.21	0.25	0.24	0	
	$\frac{\|C^m - C^*\|}{C^*}$	.0593	.3086	.0456	0	.1034

Error = $C^m - C^*$
Call price data taken from the *Wall Street Journal*, October 19, 1990.
Interest rates used are the 30-day CP rate of 8.16% and the 120-day CP rate of 7.92%.

prices and its applications. Before we examine these topics, we should emphasize that the B-S model, or the BOPM with large n, is based on several assumptions.

First, with the hedge ratio continuously changing with the passage of time and in response to stock price changes, the risk germane to the hedged portfolio cannot be eliminated totally. Thus, it may be more correct to think of the B-S option model and the BOPM with large n as being derived from quasi-arbitrage strategies, instead of as a pure arbitrage strategy with absolutely no risk. The fact that arbitrageurs cannot adjust continuously does not by itself invalidate the B-S OPM as an equilibrium pricing model. For one, the Central Limits Theorem in statistics would suggest that, even if arbitrageurs adjust discretely, if a sufficient number of periods to expiration exist, then riskless portfolios conceivably can be formed. Second, and perhaps a more compelling reason for the validity of the B-S OPM, is that the model may only require the assumption that the market "behaves as if" it adjusts continuously. The requirement for this condition is that arbitrageurs and investors collectively adjust continuously, even though individually they may not.

A second underlying assumption of the B-S and binomial models is that the variance is stable. In the B-S OPM, the equilibrium call price depends only on the underlying stock's variance. This also is the case in the BOPM when *n* is large. Since the variance is the only parameter in the OPM that must be estimated, the validity of the model depends, in part, on the variance's being stable. Moreover, the equilibrium option price is quite sensitive to changes in the underlying stock's variability. As a result, if there is considerable disagreement in the market about the size of the stock's variance or if the variance is in fact unstable—changing frequently over time and with different stock prices—then one prevailing option price will not exist, and the OPM will not be capable of determining the equilibrium price of an option. Other option models have been developed to account for cases in which the assumption of a constant variance over time and stock prices does not hold. Merton's mixed diffusion-jump model, for example, accounts for the possibilities of infrequent jumps in stock prices, and Cox and Ross's constant elasticity of variance model accounts for cases in which the variance is inversely related to the stock price. The interested reader is encouraged to examine these and other models listed in this chapter's Selected References.

Finally, the model is derived by assuming that the distribution of the underlying stock's logarithmic return is normal. Thus, the B-S OPM may not hold strictly for cases in which a stock's distribution in its rate of return is characterized by skewness or other higher statistical moments.

KEY TERMS

delta

gamma

theta

vega

rho

pseudo-American call model

continuous dividend adjustment model

pseudo-American put model

Barone-Adesi and Whaley model

implied variance

SELECTED REFERENCES

Ball, C., and Torous, W. "On Jumps in Common Stock Prices and Their Impact on Call Pricing." *Journal of Finance* 40 (1985): 155–173.

Barone-Adesi, G., and Whaley, R. "Efficient Analytic Approximation of American Option Values." *Journal of Finance* 42 (June 1987): 301–320.

Beckers, S. "Standard Deviations Implied in Option Prices as Predictors of Future Stock Price Variability." *Journal of Banking and Finance* 5 (Sept. 1981): 363–382.

Black, F. "Fact and Fantasy in the Use of Options." *Financial Analysis Journal* 31 (July–Aug. 1975): 36–41, 61–72.

Black, F., and Scholes, M. "The Pricing of Options and Corporate Liabilities." *Journal of Political Economy* 81 (May–June 1973): 637–659.

Cox, J., and Ross, S. "The Valuation of Options for Alternative Stochastic Processes." *Journal of Financial Economics* 3 (Jan.–Mar. 1976): 145–166.

Cox, J., Ross, S., and Rubinstein, M. "Option Pricing: A Simplified Approach." *Journal of Financial Economics* (Sept. 1979): 229–263.

Cox, J., and Rubinstein, M. "A Survey of Alternative Option Pricing Models." In *Option Pricing*, edited by Menachem Brenner. Lexington, Mass.: Heath, 1983.

Geske, R. "Pricing of Options with Stochastic Dividend Yield." *Journal of Finance* 33 (May 1978): 618–625.

———. "A Note on an Analytic Formula for Unprotected American Call Options on Stocks with Known Dividends." *Journal of Financial Economics* 7 (Dec. 1979): 375–380.

Geske, R., and Johnson, H. "The American Put Option Valued Analytically." *Journal of Finance* 39 (Dec. 1984): 1511–1524.

Geske, R., and Roll, R. "On Valuing American Call Options with the Black-Scholes Formula." *Journal of Finance* 39 (June 1984): 443–455.

Itô, K. "On Stochastic Differential Equations." *American Mathematical Society* 4 (Dec. 1951): 1–51.

Lantane, H., and Rendleman, R., Jr. "Standard Deviations of Stock Price Ratios Implied in Option Prices." *Journal of Finance* 31 (May 1976): 369–382.

Merton, R. "Option Pricing When Underlying Stock Returns Are Discontinuous." *Journal of Financial Economics* 3 (Jan.–Feb. 1976): 125–144.

Rogalski, R. "Variances of Option Prices in Theory and Evidence." *Journal of Portfolio Management* 4 (Winter 1978): 43–51.

Roll, R. "An Analytic Valuation Formula for Unprotected American Call Options on Stocks with Known Dividends." *Journal of Financial Economics* 5 (Nov. 1977): 251–258.

Schmalensee, R., and Trippi, R. "Common Stock Volatility Expectations Implied by Option Premia." *Journal of Finance* 33 (Mar. 1978): 129–147.

Sterk, W. "Comparative Performance of the Black-Scholes and Roll-Geske-Whaley Option Pricing Models." *Journal of Financial and Quantitative Analysis* 18 (Sept. 1983): 345–354.

Whaley, R. "On the Valuation of American Call Options on Stocks with Known Dividends." *Journal of Financial Economics* 9 (June 1981): 207–212.

———. "Valuation of American Call Options on Dividend Paying Stocks: Empirical Tests." *Journal of Financial Economics* 10 (Mar. 1982): 29–58.

PROBLEMS AND QUESTIONS

1. Suppose ABC stock currently is trading at $60 per share, has an annualized standard deviation of .35, and will not pay any dividends over the next three months; also suppose that the continuously compounded annual risk-free rate is 6%.

   a. Using the Black-Scholes OPM, calculate the equilibrium price for a three-month ABC 60 European call option.

   b. Using the Black-Scholes OPM, calculate the equilibrium price for a three-month ABC 60 European put option.

c. Show the Black-Scholes put price is the same price obtained using the put-call parity model.

d. Describe the arbitrage strategy you would pursue if the ABC 60 call was overpriced and if it was underpriced.

e. Describe the arbitrage strategy you would pursue if the ABC 60 put was overpriced and if it was underpriced.

f. What would be the new equilibrium prices of the ABC call and put if ABC stock increased to $60.50?

2. Suppose the ABC call in Problem 1 is priced at $4.91 when ABC stock is at $60.

a. Define the arbitrage strategy you would set up.

b. Show what would happen if you closed the position a short time later when the stock was at $60.50 and the price of the call was equal to its equilibrium value (assume the change in time is negligible).

3. Suppose the ABC put in Problem 1 is priced at $3.91 when ABC stock is at $60.

a. Define the arbitrage strategy you would set up.

b. Show what would happen if you closed the position a short time later when the stock was at $60.50 and the price of the call was equal to its equilibrium value (assume the change in time is negligible).

4. Suppose the ABC stock describe in Problem 1 is expected to go ex-dividend in exactly one month, with the value of the dividend on that date expected to be $1.50. Using the pseudo-American option model, calculate the equilibrium prices of the call and put options described in Problem 1.

5. Using the continuous dividend-adjusted option model, calculate the dividend-adjusted stock price, dividend-adjusted call price, and dividend-adjusted put price for the ABC stock and options described in Problem 1. In your calculations assume an annual dividend yield of 10%.

6. Given the following information:

$$S_0 = \$36 \qquad X = \$35 \qquad T = .5 \qquad R = .08 \qquad \sigma = .25$$

a. Determine the equilibrium European call price using the B-S OPM.

b. Determine the equilibrium European put price using the B-S OPM or put-call parity model.

7. Discuss the applicability of the pseudo-American model for pricing American call options and American put options.

8. Discuss the assumptions of the B-S OPM and their applicability.

9. Compare and contrast the B-S OPM with the BOPM.

10. Given a T-bill with 180 days to maturity, a quoted annual bid yield of 7.5%, and an ask yield of 7.35%, calculate the following rates.

a. The continuously compounded risk-free rate

b. The simple annual rate

11. Explain the idea of the implied variance's being the market's consensus of the correct variance.

COMPUTER PROBLEMS

1. Using the B-S OPM program, calculate the call option price for each of the following stock prices. Assume $R = 6\%$, $\sigma = .15$, $T = .25$ per year, and $X = \$50$.

   $S_0 = 42, 44, 46, 48, 49, 50, 51, 52, 53, 54, 55, 56, 58$, and 60.

   Show your results graphically. Comment on the ability of the B-S OPM to capture the features of the call and stock price relations described in Chapter 4.

2. Using the B-S OPM computer program, calculate the call option price for each of the following annualized standard deviations. Assume $R = 6\%$, $S_0 = \$50$, $T = .25$, and $X = \$50$.

   $\sigma = .13, .14, .15$, and $.16$.

   Show your results graphically. Comment on the relationship.

3. Using the B-S OPM computer program, calculate the call option price for each of the following interest rates. Assume $S_0 = \$50$, $\sigma = .15$, $T = .25$, and $X = \$50$.

   $R = .06, .062, .064, .066, .068$, and $.070$.

   Show your results graphically. Comment on the relationship.

4. Using the B-S OPM computer program, calculate the call option price for each of the following time to expiration values (use 365-day year). Assume $S_0 = \$50$, $\sigma = .15$, $R = 6\%$, and $X = \$50$.

   $T = 90, 88, 86, 84, 82, 80, 78, 76, 74, 72$, and 70 days.

   Show your results graphically. Comment on the relationship.

5. Given the following four options on ABC stock, a current price on ABC stock of $48, a 90-day risk-free rate of 8%, and 180-day rate of 8.1%, calculate for each option the implied variance for ABC stock using the average implied variance approach. Use implied variance computer program.

   a. ABC 50 call expiring in 90 days priced at $1.92

   b. ABC 50 call expiring in 180 days priced at $3.73

   c. ABC 45 call expiring in 90 days priced at $4.80

   d. ABC 45 call expiring in 180 days priced at $6.44

6. Using the WSJ option prices and bid and ask T-bill yields, select a stock (preferably one not paying a dividend) and calculate its implied variances using the average approach. Use at least three options in your calculations and the nearest T-bill rate. Once you have estimated the implied variance, determine the equilibrium price using the B-S model. Explain why your price differs from the WSJ price on that day.

Mathematical Foundation of the Black-Scholes Option Pricing Model

The first step in deriving the B-S model is to construct a portfolio consisting of the stock and call that yields a return that is invariant to stock price changes per period of time. The value of the portfolio (V_h) is:

$$V_h = n_s S + n_c C, \qquad (7.A\text{-}1)$$

where:

n_c = number of calls

n_s = number of shares.

To make the portfolio invariant to small stock price changes requires finding the n_c and n_s values in which the derivative of Equation (7.A-1) with respect to S is zero: $\partial V_h/\partial S = 0$. To this end, we first take the partial derivative of Equation (7.A-1) with respect to S and set it equal to zero. That is:

$$\frac{\partial V_h}{\partial S} = n_s \frac{\partial S}{\partial S} + n_c \frac{\partial C}{\partial S} = 0 \qquad (7.A\text{-}2)$$

$$n_s + n_c \frac{\partial C}{\partial S} = 0.$$

Next, we constrain the portfolio to one written call by setting $n_c = -1$ in Equation (7.A-2), then solve it for n_s to obtain the n_s value that makes $\partial V_h/\partial S = 0$. That is:

$$n_s - 1\frac{\partial C}{\partial S} = 0$$

Note: This appendix requires calculus.

$$n_s = \frac{\partial C}{\partial S}. \tag{7.A-3}$$

Thus, the hedge portfolio is defined by Equation (7.A-1) with $n_c = -1$ and $n_s = \partial C/\partial S$. Since this portfolio is invariant to stock price changes, in equilibrium it should yield a riskless rate of return per period of time. Thus, in equilibrium the proportional change in the portfolio, dV_h/V_h, should equal the risk-free rate of return (R_f) per time (dt). Thus, our equilibrium condition is:

$$\frac{dV_h}{V_h} = R_f dt. \tag{7.A-4}$$

For example, if the annual continuously compounded risk-free rate (R_f) is 6% and the length of the time period is a day, implying a daily risk-free rate (R_f) of $(1.06)^{(1/360)} - 1 = .000162$, then a hedged portfolio worth \$100 should, in equilibrium, increase in value by \$0.0162 per day [.000162(\$100) per day], or grow at a daily rate of .0162%.

The equilibrium change in the call price, dC, can be found by first taking the total derivative of Equation (7.A-1):

$$dV_h = n_s dS + n_e dC. \tag{7.A-5}$$

Next, we substitute Equation (7.A-4) into Equation (7.A-5), to constrain the change in the portfolio value to equal its equilibrium change, and we set $n_c = -1$ and $n_s = \partial C/\partial S$ to make the portfolio riskless. Doing this we obtain:

$$R_f V_h dt = n_s dS + n_c dC \tag{7.A-6}$$

$$R_f(n_s S + n_c C)dt = n_s dS + n_c dC$$

$$R_f\left(\frac{\partial C}{\partial S}S - C\right)dt = \frac{\partial C}{\partial S}dS - dC.$$

Last, we solve for Equation (7.A-6) for dC:

$$dC = -R_f\frac{\partial C}{\partial S}Sdt + R_f Cdt + \frac{\partial C}{\partial S}dS. \tag{7.A-7}$$

Equation (7.A-7) defines the equilibrium change in the call price in terms of the rate of change in the value of a hedged portfolio set equal to the rate earned on a risk-free security.

Given Equation (7.A-7), the last step is to define the rate of change in the stock price per time, then translate that into the rate of change in the call price per time. Here, Black and Scholes assume the change in the stock price through time follows a geometric Weiner process. When applied to stock prices, this process implies that the proportional change in stock prices (dS/S) grows along the path of its expected logarithmic return, known as a *drift component*, with the actual price being above or below the path at any time, with the extent of the deviation determined by the stock's variability. Thus, the proportional change in the stock price per time depends on the mean and variance of the stock's logarithmic return and, in a geometric Weiner process, is defined as:

$$\frac{dS}{S} = \sqrt{\mu}\,dt + \sigma dZ \tag{7.A-8}$$

where:

μ = mean logarithmic return

σ = standard deviation of the logarithmic return

Z = standard normally distributed random variable.

Given the proportional change in the stock price, Black and Scholes next used a technique known as *Ito's lemma* to determine the rate of change in the call. Specifically, by Ito's lemma, if the stock price change follows a Weiner process and the call price is a function of the stock price and time [$C = f(S, t)$], then the total differential of the call function is given as:

$$dC = \frac{\partial C}{\partial S}dS + \frac{\partial C}{\partial t}dt + \frac{1}{2}\frac{\partial^2 C}{\partial S^2}\sigma^2 S^2 dt. \qquad (7.A\text{-}9)$$

Equation (7.A-9) defines the process by which the call price changes. Substituting Equation (7.A-9) for dC in Equation (7.A-7), then solving for $\partial C/\partial t$, we obtain the the equilibrium change in the call price per time that makes the hedge portfolio grow at the risk-free rate. That is:

$$\frac{\partial C}{\partial S}dS + \frac{\partial C}{\partial t}dt + \frac{1}{2}\frac{\partial^2 C}{\partial S^2}\sigma^2 S^2 dt = \frac{\partial C}{\partial S}dS - R_f S\frac{\partial C}{\partial S}dt + R_f C dt.$$

Dividing through by dt and solving for $\partial C/\partial t$, we obtain:

$$\frac{\partial C}{\partial t} = -R_f S\frac{\partial C}{\partial S} - \frac{1}{2}\frac{\partial^2 C}{\partial S^2}\sigma^2 S^2 + R_f C. \qquad (7.A\text{-}10)$$

Equation (7.A-10) is a differential equation. It can be solved, subject to a boundary condition that the price of the call equals its intrinsic value at expiration. Black and Scholes solve Equation (7.A-10) for C with that constraint using the heat exchange equation from physics to obtain Equation (7.2-1).

Black-Scholes Arbitrage/Hedging Portfolio

7.B.1   Black-Scholes Hedged Portfolio for Calls

In the B-S model, an arbitrage portfolio can be constructed by finding the proportion of shares of stock (n_s) per written call (n_c) that makes the value of a hedged portfolio (V_h) invariant to small changes in the stock price (this type of derivation also is done in Appendix 7A to obtain the B-S equation). The value of the hedged portfolio is:

$$V_h = n_c C + n_s S, \qquad (7.B-1)$$

where:

n_s = number of shares of stock.

n_c = number of calls.

Mathematically, the hedged portfolio is found by setting $n_c = -1$ in Equation (7.B-1) to constrain the portfolio to consist of one written call, then solving for the n_s value that makes the partial derivative of Equation (7.B-1) with respect to changes in S equal to zero: $\partial V_h / \partial S = 0$. Specifically, the partial derivative of Equation (7.B-1) with respect to S is:

$$\frac{\partial V_h}{\partial S} = n_c \frac{\partial C}{\partial S} + n_s \frac{\partial S}{\partial S}. \qquad (7.B-2)$$

Note: This appendix requires calculus.

242

Setting $n_c = -1$ and $\partial V_h / \partial S = 0$ then solving for n_s yields the number of shares needed to purchase per written call that makes the hedged portfolio invariant to small stock price changes:

$$0 = (-1)\frac{\partial C}{\partial S} + n_s$$

$$n_s = \frac{\partial C}{\partial S}. \qquad\qquad (7.B\text{-}3)$$

In the B-S model, $\partial C / \partial S$ is equal to $N(d_1)$. Thus, in the B-S model a hedged portfolio can be formed by selling a call ($n_c = -1$) and buying $N(d_1)$ shares of stock [$n_s = \partial C / \partial S = N(d_1)$] or a multiple of this strategy. For example, in our B-S pricing example (Section 7.2.3), $N(d_1)$ is .4066 when ABC stock is trading at \$45 and the OPM price for the ABC 50 call is \$2.88. To form a hedged portfolio therefore would require selling the ABC 50 call and buying $N(d_1) = .4066$ shares of stock. If we assume the market price of the call equals the B-S OPM price, then a \$1 increase (decrease) in the price of the stock would lead to a \$0.4066 increase (decrease) in the value of the stock position; however, this increase (decrease) would be offset by a \$0.4066 decrease (increase) in the short call position as the call increased (decreased) in price by $\partial C / \partial S = N(d_1) = .4066$. Thus, the value of the portfolio would not change in response to a relatively small change in the price of the stock, although it would change with the passage of time.

7.B.2   Black-Scholes Arbitrage Strategy

If the market price of the call is not equal to the B-S equilibrium price, then an arbitrage return could be earned from the arbitrage/hedging portfolio. For example, if the ABC 50 call was trading at \$3.00 instead of the OPM value of \$2.88, arbitrageurs could form an arbitrage portfolio by buying .4066 shares of ABC stock at \$45 per share, selling the ABC 50 call for \$3.00, and borrowing \$15.30 [.4066(\$45) − \$3.00] at the continuously compounded annualized rate of 6%. As shown in Table 7.B-1, if ABC stock increases from \$45 to \$46 an hour after the strategy is initiated and as a result the market price of the ABC 50 call increases from \$3.00 to the B-S OPM price of \$3.30, then arbitrageurs could realize a return of \$0.10 by closing their positions—the same cash flow earned from the arbitrage portfolio formed with the replicating portfolio (Section 7.3). However, if the ABC call is overpriced ($C_0^m > C_0^*$), then to avoid potential losses or a suboptimal return, arbitrageurs would need to readjust their hedge. In this example, the $N(d_1)$ associated with the stock price of \$46 (with $T \approx .25$) is .4412. Thus, arbitrageurs would need to borrow \$1.59 to buy an additional .0346 shares at \$46 per share to move to the new hedge of .4412 shares of stock. They, in turn, would continue to readjust until that period is reached when the call is equal or below its OPM value. In contrast, if the call is underpriced initially ($C_0^m < C_0^*$), then the arbitrage strategy and the readjustment rules are the opposite of the initially overpriced one.

TABLE 7.B-1

Arbitrage Strategy Using the Black-Scholes OPM	
$C_0^m = \$3.00,\ S_0 = \$45,\ X = \$50,\ C_0^* = \$2.88$	
INITIAL POSITION	CASH FLOW
Long $N(d_1)$ Shares of Stock: $-(.4066)(\$45)$	$-\$18.30$
Short One Call: $(1)(\$3.00)$	3.00
Borrow $N(d_1)S_0 - C_0^m$ Funds: $(.4066)(\$45) - \$3.00$	15.30
Cash Flow	0

Closing position when $C_t^m = C_t^*:\ S_t = \$46,\ T \approx .25,$ and $C_t^m = C_t^* = \$3.30$	
POSITION	CASH FLOW
Stock Sale: $(.4066)(\$46)$	$\$18.70$
Call Purchase: $(-1)(\$3.30)$	$-\ 3.30$
Debt Repayment: $-(\$15.30)(1.000026)^*$	$-\ 15.30$
Cash Flow	$\$\ \ 0.10$

*The rate of .000026 represents the approximate hourly rate given a 6% annual rate.

7.B.3   Black-Scholes Arbitrage Portfolio for Puts

The arbitrage put portfolio also can be formed with an arbitrage portfolio. Like the call portfolio, this portfolio is constructed by finding the proportion of shares of stock (n_s) per puts purchased (n_p) that makes the change in the value of a hedged portfolio consisting of the stock and put invariant to changes in the stock price. That is, given the current value of the hedge put portfolio as:

$$V_p = n_p P + n_s S, \tag{7.B-4}$$

where:

n_p = number of puts

n_s = number of shares of stock,

the proportion is found by setting $n_p = 1$, to constrain the portfolio to one put purchase, then solving, as follows, for the n_s that makes the partial derivative of Equation (7.B-4) with respect to S equal to zero ($\partial V_p / \partial S = 0$):

$$\frac{\partial V_p}{\partial S} = n_p \frac{\partial P}{\partial S} + n_s \frac{\partial S}{\partial S} \tag{7.B-5}$$

$$0 = (1)\frac{\partial P}{\partial S} + n_s,$$

$$n_s = -\frac{\partial P}{\partial S}.$$

In the B-S put model, $\partial P/\partial S = -[1 - N(d_1)]$. Thus, to form a hedged portfolio that does not change in response to small stock price changes, a hedged ratio of $n_s/n_p = (-\partial P/\partial S)/1 = [1 - N(d_1)]/1$ is required. In our put example (Section 7.5.1), $[1 - N(d_1)] = .5934$. If the put is equal to the B-S put price, then a portfolio consisting of one put and .5934 share of stock would be immunized against a small stock price change per given time period. For example, if the stock decreased (increased) by \$1, then the stock position would decrease (increase) by \$0.5934; this change, though, would be offset by a \$0.5934 increase (decrease) in the value of the put, leaving the value of the hedged portfolio unchanged.

7.B.4   Arbitrage Put Portfolio

Given the hedge ratio, if the put is overpriced, then the arbitrage portfolio can be formed by buying one put and $[1 - N(d_1)]$ shares of stock at S_0, totally financed by borrowing. If the put is underpriced, then the strategy consists of selling one put and $[1 - N(d_1)]$ shares of stock short and investing the proceeds in a risk-free security. These strategies then are readjusted each period until it is profitable to close using the multiple-period readjustment rules defined earlier for the BOPM for puts.

Barone-Adesi and Whaley American Option Pricing Model

The Barone-Adesi and Whaley (BAW) model is an American option pricing model used for estimating the price of an American call or put option. The BAW model prices an American option as the sum of its European option value, as determined by the B-S OPM, and an early-exercise premium if the stock price exceeds a critical stock price (S^c) determined by the new model.

For a call option, the BAW model is:

$$C_0^a = C_0^e + A_0 \left(\frac{S_0}{S^c}\right)^{q_0}, \qquad \text{for } S_0 < S^c \qquad (7.C\text{-}1)$$

$$C_0^a = S_0 - X, \qquad \text{for } S_0 \geq S^c,$$

where:

$$A_0 = \left(\frac{S^c}{q_0}\right)[1 - (e^{-\Psi T})N(d_1^c)].$$

C_0^e = B-S OPM value defined by S_0, X, T, R, and Ψ.

$N(d_1^c)$ = delta value defined by the critical stock price S^c.

Ψ = annual dividend yield = $\dfrac{D^A}{S_0}$.

$$q_0 = \frac{1}{2}\left[-(Q_0 - 1) + \sqrt{(Q_0 - 1)^2 + \frac{4Q_1}{Q_2}}\right] \qquad (7.C\text{-}2)$$

$$Q_0 = \frac{2(R_f - \Psi)}{\sigma^2}$$

$$Q_1 = \frac{2R_f}{\sigma^2}$$

$$Q_2 = 1 - \frac{1}{e^{RT}}.$$

The critical stock price S^c is found implicitly by finding the S^c in which

$$S^c - X = C_0^c + \frac{1 - (e^{-\Psi T})N(d_1^c)}{q_0} S^c, \qquad (7.\text{C-}3)$$

when C_0^c is the B-S OPM value found using the critical stock price S^c adjusted for dividends by using the continuous dividend-adjusted model ($Se^{-\Psi T}$). S^c should be found using a computer.

As an example, consider an American call option in which $S_0 = \$50, X = \$50$, $\sigma = .5, T = .25, R = .06$, and $\Psi = .09$. q_0 for the call would be 6.3318:

$$Q_0 = \frac{2(.06 - .09)}{.5^2} = -0.24$$

$$Q_1 = \frac{2(.06)}{.5^2} = .48$$

$$Q_2 = 1 - \frac{1}{e^{(.06)(.25)}} = .01488806$$

$$q_0 = \frac{1}{2}\left[-(-.24 - 1) + \sqrt{(-.24 - 1)^2 + \frac{4(.48)}{.0148886}}\right] = 6.3318.$$

The critical stock price S^c that satisfies Equation (7.C-3) is $76.952. That is, when $S^c = \$76.952, C^c = \$26.2755, N(d_1^c) = 0.96583$, and

$$S^c - X = \$76.952 - \$50 = \$26.952,$$

$$C_0^c + \frac{1 - (e^{\Psi t}) N(d_1^c)}{q_0} S^c$$

$$= \$26.2755 + \frac{1 - [e^{-(.09)(.25)}].96583}{6.3318}\$76.952 = \$26.952.$$

Since $S_0 < S^c$, C_0^a is therefore:

$$C_0^a = C_0^e + A_0\left(\frac{S_0}{S^c}\right)^{q_0}$$

$$C_0^a = \$4.67856 + \left(\frac{\$76.952}{6.3318}\right)[1 - (e^{-(.09)(.25)}).96583]\left(\frac{\$50}{\$76.952}\right)^{6.3318}$$

$$C_0^a = \$4.67856 + (.67643)\left(\frac{\$50}{\$76.952}\right)^{6.3318}$$

$$C_0^a = \$4.67856 + .044 = \$4.72.$$

Thus, the American call is equal to $4.72, with an early-exercise premium of $0.044.

The BAW model for puts is similar. The American price is:

$$P_0^a = P_0^e + A_1\left[\frac{S_0}{S_p^c}\right]^{q_1}, \qquad \text{for } S_0 > S_p^c \qquad (7.\text{C-}4)$$

$$P_0^a = X - S_0, \qquad \text{for } S_0 \le S_p^c$$

where:

P_0^e = B-S OPM put price defined by S_0, X, T, R, and Ψ.

$$A_1 = \left[\frac{-S_p^c}{q_1}\right]\{[1 - (e^{-\Psi T})][1 - N(d_1^c)]\}.$$

$$q_1 = \frac{1}{2}[-(Q_0 - 1) - \sqrt{(Q_0 - 1)^2 + \frac{4Q_1}{Q_2}}].$$

S_p^c = critical stock price. If $S_0 < S_p^c$, then the put is exercised and worth $X - S_0$.

$1 - N(d_1^c)$ = delta value defined by S_p^c.

S_p^c is obtained by finding that stock value for which:

$$X - S_p^c = P_0^c - \frac{1 - (e^{-\Psi T})[1 - N(d_1^c)]}{q_1} S_p^c,$$

where P^c and $1 - N(d_1^c)$ are, respectively, the put and delta values associated with the critical stock price.

Extending the preceding call example to a comparable put, we find $q_1 = -5.09$ and $S_p^c = \$26$. With $S_p^c = \$26$, $P^c = \$23.8378$, $1 - N(d_1^c)) = .99401$, and

$$X - S_p^c = \$50 - \$26 = \$24,$$

$$P_0^c - \frac{1 - (e^{-\Psi T})[1 - N(d_1^c)]}{q_1}S_p^c$$

$$= \$23.8378 - \frac{1 - (e^{-(.09)(.25)}).99401}{-5.09}\$26 = \$23.9814,$$

a slight difference of $0.0186. Since $S_0 > S_p^c$, the price of the American put is $5.0516. That is:

$$P_0^a = P_0^e + A_1\left(\frac{S_0}{S_p^c}\right)$$

$$P_0^a = P_0^e + \left(\frac{-\$26}{-5.09}\right)\{1 - [e^{-(.09)(.25)}][.99401]\}\left(\frac{\$50}{\$26}\right)^{-5.09}$$

$$P_0^a = \$5.04660 + (.1435)\left(\frac{\$50}{\$26}\right)^{-5.09} = \$5.04660 + \$0.005 = \$5.0516.$$

The early-exercise premium in this case is only $0.005.

COMPUTER PROBLEM

1. Using the BAW computer program, determine the prices of an American call option and American put option and their early-exercise premiums. Assume S_0 = \$100$, $X = \$100$, $\sigma = .4$, $T = .25$, $R = .06$, and $\Psi = .10$.

CHAPTER 8

Empirical Tests and Applications of the Option Pricing Model

8.1 INTRODUCTION

To have confidence in applying any pricing model, we must determine whether the model's prices generally conform to market prices. This comparison leads us either to accept or to reject the theory as valid. In this chapter, we will describe the methodologies and results of some of the empirical studies that have examined the B-S OPM. As we shall see, these studies lead to the general conclusion that the B-S OPM is good at pricing options, especially when some time to expiration exists and the option is near the money. After examining the empirical studies, we will conclude the chapter, as well as our analysis of option pricing models, by describing some of the models' applications.

8.2 EMPIRICAL TESTS OF THE OPTION PRICING MODEL

Two types of empirical tests have been applied to the B-S OPM. The first can be described as an efficient-market test. In it, researchers try to determine whether or not excess returns can be earned by employing the arbitrage trading strategies that underlie the OPM. The second test involves comparing the OPM prices with observed prices while trying to control for some of the biases that can be associated with such tests.

8.2.1 Efficient-Market Tests

In the preceding chapters, we examined how arbitrageurs could force the market price of the option to equal the OPM value. If arbitrageurs act as we have described, then not only would the market price of the option equal its equilibrium value, but no opportunities would exist for abnormal returns to be earned from the arbitrage strategies delineated in the previous chapters. In academic literature, a market in which a security's market price is equal to its investment or true value is said to be efficient. Thus, an efficient option market would exist if professional investors, market makers, and other investors pursue arbitrage trading strategies (or behave as if they do) and, by so doing, ensure that the market price is equal to the OPM value.

In conducting empirical tests of the OPM, researchers need to consider whether the market truly is efficient, that is, to conduct **efficient-market tests**. Significant differences between actual call prices (C_t^m) and OPM prices (C_t^*) do not necessarily invalidate the B-S model, since such disparities also could be explained by an inefficient market, in which traders do not seek or are not aware of abnormal return opportunities. Thus, in testing the validity of OPM, researchers face the problem that two hypotheses are being tested simultaneously: (1) The model is valid, and (2) the market is efficient. Given this problem, the standard procedure is to conduct an efficient-market test in which the OPM is used to identify mispriced options and to define arbitrage trading rules. If no abnormal returns are observed from applying the strategies, then we could infer that the market is efficient and the OPM correct. If abnormal returns are observed, then an inefficient market could exist, and the OPM could be used to construct profitable trading strategies.

One of the first efficient-market studies was conducted by Black and Scholes (1972). Using option price data from the over-the-counter (OTC) market, they simulated trading strategies, using their model on approximately 550 options traded between 1966 and 1969. In their simulation, if the market price of a call was below its B-S OPM value, they assumed the call was purchased and hedged by selling $N(d_1)$ shares of stock short. On the other hand, if the call was overpriced relative to the B-S's values, then they assumed the call was sold and hedged by purchasing $N(d_1)$ shares. Black and Scholes also posited that the initial positions were adjusted daily by buying and selling shares necessary to maintain $N(d_1)$. From the simulations, they found opportunities for abnormal returns existed on a before-commission cost basis. However, when transaction costs were included, they found the abnormal returns disappeared. Thus, the results of their study suggested that the differences in observed and model values were significant statistically perhaps, but not economically.

In a 1977 study, Galai found results similar to Black and Scholes'. In his study, he replicated the Black-Scholes simulation tests using data on options traded on the CBOE during a seven-month period in 1973. Galai, in turn, found excess returns from the hedging strategies on a before-transaction cost basis, but discovered they disappeared once such costs were included. Hence, the Galai study, like that of Black and Scholes, suggested that applying arbitrage trading strategies based on the B-S model would not generate excess returns for nonmembers.*

Galai also conducted an ex-ante test, in which the trading strategies were defined in terms of closing prices on day t but were not executed until the next day, using closing prices for day $t + 1$. In contrast to the result from the first

---

*Abnormal returns to market makers and other members of the exchange could decrease and perhaps disappear when the cost of an exchange seat is included.

tests—ex-post tests—in which strategies were defined and executed with the same closing prices on day t, Galai found lower returns from the ex-ante tests. This finding suggested that option prices tend to adjust toward their theoretical values.

8.2.2   Price Comparisons

The second method for testing the OPM is to compare the prices obtained from the OPM to observed market prices. This was the approach used by MacBeth and Merville (1979). They compared the B-S prices, computed using implied variances, with daily closing prices on six corporations for the year 1975. They found that the B-S model tended to underprice in-the-money calls and overprice out-of-the money calls, with the degree of mispricing being greater the shorter the option's time to expiration. MacBeth and Merville did find, though, that the B-S model was good at pricing on-the-money calls with some time to expiration.

In a more recent study comparing observed and B-S model prices, Rubinstein (1981) also found that in-the-money options were mispriced. Rubinstein also compared the market prices with values obtained from other option models and found that the B-S model yielded consistently better results than did the other models.*

8.2.3   Estimating Errors

Even with a model as highly detailed as the OPM, we should not expect empirical tests to show a strict conformity between theoretical and observed values. Two types of errors can result from conducting empirical tests: ***measurement errors*** and ***stochastic errors***.

In such early empirical studies of the OPM as Galai's, measurement errors often resulted from the use of closing prices. When closing price data (such as found in the *Wall Street Journal*) are used, a timing problem, commonly referred to as a ***nonsimultaneity problem***, can exist. For example, suppose the reported closing prices on a call and its underlying stock were $7 and $100, respectively. Using these prices, a researcher estimating an OPM value of $6.35 might conclude that the option is overpriced. However, it could be that the $7 call price was the price on a last trade of the day that occurred some time before the last trade on the stock. The researcher should not assume that the market price of the call necessarily would have been the reported $7 when the stock closed trading at $100; thus, an inference that the call is mispriced or the OPM invalid cannot be deduced without some reservation.

If market activity in the stock and option market is heavy (to the extent that nonsimultaneity problems just discussed are minimal), researchers still have another problem using closing prices: They often do not know whether the prices reported are bid or ask prices or in between. For example, suppose the bid-ask spread is ½ point and the reported closing price is $6. If the closing price was based

---

*Some of the other models tested were Cox and Ross's (1976) constant elasticity of variance model and Merton's diffusion-jump model.

on a bid price, the bid-ask spread would be 6–6½, and if it was based on an ask, the spread would be 5½–6. So, a researcher using a closing price of $6 could have an error of 8.333% ($0.50/$6.00) above or below the reported $6 closing price. Thus, any empirical research using closing prices that showed abnormal returns would have to be discounted to account for the bid-ask spread differential before conclusions regarding market inefficiencies could be drawn.

In the Rubinstein study and other more current empirical studies on the OPM, the nonsimultaneity and bid-ask problems were minimized by the researchers using CBOE-recorded data. This database provides traded prices, quotes, and volume data to the nearest second. (This data later was consolidated into the Berkeley Option Data Base.) However, these studies, like the Black and Scholes and Galai studies, suffer from measurement errors resulting from using estimates of the underlying stock's volatility in determining the OPM value. In fact, Geske and Roll (1984) argue that most errors in estimating the OPM are due primarily to incorrect estimates of the variance.

The second type of error is a stochastic one. This error can result from the exclusion of important explanatory variables and/or an incorrect mathematical specification of the model. In the Black and Scholes and Galai studies, one omission was the treatment of dividends. Not surprisingly, Whaley (1982) and Sterk (1982) found less measurement error associated with the B-S OPM with dividend adjustments than without such corrections. Thus, for the Galai study, the nontreatment of dividends on options on dividend-paying stocks probably did lead to errors. The Black and Scholes study, however, was not subject to such errors, since they used OTC options that were dividend-protected; that is, if the stock price went ex-dividend, then the exercise price of the OTC call was lowered by the amount of the dividend.

Stochastic errors resulting from model misspecifications were examined in a 1980 study by Bhattacharya (1980). Bhattacharya calculated the rates of return resulting from theoretical hedged portfolios formed using the B-S OPM and also B-S prices instead of market prices. Portfolio values were calculated from observed stock prices, interest rates, and estimated variances, but used the B-S model's call values instead of market prices. Bhattacharya found that, with the exception of near-the-money calls with short periods to expiration, no significant mispricing by the B-S OPM existed, thus supporting the theoretical soundness of the B-S OPM.

Finally, stochastic errors could be due to assuming that the variance is constant. MacBeth and Merville (1980) have provided evidence showing that the variance tends to change as the stock price changes. If this is the case, then an option pricing model such as Merton's diffusion-jump model or Cox and Ross's constant elasticity of substitution model could yield better results than the B-S OPM.

8.2.4   Summary

Empirical studies provide general support for the B-S model as a valid pricing model, especially for near-the-money options. The observed errors could be the result of problems in estimating the variance or in using closing price data. The overall consensus, though, is that the B-S OPM is a useful pricing model. In fact, aside from empirical studies (many of which are biased by errors), the strongest endorsement of the B-S OPM comes from its ubiquitous use. Today, the OPM may be the most widely accepted model in the field of finance.

8.3   APPLICATIONS OF THE OPTION PRICING MODEL

The OPM can be used to evaluate option positions with different holding periods and to define an option's expected rate of return (*option expected return*) and risk (*option risk*).

8.3.1   Option Positions with Different Holding Periods

In Chapter 3, we examined a number of option strategies in terms of their profit and stock price relations. These strategies, though, were evaluated at expiration in terms of the option's intrinsic value. With the OPM, we now can examine these strategies in terms of their profit and stock price relations prior to expiration. The tables in Exhibit 8.3-1 show the stock price and profit relations for the long call, put, and straddle positions. The relations are defined for three points in time—t_1, t_2, and T. T is the time to expiration; t_1 and t_2 are the times to dates prior to expiration, with t_1 earlier than t_2. In determining the profits at t_1 and t_2, the B-S OPM is used to estimate the price of the call for each stock price, with the times to expiration being $T - t_1$ and $T - t_2$ when the positions are closed. The put-call parity model, in turn, is used to estimate put prices prior to expiration. In the tables, the call and put options evaluated have exercise prices of $50 and expirations of three months ($T = .25$ per year); the options' underlying stock is initially priced at $S_0 = \$50$ and has a volatility of $\sigma = .5$ and no dividends; the annual (continuously compounded) risk-free rate is 5%; the price of the call using the B-S OPM is $5.33 and the price of the put is $4.77; and the holding periods evaluated are one month, two months, and three months.

In examining the call and put purchase strategies (Tables a and b), note that the profit is greater at each stock price the shorter the holding period. This relationship reflects the fact that the earlier a call or put is sold, the greater its time value premium. Be careful, though, in quickly concluding that short holding periods for long positions in calls and puts are superior to longer ones. Specifically, though a shorter holding period does provide a greater time premium than a longer one, the shorter period also means that the range in possible stock prices is more limited than the price range for a longer time period. Thus, the shorter the holding period, the less time available for the stock to move to a profitable position. In contrast, the naked call and put write positions yield greater profits per stock price the longer the holding period. This, of course, is because the option's time value premium is smaller the closer the option is to expiration. As a result, the cost of closing the short position is less per stock price.

One strategy we were not able to analyze in Chapter 3 was the time (calendar or horizontal) spread. With the OPM we now can evaluate this spread by using this model to determine either the prices and profits from a longer-term option at the expiration of a shorter-term one or the prices of both options when the holding period is shorter than the expiration of the shorter-term option.

A horizontal spread evaluated using the OPM is shown in Table 8.3-1. The table shows the profit and stock price relation for the case of a spreader who forms a calendar spread consisting of a short position in a July ABC 50 call and a long position in an October ABC 50 call. The spread is evaluated at the expiration of the

EXHIBIT 8.3-1

Option Strategies with Different Holding Periods

$S_0 = \$50$, $X = \$50$,
$\sigma = .5$, $R = .05$, $T = .25$,
$C_0^* = \$5.33$, $P_0^* = \$4.77$

Table a: Call Purchase

	HOLDING PERIOD					
	ONE MONTH (t_1)		TWO MONTHS (t_2)		THREE MONTHS (T)	
S_t	C^*	PROFIT	C^*	PROFIT	C^*	PROFIT
$40	$ 0.68	− $4.65	$ 0.18	− $5.15	0	− $5.33
45	1.98	− 3.35	0.97	− 4.36	0	− 5.33
50	4.32	− 1.01	3.04	− 2.29	0	− 5.33
55	7.50	2.17	6.31	0.98	5	− 0.33
60	11.47	6.14	10.58	5.25	10	4.67

Table b: Put Purchase

	HOLDING PERIOD					
	ONE MONTH (t_1)		TWO MONTHS (t_2)		THREE MONTHS (T)	
S_t	P^*	PROFIT	P^*	PROFIT	P^*	PROFIT
$40	$10.26	$5.49	$9.97	$5.20	$10	$5.23
45	6.56	1.79	5.76	0.99	5	0.23
50	3.90	− 0.87	2.83	− 1.94	0	− 4.77
55	2.08	− 2.69	1.10	− 3.67	0	− 4.77
60	1.05	− 3.72	0.37	− 4.40	0	− 4.77

Table c: Straddle Purchase

	HOLDING PERIOD								
	ONE MONTH (t_1)			TWO MONTHS (t_2)			THREE MONTHS (T)		
S_t	C^*	P^*	PROFIT	C^*	P^*	PROFIT	C^*	P^*	PROFIT
$40	$ 0.68	$10.26	$0.84	$ 0.18	$9.97	$0.05	0	$10	− $ 0.10
45	1.98	6.56	− 1.56	0.97	5.76	− 3.37	0	5	− 5.10
50	4.32	3.90	− 1.88	3.04	2.83	− 4.23	0	0	− 10.10
55	7.50	2.08	− 0.52	6.31	1.10	− 2.69	5	0	− 5.10
60	11.47	1.05	2.42	10.58	0.37	0.85	10	0	− 0.10

July call, in which the October call is assumed to be closed at a price equal to the B-S OPM value. Since the longer-term call is more valuable than the shorter-term one (or an arbitrage opportunity would exist), the 50 July/October spread involves a cost. In the example in the table, it is assumed that ABC stock is priced at $50, has no dividends, and has a volatility of $\sigma = .5$, and that the spreader buys the spread three months prior to the July expiration at a cost of $2.36. The $2.36 price is based on the B-S OPM in which the July 50 call, expiring in three months $(T = .25)$, is $5.30 and the October 50 call, expiring in six months $(T = .5)$, is

TABLE 8.3-1

	Calendar Spread			
Short July Call: $T = .25$, $\sigma = .50$, $X = \$50$, $C^* = \$5.30$				
Long October Call: $T = .5$, $\sigma = .5$, $X = \$50$, $C^* = \$7.66$				
PROFIT AND STOCK PRICE RELATION EVALUATED AT JULY EXPIRATION				
S_t	PROFIT FROM SHORT JULY 50 CALL	OCTOBER CALL PRICE C_t^*	PROFIT FROM LONG OCTOBER 50 CALL	TOTAL PROFIT
$30	$ 530	$ 0.0841	− $ 757.59	− $227.59
35	530	0.4163	− 724.37	− 194.37
40	530	1.2408	− 641.92	− 111.92
45	530	2.8756	− 478.44	51.56
50	530	5.2999	− 236.01	293.99
55	30	8.5584	89.84	119.84
60	− 470	12.3857	472.57	2.57
65	− 970	16.6919	903.19	− 66.81
70	− 1470	21.2865	1362.65	− 107.35

$7.66. As shown in the table, the calendar spread produces the greatest profit when the stock is stable. This is because the longer-term call sells at a higher time value premium when it is on or near the money. If the investor expected the stock to move dramatically up or down, then the calendar spread should be reversed, with the spreader taking a long position in the near-term call and a short position in the longer-term one.

8.3.2 Option Return-Risk Characteristics

Investors often evaluate and select securities and portfolios in terms of their expected return and risk characteristics. To evaluate and select options, investors need to be able to define these securities in terms of these characteristics. To this end, the OPM can be used to derive the equations for an option's expected rate of return and risk.

For a call option, the OPM prices the option by determining the value of the call's replicating portfolio. Recall that the replicating call portfolio consists of the purchase of H_0^* shares of stock, partially financed by borrowing B_0^* dollars. For a no-dividend case, the expected rate of return on the call, $E(R_c)$, in equilibrium is equal to the expected rate of return on the replicating call portfolio, $E(Z_c)$. This rate is:

$$E(R_c) = E(Z_c) = w_s E(R_s) + w_r R_f, \qquad (8.3\text{-}1)$$

where:

w_s = proportion of investment funds allocated to the stock

w_r = proportion of investment funds allocated to the risk-free security

$$E(R_s) = \text{expected rate of return of the stock}$$
$$1 = w_r + w_s.$$

The total investment in the replicating call portfolios is $H_0^* S_0 - B_0^*$, which in equilibrium is equal to the call value (C_0^*); the investment in the stock is $H_0^* S_0$; the risk-free investment is $-B_0^*$ (i.e., negative investment, or borrowing). Thus, Equation (8.3-1) can be written as

$$E(R_c) = E(Z_c) = \left(\frac{H_0^* S_0}{C_0^*}\right) E(R_s) + \left(\frac{-B_0^*}{C_0^*}\right) R_f. \tag{8.3-2}$$

The risk of a portfolio's consisting of risky and risk-free securities can be defined in terms of the portfolio's standard deviation or beta (for an explanation of the portfolio return and risk equations, see Appendix G at the end of the book). The standard deviation and beta for the call or, equivalently, for the replicating portfolio are:

$$\sigma(R_c) = \sigma(Z_c) = w_s \sigma(R_s) = \left(\frac{H_0^* S_0}{C_0^*}\right) \sigma(R_s) \tag{8.3-3}$$

$$\beta_c = \beta_z = w_s \beta_s = \left(\frac{H_0^* S_0}{C_0^*}\right) \beta_s, \tag{8.3-4}$$

in which $\beta_s = $ beta of the stock.

Equation (8.3-2) and Equations (8.3-3) and (8.3-4) can be used to define the expected rate of return and risk of a call option. In the equations, the OPM is needed to determine H_0^* [equal to $N(d_1)$ in the B-S model], C_0^*, and B_0^* [$(X/e^{(RT)})N(d_2)$ in the B-S model].

For a put, the equilibrium expected rate of return [$E(R_p)$] is equal to the expected rate of return of a replicating put portfolio formed by selling H_0^{p*} shares of stock short and investing I_0^* in a risk-free security. The total investment in the replicating put portfolio is $H_0^{p*} S_0 + I_0^*$ (with $H_0^{p*} < 0$), which, in equilibrium, is equal to P_0^*. Thus, a put's expected rate of return, standard deviation, and beta can be defined as:

$$E(R_p) = E(Z_p) = w_s E(R_s) + w_r R_f \tag{8.3-5}$$

$$E(R_p) = E(Z_p) = \left(\frac{H_0^{p*} S_0}{P_0^*}\right) E(R_s) + \left(\frac{I_0^*}{P_0^*}\right) R_f$$

$$\sigma(R_p) = \sigma(Z_p) = \sqrt{w_s^2 \sigma(R_s)^2} = \sqrt{\left(\frac{H_0^{p*} S_0}{P_0^*}\right)^2 \sigma(R_s)^2} \tag{8.3-6}$$

$$\beta_p = \beta_z = w_s \beta_s = \frac{H_0^{p*} S_0}{P_0^*} \beta_s. \tag{8.3-7}$$

In the B-S put model, $H_0^{p*} = -[1 - N(d_1)]$ and $I_0^* = [X/e^{(RT)}][(1 - N(d_2)]$. It should be noted that with $H_0^{p*} < 0$, the put has a negative beta. The negative sign is consistent with our a priori expectations. That is, we should expect an inverse relationship between the rate of return on a put and the market's rate of return.

To illustrate, consider the example of the 50 call with $T = .25$ per year described in Section 7.2.3 and the 50 put with $T = .25$ described in Section 7.5.1. Using the B-S model, the call's price, hedge ratio, and B_0^* were found in Chapter

7 to be $C^* = \$2.88$, $H_0^* = N(d_1) = 0.4066$, and $B_0^* = \$15.42$, given $S_0 = \$45$, $\sigma(R_s) = .5$, and $R_f = .06$. Similarly, the price, hedge ratio, and I_0^* for the put were found to be $P_0^* = \$7.13$, $H_0^{p*} = -[1 - N(d_1)] = -.5934$, and $I_0^* = \$33.83$. If the underlying stock has an expected rate of return of $E(R_s) = .10$, standard deviation of $\sigma(R_s) = 0.5$, and a beta of $\beta = 1.5$, then the 50 call and 50 put would have the following return-risk characteristics:

Call:

$$E(R_c) = \left(\frac{H_0^* S_0}{C_0^*}\right) E(R_s) + \left(\frac{-B_0^*}{C_0^*}\right) R_f$$

$$= \frac{.4066(\$45)}{\$2.88}(.10) + \frac{-\$15.42}{\$2.88}(.06) = .314$$

$$\sigma(R_c) = \left(\frac{H_0^* S_0}{C_0^*}\right) \sigma(R_s) = 6.353(.5) = 3.1765$$

$$\beta_c = \left(\frac{H_0^* S_0}{C_0^*}\right) \beta_s = 6.353(1.5) = 9.5295.$$

Put:

$$E(R_p) = \left(\frac{H_0^{p*} S_0}{P_0^*}\right) E(R_s) + \frac{I_0^*}{P_0^*} R_f$$

$$= \frac{-.5934(\$45)}{\$7.13}(.10) + \frac{\$33.83}{\$7.13}(.06) = -.0898$$

$$\sigma(R_p) = \sqrt{\left(\frac{H_0^{p*} S_0}{P_0^*}\right)^2} \sigma(R_s) = 3.745(.5) = 1.8725$$

$$\beta_p = w_s \beta_s = \left(\frac{H_0^{p*} S_0}{P_0^*}\right) \beta_s = -3.745(1.5) = -5.6175.$$

Compared to the stock, the call and put yield higher expected returns and risks, with the put's negative expected return implying that the price of the stock must decline for a long position in the put to be profitable. The higher return-risk characteristics should not be surprising, given that a call is equivalent to a leveraged stock position and a put is equivalent to a leveraged short sale.*

It is important to note that the preceding measures for an option's return and risk hold only for a small time period and for small stock price changes. The equations for the expected return and risk using the B-S OPM therefore are defined more appropriately as *instantaneous* expected rates of return, standard deviations, and betas. Nevertheless, the equations for the parameters still provide us with a method for estimating an option's return and risk characteristics.

---

*The w_s term in the preceding equations is equal to the option's price elasticity with respect to a change in the stock's price (ϵ). That is, for a call:

$$\epsilon_c = \frac{\%\Delta C}{\%\Delta S} = \left(\frac{\Delta C}{\Delta S}\right)\left(\frac{S}{C}\right) = \frac{H_0^* S_0}{C_0^*} = w_s;$$

for a put:

$$\epsilon_p = \frac{\%\Delta P}{\%\Delta S} = \left(\frac{\Delta P}{\Delta S}\right)\left(\frac{S}{P}\right) = \frac{H_0^{p*} S_0}{P_0^*} = w_s.$$

TABLE 8.4-1

	Derivatives of the B-S Model for European Call Options	
	CALL ON STOCK PAYING NO DIVIDENDS	CALL ON STOCK PAYING ANNUAL DIVIDEND YIELD OF Ψ
Delta	$\Delta = \frac{\partial C}{\partial S} = N(d_1)$	$\Delta = e^{-\Psi T}N(d_1)$
Gamma	$\Gamma = \frac{\partial \Delta}{\partial S} = \frac{N'(d_1)}{S_0 \sigma \sqrt{T}}$	$\Gamma = \frac{N'(d_1)e^{-\Psi T}}{S_0 \sigma \sqrt{T}}$
Theta	$\Theta = -\frac{\partial C}{\partial T} = -\frac{S_0 N'(d_1)\sigma}{2\sqrt{T}}$ $- RXe^{-RT}N(d_2)$	$\Theta = -\frac{S_0 N'(d_1)\sigma e^{-\Psi T}}{2\sqrt{T}}$ $+ \Psi S_0 N(d_1)e^{-\Psi T}$ $- RXe^{-RT}N(d_2)$
Vega (Kappa)	$\Lambda = \frac{\partial C}{\partial \sigma} = S_0\sqrt{T}N'(d_1)$	$\Lambda = S_0\sqrt{T}N'(d_1)e^{-\Psi T}$
Rho	$\frac{\partial C}{\partial R} = XTN(d_2)e^{-RT}$	$\frac{\partial C}{\partial R} = XTN(d_2)e^{-RT}$

$N'(d) = \frac{1}{\sqrt{2\pi}}e^{-(d^2/2)}$

8.4   DELTA, GAMMA, AND THETA*

In addition to defining the profit relations of option positions prior to expiration and measuring an option's return-risk characteristic, the OPM also can be used to measure the delta, gamma, theta, vega, and rho values for call and put options. Recall from Chapter 7, the option's delta (Δ) measures the change in the option's price per small change in the stock price, with other factors constant; the option's gamma (Γ) defines the change in the option's delta per small change in the stock price; the option's theta (Θ) measures the change in the option's price per small change in the time to expiration; and the option's vega (Λ) and rho measure price changes per small changes in variability and interest rates, respectively. The equations for determining the delta, gamma, theta, vega, and rho values using the B-S model are shown in Table 8.4-1 for European calls on non-dividend and dividend-paying stock and in Table 8.4-2 for puts.

8.4.1   Delta

Delta is used to measure an option's price sensitivity to a small change in the price of the underlying stock. The delta (Δ) for a European call on a non-dividend-paying stock is $N(d_1)$, and for a European put is $N(d_1) - 1$. As shown in Figure 8.4-1(a), the delta for a call is positive, ranging in value from approximately 0 for deep out-of-the-money calls to approximately 1 for deep in-the-money ones. In contrast,

---

*This section makes use of calculus.

TABLE 8.4-2

	Derivatives of the B-S Model for European Put Options	
	PUT ON STOCK PAYING NO DIVIDENDS	PUT ON STOCK PAYING ANNUAL DIVIDEND YIELD OF Ψ
Delta	$\Delta = \dfrac{\partial P}{\partial S} = N(d_1) - 1$	$\Delta = e^{-\Psi T}[N(d_1) - 1]$
Gamma	$\Gamma = \dfrac{\partial \Delta}{\partial S} = \dfrac{N'(d_1)}{S_0 \sigma \sqrt{T}}$	$\Gamma = \dfrac{N'(d_1)e^{-\Psi T}}{S_0 \sigma \sqrt{T}}$
Theta	$\Theta = -\dfrac{\partial P}{\partial T} = -\dfrac{S_0 N'(d_1)\sigma}{2\sqrt{T}}$ $+ RXe^{-RT}N(-d_2)$	$\Theta = -\dfrac{S_0 N'(d_1)\sigma e^{-\Psi T}}{2\sqrt{T}}$ $- \Psi S_0 N(-d_1)e^{-\Psi T}$ $+ RXe^{-RT}N(-d_2)$
Vega (Kappa)	$\Lambda = \dfrac{\partial P}{\partial \sigma} = S_0 \sqrt{T} N'(d_1)$	$\Lambda = S_0 \sqrt{T} N'(d_1)e^{-\Psi T}$
Rho	$\dfrac{\partial P}{\partial R} = XTN(-d_2)e^{-RT}$	$\dfrac{\partial P}{\partial R} = XTN(-d_2)e^{-RT}$

$N'(d) = \dfrac{1}{\sqrt{2\pi}}e^{-(d^2/2)}$

the delta for a put is negative, ranging from approximately 0 to -1. Deltas change in response not only to stock price changes, but also to the time to expiration. As shown in Figure 8.4-1(b) and (d), as the time to expiration *decreases*, the delta of an in-the-money call or put increases, while an out-of-the-money call or put tends to decrease.

In addition to measuring a derivative security's price sensitivity to a change in the stock price, an option's delta also can be used to measure the probability that the option will be in the money at expiration. Thus, the call with a $\Delta = N(d_1) = .40$ has an approximately 40% chance that its stock price will exceed the option's exercise price at expiration.

8.4.2   Theta

As noted, theta (Θ) is the change in the price of an option with respect to changes in its time to expiration, with all other factors constant. It is a measure of the option's time decay. Since theta measures the time decay of an option, it is usually defined as the negative of the partial derivative of the option's price with respect to expiration [$\Theta = -(\partial C/\partial T)$ or $\Theta = -(\partial P/\partial T)$]. Except for the case of a deep in-the-money European put when interest rates are high, the thetas on options are negative.

Using our illustrative call and put examples (Sections 7.2.3 and 7.5.1), in which $S_0 = \$45, X = \$50, T = .25, \sigma = .5, R = .06, N(d_1) = N(-.2364) = .4066, N(d_2) = N(-.4846) = .3131,$ and $N'(d_1) = (1/\sqrt{2\pi})e^{-(-.2364^2/2)} = 0.3879,$ the call would have a theta of $-7.8024,$ and the put would have a theta of -6.698:

FIGURE 8.4-1

**Delta Relations
to Stock Prices
and Time to Expiraton**

Call

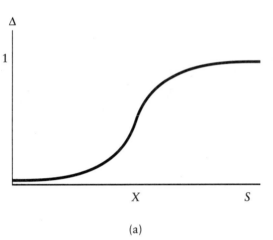

(a)

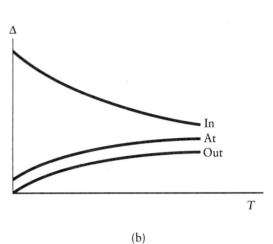

(b)

Put

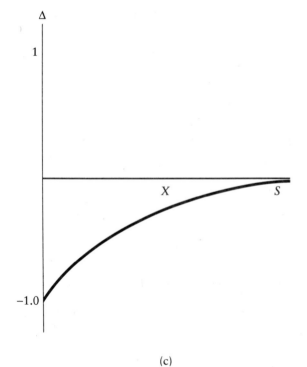

(c)

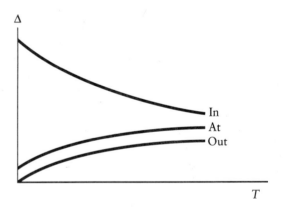

(d)

Call:

$$\Theta = -\frac{S_0 N'(d_1)\sigma}{2\sqrt{T}} - RXe^{-RT}N(d_2)$$

$$\Theta = -\frac{(\$45)(.3879)(.5)}{2\sqrt{.25}} - (.06)(\$50)e^{-.06(.25)}(.3131) = -7.8024.$$

Put:

$$\Theta = -\frac{S_0 N'(d_1)\sigma}{2\sqrt{T}} + RXe^{-RT}N(-d_2)$$

$$\Theta = -\frac{(\$45)(.3879)(.5)}{2\sqrt{.25}} + (.06)(\$50)e^{-.06(.25)}(.6869) = -6.698.$$

This means that if the option is held 1% of a year (approximately 2.5 trading days) and there is no change in the stock's price, then the call would decline in value by approximately $0.078 and the put would decrease by $0.06698.

Like delta, theta changes in response to changes in the stock price and time to expiration. These relationships are presented in Figures 8.4-2.

FIGURE 8.4-2

Theta Relations to Stock Price and Time to Expiration

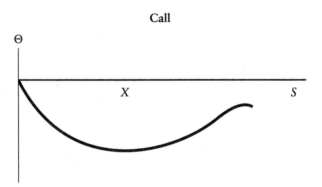

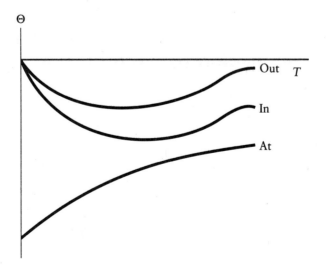

8.4.3   Gamma

Gamma (Γ) measures the change in an option's delta for a small change in the stock price. It is the second derivative of the option price with respect to the stock price. In our illustrative example, the gamma for the call or put is .03448:

$$\Gamma = \frac{N'(d_1)}{S_0\sigma\sqrt{T}} = \frac{.3879}{(45)(.5)\sqrt{.25}} = .03448.$$

Thus, a \$1 increase in the stock price would increase the delta of the call or put by approximately 0.03448.

As shown in Figure 8.4-3, the gamma of a call or put varies with respect to the stock price and time to expiration.

8.4.4   Position Delta, Gamma, and Theta Values

The description of call and put options in terms of their delta, gamma, and theta values can be extended to option positions. For example, consider an investor who

FIGURE 8.4-3

Gamma Relations to Stock Price and Time to Expiration

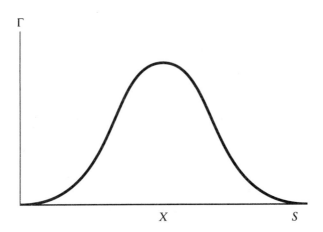

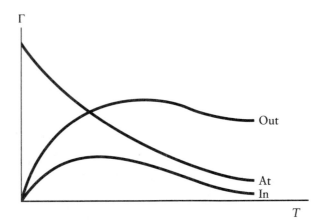

purchases n_1 calls at a price of C_1 per call and n_2 calls on another option on the same stock at a price of C_2 per call. The value of this portfolio (V) is:

$$V = n_1 C_1 + n_2 C_2. \tag{8.4-1}$$

The call prices are functions of S, T, σ, and R_f. Taking the partial derivative of Equation (8.4-1) with respect to S yields the position's delta, Δ_p. That is:

$$\Delta_p = \frac{\partial V}{\partial S} = n_1\left(\frac{\partial C_1}{\partial S}\right) + n_2\left(\frac{\partial C_2}{\partial S}\right) \tag{8.4-2}$$

$$\Delta_p = n_1 \Delta_1 + n_2 \Delta_2,$$

where:

$$\Delta_1 = \frac{\partial C_1}{\partial S} = H_1^* = N(d_1)_1$$

$$\Delta_2 = \frac{\partial C_2}{\partial S} = H_2^* = N(d_1)_2.$$

The position delta measures the change in the position's value in response to a small change in the stock price, with other factors being constant. Moreover, by setting Equation (8.4-2) equal to zero and solving for n_1 in terms of n_2 (or vice versa), a neutral position delta can be constructed with a value invariant to small changes in the stock price. That is:

$$0 = n_1 \Delta_1 + n_2 \Delta_2. \tag{8.4-3}$$

$$n_1 = -\left(\frac{\Delta_2}{\Delta_1}\right) n_2 \tag{8.4-4}$$

$$n_1 = -\left[\frac{N(d_1)_2}{N(d_1)_1}\right] n_2.$$

The position gamma (Γ_p) defines the change in the position's delta for a small change in the stock price, with other factors being constant. The gamma of the preceding call portfolio is found by taking the partial derivative of Equation (8.4-2) with respect to S to obtain:

$$\Gamma_p = \frac{\partial \Delta_p}{\partial S} = n_1\left(\frac{\partial \Delta_1}{\partial S}\right) + n_2\left(\frac{\partial \Delta_2}{\partial S}\right) \tag{8.4-5}$$

$$\Gamma = n_1 \Gamma_1 + n_2 \Gamma_2.$$

Knowing a portfolio's gamma and delta positions can be helpful in defining an investor's risk-return exposure. For example, suppose a delta-neutral portfolio is formed. If this portfolio has a positive gamma, then the portfolio will decline in value if there is little or no change in the stock price and increase in value if there is a large positive or negative change in the stock price. On the other hand, if the delta-neutral portfolio has a negative gamma, the portfolio value will increase if there is little or no change in the stock price and decrease in value if there is a large positive or negative change in the stock price. These relations are depicted in Figure 8.4-4, where the relations between the change in the portfolio value, ΔV, and ΔS

FIGURE 8.4-4

Relation Between ΔV and ΔS for Delta-Neutral Portfolio Stock Prices and Time to Expiration

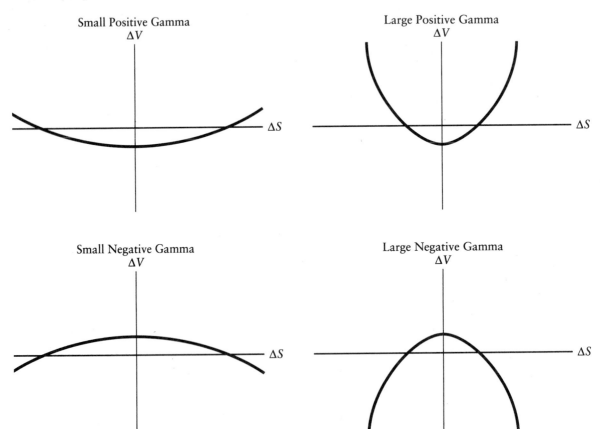

are shown for different position gammas given a delta-neutral portfolio. In addition, the graphs in Figure 8.4-4 also show that the responsiveness of ΔV to ΔS is greater the greater the absolute value of gamma.

Finally, the partial derivative of Equation (8.4-1) with respect to the time to expiration, T, gives us the call position's theta (Θ_p). That is:

$$\Theta_p = \frac{\partial V}{\partial T} = n_1\left(\frac{\partial C_1}{\partial T}\right) + n_2\left(\frac{\partial C_2}{\partial T}\right) \qquad (8.4\text{-}6)$$

$$\Theta_p = n_1\Theta_1 + n_2\Theta_2.$$

In general, the larger a position's theta, the greater its time value decay. Thus, taking a short position in an option portfolio with a large time value decay may be a profitable strategy, especially if the position also has low delta and gamma values. If a position has a theta that is large in absolute value, then either its delta or its gamma must be large. Thus, for a delta-neutral portfolio, if the portfolio's theta is large and negative, gamma tends to be large and positive, and if its theta is large and negative, its gamma tends to be large and positive.

8.4-5 Neutral Ratio Spread

A popular neutral delta strategy is the **neutral ratio spread**. This spread position is formed with a time, money, or diagonal spread, with the proportion of short calls (or puts) to long being such that the portfolio is invariant to stock price changes (i.e., a position delta of zero). Equation (8.4-4) shows that a riskless ratio spread can be formed by purchasing (selling) $n_2 = 1$ call and selling (purchasing) $n_1 = N(d_1)_2/N(d_1)_1$ of the other call or a multiple of this strategy [the negative sign in Equation (8.4-4) indicates opposite positions]. For example, if the hedge ratio for a July 50 call is $N(d_1)_1 = .570$ and the hedge ratio for a July 60 call on the same stock is $N(d_1)_2 = .292$, then the ratio spread (also referred to as a delta spread) needed to form a riskless position is:

$$-\frac{N(d_1)_2}{N(d_1)_1} = -\frac{.292}{.570} = -.5123.$$

A riskless ratio spread therefore could be constructed by purchasing one July 60 call and selling .5123 July 50 calls. If the stock increased by $1.00, the value of the long position in the July 60 call would increase by $0.292. This, however, would be offset by the decrease of $(.5123)(.570) = \$0.292$ in the value of the short position in the October 50 call. Thus, a small change in the price of the stock would not change the value of this ratio spread.

The riskless ratio spread sometimes is used with the OPM to define arbitrage or quasi-arbitrage strategies, for example, a neutral ratio spread formed by buying an underpriced call and selling an overpriced or equal-in-value call on the same stock. Given that $N(d_1)$ changes as the stock price and time change, this ratio spread strategy would need to be readjusted each period to keep the spread riskless until it is profitable to close. Thus, the riskless ratio spread can be thought of as an alternative arbitrage strategy to the arbitrage portfolio defining the B-S OPM; in fact, with the latter strategy often involving short sales and margin requirements, the ratio spread may in some cases be a better strategy to implement.

8.5 CONCLUSION

In this chapter, we have discussed some of the empirical studies that have examined the validity of the OPM, and we have shown how the B-S model can be used to define option positions prior to expiration and how it can be used to describe the characteristics of an option and option position. This completes our analysis of option pricing.

As we will see, though, the OPM can be easily adapted to price nonstock options and to measure their characteristics. We now turn our attention to the markets, uses, and pricing of nonstock options.

KEY TERMS

efficient-market test
measurement errors
stochastic errors
nonsimultaneity problem

option expected return
option risk
option beta
neutral ratio spread

SELECTED REFERENCES

Beckers, S. "The Constant Elasticity of Variance Model and Its Implications for Option Pricing." *Journal of Finance* 35 (June 1980): 661–673.

————. "Standard Deviations Implied in Option Prices as Predictors of Future Stock Price Variability." *Journal of Banking and Finance* 5 (Sept. 1981): 363–382.

Bhattacharya, M. "Empirical Properties of the Black-Scholes Formula Under Ideal Conditions." *Journal of Financial and Quantitative Analysis* 15 (Dec. 1980): 1081–1095.

————. "Transaction Data Tests of Efficiency of the Chicago Board Options Exchange." *Journal of Financial Economics* 12 (1983): 161–185.

Black, F. "Fact and Fantasy in the Use of Options." *Financial Analysis Journal* 31 (July–Aug. 1975): 36–41, 61–72.

Black, F., and Scholes, M. "The Valuation of Option Contracts and a Test of Market Efficiency." *Journal of Finance* 27 (May 1972): 399–418.

Boyle, P., and Ananthanarayanan, A. "The Impact of Variance Estimation in Option Valuation Models." *Journal of Financial Economics* 5 (Dec. 1977): 375–388.

Cornell, B. "Using the Option Pricing Model to Measure the Uncertainty Producing Effect of Major Announcements." *Financial Management* 7 (Spring 1978): 54–59.

Cox, J., and Ross, S. "The Valuation of Options for Alternative Stochastic Processes." *Journal of Financial Economics* 3 (Jan.–Mar. 1976): 145–166.

Galai, D. "Tests of Market Efficiency of the Chicago Board Options Exchange." *Journal of Business* 50 (Apr. 1977): 167–197.

————. "Empirical Tests of Boundary Conditions for CBOE Options." *Journal of Financial Economics* 6 (June–Sept. 1978): 187–211.

————. "A Convexity Test for Traded Options." *Quarterly Review of Economics and Business* 19 (Summer 1979): 83–90.

————. "A Survey of Empirical Tests of Option Pricing Models." In *Option Pricing*, edited by M. Brenner. Lexington, Mass.: Heath, 1983, pp. 45–80.

Geske, R., and Roll, R. "On Valuing American Call Options with the Black-Scholes Formula." *Journal of Finance* 39 (June 1984): 443–455.

Klemkosky, R. and Resnick, B. "An *Ex Ante* Analysis of Put-Call Parity." *Journal of Financial Economics* 8 (1980): 363–378.

MacBeth, J., and Merville, L. "An Empirical Examination of the Black-Scholes Call Option Pricing Model." *Journal of Finance* 34 (Dec. 1979): 1173–1186.

————. "Tests of the Black-Scholes and Cox Call Option Valuation Models." *Journal of Finance* (May 1980): 285–300.

Manaster, S., and Rendleman, R., Jr. "Option Prices as Predictors of Equilibrium Stock Prices." *Journal of Finance* 37 (Sept. 1982): 1043–1058.

Ritchken, Peter. *Options: Theory, Strategy, and Applications*, Glenview, Ill.: Scott, Foresman, 1987, ch. 8–10.

Rubenstein, M. "Nonparametric Tests of Alternative Option Pricing Models." Working Paper No. 117. University of California, Berkeley, Research Program in Finance, 1981.

————. "Nonparametric Tests of Alternative Option Pricing Models Using All Reported Trades and Quotes on the 30 Most active CBOE Option Classes from August 23, 1976 through August 31, 1978." *Journal of Finance* 40 (June 1985): 455–480.

Sterk, W. "Tests of Two Models for Valuing Call Options on Stocks with Dividends." *Journal of Finance* 37 (Dec. 1982): 1229–1238.

Trennepohl, G. "A Comparison of Listed Option Premiums and Black-Scholes Model Prices: 1973–1979." *Journal of Financial Research* 4 (Spring 1981): 11–20.

Trippi, R. "A Test of Option Market Efficiency Using a Random-Walk Valuation Model." *Journal of Economics and Business* 29 (Winter 1977): 93–98.

Whaley, R. "Valuation of American Call Options on Dividend-Paying Stocks: Empirical Tests." *Journal of Financial Economics* 10 (Mar. 1982): 29–58.

EXERCISES

Consider a two-state, two-period economy in which ABC stock is priced at $100 and the period risk-free rate is 2.5%. Suppose the market incorrectly estimates u and d to be 1.0583 and .9449, respectively, while you correctly estimate the up and down parameters as $u = 1.0488$ and $d = .9747$.

1. Using the BOPM, price an ABC European call using the market's u and d values and your u and d values.

2. Given the market's call price, define the arbitrage strategy you would employ. What would be your cash flow next period if the price of ABC stock increased according to your estimated u value and the market adjusted its u and d values such that they equaled your values?

3. What would be the market price of the call in period 1 if the stock price increased according to your estimate of u but the market continued to use its incorrect u and d values?

4. Based on your answer to Exercise 3, what adjustment would you need to make to your initial arbitrage position? Show what your cash flow would be at expiration when you close. Continue to assume you have the correct u and d estimates.

5. Based on Exercises 1–4, comment on the option pricing model and market efficiency.

PROBLEMS AND QUESTIONS

1. Explain the following studies:

   a. Black-Scholes (1972)

   b. Galai (1977)

   c. MacBeth and Merville (1979)

2. Explain some of the problems researchers have in testing the validity of the OPM.

3. Determine the profits from a time spread formed with a long position in an ABC 60 call expiring in six months ($T = .5$) and trading at $5.46 and a short position in an ABC 60 call expiring in three months ($T = .5$) and trading at $3.49. Assume the spread is closed at the expiration of the short-term call when ABC is trading at $65. Assume $\sigma = .35$, no dividends, and $R = .05$.

4. What would be your profit if you sold a six-month 70 call at $5.79, then closed it three months later ($T = .25$) when the stock was trading at $70? Assume ABC stock has $\sigma = .25$ and pays no dividends and $R = .05$.

5. Suppose ABC stock is trading at $50, its annualized standard deviation is 0.175, and the continuously compounded risk-free rate is 6% (annual).

   a. Calculate the B-S equilibrium call prices for an ABC 50 European call expiring in 90 days ($T = .25$) and an ABC 48 European call expiring in 90 days.

   b. Construct a neutral ratio spread with the 50 and 48 calls. What would be your initial cash flow if the calls were priced equal to their OPM values?

   c. What would happen to your neutral ratio hedge if the stock immediately increased by $1 and you closed your positions at call prices equal to their equilibrium values? What would happen if you closed your position after the stock decreased by $1?

6. Define the arbitrage strategy using the neutral delta strategy you could employ if the price of the ABC 48 call in Problem 5 was equal to its equilibrium value but the 50 call was underpriced at $2.05. Show the initial cash flow from closing the position shortly afterward at $S_t = \$51$ and $S_t = \$49$ and at call values equal to the equilibrium values you used in Problem 5.

7. Describe the arbitrage strategy you could use if the 50 call in Problem 5 was overpriced at $2.25.

8. If the ABC stock described in Problem 5 had a $\beta = .35$, what would be the β of the ABC 50 call?

9. What would be the expected rate of return and standard deviation of the ABC 50 call described in Problem 5 if the expected return and standard deviation of ABC stock were .10 and .175, respectively?

10. Briefly comment on relative sizes of the expected returns, standard deviations, and β of the ABC call and stock in Problems 8 and 9.

11. If the price of the ABC stock in Problem 5 increased by 2%, what would be the approximate percentage change in the price of the ABC 50 call?

12. Given the information on the ABC stock in Problem 5: $S_0 = \$50$, $\sigma = .175$, $R = .06$, $\beta_s = .35$, and $E(R_s) = -.10$, determine the following characteristics of an ABC 50 European put with expiration of $T = .25$:

   a. Equilibrium OPM put price

   b. Expected rate of return and standard deviation

   c. Beta

13. Suppose XYZ stock is trading at $100, its annualized standard deviation is $\sigma = .25$, and the continuous compounded risk-free rate is 6%.

   a. Determine the B-S equilibrium call prices for an XYZ European 100 call expiring in 90 days ($T = .25$) and for an XYZ European 105 call expiring in 90 days.

   b. Determine the delta, theta, and gamma for the 100 call and the 105 call.

   c. How would you construct a neutral-delta hedged portfolio? What is the value of the portfolio? What would be your position theta and gamma?

   d. Given your neutral-delta hedged portfolio, what would you expect the change in the portfolio's value to be over a short period of time if there were no changes in the price of XYZ stock? What would you expect the change in value to be if there was a positive change or a negative change in the stock price?

   e. What would be the portfolio's profit or loss if the price of XYZ stock increased to $105 and the 100 call and 105 call traded at their B-S values of $8.9597 and $6.0162, respectively? What would be the portfolio's profit or loss if the price of the XYZ stock decreased to $95 and the 100 call and 105 call traded at their B-S values of $3.2890 and $1.8133, respectively? Are your results consistent with your answer to part (d)?

COMPUTER PROBLEMS

1. Using the B-S OPM computer program, show the profit and stock price relation graphically and in a table for a diagonal time spread formed by going short in a July 60 call and long in an October 50 call. Assume the July call expires 90 days from the present, there is 90 days between the expiration of the July call and the October call, the current stock price is $50, $\sigma = .5$, the

risk-free rate is 6%, the possible stock prices at the July expiration are 30, 35, 40, 45, 50, 55, 60, 65, 70, 75, and 80, and both calls are currently priced equal to their B-S values.

2. Assume: $S_0 = \$50$, $\sigma = .5$, $X = \$50$, $R = 5\%$, and $T = .5$. Using the B-S computer program, and assuming all call and put options equal their B-S values, evaluate the profit and stock price relations at $S_t = 35, 40, 45, 50, 55, 60$ and 65, for holding periods of one month, three months, and six months for the following strategies:

- Straddle purchase
- Straddle sale
- Covered call write
- Covered put write
- Naked call write
- Naked put write

PART III

Nonstock
Options

CHAPTER 9

Stock Index and Debt Options

9.1 INTRODUCTION

Since the early 1980s, the financial markets have seen a proliferation of option securities. Innovations include different stock index options, various interest rate options, options on a number of currencies, and options on futures contracts. In this chapter, we begin our analysis of these nonstock options by examining the markets, strategies, and pricing relationships of index and debt options. In Chapter 10, we will continue the analysis by examining foreign currency options, and in Chapter 11 we will explore the option features of corporate securities. Options on futures contracts will be delineated in Chapter 16, after we've examined futures contracts in Chapters 12–15.

9.2 STOCK INDEX OPTIONS*

9.2.1 Market

Trading in stock index options began in March 1983, when the CBOE introduced an option on the Standard and Poor's 100 index (SP 100). Because of its hedging uses by institutional investors, this option (often referred to by its ticker symbol as the OEX option) quickly became one of the most highly traded options, with an annual volume exceeding the total volume of all CBOE listed stock options.

---

*See Appendix F for a description of how various stock indices are constructed.

273

In late April 1983, the American Stock Exchange began offering trading on an option on the Major Market Index (MMI), an index similar to the Dow Jones Industrial Average (DJIA). The introduction of the AMEX's option soon was followed by the New York Stock Exchange's listing of the NYSE stock index option and the Philadelphia exchange's Value Line index option (index of 1700 stocks) and the National Over-the-Counter index option (index of 100 OTC stocks).

Each of these stock indices is constructed so the rate of change in the index correlates over time with the rate of change in the average stock comprising the overall market the index represents. These are referred to as *broad-based* indices. Options also are traded on indices constructed for specific sectors; these are called *narrow-based* indices. As shown in Table 9.2-1, narrow-based indices include the Gold/Silver index (index of seven mining stocks), Financial News Composite index (30 blue-chip stocks), Utilities index (20 electric utilities stocks), Oil index (150 oil stocks), Computer Technologies index (30 computer stocks), and Institutional index (75 stocks commonly held by institutional investors). The rate of change in each of these indices, in turn, is designed to reflect the rate of change of the stocks that make up the particular sector.

9.2.2   Stock Index Options Defined

Theoretically, an index option can be thought of as an option to buy (call) or sell (put) a portfolio of stocks comprising the index, in their correct proportions. Unlike stock options, index options have a *cash settlement feature*. When such an option is exercised, the assigned writer pays the exercising holder the difference between the exercise price and the spot index at the close of trading on the exercising day. Thus, an index option is viewed more correctly as an option giving the holder the right to purchase (call) or sell (put) cash at a specific exercise price.

Specifically, a *call option on a stock index* gives the holder the right to purchase an amount of cash equal to the closing spot index (S_t) on the exercising day at the call's exercise price. To settle, the exercising holder receives a cash settlement of $S_t - X$ from the assigned writer.

For example, a May 350 SP 100 call gives the holder the right to buy cash equal to the closing spot index on the exercising day for $350 (as discussed later, there also is a multiplier). If the holder exercises when the spot index is 360, she in effect

TABLE 9.2-1

Index Options			
BROAD-BASED INDICES		**NARROW-BASED INDICES**	
INDEX	EXCHANGE	INDEX	EXCHANGE
SP 100	CBOE	Gold/Silver Index	PHLX
SP 500	CBOE	Utilities Index	PHLX
Major Market Index (MMI)	AMEX	Institutional Index	AMEX
		Oil Index	AMEX
NYSE Composite	NYSE	Computer Technology Index	AMEX
National OTC Index	PHLX	Financial News Composite Index	PSE
Value Line Index	PHLX		

is exercising the right to buy $360 of cash for $X = \$350$. With cash settlement, the assigned writer simply pays the holder $10.

The put option on a stock index, on the other hand, gives the holder the right to sell cash equal to the spot index value. That is, a **put option on a stock index** gives the holder the right to sell cash equal to the closing spot index on the exercising date at the put's exercise price. To settle, the exercising holder receives a cash settlement amount of $X - S_t$ from the assigned writer. Thus, the holder of a May 350 SP 100 put who exercises the put when the spot index is at 340 could view exercising as the equivalent to selling $340 cash to the assigned writer for $350. The writer would settle by paying the holder $X - S_t = \$10$.

9.2.3 Characteristics of Index Options

The cash settlement feature of index options is one characteristic that differentiates them from stock options. Several other differentiating features of index options should be noted.

First, the size of an index option is equal to a multiple of the index value. The SP 100 and SP 500 index options, for example, have contract multiples of $100. Thus, the actual exercise price on the preceding May 350 put contract on the SP 100 is $(350)(\$100) = \$35,000$.

Second, the expiration features on many index options are similar to stock options, with most expiring on the third Friday of the expiration month. However, some index options, like the SP 100, have a shorter expiration cycle, consisting of the current month, the next month, and third month from the present. Also, while most index options are American, several exceptions exist. For example, the SP 500 index option and the Financial News Composite index are both European.

Third, index options have an **end-of-the-day exercise feature**. When an index option is exercised, the closing value of the spot index on the exercising day is used to determine the cash settlement. Since the spot index is computed continuously throughout the day, it is possible for a holder to exercise an in-the-money call early in the day, only to have it closed at the end of the day out of the money (in such a case the holder pays the writer the difference between X and S_t). Thus, an index option holder should wait until late in the day before giving his exercise notice. The assigned writer, in turn, is notified of the option assignment on the subsequent business day, at which time she is required to pay the difference between the exercise price and the closing index price.

Fourth, unlike stock options, hedging index options is not as simple as buying or selling short the underlying stock. This is because the underlying security in an index option is a portfolio. To construct an exact long hedge with the SP 100 would require both the simultaneous purchase of the index's 100 stocks, in their correct proportions, and the correct reinvestment of each stock's dividends for the option period. In practice, many hedgers and arbitrageurs form smaller proxy portfolios, with the stock allocations determined so as to maximize the correlation between the returns of the proxy portfolio and the spot index.

Fifth, the tax treatment on index option positions differs from that on stock options, in that all realized and unrealized gains on index options that occur during the year are subject to taxes, and all realized and unrealized losses occurring during the year can offset an investor's capital gains.

EXHIBIT 9.2-1

Index Option Quotes

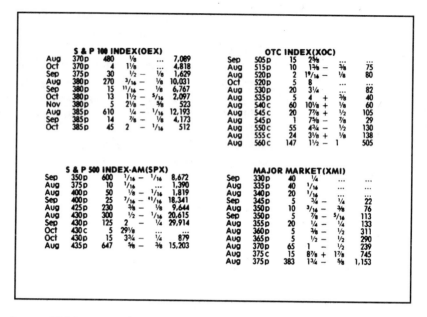

SOURCE: *Wall Street Journal*, March 31, 1994

EXHIBIT 9.2-2

Profit and Spot Index Relation

350 SP 100 Call
Purchased at 12

SPOT INDEX S_T	PROFIT
320	− $1200
330	− 1200
340	− 1200
350	− 1200
360	− 200
362	0
370	800
380	1800
390	2800

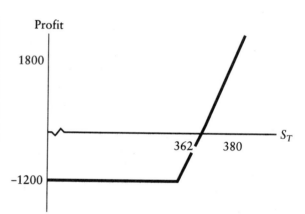

EXHIBIT 9.2-3

Profit and Spot Index Relation

350 SP 100 Put
Purchased at 1⅝

SPOT INDEX S_T	PROFIT
320	$2837.5
330	1837.5
340	837.5
348.375	0
350	− 162.5
360	− 162.5
370	− 162.5
380	− 162.5
390	− 162.5

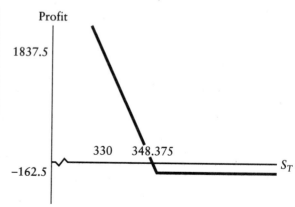

Finally, the margin requirements for index options are similar to those for stock options, except for covered write positions, which have the same margin requirements as naked index option positions.

9.2.4 Option Quotes and Fundamental Strategies

In Exhibit 9.2-1, several stock index option contracts are shown as they appear in the *Wall Street Journal* (WSJ). The quoted option premiums appearing in the WSJ are stated in points, with each point equal to $100. Thus, a May 350 SP 100 call priced at 12 costs $1200. Exhibit 9.2-2 shows the profit and spot index (S) relation for the 350 SP 100 call, when the option is assumed to be closed at expiration (T) at its intrinsic value. Exhibit 9.2-3 shows the profit and spot index relation for the May 350 SP 100 put trading initially at 1⅝ points.

9.3 HEDGING WITH INDEX OPTIONS

Part of the reason for the popularity of stock index options is that they can be used as a hedging tool by stock portfolio managers. To illustrate, consider the case of a stock portfolio manager who in January feels that he may be required to liquidate his stock portfolio in May and would like to ensure a minimum value of the portfolio for the latter part of that month. Assume that the portfolio currently is worth $1.5 million, is well-diversified (no unsystematic risk), is perfectly correlated with the SP 100, and has a beta (β) of 1. Also assume the current spot SP 100 index is at 300. To ensure a minimum portfolio value, the manager could hedge the portfolio by buying a May put option on the SP 100. If a May 300 SP 100 put is selling at 5, the manager would need to buy $N_p = 50$ puts at a total cost of $(50)(5)(\$100) = \$25,000$ to hedge the portfolio. That is:

$$N_p = \frac{\$1,500,000}{(300)(\$100)} = 50.$$

As shown in Table 9.3-1, if the market (as measured by the SP 100 spot) is 300 or less at expiration, the value of the hedged portfolio (stock portfolio value plus put profit) would be $1,475,000; if the market is above 300, the value of the hedged portfolio would increase as the market rises. In this example the hedged portfolio is able to capture 98% of the portfolio value if it is not hedged. The percentage of the hedged portfolio value relative to the unhedged portfolio value when the market increases is referred to as the *upside capture*. An upside capture of 98% implies that the opportunity costs of the hedge is a 2% loss in capital gains if the market increases. Thus, by purchasing index puts, the portfolio manager in this example can attain portfolio insurance (downside protection), with the possibility of capital gains equal to 98% of the increase in the unhedged portfolio value if the market rises.

This example is an illustration of portfolio insurance in which an index put option is used to ensure the minimum value of a portfolio. Another portfolio insurance strategy that can be employed that replicates the portfolio and index

TABLE 9.3-1

					Stock Portfolio Hedged with Puts
(1)	(2)	(3)	(4)	(5)	(6)
SP 100 SPOT INDEX S_T	PROPORTIONAL CHANGE IN THE PORTFOLIO VALUE: $g = \frac{S_T - 300}{300}$	PORTFOLIO VALUE $\$1.5M(1 + g)$	PUT PROFIT*	HEDGED PORTFOLIO VALUE (3) + (4)	UPSIDE CAPTURE (5)/(3)
210	$-$ .3	$1,050,000	$425,000	$1,475,000	—
240	$-$ .2	1,200,000	275,000	1,475,000	—
270	$-$ .1	1,350,000	125,000	1,475,000	—
300	0	1,500,000	$-$ 25,000	1,475,000	.983
330	.1	1,650,000	$-$ 25,000	1,625,000	.985
360	.2	1,800,000	$-$ 25,000	1,775,000	.986
390	.3	1,950,000	$-$ 25,000	1,925,000	.987

*Put profit $= 50 \ Max[(\$100)(300 - S_T), 0] - (50)(5)(\$100)$

strategy consists of an index call option and a riskless bond. This portfolio insurance strategy is referred to as a *fiduciary call* or a **call/Treasury-bill insurance strategy**. The equivalence between the positions is predicated on the put-call parity model. That is:

$$S_0 + P_0 = PV(X) + C_0.$$

In terms of our example, suppose the annual rate of return on a riskless pure discount bond is 6% and the time period between January and the May option's expiration is 120 days. By the put-call parity model, the equilibrium price of a May 300 call option on the SP 100 is 10.69237:

$$C_0 = S_0 + P_0 - PV(X)$$

$$C_0 = 300 + 5 - \frac{300}{(1.06)^{120/365}} = 10.69237.$$

For the portfolio manager to attain the same minimum portfolio value with a fiduciary call as he did with an index put, the manager would need to (1) liquidate the $1.5 million portfolio in January, (2) invest the proceeds in pure discount bonds for 120 days at 6%, and (3) purchase $N_c = \$1,500,000/(\$100)(300) = 50$ May 300 call options at 10.69237 per call. As shown in Table 9.3-2, this fiduciary call strategy yields approximately the same portfolio values per index value as the put and portfolio strategy.

In addition to protecting the value of a portfolio, index call options also can be used to hedge future stock portfolio purchases. For example, suppose our portfolio manager was anticipating a cash inflow of over $1.5 million in May, which he planned to invest in a well-diversified portfolio with a β of 1 that was currently worth $1.5 million. If the spot SP 100 is at 300, then the portfolio manager could view the investment as one of buying $1,500,000/300 = 5000 hypothetical shares of the SP 100 at $300 per share. Suppose the manager was fearful of a bull market's

TABLE 9.3-2

	Fiduciary Call		
(1) SP 100 SPOT INDEX S_T	(2) CALL PROFIT*	(3) VALUE OF BOND†	(4) INVESTMENT VALUE (2) + (3)
210	− $53,462	$1,529,012	$1,475,550
240	− 53,462	1,529,012	1,475,550
270	− 53,462	1,529,012	1,475,550
300	− 53,462	1,529,012	1,475,550
330	96,538	1,529,012	1,625,550
360	246,538	1,529,012	1,775,550
390	396,538	1,529,012	1,925,550

*Call Profit = 50 Max[($100)($S_T$ − 300), 0] − 50(10.69237)($100)
†Bond Value = ($1,500,00)(1.06)$^{120/365}$

TABLE 9.3-3

	Value of Stock Portfolio Purchased with $1.5M Cash Inflow and Call Profit			
(1) SP 100 SPOT INDEX	(2) CASH INFLOW	(3) CALL PROFIT*	(4) NUMBER OF HYPOTHETICAL INDEX SHARES: [(2) + (3)]/(1)	(5) PORTFOLIO VALUE (4) × (1)
210	$1,500,000	− $53,462	6888.2762	$1,446,538
240	1,500,000	− 53,462	6027.2417	1,446,538
270	1,500,000	− 53,462	5357.5481	1,446,538
300	1,500,000	− 53,462	4821.7933	1,446,538
330	1,500,000	96,538	4837.9939	1,596,538
360	1,500,000	246,538	4851.4944	1,746,538
390	1,500,000	396,538	4862.9179	1,896,538

*Call profit = 50($100)[Max($S_T$ − 300, 0)] − (50)($100)(10.69237)

pushing stock prices up, which in turn would limit the number of shares he could purchase. To hedge against this, the manager could lock in a minimum number of hypothetical index shares by purchasing 50 May 300 SP 100 index calls at 10.69237. As shown in Table 9.3-3, if the spot index is 300 or higher at expiration, the manager will be able to purchase between 4822 and 4863 hypothetical shares from his $1.5M inflow plus the profit from the calls. This equates to portfolios worth approximately $1.447M, $1.597M, $1.747M, and $1.897M when the market is at 300, 330, 360, and 390, respectively. On the other hand, if the index is 300 or less, the manager will be able to buy more hypothetical shares with the $1.5M inflow, but will incur a $53,462 loss from the calls, yielding a fixed portfolio value of $1,446,538.

Locking in stock portfolios values with call and puts represents two uses of stock index options. In Chapter 13, we will explore some of the uses of stock index futures. As we will see, many of the hedging applications using futures also hold for index options.

9.4 PRICING INDEX OPTIONS

In general, the arbitrage pricing relationships and models governing stock options that were delineated in Chapters 4 through 8 can be extended to establish the price relationships for index options. However, in extending stock option pricing relationships to index options, three features unique to index options need special consideration: the cash settlement clause, the portfolio underlying the option, and the dividends from the stocks making up the index portfolio.

9.4.1 Cash Settlement

Many of the arbitrage strategies governing the price relationships for stock options involve taking an actual position in the underlying stock. Recall, for example, the arbitrage strategy used when an American call option on a stock is priced below its intrinsic value: The strategy required purchasing the call and the stock and exercising the option. As previously noted, when an index option is exercised, the assigned writer pays the exercising holder cash equal to the difference between the closing-day spot index price and the exercise price. Because of this cash settlement feature, the arbitrage strategy for index options priced below their intrinsic values does not require taking an actual position in the underlying security. For example, if a 225 SP 100 call was trading at 4½ at the close of trading and the closing spot index was at 230, then an arbitrageur could buy the call contract for $450, then exercise to receive a $500 cash settlement from the assigned writer.

Note that the end-of-the-day exercise rule associated with index options implies that the arbitrage strategy holds only for closing index prices. That is, arbitrageurs can be assured of an arbitrage profit if the price of an index option is below its intrinsic value as determined by the closing index price.

9.4.2 Spot Portfolios

Determining the equilibrium value of an index option by the put-call parity model, the BOPM, and the B-S option pricing models requires defining arbitrage strategies involving positions in the underlying portfolio. As already indicated, because of the cost of and difficulties in constructing a portfolio that replicates the spot index exactly, many arbitrageurs instead form proxy portfolios. A proxy portfolio could be built with a small number of securities whose allocations in the portfolio are determined so as to maximize the correlation between the portfolio's returns and the spot indices'. A proxy portfolio also might be formed with a highly diversified mutual fund.

Whether it is a mutual fund or a smaller-sized, highly correlated portfolio, the proxy portfolio can be viewed as a position in the index. For example, as noted earlier, if the spot SP 100 was at 300, a highly diversified mutual fund currently valued at $1.5 million can be thought of as equivalent to a hypothetical spot portfolio consisting of $N_0 = 5000$ hypothetical shares of the index, priced at $S_0 = \$300$ per index share. Such a portfolio, in turn, could be used to price index options and determine arbitrage strategies when the index option is mispriced.

To illustrate the relationship between index pricing and proxy portfolios, consider the pricing of an index call option using the single-period BOPM. In terms of the BOPM, the equilibrium price of the index call is equal to the value of a replicating portfolio consisting of H_0^* hypothetical shares of the spot index, partially financed by borrowing B_0^* dollars. As shown in Exhibit 9.4-1, if $u = 1.0227$, $d = .9778$, $R_f = .005$, and the current spot SP 100 index is $S_0 = 310$, then the equilibrium price of a 305 SP 100 call option would be $7.26. In this case, the replicating portfolio would consist of $H_0^* = .8648$ hypothetical shares of the index, partially financed by borrowing $B_0^* = \$260.829$ (for simplicity, we are excluding the $100 multiple).

If the market price of the index call did not equal $7.26, an arbitrage portfolio could be formed by taking a position in the call and an opposite position in the replicating portfolio. In practice, the .8648 index shares priced at $S_0 = 310$ would be equivalent to buying $(.8648)(310) = \$268.088$ worth of a diversified proxy portfolio and borrowing $B_0^* = \$260.829$.

EXHIBIT 9.4-1

Pricing 305 SP 100 Call with Single-Period BOPM

$u = 1.0227, d = .9778,$
$R_f = .005, X = 305,$ Spot
SP 100 Price $= S_0 = 310$

$$S_u = uS_0 = 1.0227(310) = 317.037$$
$$C_u = \text{Max}[317.037 - 305, 0] = 12.037$$

$$S_0 = 310$$
$$C_0 = 7.259$$

$$S_d = dS_0 = .9778(310) = 303.118$$
$$C_d = \text{Max}[303.118 - 305, 0] = 0$$

$$C_0^* = H_0^* S_0 - B_0^*$$
$$C_0^* = .8648(310) - 260.829 = 7.26$$

where:

$$H_0^* = \frac{C_u - C_d}{S_u - S_d} = \frac{12.037 - 0}{317.037 - 303.118} = .8648$$

$$B_0^* = \frac{C_u(S_d) - C_d(S_u)}{r_f[S_u - S_d]} = \frac{12.037(303.118) - (0)(317.037)}{1.005(317.037 - 303.118)} = 260.829$$

or

$$C_0^* = \frac{1}{1.005}[pC_u + (1 - p)C_d]$$

$$C_0^* = \frac{1}{1.005}[.6058(12.037) + (.3942)(0)] = 7.26$$

where:

$$p = \frac{r_f - d}{u - d} = \frac{1.005 - .9778}{1.0227 - .9778} = .6058.$$

It should be kept in mind that for the more realistic multiple-period case, arbitrageurs would need to readjust their proxy portfolios each period (see end-of-the-chapter Problems and Questions).* With frequent revisions, arbitrageurs may find it advantageous to use a proxy portfolio consisting of only a few stocks or a mutual fund that is both highly correlated with the spot index and liquid. Also, since futures contracts are traded on some optioned indices, arbitrageurs alternatively could take positions in stock index futures instead of proxy spot portfolios. The relationship between options and futures is examined in Chapter 16.

9.4.3   Dividend Adjustments

As discussed in Chapter 6, stock options are not dividend-protected. As a result, when the underlying stock pays a dividend, the option pricing models must be adjusted to account for the decrease in call prices or the increase in put prices that can occur on ex-dividend dates; and in the case of American call options, the models need to be adjusted to account for the early exercise premium. For options on individual stocks, the amount of the dividend and the ex-dividend date often can be predicted with some degree of accuracy. For a stock index option, though, the stocks comprising the index portfolio may pay dividends such that the index portfolio approaches paying dividends continuously during the period. These dividends, in turn, represent part of the return earned on the replicating portfolio. To incorporate dividends into the discrete BOPM, the total dividend payments that are expected to accrue during the period (D_T), expressed as a proportion of the number of hypothetical index shares (N_0), need to be subtracted from the index price at each node, similar to the way dividend adjustments were made in Chapter 6.

Note, when dividend payments are continuous or approximate a continuous stream, they often are expressed in terms of an annual dividend yield (Ψ); that is, annual dividends per share expressed as a proportion of the current index price: Ψ = (annual dividend/N_0)/S_0. Thus, if the spot index is 150, then an index with annual dividend yield of 5% would pay approximately ΨS_0 = .05(150) = \$7.50 in annual dividends per share. If we are pricing a six-month option with the BOPM, then the dividends for the total period would be \$3.75; if we divide the total period into six one-month periods, then the subperiod dividends would be \$0.625. Thus, we would subtract \$0.625 from index price at each node in determining the BOPM's call value for this case.

Options on assets that generate a continuous flow of benefits, such as an index option, are referred to as *continuous-leakage options*. If the underlying asset on the options engenders benefits only discretely, such as an option on a stock making one dividend payment during the period, the option is referred to as a *discrete-leakage option*. If the option's underlying asset generates no benefits, it is called a *zero-leakage option*.

---

*An alternative arbitrage portfolio could be formed by taking a position consisting of one share of the spot portfolio and a proportion of calls (instead of one call and a proportion of the spot portfolio). This portfolio would be easier to adjust each period. For details, see Copeland and Weston (1983): 245–253.

9.4.4 Black-Scholes Option Pricing Model Applied to European Stock Index Options

If the dividend payments on the index portfolio approximate a continuous stream, the continuous dividend-adjusted B-S model can be used to determine the equilibrium price of a European index option (see Section 7.4.2). In this case, instead of the spot index (S_0), a dividend-adjusted spot index (S_d) is used in which:

$$S_d = S_0 e^{-\Psi T}, \qquad (9.4\text{-}1)$$

where:

Ψ = annual dividends per index share paid by all stocks comprising the index (properly weighted) divided by the current index.

To illustrate, suppose the current SP 100 spot index is at 300, has a variability of $\sigma = .2$ and an annual dividend yield of $\Psi = .05$, and the annual risk-free rate is 5%. Using the dividend-adjusted B-S model, the equilibrium price of a 300 SP 100 call expiring in three months would be 14.77. That is:

$$S_d = S_0 e^{-\Psi T} = 305 e^{-(.05)(.25)} = 301.23$$

$$d_1 = \frac{\log_e(S_d/X) + (R + .5\sigma^2)T}{\sigma\sqrt{T}}$$

$$d_1 = \frac{\log_e(306.149/305) + [.05 + .5(.04)].25}{.2\sqrt{.25}} = .05$$

$$d_2 = d_1 - \sigma\sqrt{T} = .2126 - .2\sqrt{.25} = -.05$$

$$N(.2126) = .58407 \quad \text{and} \quad N(.1126) = .5446$$

$$C_0^* = S_d N(d_1) - X e^{-RT} N(d_2)$$

$$C_0^* = (306.149)(.58407) - 305 e^{-(.05)(.25)}(.5446) = 12.01.$$

Given the equilibrium price of a call, the value of a corresponding European put can be obtained by using the put-call parity model. Thus, the price of a 305 European SP 100 put expiring in three months would be 9.83:

$$P_0^* = PV(X) - S_d + C_0^*$$

$$P_0^* = \frac{305}{e^{(.05)(.25)}} - 306.149 + 14.77 = 8.22.$$

9.4.5 American Index Options

While some index options are European (e.g., SP 500 and the Financial News Composite index), most are American. Recall that in Chapter 7 we described the pseudo-American OPM to price American call options on dividend-paying stocks. Also recall, though, that this model requires identification of the likely dates for early exercise, which for a stock call option was the stock's ex-dividend date. For index options in which continuous dividend payments and ex-dividend dates may exist, an identifiable early-exercise reference date may be difficult to specify. Consequently, the pseudo-American model may not be applicable in pricing American index options. However, for the early exercise of an index call to be profitable, the dividend yield has to be relatively large (exceeding at least the risk-free rate). Historically, dividend yields on stock indices are considerably less than the rates on risk-free securities. Thus, an early-exercise premium associated with American index call options may be relatively small. As a result, the continuous dividend-adjusted B-S OPM described earlier or the European BOPM could be used to estimate the price of an American index call option.

In contrast to index calls, the early exercise of an American put is advantageous if the dividend yield is less than the risk-free rate and the put is deep in the money. Thus, chances are better that an American index put could be exercised earlier than could an American index call. Instead of the B-S OPM, the American BOPM (in which each put price is constrained to be either the maximum of the European value, as determined by the BOPM, or its intrinsic value) could be used, or the Barone-Adesi and Whaley (BAW) model described in Appendix 7C could be used to estimate the price of an American put or call index option.

9.5 PORTFOLIO INSURANCE

As described in Section 9.3, portfolio insurance is an investment strategy designed to ensure that a minimum portfolio value is attained while at the same time leaving the chance for gains in value to occur if certain states are realized. For a stock portfolio, the simplest strategy to ensure a minimum value is to buy put options on stock indices or to construct a fiduciary call. Some institutional investors, though, may find it difficult to use either of these strategies because the position limits on index options often are too small to allow them to hedge their large-size portfolios properly, and/or the time period they want for protection often exceeds the put's expiration period. As a result, portfolio managers can use more dynamic strategies. For example, instead of using options, managers could form portfolios consisting of a stock portfolio and a risk-free security, then use the binomial model framework to adjust the portfolio each period to attain end-of-the-period objectives. In this section we examine *dynamic portfolio insurance* strategies using stock indices and stock-and-bond portfolios.

9.5.1 Dynamic Portfolio Insurance Strategy Using Index Puts

To illustrate the construction of a dynamic portfolio insurance strategy, let us first consider the case of a stock portfolio hedged with index put options using a binomial framework. In this case, assume a portfolio manager wants insurance for a diversified $2.5 million stock portfolio. Suppose the manager wants to form a portfolio insurance policy and divides the total period in which she wants insurance into two subperiods, estimating the proportional period increase and decrease for the spot index to be $u = 1.1$ and $d = 1/1.1$. Also, assume the current spot index is at 150, the portfolio pays no dividends during the period, and the rate on a risk-free bond is 5% per subperiod. Table 9.5-1 shows the possible values of the portfolio and the spot index given the manager's estimated u and d values.

Given the three possible portfolio values at the end of period 2, suppose the manager would like a minimum portfolio value of at least $2.5 million at the end of the period, with the possibility of a portfolio worth $3.025 million if the spot index reaches 181.5. To achieve these dual objectives, suppose the manager decides to purchase index put options with a 150 exercise price and expiring at the end of period 2. Table 9.5-2 shows the possible values of this put option at the end of periods 1 and 2 using the BOPM for put options (for simplicity, we will disregard the $100 multiplier).

To ensure the $2.5 million portfolio, the manager would need to purchase N_0 = $2,500,000/150 = 16,667 stock index puts. As shown in Table 9.5-3, if the spot index increases to 165 at the end of period 1, then the puts would be worthless but the stock would be worth $2.75 million, and one period later the stock portfolio would be worth either $3.025 million or $2.5 million. On the other hand, if the index decreases to 136.3636, the stock portfolio would be worth only $2.2727 million but the puts would be worth $0.108 million, yielding an insured portfolio worth $2.381 million. The next period the insured portfolio would be worth $2.5 million at either index value (150 or 123.97). Note: At the end of period 1, the manager could have liquidated the portfolio and put options when the index was at 136.3636 and invested the proceeds of $2.381 million in a risk-free security at 5%. Doing this also would have yielded $2.5 million in the next period, regardless of the index values.

TABLE 9.5-1	Portfolio and Spot Index (S)		
$u = 1.1, d = 1/1.1, n = 2$			
			Portfolio = $3.025M $S_{uu} = 181.5$
		Portfolio = $2.75M $S_u = 165$	
Portfolio = $2.5M $S_0 = 150$			Portfolio = $2.5M $S_{ud} = 150$
		Portfolio = $2.2727M $S_d = 136.3636$	
			Portfolio = $2.066M $S_{dd} = 123.97$
0		1	2

TABLE 9.5-2

		BOPM for Stock Index Puts		
		$u = 1.1, d = 1/1.1, R_f = .05, X = 150, p = (r_f - d)/(u - d), p = .738$		

$$P_{uu} = \text{Max}[X - S_{uu}, 0]$$
$$P_{uu} = \text{Max}[150 - 181.5, 0] = 0$$

$$P_u = \frac{(1 - p)P_{ud} + pP_{dd}}{r_f}$$
$$P_u = \frac{.262(0) + .738(0)}{1.05} = 0$$

$$P_0 = \frac{(1 - p)P_d + pP_u}{r_f}$$
$$P_0 = \frac{.262(6.49) + .738(0)}{1.05} = 1.619$$

$$P_{ud} = \text{Max}[X - S_{ud}, 0]$$
$$P_{ud} = \text{Max}[150 - 150, 0] = 0$$

$$P_d = \frac{(1 - p)P_{dd} + pP_{ud}}{r_f}$$
$$P_d = \frac{.262(26.03) + .738(0)}{1.05} = 6.49$$

$$P_{dd} = \text{Max}[X - S_{dd}, 0]$$
$$P_{dd} = \text{Max}[150 - 123.97] = 26.03$$

0	1	2

9.5.2 Dynamic Portfolio Insurance Strategy Using Bonds

If the type of put needed to provide insurance is not available, or position limits and the size of the portfolio make it impossible to use index puts for insurance, the portfolio manager in our earlier case could obtain the same type of protection alternatively with a stock portfolio and an investment in a risk-free bond (I_0).

To determine the correct stock portfolio and bond investments, let us define the value of the manager's stock portfolio (V_0) in terms of hypothetical shares of the SP 500 (N_0) times the spot index price. Since the $2.5M portfolio is well diversified, it can be viewed as an investment in $N_0 = \$2,500,000/150 = 16,667$ hypothetical shares of the index, with each share worth $S_0 = \$150$ per share. That is:

$$V_0 = N_0 S_0$$

$$V_0 = (16,667)(\$150) = \$2.5M.$$

Using the BOPM framework, at the end of the first period this spot index portfolio would be worth either $2.75M or $2.2727M. That is:

$$V_u = N_0(uS_0) = (16,667)(\$165) = \$2.75M,$$

or

$$V_d = N_0(dS_0) = (16,667)(\$136.3636) = \$2.2727M.$$

TABLE 9.5-3

Portfolio Insurance Strategy Using Index Puts in BOPM Framework

		$S_{uu} = 181.5$ Portfolio = \$3.025M Puts = (16,667)(0) = 0 Insured portfolio = \$3.025M
	$S_u = 165$ Portfolio = \$2.75M Puts = (16,667)(0) = 0 Insured portfolio = \$2.75M	
$S_0 = 150$ Portfolio = \$2.5M Insurance: buy 16,667 Index puts with $X = 150$ at $P_0 = 1.619$		$S_{ud} = 150$ Portfolio = \$2.5M Puts = (16,667)(0) = 0 Insured portfolio = \$2.5M
	$S_d = 136.3636$ Portfolio = \$2.2727M Puts = (16,667)(\$6.49) = \$0.108M Insured portfolio = \$2.381M	
		$S_{dd} = 123.97$ Portfolio = \$2.066M Puts = (16,667)(\$26.03) = \$0.434M Insured portfolio = \$2.5M
0	1	2

Given the dual objectives of attaining at the end of period 2 a minimum \$2.5M stock portfolio value if the market stays the same or declines and a \$3.025M value if the market increases to 181.5, the manager needs to construct an insured portfolio consisting of the stock portfolio and the risk-free bond that at the end of period 1 would be worth $V_u = $ \$2.75 million if the index is at 165 and $V_d = $ \$2.5M/1.05 = \$2.381 million if the index is at 136.3636. This portfolio can be found by solving for the N_0^* and I_0^* where:

$$N_0(uS_0) + I_0 r_f = V_u \qquad (9.5\text{-}1)$$

$$N_0(dS_0) + I_0 r_f = V_d,$$

or in terms of the example:

$$N_0(165) + I_0(1.05) = \$2.75\text{M}$$

$$N_0(136.3636) + I_0(1.05) = \$2.381\text{M}.$$

Solving (9.5-1) simultaneously for N_0^* and I_0^* yields:

$$N_0^* = \frac{V_u - V_d}{S_0(u - d)} = \frac{\$2.75M - \$2.381M}{\$150(1.1 - .9091)} = 12,886 \text{ index shares}$$

$$I_0^* = \frac{u(V_d) - d(V_u)}{r_f(u - d)} = \frac{1.1(\$2.381M) - .9091(\$2.75M)}{1.05(1.1 - .9091)}$$

$$I_0^* = \$0.5940M.$$

Thus, to have the same type of portfolio insurance protection obtained with puts, the manager would need a stock portfolio that is the equivalent of an index portfolio consisting of $N_0^* = 12,886$ index shares; this index portfolio, in turn, would be equivalent to investing $(12,886)(\$150) = \$1.933M$ in a diversified portfolio. The manager also would need to invest $\$0.5940M$ in a risk-free bond. The total cost of the portfolio would be $\$2.527M$, which is equal to the value of the original $\$2.5$ million portfolio and the cost of buying protective puts: $(16,667)(\$1.619) = \$26,984$. As shown in Table 9.5-4, next period this insured portfolio would be worth either $\$2.75M$ (if the index is at 165) or $\$2.381M$ (if the index is at 136.3636). If it is worth $\$2.75$ million, then the manager could convert the insured portfolio to an all-stock portfolio, which be worth either $\$3.025$ million or $\$2.5$ million at the end of period 2. If the portfolio is worth $\$2.381M$, the manager then could convert the insured portfolio to risk-free bonds, which would be worth $\$2.5$ million at the end of the next period. Thus, using a

TABLE 9.5-4

Dynamic Portfolio Insurance Strategy Using Bonds

		$S_{uu} = 181.5$ Portfolio = $3.025M

	At $S_u = 165$:
	    $(165)(12,886) + \$0.5940M(1.05) = \$2.75M$,
	or
	    $(\$1.933M)(1.1) + \$0.5940M(1.05) = \$2.75M$
	Strategy: Convert to all-stock portfolio	

Stock portfolio: $N_0 S_0 = (12,886)(150) = \$1.933M$ Bond investment: $0.5940M		$S_{ud} = 150$ Portfolio = $2.5M

	At $S_d = 136.3636$:
	    $(136.3636)(12,886) + \$0.5940M(1.05) = \$2.381M$
	or
	    $(\$1.933M)(.9091) + \$0.5940(1.05) = \$2.381M$
	Strategy: Convert to all bonds	

		$S_{dd} = 129.97$ Portfolio = $2.5M
0	1	2

stock-and-bond portfolio with readjustments at the end of the first period, the manager can obtain the same portfolio protection provided by puts. Moreover, if the correct puts are not available or unattainable because of position limits, this dynamic put strategy with bonds represents a feasible alternative for attaining portfolio insurance. (In Chapter 13, we will show how this same portfolio insurance strategy can be replicated with stock index futures contracts.)

In practice, dynamic portfolio insurance strategies are constructed using a number of time periods, which require frequent revisions. The rules for portfolio revising or rebalancing vary from strategies that adjust the portfolio each week to those that rebalance only after the portfolio has changed by a certain percentage (a three-period portfolio insurance case is included as one of the end-of-the-chapter problems). In general, the management of a dynamic portfolio insurance strategy involves selling stock and investing in riskless securities after stock prices have fallen and buying stock and selling riskless securities after stock prices have increased.

9.6 DEBT OPTIONS*

Options on treasury debt securities were introduced in the early 1980s. Trading in such securities, however, has been very thin. Understanding the characteristics and uses of options on spot Treasury securities, though, is still helpful in developing an understanding of options on Treasury futures contracts and interest rate options, which are examined in Chapters 16 and 17.

A debt option gives the holder the right to buy (call) or sell (put) a debt security at a specific price on or before a specific date. Debt options include T-bill options (offered by AMEX), options on Eurodollar deposits (Chicago Mercantile Exchange), Treasury-note options (AMEX), and options on Treasury bonds (CBOE). In addition to Treasury options, options on other fixed-income securities also are available through dealers on the OTC market. These so-called dealer options often are written to meet specific hedging needs of institutional investors. As a result, they are not as marketable as listed Treasury options.

9.6.1   Options on Treasury Bills

The AMEX's T-bill option gives the holder the right to buy (call) or sell (put) a T-bill with a face value (F) of $1 million and maturity of 91 days at a given exercise price. The exercise price on the T-bill option is specified either in terms of an index price (IN_0) or an annual discount yield (R_D), where the index is equal to 100 minus the quoted discount yield. Given the quoted index or discount yield, the actual exercise price on the 91-day T-bill can be found via the following formula:

$$X = \frac{100 - (100 - IN_0)(90/360)}{100}(\$1,000,000).$$

---

*This section requires some knowledge of fixed-income securities. See Appendix E for an overview of fixed-income security analysis.

Thus, the June 90 T-bill call option gives the holder the right to buy a 91-day, $1 million T-bill at an exercise price of $X = \$975,000$. That is:

$$X = \frac{100 - (100 - 90)(90/360)}{100}(\$1,000,000) = \$975,000.$$

The exercise price is based on a 90-day maturity and on a 360-day year. If the 91-day T-bill is purchased on the call option, its implied rate or yield to maturity (YTM) needs to be computed using the 365-day calendar year and the actual maturity of 91 days. The implied YTM on the T-bill purchased on the June 90 T-bill call option, in turn, would be 10.69%:

$$\text{YTM} = \left(\frac{F}{X}\right)^{365/91} - 1$$

$$\text{YTM} = \left(\frac{\$1,000,000}{\$975,000}\right)^{365/91} - 1 = .1069.$$

The premiums on T-bill options are quoted in terms of annualized basis points (PT). The actual option price is found with the following formula:

$$\text{Option premium} = \left(\frac{PT}{100}\right)\left(\frac{90}{360}\right)(\$1,000,000).$$

Thus, the actual price of the June 90 T-bill call quoted at .92 point is $2300:

$$C_0 = \left(\frac{.92}{100}\right)\left(\frac{90}{360}\right)(\$1,000,000) = \$2300.$$

9.6.2   Uses of Treasury-Bill Options

Speculation
A T-bill option can be used to speculate on movements in short-term interest rates. For example, suppose a speculator believes the Federal Reserve System will lower short-term interest rates in the near future to stimulate the economy. Since lower T-bill rates would imply greater T-bill prices, the speculator could profit (if his expectation is correct) by taking a long position in a T-bill call. Table 9.6-1 shows the profit and index price [and discount yield (R_D)] relation at expiration from closing a June 90 T-bill call purchased at .92. As shown, if rates as measured by R_D are 10% or higher at expiration, then the speculator would lose the premium of $2300; if $R_D = 9.08\%$, then the speculator breaks even; if rates are lower than 9.08%, then the speculator profits.

In contrast, if a speculator believes that short-term interest rates are going to increase in the near future, then he should take a long position in a T-bill put option. Table 9.6-2 shows the profit and index (and R_D) relation at expiration from closing a long position in a June 90 T-bill put purchased at .92.

Hedging
In addition to using T-bill options to speculate on short-term interest rate movements, these options also can be used by money managers as a hedging tool to lock in either a maximum interest rate on an anticipated short-term debt obligation or the minimum rate on a future short-term investment.

TABLE 9.6-1

Profit and Interest Rate Relation at Expiration from Closing a Long June 90 T-Bill Call Position Purchased at .92

Spot R_D	Spot Index $100 - R_D$	Spot Price of T-Bill (S_T)	Call Profit
20%	80	$950,000	- $2,300
15	85	962,500	- 2,300
10	90	975,000	- 2,300
9.08	90.92	977,300	0
8	92	980,000	2,700
5	95	987,500	10,200

$$S_T = \frac{[100 - R_D(90/360)](\$1,000,000)}{100}$$

$$X = \frac{[100 - (100 - 90)(90/360)](\$1,000,000)}{100} = \$975,000$$

$$C_0 = \left(\frac{.92}{100}\right)\left(\frac{90}{360}\right)(\$1,000,000) = \$2300$$

$$\text{Profit} = \text{Max}[S_T - X, 0] - C_0$$

TABLE 9.6-2

Profit and Interest Rate Relation at Expiration from Closing a Long June 90 T-Bill Put Position Purchased at .92

Spot R_D	Spot Index $100 - R_D$	Spot Price of T-Bill (S_T)	Put Profit
20%	80	$950,000	$ 22,700
15	85	962,500	10,200
10.92	89.08	972,700	0
10	90	975,000	- 2,300
8	92	980,000	- 2,300
5	95	987,500	- 2,300

$$S_T = \frac{[100 - R_D(90/360)](\$1,000,000)}{100}$$

$$X = \frac{[100 - (100 - 90)(90/360)](\$1,000,000)}{100} = \$975,000$$

$$P_0 = \left(\frac{.92}{100}\right)\left(\frac{90}{360}\right)(\$1,000,000) = \$2300$$

$$\text{Profit} = \text{Max}[X - S_T, 0] - P_0$$

To illustrate, consider the case of a corporate treasurer who in June anticipates a cash inflow of over $975,000 in September (the company's peak selling period). Suppose the treasurer plans to invest the September funds in a 91-day T-bill. Assume that in June, 91-day T-bills are trading at a spot index of 90 ($S_0 = \$975,000$), implying a YTM of 10.69% [that is, YTM $= (\$1,000,000/\$975,000)^{(365/91)} - 1 = .1069$]. Suppose the treasurer would like to earn a minimum rate on her September investment that is only marginally below the current T-bill YTM of 10.69%, with the possibility of higher yields if short-term rates increase. To achieve these objectives, the treasurer could take a long position in September T-bill call options. For example, suppose the treasurer buys one September 90 T-bill call option at .5 ($X = \$975,000$, $C_0 = \$1250$) in June, with plans to close the call at expiration at its intrinsic value and then to purchase a spot T-bill. Table 9.6-3 shows the effective investment expenditures at expiration (costs of the T-bill minus the profit of the T-bill call) and the hedged YTM earned from those expenditures [YTM = $(F/\text{effective investment})^{(365/91)}$]. As shown, by hedging with the T-bill call, the treasurer is able to obtain at least a 10.12% YTM, with the potential to earn higher returns if interest rates on T-bills increase.

If, instead of investing funds in the future, the treasurer was planning to borrow short-term funds in anticipation of a future cash deficiency, then she could take a long position in a T-bill put. The long put position would, in turn, enable the treasurer to obtain a maximum hedged borrowing rate with the possibility of lower borrowing rates if short-term rates decline (this case is included as one of the end-of-the-chapter problems).

To summarize, T-bill options provide a useful hedging tool for short-term positions. As such, they can be used by corporate treasurers, dealers, and financial institutions in managing short-term assets and liabilities. In practice, though, using such options as a hedging tool is somewhat more complex than the examples we presented. Problems often arise because the underlying security on the option and the security to be hedged are not identical, the expiration on the option and the

TABLE 9.6-3

	Hedging the Cost of a September T-Bill Purchase with a September T-Bill Call				
(1) SPOT R_D	(2) SPOT PRICE OF 91-DAY T-BILL S_T	(3) PROFIT ON T-BILL CALL	(4) EFFECTIVE COSTS (2) − (3)	(5) HEDGED YTM	(6) YTM WITHOUT HEDGE
7%	$982,500	$6250	$976,250	.1012	.0734
8	980,000	3750	976,250	.1012	.0844
9	977,500	1250	976,250	.1012	.0956
10	975,000	− 1250	976,250	.1012	.1069
11	972,500	− 1250	973,750	.1126	.1183
12	970,000	− 1250	971,250	.1241	.1299
13	967,500	− 1250	968,750	.1358	.1417

$$S_T = \frac{[100 - R_D(90/360)](\$1,000,000)}{100}$$

$$X = \frac{[100 - (100 - 90)(90/360)](\$1,000,000)}{100} = \$975,000$$

$$C_0 = \left(\frac{.5}{100}\right)\left(\frac{90}{360}\right)(\$1,000,000) = \$1250$$

$$\text{Profit} = \text{Max}[S_T - X, 0] - C_0$$

$$\text{Hedged YTM} = (\$1,000,000/\text{effective cost})^{365/91} - 1$$

$$\text{YTM without hedge} = \left(\frac{\$1,000,000}{S_T}\right)^{365/91} - 1$$

time to buy or sell the security often are not the same, and the size of the funds to hedge and the option contract may not be equal. In Chapter 12 we will address some of these issues when we examine hedging with futures.

9.6.3 Treasury-Bond Options

An option on a T-bond gives the holder the right to buy (call) or sell (put) a specified T-bond at a given price. Several features of T-bond options make them different than T-bill options.

First, the T-bond option contract requires the purchase (call) or sale (put) of a specific T-bond. For example, a June T-bond call option might give its holder the right to buy either a T-bond maturing in the year 2016 and paying a 9¼ coupon with a face value of $100,000 or the one maturing in 2015, paying 7½% coupon interest with a face value of $100,000. Because the option contract specifies a particular underlying bond, the maturity of the bond, as well as its value, will be changing during the option's expiration period. For example, a one-year call option on a five-year bond, if held to expiration, would be a call option to buy a four-year bond. Note, that a T-bill option contract, in contrast, calls for the delivery of a T-bill meeting the specified criteria (principal = $1 million, maturity = 91 days). With this *fixed deliverable bond clause*, a T-bill option is referred to as a fixed deliverable bond; and unlike specific-security T-bond options, which include a *specific-security bond clause*, T-bill options can have expiration dates that exceed the T-bill's maturity.

A second differentiating feature of T-bond options is that the underlying bond can pay coupon interest during the option period. As a result, if a T-bond option holder exercises on a noncoupon-paying date, the accrued interest (Acc Int) on the underlying bond must be accounted for. For T-bond options, this is done by including the accrued interest as part of the exercise price (for further discussion on accrued interest, see Appendix E). The exercise price on a T-bond option is quoted as an index (IN_0) equal to a proportion of a bond with a face value of $100 (e.g., 90). If the underlying bond has a face value of $100,000, then the exercise price would be:

$$X = \left(\frac{IN_0}{100}\right)(\$100,000) + \text{Acc Int.} \tag{9.6-1}$$

Finally, the prices of T-bonds and T-bond options are quoted in terms of points (PT) and 32nds of a point. Thus, the price of the June 90 T-bond call option quoted at 1⁵⁄₃₂ is $1,156.25. That is:

$$C_0 = \left(\frac{PT}{100}\right)F \tag{9.6-2}$$

$$C_0 = \left(\frac{1.15623}{100}\right)(\$100,000) = \$1156.25.$$

TABLE 9.6-4

Profit and Bond Price Relation on September 95 T-Bond Put		
T-Bond: Maturity of 15 Years at Expiration, 10% Coupon Put: 95 T-Bond Put Purchased at $1156		
SPOT T-BOND INDEX S_T	ESTIMATED YTM	PUT PROFIT
91	.1110	$2844
92	.1097	1844
93	.1085	844
93.844	.1074	0
94	.1072	− 156
95	.1060	− 1156
96	.1048	− 1156
97	.1035	− 1156

$$\text{Est YTM} = \frac{\text{Annual coupon interest} + [\$100,000 - (S_T/100)\$100,000]/15}{[\$100,000 + (S_T/100)(\$100,000)]/2}$$

$$\text{Put profit} = \text{Max}\left[\left(\frac{95 - S_T}{100}\right)(\$100,000), 0\right] - \$1156$$

9.6.4   Uses of Treasury-Bond Options

Speculation

T-bond options can be used as a tool for speculating on changes in long-term rates. For example, suppose in June a speculator believes that the current economic growth will push long-term interest rates up (and therefore the price on long-term bonds down) over the next three months. To profit from this expectation, the speculator buys a September 95 T-bond put at $1156, with the underlying T-bond having a maturity of 15.25 years, 10% coupon (semiannual payment), and face value of $100,000. Table 9.6-4 shows the possible profits per spot T-bond index from closing the put at expiration at its intrinsic value when the bond is assumed to have exactly 15 years to maturity and no accrued interest. As shown in the table, if long-term interest rates increase (S_T decreases), the speculator can profit; if rates decrease, his losses are limited to the put premium of $1156.*

In contrast, if speculators believe that long-term rates will fall in the future, then they should speculate by taking a long position in a T-bond call.

Hedging

T-bond options also can be used to hedge future long-term bond positions. As an example, suppose in June a portfolio manager anticipates selling a T-bond from her fixed-income portfolio in September to meet forecasted liquidity needs. Also

---

*Normally, T-bond options would be closed or exercised on noncoupon dates. As a result, accrued interest would need to be included in determining the exercise price. If we assume in this example that the expiration date represents a point halfway between semiannual coupon dates, then given a 10% semiannual coupon, an accrued interest of $2500 would need to be added to the exercise price in determining the put's intrinsic value.

suppose that the T-bond the manager plans to sell pays a 10% interest, will have 15 years to maturity and no accrued interest at the anticipated selling date in September, and currently is priced at 95. By buying a September T-bond put, the manager can attain insurance against possible increases in long-term interest rates. In this case, suppose the manager buys a September 95 T-bond put for $1156, with the underlying T-bond on the put being the same as the T-bond she plans to sell. Table 9.6-5 shows the manager's revenue from selling the T-bond and closing the put at the put's September expiration date. As shown in the table, the manager would be able to realize a minimum revenue of $93,844, if rates on 15-year T-bonds are 10.60% or more, and revenues that increase with higher bond prices if rates are below 10.60%. In this case, the fixed-income portfolio manager has attained insurance on a long-term bond position using a T-bond put. Such a strategy represents a bond insurance strategy analogous to the portfolio insurance strategies using stock index options. In contrast, if the portfolio manager was planning to buy long-term bonds in the future and was worried about higher bond prices (lower rates), she could hedge the future investment by buying T-bond calls.

As with T-bill options, T-bond options can be used by fixed-income portfolio managers, investment bankers, and dealers to hedge long-term debt positions. The hedging applications, though, are not as simple as the case just presented, in which the bond being hedged was identical with the option's underlying bond and the timing of the hedge and the option's expiration coincided. Hedging is discussed in more detail in Chapter 12.

9.6.5 Marketability of Debt Options

Unlike stock index options, the market for debt options, as noted, has not grown dramatically. The relatively poor growth of the debt option market is somewhat surprising (at least at first glance), given the speculative and hedging uses of this

TABLE 9.6-5

Hedging Future T-Bond Sale				
T-Bond: Maturity of 15 Years at Expiration, 10% Coupon Put: 95 T-Bond Put Purchased at $1156				
(1) SPOT T-BOND INDEX S_T	(2) ESTIMATED YTM	(3) PUT PROFIT	(4) BOND PRICE	(5) REVENUE (3) + (4)
91	.1110	$ 2844	$91,000	$93,844
92	.1097	1844	92,000	93,844
93	.1085	844	93,000	93,844
94	.1072	− 156	94,000	93,844
95	.1060	− 1156	95,000	93,844
96	.1048	− 1156	96,000	94,844
97	.1035	− 1156	97,000	95,844

Est YTM $= \dfrac{\text{Annual coupon interest} + [\$100,000 - (S_T/100)\$100,000]/15}{[\$100,000 + (S_T/100)(\$100,000)]/2}$

Put profit $= \text{Max}\left[\left(\dfrac{95 - S_T}{100}\right)(\$100,000),\ 0\right] - \$1156$

option. However, fixed-income portfolio managers, investment bankers, and money managers who speculate and hedge debt positions are more likely to use options on futures contracts on debt securities than options on the actual security. This is because options on the futures contracts are more liquid than options on the spot debt security. Options on futures are examined in Chapter 16.

9.6.6 Pricing Debt Options

The B-S model and the BOPM can be used to estimate the equilibrium price of a debt option. However, unlike stock options and stock index options, using the standard OPMs poses several problems. First, recall that the OPMs are based on the assumption of a constant variance. In the case of a bond, though, its variability tends to decrease as its maturity becomes shorter. Second, the OPM assumes that the interest rate is constant. For debt options, an inherent inverse relationship between interest rates and the price of the underlying bond exists. Finally, in the case of T-bond options, the underlying bond changes maturity and value over time, and the accrued interest must be incorporated into the valuation model. Because of these problems, mispricing can result when determining the equilibrium price of a debt option with the B-S OPM or the BOPM. Several debt option models exist [Rendleman and Bartter (1980), Brennen and Schwartz (1980; 1982; Sept. 1982), and Ball and Torous (1983)]. Most of these models differ in terms of the assumptions they make regarding the behavior of interest rates and the variance over time; each, in turn, redresses some of the limitations associated with applying the B-S OPM and the BOPM to the pricing of debt options.

9.6.7 Dealer Options

The OTC market has a number of dealers who specialize in offering *dealer options* on debt securities. Many of these dealers also deal in different bonds, and often write options on the bonds they deal in order to provide sweeteners for their clients (when the dealers do this, they also might take an opposite position in an exchange-traded Treasury option or futures option to hedge their position partially). In the Dealer's Option Market, option contracts are negotiable, with buyers and sellers entering directly into an agreement. Thus, the dealer's market provides option contracts tailor-made to meet the holder's or writer's specific needs. The market, though, lacks both a clearinghouse to intermediate and guarantee the fulfillment of the terms of the option contract, and market makers or specialists to ensure continuous markets; the options, therefore, lack marketability.

9.7   CONCLUSION

In this chapter we've extended our analysis of options from stocks to stock indices and debt securities. In general, most of the relations and strategies we delineated for stock options apply to these nonstock options as well. Consequently, the availability of such options makes it possible to extend the speculative, hedging, and arbitrage strategies delineated in Parts I and II to include stock portfolios and debt securities.

In the next chapter, we continue our analysis of nonstock options by examining options on foreign currencies.

KEY TERMS

cash settlement feature
call option on a stock index
put option on a stock index
end-of-the-day exercise feature
call/Treasury-bill insurance strategy
continuous-leakage option
discrete-leakage option

zero-leakage option
dynamic portfolio insurance
Treasury-bill options
Treasury-bond options
fixed deliverable bond clause
specific-security bond clause
dealer options

SELECTED REFERENCES

The option exchanges publish a number of booklets explaining the characteristics and uses of index and debt options. For a good discussion on the fundamentals of debt options and their applications, see Faboozi (1985); for a similar discussion on stock indices, see Faboozi, Gastineau, and Madansky (1984). For an analysis of dynamic portfolio insurance strategies using stock and cash positions, see Rubinstein and Leland (1981), Leland (1980), and O'Brien (1988).

Asay, M., and Edeslburg, C. "Can a Dynamic Strategy Replicate the Returns of an Option?" *Journal of Futures Markets* 6 (Spring 1986): 63–70.

Baily, W., and Stulz, R. "The Pricing of Stock Index Options in a General Equilibrium Model." *Journal of Financial and Quantitative Analysis* 24 (Mar. 1989): 1–12.

Ball, C., and Torous, W. "Bond Price Dynamics and Options." *Journal of Financial and Quantitative Analysis* 18 (Dec. 1983): 517–531.

Barone-Adesi, G., and Whaley, R. "Efficient Analytic Approximation of American Option Values." *Journal of Finance* 42 (June 1987): 301–320.

Benninga, A., and Blume, M. "On the Optimality of Portfolio Insurance." *Journal of Finance* 40 (Dec. 1985): 1341–1352.

Brennan, M., and Schwartz, E. "Conditional Predictions of Bond Prices and Returns." *Journal of Finance* (May 1980): 405–417.

————. "Alternative Methods for Valuing Debt Options." Working Paper 888, University of British Columbia, Vancouver, B.C., 1982.

————. "An Equilibrium Model of Bond Pricing and a Test of Market Efficiency." *Journal of Financial and Quantitative Analysis* 17 (Sept. 1982): 301–329.

Chance, D. "Empirical Tests of the Pricing of Index Call Options." *Advances in Futures and Options Research* 1 (1986): 141–166.

Copeland, T. E., and Weston, J. F. *Financial Theory and Corporate Policy.* Reading, Mass.: Addison-Wesley, 1983, pp. 230–275.

Courtadon, G. "The Pricing of Options on Default-Free Bonds." *Journal of Financial and Quantitative Analysis* (Mar. 1982): 75–100.

Cox, J., Ingersoll, J., and Ross, S. "An Analysis of Variable Rate Loan Contracts." *Journal of Financial Economics* (Mar. 1978): 59–69.

Ervine, J., and Rudd, A. "Index Options: The Early Evidence." *Journal of Finance* 40 (July 1985): 743–756.

Etzioni, E. "Rebalance Disciplines for Portfolio Insurance." *Journal of Portfolio Management* 13 (Fall 1986): 59–62.

Faboozi, F. *Winning the Interest Rate Game: A Guide to Debt Options.* Chicago: Probus, 1985.

Faboozi, F., Gastineau, G., and Madansky, A. "Options on Stock Indexes and Stock Index Futures: Pricing Determinants, Role in Risk Management, and Options Evaluation." In *Stock Index Futures*, edited by F. Faboozi and G. Kipnis. Homewood, Ill.: Dow Jones-Irwin, 1984.

Faboozi, F., Gastineau, G., and Wunsch, S. "Introduction to Options on Stock Indexes and Stock Index Futures Contracts." In *Stock Index Futures*, edited by F. Faboozi and G. Kipnis. Homewood, Ill.: Dow Jones-Irwin, 1984.

Leland, H. "Who Should Buy Portfolio Insurance?" *Journal of Finance* 35 (May 1980): 581–594.

O'Brien, T. "The Mechanics of Portfolio Insurance?" *Journal of Portfolio Management* (Spring 1988): 40–47.

Pozen, R. "The Purchase of Protective Puts by Financial Institutions." *Financial Analysts Journal* 34 (July–Aug. 1978): 47–60.

Rendleman, R. "Some Practical Problems in Pricing Debt Options." Working Paper, Fugue School of Business, Duke University, August 1982.

Rendleman, R., and Bartter, B. "The Pricing of Options on Debt Securities." *Journal of Financial and Quantitative Analysis* (Mar. 1980): 1124.

Rendleman, R., and McEnally, R. "Assessing the Costs of Portfolio Insurance." *Financial Analysts Journal* 43 (May–June 1987): 27–37.

Rubinstein, M. "Alternative Paths to Portfolio Insurance." *Financial Analysts Journal* 41 (July–Aug. 1985): 42–52.

Rubinstein, M., and Leland, H. "Replicating Options with Positions in Stock and Cash." *Financial Analysts Journal* 37 (July–Aug. 1981): 63–71.

Singleton, C., and Grieves, R. "Synthetic Puts and Portfolio Insurance Strategies." *Journal of Portfolio Management* 10 (Spring 1984): 63–69.

PROBLEMS AND QUESTIONS

1. Evaluate the following index option positions in terms of their profit and spot index relations at expiration.

   a. A long straddle formed with a 300 SP 100 call trading at 12 and a 300 SP 100 put trading at 8. Evaluate at spot index prices of 265, 270, 275, 280, 285, 290, 295, 300, 305, 310, 315, 320, 325, 330, and 335.

   b. A simulated long index position formed by purchasing a 300 SP 100 call at 12 and selling a 300 SP 100 put at 8. Evaluate at spot index prices of 275, 280, 285, 290, 295, 300, 304, 305, 310, 315, 320, and 325.

2. Define and evaluate a portfolio insurance strategy for a stock portfolio currently worth $10 million. Assume that an SP 500 put option is available with an exercise price of 250, expiring in 180 days, and priced at 10. Also assume that the stock portfolio is perfectly positively correlated with the SP 500 index and the current spot SP 500 index is at 250. Evaluate the portfolio insurance strategy at possible spot index values at expiration of 230, 235, 240, 245, 250, 255, 260, 265, and 270.

3. Show how the put-insured portfolio in Problem 2 could be replicated approximately with a fiduciary call. Assume that an SP 500 call is available with an exercise price of 300 and expiration at the end of 180 days, that the risk-free rate is 6% (annual), and that the market prices of index options are governed by the put-call parity model.

4. Given a spot SP 500 index of 350, describe a $3.5 million, well-diversified stock portfolio as a hypothetical SP spot portfolio.

5. Given the following:

   - Spot SP 500 index = 320
   - Annualized standard deviation in the SP 500's logarithmic returns = .25
   - Annual dividend yield of the SP 500 = 4%
   - Continuously compounded annual risk-free rate = 5%
   - SP 500 call option with an exercise price of 315 and expiring in 90 days (T = .25)
   - SP 500 put option with an exercise price of 315 and expiring in 90 days (T = .25)

   a. What is the equilibrium price of the SP 500 call and of the SP 500 put? Use the continuous dividend-adjusted B-S OPM.

   b. What is a replicating portfolio for the call and for the put?

   c. What is the major problem in constructing a replicating portfolio for an index option? How can the problem be resolved?

6. Given the following:

   - SP 100 put with X = 250 and n = 2
   - SP 100 call with X = 250 and n = 2

- SP 100 spot index = 250
- $u = 1.075, d = 1/1.075$
- Period risk-free rate of $R = 1\%$

a. Assuming a BOPM process, construct an event tree showing the values of the spot index, index call, and index put at each node.

b. Show the values at each node of a well-diversified stock portfolio currently worth $5 million.

c. How many put contracts would be needed to insure the stock portfolio (remember $100 multiplier)?

d. Show the values at each node of a put-insured portfolio. Assume put prices equal their BOPM values.

e. Assuming the call prices equal their BOPM values, construct a fiduciary call position that replicates the put-insured portfolio. Show the values of the fiduciary call at each node.

f. What model governs the relationship between a put-insured portfolio and a fiduciary call?

7. Construct a dynamic stock portfolio and risk-free bond strategy that will replicate the put-insured portfolio in Problem 6. Show the portfolio's stock portfolio and bond composition at each node and the adjustments required.

8. Assume the following:

- SP 500 index follows a binomial process in which $u = 1.05$ and $d = 1/1.05$ and the current spot index is $S_0 = 300$
- SP 500 put is available with $X = 300$ and expiration at the end of three periods, $n = 3$
- Period risk-free rate of $R = 1\%$

a. Construct an event tree showing the possible values of the spot index and index put at each node.

b. Construct an event tree showing the values at each node of a well-diversified stock portfolio currently worth $30M.

c. How many index put contracts would be needed to insure the stock portfolio?

d. Using the index put and the stock portfolio, construct an event tree showing the values at each node of a put-insured portfolio.

9. Construct a dynamic stock portfolio and risk-free bond strategy that will replicate the put-insured portfolio in Problem 8. Show the portfolio's bond-and-stock portfolio composition at each node and the adjustments required.

10. What is the major problem facing large institutional investors in insuring their stock portfolio's with put options?

11. Evaluate the following T-bill option positions in terms of their profit and interest rate relation at expiration (use the annual discount yield as your interest rate).

a. A long position in a September 90 T-bill call (M = 91 days and F = $1M) purchased at .5 (PT) when the spot T-bill was trading at R_D = 9.7 (or $975,750). Evaluate at spot index yields of 12, 11.5, 11, 10.5, 10, 9.5, 9, 8.5, and 8.

b. A long position in a September 90 T-bill put (M = 91 days and F = $1M) purchased at .2 (PT) when the spot T-bill was trading at R_D = 9.7 (or $975,750). Evaluate at spot index yields of 12, 11.5, 11, 10.5, 10, 10.2, 9.5, 9, 8.5, and 8.

12. Suppose the September T-bill put described in Problem 11(b) expires in exactly 90 days. Show how a money market manager could attain put insurance for a 181-day T-bill (F = $1M) in his portfolio, which he plans to sell 90 days from the present. Evaluate at spot index yields of 12, 11.5, 11, 10.5, 10, 9.5, 9, 8.5, and 8.

13. Suppose the September T-bill call described in Problem 11(a) expires in exactly 90 days. Show how a money market manager planning to purchase a 91-day T-bill (F = $1M) 90 days from the present could lock in a minimum price with the T-bill call. Evaluate at spot index yields of 12, 11.5, 11, 10.5, 10, 9.5, 9, 8.5, and 8. Also, show the implied YTM the manager would be locking in at each yield.

14. Evaluate a long position in a December 97 T-bond Call option purchased at 1.6 (1⁶/₃₂). Evaluate in terms of the profit at T-bond index values at expiration of 95, 96, 97, 98, 99, 100, and 101. Assume no accrued interest. What is the break-even index price?

15. Evaluate a long position in a December 97 T-bond put option purchased at 0.25 (0²⁵/₃₂). Evaluate in terms of the profit at T-bond index values at expiration of 94, 95, 96, 97, 98, 99, and 100. Assume no accrued interest. What is the break-even price?

16. Show that the December 97 T-bond call and put options in Problems 14 and 15 conform to the put-call parity model. Assume the T-bond underlying the option currently is priced at 96, the December expiration is exactly .25 year from the present, and the annual risk-free rate on securities maturing in 90 days is 6.0154%.

17. Suppose a fixed-income portfolio manager plans to sell a T-bond identical to the T-bond underlying the December 97 T-bond option described in Problems 14 and 15. Show the revenue and T-bond index relation the manager would attain if she insured the T-bond with the T-bond put. Assume the bond is sold at the option's expiration, and evaluate at 94, 95, 96, 97, 98, 99, and 100.

18. Using the information from Problem 16, show how the fixed-income portfolio manager in Problem 17 could attain approximately the same results as the put-insured T-bond by liquidating his T-bond at 96, investing in risk-free bond at 6.0154% for .25 per year (90 days), and going long in the December 97 T-bond call (C_0 = 1⁶/₃₂).

19. Explain some of the difficulties in developing an OPM for interest rate options.

CHAPTER 10

Foreign Currency Options

10.1 INTRODUCTION

In 1982, the Philadelphia Stock Exchange (PHLX) became the first organized exchange to offer trading in foreign currency options. Since then, currency option trading has grown dramatically, from less than .5 million contracts in 1983 to approximately 10 million in 1987. Today, foreign currency options are traded on a number of other exchanges as well, including ones in Toronto, Montreal, and Amsterdam. And a sophisticated dealer's market exists that offers tailor-made option contracts primarily to multinational corporations. In this chapter, we examine the currency option market, some of the option's speculative and hedgings uses, and its pricing. As background, we begin with an overview of the foreign currency market.

10.2 FOREIGN CURRENCY MARKET

The international buying and selling of goods and services creates a market in which individuals, businesses, and governments trade currencies. Most of the currency trading takes place in the *interbank foreign exchange market*. This market consists primarily of major banks, which act as currency dealers, maintaining inventories of foreign currency to sell to or buy from their customers (corporations, governments, or regional banks). The banks are linked by a sophisticated telecommunications system and operate by maintaining accounts with one another, enabling them to trade currency simply by changing computerized book entries.

Transactions occurring in the interbank market can include both spot and forward trades. In the spot market, currencies are delivered immediately (book entries changed); in the forward market, the price for trading or exchanging the currencies (forward rate) is agreed upon in the present, with the actual delivery or exchange taking place at a specified future date. The price of foreign currency—the exchange rate—is defined as the number of units of one currency that can be exchanged for one unit of another.

In Exhibit 10.2-1, spot and forward exchange rates are shown as they appear in the WSJ. The rates are quoted in terms of both the U.S. dollar price per unit of foreign currency (FC) and the FC price per U.S. dollar. The exchange rates represent the closing quotes made by one bank to another. For example, on July 28, 1994, the spot exchange rate (E_0) for the British pound (BP) was \$1.5268/BP, and the 90-day and 180-day forward exchange rates (E_{f0}) were \$1.5251/BP and

EXHIBIT 10.2-1

Spot and Forward Exchange Rates

EXCHANGE RATES

Thursday, July 28, 1994

The New York foreign exchange selling rates below apply to trading among banks in amounts of \$1 million and more, as quoted at 3 p.m. Eastern time by Bankers Trust Co., Dow Jones Telerate Inc. and other sources. Retail transactions provide fewer units of foreign currency per dollar.

Country	U.S. \$ equiv. Thurs.	Wed.	Currency per U.S. \$ Thurs.	Wed.
Argentina (Peso)	1.01	1.01	.99	.99
Australia (Dollar)	.7385	.7393	1.3541	1.3526
Austria (Schilling)	.08928	.09024	11.20	11.08
Bahrain (Dinar)	2.6522	2.6522	.3771	.3771
Belgium (Franc)	.03052	.03086	32.76	32.40
Brazil (Real)	1.0638298	1.0695187	.94	.94
Britain (Pound)	1.5268	1.5325	.6550	.6525
30-Day Forward	1.5259	1.5316	.6554	.6529
90-Day Forward	1.5251	1.5308	.6557	.6533
180-Day Forward	1.5249	1.5306	.6558	.6533
Canada (Dollar)	.7243	.7246	1.3807	1.3801
30-Day Forward	.7235	.7239	1.3821	1.3815
90-Day Forward	.7221	.7224	1.3849	1.3843
180-Day Forward	.7188	.7191	1.3913	1.3907
Czech. Rep. (Koruna)				
Commercial rate	.0354246	.0353282	28.2290	28.3060
Chile (Peso)	.002427	.002427	411.99	411.99
China (Renminbi)	.115221	.115221	8.6790	8.6790
Colombia (Peso)	.001225	.001225	816.00	816.00
Denmark (Krone)	.1599	.1615	6.2526	6.1913
Ecuador (Sucre)				
Floating rate	.000457	.000457	2190.00	2190.00
Finland (Markka)	.19092	.19303	5.2377	5.1804
France (Franc)	.18399	.18575	5.4350	5.3835
30-Day Forward	.18383	.18559	5.4397	5.3882
90-Day Forward	.18365	.18541	5.4450	5.3935
180-Day Forward	.18358	.18533	5.4473	5.3958
Germany (Mark)	.6281	.6351	1.5920	1.5746
30-Day Forward	.6278	.6348	1.5928	1.5754
90-Day Forward	.6278	.6348	1.5928	1.5754
180-Day Forward	.6287	.6357	1.5905	1.5731

SOURCE: *Wall Street Journal*, July 29, 1994

$1.5249/BP. The FC price of a dollar is the reciprocal of E_0; thus, the spot BP price of a dollar is $1/E_0 = 1/(\$1.5268/BP) = 0.6550\ BP/\$$.

In addition to the spot and forward markets for foreign currencies, a futures market for currencies also exists. The foreign currency futures market began in 1972, when the International Monetary Market (IMM) of the Chicago Mercantile Exchange (CME) began offering trading in standardized futures contracts on several currencies. This market will be examined in Chapter 15.

10.3 FOREIGN CURRENCY OPTION MARKET

10.3.1 Exchange-Traded Currency Options

The PHLX offers foreign currency option trading on the British pound (BP), Deutsche mark (DM), Japanese yen (JY), Swiss franc (SF), French franc (FF), Australian dollar (AD), and Canadian dollar (CD). It also offers trading on options on the European Currency Unit (ECU), a weighted-average index of the exchange rates of countries comprising the European Economic Community.

Exhibit 10.3-1 summarizes the characteristics of the foreign currency options traded on the Philadelphia Exchange. The contract sizes for many of the options are equal to half the size of the currency's futures listed on the International Monetary Market. For example, the foreign currency call option contract on the British pound requires (upon exercise) the purchase of 31,250 British pounds, while a long BP futures contract requires the purchase of 62,500 BP. The expiration months for PHLX's currency options are the next two months from the present and also the months of March, June, September, and December. The expiration date is the Saturday before the third Wednesday of the expiration month, with the third Wednesday of the expiration month being the settlement date. If a foreign currency call (put) is exercised, the exercising holder is required

EXHIBIT 10.3-1

Currency Options Listed on the PHLX

CURRENCY	CONTRACT SIZE	TYPE
Australian dollar	50,000	Amer, Eur
British pound	31,250	Amer, Eur
Canadian dollar	50,000	Amer, Eur
Deutsch mark	62,500	Amer, Eur
French franc	125,000	Amer, Eur
Japanese yen	6,250,000	Amer, Eur
Swiss franc	62,500	Amer, Eur
European currency unit	62,500	Amer

1. Expiration months: Two nearest months, and March, June, September, and December.
2. Position limits = 50,000 contracts.

EXHIBIT 10.3-2

PHLX Currency Option Quotes

CURRENCY TRADING

PHILADELPHIA OPTIONS

OPTIONS — PHILADELPHIA EXCHANGE

		Calls Vol.	Calls Last	Puts Vol.	Puts Last
FFranc					183.86
250,000 French Franc EOM-European style.					
18¼	Jul	1000	3.40	...	...
18½	Jul	1400	0.68	400	0.60
JYen					99.94
6,250,000 Japanese Yen EOM-European style.					
100½	Jul	...	...	10	0.10
101	Jul	...	...	10	0.50
DMark					62.81
62,500 German Marks EOM-European style.					
65½	Sep	100	0.54	...	...
Australian Dollar					73.72
50,000 Australian Dollars-European Style.					
73	Aug	...	...	25	0.29
50,000 Australian Dollars-cents per unit.					
72	Dec	10	2.32	...	...
74	Aug	304	0.41	...	...
75	Aug	300	0.18	...	...
75	Dec	...	...	10	2.52
British Pound					152.66
31,250 British Pound EOM-cents per unit.					
155	Aug	4	0.68	...	...
31,250 British Pounds-European Style.					
152½	Dec	8	3.60	...	...
31,250 British Pounds-cents per unit.					
150	Aug	103	2.96	...	...
150	Sep	...	...	10	0.85
152½	Sep	...	...	75	1.85
155	Aug	20	0.48	...	...
British Pound-GMark					242.06
31,250 British Pound-German Mark cross.					
238	Sep	...	...	10	1.16
Canadian Dollar					72.46
50,000 Canadian Dollars-cents per unit.					
73	Aug	5	0.11	...	...
French Franc					183.86
250,000 French Franc-European style.					
18	Aug	...	...	100	0.34
250,000 French Francs-10ths of a cent per unit.					
18¼	Dec	11	6.50	15	3.94
250,000 French Francs-European Style.					
19	Aug	200	0.56	...	...
GMark-JYen					62.88
62,500 GMark-JYen cross EOM.					
61½	Aug	...	...	960	0.42
63½	Aug	960	0.39	...	...
German Mark					62.81
62,500 German Marks EOM-cents per unit.					
62½	Jul	10	1.12	130	0.09
63	Jul	318	0.17	1610	0.39
63½	Jul	20	0.31	815	0.52
64	Jul	629	0.05	11	0.38
64½	Jul	...	...	14	0.95

		Calls Vol.	Calls Last	Puts Vol.	Puts Last
62,500 German Marks-European Style.					
58	Dec	...	...	100	0.22
62	Sep	...	...	30	0.49
62	Dec	...	...	100	1.10
62½	Sep	...	...	30	0.65
63	Sep	...	...	15	0.85
63½	Sep	...	...	15	1.06
64½	Sep	10	0.78	...	...
67	Aug	100	0.03	...	...
67½	Aug	150	0.03	...	...
68	Aug	175	0.02	...	...
68½	Aug	50	0.02	...	...
69	Aug	50	0.01	...	...
62,500 German Marks-cents per unit.					
59	Sep	...	...	7	0.08
60	Aug	2	3.35	...	...
61	Aug	2	2.51	20	0.10
61	Sep	4	2.28	40	0.35
61½	Aug	...	...	174	0.13
62	Aug	10	1.67	20	0.32
62	Sep	2	1.60	216	1.58
62	Dec	...	...	19	1.37
62½	Aug	6	0.78	280	0.44
62½	Sep	...	...	40	0.88
63	Aug	111	0.54	410	0.70
63	Sep	100	1.42	57	1.13
63	Dec	6	2.22	6	1.50
63½	Aug	27	0.52	291	0.99
63½	Sep	55	0.94	217	1.46
64	Aug	410	0.51	6	0.83
64	Sep	22	0.76	...	...
64	Dec	...	...	9	2.25
64½	Aug	14	0.13	...	...
64½	Sep	...	...	5	1.55
65	Aug	15	0.18	...	...
65½	Aug	...	...	10	2.03
66	Aug	...	...	10	2.53
66	Sep	3	0.34	...	...
66	Dec	100	0.95	...	...
Japanese Yen					99.94
6,250,000 Japanese Yen -100ths of a cent					
108	Dec	4	1.23	...	...
6,250,000 Japanese Yen EOM-100ths of a cent per unit.					
102	Jul	200	0.17	...	...
6,250,000 Japanese Yen EOM.					
100½	Jul	25	1.02	...	...
101½	Jul	...	...	60	0.36
6,250,000 Japanese Yen-100ths of a cent per unit.					
96	Sep	...	...	5	0.25
97	Sep	10	3.70	20	0.37
97	Dec	...	...	4	1.00

		Calls Vol.	Calls Last	Puts Vol.	Puts Last
98	Dec	...	...	27	1.43
98½	Sep	5	3.08	11	0.92
99	Aug	...	...	150	0.25
99	Dec	...	...	26	1.57
99½	Aug	...	...	20	0.37
100	Aug	...	...	147	0.96
100	Sep	...	...	269	1.35
100	Dec	...	...	5	2.60
100½	Aug	...	...	5	0.70
101	Aug	...	...	18	1.61
101	Sep	...	...	2	1.68
101½	Aug	...	...	16	1.90
101½	Sep	...	...	55	1.94
102	Aug	35	0.35	5	2.00
102	Sep	...	...	10	1.84
102	Dec	...	...	60	3.20
102½	Aug	10	0.49	...	...
102½	Sep	...	...	8	2.43
104	Sep	100	0.98	...	...
104½	Sep	3	0.67	...	...
105	Sep	16	0.55	...	...
6,250,000 Japanese Yen-European Style.					
92	Dec	...	...	20	0.28
97	Aug	10	4.78	...	...
99	Sep	10	3.20	...	...
100	Aug	...	...	3	0.47
102	Sep	...	...	5	2.68
Swiss Franc					74.08
62,500 Swiss Franc EOM-cents per unit.					
74	Jul	...	...	60	0.10
62,500 Swiss Francs-European Style.					
71½	Aug	25	3.64	...	...
74	Sep	24	1.93	4	0.85
74½	Aug	80	1.28	...	...
75	Aug	45	0.62	...	...
75	Sep	...	...	24	1.27
76	Sep	...	...	5	1.80
62,500 Swiss Francs-cents per unit.					
70	Dec	...	...	6	0.50
71	Sep	10	4.10	...	...
72	Dec	...	...	50	1.17
73	Sep	12	2.11	...	...
73	Dec	...	...	203	1.48
73½	Aug	3	1.10	...	...
74	Sep	5	0.98	7	0.66
74	Dec	...	...	3	1.58
74½	Aug	15	0.85	100	0.69
74½	Sep	...	...	15	1.35
75	Aug	4	0.70	8	0.86
75	Dec	...	...	2	2.20
75½	Aug	5	0.57	3	0.80
76	Sep	1	0.90	5	1.77
78	Sep	60	0.25	...	...
Call Vol 8,455	Open Int ... 679,924				
Put Vol 8,499	Open Int ... 536,268				

SOURCE: *Wall Street Journal*, July 29, 1994

to deliver dollars (foreign currency) to a bank designated by the OCC. The assigned writer is required to deliver the foreign currency (dollars) to the bank.*

Exhibit 10.3-2 shows the price quotes on some of the currency options trading on the PHLX as they appeared in the WSJ on July 29, 1994. In examining the

---

*The margin requirements on currency options also differ from those on stock options. For example, the maximum margin on a naked call write is the option premium, plus 4% of the underlying contract value, less the amount the call is out of the money. This minimum requirement is the option premium plus 75% of the underlying contract value.

exhibit, note that both the exercise price and the option premium are quoted in terms of cents per unit of foreign currency for the AD, BP, CD, DM, and SF, in tenths of a cent for the FF, and hundredths of a cent for the JY. Thus, the August 150 American call option on BP shown in the exhibit selling for 1.50 on July 28 would have given a holder the right to buy 31,250 BP at an exercise price of $1.50 per BP [total exercise costs of ($1.50/BP)(31,250 BP) = $46,875], with the costs of the option being $0.0296 BP [total option costs = ($0.0296/BP)(31,250 BP) = $925].

Two unique features of the PHLX should be noted. First, the PHLX was the first U.S. security exchange to offer early morning and evening trading. This was done to accommodate foreign currency traders in other countries who wanted to use the PHLX currency option market to hedge their exchange positions (early-morning hours for European traders and evening hours for Far Eastern traders). Second, the PHLX offers side-by-side trading in both American and European options listed on the same currency. The PHLX's European options originally were listed on the American exchange. After experiencing thin trading, though, the AMEX suspended trading in these options; the PHLX subsequently took over these European options, resulting in the side-by-side listing of both types of currency options.

As noted earlier, foreign currency options also are traded on a number of foreign security exchanges. From an American resident's perspective, some of these exchanges are unique, in that the options are specified in terms of the foreign currency price on the U.S. dollar instead of the dollar price of a unit of foreign currency. Finally, in addition to offering foreign currency futures, the International Monetary Market also offers options on foreign currency futures; these options will be discussed in Chapter 16.

10.3.2   Interbank Currency Options Market

The *interbank currency options market* is part of the interbank foreign exchange market. In this dealer's market, banks provide tailor-made foreign currency option contracts for their customers. Compared to exchange-traded options, options in the interbank market are larger in contract size, often European, and are available on more currencies. Because these options are tailor-made to fit customer needs, a significant secondary market for the options does not exist.* The interbank currency option market also provides a number of unique option products. For instance, Citibank and Salomon Brothers offer what is referred to as the *range-forward* instrument, which consists of both a long position in a currency put and a short position in a currency call and which is useful as a hedging tool for an exporter planning to sell foreign currency in the future.†

---

*In turn, some bankers who take positions in the interbank currency option market on behalf of their clients take opposite positions in currencies options traded on the organized exchanges, to hedge their exposure.

†For a further discussion of range-forward options and such other option instruments as currency cylinder options and bounder-payoff puts, see Gendreau (1984).

10.4 USES OF FOREIGN CURRENCY OPTIONS

10.4.1   Speculation

Figure 10.4-1 shows the profit and spot exchange rate (E) relation at expiration (T) for a long call position. The call option in this figure costs gives the holder the right to buy one unit of foreign currency (FC) at $X = \$1.50$, and it costs $C_0 = \$0.05/FC$. This long currency call position could be used by speculators who believe that the exchange rate will increase, or, equivalently stated, that the dollar will depreciate. A dollar depreciation might occur when the U.S. economy is expected to grow, with the economic growth possibly accompanied by inflation. That is, when an economy is growing, the demand for imported goods and services often increases, and if inflation accompanies the economic growth, exports may decline. The increase in imports and decrease in exports would result in an excess demand for foreign currency, which would cause the price of the foreign currency (\$/FC exchange rate) to increase.

In contrast, if the exchange rate was expected to fall in the near future (dollar appreciation), a speculator could take a long currency put position. Figure 10.4-2 shows the profit and exchange rate relation at expiration for a put with $X = \$1.50/FC$ and costing $P_0 = \$0.05/FC$. An exchange rate decrease could occur if an economic recession, possibly accompanied by lower prices for goods and services, was expected. The recession would tend to cause a decrease in import demand, and lower prices would tend to reduce imports and augment exports, both effects leading to an excess supply of foreign currency (or excess demand for dollars), which would serve to lower the \$/FC exchange rate.

10.4.2   Covered Option Write Positions

Since foreign currency can be used to purchase foreign securities, which pay interest, foreign currency options represent a continuous-leakage option. Because

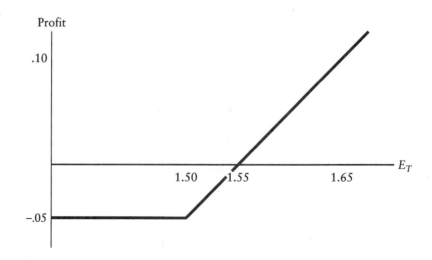

FIGURE 10.4-1

Profit and Exchange Rate Relation at Expiration for Long Currency Call Position

$X = \$1.50/FC$,
$C_0 = \$0.05/FC$

FIGURE 10.4-2

Profit and Exchange Rate Relation at Expiration for Long Currency Put Position

$X = \$1.50/FC$,
$P_0 = \$0.05/FC$

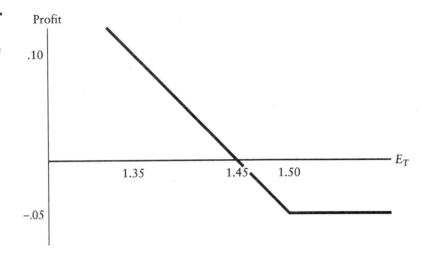

of the foreign interest earned, the covered write positions for foreign currency options are set up differently than are those for stock options.

A short foreign currency call position can be covered by borrowing a specific amount of dollars and converting it to foreign currency. To illustrate, assume for simplicity that the U.S. annual risk-free rate (R_{US}) is equal to the foreign risk-free rate (R_F) and there is a European foreign currency call option expiring at T, with an exercise price equal to the current exchange rate (E_0). From the perspective of a U.S. resident, a short currency call position can be covered by:

1. Borrowing $E_0(1 + R_{US})^{-T}$ dollars.
2. Converting the dollars to $(1 + R_{US})^{-T}$ units of foreign currency (FC) at the current exchange of E_0.
3. Investing the currency in a foreign risk-free security at a rate R_F for the period.

At expiration, the foreign currency investment would be worth one unit of FC (given $R_{US} = R_F$):

$$\text{Foreign investment at } T = (1 + R_{US})^{-T}(1 + R_F)^T = 1 \text{ FC, for } R_{US} = R_F;$$

the principal and interest on the U.S. dollar loan would be equal to E_0 dollars:

$$\text{U.S. debt at } T = E_0(1 + R_{US})^{-T}(1 + R_{US})^T = E_0.$$

Accordingly, if $E_T > X (= E_0)$, the covered call writer could cover a call assignment by selling the foreign currency to the exercising holder at $X = E_0$ dollars, then use the E_0 dollars to repay the principal and interest on his U.S. loan. On the other hand, if $E_T \leq X$ at expiration, the call would be worthless, but the covered call writer would break even or lose on the foreign currency position when the unit of FC from the foreign investment is converted to only E_T dollars. In this case, the covered call writer would have to raise additional funds equal to $E_0 - E_T$ to pay the U.S. debt.

Table 10.4-1 shows the profit and exchange rate relation for a covered call write position formed by selling a $1.50 FC call with an expiration of $T = .25$ per year at $C_0 = \$0.05/FC$. The call is assumed to be sold when the exchange rate is at $E_0 = \$1.50/FC$ and R_{US} and R_F equal 5% (annual), and the short position is assumed to be hedged by:

1. Borrowing $E_0(1 + R_{US})^{-T} = \$1.50(1.05)^{-.25} = \$1.4818$.
2. Converting the dollars at $E_0 = \$1.50/FC$ to .9879 FC[$= (1.05)^{-.25}$FC].
3. Investing the .9879 FC in foreign securities at an interest rate of $R_F = 5\%$.

At expiration, the covered call writer would have one unit of FC and would owe $E_0 = \$1.50$. The table shows the profits and losses from closing the call at expiration at a price equal to the call's intrinsic value (IV = Max[$E_T - X$, 0]) and the profits and losses from converting the FC at expiration to E_T dollars and repaying the U.S. debt of E_0 dollars. Aggregating the profits and losses from each position at each exchange rate, we see the standard limited profit and unlimited loss feature that characterizes all covered call write positions.

To cover a short put position, the writer (a U.S. resident) does the opposite of the covered call write case. Specifically, in this case the writer:

1. Borrows $(1 + R_F)^{-T}$ FC at rate R_F.
2. Converts the FC to dollars at E_0.
3. Invests $E_0(1 + R_F)^{-T}$ dollars in a U.S. risk-free security at rate R_{US}.

TABLE 10.4-1

	Foreign Currency Covered Call Write		
Call: $X = \$1.50/FC$, $T = .25$, $C_0 = \$0.05/FC$, $E_0 = \$1.50$, $R_{US} = R_F = .05$ (annual)			
EXCHANGE RATE AT EXPIRATION E_T	CALL WRITE PROFIT $-\text{MAX}[E_T - X, 0] + C_0$	CONVERTING FC AND REPAYING U.S. DEBT $E_T - E_0$	TOTAL PROFIT
$1.30/FC	$ .05	− $.20	− $.15
1.40	.05	− .10	− .05
1.45	.05	− .05	.00
1.50	.05	.00	.05
1.60	− .05	.10	.05
1.70	− .15	.20	.05
Hedge: Borrow $E_0(1 + R_{US})^{-T} = \$1.50(1.05)^{-.25} = \$1.4818$; convert to .9879 FC at $E_0 = \$1.50/FC$ and invest in foreign security at $R_F = 5\%$.			
End of the period: Investment = (.9879 FC)(1.05)$^{.25}$ = 1 FC. Debt = ($1.4818)(1.05)$^{.25}$ = $1.50 = E_0.			

If $R_F = R_{US}$, then at expiration, the covered put writer would owe one unit of FC on the foreign loan and would have earned principal and interest equal to E_0 dollars on the U.S. investment. If the covered put writer is assigned [$E_T < X$ (= E_0)], she could buy the FC at $X = E_0$ from the exercising holder with the E_0 dollars from her U.S. investment, then use the unit of FC to pay the foreign debt. If $E_T \geq X$ (where $X = E_0$), the put is worthless. Since the covered put writer only has E_0 dollars, though, she will have to raise $E_T - E_0$ additional dollars to buy the one FC needed to repay the foreign debt; thus, the writer would incur a dollar loss of $E_T - E_0$ when $ET \geq X$. Table 10.4-2 shows the profit and exchange rate relation at expiration for the covered put write position formed with a $1.50 FC put option sold at $P_0 = \$0.05$ when the spot exchange rate is at $E_0 = \$1.50/FC$ and $R_{US} = R_F = .05$ (annual).

In describing these covered write positions on foreign currency options, it should be noted that covering a call or put write position can be done alternatively by using currency futures positions. As we will discuss in Chapter 16, hedging short option positions with futures is easier than taking an actual position in the currency.

10.4.3 Hedging Currency Positions with Foreign Currency Options

Since the reestablishment of the flexible exchange rate system in 1972, multinational corporations, international banks, and governments have had to deal with the problem of exchange rate risk. Until the introduction of currency options, exchange rate risk usually was hedged with foreign currency forward or futures contracts. Hedging with these instruments allows foreign exchange participants to

TABLE 10.4-2

Foreign Currency Covered Put Write			
Put: $X = \$1.50/FC$, $T = .25$, $P_0 = \$0.05/FC$, $E_0 = \$1.50$, $R_{US} = R_F = .05$ (annual)			
EXCHANGE RATE AT EXPIRATION E_T	PUT WRITE PROFIT $-$MAX$[X - E_T, 0] + P_0$	EARNING E_0 DOLLARS AND PAYING E_T DOLLARS $E_0 - E_T$	TOTAL PROFIT
$1.30/FC	− $.15	$.20	$.05
1.40	− .05	.10	.05
1.45	.00	.05	.05
1.50	.05	.00	.05
1.55	.05	− .05	.00
1.60	.05	− .10	− .05
1.70	.05	− .20	− .15
Hedge: Borrow $(1 + R_F)^{-T} = 1$ FC$(1.05)^{-.25} = .9879$ FC; convert to $1.4818 at $E_0 = \$1.50/FC$, and invest in U.S. security at $R_{US} = 5\%$ (annual).			
End of the period: Investment $= (\$1.4818)(1.05)^{.25} = \$1.50$. Debt $= (.9879$ FC$)(1.05)^{.25} = 1$ FC; thus, E_T dollars needed to buy 1 FC.			

lock in the local currency values of their revenues or expenses. However, with exchange-traded currency options and dealer's options, hedgers, for the cost of the options, can obtain not only protection against adverse exchange rate movements, but (unlike forward and futures positions) benefits if the exchange rates move in favorable directions.

To illustrate the use of currency options as a hedging tool, consider the case of a U.S. computer corporation that sells one of its mainframe computers to a German manufacturing company for 625,000 DM, with the payment to be made in Deutsche marks by the German company to the U.S. company at the end of three months. Suppose the current exchange rate is $.40/DM. Thus, if the U.S. company were paid immediately and the marks were converted, it would receive $250,000. Since payment is not due for three months, the U.S. company faces both the risk that the $/DM exchange rate could decrease, resulting in fewer dollars, and the possibility of greater dollar returns if the $/DM exchange rate increases. For the costs of DM put options, the U.S. company can protect its dollar revenues from possible exchange rate decreases while still benefiting if the exchange rate increases.

For example, suppose a 40-DM put is available at 1 ($X = \$0.40/DM$ and $P_0 = \$0.01/FC$), with an expiration coinciding with the date the U.S. company is to receive its 625,000 DM. To hedge its future dollar revenue, currently worth ($.40/DM)(625,000 DM) = $250,000, against exchange risk, the U.S. computer company would need to buy 10-DM put contracts (contract size on a DM option is 62,500) expiring at the end of three months. Table 10.4-3 shows the net revenues the U.S. company would receive three months later from converting its receipts of 625,000 DM to dollars at the spot exchange rate (E_T) and closing its 10 put contracts at a price equal to the DM put's intrinsic value. As shown, if the exchange rate is less than $.40/DM, the company would receive less than $250,000 when it converts the 625,000 DM to dollars; these lower revenues, however, would be offset by the profits from the put position.

TABLE 10.4-3

Hedging Future DM Receipts with DM Put Options			
DM revenue at expiration = 625,000 DM Hedge: long in ten, 40-DM puts Put contract = 62,500 DM, cost of put = $.01/DM, or $625 per contract			
(1) SPOT EXCHANGE RATE AT EXPIRATION $E_T = \$/DM$	(2) PUT PROFIT*	(3) DOLLAR VALUE OF 625,000 DM: $E_T(625,000 DM)$	(4) DOLLAR RECEIPTS (2) + (3)
$.30/DM	$56,250	$187,500	$243,750
.35/DM	25,000	218,750	243,750
.40/DM	− 6,250	250,000	243,750
.45/DM	− 6,250	281,250	275,000
.50/DM	− 6,250	312,500	306,250

*Put profit = 10 Max[$.40/DM − E_T, 0](62,500 DM) − 10($.01/DM)(62,500 DM)

For example, at a spot exchange rate of $0.30/DM, the company would receive only $187,500 from converting the 625,000-DM payment, but would earn from the puts a profit of

$$10 \, \text{Max}[\$0.40/DM - \$0.30/DM, 0](62,500 \, DM)$$
$$- 10(\$0.01/DM)(62,500 \, DM) = \$56,250.$$

This would result in a combined receipt of $243,750. As shown in the table, if the exchange rate is $0.40/DM or less, the company would receive $243,750. This amount equals the hedged amount ($250,000) minus the costs of the put options. On the other hand, if the exchange rate at expiration exceeds $0.40/DM, the U.S. company would realize a dollar gain when it converts the 625,000 DM at the higher spot, while its losses on the put would be limited to the amount of the premium. Thus, by hedging with currency put options, the company is able to obtain exchange rate risk protection in the event the exchange rate decreases while still retaining the potential for increased dollar revenues if the exchange rate rises.

Suppose that instead of receiving foreign currency, a company had to make a foreign currency payment at some future date. To protect itself against possible increases in the exchange rate while still benefiting if the exchange rate decreases, the company could hedge the position by taking a long position in a currency call option. For example, suppose a U.S. importer bought 10 German automobiles for 62,500 DM each, with the total payment of 625,000 DM to be made at the end of three months. If the current exchange rate again is $0.40/DM, then the importer's total dollar expenditure would be $250,000 if the exchange rate did not change. If the exchange rate increased, though, the importer would pay more, and if it decreased, he would pay less.

To benefit from the lower exchange rates and still limit the dollar costs of purchasing 625,000 DM in the event the $/DM exchange rate rises, the importer could buy DM call options expiring at the end of the three months. Table 10.4-4 shows the costs of purchasing 625,000 DM at different exchange rates and the

TABLE 10.4-4				

Hedging Future DM Purchase with DM Call Options				
DM costs at expiration = 625,000 DM				
Hedge: long in ten 40-DM calls				
Call contract = 62,500 DM, cost of call = $.01/DM, or $625 per contract				

(1) SPOT EXCHANGE RATE AT EXPIRATION $E_T = \$/DM$	(2) CALL PROFIT*	(3) DOLLAR COST OF 625,000 DM: $E_T (625,000 \, DM)$	(4) DOLLAR COSTS (3) − (2)
$.30/DM	− $ 6,250	$187,500	$193,750
.35/DM	− 6,250	218,750	225,000
.40/DM	− 6,250	250,000	256,250
.45/DM	25,000	281,250	256,250
.50/DM	56,250	312,500	256,250

*Call profit = 10 Max$[E_T − \$.40/DM, 0](62,500 \, DM) − 10(\$.01/DM)(62,500 \, DM)$

profits and losses from purchasing 10 three-month 40-DM calls at 1 and closing them at expiration at a price equal to the call's intrinsic value. As shown in the table, for cases in which the exchange rate is greater than \$.40/DM, the importer has dollar expenditures exceeding \$250,000; the expenditures, though, are offset by the profits from the calls. On the other hand, when the exchange rate is less than \$.40/DM, the dollar costs of purchasing 625,000 DM decreases as the exchange rate decreases, while the losses on the call options are limited to the option premium.

10.5 FOREIGN CURRENCY OPTION PRICING RELATIONS

Since foreign currency can be invested in interest-bearing foreign securities, currency options represent a continuous-leakage option. As a result, the option pricing relationships for currency options differ from the option price relationships for stocks and other zero-leakage or discrete-leakage securities by the inclusion of the foreign interest rate. In this section, we will examine four currency option pricing relationships in which the foreign interest rate is a factor: the boundary conditions for the minimum prices of currency calls and puts, the foreign currency put-call parity model, the currency BOPM, and the B-S OPM for currency options.

10.5.1 Minimum Values of Currency Options

The minimum-price condition for a European or an American call option on a currency can be found by comparing two investments (for a U.S. resident):

1. The dollar purchase of $E_0(1 + R_F)^{-T}$ units of foreign currency, with the FC funds invested for the period T in a foreign risk-free security yielding a rate R_F.

2. The purchase of a European currency call option for C_0 and the purchase of a pure discount bond maturing at the option's expiration date, with a face value (F) equal to the option's exercise price and yielding a risk-free rate of R_{US} for the period.

As shown in Table 10.5-1, at expiration, the values of each investment depend on the spot exchange rate, E_T. The first investment would be worth 1 FC at expiration and E_T dollars when converted; the second investment is equal to the exercise price if $E_T \leq X$, and is worth E_T if $E_T > X$. Comparing the two, the second investment yields the same return as the first in some cases and a better return in others. A priori, we would expect the market to value the second investment more than the first. Hence:

$$C_0 + X(1 + R_{US})^{-T} > E_0(1 + R_F)^{-T}. \qquad (10.5\text{-}1)$$

Expressing Inequality (10.5-1) as an equality in terms of C_0, with a constraint that C_0 not be negative, we obtain the minimum value of a currency call:

TABLE 10.5-1

			DOLLAR CASH FLOW AT EXPIRATION		
	INVESTMENT	CURRENT DOLLAR INVESTMENT	$E_T < X$	$E_T = X$	$E_T > X$
1	Investment in foreign security	$E_0(1 + R_F)^{-T}$	E_T	E_T	E_T
2	Call Bond	C_0 $X(1 + R_{US})^{-T}$	0 X	0 X	$E_T - X$ X
			X	X	E_T
		Preference:	2	Indifferent	Indifferent

The table is titled **Minimum Value of a Currency Call**.

Since Investment 2 yields the same cash flow as Investment 1 in some cases and better in other cases, it should be valued greater. Thus:

$$C_0 + X(1 + R_{US})^{-T} > E_0(1 + R_F)^{-T},$$

and

$$\text{Min } C_0 = \text{Max}[E_0(1 + R_F)^{-T} - X(1 + R_{US})^{-T}, 0].$$

$$\text{Min } C_0 = \text{Max}[E_0(1 + R_F)^{-T} - X(1 + R_{US})^{-T}, 0]. \quad (10.5\text{-}2)$$

If the market price of a currency call (C_0^m) is less than the minimum price, an arbitrage opportunity exists by taking a short position in the foreign security, borrowing $(1 + R_F)^{-T}$ FC and converting it to dollars at E_0, then using the dollars to buy the call and a U.S. risk-free security with a face value of X and maturity of T. As shown in Exhibit 10.5-1, this strategy would yield an initial positive cash flow of $E_0(1 + R_F)^{-T} - [X(1 + R_{US})^{-T} + C_0^m]$ and no liabilities at expiration.

For American currency puts, the minimum-price condition is defined by the put's intrinsic value. For European currency puts, the minimum-price condition is established by comparing the following investments:

1. Investment in a domestic risk-free pure discount bond with a face value of X and maturity of T.

2. Investment in a European currency put (P_0^e) and a foreign risk-free investment in which $E_0(1 + R_F)^{-T}$ dollars are converted into $(1 + R_F)^{-T}$ units of FC and invested in a foreign security yielding a rate R_F for the period. The foreign investment would be worth one unit of FC or E_T dollars at expiration.

As shown in Table 10.5-2, the second investment is either equivalent to or better than the first investment. Thus:

$$P_0^e + E_0(1 + R_F)^{-T} > X(1 + R_{US})^{-T} \quad (10.5\text{-}3)$$

$$\text{Min } P_0^e = \text{Max}[X(1 + R_{US})^{-T} - E_0(1 + R_F)^{-T}, 0]. \quad (10.5\text{-}4)$$

EXHIBIT 10.5-1

Arbitrage Strategy When
$C_0^m < E_0(1 + R_F)^{-T} - X(1 + R_{US})^{-T}$

Strategy: $\{+C_0^m, -[E_0(1 + R_F)^{-T} - X(1 + R_{US})^{-T}]\}$

STRATEGY	DETAILS	CURRENT CASH FLOW
Short $E_0(1 + R_F)^{-T}$	Borrow $(1 + R_F)^{-T}$ FC, convert to dollars at E_0 (owe 1 FC at T)	$E_0(1 + R_F)^{-T}$
Long $X(1 + R_{US})^{-T}$	Buy U.S. pure discount bond with face value of X and maturity of T	$-X(1 + R_{US})^{-T}$
Long call	Buy call	$-C_0^m$
Initial Cash Flow		$E_0(1 + R_F)^{-T} - X(1 + R_{US})^{-T} - C_0^m > 0$

	EXPIRATION		
	DOLLAR CASH FLOW AT EXPIRATION		
POSITION	$E_T < X$	$E_T = X$	$E_T > X$
Short foreign security: dollar costs of repaying debt of 1 FC: E_T Long bond Long call	$-E_T$ X 0	$-E_T$ X 0	$-E_T$ X $E_T - X$
Cash Flow	$(X - E_T) > 0$	0	0

TABLE 10.5-2

	Minimum Value of European Currency Put				
			DOLLAR CASH FLOW AT EXPIRATION		
	INVESTMENT	CURRENT DOLLAR INVESTMENT	$E_T < X$	$E_T = X$	$E_T > X$
1	Bond	$X(1 + R_{US})^{-T}$	X	X	X
2	Put Foreign bond	P_0^e $E_0(1 + R_F)^{-T}$	$X - E_T$ E_T	0 E_T	0 E_T
			X	E_T	E_T
		Preference:	Indifferent	Indifferent	2

Since Investment 2 yields the same cash flow as Investment 1 in some cases and better in other cases, it should be valued greater. Thus:

$$P_0^e + E_0(1 + R_F)^{-T} > X(1 + R_{US})^{-T},$$

and

$$\text{Min } P_0^e = \text{Max}[X(1 + R_{US})^{-T} - E_0(1 + R_F)^{-T}, 0].$$

As shown in Exhibit 10.5-2, if this minimum-price condition is violated, then an arbitrage opportunity exists by shorting a U.S. bond, buying a foreign bond, and purchasing the currency put.

10.5.2   Foreign Currency Put-Call Parity Model

Recall that the put-call parity model for stock options was derived by determining the European call and put prices in which the arbitrage profit from a conversion and risk-free bond strategy was zero. For European currency options, a conversion is formed via the following strategy.

1. Take a long position in the foreign currency in which $E_0(1 + R_F)^{-T}$ dollars are converted to foreign currency and invested in a foreign risk-free security at a rate of R_F.

2. Form a synthetic short position in foreign currency by taking a short position in a European currency call and a long position in a European currency put.

As shown in Table 10.5-3, at expiration the foreign currency conversion yields a certain return equal to the exercise price on the options. As a result, in equilibrium the value of the conversion should equal the present value of a domestic (U.S.) riskless bond with a face value equal to X. Thus, the put-call parity relation for European currency options is:

$$P_0^e - C_0^e + E_0(1 + R_F)^{-T} = X(1 + R_{US})^{-T} \qquad (10.5\text{-}5)$$

$$P_0^e = C_0^e - E_0(1 + R_F)^{-T} + X(1 + R_{US})^{-T}$$

$$C_0^e = P_0^e + E_0(1 + R_F)^{-T} - X(1 + R_{US})^{-T}.$$

10.5.3   Foreign Currency Binomial Option Pricing Model

In terms of the BOPM, the equilibrium price of a European currency call option is equal to the value of a replicating portfolio formed by borrowing B_0^* dollars to finance partially the purchase of H_0^* units of foreign currency at an exchange rate E_0, with the currency then invested in a foreign risk-free security for the period.

To derive the currency option's replicating portfolio for a single period, assume:

1. The underlying exchange rate can either increase to equal a proportion u times its initial value or decrease to equal d times the initial value.

2. The call option on the foreign currency is European and expires at the end of the period.

EXHIBIT 10.5-2

Arbitrage Strategy When $P_0^m < X(1 + R_{US})^{-T} - E_0(1 + R_F)^{-T}$

Strategy: $\{+P_0^m, -[X(1 + R_{US})^{-T} - E_0(1 + R_F)^{-T}]\}$

STRATEGY	DETAILS	CASH FLOW
Short $X(1 + R_{US})^{-T}$	Borrow $X(1 + R_{US})^{-T}$ dollars	$X(1 + R_{US})^{-T}$
Long $E_0(1 + R_F)^{-T}$	Convert $E_0(1+R_F)^{-T}$ dollars to $(1 + R_F)^{-T}$ FC at exchange rate E_0 and buy foreign bond for $(1 + R_F)^{-T}$ (receive 1 FC at T)	$-E_0(1 + R_F)^{-T}$
Long put	Buy put	$-P_0^m$
Initial Cash Flow		$X(1 + R_{US})^{-T} - E_0(1 + R_F)^{-T} - P_0^m > 0$

	EXPIRATION		
	DOLLAR CASH FLOW AT EXPIRATION		
POSITION	$E_T < X$	$E_T = X$	$E_T > X$
Short bond	$-X$	$-X$	$-X$
Long foreign bond: dollar value of 1 FC = E_T	E_T	E_T	E_T
Long put	$X - E_T$	0	0
Cash Flow	0	0	$(E_T - X) > 0$

TABLE 10.5-3

Foreign Currency Conversion			
Investment: 1. Convert $E_0(1 + R_F)^{-T}$ dollars to $(1 + R_F)^{-T}$ units of foreign currency and invest in foreign risk-free security; the investment is worth 1 FC and E_T dollars at expiration. 2. Sell FC call and buy FC put.			
	DOLLAR VALUE OF CONVERSION AT EXPIRATION		
POSITION	$E_T < X$	$E_T = X$	$E_T > X$
Dollar value of foreign investment	E_T	E_T	E_T
Short call	0	0	$-(E_T - X)$
Long put	$X - E_T$	0	0
Total	X	X	X

3. The domestic (U.S.) risk-free security pays a rate of R_{US} for the period with a terminal value of $r_{US} = 1 + R_{US}$, and the foreign risk-free security pays a rate R_F for the period with a terminal value of $r_F = 1 + R_F$.

The first two assumptions suggest the following exchange rate and currency option values:

$$
\begin{array}{|c|c|}
\hline
& \begin{array}{l} E_u = uE_0 \\ C_u = \text{Max}[uE_0 - X, 0] \end{array} \\
\hline
\begin{array}{l} E_0 \\ C_0 \end{array} & \\
\hline
& \begin{array}{l} E_d = dE_0 \\ C_d = \text{Max}[dE_0 - X, 0] \end{array} \\
\hline
\end{array}
$$

At the end of the period, the replicating portfolio would have a debt obligation of $r_{US}B_0$ dollars and the foreign investment would be worth $H_0(r_F)$ units of FC, which would be converted to dollars at an exchange rate of either uE_0 or dE_0. Thus, at expiration the replicating portfolio would have one of the following values:

$$
\begin{array}{|c|c|}
\hline
& (H_0r_F) uE_0 - B_0r_{US} \\
\hline
H_0E_0 - B_0 & \\
\hline
& (H_0r_F)dE_0 - B_0r_{US} \\
\hline
\end{array}
$$

Solving for the H_0^* value and the B_0^* value, in which:

$$H_0(r_F)uE_0 - B_0r_{US} = C_u \qquad (10.5\text{-}6)$$

$$H_0(r_F)dE_0 - B_0r_{US} = C_d, $$

we obtain

$$H_0^* = \frac{C_u - C_d}{E_0r_F(u - d)} \qquad (10.5\text{-}7)$$

$$B_0^* = \frac{C_u(dE_0) - C_d(uE_0)}{r_{US}E_0(u - d)}. \qquad (10.5\text{-}8)$$

The equilibrium currency call price is therefore:

$$C_0^* = H_0^*E_0 - B_0^*, \qquad (10.5\text{-}9)$$

or upon substituting Equations (10.5-7) and (10.5-8) into Equation (10.5-9) and rearranging:

$$C_0^* = \frac{pC_u + (1 - p)C_d}{r_{US}}, \qquad (10.5\text{-}10)$$

where:

$$p = \frac{r_{US} - r_F d}{r_F(u - d)}.$$

The arbitrage strategy used when the market price of the currency option does not equal the BOPM value involves taking opposite positions in the call and the replicating portfolio. For example, suppose $u = 1.1$, $d = .95$, $R_{US} = .05$, $R_F = .03$, and $E_0 = \$1.50/FC$. Using the same single-period currency BOPM, the equilibrium price of a \$1.50 FC call option expiring at the end of the period would be \$0.066 by the single-period model. As shown in Table 10.5-4, if the market price of the currency call was \$0.075, an arbitrageur could profit by selling the call and going long in the replicating portfolio: Borrow $B_0^* = \$0.90476$, then buy $H_0^* = .6472$ FC at $E_0 = \$1.50$, with the FC invested in the foreign risk-free security at $R_F = .03$. As shown in the table, at expiration the arbitrageur would

TABLE 10.5-4	Single-Period Overpriced Arbitrage Strategy

Single-Period Overpriced Arbitrage Strategy
$u = 1.1$, $d = 0.95$, $R_{US} = .05$, $R_F = .03$, $E_0 = \$1.50/FC$, $X = \$1.50/FC$, $C_u = \text{Max}[uE_0 - X, 0] = \$0.15$, $C_d = \text{Max}[dE_0 - X, 0] = 0$, $$H_0^* = \frac{C_u - C_d}{E_0 r_F(u - d)} = \frac{\$0.15 - 0}{\$1.50(1.03)(1.1 - .95)} = .6472,$$ $$B_0^* = \frac{C_u(dE_0) - C_d(uE_0)}{r_{US}E_0(u - d)} = \frac{\$0.15(.95)(\$1.50) - 0(1.1)(\$1.50)}{(1.05)(\$1.50)(1.1 - .95)} = \$.90476,$$ $C_0^* = H_0^* E_0 - B_0^* = .6742(\$1.50) - \$0.90476 = \$0.066, C_0^m = \$0.075$

STRATEGY	CASH FLOW
Purchase H_0^* units of foreign currency at E_0 with the FC invested in foreign security: $H_0^* E_0 = .6472(\$1.50)$	− \$0.9708
Borrow B_0^* dollars: $B_0^* = \$0.90476$	0.90476
Sell call: $C_0^m = \$.075$	0.075
Initial Cash Flow	\$0.00896

	END-OF-THE-PERIOD CASH FLOW	
CLOSING POSITION	$E_T = 1.1(\$1.50/FC)$ = \$1.65/FC $C_T = \$0.15$	$E_T = .95(\$1.50/FC)$ = \$1.425/FC $C_T = 0$
Convert $H_0^*(r_F)$ FC to dollars at E_T: $E_T(.6472)(1.03)$ FC	\$1.10	\$0.95
Repay debt: $-r_{US}B_0^* =$ $(1.05)(-\$0.90476)$	− 0.95	− 0.95
Purchase call: C_T	− 0.15	0
Value of initial cash flow: (\$.00896)(1.05)	0.0094	0.0094
Cash Flow	\$0.0094	\$0.0094

earn a profit of $0.0094, regardless of whether the exchange rate was $E_T = uE_0$ = 1.1($1.50/FC) = $1.65/FC or $E_T = dE_0$ = .95($1.50/FC) = $1.425/FC.

In contrast, if the currency option was underpriced at $0.05, an arbitrageur could buy the call and short the replicating portfolio: Borrow H_0^* = .6472 FC at foreign rate of R_F = .03, convert at E_0 = $1.50/FC to $0.9708, and use the dollars to buy the call and a U.S. risk-free security paying R_{US} = .05. Table 10.5-5 shows that the arbitrageur would earn a certain return of $0.0168 at expiration from implementing this strategy.

For multiple periods, the BOPM for currency options is derived with the same recursive methodology used to derive the BOPM for stock options. An example of a two-period model is shown in Table 10.5-6 in which the previous $1.50 currency call is priced assuming the same parameter values as in the preceding single-period example. In the multiple-period model, the same arbitrage strategies and multiple-period readjustment rules described in Chapter 5 for mispriced stock options apply here for currency call options (see end-of-the-chapter problems). Also, the BOPM

TABLE 10.5-5	**Single-Period Underpriced Arbitrage Strategy**

u = 1.1, d = 0.95, R_{US} = .05, R_F = .03, E_0 = $1.50/FC, X = $1.50/FC,
$C_u = \text{Max}[uE_0 - X, 0]$ = $0.15, $C_d = \text{Max}[dE_0 - X, 0]$ = 0,

$$H_0^* = \frac{C_u - C_d}{E_0 r_F(u - d)} = \frac{\$0.15 - 0}{\$1.50(1.03)(1.1 - .95)} = .6472,$$

$$B_0^* = \frac{C_u(dE_0) - C_d(uE_0)}{r_{US}E_0(u - d)} = \frac{\$0.15(.95)(\$1.50) - 0(1.1)(\$1.50)}{(1.05)(\$1.50)(1.1 - .95)} = \$.90476,$$

$C_0^* = H_0^*E_0 - B_0^*$ = .6472($1.50) − $0.90476 = $0.066, C_0^m = $0.050

STRATEGY	CASH FLOW
Borrow H_0^* units of foreign currency and convert to dollars at E_0: $H_0^*E_0$ = .6472($1.50)	$0.9708
Invest B_0^* dollars in domestic risk-free security: B_0^* = $0.90476	− 0.90476
Buy call: C_0^m = $.05	− 0.05
Initial Cash Flow	$0.016

	END-OF-THE-PERIOD CASH FLOW	
CLOSING POSITION	E_T = 1.1($1.50/FC) = $1.65/FC C_T = $0.15	E_T = .95($1.50/FC) = $1.425/FC C_T = 0
Repay foreign debt: $E_T[H_0^*(r_F)] = E_T(.6472)(1.03)$ FC	− $1.10	− $0.95
Investment return: $B_0^*r_{US}$ = (1.05)($0.90476)	0.95	0.95
Call sale: C_T	0.15	0
Value of initial cash flow: ($.016)(1.05)	0.0168	0.0168
Cash Flow	$0.0168	$0.0168

TABLE 10.5-6   **Two-Period BOPM for Currency Call Options**

$u = 1.1$, $d = 0.95$, $R_{US} = .05$, $R_F = .03$, $p = .46278$, $E_0 = \$1.50$, $X = \$1.50$, $n = 2$

		$u^2E_0 = \$1.815$ $C_{uu} = \$0.315$
	$uE_0 = \$1.65$ $C_u = \$0.17$ $H_u = .97087$ $B_u = \$1.43$	
$E_0 = \$1.50$ $C_0^* = \$0.09$ $H_0 = .6041$ $B_0^* = \$.81515$		$udE_0 = \$1.5675$ $C_{ud} = \$0.0675$
	$dE_0 = \$1.424$ $C_d = \$0.03$ $H_d = .3068$ $B_d = \$0.407$	
		$d^2E_0 = \$1.35375$ $C_{dd} = 0$
0	1	2

for currency puts is the same as the BOPM for stock options described in Chapter 6, except for the inclusion of the foreign interest rate. The derivation of the BOPM for currency put options is included as one of the end-of-the-chapter problems.

In describing the BOPM for currency options, several points should be kept in mind. First, with the multiple-period BOPM it is possible to obtain an option value in a period that is less than the option's intrinsic value. While this is not the case in the multiple-period example shown in Table 10.5-6, such a situation could occur if the call is in the money, $R_F > R_{US}$, the foreign interest rate is relatively large, and the time to expiration is small.* Given these possibilities, if the currency call option is American, then the BOPM needs to be adjusted by constraining each price to be the maximum of either its European value, as determined by the BOPM, or its intrinsic value. It is also possible for European puts to be less than the IV. For puts, this could occur if $R_F > R_{US}$, the foreign rate is relatively low, and the put is deep in the money. If the put is American, the BOPM for puts needs to be adjusted similarly to account for the early-exercise premium.†

---

*Such a case is analogous to a call option on a dividend-paying stock.

†The side-by-side trading of American and European options on the Philadelphia Exchange makes it possible to determine whether American currency options trade at premiums above comparable European values. In a 1989 study, Allan Tucker compared such options and found American options did trade at a premium above European options, implying that an early-exercise premium does exist.

Second, the methodology for estimating u and d that was delineated in Chapter 5 also can be used to estimate the u and d values for the spot exchange rate. In extending the estimating approach to exchange rates, you need to assume that the distribution of logarithmic returns for exchange rates $[\log_e(E_t/E_{t-1})]$ is symmetrical. For exchange rates, though, some empirical evidence suggests that the distribution of logarithmic returns of exchange rates is not normal. Thus, using the BOPM to price options with u and d estimated in such a way, as well as using the B-S OPM, may lead to mispricing.

Finally, note that the currency BOPM and its underlying arbitrage strategy can be defined more easily in terms of foreign currency futures or forward contract positions, instead of the spot exchange rate and foreign security positions. The BOPM derived in terms of currency futures is examined in Chapter 16.

10.5.4   Black-Scholes Option Pricing Model for Currency Options

As previously noted, a foreign currency option is similar to an option on a stock or a stock index paying a continuous dividend. Thus, the currency BOPM with the inclusion of the foreign interest rate that was derived earlier can be viewed as a variation of the dividend-adjusted stock option model. This variation was first noted by Garman and Kohlhagen (G-K) (1983), who extended the continuous-time B-S OPM to the pricing of currency options. The G-K currency OPM uses a foreign-interest-rate-adjusted exchange rate, E_d (analogous to the continuous dividend-adjusted stock price), as the price of the underlying asset in the B-S equation to obtain:

$$C_0^* = E_d N(d_1) - Xe^{-R_{us}T}N(d_2) \qquad (10.5\text{-}11)$$

$$d_1 = \frac{\log_e(E_d/X) + (R_{us} + .5\sigma^2)T}{\sigma\sqrt{T}}$$

$$d_2 = d_1 - \sigma\sqrt{T}$$

$$E_d = E_0 e^{-R_F T},$$

where:

R_F = annual continuously compounded foreign risk-free rate

R_{US} = annual continuously compounded domestic risk-free rate

σ = standard deviation of the logarithmic rate of return on the spot exchange rate.

To illustrate, suppose the current \$/DM exchange rate is \$0.42/DM, the volatility of the exchange rate is $\sigma = .10$, and the annual U.S. and German continuously compounded risk-free rates are $R_{US} = .06$ and $R_F = .08$. Using the

G-K OPM, the equilibrium price of a 40-DM European call with three months to expiration ($T = .25$) is $0.01973/DM:

$$E_d = \$0.42e^{-(.08)(.25)} = \$0.41168/DM$$

$$d_1 = \frac{\log_e(\$.41168/\$.40) + [.06 + .5(.10^2)].25}{.10\sqrt{.25}} = .90064$$

$$d_2 = .90064 - .10\sqrt{.25} = .85064$$

$$N(.90064) = .81595 \quad \text{and} \quad N(.85064) = .80240$$

$$C_0^* = (\$0.41168)(.81595) - \$0.40e^{-(.06)(.25)}(.80240)$$

$$C_0^* = \$0.01973.$$

The G-K model also can be substituted into the put-call parity model [Equation (10.5-5)] to determine the equilibrium price of a currency put:

$$P_0^* = C_0^* + Xe^{-RT} - E_de^{-R_FT}. \tag{10.5-12}$$

Using the preceding example, the value of the corresponding 40-DM European put is $0.01025/DM:

$$P_0^* = \$0.01973/DM + \$.40/DM[e^{-(.06)(.25)}] - \$0.41168/DM[e^{-(.08)(.25)}]$$
$$= \$0.01025/DM.$$

Note: The equilibrium currency call option price in this example is valued below its intrinsic value ($C^* = \$0.01973/DM$, IV = $.02/DM$). If the call was American, an arbitrage opportunity would exist by buying the 40-DM call at $0.01973, exercising the call to obtain a DM for $0.40, and selling the DM for $0.42. Thus, as we noted earlier with the BOPM, using the B-S model to value American options can lead to mispricing. Under certain conditions, American currency options should be priced using either the American BOPM or the Borone-Adesi and Whaley (BAW) model described in Appendix 7C.*

10.6   CONCLUSION

In this chapter, we've extended our analysis of nonstock options to currency options. Currency options can be used for speculating on exchange rate movements, and they can be used to hedge the dollar values or costs of future currency cash flows against exchange rate risk. Also, since foreign currency can be invested in interest-bearing foreign securities, these options have a continuous-leakage

---

*In two 1987 studies, one by Bodurtha and Courtadon and one by Shastri and Wethyarivorn, mispricing was found using the B-S OPM to price currency options.

characteristic similar to the continuous-dividend characteristic associated with index options. As a result, the pricing relations for currency options differ from stock options relations by the inclusion of a foreign interest rate.

Foreign currency options, as well as stock index and debt options, represent relatively new types of options. For many years, though, corporations have offered option securities in the form of convertible bonds, warrants, and rights, and there are a number of features of common stock and debt securities that are similar to options.

In the next chapter, we complete our analysis of nonstock options by examining the options of corporations and the option characteristics embedded in corporate securities.

KEY TERMS

interbank foreign exchange market
interbank currency options market
foreign currency put-call parity model
foreign currency binomial option pricing model
Black-Scholes option pricing model for currency options

SELECTED REFERENCES

Bodurtha and Courtadon (1986) empirically examine currency option boundary conditions. Bodurtha and Courtadon (1987) also examine the B-S OPM pricing of currency options. For a discussion of foreign currency option pricing models, see Biger and Hull (1983) and Garman and Kohlhagen (1983).

Biger, N., and Hull, J. "The Valuation of Currency Options." *Financial Management* (Spring 1983): 24–29.

Bodurtha, J., and Courtadon, G. "Efficiency Tests of the Foreign Currency Options Market." *Journal of Finance* 41 (Mar. 1986): 151–162.

———. "Tests of an American Option Pricing Model on the Foreign Currency Options Market." *Journal of Financial and Quantitative Analysis* 22 (June 1987): 153–167.

Borensztein, E., and Dooley, M. "Options of Foreign Exchange and Exchange Rate Expectations." *International Monetary Fund Staff Papers* 34 (Dec. 1987): 643–680.

Feiger, G., and Jacquillat, B. "Currency Option Bonds, Puts and Calls on Spot Exchange, and the Hedging of Contingent Foreign Earnings." *Journal of Finance* 5 (Dec. 1979): 1129–1139.

Garman, M., and Kohlhagen, W. "Foreign Currency Option Values." *Journal of International Money and Finance* 2 (Dec. 1983): 231–237.

Gendreau, B. "New Markets in Foreign Currency Options." *Business Review* (July–Aug. 1984): 3–12.

Johnson, L. "Foreign Currency Options, Ex Ante Exchange Rate Volatility, and Market Efficiency: An Empirical Test." *Financial Review* (Nov. 1986): 433–450.

Johnson, R. S., Zuber, R., and Loy, D. "An Investigation into Currency Options." *International Review of Economics and Business* (Oct.–Nov. 1986): 1077–1093.

Madura, J., and Veit, T. "Use of Currency Options in International Cash Management." *Journal of Cash Management* (Jan.–Feb. 1986): 42–48.

Shastri, K., and Wethyavivorn, K. "The Valuation of Currency Options for Alternative Stochastic Processes." *Journal of Financial Research* 4 (Dec. 1985): 455–468.

Tucker, A. "Empirical Tests of the Efficiency of the Currency Option Market." *Journal of Financial Research* (Winter 1985): 275–285.

———. "Market-Determined Premia for American Currency Spot Options." Working paper. Temple University (1989).

PROBLEMS AND QUESTIONS

1. Evaluate the following strategies in terms of their profit and exchange rate relations at expiration (use standard contract sizes).

   a. The purchase of a 33(¢)-DM call contract for $0.02 and the sale of a 35(¢)-DM call for $0.01 (contract size 62,500 DM). Evaluate at expiration exchange rates of $.30/DM, $.31, $.33, $.34, $.35, $.36, $.38, and $.40.

   b. The purchase of a 110(¢)-BP call contract for $.02 and the purchase of a 110(¢)-BP put contract at $0.01 (BP option contract size is 31,250). Evaluate at expiration exchange rates of $.95/BP, $1.00, $1.05, $1.07, $1.10, $1.13, $1.15, $1.20, and $1.25.

   c. The purchase of a 33(¢)-DM call contract for $0.0075 and the sale of a 33(¢)-DM put contract for $0.015 (contract size = 62,500 DM). Evaluate at $0.28/DM, $0.30, $0.31, $0.33, $0.34, $0.35, and $0.36.

2. ABC International Investments has investments in British bonds. The bond portfolio pays approximately 625,000 BP in interest every six months, which the company converts to dollars. Recently the $/BP exchange rate has become more volatile. ABC expects, though, that the $/BP exchange rate will increase from its current level of $1.15/BP. Explain how ABC could hedge its next interest payment of 625,000 BP to be paid at the end of March against exchange rate risk, while still gaining if the spot $/BP exchange rate increases, by buying a 115(¢) March BP put for $0.05. Assume the interest payment date and option expiration date are the same. Evaluate at $E_T = $1.00/BP$, $1.05, $1.10, $1.15, $1.20, and $1.25.

3. The James Company, a U.S. corporation, has just purchased machinery from a British company for 937,500 BP. The present $/BP spot rate is $E_0 = $1.10/BP$. The machinery is to be delivered at the end of June, with

payment due at that time. The James Company believes that the U.S. dollar will strengthen against the pound (E_0 decrease) and would like to benefit by paying less in dollars for the machine. At the same time the company does not want to be subject to exchange rate risk. Show how the company could meet its dual objectives by purchasing June 110 BP call contracts trading at $.04/BP. Assume the payment date and June expiration date are the same. Evaluate at $0.95/BP, $1.00, $1.05, $1.10, $1.15, $1.20, and $1.25.

4. Prove the following boundary conditions hold for currency options by showing the arbitrage profits that could occur if the condition is violated and by showing that no liabilities exist at expiration:

a. $C_0 \geq E_0(1 + R_F)^{-T} - X(1 + R_{US})^{-T}$

b. $C_0^a \geq E_0 - X$

c. $P_0^e \geq X(1 + R_{US})^{-T} - E_0(1 + R_F)^{-T}$

d. $P_0^a \geq X - E_0$

e. $P_0^e + E_0(1 + R_F)^{-T} = C_0^e + X(1 + R_{US})^{-T}$

5. Prove that the cash flows at expiration from a reversal formed with currency options are equal to $-X$.

6. Using the put-call parity model, explain how you can form a synthetic long position in a foreign currency using European currency call and put options and a position in a U.S. risk-free bond. Show that your expiration values always equal $E_T(1 + R_F)^T$.

7. Explain what an arbitrageur would do in the following circumstances.

a. $/DM exchange rate is $0.51/DM, the German risk-free rate is 4% (annual), the U.S. risk-free rate is 6%, and a DM call option with an exercise price of $0.50/DM and a three-month expiration ($T = .25$) is trading at $0.01/DM.

b. $/DM exchange rate is $0.48/DM, the German risk-free rate is 4% (annual), the U.S. risk-free rate is 6%, and a European DM put with an exercise price of $0.50/DM and a three-month expiration ($T = .25$) is trading at $0.01/DM.

c. $/DM exchange rate is $0.52/DM, the German risk-free rate is 4% (annual), the U.S. risk-free rate is 6%, and a DM put with an exercise price of $0.50/DM and with an expiration of three months is trading at $0.0075, and a DM call with similar terms is trading at $0.04.

8. Assume the following:

- German risk-free rate (simple annual rate) = .058
- U.S. risk-free rate = .075
- $/DM spot exchange rate = E_0 = $0.32/DM
- Mean logarithmic return (for the $/DM exchange rate) = $\mu = 0$
- Annualized variance = $V[\log_e(E_t/E_{t-1})] = V_e^A = .02777$

a. Using the single-period foreign currency BOPM, determine the price on a DM European call option with an exercise price of $0.33/DM and expiring in two months ($T = .16667$ per year). Note: The period rate is $(1 + R_{Annual})^T - 1$.

b. Explain what an arbitrageur would do if the DM call was priced at $.0075. Show what the arbitrageur's cash flows at expiration would be at $E_T = uE_0$ and $E_T = dE_0$.

c. Explain what an arbitrageur would do if the DM call was priced at $.0045. Show what the arbitrageur's cash flows at expiration would be at $E_T = uE_0$ and $E_T = dE_0$.

9. a. Assuming a foreign period (two-month) risk-free rate of $R_F^{Period} = .00471$ and U.S. rate of $R_{US}^{Period} = .00604$, determine the equilibrium price of the call in Problem 8 using a two-period model.

b. Explain what an arbitrageur would do if the call was priced at $.0075. What would be the arbitrageur's cash flows at the end of period 1 if she closed the positions at $C_1^m = $.015$ when $E_t = uE_0$?

c. Explain how the arbitrageur should readjust the position, and after readjusting, what his cash flow at expiration would be upon closing at $E_T = u^2E_0$ or $E_T = udE_0$.

d. What adjustment would you make if the option was American?

10. Derive the single-period BOPM for foreign currency European put options.

11. Using the single-period foreign currency model for puts derived in Problem 10, price a 33-DM European put option that is comparable to the DM call option described in Problem 8. Is your answer consistent with the put-call parity model?

12. Explain what an arbitrageur would do if the put in Problem 11 was priced at $.0175. Show what the arbitrageur's cash flow at expiration would be at $E_T = uE_0$ and $E_T = dE_0$.

13. Given:

- Continuously compounded British annual risk-free rate $= .12$
- Continuously compounded U.S. annual risk-free rate $= .076$
- $E_0 = $/BP = $1.10/BP$
- $X = 1.10
- Annualized variance $= .0756$

Use the Garman-Kohlhagen currency OPM to determine the equilibrium price of a call option on the BP with an exercise price of $1.10 and expiration of three months ($T = .25$).

COMPUTER PROBLEMS

1. Using information from the *Wall Street Journal* or similar financial source, analyze the following strategies using the software program OPTIONS.

   a. Bull spread with foreign currency call options
   b. Bear spread with foreign currency put options
   c. Straddle purchase with foreign currency options
   d. Strap write with foreign currency options
   e. Combination purchase with foreign currency options

2. Using the BOPM computer program for currency options, determine the equilibrium price of the DM European call in Problem 8 ($E_0 = \$.32$, $X = \$.33$, $T = .16667$, annualized variance $= .02777$, annualized mean $= 0$, $R_F^A = .058$, $R_{US}^A = .075$) when the time to expiration is subdivided into the following subperiods: $n = 1, 2, 10, 20, 100$.

3. Using the G-K currency OPM program, determine the equilibrium BP call prices for each \$/BP exchange rate shown below. Assume $R_F = .12$, $R_{US} = .076$, $X = \$1.10$, $\sigma = .27495$, $T = .25$.

   $E_0 = \$1.00/BP, 1.02, 1.04, 1.06, 1.07, 1.08, 1.09, 1.10, 1.11, 1.12, 1.14, 1.16, 1.18,$ and 1.20.

   Show your results graphically. Comment on the relation.

4. Using the G-K currency OPM program, determine the equilibrium BP put prices for each \$/BP exchange rate shown below. Assume $R_F = .12$, $R_{US} = .076$, $X = \$1.10$, $\sigma = .27495$, $T = .25$.

   $E_0 = \$1.00/BP, 1.02, 1.04, 1.06, 1.07, 1.08, 1.09, 1.10, 1.11, 1.12, 1.14, 1.16, 1.18,$ and 1.20.

   Show your results graphically. Comment on the relation.

5. Given the four following options on the BP, a current spot exchange rate of \$1.10/BP, a 90-day British risk-free rate of .08 and 180-day rate of .082, and U.S. risk-free rates of .05 (90 days) and .053 (180 days), calculate the implied variance for the \$/BP exchange rate using the average implied variance approach.

   a. BP 110 call expiring in 90 days at .05
   b. BP 110 call expiring in 180 days at .055
   c. BP 108 call expiring in 90 days at .063
   d. BP 108 call expiring in 180 days at .066

CHAPTER 11

Option Features
of Corporate Securities

11.1 INTRODUCTION

Our examination of options to this point has focused almost exclusively on exchange-traded options. Many of the characteristics germane to exchange options, though, are embedded in the equity and debt securities of corporations. For example, the call and put features on corporate debt securities, the conversion clauses on convertible bonds, and the preemptive rights of existing stockholders are all optionlike characteristics associated with corporate securities. In fact, the stock of a corporation with debt (a leveraged corporation) can be regarded as an option; that is, a company's stock in effect gives its shareholders the right to buy the firm from the company's creditors at an exercise price equal to the face value of the debt. If the company is successful, causing the value of the firm's assets to grow, then the shareholders will exercise their equity right and buy the company from the creditors at the exercise price equal to the debt's face value. If the value of the firm is less than the debt's face value, then the shareholders will choose not to exercise their option to reclaim the firm from the bondholders.

In this chapter, we will examine the option features embedded in corporate securities. The analysis of the option characteristics of corporate securities, referred to as **contingent claims analysis**, was first examined in the seminal Black and Scholes (1973) option pricing article. We begin our analysis by looking at how a corporation's common stock and debt can be viewed as call options (in Appendix 11A, we analyze stock and debt as put options). This is followed by an analysis of the option features of corporate bonds. Finally, we complete the chapter by examining warrants, rights, and convertible securities and showing how the option pricing methodology can be used as a capital budgeting tool.

11.2 CORPORATE STOCK AND DEBT AS OPTIONS

11.2.1 Equity and Debt as Call Option Positions

The limited-liability feature of common stock enables the stockholders of a leveraged corporation to view their equity position as a call option on the assets of the corporation, with the corporation's creditors being seen as the writers of the call option and the owners of the firm. To illustrate, suppose a company has debt consisting only of a pure discount bond with a face value of F and maturing at time T. The stockholders of the company can view their equity as a call option in which they can buy the company from the bondholders at an exercise price equal to the face value of the debt, with an expiration date equal to the bond's maturity. As shown in Figure 11.2-1(a), if the value of the assets of the firm (V^A) exceeds F at maturity ($V_T^A > F$), then the shareholders of the company would exercise their option and purchase the company from the bondholder at the exercise price of F. If $V_T^A < F$ at maturity, then the shareholders would not (or could not) exercise. Thus, at expiration the total value of equity of the company (V_T^E) would be:

$$V_T^E = \text{Max}[V_T^A - F, 0]. \tag{11.2-1}$$

The bondholders' position, as noted, can be viewed as a covered call write position in which they (1) own the assets of the firm and (2) have a short position on a call option on the firm's assets. As shown in Figure 11.2-1(b), at expiration if $V_T^A < F$, the call (or equity) position is worthless, and the bondholders retain their ownership of the company. If $V_T^A > F$, though, then the stockholders will buy the

FIGURE 11.2-1

Equity and Debt Values at Maturity

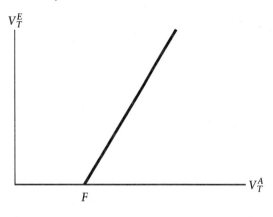

Value of Equity
at Maturity
(a)

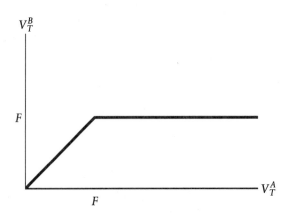

Value of Debt
at Maturity
(b)

company from the bondholders at the exercise price of F. In this case the value of the bond (V_T^B) is equal to F. Thus, the value of the bondholders' position at maturity is equal to the minimum of either F or V_T^A:

$$V_T^B = \text{Min}[V_T^A, F]. \qquad (11.2\text{-}2)$$

This minimum condition can be stated equivalently in terms of the following maximum condition:

$$V_T^B = V_T^A - \text{Max}[V_T^A - F, 0]. \qquad (11.2\text{-}3)$$

That is:

	$\text{Min}[V_T^A, F]$	$V_T^A - \text{Max}[V_T^A - F, 0]$
If $V_T^A \geq F$	F	$V_T^A - (V_T^A - F) = F$
If $V_T^A < F$	V_T^A	$V_T^A - 0 = V_T^A$

Equation (11.2-3) shows that the expiration value of the debt is equal to the value of the firm minus the intrinsic value of the call, which is equal to the expiration value of a covered call write position.

Prior to maturity, the value of the stock (V_t^E) would equal its intrinsic value [Equation (11.2-1)] plus a time value premium, and the value of the debt would equal the value of the firm minus the equity value. Figure 11.2-2 shows the values of equity and debt as functions of the value of the firm. In the figure, the IV line depicts the intrinsic value of the equity, the 45° line shows the maximum equity value, the curve in between shows the familiar call price curve, representing the value of the equity, and the vertical distance between the 45° line (V_t^A) and the equity curve (V_t^E) shows the value of the debt.

FIGURE 11.2-2

Equity and Debt Values

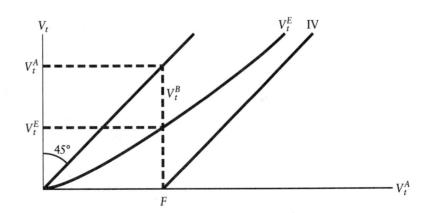

11.2.2   Valuing Equity as a Call Option with the Black-Scholes Option Pricing Model

The value of equity can be estimated using the B-S OPM. Specifically:

$$V_0^E = V_0^A N(d_1) - Fe^{-RT}N(d_2) \tag{11.2-4}$$

$$d_1 = \frac{\log_e(V_0^A/F) + (R + .5\sigma^2)T}{\sigma\sqrt{T}}$$

$$d_2 = d_1 - \sigma\sqrt{T}.$$

As an example, suppose the ABC Company currently is worth $15 million, has a debt obligation consisting of a pure discount bond maturing in two years with a face value of $10 million, and has an asset variability of $\sigma = .5$. If the annual risk-free rate is 6%, then the value of ABC stock, using the B-S OPM, would be $7.17 million, and the value of its debt would be $7.83 million. That is:

$$d_1 = \frac{\log_e(\$15M/\$10M) + [.06 + .5(.5^2)]2}{.5\sqrt{2}} = 1.09667$$

$$d_2 = 1.09667 - .5\sqrt{2} = .38957$$

$$N(1.09667) = .86338 \quad \text{and} \quad N(.38957) = .65175$$

$$V_0^E = \$15M(.86338) - (\$10M)e^{-(.06)(2)}.65175 = \$7.17M$$

$$V_0^B = V_0^A - V_0^E = \$15M - \$7.17M = \$7.83M.$$

Note that the value of the stock is an increasing function of the variability of the firm's assets when equity is valued as an option. This direct relation reflects the fact that equity provides an unlimited profit potential and a limited-loss (or limited-liability) characteristic. Given the direct relationship between equity value and variability, it follows that if the objective of the company's managers is to maximize the wealth of its shareholders, then with other factors constant, managers in selecting among mutually exclusive investment projects should select the riskier one. If the market, in turn, values stock as a call option, then managers can augment the equity values of their company by selecting riskier investments (and finding creditors to help finance them).

11.2.3   Subordinated Debt

In the preceding section, we assumed that the corporation had only one class of debt. Consider now the case in which the company has the following two debt classes:

1. A pure discount bond with a priority or senior claim on the company's assets, a face value of F^s, and a current value of V_0^{Bs}.

2. A pure discount bond with a claim to the company's assets that is subordinate (or second) to the senior bond's claim, a face value of F^j, and a current value of V_0^{Bj}.

For simplicity, assume that both bonds mature at the same time and that the company will not pay any dividends until the principals on the bonds have been paid.

With these two debt obligations, the value of the firm is now defined as:

$$V_0^A = V_0^E + V_0^{Bs} + V_0^{Bj}. \tag{11.2-5}$$

As before, the stockholders' position is equivalent to a long call option in which they have the right to buy the company from the bondholders. In this case, the exercise price is equal to the sum of F^s and F^j, and the value of the stockholders' position at maturity is:

$$V_T^E = \text{Max}[V_T^A - (F^s + F^j), 0]. \tag{11.2-6}$$

The senior bondholders' position is the same as in the preceding section: a covered call position in which they own the asset and are short in a call option with an exercise price equal to F^s. At maturity, the value of their position is:

$$V_T^{Bs} = \text{Min}[V_T^A, F^s] \tag{11.2-7}$$

$$V_T^{Bs} = V_T^A - \text{Max}[V_T^A - F^s, 0].$$

Finally, the subordinated bondholders have a position equivalent to a portfolio with a long call position on the firm with an exercise price of F^s and a short call position on the firm with an exercise price of $F^s + F^j$. At expiration, the value of their position is:

$$V_T^{Bj} = \text{Max}[V_T^A - F^s, 0] - \text{Max}[V_T^A - (F^s + F^j), 0]. \tag{11.2-8}$$

This equivalence can be seen below in Table 11.2-1, which shows: If $V_T^A > (F^s + F^j)$ at maturity, then the junior bondholders receive F^j; if $F^s < V_T^A < (F^s + F^j)$, then the senior bondholders receive F^s, with $V_T^A - F^s$ left to the junior bondholders; finally, if $V_T^A < F^s$, then the senior bondholders retain the company, and the junior bondholders, as well as the shareholders, receive nothing. These three positions are summarized graphically in Figure 11.2-3.

TABLE 11.2-1	**Subordinate Debt Position**	
	$V_T^{Bj} = \text{Max}[(V_T^A - F^s), 0] - \text{Max}[V_T^A - (F^s + F^j), 0]$	
	If $V_T^A > (F^s + F^j)$	$V_T^{Bj} = V_T^A - F^s - (V_T^A - (F^s + F^j)) = F^j$
	If $F^s < V_T^A < (F^s + F^j)$	$V_T^{Bj} = V_T^A - F^s - 0 = V_T^A - F^s$
	If $V_T^A < F^s$	$V_T^{Bj} = 0$

FIGURE 11.2-3

Equity, Senior Debt, and
Junior Debt Positions
at Expirations

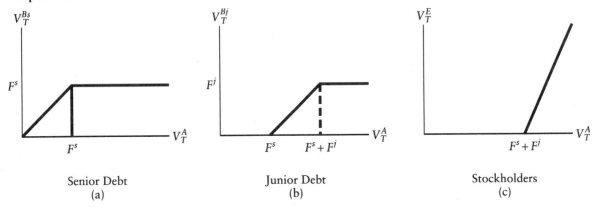

Senior Debt
(a)

Junior Debt
(b)

Stockholders
(c)

11.3   OPTION FEATURES OF BONDS

The default-risk characteristic of the bonds just described represent an optionlike feature inherent to the bonds. Other embedded option characteristics of bonds also exist, including coupon payments, the call rights of the issuer, and the put rights of the bondholders.

11.3.1   Coupon Bonds

In describing the preceding option characteristics of the stockholders' and creditors' positions, we assumed the debt claims were pure discount bonds. If the company's bonds pay coupons, then Equation (11.2-3) for valuing debt and Equation (11.2-1) for valuing equity only approximate the debt and equity values of the company.

A more precise model is found by viewing the shareholders as having a long position and the bondholders a short position in a **compound option**: an option on an option. That is, for a coupon bond in which the principal is paid at maturity, the shareholders have the right to buy the company from the bondholders at an exercise price equal to the bond's face value ($X = F$) at expiration (T). The period before expiration ($T - 1$), the stockholders are responsible for paying the period coupon. This payment can be viewed by the stockholders as a call option, with an exercise price equal to the coupon payment, giving them the right to buy the call option with $X = F$ expiring at maturity—an option on an option. Similarly, the coupon payment two periods from maturity ($T - 2$) also is a call option, giving the stockholders the right to buy the call option on the option in period $T - 1$ at an exercise price equal to the coupon payment. Thus, when the debt of the company consists of a coupon bond, the stockholders have a long position and the bondholders a short position on a compound call option.*

11.3.2   Callable Bonds

Callable bonds have features that give the issuer the right to buy back the bond from the bondholders at a specified price. This feature is a benefit to the issuer. If interest rates decrease in the market, then the issuer can reduce his interest costs of financing assets by borrowing funds at the lower rates and using the proceeds to call the bond issue. When a bond issue is called, the bondholders sell their bonds back to the issuer, usually at a premium above the face value of the bond, the amount of the premium being specified in the bond indenture. While the bondholders benefit from receiving the call premium, they also are in a situation in which they have to reinvest their funds in a market with lower interest rates.

Conceptually, when an investor buys a callable bond, she implicitly is selling a call option to the issuer, giving the issuer the right to buy the bond from the bondholder before maturity at a specified price. Theoretically, a callable bond can be priced as the sum of the value of an identical, but noncallable, bond minus the value of the call feature.

For example, suppose a three-year, noncallable bond with a 10% annual coupon is selling at par ($F = 100$), or a yield to maturity (YTM) of 10%. A callable bond that is identical in all respects except for its call feature should sell at 100 minus the call premium. An approximate value of the embedded call option can be estimated using the B-S OPM.[†] In this case, suppose the call feature gives the issuer the right to buy back the bond at any time during the bond's life at an exercise price of 115. Assuming a risk-free rate of 6% and a variability of $\sigma = .10$ on the noncallable bond's natural logarithmic return, the call premium using the Black-Scholes model would be 8.95. That is:

$$d_1 = \frac{\log_e(V_0^B/X) + (R + .5\sigma^2)T}{\sigma\sqrt{T}}$$

$$= \frac{\log_e(100/115) + [.06 + .5(.10^2)]3}{.10\sqrt{3}} = .31892$$

$$d_2 = d_1 - \sigma\sqrt{T} = .31892 - .10\sqrt{3} = .14571$$

$$N(d_1) = N(.31892) = .62519$$

$$N(d_2) = N(.14571) = .55772$$

---

*Since a coupon bond represents a portfolio of pure discount bonds with face values equal to the coupons, it would seem that a coupon bond would consist of a portfolio of short call option positions. This approach, though, fails to account for the dependency between coupon payments.

[†]The call features on many callable bonds allow the issuer to call the bond at any time. As a result, the bond's embedded call option is American. Also, as noted in Chapter 7, the B-S OPM assumes interest rates are constant. For most bonds, though, the change in their value is due to interest rate changes. Thus, the use of the B-S OPM (defined for European options and with a constant interest rate) to value the call option embedded in a bond should be viewed only as an approximation.

$$C_0^* = V_0^B N(d_1) - Xe^{-RT}N(d_2) = 100(.62519)$$
$$- 115e^{-(.06)(3)}(.55772) = 8.95.$$

Thus, the price of the callable bond is 91.05:

Price of callable bond = Price of noncallable bond − Call premium

Price of callable bond = 100 − 8.95 = 91.05.

As an investment strategy, the buyer of a callable bond hopes that the price of the bond stays slightly below the exercise price and that interest rates are stable. If interest rates decrease, then the price of the callable bond may increase above the exercise price, leading to a call on the bond and forcing the bondholder to reinvest in a market with lower rates. On the other hand, if rates increase, the price of the bond would decrease, resulting in a capital loss if the bondholder has to liquidate before maturity.

11.3.3   Putable Bonds

A *putable bond*, or *put bond*, gives the bondholder the right to sell the bond back to the issuer at a specified price. In contrast to callable bonds, putable bonds benefit the holder: If the price of the bond decreases below the exercise price, the bondholder can sell the bond back to the issuer. From the bondholders' perspective, a put bond is analogous to a protective put position. If interest rates decrease in the market, then the bondholder benefits from the resulting higher bond price; if interest rates increase, the holder can exercise, thus giving him downside protection. Conceptually, with a put bond the holder is buying an identical, but nonputable, bond plus a put option on the bond. Such a bond could be priced by determining the values of the nonputable bond and the put option, with the value of the option being estimated by the OPM for puts.

11.4   CONVERTIBLE SECURITIES

Warrants, rights, convertible bonds, and convertible preferred stock can be classified as convertible securities. These instruments give the holders the right to convert one security into another.

11.4.1   Warrants

A *warrant* is a call option giving the holder the right to buy a specified number of shares of another security at a specific price, on or before a specific date. Most warrants are sold by corporations, usually giving the holder the right to buy a specified number of shares of the company's common stock any time on or before expiration, with expiration ranging between three and five years.* As such, warrants represent a long-term American call option written by the corporation. Like exchange-traded call options, warrants are protected against stock splits and dividends, but not against cash dividends.

Corporations often issue warrants as a "sweetner" with other securities (e.g., subordinate bond or preferred stock). When they are issued with another security, they can be either nondetachable or detachable. If the holder of a **nondetachable warrant** wants to sell the warrant, she would have to sell the accompanying security with it or exercise the warrant. A **detachable warrant**, though, can be sold separately. Most outstanding warrants trade on the over-the-counter market, although a number of warrants are listed on the New York, Pacific, and American stock exchanges.

Most of the contractual characteristics of warrants (exercise price, expiration, etc.) are similar to those of call options on a stock. The fundamental difference between a call on a stock and a warrant on the same stock is that the writer of the warrant is the corporation, while the writer of a call option is an individual investor. This difference implies that when a warrantholder exercises, the corporation must issue new shares of stock. When the company, in turn, sells the shares on the warrant contract, it will receive cash from the warrantholders, which it can use to finance its capital formation; however, the company also will have its stock diluted. In contrast, when an exchange-traded call option on the stock is exercised, the writer sells his shares (if the writer is covered) or buys existing shares in the market (if naked) and sells them to the holder. Thus, exercising a call neither dilutes the company's stock nor increases its cash flows.

To illustrate the difference between warrants and call options, consider the case of the LM corporation, which owns a small crude-oil well currently worth $100,000. Assume the LM company is an all-equity company, has 100 shares of stock outstanding (n_0), with each share worth $1000, and is owned by four shareholders, A, B, C, and D, each with 25 shares.[†]

To see the implications of a call option on the LM company, suppose that shareholder D sells a call option to investor E, giving the investor the right to buy 25 shares of LM stock at $X = \$1100$ per share. After the call option is sold, suppose the value of the oil well company increases from $100,000 to $120,000, raising the price of a share of LM stock from $1000 to $1200. If, after the increase in value, investor E exercises her call option, shareholder D simply would sell his 25 shares to E at $1100 per share. For the LM corporation, the exercise of this call option would have no impact on the company's total number of shares of 100.

Now suppose that instead of shareholder D's selling a call option when the company is worth $100,000, the LM corporation sells a warrant to investor E, giving E the right to buy $n_w = 25$ shares at $1100 per share. Again suppose that the value of the company increases to $120,000 and that E exercises her warrant. When E exercises, the LM corporation will have to print 25 new shares of stock and sell them to E. This, in turn, will dilute the company's equity shares. This dilution effect, though, will be offset partially by the receipt of (25 shares)($1100

---

*Some warrants can be converted into preferred stock and bonds, and some warrants can be converted into the stock of another corporation (this is usually when a merger is pending).

†This example is based on a similar one presented by Ross, Westerfield, and Jaffe (1991).

per share) = $27,500 in cash from E. Thus, in this case the exercise of the warrant affects the number of shares of the LM company and its value. Specifically, the new value of the LM company (V^{LM}) is $147,500 [the value of the oil well (V^{oil}) plus the cash]:

$$V^{LM} = V^{oil} + \text{Cash from the exercised warrant}$$

$$V^{LM} = \$120,000 + \$27,500 = \$147,500.$$

The LM company now has $n_0 + n_w = 125$ shares of stock, with each share worth $1180:

$$\frac{\text{Stock value}}{\text{Shares}} = \frac{V^{LM}}{n_0 + n_w}$$

$$\frac{\text{Stock value}}{\text{Shares}} = \frac{\$147,500}{125} = \$1180.$$

For investor E, the dilution effect associated with the warrant causes the gain from exercising the warrant to be less than the gain from exercising the call. That is, E's return from exercising the call is $25(\$1200 - \$1100) = \$2500$, while her return from exercising the warrant is only $25(\$1180 - \$1100) = \$2000$. Formally, the difference between the two options can be seen by comparing their intrinsic values (IV_c and IV_w). That is:

$$IV_c = \text{Max}\left[\frac{V^{oil}}{n_0} - X, 0\right] \tag{11.4-1}$$

$$IV_w = \text{Max}\left[\frac{V^{oil} + Xn_w}{n_0 + n_w} - X, 0\right]. \tag{11.4-2}$$

IV_w expressed in terms of IV_c is:

$$IV_w = \left(\frac{n_0}{n_0 + n_w}\right)IV_c. \tag{11.4-3}$$

The term $n_0/(n_0 + n_w)$ is a **dilution factor**. In the example, it is equal to $100/125 = .8$. Thus, Equation (11.4-3) shows that the intrinsic value of a warrant is equal to the intrinsic value of a call option on the same underlying stock times the dilution factor. Since warrants and call options on the same stock are perfectly correlated (they both derive their values from the same asset), the current warrant price (W_0), in turn, should equal the current call value times the dilution factor. That is:

$$W_0 = \left(\frac{n_0}{n_0 + n_w}\right)C_0. \tag{11.4-4}$$

Accordingly, to price a warrant we can use the OPM to value the warrant as a call, then multiply that value by the dilution factor to determine the value of the warrant.

11.4.2 Rights

Most state laws give the stockholders of a corporation **rights** to maintain their shares of ownership in the corporation. This **preemptive right** implies that when a company issues new shares of stock, the existing shareholders must be given the first right of refusal. Corporations accomplish this by issuing each stockholder a certificate, known as a right (or subscription warrant). The right entitles the existing shareholder to buy new issues of common stock at a specified price, known as the **subscription price**, for a specified period of time before the stock is sold to the general public. To maintain ownership proportionality, each share of stock receives one right; and to facilitate the new stock sale, the subscription price usually is set below the current stock price. After a company issues rights to its shareholders, the existing shares of stock sell cum rights (buyers of the stock are entitled to the right) to a specified ex-rights date, after which the stock sells without the right.

A right is similar to a warrant. Technically, it is a call option issued by the corporation, giving the holder the right to buy stock at a specified price (subscription price) on or before a specific date. Like warrants, when a right is exercised, new shares are created, and the company has additional capital. Also like warrants, rights can be sold in a secondary market; the rights for large companies often are traded on organized exchanges, while smaller companies have their rights traded on the over-the-counter exchange. Rights differ from warrants in that their expiration periods are shorter (e.g., one to three months compared to three to five years for a warrant), and their exercise prices usually are set below their stock prices, while warrants usually have exercise prices above. Also, because of their short expiration periods, rights are usually not adjusted for stock splits and stock dividends.

To illustrate the characteristics of rights, consider the case of the ABC corporation, which is planning to raise $10 million in equity to finance the construction of a new plant. The company currently is worth $100 million, has no debt, and has 1 million shares of stock outstanding (n_0), with each share trading at $100. Because of the preemptive rights of shareholders, ABC plans to finance its $10 million investment with a **rights offering** in which its existing shareholders will be given the opportunity to buy new shares of stock at a subscription price of $80, with each shareholder to receive one right for each share he owns.

The key question for the ABC company is how many rights will be needed to purchase one new share of ABC stock at $80 per share. This can be found by first determining the number of shares that need to be sold to raise the desired capital. In this example, with a planned $10 million investment expenditure and a subscription price of $80, ABC would need to sell 125,000 new shares:

$$\text{Number of new shares} = N_n = \frac{\text{Investment expenditure}}{\text{Subscription price}}$$

$$N_n = \frac{\$10{,}000{,}000}{\$80/\text{share}} = 125{,}000 \text{ shares.}$$

Since one right is given for each existing share and ABC has 1 million existing shares, eight rights would be needed (N_r) to purchase one new share:

$$\begin{matrix} \text{Number of rights} \\ \text{needed to buy} \\ \text{one share} \end{matrix} = N_r = \frac{\text{Number of existing shares}}{\text{Number of new shares}}$$

$$N_r = \frac{1,000,000}{125,000} = 8 \text{ rights.}$$

Thus, shareholders would surrender eight rights and $80 to buy one new share. This rights offering, in turn, would provide ABC $10 million in cash to finance its investment, and would create 125,000 additional shares.

The intrinsic value of the right (IV_r) is equal to the difference between the market price of the stock (S_T) and the subscription price (X_s) divided by the number of rights needed to purchase one share:

$$\text{Intrinsic value of the right} = IV_r = \frac{S_T - X_s}{N_r}.$$

With 125,000 additional shares and $10 million cash inflow, the estimated price of ABC stock would be $97.78:

$$S_T = \frac{\text{Existing equity value} + \text{Investment value}}{\text{Old shares} + \text{New shares}}$$

$$S_T = \frac{\$100,000,000 + \$10,000,000}{1,000,000 + 125,000} = \$97.78.$$

With an $80 subscription price, eight rights would be worth $97.78 − $80 = $17.78, and one right would be worth $2.22:

$$\frac{S_T - X_s}{N_r} = \frac{\$97.78 - \$80}{8} = \$2.22.$$

11.4.3   Convertible Bonds

A *convertible bond* is similar to a bond with a nondetachable warrant. Like a regular bond, it pays interest and principal; and like a warrant, it can be exchanged for a specified number of shares of common stock.

Convertible bonds often are sold as subordinate issues by smaller, riskier companies. The conversion feature of the bond, in turn, serves as a "sweetner" to the debt issue. To investors, convertible bonds offer the potential for high rates of return if the corporation does well, while still providing a downside protection with the bond. Convertible bonds usually sell at a lower YTM than similar nonconvertible bonds and usually are callable.

Convertible Bond Terms

Consider the ABC corporation's convertible bond, which pays an annual coupon of 5%, a par value of $1000, matures in 10 years, can be called at any time by the issuer at an exercise price (X_B) of $1050, and can be converted by the holder at any time into 25 shares of ABC stock. The convertible features of the ABC bond include conversion ratio, conversion price, conversion value, and straight debt value.

The *conversion ratio* (CR) is the number of shares of stock that can be acquired when the bond is tendered for conversion. The ABC convertible's conversion ratio is 25 shares of ABC stock for each bond. Note that the conversion ratio on some convertible bonds can change over time. Also, some convertible bonds allow conversion to be done either by tendering over the bond or paying a specified amount of cash (or some combination). For example, a convertible could stipulate that 25 shares of stock can be obtained in exchange for the bond or for cash equal to a specific proportion of the company's stock value, whichever is smaller.

The *conversion price* (CP) is the bond's par value divided by the conversion ratio:

$$CP = \frac{F}{CR}. \tag{11.4-5}$$

The conversion price of the ABC convertible is $40. The conversion price is applicable only when the bond is trading at par. Many convertible bond contracts, though, specify changes in the conversion ratio over time by specifying changes in the conversion price instead of in the conversion ratio.

The *conversion value* (CV) is the convertible bond's value as a stock. At a given point in time (t), the conversion value is equal to the product of the conversion ratio and the market price of the stock (S_t):

$$CV_t = (CR)S_t. \tag{11.4-6}$$

If the current price of ABC stock is $25, the conversion value of ABC's convertible bond is (25)($25) = $625. If the price of the stock is expected to grow at a constant rate over time, the expected conversion values can be expressed as a function of time, in which:

$$CV_t = (CR)(S_0)(1 + g)^t \tag{11.4-7}$$

where:

g = annual expected growth rate of the stock's price*

t = years

S_0 = current stock price.

Table 11.4-1 and Figure 11.4-1 show the conversion values of the ABC convertible per year given an assumed annual growth rate of 7%.

The *straight debt value* (SDV) is the convertible bond's value as a nonconvertible bond. The SDV is found by discounting the convertible's cash flows by the YTM on an identical, but nonconvertible, bond. Thus, in the case of the ABC convertible, if the YTM on a 10-year, 5% (coupon) callable bond with the same default risk as ABC was trading at a YTM of 10%, then the current SDV of the ABC convertible would be $692.77:

$$SDV_0 = \sum_{t=1}^{M} \frac{Coupon_t}{(1 + YTM)^t} + \frac{F}{(1 + YTM)^M} \tag{11.4-8}$$

$$SDV_0 = \sum_{t=1}^{10} \frac{\$50}{(1.10)^t} + \frac{\$1000}{(1.10)^{10}} = \$692.77.$$

---

*If a company has a constant price-earnings ratio over time, then the growth rate in its stock price would be related directly to the company's earnings growth rate.

TABLE 11.4-1

	Conversion Values and Straight Debt Values over Time		
t (YEAR)	STOCK PRICE S_T	CV_t	SDV_t
0	$25.00	$ 625.00	$ 692.77
1	26.75	668.75	712.05
2	28.62	715.56	733.25
3	30.63	765.65	756.58
4	32.77	819.25	782.24
5	35.06	876.59	810.46
6	37.52	937.96	841.51
7	40.14	1003.61	875.66
8	42.95	1073.87	913.22
9	45.96	1149.04	954.54
10	49.18	1229.47	1000.00

$$CV_t = (CR)(S_0)(1 + g)^t = (25)(\$25)(1.07)^t$$

$$SDV = \sum_{t=1}^{M} \frac{Coupon_t}{(1 + YTM)^t} + \frac{F}{(1 + YTM)^M} = \sum_{t=1}^{10} \frac{\$50}{(1.10)^t} + \frac{\$1000}{(1.10)^{10}}$$

FIGURE 11.4-1

Conversion Values and
Straight Debt Values over
Time

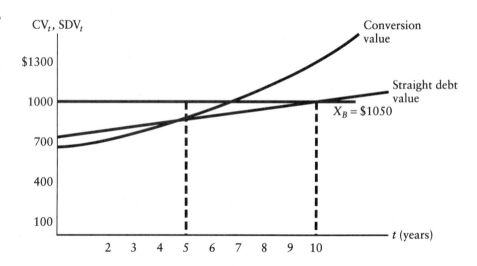

As shown in Table 11.4-1 and Figure 11.4-1, if the yield curve is flat and constant over time, then the SDV_t will grow at constant rate over time, equaling its face value at maturity.

Minimum and Maximum Convertible Bond Prices
Arbitrage forces ensure that the **minimum convertible bond price** (P_t^{cb}) is the greater of either the bond's straight debt value or its conversion value. Thus, the minimum price of a convertible bond is:

$$\text{Min } P_t^{cb} = \text{Max}[CV_t, SDV_t]. \qquad (11.4\text{-}9)$$

If a convertible bond is priced below its conversion value, arbitrageurs could buy it, convert to stock, then sell the stock in the market to earn an abnormal profit of $CV - P_t^{cb}$. Arbitrageurs seeking such opportunities would push up the price of the convertible until it is at least equal to its conversion value. Similarly, if a convertible is priced below its SDV, then you could profit by buying the convertible and selling it as a regular bond. Thus, the dominant CV or SDV curve depicted in Figure 11.4-1 defines the minimum boundary condition for the ABC convertible bond.

In addition to a minimum price, if the convertible bond has a call feature, the exercise price at which the issuer can redeem the bonds (X_B) places a maximum limit on the price of the convertible. That is, for most issuers it is advantageous to buy back the convertible bond once its price is equal to the exercise price. Buying back the bond, in turn, frees the company to sell new stock and debt at prices higher than the stock or straight debt values associated with the convertible. Thus, the maximum price of a convertible bond is its exercise price:

$$\text{Max } P_t^{cb} = X_B. \tag{11.4-10}$$

The maximum price for the ABC convertible is depicted in Figure 11.4-1 by the horizontal line at $X_B = \$1050$.

The actual price of a convertible usually will be at a premium above its minimum value but below the maximum:

$$X_B > P_t^{cb} > \text{Max}[SDV_t, CV_t]. \tag{11.4-11}$$

Pricing a Convertible with the Option Pricing Model

Conceptually, the price of the convertible can be thought of as the sum of its straight debt value plus the value of the call option on the stock. To estimate the call value using the OPM, an exercise date, as well as an appropriate exercise price, needs to be specified. In addition, you also need to consider the possible impact a conversion would have on the firm's capital structure (since the conversion will change the company's debt/equity mix) and the possible dilution effect on the company's stock. For these reasons, valuing the call feature of a convertible bond with the OPM can yield only an approximate value.

11.5 USING OPTIONS AS A CAPITAL BUDGETING TOOL

Many investment projects have optionlike characteristics that traditional capital budgeting tools are unable to value. To see this, consider the case of East Side Developers (ESD): a development company that is thinking of purchasing and developing a 50-acre farm to sell eventually to area housing developers. The cost of the land is $0.5 million, and a number of developers other than ESD are interested in the property. ESD estimates with a high degree of certainty that the development expenditures for clearing, road construction, utility installation, and the like will be $2 million and that development will take one year to complete. ESD also projects that the expected revenue (after taxes) from selling the developed lots will be $3 million and will occur one year after their development.

Because of the uncertainty over the expected $3 million revenue from the lot sales, ESD requires a rate of return on the project (cost of capital) of 20%. As a result, the net present value (NPV) of the project is a negative $0.0833M, and so the project should be rejected. That is:

$$NPV = -\$0.5M - \frac{\$2M}{1.20} + \frac{\$3M}{1.20^2} = -\$0.08333M.$$

However, the risk of the project can be attributed directly to the uncertainty over whether a shopping mall will be developed near the proposed development location. Furthermore, ESD knows that if the mall developers are able to secure an anchor tenant, they will be able to obtain their financing, and the mall will be developed. If this occurs, ESD is certain it will be able to sell the lots for a total of $6 million; however, if the mall is not developed, they see no chance of selling the lots. The information about the anchor tenant will not be known for another year, and ESD currently estimates there is a 50/50 chance a tenant will be secured.

Given these contingencies, ESD alternatively can view the project as one in which it could pay $0.5 million for the land (assuming that other developers remain interested), then wait one year before it decides on developing the lots, at which time the status of the mall will be known. If the mall project is accepted, then ESD will be able to earn an almost certain revenue of $6M. Given the acceptance of the mall project, the NPV of ESD's project would be the present value of $6M, with the discount rate being the risk-free rate (or at least a lower discount rate than 20%, since the project risk has been reduced), minus the $2M land development expenditures. If ESD uses a 10% discount rate, then the NPV of its project at year 1 would be $3.454M, assuming the mall project is accepted. That is:

$$NPV_1 = -\$2M + \frac{\$6M}{1.10} = \$3.454M.$$

Thus, by waiting, the investment project now can be viewed as a call option costing $0.5 million (the purchase of the land), giving the developers the right to develop the project for an exercise price of $2M and a certain future return of $6M, with an expiration of one year. If the mall is developed, ESD will exercise its call, realizing a gain in value of $3.454M; if the mall is not developed, the call is worthless, and ESD will not exercise, losing its call premium of $0.5M.*

In summary, the example illustrates how investment projects can be viewed as options. Using an option perspective allows more flexibility in investment decisions than do traditional capital budgeting approaches.

11.6 CONCLUSION

In this chapter, we've examined the option features embedded in corporate securities. Our analysis of the contingent claims of corporations has included the

---

*If the mall is not developed but the developer can sell the undeveloped land for some amount, then the project could also be viewed as having putlike characteristics.

option positions inherent in the equity and debts positions of leveraged corporations; call and put features of bonds; the option-conversion features of warrants, rights, and convertible securities; and the application of option methodology to capital budgeting.

KEY TERMS

contingent claims analysis
compound option
callable bond
putable bond
warrant
nondetachable warrant
detachable warrant
dilution factor
rights

preemptive right
subscription price
rights offering
convertible bond
conversion ratio
conversion price
conversion value
straight debt value
minimum convertible bond price

SELECTED REFERENCES

Black, F., and Scholes, M. "The Pricing of Options and Corporate Liabilities." *Journal of Political Economy* 81 (1973): 637–659.

Brennan, M., and Schwartz, E. "Convertible Bonds: Valuation and Optimal Strategies for Call Conversion." *Journal of Finance* 32 (Dec. 1977): 1699–1716.

―――. "Evaluating Natural Resource Investments." *Journal of Business* 58 (1985): 135–157.

Constantinides, G. "Warrant Exercise and Bond Conversion in Competitive Markets." *Journal of Financial Economics* 13 (Sept. 1984): 371–397.

Galai, D., and Schneller, M. "Pricing Warrants and the Value of the Firm." *Journal of Finance* 33 (Dec. 1978): 1333–1342.

Geske, R. "The Valuation of Compound Options." *Journal of Financial Economics* 7 (Mar. 1979): 63–81.

Hsia, C. "Optimal Debt of a Firm: An Option Pricing Approach." *Journal of Financial Research* 4 (Fall 1981): 221–231.

Ingersoll, J. "A Contingent-Claims Valuation of Convertible Securities." *Journal of Financial Economics* 4 (May 1977): 289–322.

Ross, S., Westerfield, R., and Jaffe, J. F. *Corporate Finance.* Homewood, Ill.: Dow Jones-Irwin, 1991, pp. 634–648.

Schwartz, E. "The Valuation of Warrants: Implementing a New Approach." *Journal of Financial Economics* 4 (Jan. 1977): 79–93.

PROBLEMS AND QUESTIONS

1. Keening Land Developers is a real estate development company with a project in the Midwest currently valued at $20M. The Keening company financed the project by borrowing from Southwest Savings and Loan. The loan called for a principal payment of $25 million at the end of four years (no coupon interest).

   a. Use the B-S OPM to determine the equity value of Keening Developers' Midwest project. Assume $R = 6\%$ and the volatility of the project is $\sigma = .3$.

   b. What is the value of the creditors' position?

   c. Show graphically the following positions: the value of the Keening equity position at the loan's maturity as it relates to the value of the asset; the value of the creditors' position at the loan's maturity as it relates to the value of the asset; the current equity and debt values as they relate to the value of the asset.

   d. Use the B-S OPM to determine the equity value of Keening Developers' Midwest project and its debt value if the volatility was $\sigma = .5$.

2. Using an option perspective, comment on the relation between stock value and variability. Provide an example or a case to illustrate the relation.

3. Given the following information on a callable bond:

   - Coupon rate = 10% (annual)
   - Face value = F = $1000
   - Maturity = 5 years
   - Callable at $1100
   - YTM on a similar noncallable bond = 10%
   - Annualized standard deviation of the noncallable bond's natural logarithmic return = .15
   - Continuously compounded, annual risk-free rate = 5%

   a. What is the value of the noncallable bond?

   b. Using the B-S OPM, what is the value of the callable bond's call feature to the issuer?

   c. What is the value of the callable bond?

4. Given the following information on a putable bond:

   - Coupon rate = 10% (annual)
   - Face value = F = $1000
   - Maturity = 5 years
   - Putable at $950
   - YTM on a similar nonputable bond = 10%
   - Annualized standard deviation of the nonputable bond's natural logarithmic return = .15

- Continuously compounded, annual risk-free rate $= 5\%$

a. What is the value of the nonputable bond?

b. Using the B-S OPM, what is the value of the putable bond's put feature to the holder?

c. What is the value of the putable bond?

5. ABC Thoroughbred Inc. is a small horsing syndicate that owns one three-year-old racehorse named Box Spread. Based on Box Spread's racing record and potential breeding value, the estimated value of the horse, and therefore of ABC Thoroughbred Inc., is $1,000,000. ABC Thoroughbred Inc. has 10 shareholders, each with 100 shares (total shares $= n = 1000$) and no debt. In addition, ABC also has a warrant it sold to Mr. Lucky giving him the right to buy 100 shares of ABC for $1300 per share.

a. What would be the intrinsic value of Mr. Lucky's ABC warrant if Box Spread won the Kentucky Cup, a major stakes race, causing the value of the horse and of ABC Inc. to increase to a value of $2,000,000?

b. Instead of an ABC warrant, suppose one of the investors for ABC sold a call option to Mr. Lucky giving him the right to buy 100 shares of ABC stock at $1300 per share. What would be the IV of the call if Box Spread won the Kentucky Cup?

c. Explain intuitively the difference between the call's IV and the warrant's IV.

d. Show the algebraic relationship between the values of a warrant and a call.

6. Make up an example similar to the one in Problem 5 that illustrates the fundamental difference between warrants and call options.

7. J.R. Inc. is a $50 million oil company. The company has 1 million shares outstanding and no debt. Expecting the price of oil to increase, J.R. Inc. is planning to raise $5 million through a rights offering to finance the purchase of an oil well. The company has decided to make the subscription price $25 on new shares, and, to comply with the state's preemption right, the company will issue one right for each share.

a. Determine the number of rights that will be needed to buy one new share.

b. What is the intrinsic value of each right?

8. Given the following features of the XYZ convertible bond:

- Coupon rate (annual) $= 10\%$
- Face value $= F = \$1000$
- Maturity $= 10$ years
- Callable at $1100
- YTM on a comparable, nonconvertible bond $= 12\%$
- Conversion ratio $= 10$ shares
- Current stock price $= S_0 = \$90$

Calculate the following:

a. XYZ's conversion price
b. XYZ's conversion value
c. XYZ's straight debt value
d. Minimum price of the convertible
e. The arbitrage strategy if the price of the convertible was $880

9. Make up a capital budgeting case that is analyzed better with an option methodology than via the traditional NPV approach.

Equity and Debt
as Put Options

In Section 11.2, we defined equity and debt in terms of their call positions. The stockholders' and bondholders' positions alternatively can be described in terms of put option positions. In this case, the stockholders' position of a leverage firm consists of: (1) ownership of the firm, (2) a default-free debt obligation to the bondholders, and (3) a put option on the firm giving them the right to sell the company to the bondholders at an exercise price equal to the face value of the debt. At the bond's maturity, if $V_T^A < F$, then the stockholders will sell the firm to the bondholders on their put option for F. Since the stockholders also owe the bondholders F on the default-free debt obligation, then instead of receiving cash of F dollars, the stockholders will be paid by having the debt obligation canceled. In contrast, if $V_T^A > F$, the put is worthless. The stockholders, though, can pay their default-free debt obligation of F and retain ownership of the company. Thus, at expiration, the value of the equity position would be:

$$V_T^E = V_T^A - F + \text{Max}[F - V_T^A, 0] = \text{Max}[V_T^A - F, 0] \qquad (11.\text{A-1})$$
$$V_T^E = V_T^A - F + P_T = C_T,$$

where:

$$P_T = \text{Max}[F - V_T^A, 0]$$
$$C_T = \text{Max}[V_T^A - F, 0],$$

and the current value would be:

$$V_0^E = V_0^A - \text{PV}(F) + P_0 = C_0. \qquad (11.\text{A-2})$$

The creditors' position, on the other hand, consists of the long debt position in the default-free bond and a short put option position on the firm. If $V_T^A < F$ at maturity, then the stockholders will sell the company on their put to the creditors, who will pay for the company by canceling their debt obligation of F; if $V_T^A > F$, then the creditors will receive F on their default-free bond from the shareholders. Thus, at maturity the value of the creditors' position is:

$$V_T^B = \text{Min}[V_T^A, F] \qquad (11.A\text{-}3)$$
$$V_T^B = F - \text{Max}[F - V_T^A, 0]$$
$$V_T^B = F - P_T,$$

and the current value is:

$$V_0^B = \text{PV}(F) - P_0. \qquad (11.A\text{-}4)$$

11.A.1   Valuing Equity as a Put Option with the Black-Scholes Option Pricing Model

Equation (11.A-4) shows that the value of the risky bond is equal to the value of a default-free bond minus the value of the put option on the firm. Using the B-S OPM for puts, the value of the put is:

$$P_0 = -V_0^A[1 - N(d_1)] + Fe^{-RT}[1 - N(d_2)]. \qquad (11.A\text{-}5)$$

In terms of the example in Section 11.2.2, the value of the put option on the ABC company using the OPM would be $1.039 million:

$$1 - N(d_1) = 1 - .86338 = .13662$$

$$1 - N(d_2) = 1 - .65175 = .34825,$$

$$P_0 = -\$15M(.13662) + (\$10M)e^{-(.06)(2)}(.34825) = \$1.039M.$$

The value of the equity would therefore be $7.17M:

$$V_0^E = \$15M - (\$10M)e^{-(.06)(2)} + \$1.039M = \$7.17M,$$

the same as obtained using the call option approach. Finally, the value of the risky debt of ABC is:

$$V_0^B = (\$10M)e^{-(.06)(2)} - \$1.039M = \$7.83M.$$

11.A.2   Put-Call Parity Model

Viewing corporate securities as either call or put positions can be reconciled via the put-call parity model. For stock options, the model is defined as:

$$S_0 + P_0 - C_0 = \text{PV}(X).$$

Extending the put-call parity model to the value of the firm, we have:

$$V_0^A + \frac{\text{Value of put}}{\text{on asset}} - \frac{\text{Value of call}}{\text{on asset}} = \frac{\text{Value of default-}}{\text{free bond}} \qquad (11.A-6)$$

Solving Equation (11.A-6) for the call value shows the shareholders' call option as equivalent to owning the company, having a debt obligation on a default-free bond, and having a long position on a put:

Stockholders' Position:

$$\frac{\text{Value of call}}{\text{on asset}} = V_0^A + \frac{\text{Value of put}}{\text{on asset}} - \frac{\text{Value of default-}}{\text{free bond}} \qquad (11.A-7)$$

In terms of the example:

$$\text{Value of call on asset} = \$15M + \$1.039M - (\$10M)e^{-(.06)(2)} = \$7.17M.$$

Similarly, rearranging Equation (11.A-6), the creditors' position in terms of the call and put positions is:

Creditors Position:

$$V_0^A - \frac{\text{Value of call}}{\text{on asset}} = \frac{\text{Value of default-}}{\text{free bond}} - \frac{\text{Value of put}}{\text{on asset}} \qquad (11.A-8)$$

In terms of the example:

$$\$15M - \$7.17M = (\$10M)e^{-(.06)(2)} - \$1.039M = \$7.83M.$$

PROBLEMS AND QUESTIONS

The following refer to the Keening company described earlier in Problem 1.

1. Describe and calculate the current value of the equity position of the Keening company, using a put option in the valuation.

2. Describe and calculate the current value of the debt position of Southwest Savings and Loan.

3. What relationship governs the call and put approaches?

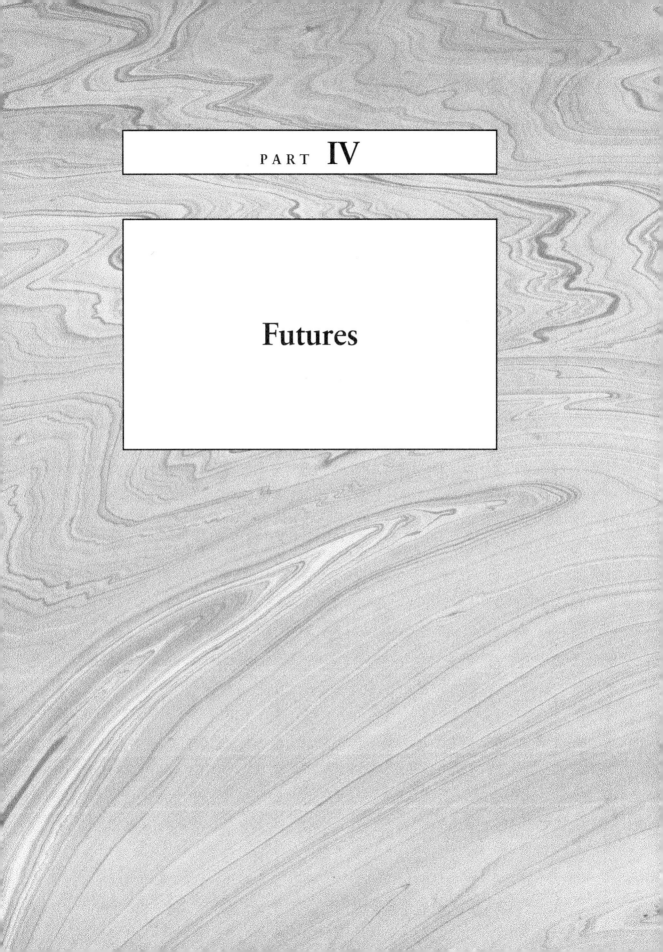

PART **IV**

Futures

CHAPTER 12

Futures and Forward Contracts

12.1 INTRODUCTION

In the 1840s, Chicago emerged as a transportation and distribution center for agriculture products. Midwestern farmers transported and sold their products to wholesalers and merchants in Chicago who often would store and later transport the products via either rail or the Great Lakes to population centers in the east. Partly because of the seasonal nature of grains and other agriculture products and partly because of the lack of adequate storage facilities, farmers and merchants began to use *forward contracts* as a way of circumventing storage costs and pricing risk. These were agreements in which two parties agreed to exchange commodities for cash at a future date, but with the terms and the price agreed upon in the present. For example, an Ohio farmer in June might agree to sell his expected wheat harvest to a Chicago grain dealer in September at an agreed-upon price. This forward contract enabled both the farmer and the dealer to lock in a September wheat price in June.

In 1848, the Chicago Board of Trade (CBT) was formed by a group of Chicago merchants to facilitate the trading of grain. This organization subsequently introduced the first standardized forward contract, called a "to-arrive" contract. Later, it established rules for trading the contracts and developed a system in which traders ensured their performance by depositing good-faith money to a third party (i.e., margin requirements). These actions made it possible for speculators as well as farmers and dealers who were hedging their positions to trade their forward contracts. By definition, *futures* are marketable forward contracts. Thus, the CBT evolved from a board offering forward contracts to the first organized exchange listing futures contracts—a futures exchange.

Since the 1840s, as new exchanges were formed in Chicago, New York, and other large cities throughout the world, the types of futures contracts have grown from grains and agricultural products to commodities and metals and finally to *financial futures*: futures on foreign currency, debt securities, and security indices. Because of their use as a hedging tool by portfolio managers, money managers, and investment bankers, the introduction of financial futures in the early 1970s led to a dramatic growth in futures trading.

Formally, a *forward contract* is an agreement between two parties to trade a specific asset at a future date with the terms and price agreed upon today. A *futures contract*, in turn, is a "marketable" forward contract, with marketability provided through futures exchanges that list hundreds of standardized contracts, establish trading rules, and provide for clearinghouses to guarantee and intermediate contracts. In contrast, forward contracts are provided by financial institutions and dealers, are less standardized and more tailor-made, are usually held to maturity, and, unlike futures, often do not require initial or maintenance margins.

Both forward and futures contracts are similar to option contracts, in that the underlying asset's price on the contract is determined in the present, with delivery and payment occurring at a future date. The major difference between these derivative securities is that the holder of an option has the right, but not the responsibility, to execute the contract (i.e., it is a contingent-claim security), whereas the holder of a futures or forward contract has an obligation to fulfill the terms of the contract. In this chapter, we begin our analysis of futures and forward contracts by examining the speculative and hedging uses of these contracts, trading arrangements, and the pricing of such contracts. In Chapters 13–15, we will focus on stock index, interest rate, and currency futures.

12.2   FUTURES MARKET

In the United States, the annual volume of futures trading grew from 30 million contracts in the early 1970s to approximately 275 million by the end of the 1980s. As noted earlier, the major cause for this dramatic growth was the introduction of financial futures. This market began formally in 1972 when the International Monetary Market (IMM), a subsidiary of the Chicago Mercantile Exchange (CME), began offering futures contracts on foreign currency. In 1976, the IMM extended its listings to include a futures contract on a Treasury bill. The Chicago Board of Trade (CBT) introduced in 1975 its first futures contract, a contract on the GNMA (Government National Mortgage Association) Pass-Throughs, and in 1977 the CBT introduced a Treasury-bond futures contract. The Kansas City Board of Trade was the first exchange to offer trading on a futures contract on a stock index, when it introduced the Value Line Composite Index (VLCI) contract in 1983.* This was followed by the introduction of the SP 500 futures contract by the CME and the NYSE index futures contract by the New York Futures Exchange (NYFE). Table 12.2-1 lists the major futures exchanges and the general types of contracts they list, and Exhibit 12.2-1 shows the price quotes and contract specification on some select futures contracts as they appear in the WSJ.

---

*Stock index futures are sometimes referred to as "pin-stripe pork bellies."

TABLE 12.2-1

Futures Exchanges		
EXCHANGE	YEAR FOUNDED	TYPES OF CONTRACT*
UNITED STATES		
Chicago Board of Trade (CBT)	1848	P, I, R
Chicago Mercantile Exchange (CME)	1919	P, I, R, FC
Coffee, Sugar, and Cocoa Exchange (N.Y.)	1882	P, I
Commodity Exchange (COMEX) (N.Y.)	1933	P
Kansas City Board of Exchange (KCBT)	1856	P, I
Mid-American Commodity Exchange (Chicago)	1880	P, R, FC
Minneapolis Grain Exchange	1881	P
New York Cotton Exchange	1870	P, I, FC
Citrus Associates of the N.Y. Cotton Exchange	1966	P
Petroleum Associates of the N.Y. Cotton Exchange	1971	P
New York Futures Exchange (NYFE)	1979	I
New York Mercantile Exchange	1872	P
Chicago Rice and Cotton Exchange	1976	P
FOREIGN FUTURES MARKETS		
International Futures Exchange (INTEX) (Bermuda)	1984	P, I
London International Financial Futures Exchange (LIFFE)	1982	I, R, FC
Tokyo Financial Futures Exchange	1985	I, R, FC
Singapore International Monetary Exchange (SIMEX)	1984	I, R, FC
Hong Kong Futures Exchange	1977	P, I
New Zealand Futures Exchange	1985	P, I, R, FC
Sydney Futures Exchange	1960	P, I, R, FC
Toronto Futures Exchange	1984	I, R, FC

SOURCES: *Wall Street Journal*; various exchanges' annual reports
*P = physical; I = index; R = interest rate; FC = currency

While the 1970s marked the advent of financial futures, the 1980s saw the globalization of futures markets with the openings of the London International Financial Futures Exchange (1982), the Singapore International Monetary Market (1986), the Toronto Futures Exchange (1984), the New Zealand Futures Exchange (1985), and the Tokyo Financial Futures Exchange (1985). The increase in the number of futures exchanges internationally led to a number of trading innovations: 24-hour world-wide trading, GLOBEX (an after-hour computer trading system introduced by the CME), multiple listings, and cooperative linkage agreements between exchanges that allow futures traders to open a position in one market and close it in another. The growth in the futures market also led to the need for more governmental oversight to ensure market efficiency and to guard against abuses. In 1974, the *Commodity Futures Trading Commission* (CFTC) was

EXHIBIT 12.2-1

Futures Quotes

FUTURES PRICES

Thursday, July 28, 1994

Open Interest Reflects Previous Trading Day.

GRAINS AND OILSEEDS

	Open	High	Low	Settle	Change	Lifetime High	Lifetime Low	Open Interest

CORN (CBT) 5,000 bu.; cents per bu.

Sept	217	217¼	214¾	216	− 1¼	292¼	214¾	46,271
Dec	218¾	219¾	217	219¼	−	277	217	120,875
Mr95	227¾	228¾	226	228	− ¼	282½	226	24,204
May	234	235	232¾	234½	− ¼	285	232½	8,892
July	238¼	239	236¾	238¾	−	285½	236½	8,180
Sept	241¼	241¼	239½	241	− ½	270½	239	587
Dec	242¼	243	241½	242½	− ¾	263	235½	4,581
Dc96			241			257	239	128

Est vol 26,000; vol Wed 25,334; open int 214,200, −218.

OATS (CBT) 5,000 bu.; cents per bu.

Sept	114½	116	113½	115½	− ½	154½	111½	6,110
Dec	117	118¾	116	118½	+ ¾	157¼	116	5,172
Mr95	122¼	124½	121½	124¼	+ 1¾	152¾	121½	473
May	125	125	123	127¼	+ 1¼	151	125	521

Est vol 1,000; vol Wed 751; open int 12,276, +72.

METALS AND PETROLEUM

COPPER-HIGH (CMX) — 25,000 lbs.; cents per lb.

Aug	109.70	110.20	109.10	109.90	− .80	116.00	75.30	768
Sept	110.20	110.60	109.40	110.30	− .85	116.90	74.90	29,963
Oct	109.75	109.75	109.70	110.25	− .75	115.05	75.20	420
Nov				110.00	− .80	112.80	77.75	322
Dec	109.70	110.00	109.00	109.80	− .85	115.20	75.75	10,782
Ja95				109.50	− .90	111.30	76.90	341
Feb				109.20	− .95	111.30	87.85	245
Mar	108.70	108.80	107.90	108.80	− 1.05	113.70	76.30	2,500
Apr				108.20	− 1.25	110.40	90.10	121
May	108.00	108.00	107.30	107.80	− 1.20	111.40	76.85	1,016
July	106.50	106.50	106.50	106.80	− 1.45	112.50	78.00	797
Sept				105.80	− 1.60	110.05	79.10	592
Dec	104.50	104.80	104.35	104.90	− 1.60	109.00	88.00	727

Est vol 10,000; vol Wed 15,423; open int 49,071, +134.

GOLD (CMX) — 100 troy oz.; $ per troy oz.

Aug	387.00	387.70	384.30	384.80	− 2.90	415.00	341.50	26,997
Oct	390.40	390.90	387.80	388.00	− 2.90	417.00	344.00	9,138
Dec	393.60	394.10	391.00	391.20	− 2.90	426.50	343.00	64,669
Fb95	397.10	397.30	396.90	394.60	− 2.90	411.00	363.50	10,559

CRUDE OIL, Light Sweet (NYM) 1,000 bbls.; $ per bbl.

Sept	19.43	19.84	19.40	19.77	+ .31	20.78	14.50	100,691
Oct	19.12	19.45	19.10	19.39	+ .24	20.73	14.65	52,696
Nov	19.06	19.22	18.94	19.16	+ .19	20.69	14.82	30,729
Dec	na	19.05	18.80	19.00	+ .16	21.25	14.93	46,050
Ja93	18.80	18.95	18.76	18.88	+ .13	20.12	15.15	20,639
Feb	18.76	18.84	18.69	18.80	+ .12	19.60	15.28	11,775

INTEREST RATE

TREASURY BONDS (CBT) — $100,000; pts. 32nds of 100%

	Open	High	Low	Settle	Change	Lifetime High	Lifetime Low	Open Interest
Sept	102-08	103-03	101-29	103-00	+ 21	118-26	90- 12	365,940
Dec	101-15	102-10	101-04	102-08	+ 22	118-08	91-19	62,885
Mr95	100-26	101-18	100-20	101-17	+ 22	116-20	98-20	4,268
June	100-00	100-28	100-00	100-28	+ 22	113-15	98-12	1,549
Sept	99-12	100-09	99-12	100-09	+ 22	112-15	97-28	672

Est vol 425,000; vol Wed 348,630; op int 435,410, −3,976.

TREASURY BONDS (MCE) — $50,000; pts. 32nds of 100%

Sept	102-04	103-03	101-29	102-30	+ 20	115-20	100-02	13,535

Est vol 4,000; vol Wed 13,581, +54.

TREASURY NOTES (CBT) — $100,000; pts. 32nds of 100%

Sept	103-13	103-31	103-04	103-28	+ 12	115-01	101-18	225,452
Dec	102-14	102-30	102-06	102-29	+ 13	114-21	100-25	14,761

Est vol 100,001; vol Wed 89,552; open int 240,282, +5,774.

INDEX

S&P 500 INDEX (CME) $500 times index

	Open	High	Low	Settle	Chg	High	Low	Open Interest
Sept	453.10	455.70	452.35	455.10	+ 1.95	485.20	436.75	203,698
Dec	455.40	458.05	455.30	457.60	+ 2.00	487.10	438.85	12,968
Mr95	461.10	461.40	458.90	461.00	+ 1.90	479.00	441.45	2,855
June				464.55	+ 1.95	472.70	449.50	1,274

Est vol 43,688; vol Wed 52,783; open int 220,795, +2,026.
Indx prelim High 454.93; Low 452.30; Close 454.24 +1.67

S&P MIDCAP 400 (CME) $500 times index

Sept	167.80	169.35	167.80	168.90	+ .70	186.70	161.50	11,882

Est vol 718; vol Wed 505; open int 11,926, +44.
The index: High 168.25; Low 167.48; Close 168.02 +.43

NIKKEI 225 STOCK AVERAGE (CME)—$5 times index

Sept	20260.	20545.	20240.	20520.	+ 300.0	21775.	16240.	22,104

Est vol 2,874; vol Wed 1,044; open int 2,779, −448.
The index: High 20262.55; Low 19993.70; Close 20247.85 +110.62

NYSE COMPOSITE INDEX (NYFE) 500 times index

Sept	250.00	251.40	249.70	251.15	+ 1.20	267.90	241.00	3,926
Dec	250.80	252.10	250.80	252.15	+ 1.20	264.50	244.15	193

Est vol 2,233; vol Wed 2,573; open int 4,225, +405.
The index: High 250.91; Low 249.71; Close 250.60 −.76

CURRENCY

	Open	High	Low	Settle	Change	Lifetime High	Lifetime Low	Open Interest

JAPAN YEN (CME) — 12.5 million yen; $ per yen (.00)

Sept	1.0193	1.0206	.9998	1.0023	− .0159	1.0408	.8942	70,300
Dec	1.0275	1.0280	1.0090	1.0100	− .0159	1.0490	.9525	10,230
Mr95	1.0250	1.0250	1.0250	1.0186	− .0159	1.0560	.9680	1,016
Jun	1.0450	1.0450	1.0350	1.0281	− .0159	1.0670	.9915	217

Est vol 35,027; vol Wed 27,374; open int 77,374, +1,626.

DEUTSCHEMARK (CME) — 125,000 marks; $ per mark

Sept	.6343	.6382	.6268	.6279	− .0065	.6595	.5364	83,092
Dec	.6360	.6385	.6275	.6284	− .0066	.6606	.5351	4,218
Mr95	.6380	.6385	.6297	.6297	− .0067	.6595	.5798	1,094

Est vol 54,675; vol Wed 33,418; open int 88,450, +515.

CANADIAN DOLLAR (CME) — 100,000 dlrs.; $ per Can $

Sept	.7225	.7240	.7220	.7239	+ .0006	.7740	.7068	32,137
Dec	.7200	.7210	.7200	.7212	+ .0007	.7670	.7038	2,514
Mr95			.7181	.7209	+ .0007	.7618	.7020	611
June	.7136	.7142	.7136	.7141	+ .0007	.7600	.6990	434

Est vol 3,383; vol Wed 3,514; open int 35,768, +169.

LIVESTOCK AND MEAT

CATTLE-FEEDER (CME) 50,000 lbs.; cents per lb.

Aug	78.90	79.02	78.45	78.55	− .52	83.00	71.10	4,022
Sept	77.65	77.80	77.27	77.32	− .40	81.70	71.00	2,590
Oct	76.85	76.90	76.55	76.67	− .42	82.35	70.95	2,709
Nov	77.85	77.85	77.40	77.45	− .40	81.85	72.40	1,665
Ja95	77.15	77.20	76.80	76.90	− .47	80.95	72.95	626
Mar	75.35	75.35	75.20	75.20	− .25	80.25	72.55	76
Apr	74.50	74.50	74.50	74.50	− .30	76.90	72.45	116

Est vol 1,325; vol Wed 1,413; open int 11,826, +23.

CATTLE-LIVE (CME) 40,000 lbs.; cents per lb.

Aug	68.20	68.65	68.02	68.35	− .07	73.87	61.65	21,843
Oct	71.35	71.62	71.20	71.30	− .22	74.10	65.70	25,671
Dec	70.75	70.85	70.47	70.55	− .45	74.30	67.20	12,644
Fb95	69.95	69.95	69.60	69.65	− .45	75.25	67.90	10,011
Apr	71.05	71.05	70.82	70.87	− .37	75.10	69.40	5,360
June	67.95	67.95	67.75	67.75	− .17	72.50	66.50	1,230
Aug	67.40	67.40	67.32	67.32	− .17	68.90	66.45	132

Est vol 11,943; vol Wed 12,853; open int 76,891, +592.

HOGS (CME) 40,000 lbs.; cents per lb.

Aug	46.05	46.12	45.50	45.95	− .15	53.40	42.45	7,098
Oct	41.65	42.20	41.25	41.97	+ .35	49.75	39.60	11,802
Dec	41.15	41.47	40.90	41.37	+ .17	50.50	39.85	4,692
Fb95	40.60	40.90	40.35	40.42	− .17	50.80	38.80	1,585
Apr	39.65	39.85	39.50	39.60	− .20	48.80	38.85	932
June	44.25	44.30	44.05	44.30	− .12	51.55	43.75	411
July	44.12	44.12	43.95	44.05	− .10	49.00	43.72	109

Est vol 6,428; vol Wed 6,253; open int 26,664, −689.

PORK BELLIES (CME) 40,000 lbs.; cents per lb.

Aug	29.00	29.30	27.20	27.62	− 1.45	59.50	27.20	3,263
Fb95	42.50	43.35	42.30	42.37	− .10	60.05	41.00	4,676
Mar	42.65	43ñ10	42.35	42.50	− .15	60.20	40.62	238

Est vol 3,691; vol Wed 3,526; open int 8,255, +65.

FOOD AND FIBER

COCOA (CSCE) — 10 metric tons; $ per ton.

Sept	1,443	1,457	1,438	1,445	− 13	1,543	1,020	33,634
Dec	1,489	1,499	1,480	1,489	− 11	1,580	1,045	19,513
Mr95	1,518	1,527	1,517	1,526	− 11	1,600	1,077	8,007
May	1,535	1,545	1,545	1,544	− 11	1,612	1,111	2,953
July				1,564	− 11	1,593	1,225	2,344
Sept				1,584	− 11	1,463	1,265	1,092
Dec				1,609	− 11	1,633	1,290	4,348
Mr96				1,634	− 11	1,664	1,350	1,444

Est vol 4,117; vol Wed 11,426; open int 73,335, −777.

COFFEE (CSCE) — 37,500 lbs.; cents per lb.

Sept	203.00	208.50	200.00	202.40	− 8.55	274.00	68.50	19,552
Dec	209.10	211.75	200.30	206.25	− 8.20	244.25	77.10	12,295
Mr95	214.50	215.00	211.50	211.50	− 6.00	244.00	78.90	5,107
May	216.50	215.00	213.30	213.30	− 6.00	244.40	82.50	1,762
July				215.00	− 6.00	245.10	85.00	337
Dec				219.10	− 6.00	242.00	194.50	225

Est vol 8,111; vol Wed 8,414; open int 39,317, +74.

ORANGE JUICE (CTN) — 15,000 lbs.; cents per lb.

Sept	93.90	95.40	93.90	95.35	+ .60	135.40	86.05	14,107
Nov	97.50	98.60	97.50	98.45	+ .15	134.00	89.10	3,237
Ja95	100.90	102.20	100.90	102.20	+ .60	132.00	93.00	3,757

created by the U.S. Congress to monitor and regulate futures trading, and the National Futures Association (NFA), a private agency, was established to oversee futures trading.*

12.3   NATURE OF FUTURES TRADING AND THE ROLE OF THE CLEARINGHOUSE

12.3.1   Futures Positions

An investor or hedger can take one of two positions on a futures contract: a long position (or futures purchase) or a short position (futures sale). In a long futures position, you agree to buy the contract's underlying asset at a specified price, with payment and delivery to occur on the expiration date (also referred to as the delivery date); in a short position, you agree to sell an asset at a specific price, with delivery and payment occurring at expiration.

To illustrate how positions are taken, suppose that in June, speculator A believes that the upcoming summer will be unusually dry in the Midwest, causing an increase in the price of wheat. With hopes of profiting from this expectation, speculator A decides to take a long position in a wheat futures contract and instructs his broker to buy one September wheat futures contract listed on the CBT (one contract is for 5000 bushels). To fulfill this order, A's broker finds a broker representing speculator B, who believes that the summer wheat harvest will be above normal and therefore hopes to profit by taking a short position in the September wheat contract. After negotiating with each other, the brokers agree to a price of $2.40/bu on the September contract for their clients. In terms of futures positions, speculator A would have a long position in which he agrees to buy 5000 bushels of wheat at $2.40/bu from speculator B at the delivery date in September, and speculator B would have a short position in which she agrees to sell 5000 bushels of wheat at $2.40/bu to A at the delivery date in September. That is:

Agreement to Deliver

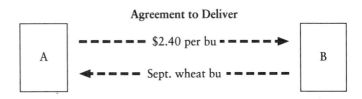

---

*The most recent justification for the need for government oversight was best demonstrated in the late 1980s when the FBI launched an investigation to see if a price-manipulation scheme known as "bucket trading" occurred on the CBT and CME. In a bucket trade, a commission broker with an order to execute tips off another broker (referred to as the "bagman") who proceeds to take a position in the futures. When conditions are favorable, the commission broker executes the order with the bagman.

If both parties hold their contracts to delivery, their profits or losses would be determined by the price of wheat on the spot market (also called cash, physical, or actual market). For example, suppose the summer turns out to be dry, causing the spot price of wheat to be $2.50/bu at the grain elevators in the Midwest at or near the delivery date on the September wheat futures contract. Accordingly, speculator A would be able to buy 5000 bushels of wheat on his September futures contract at $2.40/bu from speculator B, then sell the wheat for $2.50/bu on the spot market to earn a profit of $500, before commission and transportation costs are included. On the other hand, to deliver 5000 bushels of wheat on the September contract, speculator B would have to buy the wheat on the spot market for $2.50/bu, then sell it on the futures contract to speculator A for $2.40/bu, resulting in a $500 loss (again, not including commission and transportation costs).

12.3.2   Clearinghouse*

To provide contracts with marketability, futures exchanges use *clearinghouses*. Like the Option Clearing Corporation, the clearinghouses associated with futures exchanges guarantee each contract and act as intermediaries by breaking up each contract after the trade has taken place. Thus, in the preceding example, the clearinghouse (CH) would come in after speculators A and B have reached an agreement on the price of September wheat, becoming the effective seller on A's long position and the effective buyer on B's short position. That is:

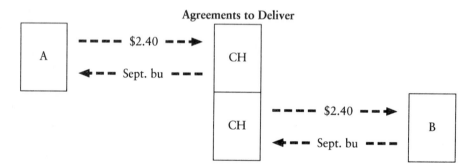

Once the clearinghouse has broken up the contract, A's and B's contracts would be with the clearinghouse. The clearinghouse, in turn, would record the following entries in its computers:

CLEARINGHOUSE RECORD
1. Speculator A agrees to buy September wheat at $2.40/bu from the clearinghouse.
2. Speculator B agrees to sell September wheat at $2.40/bu to the clearinghouse.

---

*In this section, the diagrams depicting the clearinghouse's function are based on those presented by William Sharpe (1981).

As discussed earlier with the Option Clearing Corporation, the intermediary role of the clearinghouse makes it easier for futures traders to close their positions before expiration. Returning to our example, suppose that the month of June is unexpectedly dry in the Midwest, leading a third speculator, speculator C, to want to take a long position in the listed September wheat futures contract. Seeing a profit potential from the increased demand for long positions in the September contract, speculator A agrees to sell a September wheat futures contract to speculator C for $2.45/bu. Upon doing this, speculator A would then be short in the new September contract, with speculator C having a long position, and there would be two contracts on September wheat. Without the clearinghouse's intermediating, the two contracts can be described as follows:

Agreements to Deliver

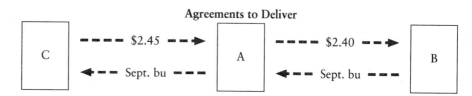

After the new contract between A and C has been established, the clearinghouse would step in and break it up. For speculator A, the clearinghouse's record would then show the following:

CLEARINGHOUSE RECORDS FOR SPECULATOR A
1. Speculator A agrees to *buy* September wheat from the clearinghouse for $2.40/bu.
2. Speculator A agrees to *sell* September wheat to the clearinghouse for $2.45/bu.

Thus:

CH - - - - $0.05 - - ➤ A

The clearinghouse accordingly would close speculator A's positions by paying him $2.45/bu − $2.40/bu = $0.05/bu, a total of (5000 bu)($0.05/bu) = $250 on the contract. Since speculator A's short position effectively closes his position, it is variously referred to as a closing, reversing out, or offsetting position or simply as an offset. Thus, the clearinghouse, like the Option Clearing Corporation, makes it easier for futures contracts to be closed prior to expiration.

Commission costs and the costs of transporting commodities cause most futures traders to close their positions instead of taking delivery. As the delivery date approaches, the number of outstanding contracts (open interest) declines, with only a relatively few contracts still outstanding at delivery. Moreover, at expiration, the contract prices on futures contracts established on that date (f_T) should equal (or approximately equal) the prevailing spot price on the underlying asset (S_T). That is:

At expiration: $f_T = S_T$.

If f_T does not equal S_T at expiration, an arbitrage opportunity would exist. Arbitrageurs could take a position in the futures contract and an opposite position in the spot market. For example, if the September wheat futures contract was available at \$2.50 on the delivery date in September and the spot price for wheat was \$2.55, arbitrageurs could go long in the September contract, take delivery by buying the wheat at \$2.50 on the futures contract, then sell the wheat on the spot market at \$2.55, to earn a riskless profit of \$0.05/bu. The arbitrageurs' efforts to take long positions, though, would drive the contract price up to \$2.55. On the other hand, if f_T exceeds \$2.55, then arbitrageurs would reverse their strategy, pushing f_T to \$2.55/bu. Thus, at delivery arbitrageurs will ensure that the prices on expiring contracts equal the spot price. As a result, closing a futures contract with an offsetting position at expiration will yield the same profits or losses as closing futures positions on the spot market by purchasing (selling) the asset on the spot market and selling (buying) it on the futures contract.

Returning to our example, suppose near the delivery date on the September contract the spot price of wheat and the price on the expiring September futures contracts are both \$2.50/bu. To close her existing short contract, speculator B would need to take a long position in the September contract, while to offset his existing contract, speculator C would need to take a short position. Suppose speculators B and C take their offsetting positions with each other on the expiring September wheat contract priced at $f_T = S_T = \$2.50$/bu. After the clearinghouse breaks up the new contract, speculator B would owe the clearinghouse \$0.10/bu, and speculator C would receive \$0.05/bu from the clearinghouse. That is:

CLEARINGHOUSE RECORDS FOR SPECULATOR B
1. Speculator B agrees to *sell* September wheat to CH for \$2.40/bu.
2. Speculator B agrees to *buy* September wheat from CH at \$2.50/bu.

Thus:

CLEARINGHOUSE RECORDS FOR SPECULATOR C
1. Speculator C agrees to *buy* September wheat at $2.45/bu.
2. Speculator C agrees to *sell* September wheat for $2.50/bu.

Thus:

To recapitulate: In this example, the contract prices on September wheat contracts went from $2.40/bu on the A and B contract, to $2.45/bu on the A and C contract, to $2.50/bu on the B and C contract at expiration. Speculators A and C each received $0.05/bu from the clearinghouse, while speculator B paid $0.10/bu to the clearinghouse, the clearinghouse with a perfect hedge on each contract received nothing (other than clearinghouse fees attached to the commission charges), and no wheat was purchased or delivered.

12.4 FUTURES HEDGING

Futures markets provide investors, businesses, and other economic entities a means for hedging their particular spot positions against adverse price movements. Two hedging positions exist: the long hedge and the short hedge. In a *long hedge* (or hedge purchase), a hedger takes a long position in a futures contract to protect against an increase in the price of the underlying asset or commodity. Long hedge positions are used, for example, by manufacturers to lock in their future costs of purchasing raw materials, by portfolio managers to fix the price they will pay for securities in the future, or by multinational corporations that want to lock in the dollar costs of buying foreign currency at some future date. In a *short hedge*, you take a short futures position to protect against a decrease in the price of the underlying asset. In contrast to long hedging, short hedge positions are used, for example, by farmers who want to lock in the price they will sell their crops for at harvest, by portfolio managers and investment bankers who are planning to sell securities in the future and want to minimize price risk, or by multinational corporations who have to convert future foreign currency cash flows into dollars and want to immunize the future exchange against adverse changes in exchange rates.

◆ **12.4.1   Long Hedge Example**

To illustrate a long hedge position, consider the case of an oil refinery that, in December, anticipates purchasing 100,000 barrels of crude oil in February. Suppose the refinery wants to avoid the price risk associated with buying crude oil on the spot market in February.* In the absence of a forward contract or futures market for crude oil, the only way the refining company could avoid price risk would be to buy the crude oil in December and store it until February. With crude oil futures contracts listed on the New York Mercantile Exchange, though, the refinery alternatively can minimize price risks by taking a long position in the February crude oil contract. With the standard size on crude oil futures of 1000 barrels, the company would need to go long in 100 February crude oil contracts to hedge its February spot purchase.

To this end, suppose the refinery purchases 100 February contracts at $20.00/ barrel. At expiration, the company would probably find it advantageous (lower transportation costs) to purchase its 100,000 barrels of crude oil on the spot market at the spot price, then close its futures position by going short in the expiring February crude oil futures contract. Given that the spot and expiring futures prices must be equal (or approximately equal), the refinery will find that any additional costs of buying crude oil above the $20.00/barrel price on the spot market will be offset by a profit from its futures position; while, on the other hand, any benefits from the costs of crude oil being less the $20.00/barrel price would be negated by losses on the refinery's futures position. As a result, the refining company's costs of buying crude oil on the spot market and closing its futures position would be $20.00/barrel, which is the initial February crude oil contract price they obtained in December.

The refining company's long hedge position is shown in Table 12.4-1. In the table, the first row shows three possible spot prices, at the February delivery date, of $18.00, $20.00, and $22.00. The second row shows the profits and losses per

---

*Oil companies often buy crude oil on contracts with producers that stipulate that the producer will deliver the crude oil at a specified price and on a specified date. These contracts represent forward contracts. The example here might best represent a case in which the refinery anticipates having to buy more crude oil than specified in its longer-term contract with a producer.

TABLE 12.4-1

Long Hedge Example		
Initial Position: Long in February crude oil futures contracts at $20.00/barrel to hedge crude oil purchases in February.		
At Delivery: Close February crude oil contract at $f_T = S_T$ and purchase crude oil on the spot market at S_T.		

POSITIONS	COST PER BARREL		
February spot price	$18.00	$20.00	$22.00
− Profit on futures	(2.00)	0.00	2.00
Net costs	$20.00	$20.00	$22.00

(Profit on futures)/barrel = (Spot price − $20.00)/barrel

barrel from the long futures position, in which the offset position has a contract price (f_T) equal to the spot price (S_T). The last row shows the net $20.00 cost per barrel resulting from purchasing the crude and closing the futures position. Thus, if the price of crude oil on the spot market is $18.00 at the February delivery date, the refinery would pay $18.00 per barrel of crude oil and $2.00 to the clearing-house to close its futures positions (i.e., the agreement to buy at $20.00 and the offsetting agreement to sell at $18.00 means the refining company must pay the clearinghouse $2.00); if the spot crude oil price is $22.00, the company will have to pay $22.00 per barrel for the crude oil, but could finance part of that expen-diture with the $2.00 per barrel it received from the clearinghouse from closing (i.e., the agreement to buy at $20.00 plus the offsetting agreement to sell at $22.00 means the clearinghouse will pay the refining company $2.00 per barrel).   ◆

◆ 12.4.2   Short Hedge Example

To illustrate how a short hedge works, consider the case of a wheat farmer who, in June, wants to lock in the price she will receive for her estimated 5000 bushels of wheat scheduled to be harvested in September. If the farmer goes short in one September wheat futures contract (contract size is 5000 bushels) priced at $2.40/bu in June, she would be able to receive $2.40/bu at the delivery date in September from selling the wheat on the spot market and closing the futures contract by going long in the expiring September contract trading at the spot price.

This can be seen in Table 12.4-2. In the table, the first row shows three possible spot prices of $2.00, $2.40, and $3.00; the second row shows the profits and losses from the futures position, and the third row shows the constant revenue per bushel of $2.40 from aggregating both positions. If the farmer receives only $2.00 per bushel for her wheat, she realizes a profit of $0.40 per bushel from her futures position (the agreement to sell September wheat for $2.40 is closed with an agreement to buy September wheat for $2.00, resulting in a $0.40 receipt from the clearinghouse). On the other hand, if the farmer is able to sell her wheat for $3.00 per bushel, she also will have to pay the clearinghouse $0.60 per bushel to close the futures position. Thus, regardless of the spot price, the farmer receives $2.40 per bushel.   ◆

TABLE 12.4-2	Short Hedge Example

Initial Position: Short in a September wheat futures contract at $2.40/bu to hedge wheat sale in September.

At Delivery: Close wheat futures contract at $f_T = S_T$ and sell the harvested wheat on the spot market at S_T.

POSITIONS	REVENUE PER BUSHEL		
Spot wheat price	$2.00	$2.40	$ 3.00
+ Profit from futures	0.40	0.00	(0.60)
Revenue	$2.40	$2.40	$ 2.40

(Profit from futures)/bu = ($2.40 − S_T)/bu

12.4.3 Hedging Risk

The preceding examples represent perfect hedging cases, in which certain revenues or costs can be locked in at a future date. In practice, perfect hedges are the exception and not the rule. There are three types of hedging risk that preclude a zero risk position: *quality risk, timing risk*, and *quantity risk*.

Quality risk exists when the commodity or asset being hedged is not identical to the one underlying the futures contract. The oil refinery in our example, for instance, may need to purchase a different grade or quality of crude oil than the one specified in the futures contract. In certain hedging cases, futures contracts written on a different underlying asset are used to hedge the spot asset. For example, a portfolio manager planning to buy corporate bonds in the future might hedge the acquisition by going long in T-bond futures. This type of hedge is known as a *cross-hedge*. Unlike *direct hedges*, in which the future's underlying assets are the same as the assets being hedged, cross-hedging cannot eliminate risk altogether but can minimize it.*

Timing risk occurs when the delivery date on the futures contract does not coincide with the date the hedged assets or liabilities need to be purchased or sold. For example, timing risk would exist in our first hedging example if the oil refining company needed crude oil the first of February instead of at the futures' expiration at the end of the month. If the spot asset or commodity is purchased or sold at a date t that differs from the expiration date on the futures contract, then the price on the futures (f_t) and the spot price (S_t) will not necessarily be equal. The difference between the futures price and the spot price is called the *basis* (B_t). The basis tends to narrow as expiration nears, converging to zero at expiration $(B_T = 0)$. Prior to expiration, the basis can vary, with greater variability usually observed the longer the time is to expiration. Given this basis risk, the greater the time difference between buying or selling the hedged asset and the futures' expiration date, the less perfect the hedge.

To minimize timing risk or basis risk, hedgers often select futures contracts that mature before the hedged asset is to be bought or sold, but as close as possible to that date. For very distant-horizon dates, though, hedgers sometimes follow a strategy known as *rolling the hedge forward*, which involves taking a futures position, then at expiration closing the position and taking a new one.

Finally, because of the standardization of futures contracts, futures hedging also is subject to quantity risk. *Quantity risk* would have been present in our second hedging example if the farmer had expected a harvest of 6000 bushels instead of 5000 bushels. With the contract size on the wheat futures contract being 5000 bushels, 1000 bushels of the farmer's harvest could not have been protected against price changes.

---

*Cross-hedging can occur when an entire group of assets or liabilities is hedged by one type of futures contract; this is referred to as macro-hedging. Micro-hedging, on the other hand, occurs when each individual asset or liability is hedged separately.

12.4.4   Hedging Models

The presence of quality, timing, and quantity risk means that pricing risk cannot be eliminated totally by hedging with futures contracts. As a result, the objective in hedging is to minimize risk. Several hedging models try to achieve this objective: price-sensitivity model, minimum variance model, naive-hedge model, and utility-based hedging model. These models have as their common objective the determination of a *hedge ratio*: the optimal number of futures contracts needed to hedge a position. In Chapters 13–15, we will define these models and examine how some of them can be used to hedge stock portfolios, debt securities, and foreign currency positions.

12.5   FUTURES SPREADS

Futures spreads are speculative strategies, not as risky as the pure speculative strategies described in Section 12.3. Like option spreads, a futures spread is formed by taking long and short positions on slightly different futures contracts simultaneously. Two general types of spreads exist: an *intracommodity spread* and an *intercommodity spread*.

12.5.1   Intracommodity Spread

An *intracommodity spread*, or *time spread*, is formed with futures contracts on the same asset but with different expiration dates; for example, a long position on a June SP 500 futures contract and a short position on a September SP 500 futures contract. Since more distant futures contracts are more price-sensitive to changes in the spot price than near-term futures, a speculator who is bullish could form an intracommodity spread by going long in a longer-term index futures contract and short in a shorter-term one.

12.5.2   Intercommodity Spread

An *intercommodity spread* is formed with two futures contracts with the same expiration dates but on different commodities; for example, opposite positions on the June SP 500 Index and the June Value Line Composite Index. In constructing intercommodity spreads, a spreader makes use of the correlation between the underlying assets. For example, suppose the relation between gold and silver prices is such that when gold prices change by 10%, silver prices change in the same direction by 9%. A mildly bullish precious metals speculator who wanted a lower return-risk combination than implied by either metal could form an intercommodity spread by going long in a gold futures contract and short in a silver futures contract. If the spread is set up on a one-to-one basis, then for a 10% increase in gold prices and a corresponding 9% increase in silver prices, the spreader would realize a 1% gain, and for a decrease of the same percentages, the spreader would lose 1%.

Many different spreads, each with different return-risk combinations, can be formed by changing the ratio of long to short positions. Futures spreads formed with stock indices, debt, and foreign currency futures will be discussed further in subsequent chapters.

12.6 OPERATIONS AND FUNCTIONS OF THE EXCHANGES

Physically, many futures exchanges are made up of several trading rooms, with each room having a number of trading pits (or rings) where exchange members go to trade contracts. While computerized trading systems such as *globex* have the potential to change the way futures are traded, most exchange trading still takes place with brokers going to a pit and using the open outcry method to execute their orders.

Floor brokers carry out most of the trading on the exchanges, buying and selling for their customers. In addition to floor brokers, most futures exchanges also have independents. Some independent members act solely as speculators or arbitrageurs trading on their own accounts. Other independents, though, engage in **dual trading**, in which they trade for both clients and themselves.* Floor brokers serve the important role of linking futures traders, while independents serve to make the market more efficient. The other important functions of the futures exchanges are standardizing contracts, providing continuous trading, establishing delivery procedures, and setting trading rules.

12.6.1 Standardization

The futures exchanges provide standardization by specifying the grade or type of each asset (e.g., type of wheat) and the size of the underlying asset (e.g., 5000 bushels of wheat or a T-bill with face value of $1 million). Exchanges also specify how contract prices are quoted. For example, the contract prices on T-bill futures are quoted in terms of the T-bill's annualized discount yield or an index equal to 100 minus the yield; a T-bond is quoted in terms of dollars and $\frac{1}{32}$s of a T-bond with a face value of $100.

12.6.2 Continuous Trading

As discussed in Chapter 2, most U.S. security exchanges use market-makers or specialists to ensure a continuous market. On most futures exchanges, continuous trading also is provided, but not with market-makers or specialists assigned by the exchange to deal in a specific contract. Instead, many futures markets provide

---

*As a matter of security law, dual traders are not allowed to trade on their own accounts when they are about to trade for their clients. With advance knowledge of a client's position, a dual trader could profit by taking a favorable position before executing the client's order. This type of price manipulation is known as *front running*.

continuous trading through independent floor traders who are willing to take temporary positions in one or more futures. These exchange members fall into one of three categories: *scalpers*, who offer to buy and sell simultaneously, profiting from a bid-ask spread; *day traders*, who hold positions for as long as a day; *position traders*, who hold positions for as long as a week before they close. Collectively, these exchange members make it possible for the futures markets to provide continuous trading.

12.6.3   Delivery Procedures

While 98% of all futures contracts are closed prior to expiration, detailed delivery procedures are nevertheless important, since they ensure that the contract prices on futures are determined by the spot price on the underlying asset. The exchanges have various rules and procedures governing the delivery of the contract and delivery dates.

Some futures contracts allow for the delivery of different assets at expiration. On T-bond futures contracts, for example, the delivered T-bond can be selected from a number of T-bonds, each differing in its maturity and/or coupon payments. In cases in which different assets can be delivered, the exchange uses a price adjustment procedure to convert the price of the deliverable asset to the price of the asset defined by the contract. Like index options, some futures have a cash-settlement delivery procedure. Futures contracts on stock indices and Eurodollar time deposits, for example, are settled in cash at delivery. In a cash-settled futures contract, a settlement price is defined that specifies how the position's closing value will be determined at delivery.

The dates when futures contracts can be delivered also vary. Many contracts call for delivery on or just after the delivery date. However, contracts such as T-bond futures can be delivered on any business day of the delivery month. In cases that have an extended delivery period, the exchange defines a delivery notification procedure that must be followed.

Finally, the lengths of futures contracts can vary. Many have the standard March, June, September, December cycle. Agriculture commodities often have delivery dates set up to coincide with the underlying commodity's harvest season. Some futures contracts have delivery dates that extend out almost two years.

12.6.4   Position Limits and Price Limits

The futures exchanges set position limits on many of their futures contracts. This is done as a safety measure both to ensure sufficient liquidity and to minimize the chances of a trader's trying to corner a particular asset. In addition to position limits, the Commodity Futures Trading Commission requires that each exchange impose *price limits* on the daily changes in contract prices. Thus, the price of a contract must be within its daily price limits, unless the exchange intervenes and changes the limit. When the contract price hits its maximum or minimum limit, it is referred to as being limited up or limited down, respectively. For example, if the daily price limit on the September wheat futures contract is $0.10 and its closing contract price the preceding day was $2.40, then the contract price that day cannot be more than $2.50 or less than $2.30.

Price limits are designed to stop destabilizing price trends from occurring. They also make it possible for margin requirements on futures contracts to be set relatively low. Unfortunately, price limits also can cause substantial opportunity losses by locking in a trader's position when the underlying contract's price is moving in her favor.

12.7 MARGINS REQUIREMENTS, TRANSACTION COSTS, AND TAXES

12.7.1 Margin Requirements

Since a futures contract is an agreement, it has no initial value. Futures traders, however, are required to post some security or good-faith money with their brokers.* Depending on the brokerage firm, the customer's margin requirement can be satisfied in the form of either cash or cash equivalents (e.g., U.S. T-bill).

You should not misconstrue the deposit of a trader securing a futures position as being a margin purchase. In a margin stock purchase, for example, part of the investor's funds are used to buy the stock, with the other part being borrowed. Since the investor does not buy or sell a futures contracts, the deposited funds stay with the broker. Thus, the margin on a futures contract represents a good-faith deposit.

Like options, futures contracts have both initial and maintenance margin requirements. The initial (or performance) margin is the amount of cash or cash equivalents that must be deposited by the investor on the day the futures position is established. The futures trader does this by setting up a commodity account with the broker and depositing the required cash or cash equivalents. The amount of the margin is determined by the margin requirement, defined as a proportion (m) of the contract value (usually 5%–10%). For example, if the initial margin requirement is 10%, then speculators A and B in our very first example would be required to deposit $1200 in cash or cash equivalents in their commodity accounts as good-faith money on their $2.40 September wheat futures contracts. That is:

$$m[\text{contract value}] = .10(\$2.40/\text{bu})(5000 \text{ bu}) = \$1200.$$

The maintenance (or variation) margin is the amount of additional cash or cash equivalents that futures traders must deposit to keep the equity in their commodity account equal to a certain percentage (e.g., 80%) of the initial margin value. The equity in an investor's commodity account is equal to the cash or the value of the cash equivalents initially deposited plus the sum of the daily changes in the value of the futures position. The changes in the position value of the account are determined each day by the settlement price on new contracts. On futures

---

*Technically, since the clearinghouse guarantees the futures contract, margins are required by the members of the clearinghouse; the clearinghouse members then require margins to be maintained by the brokerage firm on their client.

contracts, the settlement price is the average price of the last several trades of the day; it is determined by the clearinghouse officials.

In our example, suppose the day after speculators A and B established their respective long and short positions, the settlement price was $2.42/bu. A's and B's equity would therefore be:

A: Equity $= .10(\$2.40/bu)(5000\ bu) + (\$2.42/bu - \$2.40/bu)(5000\ bu) = \$1300$

B: Equity $= .10(\$2.40/bu)(5000\ bu) + (\$2.40/bu - \$2.42/bu)(5000\ bu) = \$1100.$

If after reaching $2.42, the next day's settlement price was $2.41, then the speculators' equity would be:

A: Equity $= .10(\$2.40/bu)(5000\ bu) + (\$2.42/bu - \$2.40/bu)(5000\ bu)$
$+ (\$2.41/bu - \$2.42/bu)(5000\ bu)$
Equity $= \$1200 + \$100 - \$50 = \$1250.$

B: Equity $= .10(\$2.40/bu)(5000\ bu) + (\$2.40/bu - \$2.42/bu)(5000\ bu)$
$+ (\$2.42/bu - \$2.41/bu)(5000\ bu)$
Equity $= \$1100 - \$100 + \$50 = \$1150.$

If the maintenance margin requirements are equal to 90% of the initial margin, then A and B would have to keep the equity values of their accounts equal to $.9(\$1200) = \$1080$. In our example, neither speculator would be required to deposit additional cash or cash equivalents.

If the equity value of either account falls below $1080, then additional cash or cash equivalents would need to be deposited. For example, if the third day after A and B established their contracts, the contract price on September wheat was $2.45, then A's and B's equity values would be:

A: Equity $= \$1200 + (\$2.45/bu - \$2.40/bu)(5000\ bu) = \$1450$

B: Equity $= \$1200 + (\$2.40/bu - \$2.45/bu)(5000\ bu) = \$950.$

In this case, B would have an undermargined account and would have to post an additional $250 in cash or cash equivalents in her account to make the equity value of the account equal the initial margin.

By depositing the required amount of cash, speculator B's account would become *marked to market*. A futures account is **marked to market** when it meets the maintenance margin requirements. If speculator B does not deposit the required margin immediately, then she would receive a **margin call** from the broker instructing her to post the required amount of funds. If speculator B does not comply with the margin call, the broker can close the position. If this occurs and the broker is able to close B's short position with an offsetting long position at $2.45, then $250 of B's $1200 initial deposit would be used to pay the clearinghouse and $950 would be returned to speculator B.

Several points should be noted in describing margin requirements. First, the low initial margin requirements on futures tend to make futures positions similar to highly leveraged security acquisitions. In fact, there is a ubiquitous argument over whether margin requirements are too low and therefore futures positions too risky. This argument resurfaced after the October 1987 market crash when stock indices dropped dramatically, causing many of the long positions on stock index futures to become undermargined. However, while low margin requirements make futures positions risky, keep in mind that one reason behind imposing price limits is to guard against accounts becoming undermargined so fast that traders are unable to close.

Second, the maintenance margin requirements on futures require constant management of your account. With daily resettlement, futures traders who are undermargined have to decide each day whether to close their positions and incur losses or to post additional collateral; similarly, those who are overmargined must decide each day whether or not they should close. One way for an investor to minimize the management of his futures position is to keep his account overmargined by depositing more cash or cash equivalents than initially required or by investing in one of a number of **futures funds**. A futures fund pools investors' monies and uses them to set up futures positions. Typically, a large percentage (e.g., 75%) of the fund's money is invested in money market securities. Thus, the funds represent overmargined futures positions.

Finally, margins are required on all futures contracts, regardless of whether the position is established by a speculator, a spreader, or a hedger. Since their positions are less risky, hedgers and spreaders do have smaller initial margin requirements than speculators; like speculators, though, their accounts are still marked to market.

12.7.2 Transaction Costs

In addition to margin requirements, transaction costs also are involved in establishing futures positions. Like options, such costs include broker commissions, clearinghouse fees, and the bid-ask spread. On futures contracts, commission fees usually are charged on a per-contract basis and for a round lot (i.e., the fee includes both opening and closing the position), and the fees are negotiable. The clearinghouse fee is relatively small and is collected along with the commission fee by the broker. Finally, the bid-ask spreads are set by floor traders and represent an indirect cost of trading futures.

12.7.3 Taxes

For tax purposes, futures positions are treated as capital gains and losses. For speculators, a marked-to-market rule applies in which the profits on a futures position are taxed in the year the contract is established. That is, at the end of the year, all futures contracts are marked to market to determine any unrealized gain or loss for tax purposes.

For example, suppose in September a futures speculator takes a long position on a March contract at a contract price of $1000. If the position is still open at the end of the year, the speculator's taxes on the position would be based on the settlement price at year's end. If the contract is marked to market at $1200 at the end of the year, then a $200 capital gain would need to added to the speculator's net capital gains to determine her tax liability. If the speculator's position is later closed, in March of the following year, at a contract price of $1100, then she would realize an actual capital gain of $100. For tax purposes, though, the speculator would report a loss equal to the difference between the settlement price at the end of the year ($1200) and the position's closing price ($1100); that is, a $100 loss. Both realized and unrealized capital losses, in turn, are deductibles that are subtracted from the investor's capital gains.*

The end-of-the-year marked-to-market rule on futures applies only to speculative positions and not to hedging positions. Also, when delivery on a futures contract takes place, taxes are applied when the commodity actually is sold.

12.8 FUTURES PRICING

12.8.1 Value of Futures and Forward Contracts

As earlier noted, the major difference between options and futures is that the former gives the holder the right but not the obligation to execute the terms of the contract, while the latter is an obligation. As a result, in an options contract the right to exercise has value, and the contract therefore has value when it is introduced; a futures or forward contract, though, is simply an agreement that has no inherent value when it is introduced.

In the case of forward contracts, there is a value to an existing contract. After its introduction, the value of a forward contract at time t should equal the present value of the difference between its initial contract price (F_0) and the contract price on a new forward contract with the same expiration date and underlying asset (F_t). That is, the value of a long position on the initial forward contract at time $t(V_t^{F_0})$ is:

$$\text{Value of long position on initial forward contract} = V_t^{F_0} = \frac{F_t - F_0}{(1 + R)^t}. \qquad (12.8\text{-}1)$$

For example, if the forward contract price on September wheat is $2.50 ($F_t$) when there is one month to expiration ($t = \frac{1}{12}$ of a year) and the annual risk-free rate is 6%, then the value of a long position on a September wheat forward contract initiated earlier at $2.40 would be $0.0995:

$$V_t^{F_0} = \frac{F_t - F_0}{(1 + R)^t}$$

---

*The marked-to-market tax rule was established in 1981. One of the reasons for the law was to stop the activities of futures spreaders who would take long and short positions in similar futures contracts, then for tax purposes at the end of the year would close the position, thus showing a loss.

$$V_t^{F_0} = \frac{\$2.50 - \$2.40}{(1.06)^{1/12}} = \$0.0995.$$

With one month to delivery, the $0.0995 value of the earlier contract reflects the $0.10 riskless return that the holder of the earlier contract can realize at the end of one month by forming an intracommodity spread through taking a short position in the new contract. At the September expiration, the spreader would be able to buy the wheat at $2.40 and sell it at $2.50.*

Like forward contracts, futures contracts also can have values after their inceptions, but only until they are marked to market. Once a futures contract is marked to market, its value reverts to zero.

12.8.2 Basis

The underlying asset price on a futures or forward contract depends primarily on the spot price of the underlying asset. As pointed out earlier, the difference between the futures price (f) or forward price (F) and the spot price is called the basis (B_t):

$$\text{Basis} = B_t = f_t - S_t. \tag{12.8-2}$$

(The basis also can be expressed as $S_t - f_t$.) For most futures contracts, the futures price exceeds the spot price before expiration and approaches the spot price as expiration nears. Thus, the basis usually is positive and decreasing over time, equaling zero at expiration ($B_T = 0$). Futures and spot prices also tend to be highly correlated with each other, increasing and decreasing together; their correlation, though, is not perfect. As a result, the basis tends to be relatively stable along its declining trend, even when futures and spot prices vacillate.

Theoretically, the relationship between the spot price and the futures or forward price can be explained by the **carrying-cost model** (or *cost-of-carry model*). In this model, arbitrageurs ensure that the equilibrium forward price is equal to the net costs of carrying the underlying asset to expiration. The model is used to describe what determines the equilibrium price on a forward contract. As we will explain later, though, if short-term interest rates are constant, futures and forward prices will be equal, and thus the carrying-cost model can be extended to price futures contracts as well.

12.8.3 Carrying-Cost Model

In terms of the carrying-cost model, the price difference between forward and spot prices can be explained by the costs and benefits of carrying the underlying asset to expiration. For financial futures, the carrying costs include the financing costs of holding the underlying asset to expiration, and the benefits include coupon interest or dividends earned from holding the asset. For commodities, the carrying costs include not only financing costs but also storage and transportation costs.

---

*At expiration, the value of a forward contract would equal the difference between the forward price and the spot price. For long positions, that would be $S_T - F_0$; for short positions, it would be $F_0 - S_T$.

Pricing a Contract on a Pure Discount Bond

To illustrate the carrying-cost model, consider the pricing of a forward contract on a pure discount bond (PDB). With no coupon interest, the underlying asset does not generate any benefits during the holding period, and the financing costs are the only carrying costs. In terms of the model, the equilibrium relationship between the forward and spot prices on the PDB is:

$$F_0 = S_0(1 + R)^T, \qquad (12.8\text{-}3)$$

where:

> F_0 = contract price on a forward contract for a PDB with a maturity of M_1
>
> T = time to expiration on the forward contract
>
> S_0 = current spot price on a PDB, identical to the forward contract's bond, except it has a maturity of $M_2 = M_1 + T$
>
> R = risk-free rate or repo rate
>
> $S_0(1 + R)^T$ = financing costs of holding a PDB.

In pricing futures or forward contracts, the *repo rate* often is used as the interest rate. The **repo rate** is the loan rate on a repurchase agreement. A repurchase agreement is a transaction in which a security holder (or short seller) sells a security, with the obligation of repurchasing it at a later date. To the holder, the repurchase agreement represents a secured loan in which he receives funds from the sale of the security, with the responsibility of purchasing the security later at a higher price that reflects the shorter time to maturity. The repo rate, in turn, is the loan rate implied on this loan. Repurchase agreements typically involve government securities, with the agreement usually specifying repayment the next day (overnight repos). Longer-term repurchase agreements also exist, however.

If Equation (12.8-3) does not hold, an arbitrage opportunity occurs. The arbitrage strategy, referred to as a **cash-and-carry arbitrage**, involves taking opposite positions in the spot and forward contracts. For example, suppose in June there is a PDB maturing in six months ($M_2 = .5$ year) priced at $95 and a forward contract on an identical PDB except that the bond has a maturity of three months ($M_1 = .25$). If the risk-free interest rate or repo rate is 8% (annualized) and the expiration of the forward contract is three months ($T = .25$), then the equilibrium price of the forward contract would be $F_0 = \$96.85$:

$$F_0 = \$95(1.08)^{.25} = \$96.85.$$

If the contract price does not equal $96.85, an arbitrage opportunity would exist by taking a position in the forward contract and an opposite position in the spot. For example, if the forward price is $98, an arbitrageur could:

1. Borrow $95 at 8% interest and buy the six-month PDB for $95; and
2. Take a short position in the PDB forward contract at the price of $98.

At expiration, the arbitrageur would receive $98 from selling her bond (which would have a maturity of three months) on the forward contract and would pay $96.85 in principal and interest on the loan, resulting in a profit of $1.15. Given this opportunity, arbitrageurs would go short in the forward contract until the contract price fell to $96.85.

If the forward contract is below the equilibrium price, then the cash-and-carry arbitrage strategy is reversed. For example, if the forward price is at $95, a money market manager holding a six-month PDB could:

1. Sell the bond for $95;

2. Invest the $95 proceeds for three months at 8% interest; and

3. Take a long position in the forward contract in order to buy back the bond three months later.

At expiration (three months later), the manager would receive $96.85 in principal and interest and would buy a three-month PDB on the forward contract for $95. Thus, the manager would earn a $1.85 arbitrage profit and still have the PDB. Given this opportunity, money managers would go long in forward contracts on the PDB until the price increased to $96.85.

Pricing a Forward Contract on a Stock Portfolio

If the underlying asset on the forward contract generates such benefits during the period as dividends, the benefits need to be subtracted from the costs of carrying the asset in determining the equilibrium price of the forward contract. That is:

$$F_0 = S_0(1 + R)^T - D_T, \qquad (12.8\text{-}4)$$

where:

D_T = the value of benefits at time T.

As an example, suppose there is a stock portfolio currently worth $S_0 = \$150$ that will pay dividends worth $1.50 at T ($D_T = \$1.50$) and a forward contract on the stock portfolio expiring in three months ($T = .25$). If the risk-free rate is $R = .08$, then the equilibrium price of the forward contract would be $151.41:

$$F_0 = \$150(1.08)^{.25} - \$1.50 = \$151.41.$$

If the actual contract price did not equal F_0, then an arbitrage opportunity could be realized by applying the same cash-and-carry arbitrage strategy described earlier for the PDB. For example, if the forward price is $154, an arbitrageur could borrow $150 at 8%, buy the portfolio with the loan proceeds, and enter a forward contract to sell the portfolio at $154 at the end of three months. At the end of the period, the arbitrageur would receive $154 from the sale of the portfolio on the forward contract and dividends worth $1.50 and would owe $152.91 in principal and interest on the debt, netting a riskless profit of $2.59. The arbitrageur would, of course, pursue this strategy until the forward price is $154.41. If the contract price is below $F_0 = \$151.41$, the arbitrageur reverses the strategy: He sells the portfolio short and takes a long position in the forward contract. This strategy also would yield a riskless return until the forward price is $151.41.

Pricing a Commodity Contract

For most commodities contracts, there usually are no benefits realized from carrying the underlying asset. There are, as noted already, storage and transportation costs. Accordingly, the carrying-cost model for a typical commodity forward contract is:

$$F_0 = S_0(1 + R)^T + KT + \text{TRC}, \qquad (12.8\text{-}5)$$

where:

K = storage costs per unit of commodity per period

TRC = transportation costs.

To illustrate, suppose in June the spot price of a bushel of wheat is $2.00, the annual storage cost is $0.30 per/bushel, the risk-free rate is 8%, and the costs of transporting wheat from the destination point specified on the forward contract to a local grain elevator, or vice versa, is $0.01/bu. By the cost-of-carry model, the equilibrium price of a forward contract on September wheat (expiration of $T = .25$) would be $2.124/bu:

$$F_0 = (\$2.00/\text{bu})(1.08)^{.25} + (\$0.30/\text{bu})(.25) + \$0.01/\text{bu} = \$2.124/\text{bu}.$$

If the actual forward price is $2.16, an arbitrageur would:

1. Take a short position in the forward contract: agree to sell a September bushel of wheat for $2.16;
2. Borrow $2 at 8% interest;
3. Use the loan proceeds to buy a bushel of wheat for $2.00, then store it for three months.

At expiration, the arbitrageur would:

1. Transport the wheat from the grain elevator to the specified destination point on the forward contract for $0.01/bu;
2. Pay the financing costs of $2.0388/bu and the storage costs of ($0.30/bu) (.25) = $0.075/bu;
3. Sell the bushel of wheat on the forward contract at $2.16/bu.

From this cash-and-carry strategy, the arbitrageur would earn a riskless return of $0.036/bu.

If the forward price on a commodity is below the equilibrium price, the strategy would need to be reversed. This would entail taking a short position in the spot commodity and a long position in the forward contract. In our wheat example, such an opportunity might be available, for example, to a mill company maintaining an inventory of wheat. Instead of holding all of its wheat, the company might sell some of it on the spot market and invest the proceeds in a risk-free security for the period, then go long in a forward contract to buy the wheat back.

For many commodities, though, this reverse strategy may not be practical. For those commodities in which the reverse cash-and-carry arbitrage strategy does not apply, the equilibrium condition for the forward contract needs to be specified as an inequality. That is:

$$F_0 < S_0(1 + R)^T + KT + \text{TRC}. \qquad (12.8\text{-}6)$$

12.8.4   Normal and Inverted Markets

For many assets the costs of carrying the asset for a period of time exceeds the benefits. As a result, the forward price on such assets exceeds the spot price prior to expiration and the basis ($F_t - S_t$) on such assets is positive. By definition, a market in which the forward price exceeds the spot price is referred to as a *contango*, or a *normal market*. In contrast, if the forward price is less then the spot price (a negative basis), then the cost of carrying the asset is said to have a *convenience yield*, in which the benefits from holding the asset exceed the costs. A market in which the basis is negative is referred to as a *backwardation*, or an *inverted market*.

For commodity futures, an inverted market often exists for unstorable commodities (e.g., eggs) or can occur in certain situations in which the existing supplies of a commodity (e.g., wheat) are limited but future supplies (e.g., the next wheat harvest) are expected to be abundant. For financial futures, an inverted market could occur if large coupon or dividend payments are to be paid during the period. For example, if the dividend in the earlier stock portfolio example had been $3.00 instead of $1.50, then F_0 would have been $149.91 instead of $151.41, and the forward market on the portfolio would have been inverted.

12.8.5   Price Relationship Between Forward Contracts with Different Expirations

The same arbitrage arguments governing the forward and spot price relation also can be extended to establish the equilibrium relationship between forward prices with different expirations. Specifically, given a distant forward contract expiring in T_2 and a nearby contract on the same asset expiring in T_1, the equilibrium relationship between the forward prices on the two contracts (F_{T2} and F_{T1}) is:

$$F_{T2} = F_{T1}(1 + R_{T1})^{T2-T1} - D_{T2} + K(T_2 - T_1) + \text{TRC}, \qquad (12.8\text{-}7)$$

where:

R_{T1} = risk-free rate or repo rate at time T_1; the rate can be locked in with a forward contract (or an implied forward rate strategy; see Chapter 14)

D_{T2} = value of benefits at time T_2 received from holding the asset for the period from T_1 to T_2.

If the market price of the forward contract with T_2 expiration (F_{T2}^m) exceeded the equilibrium price, an arbitrageur could profit by forming an intracommodity spread by:

1. Taking a long position in the T_1 forward contract;
2. Taking a short position in the T_2 forward contract; and
3. Entering a forward contract to borrow at time T_1, F_{T1} dollars at rate R_{T1} for the period from T_1 to T_2.

At T_1 expiration, the arbitrageur would:

1. Borrow F_{T1} dollars at a rate of R_{T1} on the forward contract;
2. Buy the asset on the T_1 forward contract for F_{T1};
3. Transport and store the asset (if necessary) for the period at a cost of $K(T_2 - T_1) + TRC$.

At the T_2 expiration, the arbitrageur would:

1. Sell the asset on the T_2 forward contract for F_{T2};
2. Receive benefits worth D_{T2} that have accrued during the $T_2 - T_1$ period;
3. Repay the loan of $F_{T1}(1 + R_{T1})^{T2-T1}$; and
4. Pay the transportation and storage costs of $K(T_2 - T_1) + TRC$.

The arbitrageur's actions would result in a riskless return of $F_{T2}^m - [F_{T1}(1 + R_{T1})^{T2-T1} - D_{T2} + K(T_2 - T_1) + TRC]$. Such actions, in turn, would continue until the equilibrium condition (12.8-7) is satisfied.

To illustrate, consider the forward price relationship for March and June lumber contracts. Suppose the following conditions are present: (1) The forward price on the March lumber contract is $F_{T1} = \$0.24$/sq ft, (2) the March forward interest rate on a three-month loan is 8% (annual), (3) the storage costs for lumber is $0.06/sq ft per year, and (4) the carrying-cost benefits and the costs of transporting lumber are zero (assume there is a storage facility at the location point specified on the lumber forward contract). If the time period between the expiration on the June lumber contract and the March contract is $T_2 - T_1 = .25$/year, then the equilibrium price on the June contract would be $0.26/sq ft:

$$F_{T2} = \$0.24(1.08)^{.25} + \$0.06(.25) = \$0.26/\text{sq ft.}$$

If the June lumber forward contract is $0.28, then an arbitrageur could earn a $0.02/sq ft profit by:

1. Entering a March forward contract to borrow $0.24 at $R_{T1} = 8\%$;
2. Going long in the March lumber contract at $F_{T1} = \$0.24$/sq ft; and
3. Taking a short position on the June lumber contract at $F_{T2} = \$0.28$.

In March, the arbitrageur would:

1. Borrow $0.24 at 8% interest on the forward contract;
2. Purchase the lumber for $0.24/sq ft on the March contract;
3. Store the lumber at an annual rate of $0.06/sq ft for .25 year.

At the June expiration the arbitrageur would realize a $0.02/sq ft profit by:

1. Selling the lumber on the June contract for $0.28/sq ft;
2. Repaying the loan of $0.24(1.08)^{.25} = 0.245; and
3. Paying the storage costs of ($0.06/sq ft)(.25) = 0.015.

If the June lumber contract is less than the equilibrium price, then this intracommodity spread strategy would need to be reversed. This would require taking a short position in the March contract, taking a long position in the June contract, and entering a forward contract to invest F_{T1} funds at rate R_{T1} for 90 days. The implementation of this reverse strategy may or may not be practical. For financial futures, for example, this reverse strategy generally can be applied. However, for many commodity futures contracts, the reverse strategy does not hold. For such commodity futures, Equation (12.8-7), in turn, needs to be expressed as an inequality.

12.8.6   Relation Between the Forward Price and the Expected Spot Price

The carrying-cost model relates the equilibrium forward price to the current spot price. The forward price also is related to an unknown expected spot price. Several expectation theories have been advanced to explain the relationship between the forward and expected spot prices.

One of the first theories was put forward by the famous British economists John Maynard Keynes (1930) and J. R. Hicks (1939). They each argued that if a spot market was dominated by hedgers who, on balance, wanted a short forward position, then for the market to clear (for supply to equal demand) the price of the forward contract would have to be less than the expected price of the spot commodity at expiration [$E(S_T)$]. According to Keynes and to Hicks, the difference between $E(S_T)$ and F_0 represents a risk premium that speculators in the market require in order to take a long forward position. For example, if F_0 is equal to or less than $E(S_T)$, then there would be too few speculators to take long positions, and an excess demand of short over long positions would occur. This excess, though, would force the contract price down, inducing speculators to take a long position. Thus, if there are more short hedgers than long, then equilibrium would require a risk premium of $E(S_T) - F_0$. Keynes and Hicks both called this market situation *normal backwardation*.

The opposite case, in which $F_0 > E(S_T)$, could occur if the market consisted of hedgers who, on balance, wanted to go long. In this case, the price of the forward contract would have to exceed $E(S_T)$ to induce speculators to take a short position. C. O. Hardy (1940) also argued for the case of $F_0 > E(S_T)$, even in a market of short hedgers. His argument, though, is based on investor's risk behavior. He maintained that since speculators were akin to gamblers, they were willing to pay for the opportunity to gamble (risk-loving behavior). Thus, a gambler's fee, referred to as a contango, or forwardation, would result in a negative risk premium.

Finally, there is a risk-neutral pricing argument, in which futures contracts, like options, represent redundant securities. In this argument, the forward price represents an unbiased estimate of the expected spot price [$F_0 = E(S_T)$] and, with risk-neutral pricing, investors purchasing an asset for S_0 and expecting an asset value at T of $E(S_T) = F_0$ require an expected rate of return equal to the risk-free rate (R). Thus:

$$S_0 = \frac{E(S_T)}{(1 + R)^T}$$

$$S_0 = \frac{F_0}{(1 + R)^T} \qquad (12.8\text{-}8)$$

Solving Equation (12.8-8) for F_0, in turn, yields the carrying-cost model:

$$F_0 = S_0(1 + R)^T.$$

Whether a risk premium exists is an empirical question. One of the first empirical studies to test for the existence of such a premium was done by Houthakker (1957), who found abnormal returns could be earned from taking positions in corn, wheat, and cotton for the period from 1937 to 1957. Telser in a 1958 study and Gray in a 1961 study, though, did not find these abnormal returns. In a more recent empirical study, Hartzmark (1987) found futures prices to be unbiased estimates of expected spot prices.

12.8.7   Relation Between Futures and Forward Prices

The price relationships we've described thus far hold only for forward contracts that have no initial or maintenance margin requirements. Under the assumption that short-term interest rates are constant over time, though, it can be shown that the prices of futures and forward contracts on the same underlying asset are the same. Accordingly, if this assumption is reasonable, the pricing relationships that we've specified for forward contracts also can be used to price futures contracts; if the assumption is not reasonable, then those pricing models for forward contracts can be used only to approximate the price of a futures contract.

To see the relationship between futures and forward prices, assume that both futures and forward contracts exist on the same asset and that each contract has two days to expiration. If the price on the futures contract with two days to expiration (f_2) exceeds the price on the forward contract (F_0), then an arbitrageur could profit by taking a long position in the forward contract and a short position in $(1 + R)^{-(1/365)}$ futures contracts. At the end of the day, the futures contract would be marked to market, and the arbitrageur could: (1) close the $(1 + R)^{-(1/365)}$ futures position at the end-of-the-day settlement price of f_1, and (2) take a new short position in a futures contract with only one day to expiration and with a contract price of f_1. If there is a profit (π) from closing the first position [$\pi = (f_2 - f_1)(1 + R)^{-(1/365)} > 0$], then the arbitrageur would invest the excess to expiration (one day); if there is a loss, she would borrow funds to finance the shortfall. If the funds are invested (borrowed) at a rate the same as the previous day's, then at expiration (one day later), the arbitrageur's profit (loss) would be:

$$\pi = (f_2 - f_1)(1 + R)^{-(1/365)}(1 + R)^{(1/365)} = f_2 - f_1.$$

At expiration (the next day), the arbitrageur would purchase the underlying asset on the forward contract at F_0, then sell the asset on the futures contract at f_1, for a profit or loss equal to $f_1 - F_0$. The arbitrageur's total profit at expiration (π_T) would therefore be:

$$\pi_T = (f_2 - f_1) + (f_1 - F_0) = f_2 - F_0.$$

Thus, if interest rates are constant over time (both days), then this strategy would yield the arbitrageur a riskless cash flow of $f_2 - F_0$. In theory, arbitrageurs would exploit this opportunity by going short in the futures contract and long in the forward contract, readjusting each day when the futures contract is marked to market, until the arbitrage profit is zero. Arbitrageurs would do this until $f_t = F_0$. Hence, if short-term interest rates are constant over time, then in equilibrium, futures and forward prices will be equal.* (The reader is encouraged to investigate the opposite arbitrage strategy in which $f_2 < F_0$.)

12.9 CONCLUSION

In this chapter we've provided an overview of futures and forward contracts. These derivative securities are very similar to options. Like options, they can be used as speculative tools to profit from changes in asset prices and as hedging tools to minimize price risk. Also like options, futures contracts are traded on organized exchanges that have many of the same trading rules and procedures that option exchanges have. Finally, futures and forward contracts, like options, are derivative securities; as such, their prices are determined by arbitrage forces.

The fundamental difference between these contracts is that options give the holders a right, while futures or forward contract holders have an obligation. As a result, potential profits and losses on pure speculative futures positions are virtually unlimited, compared to limited profit-and-loss potentials on fundamental speculative option positions. Hedging strategies with futures, while capable of eliminating downside risk, can also affect the upside potential, as compared to option hedging, which can provide minimum and maximum limits.

Given this background in futures and forward contracts, we now turn our focus to three specific types of financial futures: stock index, interest rates, and foreign currency.

---

*Several empirical studies have examined the differences between futures and forward prices. The results, though, are mixed. Cornell and Reinganum (1981), for example, found no significant difference between futures and forward prices on currencies, while French (1983) found a significant difference between futures and forward prices on silver.

KEY TERMS

forward contracts	basis	margin call
futures	quantity risk	futures funds
financial futures	hedge ratio	carrying-cost model
Commodity Futures	intracommodity spread	repo rate
Trading Commission	intercommodity spread	cash-and-carry
clearinghouse	dual trading	arbitrage
long hedge	scalper	coutango
short hedge	day trader	normal market
quality risk	position trader	convenience yield
cross-hedge	price limits	backwardation
direct hedge	marked to market	inverted market
timing risk		

SELECTED REFERENCES

Agmon, T., and Amihud, Y. "The Forward Exchange Rate and the Prediction of the Future Spot Rate." *Journal of Banking and Finance* (Sept. 1981): 425–437.

Arrow, K. "Futures Markets: Some Theoretical Perspectives." *Journal of Futures Markets* 1 (Summer 1981): 107–116.

Black, F. "The Pricing of Commodity Contracts." *Journal of Financial Economics* 3 (Jan.–Feb. 1976): 167–179.

Brennan, M. "A Theory of Price Limits in Futures Markets." *Journal of Financial Economics* 16 (1988): 213–233.

Carlton, D. "Futures Markets: Their Purpose, Their History, Their Successes and Failures." *Journal of Futures Markets* 4 (Fall 1984): 237–271.

Chance, D. *Options and Futures*. Chicago: Dryden Press, 1991, pp. 239–274.

Chang, E. "Returns to Speculators and the Theory of Normal Backwardation." *Journal of Finance* 40 (Mar. 1985): 193–208.

Chicago Board of Trade. *Commodity Trading Manual*. Chicago: Board of Trade of the City of Chicago, 1989.

Cornell, B., and Reinganum, M. "Forward and Futures Prices: Evidence from the Foreign Exchange Markets." *Journal of Finance* 36 (Dec. 1981): 1035–1045.

Cox, J., Ingersoll, J., and Ross, S. "The Relation Between Forward and Futures Prices." *Journal of Financial Economics* 10 (Dec. 1981).

Duffie, D. *Futures Markets*. Englewood CLiffs, N.J.: Prentice-Hall, 1989, ch. 7.

Easterbrook, F. "Monopoly, Manipulation and the Regulation of Futures Markets." *Journal of Business* 59 (1966): 103–127.

Edwards, F. "The Clearing Association in Futures Markets: Guarantor and Regulator." *Journal of Futures Markets* 3 (Winter 1983): 369–392.

Fishe, R., and Goldberg, L. "The Effects of Margins on Trading in Futures Markets." *Journal of Futures Markets* 6 (Summer 1986): 261–271.

Francis, J. *Investments: Analysis and Management*. New York: McGraw-Hill, 1991, pp. 751–784.

French, K. "A Comparison of Future and Forward Prices." *Journal of Financial Economics* 12 (Nov. 1983): 311–342.

Gray, R. "The Search for a Risk Premium." *Journal of Political Economy* 69 (June 1961): 250–260.

Hansell, S. "The Computer That Ate Chicago." *Institutional Investor* (Feb. 1989): 181–188.

Hardy, C. *Risk and Risk Bearing*. Chicago: University of Chicago Press, 1940, pp. 67–69.

Hardy, C., and Lyon, L. "The Theory of Hedging." *Journal of Political Economy* 31 (1923): 271–287.

Hartzmark, M. "The Effects of Changing Margin Levels on Futures Market Activity, the Composition of Traders in the Market, and Price Performance." *Journal of Business* 59 (1986): 147–180.

———. "Return to Individual Traders: Aggregate Results." *Journal of Political Economy* 95 (1987): 1291–1306.

Hicks, J. *Value and Capital*, 2nd ed. Oxford: Clarendon Press, 1939.

Horn, F. *Trading in Commodity Futures*. New York: New York Institute of Finance, 1984.

Houthakker, H. "Can Speculators Forecast Prices?" *Review of Economics and Statistics* 39 (1957): 143–151.

Hull, J. *Options, Futures, and Other Derivation Securities*. Englewood Cliffs, N.J.: Prentice-Hall, 1989, ch. 1.

Irwin, S., and Brorsen, B. "Public Futures Funds." *Journal of Futures Markets* 5 (1985): 463–485.

Jarrow, R., and Oldfield, G. "Forward Contracts and Futures Contracts." *Journal of Financial Economics* (Dec. 1981): 373–382.

Kaldor, N. "Speculation and Economic Stability." *Review of Economic Studies* 7 (1939–1940).

Kaufman, P. *Handbook of Futures Markets*. New York: Wiley, 1984, ch. 1–6, 10.

Keynes, J. *A Treatise On Money*. London: Macmillan, 1930.

Kolb, R. *Understanding Futures Markets*, Glenview, Ill.: Scott, Foresman, 1988, pp. 1–26.

Kolb, R., Gay, G., and Jordan, J. "Futures Prices and Expected Future Spot Prices." *Review of Research in Futures Markets* 2 (1983): 110–123.

Kramer, Andrea S. *Taxation of Securities, Commodities and Options*. New York: Wiley, 1987.

Park, H., and Chen, A. "Differences Between Futures and Forward Prices: A Further Examination of the Marking-to-the-Market Effects." *Journal of Futures Markets* (Spring 1985): 77–88.

Powers, M. *Inside the Financial Futures Markets*, 2nd ed. New York: Wiley, 1984, ch. 11, 12, 15, 18.

Schwarz, E., Hill, J., and Schneewis, T. *Financial Futures: Fundamentals, Strategies and Applications*. Homewood, Ill.: Irwin, 1986, ch. 6, 7.

Sharpe, W. *Investments*, Englewood Cliffs, N.J.: Prentice Hall, 1981, pp. 460–463.

Siegel, D., and Siegel, D. *Futures Markets*, Chicago: Dryden Press, 1990, pp. 1–105.

Silber, W. "Marketmaker Behavior in an Auction Market: An Analysis of Scalpers in Futures Markets." *Journal of Finance* 39 (Sept. 1984): 937–953.

Strong, R. *Speculative Markets*, Chicago: Longman Financial Services, 1989.

Telser, L. "Futures Trading and the Storage of Cotton and Wheat." *Journal of Political Economy* 66 (June 1958): 233–255.

———. "Margins and Futures Contract." *Journal of Futures Markets* 1 (Fall 1981): 225–253.

Tucker, A. *Financial Futures, Options and Swaps*, St. Paul: West, 1991, pp. 79–99.

Working, H. "The Theory of Price of Storage." *American Economic Review* (Dec. 1949): 1262–1280.

PROBLEMS AND QUESTIONS

1. Explain the differences between forward contracts and option contracts.

2. Explain the differences between forward and futures contracts.

3. Define and explain the functions provided by futures exchanges.

4. Answer the following questions regarding the functions of the clearinghouse:

   a. Explain how the clearinghouse would record the following:

      (1) Mr. A buys a September wheat futures contract from Ms. B for $3.00/bu on June 20.

      (2) Mr. D buys a September wheat futures contract from Mr. E for $2.98/bu on June 25.

      (3) Ms. B buys a September wheat futures contract from Mr. D for $2.97/bu on June 28.

      (4) Mr. E buys a September wheat futures contract from Mr. A for $3.02/bu on July 3.

   b. Show the clearinghouse's payments and receipts needed to close each position.

5. Explain why the price on an expiring futures contract must equal or approximately equal the spot price on the contract's underlying asset.

6. What is the major economic justification of the futures market?

7. Mr. Woody is the chief financial officer of the Corso Company, a large metropolitan real estate developer. In January, Mr. Woody estimates that the company will need to purchase 30,000 square feet of plywood in June to meet its material needs on one of its office construction jobs.

a. Suppose there is a June plywood contract trading at f_0 = $0.20/sq ft (contract size is 5000 square feet). Explain how Mr. Woody could hedge the company's June plywood costs with a position in the June plywood contract.

b. Show in a table Mr. Woody's net costs, at the futures' expiration date, of buying plywood on the spot market at possible spot prices of 0.18/sq ft, 0.20/sq ft, 0.22/sq ft, and 0.24/sq ft and closing the futures position. Assume no quality, quantity, and timing risk.

c. Define the three types of hedging risk, and give an example of each in the context of the problem just stated.

d. How much cash or risk-free securities would Mr. Woody have to deposit to satisfy an initial margin requirement of 5%?

8. In May, Mr. Jones planted a wheat crop he expects to harvest in September. He anticipates the September harvest to be 10,000 bushels and would like to hedge the price he can get for his wheat by taking a position in a September wheat futures contract.

a. Explain how Mr. Jones could lock in the price at which he sells his wheat with a September wheat futures contract trading in May at f_0 = $4.20/bu (contract size of 5000 bushels).

b. Show in a table Mr. Jones' revenue, at the futures' expiration date, from closing the futures position and selling 10,000 bushels of wheat on the spot market at possible spot prices of $4.00/bu, $4.20/bu, and $4.40/bu. Assume no quality, quantity, or timing risk.

c. Give examples of the three types of hedging risk in the context of Problem (b).

d. How much cash or risk-free securities would Mr. Jones have to deposit to satisfy an initial margin requirement of 5%?

9. Ms. Smith is an orange juice distributor who, in January, signed a contract to deliver 60,000 pounds of frozen orange juice to Churchill Downs on Kentucky Derby Day (first Saturday in May). Ms. Smith plans to buy the orange juice from a local distributor in May. With a small profit margin, though, Ms. Smith is afraid she might incur a loss if orange juice prices increase.

a. Explain how Ms. Smith could lock in her orange juice costs with a May frozen orange juice futures contract trading in January at f_0 = $0.95/lb (contract size of 15,000 pounds).

b. Show in a table Ms. Smith's net costs, at the futures' expiration date, from closing the futures position and buying 60,000 pounds of frozen orange juice on the spot market at possible spot prices of $0.90/lb, $0.95/lb, and $1.00/lb. Assume no quality, quantity, or timing risk.

c. How much cash or risk-free securities would Ms. Smith have to deposit to satisfy an initial margin requirement of 5%?

10. Ms. Hunter is a money market manager. In July, she anticipates needing cash in September that she plans to obtain by selling 10 T-bills she currently holds,

each T-bill having a face value of $1M. At the time of the anticipated September sale, the T-bills will have a maturity of 91 days. Suppose there is a September T-bill futures contract with the contract's underlying T-bill having a maturity of 91 days and a face value of $1M and trading a discount yield of $R_D = 10\%$ or

$$f_0 = \left[\frac{100 - (10)(.25)}{100}\right](\$1,000,000) = \$975,000.$$

a. Assuming Ms. Hunter is fearful that short-term interest rates could increase, how could she lock in the selling price on her T-bills?

b. Show in a table Ms. Hunter's net revenue, at the futures' expiration date, from closing the futures position and selling her 10 T-bills at possible discount yields of 9%, 10%, and 11%. Assume no quality, quantity, or timing risk.

11. Explain the similarities between a gambler who bets the Bulls over the Suns when the Las Vegas point spread line is the Bulls' by 10 points and a speculator who goes long in September wheat futures at $4.20/bu.

12. What spread positions would you form in the following cases?

a. In July, you expect the spot price of wheat to increase, and September and October wheat futures contracts are available.

b. In April, you expect long-term interest rates to increase, and June and September T-bond futures contracts are available.

c. The estimated relationship between the percentage changes in the price of copper (P_c) and the price of lead (P_L) is: $\% \Delta P_c = .9(\% \Delta P_L)$. You expect a decrease in the price of metals, and futures contracts are available on both metals.

13. Define price limits, and explain why they are used.

14. Suppose that on March 1 you take a long position in a June crude oil futures contract at $20/barrel (contract size = 1000 barrels).

a. How much cash or risk-free securities would you have to deposit to satisfy an initial margin requirement of 5%?

b. Calculate the values of your equity account on the following days, given the following settlement prices:

3/2	$20.50
3/3	20.75
3/4	20.25
3/5	19.50
3/8	19.00
3/9	20.00

c. If the maintenance margin requirement specifies keeping the value of the equity account equal to 100% of the initial margin requirement each day, how much cash would you need to deposit in your commodity account each day?

15. Define the basis and its relationship to the time to expiration. Define normal and inverted markets.

16. What would be the value on July 1 of a forward contract initiated on June 1 to purchase crude oil for $20/barrel on September 1 if the same contract was available on July 1 but with a contract price of $25/barrel? Assume that on July 1 there are exactly two months to expiration, the risk-free rate is 6% (annual), and the forward contracts are not marked to market. What arbitrage strategy could the holder of the June contract employ if the contract price in July is not correctly priced?

17. Why is the value of a forward contract or futures contract at the time of its origination equal to zero?

18. Suppose the forward price on a crude oil contract expiring in one year was $18 per barrel. What would this forward contract be worth six months later if at that time a new contract on crude oil with a six-month expiration was priced at $20 and the risk-free rate was 8% (annual)? Explain your answer.

19. Using the carrying-cost model, determine the equilibrium prices of each of the following forward contracts, and describe the cash-and-carry arbitrage strategy governing the equilibrium relationships when the contract prices are above and below the equilibrium levels.

    a. A forward contract on a 90-day pure discount bond (PDB) with a face value of $1M and expiring in 180 days. Assume the price on a similar 270-day spot PDB is $954,484 and the risk-free rate on 90-day investments is 6% (annual).

    b. A forward contract on ABC stock expiring in 90 days. Assume the current stock price is $100, the stock will pay dividends worth $0.50 at expiration, and the risk-free rate on 90-day investments is 6% (annual).

    c. A forward contract on a barrel of crude oil expiring in 90 days. Assume the current spot price of crude oil is $22/barrel, the risk-free rate on 90-day investments is 6% (annual), storage costs are $2/barrel per year, and the total transportation cost from supplier to storage facility and to the destination point on the forward contract is $0.20/barrel.

    d. A forward contract on ABC stock expiring in 180 days. Assume the forward price on an ABC stock expiring in 90 days is 96, the forward risk-free rate on 90-day investments or loans made 90 days from the present is 6% (annual), and the stock pays no dividends.

20. Explain what a contango market and a backwardation market are in terms of the carrying-cost model.

21. Explain the relationship between the expected spot price on an asset $[E(S_T)]$ and the futures prices for the following markets in which there are more short hedgers than long:

    a. Risk-averse (Keynes-Hicks normal backwardation market)

    b. Risk-loving (Hardy's gambler's market)

    c. Risk-neutral

22. Suppose that on June 1 the spot price on crude oil was $18 per barrel and the price of September crude oil futures was $19. If the market was risk-neutral, what would investors expect the spot price of crude oil to be at the September futures expiration date? If the market was risk-averse, would investors expect the September spot price to be greater or less than the futures price?

23. Suppose that the price on a futures contract on ABC stock that is expiring in two days is $100 and the price on a forward contract on ABC stock that is expiring in two days is $97.

    a. Show how an arbitrageur could earn a certain $3 profit if short-term interest rates were constant. Assume that the current and next-day rates are 6% (annual).

    b. What would be the market impact on the prices as a result of the arbitrageur's actions?

    c. Comment on the conditions necessary for futures and forward prices to be equal.

24. Briefly comment on the following.

    a. The importance of the delivery procedure on futures contracts, even though most futures contracts are closed by offsetting positions

    b. The advantages and disadvantages of price limits

    c. The marked-to-market tax rule on speculative futures positions

    d. The benefits of futures funds

    e. The role of floor traders in ensuring a continuous futures market

CHAPTER 13

Stock Index Futures

13.1 INTRODUCTION

The annual volume of stock index futures trading has grown from less than 5 million contracts in the early 1980s to over 30 million by the end of that decade. Like the growth in stock index options, the growth in stock index futures' popularity can be attributed to their use as a stock portfolio management tool.

Currently, four futures contracts are actively traded: the SP 500 [Chicago Mercantile Exchange (CME)], the NYSE Composite Index [New York Futures Exchange (NYFE)], the Major Market Index, MMI [Chicago Board of Trade (CBT)], and the VLCI [Kansas City Board of Trade (KCBT)]. The most popular of these index futures is the SP 500, which encompasses approximately 75% of the index futures trading. The characteristics of these and several other selected futures contracts are shown in Table 13.1-1. These index futures have many of the same characteristics as index options. For instance, like index options, the size of index futures contracts is equal to a multiple of the index value (the multiples for the SP 500, NYSE, and VLCI are $500, while the multiple for the MMI is $250); and like index options, index futures are cash-settled contracts.

In this chapter, we will examine the speculative and hedging uses of these contracts, how they are priced, and the arbitrage strategy known as program trading that is used when index futures contracts are not priced correctly.

TABLE 13.1-1

Characteristics of Select Index Futures			
INDEX	EXCHANGE*	CONTRACT MULTIPLIER	DELIVERY MONTH
Major Market Index (MMI)	CBT	250	Monthly
SP 500	CME	500	March/June/ Sept./Dec.
SP 100	CME	500	Next four months and March/June/ Sept./Dec.
SP Over-the-Counter Index	CME	500	March/June/ Sept./Dec.
VLCI	KCBT	500	March/June/ Sept./Dec.
Mini-VLCI	KCBT	100	March/June/ Sept./Dec.
NYSE Composite	NYFE	500	March/June/ Sept./Dec.

*CBT = Chicago Board of Trade; CME = Chicago Mercantile Exchange; KCBT = Kansas City Board of Trade; NYFE = New York Futures Exchange.

13.2   SPECULATIVE STRATEGIES

As a speculative tool, stock index futures represent an inexpensive and highly liquid short-run alternative to speculating on the stock market. Instead of purchasing the stocks that make up an index or a proxy portfolio, a bullish (bearish) speculator can take a long (short) position in an index futures contract, then purchase Treasury securities to satisfy the margin requirements. A long or short speculative futures position is referred to as a pure speculative position, or a *naked (outright) position*. A speculator who wants to profit from directional changes in the market but who does not want to assume the degree of risk associated with an outright position could instead form either an intracommodity or intercommodity spread with stock index futures.

Since most longer-term futures contracts are more price-sensitive to spot market changes than are shorter-term ones, a risk-averse spreader who is bullish on the stock market could form an intracommodity spread by taking a short position in a nearer-term index futures contract and a long position in a longer-term one. If the market subsequently rises, the percentage gain in the long position on the distant contract will exceed the percentage loss on the short position on the nearby contract. In this case, the spreader will profit, but not as much as he would with a pure speculative long position. On the other hand, if the market declines, the percentage losses on the long position will exceed the percentage gains from the short position. In this situation, the spreader will lose, but not as much as he would have if he had had an outright long position.

Instead of an intracommodity spread, a spreader could form an intercommodity spread by taking opposite positions in different index futures. For example, suppose the relation between the MMI and the SP 500 is such that when the MMI changes by 10%, the SP 500 changes by 9.5%. A risk-averse investor who is bearish on the market could set up an intercommodity spread by going short in the MMI futures contract and long in the SP 500 contract.

Similar to option spreads, index futures spreads allow investors to attain lower return-risk combinations than pure speculative positions. Moreover, by changing the ratios from one long to one short or by forming intercommodity spreads with different correlations, spreaders can attain a number of different return-risk combinations.

13.3   HEDGING WITH STOCK INDEX FUTURES

Several different types of hedging models can be applied to stock index futures. Depending on the underlying asset to be hedged, the most popular models are the *naive hedging model* and the *price-sensitivity model*.

13.3.1   Naive Hedging Model

In the hedging cases presented in the last chapter, we assumed ideal conditions in which there was no quantity, quality, or timing risk extant. In such rare cases, a perfect hedge, in which the value of the spot position is unchanged at expiration, can be attained using a *naive hedging model*. In this model, the number of futures contracts (n_f) is found simply by dividing the current value of the spot position (V_0) by the price of the futures contract (f_0):

$$\text{Naive hedge:} \quad n_f = \frac{V_0}{f_0}. \qquad (13.3\text{-}1)$$

A portfolio manager who wants to lock in a $2.5 million portfolio when the futures price on the SP 500 futures contract is 200 could do so by going short in $n_f = 25$ SP 500 futures contracts:

$$n_f = \frac{V_0}{f_0} = \frac{\$2,500,000}{(200)(\$500)} = 25 \text{ contracts.}$$

Under ideal conditions, the combined value of the portfolio and the cash flows from the futures position would be worth $2.5 million at the futures delivery date.

In practice we would expect some quality, quantity, and/or timing risk to exist in hedging a portfolio with index futures. For example, the $2.5M portfolio may not be perfectly positively correlated with the SP 500 spot index (quality risk). With less than perfect positive correlation, the percentage changes in the portfolio value would differ from those of the index. In such a case, a naive hedging model will not provide a perfect hedge. Also, in most hedging applications, the time period for hedging the portfolio differs from the time period on the futures contract (timing risk), and the relative prices of the portfolio and futures contract usually do not yield a hedge ratio with a round number like 25 (quantity risk). For a manager wanting to hedge a stock portfolio with index futures in which such hedging risk exists, the price-sensitivity model may be more effective in reducing price risk than the naive hedging model.

13.3.2 Stock Index Price-Sensitivity Model

The *stock index price-sensitivity model* determines the number of stock index futures contracts that will minimize the variability of the profits from a hedged portfolio consisting of the stock portfolio and stock index futures contracts. The model is derived in Appendix 13A at the end of this chapter. In this model, the number of futures contracts or hedge ratio that will minimize the variability is:

$$n_f^* = - \beta \frac{V_0}{f_0}, \qquad (13.3\text{-}2)$$

where:

V_0 = current value of stock portfolio

f_0 = price on futures contract

β = beta of stock portfolio

Negative sign indicates opposite positions in the futures contract and the portfolio.

Thus, if a June SP 500 futures contract is available at 300, a portfolio manager wanting to hedge a $2.5 million portfolio with a beta of 1.5 would need 25 short contracts.*

$$n_f^* = - \frac{(1.5)(\$2,500,000)}{(\$500)(300)} = -25.$$

The stock index price-sensitivity model easily can be extended to determining the optimum number of stock index *option* contracts needed to hedge a portfolio. When stock index options are used instead of futures to hedge a portfolio, the hedge ratio (n^*) is found by substituting the option's exercise price for the futures price in Equation (13.3-2). That is:

$$n^* = \frac{\beta V_0}{X}. \qquad (13.3\text{-}3)$$

---

*A diversified portfolio with a β greater than 1 can be thought of as a leveraged investment in the SP 500. The number of hypothetical SP 500 shares would be $n_f^* = \beta V_0/S_0$, where S_0 is the spot SP 500 index, and the amount of debt used to finance the index stock would be the present value of $n_f^* S_0 - V_0$. Thus, if the spot SP 500 index is at 100, a $2.5M portfolio with β = 1.5 would be the equivalent to buying n_f^* = 1.5($2.5M)/100 = 37,500 index shares at $100 per share ($3.75M) and borrowing an amount equal to the present value of $3.75M − $2.5M = $1.25M.

◆ **13.3.3** **Short Index Hedging Example**

To illustrate the use of the price-sensitivity model, consider the case of a stock portfolio manager who in January feels that she may be required to liquidate her stock portfolio in June. Because of this concern, the manager decides to hedge the value of the stock portfolio by taking a short position in the June SP 500 futures contract. The portfolio is well diversified (no unsystematic risk), has a $\beta = 1.5$, and in January is worth $2,500,000 when the SP 500 spot index (S_0) is at 300. Finally, a June SP 500 futures contract priced at 300 is available.

To hedge the portfolio using the price-sensitivity model, the manager would need to go short in 25 SP 500 contracts. That is:

$$n_f^* = -1.5\frac{\$2,500,000}{(300)(\$500)} = 25 \text{ short contracts.}$$

As shown in Table 13.3-1, at the June expiration the value of the futures-hedged portfolio would be $2,500,000, regardless of the market index level.

In this example we have a perfect hedge. This is because we've assumed the portfolio is well diversified and the futures price and portfolio value are such that exactly 25 contracts are needed. In most cases, we would not expect such conditions to exist. Also, if the carrying-cost model holds, we would not expect any difference to exist between locking in the June value of the portfolio with index futures and locking in the June portfolio value by selling the portfolio in January and investing the proceeds in a risk-free security for the period. Thus, if the portfolio manager actually knew she would be liquidating the portfolio in June, then selling 25 futures contracts in January and closing the contracts and liquidating the portfolio in June should be equivalent to selling the portfolio in January and investing the funds in a risk-free security for the period. If this equivalence did not hold, an arbitrage opportunity would exist (this will be discussed further in Section 13.7).

Suppose that instead of locking in a future portfolio value, the portfolio manager wanted portfolio insurance so that she had downside protection in case

TABLE 13.3-1

		Value of the Hedged Stock Portfolio		
(1)	(2)	(3)	(4)	(5)
SP 500 Spot Index at Expiration: $S_T = f_T$	Proportional Change in Portfolio Value (βg): $\beta g = 1.5\frac{S_T - 300}{300}$	Portfolio Value: $(1 + \beta g)\$2.5\text{M}$	Futures Profit: $25(\$500)(300 - f_T)$	Hedged Portfolio Value $(3) + (4)$
240	− .3	$1,750,000	$750,000	$2,500,000
260	− .2	2,000,000	500,000	2,500,000
280	− .1	2,250,000	250,000	2,500,000
300	0	2,500,000	0	2,500,000
320	.1	2,750,000	− 250,000	2,500,000
340	.2	3,000,000	− 500,000	2,500,000
360	.3	3,250,000	− 750,000	2,500,000

$$n_f^* = \frac{-\beta V_0}{f_0} = \frac{-(1.5)(\$2,500,000)}{(\$500)(300)} = 25 \text{ short contracts}$$

the market declined but still could profit if the market increased. In terms of the example, if a June 300 SP 500 put option trading at 10 exists (recall that the multiple on SP 500 options is $100), then $X = (\$100)(300) = \$30,000$ and $P_0 = \$1000$. Using the price-sensitivity model, the manager could attain portfolio insurance by buying 125 put contracts [total cost of $(125)(10)(\$100) = \$125,000$]:

$$n_p^* = 1.5\frac{\$2,500,000}{(300)(\$100)} = 125 \text{ put contracts.}$$

As shown in Table 13.3-2, if the market is at 300 or less at the June expiration, the value of the put-hedged portfolio would be $\$2,500,000 - \$125,000 = \$2,375,000$. If the market is above 300, the value of the hedged portfolio would rise as the market increases. Thus, for the costs of the puts, the portfolio manager can attain portfolio insurance: downside protection, with the possibility of capital gains if the market rises. ◆

◆ 13.3.4 Long Index Hedging Example

A portfolio manager who was planning to invest a future inflow of cash in a stock portfolio could lock in the purchase price of the portfolio by going long in a stock index futures contract. For example, suppose that in January the portfolio manager in the preceding example was anticipating an inflow of cash in June and was planning to invest the cash in a stock portfolio with $\beta = 1.5$ and currently worth $\$2,500,000$. If the June SP 500 futures contract is at $f_0 = 300$, the manager could hedge the purchase price by going long in 25 contracts:

$$n_f^* = 1.5\frac{\$2,500,000}{(300)(\$500)} = 25 \text{ long contracts.}$$

As shown in Table 13.3-3, the long hedge position enables the manager to lock in a net cost of $2.5M for purchasing the portfolio and closing the futures position.

TABLE 13.3-2					
	Value of Put-Hedged Stock Portfolio				
(1) SP 500 SPOT INDEX AT EXPIRATION: S_T	(2) PROPORTIONAL CHANGE IN PORTFOLIO VALUE: $\beta g = 1.5\frac{S_T - 300}{300}$	(3) PORTFOLIO VALUE: $\$2.5M(1 + \beta g)$	(4) PUT PROFIT*	(5) HEDGED PORTFOLIO VALUE (3) + (4)	
240	− .3	$1,750,000	$625,000	$2,375,000	
260	− .2	2,000,000	375,000	2,375,000	
280	− .1	2,250,000	125,000	2,375,000	
300	0	2,500,000	− 125,000	2,375,000	
320	.1	2,750,000	− 125,000	2,625,000	
340	.2	3,000,000	− 125,000	2,875,000	
360	.3	3,250,000	− 125,000	3,125,000	

*$n_p^* = 1.5\frac{\$2,500,000}{(300)(\$100)} = 125$ put contracts

Put profit $= n_p^*(IV - P_0) = 125\{\text{Max}[\$100(300 - S_T), 0] - 10(\$100)\}$

TABLE 13.3-3

Future Portfolio Purchase Hedged with Index Futures and Hedged with Index Options						
(1) SP 500 SPOT INDEX: S_T	(2) PROPORTIONAL CHANGE IN PORTFOLIO VALUE: $\beta g = \frac{1.5(S_T - 300)}{300}$	(3) PORTFOLIO COSTS: $2.5M(1 + \beta g)$	(4) FUTURES PROFIT*	(5) CALL PROFIT†	(6) PORTFOLIO COSTS WITH FUTURES (3) − (4)	(7) PORTFOLIO COSTS WITH CALLS (3) − (5)
240	− .3	$1,750,000	− $750,000	− $125,000	$2,500,000	$1,875,000
260	− .2	2,000,000	− 500,000	− 125,000	2,500,000	2,125,000
280	− .1	2,250,000	− 250,000	− 125,000	2,500,000	2,375,000
300	0	2,500,000	0	− 125,000	2,500,000	2,625,000
320	.1	2,750,000	250,000	125,000	2,500,000	2,625,000
340	.2	3,000,000	500,000	375,000	2,500,000	2,625,000
360	.3	3,250,000	750,000	625,000	2,500,000	2,625,000

*Futures profit $= 25[(\$500)(S_T - 300)]$
†Call profit $= 125\{Max[100(S_T - 300), 0] - (\$100)(10)\}$

In addition to an anticipatory hedge, the manager also could lock in a maximum portfolio cost or minimum number of shares with the possibility of lower costs or more shares if the market declines by purchasing an index call option. Column 7 of Table 13.3-3 shows the costs of purchasing the portfolio and closing $n_c^* = 125$ June 300 call options purchased at 10, where

$$n_c^* = \frac{\beta S_0}{X} = \frac{(1.5)(\$2,500,000)}{(300)(\$100)}.$$

As shown in the table, if the index is at 300 or higher, the costs of purchasing the portfolio and closing the call options are limited to $2,625,000 ($2,500,000 plus cost of the calls); if the index is less than 300, the net cost declines as the index decreases. ◆

13.4 MARKET TIMING

Instead of immunizing a portfolio against market or systematic risk, suppose a manager wanted to change his portfolio's exposure to the market. For example, a stock portfolio manager who is very confident of a bull market may want to give his portfolio more exposure to the market by increasing the portfolio's beta. Changing a portfolio's beta to profit from an expected change in the market is referred to as **market timing**.

Without index futures (or options), the beta of a portfolio can be changed only by altering the portfolio's allocations of securities. With index futures, though, a manager can change the portfolio beta, β_0, to a new one, referred to as a target beta, β_{TR}, simply by buying or selling futures contracts. The number of futures contracts needed to move the portfolio beta from β_0 to β_{TR} can be determined via the price-sensitivity model, in which:*

$$n_f = \frac{V_0}{f_0}(\beta_{TR} - \beta_0), \qquad\qquad (13.4\text{-}1)$$

where:

if $\beta_{TR} > \beta_0$, long in futures

if $\beta_{TR} < \beta_0$, short in futures.

◆ 13.4.1   Market-Timing Example

Consider the case of a stock portfolio manager who in September is confident the market will increase over the next three months, and as a result wants to change her portfolio's beta from its current value of $\beta_0 = .9$ to $\beta_{TR} = 1.25$. Suppose the portfolio currently is worth \$4 million, the spot SP 500 index is at 185, and the price on the December SP 500 futures contract is 190. To adjust the portfolio beta from .9 to 1.25, the manager would need to buy $n_f = 15$ December SP 500 index futures:

$$n_f = \frac{V_0}{f_0}(\beta_{TR} - \beta_0) = \frac{\$4,000,000}{(190)(\$500)}(1.25 - .90) = 14.74.$$

As shown in Table 13.4-1, if the market increases, the manager earns higher rates of return from the futures-adjusted portfolio than from the unadjusted portfolio. If the market declines, though, she incurs greater losses with the adjusted portfolio than with the unadjusted. This greater return-risk from the futures-adjusted portfolio is consistent with the characteristics of a portfolio with a larger beta.† ◆

13.5 SPECULATING ON UNSYSTEMATIC RISK

The price movements of an individual stock are affected by both systematic factors (market factors that affect all stocks) and unsystematic factors (factors unique to the securities of a particular industry or firm). Given this, suppose an investor is very confident that firm or industry factors in the future will lead to a stock price increase. However, suppose the investor also is bearish about the market, fearing that a general price decline in all securities would negate the anticipated positive

---

*Portfolio exposure also can be changed by buying index call or put options. The number of options needed to change the beta is: $n = (V_0/X)(\beta_{TR} - \beta_0)$. If $\beta_{TR} > \beta_0$, index calls are purchased; if $\beta_{TR} < \beta_0$, index puts are purchased.

†The manager also could increase her portfolio's exposure by buying index calls. For example, if there is a December 190 SP 500 call option available, the manager could increase her market exposure by buying 74 calls:
$$n_c = \frac{V_0}{X}(\beta_{TR} - \beta_0) = \frac{\$4,000,000}{(190)(\$100)}(1.25 - .90) = 73.68.$$

TABLE 13.4-1

		Market Timing		
(1)	(2)	(3)	(4)	(5)
SP 500 Spot Index: $S_T = f_T$	Proportional Change: $g = \frac{S_T - 185}{185}$	Futures Profit*	Portfolio Value: $4M(1 + .9g)$	Portfolio Value with Futures (3) + (4)
170	−.081081	− \$150,000	\$3,708,108	\$3,558,108
180	−.027027	− 75,000	3,902,703	3,827,703
190	.027027	0	4,097,297	4,097,297
200	.081081	75,000	4,291,892	4,366,892
210	.135135	150,000	4,486,486	4,636,486
220	.189189	225,000	4,681,080	4,906,080

	Portfolio Rates of Return†	
SP 500 Spot Index: S_T	Unadjusted	Futures-Adjusted
170	−.073	−.110
180	−.024	−.043
190	.024	.024
200	.073	.092
210	.122	.159
220	.170	.226

$S_0 = 185, \quad f_0 = 190,$
$n_f = \frac{V_0}{f_0}(\beta_{TR} - \beta_0) = \frac{\$4,000,000}{(190)(\$500)}(1.25 - .90) \cong 15.$
*Futures profit $= 15(\$500)(S_T - 190).$
†Portfolio rates $=$ (Portfolio value $-$ \$4,000,000)/\$4,000,000.

impacts on the stock's price resulting from the specific firm and industry factors. The investor would like to eliminate the stock's systematic factors, leaving her investment exposed only to the unsystematic factors. With index futures (and options), an investor can accomplish *speculating on unsystematic risk* by hedging away the systematic risk of the stock.

◆ **13.5.1   Example of Speculating on Unsystematic Risk**

To illustrate how speculating on unsystematic risk works, consider the case of a bank trust department that in June identifies the ABC company as a good candidate for takeover by a leveraged buyout firm. Based on this expectation, the bank is considering purchasing 50,000 shares of ABC stock, but it is hesitant because of fear the stock market could decline over the next six months (the time period it is believed the takeover could happen). To hedge against the systematic risk, the trust department could go short in December index futures (or purchase December stock index put options). In this case, suppose ABC stock has a beta of 1.2 and is trading at \$20 per share, the spot SP 500 is at 198, and the December SP 500 futures contract is at 200. The trust department could speculate on the stock's unsystematic risk while hedging the systematic risk by buying 50,000 shares of the ABC stock and going short in 12 December index futures contracts:

$$n_f = -\beta \frac{V_0}{f_0} = -(1.2)\frac{(50,000)(\$20)}{(200)(\$500)} = 12 \text{ short contracts.}$$

To see the possible impacts of using this strategy, consider the following three scenarios occurring in mid-December:

Scenario A: The takeover of ABC and a bull market cause the price of ABC stock to increase by 15% to $23 and the spot SP 500 to increase to 213.

Scenario B: The takeover of ABC and a bear market cause ABC stock to increase by 5% to $21 and the spot SP 500 to decrease to 190.

Scenario C: No takeover of ABC and a bear market cause ABC stock to decrease by 12% to $17.60 and the spot SP 500 to decrease to 190.

Table 13.5-1 shows the values and rates of return for both the futures-hedged stock position and the unhedged stock position for each of the three cases. As shown in the table, the highest returns are earned on the hedged stock if scenario B occurs: The takeover takes place during a bear market. In this case, the trust department would gain both from speculating on the takeover and from the short futures position, earning an 11% rate of return. If the trust department had not hedged, then its rate of return would have been only 5%. The bear market in this

TABLE 13.5-1

				Speculating on Unsystematic Risk
	(1)	(2)	(3) STOCK VALUE (PRICE OF ABC STOCK)	(4) STOCK VALUE HEDGED WITH FUTURES
	SCENARIO	FUTURES PROFIT*	(50,000 SHARES)	(2) + (3)
A	ABC stock: $23 Bull market: $S_T = 213$	− $78,000	$1,150,000	$1,072,000
B	ABC stock: $21 Bear market: $S_T = 190$	60,000	1,050,000	1,110,000
C	ABC stock: $17.60 Bear Market: $S_T = 190$	60,000	880,000	940,000

	RATE OF RETURN†	
SCENARIO	UNHEDGED STOCK	FUTURES-HEDGED STOCK
A	15%	7.2%
B	5%	11 %
C	− 12%	− 6 %

$f_0 = 200,$ $S_0 = 198.$

*Futures profit $= 12(\$500)(200 - S_T).$

†Rate of return $= \dfrac{\text{Stock value} - (\$20)(50,000)}{(\$20)(50,000)}$

case partially offsets the price gain resulting from the takeover. Positive rates of return on the hedged stock position also are realized in scenario A, in which ABC stock rises during a bull market. Since the trust department has hedged away the systematic factors, the hedged returns are not as high as the unhedged position in this scenario. Finally, in scenario C, in which the takeover does not occur and the market declines, the hedged stock position loses, but not as much as the unhedged. Thus, the best scenario for the trust department is B, in which both of the department's expectation occur—takeover and bear market.* ◆

13.6 STOCK INDEX FUTURES PRICING: CARRYING-COST MODEL

The equilibrium futures price on a stock index futures contract can be determined via the carrying-cost model described in the last chapter. In terms of the model, the index futures price is equal to the net costs of carrying a spot index portfolio or proxy portfolio to expiration at time T. For stock index futures, transportation or storage costs do not exist, but dividends from holding the index portfolio do. Thus, the equilibrium price for an index futures is:[†]

$$f_0^* = S_0(1 + R)^T - D_T, \tag{13.6-1}$$

where:

S_0 = current spot index value

D_T = value of stock index dividends at time T.

If the equilibrium condition defined by Equation (13.6-1) does not hold, an arbitrage opportunity will exist by taking a position in the spot portfolio and an opposite one in the futures contract. For example, if the market price on the futures contract (f_0^m) exceeds the equilibrium price, an arbitrageur could earn a riskless profit of $f_0^m - f_0^*$ with an *index arbitrage* strategy in which he borrows S_0 dollars at the risk-free rate of R, buys the spot index portfolio for S_0, and locks in the selling price on the portfolio at time T by going short in the index futures at f_0^m.

The carrying-costs model for index futures also can be described as an investment in a riskless stock index portfolio paying a certain dividend. That is, an investor who purchases a spot index portfolio (at S_0) paying a certain dividend worth D_T at T and who then locks in the portfolio's selling price at time T by

---

*Hedging the systematic risk of a stock does not eliminate the unsystematic risk. Thus, this type of strategy is subject to risk.

[†]The carrying-cost model defined for continuous time is:

$f_0 = S_0 e^{RT} e^{-\Psi T}$,

where R = continuously compounded annual risk-free rate, T = time to expiration as a proportion of the year, and Ψ = annual dividend yield.

going short in an index futures contract at f_0 will earn a riskless one-period rate of return of:

$$\text{Rate} = \frac{(f_0 - S_0) + D_T}{S_0}. \tag{13.6-2}$$

Since this investment is riskless, in equilibrium the futures and spot prices should be such that the rate of return on the investment is equal to a riskless rate (if not, abnormal rates of return could be earned from this investment). Thus, setting Equation (13.6-2) equal to the risk-free rate, then solving for f_0, we obtain the carrying-cost model [Equation (13.6-1)], and solving for S_0 we obtain:

$$S_0 = \frac{f_0 + D_T}{(1 + R)^T}. \tag{13.6-3}$$

Hence, if the carrying-cost model holds, then in equilibrium the rate of return from an investment in a spot portfolio with the selling price locked in with a futures contract is equal to the risk-free rate, and the spot portfolio price is equal to the present value of the futures price and the portfolio's dividends, with the discount rate being equal to the risk-free rate [Equation (13.6-3)].

13.7   PROGRAM TRADING AND INDEX ARBITRAGE

13.7.1   Program Trading

Introduced to the financial vernacular in the 1980s, **program trading** refers to the use of computers in constructing and executing security portfolio positions. Program trading often involves using computer programs to: (1) monitor real-time data of stocks, futures, and option prices to identify any mispricing of stock portfolio values relative to the values of index futures or option positions; (2) define appropriate arbitrage strategies given mispriced portfolios and futures and option positions; and (3) execute orders so securities can be bought or sold quickly and simultaneously when arbitrage advantages exist.

A number of stock portfolio arbitrage and hedging strategies involve monitoring and periodic portfolio adjustments that can be classified as program trading. One group of these strategies is the dynamic portfolio insurance strategies discussed in Chapter 9. A second group is the index arbitrage strategies.

13.7.2   Index Arbitrage

Index arbitrage strategies can be formed with stock index futures contracts and a portfolio consisting of the stocks comprising the index in their proper allocation or a proxy portfolio. To illustrate an index arbitrage strategy, consider a proxy portfolio that is highly diversified, has a beta of 1, is valued at $2.5 million, and is expected to pay dividends worth $62,500 at the end of six months. If the spot SP 500 index is at 300, the portfolio can be viewed as a proxy portfolio consisting of 8,333.333 hypothetical shares of the index, with each share priced at $300 and paying a dividend of $62,500/8,333.333 = $7.50 per index share.

Given the proxy portfolio, suppose the risk-free rate is 8% (annualized) and an SP 500 futures contract exists that expires in six months. In terms of the carrying-cost model, the equilibrium price on the futures contract would be $304.2691:

$$f_0^* = S_0(1 + R)^T - D_T$$

$$f_0^* = \$300(1.08)^{.5} - \$7.50 = \$304.2691.$$

If the actual futures price is above the equilibrium—for example at $f_0^m = 310$, an arbitrageur could earn a riskless profit of $310 − $304.2691 per index share, with an index arbitrage strategy formed by borrowing $300 at 8%, buying an SP 500 spot index share, and going short in the SP 500 futures contract at 310. As a program trading strategy using the proxy portfolio, the index arbitrage strategy would consist of borrowing $2.5 million at 8%, purchasing the proxy portfolio, and going short in 8,333.333/500 = 16.6667 SP 500 futures contracts (assume perfect divisibility) expiring at the end of six months. As shown in Table 13.7-1, with the contract price on the expiring futures contract equal to the spot SP 500 index at expiration, this strategy would yield a riskless profit of ($310 − $304.2691)8,333.333 = $47,757 at expiration, regardless of the value of the index.

If the contract price on the futures contract is below $304.2691, this index arbitrage strategy is reversed. In that case an arbitrageur would take a short position in the spot portfolio, a long position in the risk-free security, and a long position in the futures contract. For example, if the index futures contract is at 300, a portfolio manager with the $2.5 million proxy portfolio could sell it and invest the proceeds in the risk-free security for six months, then go long in 16.6667 SP 500 futures contracts. As shown in Table 13.7-2, at expiration the manager could repurchase the same portfolio and close the futures position for a total cost of $2.5 million. The manager would have earned $98,076 during the period from the investment in the risk-free security; this $98,076, in turn, is $35,576 greater than the $62,500 in dividends foregone by selling the portfolio. By implementing this

TABLE 13.7-1	Index Arbitrage When $f_0^m > f_0^*$		
	$f_0^* = 304.2691$, $f_0^m = 310$, $S_0 = 300$ Strategy: Borrow $2.5 million at 8% interest for six months; purchase $2.5 million proxy portfolio; sell 16.6667 SP 500 futures contracts expiring at the end of six months		
	CLOSING POSITION	INDEX DECREASES 10%: $S_T = f_T = 270$	INDEX INCREASES 10%: $S_T = f_T = 330$
	Debt: $2.5M(1.08)^{.5}$ Portfolio: $S_T(8,333.333)$ Futures: $500(310 − f_T)(16.6667)$ Dividends: $7.50(8,333.333)$	− $2,598,076 2,250,000 333,333 62,500	− $2,598,076 2,750,000 − 166,667 62,500
	Arbitrage Cash Flow	$ 47,757	$ 47,757

TABLE 13.7-2

Index Arbitrage When $f_0^m < f_0^*$		
$f_0^* = 304.2691$, $f_0^m = 300$, $S_0 = 300$ Strategy: Sell \$2.5 million proxy portfolio; invest \$2.5 million in risk-free security at 8%; buy 16.6667 SP 500 futures contracts expiring at the end of six months		
CLOSING POSITIONS	INDEX DECREASES 10%: $S_T = f_T = 270$	INDEX INCREASES 10%: $S_T = f_T = 330$
Portfolio purchase: $-S_T(8,333.333)$ Futures: \$500$(f_T - 300)$(16.6667) Investment: \$2.5M$(1.08)^{.5}$ Dividends foregone: $-\$7.50(8,333.333)$	$-\$2,250,000$ $-$ 250,000 2,598,076 $-$ 62,500	$-\$2,750,000$ 250,000 2,598,076 $-$ 62,500
Arbitrage Cash Flow	\$ 35,576	\$ 35,576

type of index arbitrage strategy, the manager would be able to earn an arbitrage profit of $(304.2691 - 300)8,333.333 = \$35,576$, regardless of any changes in the market.

13.7.3   Stock Volatility and the Triple Witching Hour

Since the price of an expiring futures contract is equal to the spot index price at expiration, program traders who have implemented an index arbitrage strategy often will wait until the expiration day on the futures contract to close their positions. As a result, during the last hour of trading on the delivery day of the index futures contract, an abnormally large volume of trading often occurs on the exchanges as program traders, other arbitrageurs, and hedgers close their futures positions and liquidate or purchase large blocks of stock. This reversing of positions has often caused large swings to occur in stock prices, with the fluctuations being particularly dramatic on the *triple witching hour*: the last hour of trading on the day when index futures, stock index options, and options on stock index futures all expire.

Finance scholars have debated over the significance of the increased volatility on expiration days resulting from program trading. Some scholars argue that program traders often liquidate stocks during a bear market and purchase them during a bull market, thus causing the market prices of stocks to overshoot their equilibrium levels, leading to market inefficiency. Other scholars, though, maintain that index arbitrageurs actually move stock prices to their equilibrium levels, and any temporary increase in volatility that may occur on the expiration date should be viewed simply as part of the costs of ensuring an efficient market.*

---

*Stoll and Whaley in a 1987 study argue that price changes on the triple witching hour are no different than price changes that occur as a result of any block trade.

13.8 PORTFOLIO INSURANCE USING STOCK INDEX FUTURES

13.8.1 Dynamic Hedge Ratio

In Chapter 9, we examined how dynamic portfolio insurance strategies could be constructed with stock index put options or risk-free bonds and managed via a binomial option pricing model. In addition to index puts and bonds, portfolio insurance strategies also can be formed with stock index futures contracts.[*] These strategies require finding the number of futures contracts, referred to as the **dynamic hedge ratio** (n_f), that will replicate the put-insured stock portfolio. The model's derivation is presented in Appendix 13B at the end of this chapter. The dynamic hedge ratio, in turn, is:

$$n_f = \left[\left(\frac{V^{SP}}{S_0 + P_0} \right)\left(1 + \frac{dP}{dS} \right) - \frac{V^{SP}}{S_0} \right] e^{-RT}, \qquad (13.8\text{-}1)$$

where:

V^{SP} = sum of value of stock portfolio and costs of put options used to ensure stock portfolio

S_0 = per-share price of stock portfolio or stock index value

P_0 = price of stock index put option

T = time to expiration on the put option.

The hedge ratio n_f can be estimated using either the continuous-time B-S OPM or the discrete BOPM. If the B-S model is used, the change in the put index price per small change in the spot index price, dP/dS, is equal to $N(d_1) - 1$, and the risk-free rate is the continuously compounded rate. If the BOPM is used, $dP/dS = H_0^p = (P_u - P_d)/S_0(u - d)$, and a discrete-period risk-free rate is used.

13.8.2 Put-Insured and Futures-Insured Portfolios

To see the equivalence between a put-insured portfolio and futures-insured one, consider a two-period binomial option pricing model case in which the spot index is currently priced at $S_0 = 150$ with $u = 1.1$ and $d = 1/1.1$, a European put option on the index exists with an exercise price of 150 and with period values determined by the BOPM, the period risk-free rate is 5%, and a futures contract on the index exists with a price determined by the carrying-cost model. For simplicity, assume there are no dividends and no multiplier on the futures contract. The period values of the spot index, put, and futures contract are shown in the top part of each node's block in Table 13.8-1, along with the put hedge ratios $[H^p = (P_u - P_d)/S(u - d)]$ and the dynamic hedge ratios, n_f [Equation (13.8-1)].

In the current period, the put-insured index value $(V_0^{SP} = S_0 + P_0)$ is 151.6194 when $S_0 = 150$; in period 1 it is either 165 when $S_u = 165$, or 142.8536 when

---

[*]The portfolio insurance strategy using index futures was first developed by Rubinstein (1985).

TABLE 13.8-1

Futures-Insured and Put-Insured Index Values

$S_0 = 150, R = .05, X = 150, u = 1.1, d = 1/1.1, n = 2; p = (r_f - d)/(u - d) = .738; f_0 = S_0(1 + R)^n = 150(1.05)^2 = 165.375$
$H_0^P = (P_u - P_d)/(S_u - S_d); n_f = \{[V^{SP}/(S + P)](1 + R)^n - 1; V^{SP} = S + P; n = \text{hypothetical indexed shares} = V^{SP}/S;$
$f_u = S_u(1 + R)^{n-1}, f_d = S_d(1 + R)^{n-1}.$

		$S_{uu} = f_{uu} = 181.5, P_{uu} = 0$ Futures-insured portfolio $= n_u S_{uu} + n_{fu}(f_u - f_{uu}) = 181.5$ Put-insured portfolio $= S_{uu} + P_{uu} = 181.5$
	$S_u = 165, P_u = 0, f_u = 173.25, H_u^P = 0, n_{fu} = 0, n_u = (S_u + P_u)/S_u = 1$ Futures-insured portfolio $= n_0 S_u + n_{f0}(f_0 - f_u) = 165$ Put-insured portfolio $= S_u + P_u = 165$ Adjustment: Sell $(n_0 - n_u)$ index shares at S_u; use proceeds of $1.78 to close futures: $n_{f0}(f_0 - f_u) = -\$1.78$ Position: $n_u = 1$ index share, $n_{fu} = 0$ futures	
		$S_{ud} = f_{ud} = 150, P_{ud} = 0$ or Futures-insured portfolio $= n_u S_{ud} + n_{fu}(f_u - f_{ud}) = 150$ Futures-insured portfolio $= n_d S_{ud} + n_{fd}(f_d - f_{ud}) = 150$ Put-insured portfolio $= S_{ud} + P_{ud} = 150$
$S_0 = 150, P_0 = 1.6194, f_0 = 165.375, H_0^P = -.2266,$ $n_{f0} = .2261$ short contracts, $n_0 = (S_0 + P_0)/S_0 = 1.010796$ Put-insured portfolio $= S_0 + P_0 = 151.619$ Futures-insured portfolio: Purchase n_0 index shares at S_0: $(1.010796)(150) = 151.619$; short n_{f0} futures at f_0		
	$S_d = 136.3636, P_d = 6.49, f_d = 143.1818, H_d^P = -1, n_{fd} = 1.0476$ short contracts, $n_d = (S_d + P_d)/S_d = 1.0476$ Futures-insured portfolio $= n_0 S_d + n_{f0}(f_0 - f_d) = 142.85$ Put-insured portfolio $= S_d + P_d = 142.85$ Adjustment: Close futures: $n_0(f_0 - f_d) = 5.02$; use futures profit of 5.02 to buy $(n_d - n_0)$ index shares at S_d: Cost $= n_d - n_0$ $S_d = 5.02$; go short n_{fd} futures at f_d Position: Long $n_d = 1.0476$ index shares, short $n_{fd} = 1.0476$ index futures at f_d	
		$S_{dd} = f_{dd} = 123.97, P_{dd} = 26.03$ Futures-insured portfolio $= n_d S_{dd} + n_{fd}(f_d - f_{dd}) = 150$ Put-insured portfolio $= S_{dd} + P_{dd} = 150$

$S_d = 136.3636$. To replicate the put-insured values for period 1 with futures and spot index positions requires:

1. Buying \$151.6194 of the spot index (investment equal to $V_0^{SP} = S_0 + P_0$) or equivalently purchasing 1.010796 hypothetical index shares at \$150 per share. That is:

$$n_0 = \frac{V_0^{SP}}{S_0} = \frac{S_0 + P_0}{S_0} = \frac{\$151.6194}{\$150} = 1.010796 \text{ index shares,}$$

2. Going short in $n_{f0} = .2261$ index futures contracts priced at $f_0 = 165.375$:

$$n_{f0} = \left[\frac{V_0^{SP}}{S_0 + P_0}(1 + H_0) - \frac{V_0^{SP}}{S_0} \right] \frac{1}{(1 + R)^{n-1}}$$

$$n_{f0} = \left[\frac{151.6194}{150 + 1.6194}(1 - .2266) - \frac{151.6194}{150} \right] \frac{1}{1.05}$$
$$= -.2261 = .2261 \text{ short contracts,}$$

where the negative sign indicates a short position.

At the end of period 1, the values of the futures-insured index would equal the put-insured index values. For example, if the spot index is at 165, then the $n_0 = 1.010796$ index shares would be worth 166.78, but there would be a \$1.78 loss on the futures positions, yielding a futures-insured index value of 165—the same as the put-insured index value. That is:

$$
\begin{aligned}
\text{Futures-insured value} &= (n_0)S_u + n_{f0}(f_0 - f_u) \\
&= (1.010796)(165) + .2261(165.375 - 173.25) \\
&= 166.78 - 1.78 = 165
\end{aligned}
$$

$$
\begin{aligned}
\text{Put-insured value} &= S_u + P_u \\
&= 165 + 0 = 165.
\end{aligned}
$$

On the other hand, if the spot index is at 136.3636, then the $n_0 = 1.010796$ index shares would be worth only 137.83, but a futures profit of \$5.02 would exist, yielding a futures-insured index value of 142.85, the same as the put-insured index value:

$$
\begin{aligned}
\text{Futures-insured value} &= (n_0)S_d + n_{f0}(f_0 - f_d) \\
&= (1.010796)(136.3636) + (.2261)(165.375 - 143.1818) \\
&= 137.83 + 5.02 = 142.85
\end{aligned}
$$

$$
\begin{aligned}
\text{Put-insured value} &= S_d + P_d \\
&= 136.3636 + 6.49 = 142.85.
\end{aligned}
$$

Like the dynamic portfolio insurance strategy using bonds that we examined in Chapter 9, the dynamic portfolio insurance strategy using futures also must be adjusted each period. To replicate the three put-insured index values in the last period, the index shares (n_0) and the dynamic hedge ratio n_{f0} set up in the initial period would need to be adjusted to equal the index shares and the hedge ratio for period 1.

As shown in Table 13.8-1, if the index is at 165, then the hedge ratio for the next period (n_{fu}) would be zero, and the number of index shares (n_u) would be $n_u = (S_u + P_u)/S_u = (165 + 0)/165 = 1$. The adjustments in this case would require selling $n_0 - n_u = 1 - 1.010796 = .010796$ share at $165 per share, then using the proceeds of $(.010796)(165) = \$1.78$ to cover the $1.78 futures obligation needed to close the contract: $.2261(165.375 - 173.25) = -1.78$. After adjusting, you would have just one index share, which next period would be worth either 181.5 or 150—the same values as the put-insured index.

On the other hand, if the index is 136.3636 at the end of period 1, then the put would be worth $P_d = 6.49$, the number of index shares (n_d) would need to be $n_d = (S_d + P_d)/S_d = (136.3636 + 6.49)/136.3636 = 1.0476$, and the required dynamic hedge ratio would also need to be $n_{fd} = 1.0476$. To move to these parameter values would require:

1. Closing the futures position for a profit of $0.2261(165.375 - 143.1818) = 5.02$;

2. Buying 0.0368 additional index share at 136.3636 per share with the $5.02 futures profit: $S_d(n_d - n_0) = 136.3636(1.0476 - 1.010796) = 5.02$;

3. Going short in $n_{fd} = 1.0476$ index futures contracts at a price of $143.1818 per share.

At the end of period 2, the adjusted futures-insured index value would be worth 150 at either spot index—150 or 123.97, the same as the put-insured index value.

At $S_{ud} = 150$:

$$\text{Futures-insured index value} = (n_d)S_{ud} + n_{fd}(f_{ud} - f_d)$$
$$= 1.0476(150) + (1.0476)(143.1818 - 150)$$
$$= 157.14 - 7.14 = 150$$

$$\text{Put-insured index value} = S_{ud} + P_{ud}$$
$$= 150 + 0 = 150.$$

At $S_{dd} = 123.97$:

$$\text{Futures-insured index value} = (n_d)S_{dd} + n_{fd}(f_{dd} - f_d)$$
$$= (1.0476)(123.97) + (1.0476)(143.1818 - 123.97)$$
$$= 129.87 + 20.13 = 150.$$

$$\text{Put-insured index value} = S_{dd} + P_{dd}$$
$$= 123.97 + 26.03 = 150.$$

◆ **13.8.3**   **Example of Dynamic Futures-Insured Portfolio**

In Chapter 9, we presented an example of a portfolio insurance strategy using both index put options and a risk-free bond in which a portfolio manager ensured a minimum value of $2.5 million on a diversified portfolio. In the example, we assumed the same two-period binomial case presented in the last section ($S_0 = 150, u = 1.1, d = 1/1.1$, 5% period risk-free rate, zero dividends, and a 150 index put option expiring at the end of two periods). In the Chapter 9 example, the portfolio manager was able to attain a minimum portfolio value of $2.5 million at the end of the period, with the possibility of the portfolios being worth $3.025 million, by purchasing 16,667 index puts (assume no multiplier): $n_0 =$ (minimum portfolio value)$/X = \$2,500,000/150$. The example is summarized in the second part of each node's block in Table 13.8-2.

Instead of using index puts, the manager alternatively could attain the same insurance using index futures contracts. Assuming the prices on the futures contract are determined by the carrying-cost model, the manager, in seeking to form a futures-insured portfolio that replicates the put-insured one, first would need to buy $2,526,984 worth of the diversified portfolio (or if she has a current $2.5M portfolio, buy an additional $26,984 worth of the portfolio). The $2,526,984 portfolio would be the equivalent of buying $n_0 = 16,846.56$ index shares at the current SP 500 index price of $150 per index share. That is:

$$n_0 = \frac{\text{Insured portfolio value} + \text{Put value}}{S_0}$$

$$n_0 = \frac{\$2,500,000 + (16,667)(\$1.619)}{\$150} = 16,846.56.$$

The additional $26,984 portfolio investment is equal to the costs of the puts; it thus represents the costs of the insurance.

In addition to the portfolio, the manager also must go short in $n_{f0} = 3768$ index futures contracts at a price of $f_0 = S_0(1 + R)^n = 150(1.05)^2 = 165.375$:

$$n_{f0} = \left[\frac{\$2,526,984}{150 + 1.619}(1 - .2266) - \frac{\$2,526,984}{150} \right] \frac{1}{1.05}$$

$$n_{f0} = -3768 \text{ contracts} = 3768 \text{ short contracts.}$$

As shown in the lower part of the blocks in Table 13.8-2, if the market decreases to 136.3636 at the end of the first period, the portfolio and futures positions would be worth $2.381 million (the same as the put-insured portfolio). In this case, the manager could:

1. Close the futures positions, realizing a cash flow of $3768(165.375 - 143.1818) = \$83,624$,

2. Invest the $83,624 in the diversified portfolio, now worth $(1/1.1)(\$2,526,984) = \$2,297,258$, making the total portfolio investment worth $2.381 million, and

3. Go short in $n_{fd} = 17,460$ index futures contracts at a futures price of 143.1818:

TABLE 13.8-2

Portfolio Insurance Strategy Using Puts and Futures

$S_0 = 150, R = .05, X = 150, u = 1.1, d = 1/1.1, n = 2; p = (r_f - d)/(u - d) = .738; f_0 = S_0(1 + R)^n = 150(1.05)^2 = 165.375$
$H_0^P = (P_u - P_d)/(S_u - S_d); n_f = \{[V^{SP}/(S + P)](1 + H^P) - (V^{SP}/S)\}/(1 + R)^{n-1}; V^{SP} = $ value of stock portfolio and puts; $n = $ hypothetical indexed shares $= V^{SP}/S; f_u = S_u(1 + R)^{n-1}, f_d = S_d(1 + R)^{n-1}$.

$S_0 = 150, P_0 = 1.619, f_0 = 165.375, H_0^P = -.2266, n_{f0} = $ 3768 short contracts, $n_0 = 16,846.56$
Put-insured portfolio: portfolio = $2.5M, put insurance: Buy 16,667 stock index puts with X = 150 at $P_0 = 1.619$: puts = (16,667)(1.619) = $26,984
$V_0^{SP} = $ insured portfolio = $2,526,984
Futures-insured portfolio: Portfolio = $2,526,984, short in $n_{f0} = $ 3768 index futures stock contracts at $f_0 = 165.375$

$S_u = 165, P_u = 0, f_u = 173.25, H_u^P = 0, n_{fu} = 0, n_u = V^{SP}/S_u = 16,667$
Put-insured portfolio: Portfolio = $2.75M; puts = (16,667)(0) = 0; $V_u^{SP} = $ insured portfolio = $2.75M
Futures-insured portfolio: Portfolio = V = $2,779,682; Futures: 3768(165.375 − 173.25) = −$29,673; insured portfolio = $2.75M
Adjustment: Liquidate $29,673 of the portfolio to finance futures closing
Stock portfolio = $2.75M and 0 futures position ($n_{fu} = 0$)

$S_{uu} = f_{uu} = 181.5, P_{uu} = 0$
Put-insured portfolio: Portfolio = $3.025M; puts = (16,667)(0) = 0; $V_{uu}^{SP} = $ insured portfolio = $3.025 M
Futures-insured portfolio = $3.025M

$S_d = 136.3636, P_d = 6.49, f_d = 143.1818, H_d^P = -1, n_{fd} = V_d^{SP}/S_d = 17,461$
17,460 short contracts, $n_d = V^{SP}/S_d = 17,461$
Put-insured portfolio: Portfolio = $2.2727M
Puts = (16,667)($6.49) = $.108M
$V_d^{SP} = $ insured portfolio = $2.381M
Futures-insured portfolio: Portfolio = $2,297,258
Futures = 3768(165.375 − 143.1818) = $83,624
Insured portfolio = $2.381M
Adjustment: Invest futures profit in stock portfolio; go short in $n_{fd} = $ 17,460 index futures at $f_d = 143.1818$,
Stock portfolio = $2.381M and 17,460 index futures

$S_{ud} = f_{ud} = 150, P_{ud} = 0$
Put-insured portfolio: Portfolio = $2.5M; puts = (16,667)(0) = 0
$V_{ud}^{SP} = $ insured portfolio = $2.5M
Futures-insured portfolio = $2.75M(1/1.1) + 0 = $2.5M
or
$2.381M(1.10) + (17,460) (f_d - f_{ud}) = $2.5M

$S_{dd} = f_{dd} = 123.97, P_{dd} = 26.03$
Put-insured portfolio: Portfolio = $2.066M
Puts = (16,667)($26.03) = $.434M
$V_{dd}^{SP} = $ insured portfolio = $2.5M
Futures-insured portfolio: $2.381M(1/1.1) + (17,460)(f_d - f_{dd}) = $2.5M

$$n_{fd} = \left[\frac{\$2,381,000}{136.3636 + 6.49}(1 - 1) - \frac{\$2,381,000}{136.3636} \right] \frac{1}{(1.05)^0}$$

$$n_{fd} = -17,460 \text{ contracts} = 17,460 \text{ short contracts.}$$

With this adjustment, the manager would ensure an investment value of $2.5 million next period.

At $S_{ud} = 150$:

Futures-insured portfolio = $2.381M(1.1) + (17,460)(143.1818 - 150)
= $2.5M.

At $S_{dd} = 123.97$:

Futures-insured portfolio = $2.381M(1/1.1) + (17,460)(143.1818
- 123.97) = $2.5M.

Alternatively, the manager could liquidate the portfolio and close the futures position in period 1, earning $2.381 million, then invest the $2.381 million proceeds in a risk-free security at 5% to ensure a $2.5 million investment value at the end of next period.

In contrast, if the market increases to 165 at the end of the first period, then the combined stock portfolio and futures position would be worth $2.75M. The stock portfolio would be worth 1.1($2,526,984) = $2,779,682, and the costs of closing the futures would be 3768(165.375 - 173.25) = $29,673. In this case, the portfolio manager could sell $29,673 of the portfolio and use the proceeds to finance the futures closing. Since no new futures are required ($n_{fu} = 0$), the manager would have a $2.75 million stock portfolio that would be worth either $3.025 million or $2.5 million at the end of the next period—the same as the put-insured portfolio. ◆

13.9   CONCLUSION

Since their introduction by the Kansas City Board of Exchange in the early 1980s, stock index futures have become a valuable tool in stock market speculation and managing stock portfolios. Index futures provide a liquid and relatively inexpensive way to speculate on the market: By forming different types of intracommodity and intercommodity spreads, speculators can use them to attain a number of return-risk investment strategies. Index futures also enable stock portfolio managers to lock in future portfolio values or to obtain portfolio insurance to ensure a minimum portfolio value. Managers also can use stock index futures to adjust the beta of a portfolio if they anticipate a bull or a bear market, thus eliminating the need to revise their portfolio allocation. Finally, managers can use index futures to eliminate a stock's systematic risk, enabling them to speculate on unsystematic factors.

Given the myriad uses of index futures, it is not surprising that such instruments have grown since their introduction. Equally impressive as the growth in index futures, though, is the increased use of interest rate futures. As we will examine in the next chapter, these contracts, like index futures, also have a number of speculative and hedging uses.

KEY TERMS

naked (outright) position

naive hedging model

stock index price-sensitivity model

market timing

speculating on unsystematic risk

index arbitrage

program trading

triple witching hour

dynamic hedge ratio

SELECTED REFERENCES

Clarke, R., and Arnott, R. "The Cost of Portfolio Insurance: Tradeoffs and Choices." *Financial Analysts Journal* 43 (Nov.–Dec. 1987): 35–47.

Eytan, T., and Harpaz, G. "The Pricing of Futures and Option Contracts on the Value Line Index." *Journal of Finance* 41 (Sept. 1986): 843–855.

Figlewski, S. "Hedging Performance and Basis Risk in Stock Index Futures." *Journal of Finance* 39 (July 1984): 657–669.

Figlewski, S., and Kin, S. "Portfolio Management with Stock Index Futures." *Financial Analysts Journal* 38 (Jan.–Feb. 1982): 52–60.

Grant, D. "How to Optimize with Stock Index Futures." *Journal of Portfolio Management* 8 (Spring 1982): 32–36.

Gressis, N., Glahos, G., and Philippatos, G. "A CAPM-based Analysis of Stock Index Futures." *Journal of Portfolio Management* 10 (Spring 1984): 47–52.

Hill, J., and Jones, F. "Equity Trading, Program Trading, Portfolio Insurance, Computer Trading and All That." *Financial Analysts Journal* 44 (July–Aug. 1988): 29–38.

Modest, D., and Sundaresan, M. "The Relationship Between Spot and Futures Prices in Stock Index Futures Markets: Some Preliminary Evidence." *Journal of Futures Markets* 3 (1983): 15–41.

Morgan, G. "Forward and Futures Pricing of Treasury Bills." *Journal of Banking and Finance* (Dec. 1981): 483–496.

O'Brien, T. "The Mechanics of Portfolio Insurance." *Journal of Portfolio Management* 14 (Spring 1985): 40–47.

Rendleman, R., Jr., and McEnally, R. "Assessing the Cost of Portfolio Insurance." *Financial Analysts Journal* 43 (May–June 1987): 27–37.

Rubinstein, M. "Alternative Paths to Portfolio Insurance." *Financial Analysts Journal* 41 (July–Aug. 1985): 42–52.

————. "Portfolio Insurance and the Market Crash." *Financial Analysts Journal* 44 (Jan.–Feb. 1988): 38–47.

Santoni, G. "Has Program Trading Made Stock Prices More Volatile?" *Review* (Federal Reserve Bank of St. Louis) 69: 18–29.

Siegel, D., and Siegel, D. *Futures Markets*. Chicago: Dryden Press, 1990, pp. 165–179.

Smith, D. "The Arithmetic of Financial Engineering." *Journal of Applied Corporate Finance* 1 (1989): 49–58.

Stoll, H., and Whaley, R. "Expiration Day Effects of Index Options and Futures," Salomon Brothers Center for the Study of Financial Institutions. Monograph Series in Finance and Economics, Monograph 1986-3.

Stoll, H., and Whaley, R. "Program Trading and Expiration Day Effects." *Financial Analysts Journal* 43 (Mar.–Apr. 1987): 16–23.

Tucker, A. *Financial Futures, Options and Swaps*. St. Paul: West, 1991, pp. 453–470.

PROBLEMS AND QUESTIONS

1. Mr. Fiore is a stock portfolio manager for the Investment Trust Company. On January 10, Mr. Fiore determines he will have to liquidate part of his stock portfolio in June, and he would like to hedge the portfolio sale. The portfolio he plans to sell is well diversified, has a β of 1.5, is expected to generate certain dividends worth $8.75M in June, and on January 10 is worth $50M. On January 10, the SP 500 spot index is at 300, a June SP 500 futures contract is at 300, and a June SP 500 put with an exercise price of 300 is trading at 15.

   a. Using the price-sensitivity model, determine how many SP 500 futures contracts Mr. Fiore would need in order to hedge the sale of his $50 million portfolio in June.

   b. Show in a table the values of the portfolio, futures profits, and the hedged portfolio values on the June expiration date for possible spot index values of 270, 280, 290, 300, 310, 320, and 330. Assume no quantity, quality, or timing risks.

   c. How many SP 500 put contracts would Mr. Fiore need if he wanted to ensure the portfolio with a portfolio insurance strategy? Use the price-sensitivity model.

   d. Evaluate the put-insured strategy at spot index prices at expiration of 270, 280, 290, 300, 310, 320, and 330. Assume no quantity, quality, or timing risks.

2. Ms. Di is a stock portfolio manager for LM Insurance Company. Ms. Di is expecting a $20M inflow of cash from premiums on June 20 and is planning to invest the cash in a portfolio of stocks with $\beta = 1$. Ms. Di is concerned there will be a strong bull market, and she would like to hedge her June investment

with a June SP 500 futures contract trading at 320. Currently, the SP 500 spot index is at 320, and there is exactly one month to the June expiration on the futures contracts.

    a. Describe Ms. Di's June portfolio purchase as an investment in hypothetical shares of the SP 500.

    b. Evaluate the June costs of Ms. Di's portfolio as a purchase of hypothetical SP 500 shares at spot index values of 305, 310, 315, 320, 325, 330, and 335.

    c. How many futures contracts would Ms. Di need to lock in her portfolio purchase such that it is equivalent to buying the portfolio at its current value?

    d. Evaluate the hedged portfolio cost at spot index prices at expiration of 305, 310, 315, 320, 325, 330, and 335.

3. Ms. Ellis manages a portfolio consisting of five stocks (A, B, C, D, and E). Table 13.P-3 shows Ms. Ellis's stocks, shares, β's, and stock prices as of March 20.

    a. How many futures contracts would Ms. Ellis need in order to hedge the value of her portfolio on September 20 if a September SP 500 futures contract, expiring on September 20, was trading at $f_0 = 315$ when the spot was at $S_0 = 310$?

    b. Determine what the September values of Ms. Ellis's unhedged and futures-hedged portfolio would be if on September 20 the market had decreased such that the spot SP 500 was at 279 and the prices of her stocks were selling at the values indicated in column 5 of Table 13.P-3. Assume no quantity, quality, or timing risks.

4. Suppose Ms. Ellis, in Problem 3, believed there would be a bull market over the next six months (March 20 to September 20), and wanted to profit by increasing her portfolio β to 1.5. Explain how Ms. Ellis could increase her β to 1.5 using the September SP 500 futures contract described in Problem 3. Compare Ms. Ellis's portfolio values on September 20 with and without the futures for possible proportional rates of change in the market from March 20 to September 20 of $-.15$, $-.10$, $-.05$, 0, .05, .10, and .15.

TABLE 13.P-3

(1) STOCKS	(2) SHARES	(3) 3/20 PRICE PER SHARE	(4) β	(5) 9/20 PRICE PER SHARE
A	20,000	$45	1.30	$39.15
B	10,000	50	.90	45.50
C	20,000	30	.75	27.75
D	5,000	15	1.20	13.20
E	15,000	35	1.40	30.10

5. On April 1, Mr. Colbert received information that General Pharmaceutical (GP) might be introducing a new acne drug the following month. In response to the information, Mr. Colbert decided to buy 10,000 shares of GP, priced at $S_g = \$50$/share and with a β of .8. Mr. Colbert, though, was concerned that the market might decline over the next month, negating any increase in GP stock.

   a. Explain how Mr. Colbert could construct a hedge with SP 500 futures contract expiring next month to reduce his exposure to systematic risk. Assume the current spot index and the futures contract are both 200.

   b. Evaluate the value of the stock and the futures for the following scenarios occurring one month later:

      (1) There is a bull market, and the new drug is introduced, causing $S_T = 225$ and $S_g = \$60$.

      (2) There is a bear market, and the new drug is introduced, causing $S_T = 175$ and $S_g = \$54$.

   c. Compare the period rates of return for each scenario that would result with and without the futures position.

6. Determine the equilibrium price of a December SP 500 futures contract available on September 20. Assume the spot SP 500 index is at 212, the risk-free rate is 6.5%, dividends worth a certain $2.62 at the December expiration, and 90 days to expiration.

7. PI investment company has formed a proxy portfolio it is using to identify arbitrage opportunities via index arbitrage strategies. The proxy portfolio consists of five stocks; the stock prices, shares, dividend values at the end of the next quarter, and β's are shown in Table 13.P-7. The current SP 500 index is at 212.03156, and the risk-free rate is 6%.

   a. Define the PI investment company's portfolio as an investment in hypothetical shares in the SP 500. What is the quarterly dividend per index share?

   b. Determine the equilibrium price of an SP 500 futures contract expiring at the end of one quarter ($T = 90$ days).

   c. Describe the index arbitrage strategy PI could employ if the SP 500 futures was trading at 215 (assume you can buy fractional contract shares).

   d. Evaluate the index arbitrage from Problem 7c at the futures' expiration by first assuming the market increases by 10%, then assuming it decreases by 10%. Assume the portfolio is perfectly correlated with the market.

TABLE 13.P-7

STOCK	SHARES	SHARE PRICE	SHARE DIVIDENDS	β
A	20,000	$60	$0.75	0.90
B	10,000	70	0.50	0.95
C	20,000	50	0.70	1.1
D	10,000	60	0.60	1.05
E	20,000	40	0.60	1.032

     e. Describe the index arbitrage strategy PI could employ if the SP 500 futures was trading at 210 (assume perfect divisibility and no short sale restrictions).

     f. Evaluate the index arbitrage from Problem 7e at the futures' expiration, first assuming the market increased by 10%, then assuming it decreased by 10%. Assume the portfolio is perfectly correlated with the market.

8. Describe program trading.

9. What is the triple witching hour?

10. The following event tree shows at each node the SP 500 index prices and the BOPM put prices and hedge ratios (H) for a European put on the SP 500 with an exercise price of 300. The prices reflect the following assumptions: $u = 1.1, d = 1/1.1, R_f = .05, n = 2, p = .738$, and no dividends.

$$
\begin{array}{l}
S_{uu} = 363 \\
P_{uu} = 0
\end{array}
$$

$$
\begin{array}{l}
S_u = 330 \\
P_u = 0 \\
H_u^P = 0
\end{array}
$$

$$
\begin{array}{l}
S_0 = 300 \\
P_0 = 3.24174 \\
H_0^P = -.226838
\end{array}
$$

$$
\begin{array}{l}
S_{ud} = 300 \\
P_{ud} = 0
\end{array}
$$

$$
\begin{array}{l}
S_d = 272.727 \\
P_d = 12.9917 \\
H_d^P = -1
\end{array}
$$

$$
\begin{array}{l}
S_{dd} = 247.934 \\
P_{dd} = \$52.066
\end{array}
$$

     a. Show with an event tree the values at each node of a well-diversified portfolio that is currently worth \$10M and is hedged with SP 500 index puts. Assume no index put multiplier.

     b. Show with an event tree the prices at each node of an SP 500 futures contract expiring at end of the second period. Assume no contract multiplier and dividends.

     c. Construct a dynamic insured portfolio with the preceding futures contracts that replicates the put-insured portfolio at expiration. Show with an event tree the values of your futures-insured portfolio at each node and the adjustments needed to keep the portfolio identical to the put-insured portfolio.

11. This question is based on Problem 8 in Chapter 9. Given the following:

     • An SP 500 index that is currently priced at $S_0 = 300$ and that follows a binomial process where $u = 1.05$ and $d = 1/1.05$. The values of the index at each node are shown in Figure 13.P-11.

FIGURE 13.P-11

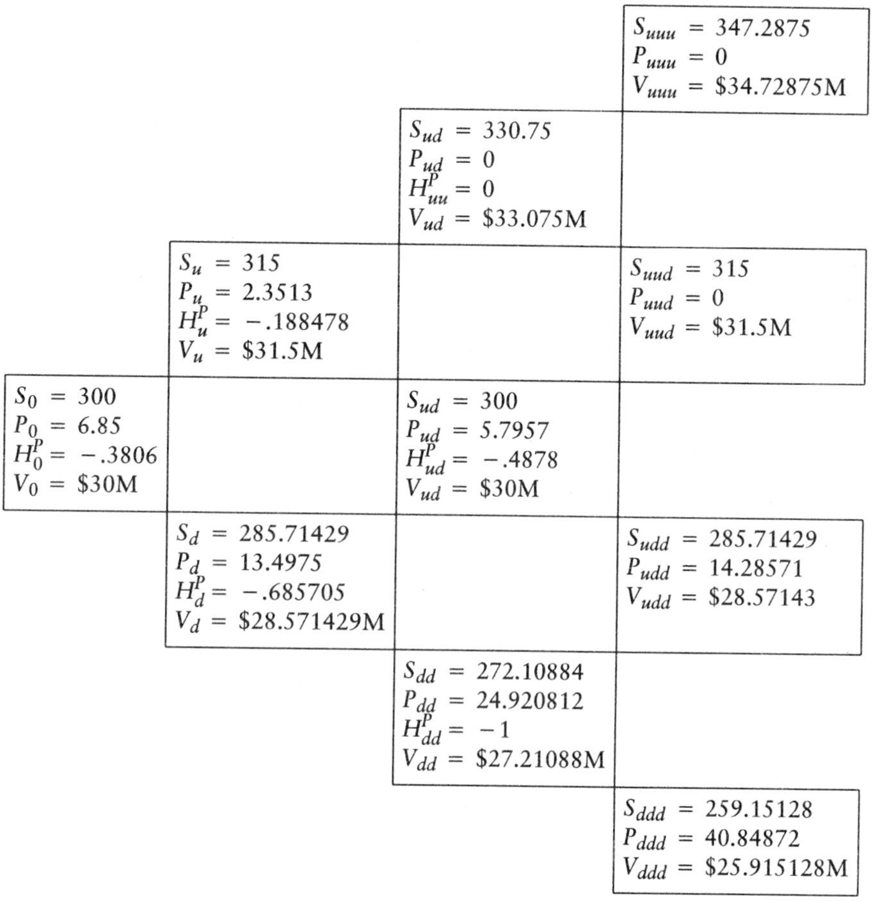

$S_{uuu} = 347.2875$
$P_{uuu} = 0$
$V_{uuu} = \$34.72875M$

$S_{ud} = 330.75$
$P_{ud} = 0$
$H_{uu}^P = 0$
$V_{ud} = \$33.075M$

$S_u = 315$
$P_u = 2.3513$
$H_u^P = -.188478$
$V_u = \$31.5M$

$S_{uud} = 315$
$P_{uud} = 0$
$V_{uud} = \$31.5M$

$S_0 = 300$
$P_0 = 6.85$
$H_0^P = -.3806$
$V_0 = \$30M$

$S_{ud} = 300$
$P_{ud} = 5.7957$
$H_{ud}^P = -.4878$
$V_{ud} = \$30M$

$S_d = 285.71429$
$P_d = 13.4975$
$H_d^P = -.685705$
$V_d = \$28.571429M$

$S_{udd} = 285.71429$
$P_{udd} = 14.28571$
$V_{udd} = \$28.57143$

$S_{dd} = 272.10884$
$P_{dd} = 24.920812$
$H_{dd}^P = -1$
$V_{dd} = \$27.21088M$

$S_{ddd} = 259.15128$
$P_{ddd} = 40.84872$
$V_{ddd} = \$25.915128M$

- An SP 500 European put is available with $X = 300$ and expiration at the end of three periods ($n = 3$); the BOPM's put values and hedge ratios (H^P) are shown in Figure 13.P-11.

- The period risk-free rate is 1%.

- There is a well-diversified stock portfolio currently worth $V_0 = \$30M$. The portfolio values at each node are shown in Figures 13.P-11.

a. Using the index put-and-stock portfolio, construct an event tree showing the values at each node of a put-insured portfolio. Use a $100 contract multiplier.

b. Show with an event tree the prices at each node of an SP 500 futures contract expiring at the end of the third period. Assume no dividends and no contract multiplier.

c. Construct a dynamic insured portfolio with the preceding futures contracts that replicates the put-insured portfolio at expiration. Show with an event tree the values of your futures-insured portfolio and the adjustment required at each node.

Derivation of the Stock Portfolio Price-Sensitivity Hedging Model

The price-sensitivity model for hedging a stock portfolio determines the number of stock index future contracts, n_f, that will minimize the variability of profits (π) on a portfolio consisting of a stock portfolio and the futures contract. The portfolio's profit is defined as:

$$\tilde{\pi} = \tilde{R}_S S_0 + n_f(\tilde{R}_F f_0), \qquad (13.A-1)$$

where:

$\tilde{R}_S$ = uncertain rate of return on stock portfolio

S_0 = current value of stock portfolio

$\tilde{R}_F$ = uncertain rate of return on futures position.

The variance of the $\tilde{\pi}$ is:

$$V(\pi) = E[\tilde{\pi} - E(\tilde{\pi})]^2$$

$$V(\pi) = E[\tilde{R}_S S_0 + n_f \tilde{R}_F f_0 - S_0 E(\tilde{R}_S) - n_f E(\tilde{R}_F) f_0]^2$$

$$V(\pi) = S_0^2 E[\tilde{R}_S - E(\tilde{R}_S)]^2 + n_f^2 f_0^2 E[\tilde{R}_F - [E(\tilde{R}_F)]^2 + 2(S_0)(n_f) f_0 E[\tilde{R}_S - E(\tilde{R}_S)][\tilde{R}_F - E(\tilde{R}_F)]$$

$$V(\pi) = S_0^2 V(R_S) + n_f^2 f_0^2 V(R_F) + 2 S_0 n_f f_0 \text{ Cov}(R_S R_F). \qquad (13.A-2)$$

The first-order condition for minimizing $V(\pi)$ is found by taking the derivative of Equation (13.A-2) with respect to n_f, setting the resulting equation equal to zero, and solving for n_f.* That is:

$$\frac{dV(\pi)}{dn_f} = 2n_f f_0^2 V(R_F) + 2S_0 f_0 \, \text{Cov}(R_S R_F) = 0. \qquad (13.A-3)$$

$$n_f = \frac{-S_0}{f_0} \frac{\text{Cov}(R_S R_F)}{V(R_F)}. \qquad (13.A-4)$$

By definition, the stock portfolio's beta is:

$$\beta = \frac{\text{Cov}(R_S R_m)}{V(R_m)},$$

where:

$V(R_m)$ = Variance of rate of return on spot market portfolio.

If we assume the rate of return on a stock index futures contract is highly correlated with the rate on the underlying spot index (R_m), then $\text{Cov}(R_S R_F)/V(R_F) = \text{Cov}(R_S R_m)/V(R_m)$. Given this assumption, beta can be substituted for $\text{Cov}(R_S R_F)/V(R_m)$ in Equation (13.A-4), and the optimum hedge can be expressed as:

$$n_f^* = \frac{-S_0}{f_0}\beta. \qquad (13.A-5)$$

Equation (13.A-5) is the same as Equation (13.3-2).

---

*The second-order derivative of Equation (13.A-2) with respect to n_f is positive, satisfying the second-order condition. That is:

$$\frac{d^2 V(\pi)}{dn_f^2} = 2f_0^2 V(R_F) > 0.$$

APPENDIX 13B

Derivation of the Dynamic Hedge Ratio

The dynamic hedge ratio is defined as the number of futures contracts (n_f) that will replicate the put-insured stock index portfolio. The value of the put-insured stock index portfolio (V^{SP}) consists of n shares of the stock index, priced at S per share, and n index put options priced at P, where the number of puts and index shares (n) are the same. That is:

$$V^{SP} = n(S + P). \qquad (13.B\text{-}1)$$

The change in the portfolio value for a small change in the stock index price is:

$$\frac{\partial V^{SP}}{\partial S} = n\frac{\partial S}{\partial S} + n\frac{\partial P}{\partial S} = n\left(1 + \frac{\partial P}{\partial S}\right). \qquad (13.B\text{-}2)$$

From Equation (13.B-1), $n = V^{SP}/(S + P)$. Substituting $V^{SP}/(S + P)$ for n in Equation (13.B-2) we obtain:

$$\frac{\partial V^{SP}}{\partial S} = \frac{V^{SP}}{S + P}\left(1 + \frac{\partial P}{\partial S}\right). \qquad (13.B\text{-}3)$$

The futures-insured portfolio that will replicate the put-insured portfolio consists of n_s shares of the stock index and n_f futures contracts priced at f. The value of the futures-insured portfolio (V^F) is:

$$V^F = n_s S + n_f f. \qquad (13.B\text{-}4)$$

For the futures-insured portfolio to provide the same portfolio protection as the put-insured portfolio, its current value must equal the put-insured portfolio's value. That is:

$$V^F = V^{SP} = n_s S + n_f f = n_s S, \qquad (13.B\text{-}5)$$

where the initial value of the futures contract is zero. Since the futures contract has no initial value, Equation (13.B-5) simplifies to:

$$n_s = \frac{V^{SP}}{S}.$$ (13.B-6)

The derivative of Equation (13.B-4) with respect to S is:

$$\frac{\partial V^F}{\partial S} = n_s + n_f \frac{\partial f}{\partial S}.$$ (13.B-7)

If we assume there are no dividends on the index portfolio, then:

$$f_0 = S_0 e^{RT},$$ (13.B-8)

and

$$\frac{df}{dS} = e^{RT}.$$ (13.B-9)

Substituting Equations (13.B-6) and (13.B-9) into Equation (13.B-7), we obtain:

$$\frac{\partial V^F}{\partial S} = \frac{V^{SP}}{S} + n_f e^{RT}.$$ (13.B-10)

For the futures-insured portfolio to replicate the put-insured portfolio, its value must change in response to the stock index price changes the same way the value of the put-insured portfolio's value does. That is, Equation (13.B-3) must equal Equation (13.B-10):

$$\frac{\partial V^{SP}}{\partial S} = \frac{\partial V^F}{\partial S}$$

$$\frac{V^{SP}}{S + P}\left(1 + \frac{\partial P}{\partial S}\right) = \frac{V^{SP}}{S} + n_f e^{RT}.$$ (13.B-11)

Given the replicating condition defined by Equation (13.B-11), the dynamic hedging ratio in which a futures-insured portfolio replicates the put-insured portfolio is found by solving Equation (13.B-11) for n_f. Doing this yields:

$$n_f = \left[\left(\frac{V^{SP}}{S + P}\right)\left(1 + \frac{\partial P}{\partial S}\right) - \frac{V^{SP}}{S}\right]e^{-RT}.$$ (13.B-12)

Equation (13.B-12) is the same as Equation (13.8-1).

CHAPTER 14

Interest Rate Futures

14.1 INTRODUCTION

During the 1970s and 1980s, the U.S. economy experienced relatively sharp swings in interest rates. Because interest rate futures contracts could be used in hedging positions that were affected by interest rate changes, the market for these instruments grew dramatically during this period. Currently, the most popular of the interest rate futures are the T-bond contract offered by the CBT and the Eurodollar futures contract, listed on the IMM. (The Eurodollar futures is a contract on a short-term instrument; it competes with T-bill futures contracts, which also are traded on the IMM.) One futures contract that has been gaining in popularity since its introduction is the CBT's Municipal Bond Index (MBI). This index, which is determined by the average value of 40 municipal bonds, is used extensively by portfolio managers, investment bankers, and dealers who trade regularly in municipal bonds.

In this chapter, we will examine the characteristics, pricing, and speculative and hedging uses of interest rate futures. Our discussion will focus on interest rate futures contracts on short-term securities (T-bill and Eurodollar contracts) and contracts on intermediate-term and long-term securities (Treasury notes and bonds).

Note: This chapter assumes some knowledge of fixed-income securities. For a primer, see Appendix E at the end of the book.

TABLE 14.2-1	Select Interest Rate Futures Contracts			
	CONTRACT	EXCHANGE*	DELIVERY MONTHS	CONTRACT SIZE
	T-bond	CBT	Mar/June/Sept/Dec	$100,000, 8% coupon
	T-note (6.5–10 yr)	CBT	Mar/June/Sept/Dec	$100,000, 8% coupon
	Municipal Bond Index	CBT	Mar/June/Sept/Dec	$1000, times Municipal Bond Index
	T-bill (91 days)	IMM	Mar/June/Sept/Dec	$1,000,000
	Certificate of deposit (91 days)	IMM	Mar/June/Sept/Dec	$1,000,000
	Eurodollar time deposits (90 days)	IMM	Mar/June/Sept/Dec; current spot month	$1,000,000
	T-bill (91 days)	MCE	Mar/June/Sept/Dec	$500,000
	T-bond	LIFFE	Mar/June/Sept/Dec	$100,000
	Eurodollar (linked to IMM)	SIMEX	Mar/June/Sept/Dec	$1,000,000

CBT = Chicago Board of Trade; IMM = International Monetary Market; MCE = Mid-American Commodity Exchange; LIFFE = London International Financial Futures Exchange; SIMEX = Singapore International Monetary Exchange.

14.2 CHARACTERISTICS OF INTEREST RATE FUTURES

The characteristics of selected interest rate futures are summarized in Table 14.2-1; price quotes on several interest rate futures contracts from the *Wall Street Journal* are shown in Exhibit 14.2-1. Of these contracts, the four most popular are the T-bond, the T-note, the Eurodollar deposit, and the T-bill. As already noted, T-bill and Eurodollar futures are listed on the IMM exchange and represent contracts on short-term debt securities; T-note and T-bond futures are traded on the CBT and represent contracts on intermediate-term and long-term securities, respectively.

14.2.1 Treasury-Bill Futures Contracts

Treasury-bill futures contracts call for the delivery (short) or purchase (long) of a T-bill with a maturity of 90, 91, or 92 days and a face value (*F*) of $1 million.* Futures prices on T-bill contracts, like the exercise price on T-bill options, are quoted in terms of the IMM index. This index is equal to 100 minus the annual percentage discount yield (R_D). Given a quoted IMM index value and a face value on the underlying T-bill of $1,000,000, the actual contract price on the T-bill futures contract is:

$$f_0 = \left[\frac{100 - R_D(90/360)}{100} \right]($1,000,000). \qquad (14.2\text{-}1)$$

*Ninety-one-day T-bills are acceptable at delivery; 90- and 92-day T-bills can be delivered with their prices adjusted.

EXHIBIT 14.2-1

Interest Rate Futures Quotes

```
                    INTEREST RATE                      TREASURY BILLS (CME)-$1 mil.; pts. of 100%
        TREASURY BONDS (CBT)-$100,000; pts. 32nds of 100%                                    Discount    Open
                                   Lifetime      Open          Open High Low Settle Chg Settle Chg Interest
           Open High Low Settle Change High Low Interest  Sept  95.20 95.22 95.16 95.21 + .01 4.79 - .01 19,860
   Sept   102-08 103-03 101-29 103-00 + 21 118-26 90- 12 365,940  Dec  94.60 94.65 94.57 94.64 + .03 5.36 - .03  9,147
   Dec    101-15 102-10 101-04 102-08 + 22 118-08 91-19 62,885  Mr95  94.31 94.38 94.30 94.38 + .04 5.62 - .04  2,008
   Mr95   100-26 101-18 100-20 101-17 + 22 116-20 98-20  4,268     Est vol 2,825; vol Wed 3,817; open int 31,016, -623.
   June   100-00 100-28 100-00 100-28 + 22 113-15 98-12  1,549        LIBOR-1 MO. (CME)-$3,000,000; points of 100%
   Sept    99-12 100-09 99-12 100-09 + 22 112-15 97-28    672  Aug   95.22 95.27 95.20 95.25 + .01 4.75 - .01 21,111
      Est vol 425,000; vol Wed 348,630; op int 435,410, -3,976.  Sept  94.98 95.03 94.95 95.02 + .02 4.98 - .02  7,266
        TREASURY BONDS (MCE)-$50,000; pts. 32nds of 100%     Oct   94.82 94.83 94.79 94.82 + .01 5.18 - .01  2,262
   Sept   102-04 103-03 101-29 102-30 + 20 115-20 100-02 13,535  Nov   94.65 94.67 94.61 94.66 + .01 5.34 - .01  2,326
      Est vol 4,000; vol Wed 3,423; open int 13,581, +54.     Dec   93.95 93.95 93.88 93.94 + .03 6.06 - .03  1,480
        TREASURY NOTES (CBT)-$100,000; pts. 32nds of 100%    Ja95  94.21 94.33 94.21 94.31 + .05 5.69 - .05    378
   Sept   103-13 103-31 103-04 103-28 + 12 115-01 101-18 225,452  Feb   94.21 94.21 94.12 94.17 + .03 5.83 - .03    106
   Dec    102-14 102-30 102-06 102-29 + 13 114-21 100-25 14,761  Mar   94.03 94.03 94.00 94.05 + .03 5.95 - .03    109
      Est vol 100,001; vol Wed 89,552; open int 240,282, +5,774.  May   93.83 93.83 93.75 93.80 + .03 6.20 - .03    200
        5 YR TREAS NOTES (CBT)-$100,000; pts. 32nds of 100%    Est vol 6,976; vol Wed 4,919; open int 35,536, +890.
   Sept   103-19 103-28 03-125 103-27 +  7 101-95 102-12 200,638   MUNI BOND INDEX (CBT)-$1,000; times Bond Buyer MBI
   Dec    02-245 103-02 02-215 103-02 + 6.5 104-18 101-26  2,726                                            Open
      Est vol 45,000; vol Wed 41,609; open int 203,364, +1,845.       Open High Low Settle Chg High Low Interest
        2 YR TREAS NOTES (CBT)-$200,000; pts. 32nds of 100%   Sept  90-06 90-28 89-24 90-26 + 18 95-17 86-13 23,125
   Sept   02-225 102-24 102-20 102-24 + 1.5 104-31 102-04 31,001   Est vol 2,800; vol Wed 2,800; open int 23,158, -48.
   Dec    .....  .....  .....  102-05 + 1.5 02-187 02-165    610   The index: Close 91-12; Yield 6.73.
      Est vol 2,000; vol Wed 1,206; open int 31,611, -79.           EURODOLLAR (CME)-$1 million; pts of 100%
        30-DAY FEDERAL FUNDS (CBT)-$5 million; pts. of 100%                                        Yield     Open
   July    95.74 95.75 95.74 95.75 + .01 96.65 95.25  3,228           Open High Low Settle Chg Settle Chg Interest
   Aug     95.50 95.54 95.49 95.53 + .02 96.58 95.05  3,828  Sept  94.76 94.78 94.72 94.77 + .01 5.23 - .01 431,981
   Sept    95.22 95.29 95.22 95.28 + .03 96.44 94.81  2,120  Dec   94.05 94.09 93.99 94.08 + .03 5.92 - .03 436,986
   Oct     95.00 95.05 94.99 95.04 + .02 95.63 94.63    423  Mr95  93.80 93.85 93.75 93.84 + .03 6.16 - .03 334,342
   Nov     94.82 94.87 94.82 94.87 + .03 95.04 94.50    225  June  93.47 93.53 93.43 93.52 + .03 5.48 - .03 241,690
      Est vol 1,030; vol Wed 1,338; open int 9,929, +7.      Sept  93.22 93.26 93.16 93.25 + .03 6.75 - .03 216,979
                                                             Dec   92.94 92.98 92.89 92.98 + .03 7.02 - .03 146,155
                                                             Mr96  92.88 92.92 92.83 92.92 + .03 7.08 - .03 129,434
```

SOURCE: *Wall Street Journal* April 19, 1994

Note that, like T-bill options, the IMM index is quoted on the basis of a 90-day T-bill with a 360-day year (thus, a 1-point move in the index would equate to a $2500 change in the futures price). The implied yield to maturity (YTM_f) on a T-bill delivered on the futures contract is found using 365 days and the actual maturity on the delivered bond (90, 91, or 92 days). For example, if the IMM index on the futures is at 92.5 ($R_D = 7.5\%$), then the futures contract price for the T-bill would be $981,250, and the implied YTM_f for a 91-day T-bill would be 7.89%. That is:

$$f_0 = \left[\frac{100 - (7.5)(90/360)}{100} \right] (\$1,000,000) = \$981,250,$$

and

$$YTM_f = \left(\frac{F}{f_0} \right)^{365/91} - 1$$

$$YTM_f = \left(\frac{\$1,000,000}{\$981,250} \right)^{365/91} - 1 = .0789.$$

Expiration months on T-bill futures are March, June, September, and December, and they extend out about two years. The last trading day occurs during the third week of the expiration month, on the business day preceding the issue of spot T-bills (T-bills are auctioned each week). Delivery can take place on that day or on any other remaining day of the expiration month.

14.2.2   Eurodollar Futures Contracts

A Eurodollar deposit is a time deposit in a bank located or incorporated outside the United States. The interest rates paid on such deposits are quoted in terms of the *London Interbank Offer Rate* (*LIBOR*), which is the average rate paid by a sample of London Eurobanks on Eurodollar deposits held for 90 days. The IMM's futures contract on the Eurodollar deposit calls for the delivery or purchase of a Eurodollar deposit with a face value of $1 million and a maturity of 90 days. Like T-bill futures contracts, *Eurodollar futures contracts* are quoted in terms of the IMM index, with the actual contract price found via Equation (14.2-1). Also, like T-bill futures, the expiration months on Eurodollar futures contracts are March, June, September, and December and extend for about two years, with the last trading day being the second business day before the Wednesday of the expiration month.

The major difference between Eurodollar and T-bill contracts is that Eurodollar contracts have cash settlement at delivery, while T-bill contracts call for the actual delivery of the instrument. When a Eurodollar futures contract expires, the cash settlement is determined by the futures price and the settlement price. The settlement price, or expiration futures index price, is 100 minus the three-month LIBOR offered by selected banks on the expiration date:

$$\text{Expiration futures price} = 100 - \text{LIBOR}. \qquad (14.2\text{-}2)$$

14.2.3   Treasury-Bond and Treasury-Note Futures Contracts

Treasury-bond futures contracts call for the delivery or purchase of a T-bond with a maturity or earliest call date of at least 15 years. *Treasury-note futures contracts* are similar, except they call for the delivery or purchase of T-notes with maturities between 6½ and 10 years. Given their similarities, we will examine the characteristics of just the T-bond contract.

The T-bond futures contract is based on the delivery of a bond with an 8% coupon (semiannual payments) and a face value of $100,000. The delivery months on the contracts are March, June, September, and December, going out approximately two years; delivery can occur at any time during the delivery month. T-bond futures prices are quoted in dollars and 32nds for T-bonds with a face value of $100. Thus, for a futures quote of $60 - 20$ (i.e., $60^{20}/_{32}$, or 60.625), the price of the T-bond (8%, 15-year T-bond with $F = \$100{,}000$) on the contract would be $60,625. Finally, to ensure liquidity, a number of T-bonds are eligible for delivery, with a conversion factor used to determine the price of the deliverable bond.

Treasury-Bond Delivery Procedure
Since T-bond futures contracts allow for the delivery of a number of T-bonds at any time during the delivery month, the CBT's delivery procedure on such contracts is more complicated than the procedures on other futures contracts.

Under the CBT's procedures, a T-bond futures trader with a short position who wants to deliver on the contract has the right to determine during the expiration month the day of the delivery and the eligible bond to deliver. The delivery process encompasses the following three business days.

Business Day 1, *position day*: The short position holder notifies the clearing-house that he will deliver.

Business Day 2, *notice of intention day*: The clearinghouse assigns a long position holder the contract (typically the holder with the longest outstanding contract).

Business Day 3, *delivery day*: The short holder delivers an eligible T-bond to the assigned long position holder, who pays the short holder an invoice price determined by the futures price and a conversion factor.

The invoice price on the deliverable bond is found first, by determining the correct conversion factor (CF). Since the futures' price is based on a 15-year, 8% coupon bond, the CBT uses a conversion factor based on discounting the deliverable bond by an 8% YTM. Specifically, the CF is based on the price of a bond with a face value of $1, a coupon rate and maturity of the deliverable bond, and a discount rate of 8%. If the number of semiannual periods making up the deliverable bond's maturity or first call date is even, the following conversion factor (CF_e) is used:

$$CF_e = \sum_{t=1}^{M} \frac{C_t}{(1.04)^t} + \frac{1}{(1.04)^M}, \qquad (14.2\text{-}3)$$

where:

C_t = semiannual payment coupon on T-bond with $F = \$1$

M = number of semiannual periods to maturity or first call.

If the number of periods to maturity or first call is odd, the conversion factor (CF_{od}) is:

$$CF_{od} = \left[\sum_{t=1}^{M} \frac{C_t}{(1.04)^t} + \frac{1}{(1.04)^M} + C_t \right] \frac{1}{\sqrt{1.04}} - .5C_t. \qquad (14.2\text{-}4)$$

To illustrate, suppose one of the eligible bonds that can be delivered on a March 1995 T-bond futures contract is a T-bond with a 10% coupon and a maturity of May 2012. (The maturity of the deliverable bond is based on the first day of the delivery month.) The deliverable bond would have 34 semiannual periods to maturity; thus, its conversion factor would be:

$$CF_e = \sum_{t=1}^{34} \frac{0.05}{(1.04)^t} + \frac{1}{(1.04)^{34}} = 1.184.$$

Given the CF, the invoice price the assigned long holder would pay the short holder on the delivery day is found by multiplying the CF by the futures settlement price (S_T) on the position day and adding any accrued interest (Acc int) on the deliverable bond. That is:

$$\text{Invoice price} = (CF)(S_T) + (\text{Acc int}). \qquad (14.2\text{-}5)$$

Trading Implications of the Treasury-Bond Delivery Process

Two trading implications resulting from the T-bond delivery procedure should be noted. First, given the number of eligible bonds, a short holder should select the

T-bond for delivery that is the least expensive to purchase. This bond is referred to as the *cheapest-to-deliver bond*. Since the short holder has the right to select this bond from an eligible bond list, she is said to have a delivery, or quality, option.

Second, since a short holder can notify the clearinghouse of her intention to deliver a bond at the end of the position day (not necessarily at the end of the futures' trading day), an arbitrage opportunity has arisen because of the futures exchange's closing time being 3:00 and the closing time on spot T-bond trading being 5:00. Thus, a short holder knowing the settlement price at 3:00 could find the price of an eligible T-bond decreasing in the next two hours on the spot market. If this occurred, she could buy the bond at the end of the day at the lower price, then notify the clearinghouse of her intention to deliver that bond on the futures contract. This feature of the T-bond futures contract is known as the *wild-card option*.

Though the T-bond delivery procedure is complex, the procedure is necessary to ensure that a sufficient number of T-bonds are available.

14.3   INTEREST RATE FUTURES PRICING

Interest rate futures can be priced using the basic carrying-cost model defined in Chapter 12. For T-bill and Eurodollar contracts, the pricing of the underlying asset is straightforward. For T-bond and note contracts, though, pricing in terms of the carrying-cost model is more complicated, due to the delivery procedures.

14.3.1   Pricing Treasury-Bill Futures

Using the carrying-cost model, the futures price on a T-bill contract expiring at T $[f_0(T)^*]$ is determined by the costs of carrying a spot T-bill with a maturity of M_2 = $M_1 + T$ and trading at $S_0(M_2)$, where M_1 is the maturity on the T-bill underlying the futures contract (M_1 = 91 days, or 91/365 per year). That is:

$$f_0(T)^* = S_0(M_2)(1 + R)^T, \qquad (14.3\text{-}1)$$

where:

R = risk-free rate or repo rate with maturity of T.

For example, if a spot T-bill with a maturity of 161 days is trading at a YTM of 5.7% (annualized) or, using a $100 face value, at an index price of $100/(1.057)^{161/365}$ = 97.5844, and the 70-day risk-free or repo rate is 6.38% (annualized), then by the carrying-cost model the equilibrium futures price on a T-bill contract expiring in 70 days would be 98.74875:

$$f_0(T)^* = S_0(M_2)(1 + R)^T$$

$$f_0(70)^* = S_0(161)(1.0638)^{(70/365)}$$

$$f_0(70)^* = 97.5844(1.0638)^{(70/365)} = 98.74875.$$

If the market price on the T-bill futures contract is not equal to 98.74875, then a cash-and-carry arbitrage opportunity would exist. For example, if the T-bill futures price is at $f_0^m = 99$, an arbitrageur could earn a riskless profit of 99 − 98.74875 = 0.25125 at the expiration date by executing the following strategy:

1. Borrow $97.5844 at the repo (or borrowing) rate of 6.38%, then buy a 161-day spot T-bill for $S_0(161) = 97.5844$;

2. Take a short position in a T-bill futures contract expiring in 70 days at the futures price of $f_0(70) = 99$.

At expiration, the arbitrageur would earn the riskless profit of $0.25125 when he:

1. Sells the T-bill on the spot futures contract at 99, and

2. Repays the principal and interest on the loan of $97.5844(1.0638)^{70/365} = 98.74875$.

If the market price on the T-bill futures contract is below the equilibrium value, then the cash-and-carry arbitrage strategy is reversed. In our example, if the futures price is below 98.74875, a money manager holding 161-day T-bills could obtain an arbitrage profit by liquidating the bills, investing the proceeds for 70 days, and going long in the T-bill futures contract expiring in 70 days.

14.3.2 Other Equilibrium Conditions Implied by the Carrying-Cost Model

For T-bill futures, the equilibrium condition defined by the carrying-cost model in Equation (14.3-1) can be redefined in terms of the following equivalent conditions: (1) The rate on a spot T-bill (or actual repo rate) is equal to the rate on a synthetic T-bill (or implied repo rate); (2) the rate implied on the futures contract is equal to the implied forward rate.

Equivalent Spot and Synthetic Treasury-Bill Rates

With the market for T-bill futures contracts, a money market manager planning to invest funds in a T-bill for a given short-term horizon period can either invest in the spot T-bill or construct a synthetic T-bill by purchasing a longer-term T-bill, then locking in its selling price by going short in a T-bill futures contract.

For example, suppose a money market manager is looking to invest current excess funds in riskless Treasury securities for the next 70 days. Using the rates from the preceding example, the manager either could buy a 70-day spot T-bill yielding a 6.38% rate of return and trading at $S_0(70) = 98.821$,

$$S_0(70) = \frac{100}{(1.0638)^{70/365}} = 98.821,$$

or could create a long position in a synthetic 70-day T-bill by buying the 161-day T-bill trading at $S_0(161) = 97.5844$, then locking in the selling price by going short in the T-bill futures contract expiring in 70 days.

Whether the manager should buy the spot or the synthetic T-bill depends on the price on the futures contract. If the futures price in the market exceeds the equilibrium value as determined by the carrying-cost model ($f_0^m > f_0^*$), then the rate of return on the synthetic T-bill (YTM_{syn}) will exceed the YTM on the spot; the manager should choose the synthetic T-bill. For example, if the futures price is 99, the manager could earn a rate of return of 7.8% on the synthetic, compared to only 6.38% from the spot. That is:

$$YTM_{syn}(70) = \left(\frac{f_0(70)}{S_0(161)}\right)^{365/70} - 1$$

$$YTM_{syn}(70) = \left(\frac{99}{97.5844}\right)^{365/70} - 1 = .078.$$

If commission costs are not a factor, then the money market manager would be better off investing funds in the synthetic 70-day T-bill than in the spot 70-day T-bill. On the other hand, if the futures price is less than its equilibrium value ($f_0^m < f_0^*$), then the YTM_{syn} will be less than the YTM on the spot; in this case, the manager should purchase the spot T-bill.

In an efficient market, money managers will drive the futures price to its equilibrium value as determined by the carrying-cost model. When this condition is realized, the YTM_{syn} will equal the YTM on the spot, and the money manager would be indifferent to either investment. In our example, this occurs when the market price on the futures contract is equal to the equilibrium value of 98.74875. At that price the YTM_{syn} is equal to 6.38%:

$$YTM_{syn}(70) = \left(\frac{98.74875}{97.5844}\right)^{365/70} - 1 = .0638.$$

Thus, if the carrying-cost model holds, the YTM earned from investing in a spot T-bill and the YTM from investing in a synthetic will be equal.

Implied and Actual Repo Rates

The rate earned from the synthetic T-bill commonly is referred to as the *implied repo rate*. Formally, the implied repo rate is defined as the rate at which the arbitrage profit from implementing the cash-and-carry arbitrage strategy is zero. That is:

$$\text{Arbitrage profit} = f_0(T) - S_0(M_2)(1 + R)^T$$

$$0 = f_0(T) - S_0(M_2)(1 + R)^T$$

$$R = \left[\frac{f_0(T)}{S_0(M_2)}\right]^{1/T} - 1. \qquad (14.3\text{-}2)$$

The actual repo rate is the one we use in solving for the equilibrium futures price in the carrying-cost model; in our example, this was the rate on the 70-day T-bill (6.38%). Thus, the equilibrium condition that the synthetic and spot T-bill be equal can be stated equivalently as an equality between the actual and the implied repo rates.

Implied Forward and Futures Rates

The other way to describe the carrying-cost equilibrium condition is in terms of the equality between the rate implied by the futures contract and what is commonly referred to as the *implied forward rate*. This condition can be stated as follows:

$$\text{Implied futures rate} = \text{Implied forward rate}$$

$$YTM_f = R_I \qquad\qquad (14.3\text{-}3)$$

$$\left[\frac{F}{f_0(T)}\right]^{1/M_1} - 1 = \left[\frac{S_0(T)}{S_0(M_2)}\right]^{1/M_1} - 1,$$

where:

    F = face value on spot T-bill

    M_1 = maturity of the futures contract's underlying T-bill (91 days)

    R_I = implied forward rate

    YTM_f = implied futures rate

    $M_2 = M_1 + T$.

The right-hand side of Equation (14.3-3) is the implied forward rate, which is determined by the current spot prices on T-bills maturing at T and at M_2. In our illustrative example, the implied forward rate is 5.18%:

$$R_I = \left[\frac{S_0(T)}{S_0(M_2)}\right]^{1/M_1} - 1$$

$$R_I = \left[\frac{S_0(70)}{S_0(161)}\right]^{365/91} - 1$$

$$R_I = \left(\frac{98.821}{97.5844}\right)^{365/91} - 1 = .0518.$$

The left-hand side of Equation (14.3-3) is the YTM implied on the futures contract. If an investor purchases a 91-day T-bill on the futures contract at the equilibrium price, then the implied futures rate will equal the implied forward rate. In terms of our example, if $f_0(T) = f_0(70) = 98.74875$, then the implied futures rate will be 5.18%:

$$YTM_f = \left[\frac{F}{f_0(T)}\right]^{1/M_1} - 1$$

$$YTM_f = \left(\frac{100}{98.74875}\right)^{365/91} - 1 = .0518.$$

Formally, the implied forward rate is the interest rate attained at a future date that is implied by current rates. For investments, the implied forward rate can be attained by a locking-in strategy consisting of a short position in a shorter-term bond and a long position in a longer-term one. For borrowing, the implied forward borrowing rate is attained by going short in the longer-term bond and long in a shorter-term one. In terms of our example, the implied forward rate on a 91-day T-bill investment to be made 70 days from the present, $R_I(91, 70)$, is obtained by:

1. Selling short the 70-day T-bill at 98.821 (or equivalently borrowing 98.821 at YTM(70) of 6.38%),

2. Buying $S_0(T)/S_0(M_2) = S_0(70)/S_0(161) = 98.821/97.5844 = 1.01267$ issues of the 161-day T-bill,

3. Paying 100 at the end of 70 days to cover the short position on the maturing bond (or the loan), and

4. Collecting 1.01267(100) at the end of 161 days from the long position.

This locking-in strategy would earn an investor a return of $101.267, 91 days after the investor expends $100 to cover the short sale. Thus, the implied forward rate on a 91-day investment made 70 days from the present is 1.267%, or 5.18% annualized:

$$R_I(91, 70) = \left(\frac{\$101.267}{\$100}\right)^{365/91} - 1 = .0518.$$

If the futures price does not equal its equilibrium value, then the implied forward rate will not equal the implied futures rate, and an arbitrage opportunity will exist from the cash-and-carry arbitrage strategy.

In summary, we have three equivalent equilibrium conditions governing futures prices on T-bill contracts: (1) The futures price is equal to the costs of carrying the underlying spot security; (2) the YTM on the spot is equal to the YTM on the synthetic security (or the implied repo rate is equal to the actual repo rate); (3) the implied rate of return on the futures contract is equal to the implied forward rate.

14.3.3   Pricing Treasury-Bond Futures

The pricing of T-bond futures is somewhat more complex than the pricing of T-bill or Eurodollar futures because of their delivery procedures. Like T-bill futures, the price on a T-bond futures contract depends on the spot price on the underlying T-bond (S_0) and the risk-free or repo rate. Given that a number of T-bonds can be delivered on the contract, the spot price to use in the carrying-cost model is the one for the cheapest bond to deliver. The price of this bond also must include any accrued interest (Acc int$_0$). The futures price, in turn, is equal to the futures price on the contract times the conversion factor on the cheapest bond to deliver (CF), plus any accrued interest on that bond at the delivery date. Thus, the carrying-cost model for T-bond futures is:

$$f_0(CF) + (Acc\ int)_T = [S_0 + (Acc\ int_0)](1 + R)^T. \qquad (14.3\text{-}4)$$

As with T-bill futures, cash-and-carry arbitrage opportunities will exist if Equation (14.3-4) does not hold.

14.4 EVALUATING ALTERNATIVE INVESTMENTS USING THE CARRYING-COST MODEL: MANAGING A BANK'S MATURITY GAP

Aside from identifying arbitrage opportunities, one of the practical uses of examining the equilibrium conditions governing interest rate futures and spot prices is that it allows us to evaluate alternative investment and financing arrangements. This can be seen by applying the conditions underlying the carrying-cost model to establish how a bank could manage its maturity gap—the difference between the maturities of its assets and those of its liabilities.

Consider the case of a commercial bank that provides a $1 million, 180-day construction loan financed by the sale of its certificates of deposit (CDs). Suppose the bank wants to eliminate (or at least minimize) its exposure to interest rate changes. To accomplish this, the bank could finance the construction loan either with a 180-day CD or with a synthetic 180-day CD formed by selling a 90-day CD now and a 90-day CD three months later, with the rate locked in with a short position in a Eurodollar futures contract expiring in three months.

The bank's choice of financing depends on whether the carrying-cost model holds. In this case, suppose 180-day CDs are selling at $S_0(180) = 96$ (as a percentage of $100 CD face value), or a YTM of 8.63%, and 90-day CDs are selling at $S_0(90) = 98.0625$, or a YTM of 8.258%. The implied forward rate on a 90-day loan made 90 days from the present $[R_I(90, 90)]$ would therefore be 9%:*

$$R_I(90, 90) = \left[\frac{S_0(90)}{S_0(180)} \right]^{1/T} - 1$$

$$R_I(90, 90) = \left(\frac{98.0625}{96} \right)^{365/90} - 1 = .09.$$

If the price on a Eurodollar futures contract expiring at the end of 90 days is greater than its equilibrium value as determined by the carrying-cost model, with the 90-day CD rate of 8.258% used as the repo rate, then the rate implied on the futures contract will be less than the implied forward rate of 9%, and the bank would find it cheaper to finance its construction loan with a synthetic 180-day CD rather than with the spot 180-day CD. However, if the futures price is less than its equilibrium value, then the implied futures rate will be greater than 9%, and the bank would find the 180-day spot CD less expensive than the synthetic.

For example, suppose the bank's 90-day CD rate is equal to the LIBOR and a Eurodollar futures contract expiring at the end of 90 days is trading at a futures price of 98.1 (as a percentage of a $100 face value), or an IMM index price of 92.4.

---

*For borrowers, the implied forward borrowing rate for 90-day funds, 90 days from now, is found by reversing the locking-in strategy defined earlier for an investment rate. In this example, the bank could lock in an implied borrowing rate with 90- and 180-day CDs by (1) selling the 180-day CD, receiving $S_0(180) = 96$, (2) buying $S_0(180)/S_0(90) = 96/98.0625 = .97897$ 90-day CDs, (3) at the end of 90 days receive $.97897(100) = 97.897$ from the 90-day CD, and (4) at the end of 180 days pay $100 to cover the 180-day CD obligation. Doing this, the bank would receive $97.897, 90 days from the present, and pay $100, 180 days from the present, for an implied forward borrowing rate of 9%:

$$R_I(90, 90) = \left(\frac{100}{97.897} \right)^{365/90} - 1 = .09.$$

In this case, the futures contract is priced above its equilibrium value of $96(1.08258)^{90/365} = 97.897$, and the implied futures rate $[\text{YTM}_f(90, 90)]$ is 8.09%:

$$\text{YTM}_f(90, 90) = \left(\frac{100}{98.1}\right)^{365/90} - 1 = .0809.$$

Thus, the bank would find it less expensive to finance the construction loan with a 90-day spot CD, rolled over 90 days later with another 90-day CD, with the latter rate locked in with a short position in a Eurodollar futures contract at 98.1 (assume the face value on the contract is $100 for this example).

At the implied futures rate of 8.09%, the rate the bank would pay on the synthetic 180-day CD would be 8.17%, compared to the 8.63% rate paid on the 180-day spot CD. To attain 8.17% financing of the $1 million construction loan, the bank would have to:

1. Sell 90-day CDs currently worth $1 million at a rate of 8.258%, yielding a principal obligation at the end of 90 days of

   $$(\$1,000,000)(1.08258)^{(90/365)} = \$1,019,758;$$

2. Sell $n_f = \$1,019,758/\$98.1 = 10,395$ Eurodollar futures contracts expiring at the end of 90 days at $f_0 = \$98.1$ (assume Eurodollar has $F = \$100$).

Ninety days later the bank would need to sell a new 90-day CD to finance the net costs of closing the futures contract and covering its principal and interest obligation of $1,019,758. As shown in Table 14.4-1, if the 90-day LIBOR at that time is 7.5% [price of $S_T(90) = \$98.23256$, with $F = \$100$], then the bank would incur a loss of $(f_0 - f_T)n_f = (98.1 - 98.23256)(10,395) = -\$1378$ on its short Eurodollar futures position and therefore would need to borrow a total of $1,021,136. The greater debt obligation, though, would be offset partially by the lower borrowing rate of 7.5% that the bank would pay on borrowed funds for the next 90 days. As a result, at the end of 180 days, the bank would end up owing $1,021,136(1.075)^{90/365} = \$1,039,509$.

On the other hand, if the CD rate was at 8.7% after 90 days [$S_T(90) = 97.96404$], then the bank would earn a $1413 profit on the futures contract. The bank therefore would need to borrow only $1,019,758 - \$1413 = \$1,018,345$. However, this lower debt obligation would be offset by the higher costs of borrowing. At an 8.7% CD rate, the bank would end up with the same debt obligation of $1,018,345(1.087)^{90/365} = \$1,039,509$ that it would have had at the 7.5% CD rate or any other CD rate. Thus, at the end of 180 days, the bank would have a certain debt obligation of $1,039,509; this obligation, in turn, equates to an effective borrowing rate of 8.17% for the period:*

$$\text{Borrowing rate (180 days)} = \left(\frac{\$1,039,509}{\$1,000,000}\right)^{365/180} - 1 = .0817.$$

---

*The 180-day synthetic CD rate can be found directly by using the geometric mean. In this example:
$\text{YTM}_{\text{syn}}(180) = \{[1 + \text{YTM}(90)]^{90/365}[1 + \text{YTM}_f(90)]^{90/365}\}^{365/180} - 1$
$\text{YTM}_{\text{syn}}(180) = [(1.08258)^{90/365}(1.0809)^{90/365}]^{365/180} - 1 = 0.0817.$

TABLE 14.4-1

Managing the Maturity Gap: Synthetic 180-Day CD		

Bank makes $1 million loan for 180 days.

The bank finances the loan by:
1. Selling 90-day CDs at the rate of 8.258%,
2. Refinancing the debt of $1,000,000(1.08258)^{90/365}$ 90 days later with the sale of 90-day CDs, and
3. Locking in the CD rate 90 days later with 10,395 short Eurodollar futures contracts priced at $f_0 = 98.1$ (assume $F = \$100$ on Eurodollar contract).

90 Days Later		
Spot CD Rate = LIBOR $[R(90)]$	.075	.087
1. Spot 90-day CD price ($F = 100$): $S_T(90) = f_T(90) = 100/[1 + R(90)]^{90/365}$	98.23256	97.96404
2. Futures profit: $10,395[98.1 - f_T(90)]$	− $ 1,378	$ 1,413
3. Debt on CD: $\$1M(1.08258)^{90/365}$	$1,019,758	$1,019,758
4. Total funds to be financed for the next 90 days with new CD: Row (3) − Row(2)	$1,021,136	$1,018,345
5. Debt obligation at the end of the period: Row (4)$[1 + R(90)]^{90/365}$	$1,039,509	$1,039,509
6. Rate paid for 180-day period: $(\$1,039,509/\$1,000,000)^{365/180} - 1$	8.17%	8.17%

If the rate implied on the futures contract exceeded the implied forward rate, then the bank would obtain a lower financing rate with a spot 180-day CD. Finally, if the carrying-cost model governing Eurodollar futures prices holds, then the rate of the synthetic will be equal to the rate on the spot; in this case, the bank would be indifferent to its choice of financing. Finally, it should be noted that the bank may be interested in hedging with futures even if no mispricing is present. For example, it may be that the bank's customers prefer 90-day CDs, while its borrowers generally prefer 180-day loans.

14.5 SPECULATING WITH INTEREST RATE FUTURES

Interest rate futures, like debt options, can be used to speculate on expected interest rate changes. A long naked or outright interest rate futures position is taken when interest rates are expected to fall, and a short position is taken when rates are expected to rise. Speculating on interest rate changes by taking outright futures positions represents an alternative to buying or short-selling a bond on the spot market. Because of the risk inherent in outright futures positions, though, many speculators form either intracommodity spreads or intercommodity spreads instead of taking a naked position.

14.5.1 Intracommodity Spread

Recall that an intracommodity spread is formed by taking long and short positions simultaneously on futures contracts on the same underlying asset but with different expirations. For example, a speculator who expected the interest rate on long-term bonds to decrease in the future could form an intracommodity spread by going short in a nearby T-bond futures contract and long in a more deferred one. This type of intracommodity spread will be profitable if the expectation of a decrease in long-term rates occurs. If rates rise (and bond prices decline), though, losses will occur on the long position; these losses will be offset partially by profits realized from the short position on the shorter-term contract. On the other hand, if a bond speculator believed rates would increase but did not want to assume the risk inherent in an outright short position, she could form a spread with a short position in a longer-term contract and a long position in the shorter-term contract.

14.5.2 Intercommodity Spread

Intercommodity spreads consist of long and short positions on futures contracts with the same expirations but with different underlying assets. A number of different intercommodity spreads can be formed with interest rate futures.

Consider the case of a spreader who is forecasting a general decline in interest rates across all maturities (i.e., a downward parallel shift in the yield curve). Since bonds with greater maturities are more price sensitive to interest rate changes than those with shorter maturities, to profit from this expectation the spreader could form an intercommodity spread by going long in a T-bond contract and short in a T-note (or T-bill) contract. On the other hand, if the spreader was forecasting an increase in rates across all maturities, he could go short in the T-bond contract and long in the T-note. Forming spreads with T-note and T-bond futures is referred to as the notes over bonds spread (*NOB spread*).

Another type of intercommodity spread involves contracts on bonds with different default risk characteristics, for example, a spread formed with contracts on a T-bond and a Municipal Bond Index (MBI) or contracts on T-bills and Eurodollar deposits. Profits from these spreads are based on the ability to forecast a narrowing or a widening of the spread between the yields on the underlying bonds.

For example, in an economic recession the demand for lower-default-risk bonds often increases relative to the demand for higher-default-risk bonds. If this occurs, then the spot yield spread for lower-grade bonds over higher-grade ones would tend to widen. A speculator forecasting an economic recession could, in turn, profit from an anticipated widening in the risk premium by forming an intercommodity spread consisting of a long position in a T-bond futures contract (no default risk) and a short position in an MBI contract (some degree of default risk). Similarly, since Eurodollar deposits are not completely riskless, whereas T-bills are, a spreader forecasting riskier times (and the resulting widening of the spread between Eurodollar rates and T-bill rates) could go long in the T-bill contract and short in the Eurodollar contract. A spread with T-bills and Eurodollars contracts is known as a *TED spread*.

14.5.3   Arbitrage Spreads

Spreads often are formed by arbitrageurs to take advantage of mispricing between futures contracts with different expirations. In Chapter 12, we defined the equilibrium pricing relationship for futures contracts expiring at times T_1 and T_2 (see Section 12.8.5). For contracts in which the carrying costs for the underlying asset do not involve storage costs and for which no convenience yield exists, the equilibrium relationship is:

$$f_{T2} = f_{T1}(1 + R_{T1})^{T2-T1}, \tag{14.5-1}$$

where:

R_{T1} = implied forward rate at time T_1, locked in by an implied forward rate strategy or with a position in a T-bill or Eurodollar futures contract.

Recall from Chapter 12 that if the market price on the futures contract with T_2 expiration exceeds the equilibrium value as specified in Equation (14.5-1), then an arbitrageur can realize a riskless profit by forming a spread consisting of (1) a long position in the T_1 futures contract, (2) a short position in the T_2 contract, and (3) a forward contract to borrow f_{T1} dollars at the implied forward rate for the T_1-T_2 period of R_{T1} (this rate could be locked in with a short position in a T-bill or Eurodollar futures contract). Thus, if the futures prices on June and September T-bonds and the implied forward rate (or futures rate on a September T-bill) are such that the price of the September T-bond contract exceeds the equilibrium value as determined by Equation (14.5-1), then an arbitrage opportunity would exist by going long in the September T-bond contract and short in the June contract and locking in the borrowing rate by a locking-in strategy (or by going short in T-bill futures contracts). This arbitrage strategy involves an intracommodity spread (June and September T-bonds) and an intercommodity spread if T-bill futures are used to lock in the borrowing rate R_{T1}. The combination of two positions on T-bond futures with different expirations and one position in a T-bill futures contract is referred to as a ***turtle spread.***

14.6   HEDGING INTEREST RATE POSITIONS WITH A NAIVE HEDGING MODEL

In Chapter 9, we examined how debt and fixed-income security positions could be hedged using call and put options on debt securities. Interest rate futures can be used in many of the same ways as debt options. Several different hedging models exist. The simplest is a naive hedging model that uses a one-to-one hedge. For interest rate positions, a naive hedge can be formed by hedging each dollar of the face value of the spot position with one market-value dollar in the futures. For example, if a T-bond futures' price is at 90, then $100/90 = 1.11$ futures contracts could be used to hedge each dollar of the face value of the bond. A naive hedge also can be formed by hedging each dollar of the market value of the spot position with one market-value dollar of the futures. Thus, if $98 were to be used to buy our T-bond at some future date, then 98/90 = 1.089 futures contracts could be purchased to hedge the position.

If the debt position to be hedged has a futures contract with the same underlying asset, then a naive hedge usually will be effective in reducing interest rate risk. Many debt positions, though, involve securities in which a futures contract on the underlying security does not exist. In such cases, an effective cross-hedge needs to be determined to minimize the price risk in the underlying spot position. Two commonly used models for cross-hedging are the regression model and the price-sensitivity model. In the regression model, the estimated slope coefficient of the regression equation is used to determine the hedge ratio. The coefficient, in turn, is found by regressing the spot price on the bond to be hedged against the futures price. The second hedging approach is to use the Kolb-Chiang (K-C) price-sensitivity model. Similar to the price-sensitivity model for stock index futures discussed in Chapter 13, the K-C model has been shown to be relatively more effective than other hedging models in reducing the variability of debt positions.[*]

In this section, we will examine cases in which the security to be hedged is either a T-bill or a bank CD and as such can be hedged with a naive model using T-bill or Eurodollar futures. In Section 14.7, we will look at cross-hedging cases in which the K-C price-sensitivity model is more applicable.

14.6.1   Hedging a Future 91-Day Treasury-Bill Investment

A long position in a T-bill or Eurodollar futures contract can be used by money market managers to lock in the purchase price and YTM on a future short-term investment in T-bills or CDs. To see this, suppose in April the treasurer of a corporation was expecting a $5 million cash inflow in June, which he was planning to invest in T-bills for 91 days. If the treasurer wanted to lock in the yield on the T-bill investment, he could do so by going long in June T-bill futures contracts. For example, if the June T-bill contract was trading at the IMM index price of 91, the treasurer could lock in a rate of return of 9.56% on a 91-day investment made at the futures' expiration date in June, $R_f(June, 91)$:

$$f_0 = \left[\frac{100 - (100 - 91)(.25)}{100}\right](\$1,000,000) = \$977,500.$$

$$R_f(June, 91) = \left(\frac{\$1,000,000}{\$977,500}\right)^{365/91} - 1 = .0956.$$

To obtain the 9.56% rate, the treasurer would need to form a naive hedge in which he bought 5.115 June T-bill futures contracts (assume perfect divisibility). That is:

$$n_f = \frac{\text{Investment in June}}{f_0} = \frac{\$5,000,000}{\$977,500} = 5.115 \text{ long contracts.}$$

At the June expiration date, the treasurer would close the futures position at the price on the spot 91-day T-bills. If the cash flow from closing is positive, the

---

[*]See Kolb and Chiang (1981) and Toevs and Jacobs (1986).

treasurer would invest the excess cash in T-bills; if it is negative, the treasurer would cover the shortfall with some of the anticipated cash inflow earmarked for purchasing T-bills.

For example, suppose at expiration the spot 91-day T-bill was trading at a YTM of 8%, or $S_T = \$1M/(1.08)^{91/365} = \$980,995$. In this case, the treasurer would realize a profit of $17,877 from closing the futures position:

$$\pi = (S_T - f_0)n_f$$

$$\pi = (\$980,995 - \$977,500)5.115 = \$17,877.$$

With the $17,877 profit on the futures, the $5 million inflow of cash (assumed to occur at expiration), and the spot price on the 91-day T-bill at $980,995, the treasurer would be able to purchase 5.1151 91-day T-bills (face value of $1 million):

$$\text{Number of 91-day T-bills} = \frac{\$5,000,000 + \$17,877}{\$980,995} = 5.1151.$$

Ninety-one days later, the treasurer would have $5,115,100, which equates to a rate of return from the $5 million inflow of 9.56%—the rate implied on the futures contract. That is:

$$\text{Rate} = \left[\frac{5.1151(\$1,000,000)}{\$5,000,000}\right]^{365/91} - 1 = .0956.$$

On the other hand, if the spot T-bill rate was 10% at expiration, or $S_T = \$1M/(1.10)^{91/365} = \$976,518$, then the treasurer would lose ($976,518 - $977,500)5.115 = -$5023 from closing the futures position. With the inflow of $5 million, the treasurer would need to use $5023 to settle the futures position, leaving him only $4,994,977 to invest in T-bills. However, with the price of the T-bill lower in this case, the treasurer would again be able to buy $4,994,977/ $976,518 = 5.1151 T-bills, and therefore realize a 9.56% rate of return from the $5 million investment.

14.6.2 Hedging a 182-Day Investment: Synthetic Futures on a 182-Day Treasury-Bill

Suppose in the preceding example that the treasurer in April was planning to invest the expected $5 million June cash inflow in T-bills for a period of 182 days instead of 91 days, and again wanted to lock in the investment rate. Since the underlying T-bill on a futures contract has a maturity of 91 days, not 182, the treasurer would need to take two long futures positions: one position expiring at the end of 91 days (the June contract) and the other expiring at the end of 182 days (the September contract). By purchasing futures contracts with expirations in June and September, the treasurer would have the equivalent of one June T-bill futures contract on a T-bill with 182-day maturity.

The implied futures rate of return earned on a 182-day investment made in June, R_f(June, 182), is equal to the average (geometric) of the implied futures rate on the contract expiring in June, $R_f(\text{June}, 91)$, and the implied futures rate on the contract expiring in September, $R_f(\text{Sept}, 91)$:

$$R_f(\text{June}, 182) = \{[1 + R_f(\text{June}, 91)]^{91/365}[1 + R_f(\text{Sept}, 91)]^{91/365}\}^{365/182} - 1. \quad (14.6\text{-}1)$$

In this example, if the IMM index on the June T-bill contract is at 91 and the index on a September T-bill contract is at 91.4, then the implied futures rate on each contract's underlying T-bills would be 9.56% and 9.1%, respectively, and the implied futures rate on 182-day investment made in June would be 9.3%:

$$f_0(\text{June}, 91) = \left[\frac{100 - (100 - 91)(.25)}{100}\right](\$1,000,000) = \$977,500$$

$$R_f(\text{June}, 91) = \left(\frac{\$1,000,000}{\$977,500}\right)^{365/91} - 1 = .0956$$

$$f_0(\text{Sept}, 91) = \left[\frac{100 - (100 - 91.4)(.25)}{100}\right](\$1,000,000) = \$978,500$$

$$R_f(\text{Sept}, 91) = \left(\frac{\$1,000,000}{\$978,500}\right)^{365/91} - 1 = .091$$

$$R_f(\text{June}, 182) = [(1.0956)^{91/365}(1.091)^{91/365}]^{365/182} - 1 = .093.$$

To actually lock in the 182-day rate for the $5 million investment, the treasurer would need to purchase 5.115 June contracts and 5.11 September contracts (again, assume perfect divisibility). That is, using a naive hedging model, the required hedging ratios would be:

$$n_f(\text{June}) = \frac{\$5,000,000}{\$977,500} = 5.115 \text{ contracts}$$

$$n_f(\text{Sept}) = \frac{\$5,000,000}{\$978,500} = 5.11 \text{ contracts}.$$

Suppose at the June expiration date, the spot 91-day T-bill is trading at 8% and the spot 182-day T-bill is trading at 8.25%. The price on the spot T-bill and expiring June T-bill futures contract would be $980,995, and the spot price on 182-day T-bill would be $961,243:

$$S(91) = f_T(\text{June}, 91) = \frac{\$1,000,000}{(1.08)^{91/365}} = \$980,995$$

$$S(182) = \frac{\$1,000,000}{(1.0825)^{182/365}} = \$961,243.$$

If the carrying-cost model holds and the repo or risk-free rate is the spot 91-day T-bill rate, then at the June expiration date the price on the September T-bill futures contract would be $979,865:

$$f(\text{Sept}, 91) = S(182)(1 + R)^{91/365}$$

$$f(\text{Sept}, 91) = \$961,243(1.08)^{91/365} = \$979,865.$$

If this is the case, then at the June expiration date the treasurer would realize a profit of $24,852 from closing both futures contracts:

$$\pi(\text{June}) = (\$980,995 - \$977,500)5.115 = \$17,877$$

$$\pi(\text{Sept}) = (\$979,865 - 978,500)5.11 = \$6975$$

Total futures profit $= \$17,877 + \$6975 = \$24,852.$

After closing both futures, the treasurer would be able to invest the $5 million cash inflow plus the $24,852 futures profit in 182-day spot T-bills. With the spot price on the 182-day T-bills at $S(182) = \$961,243$, the treasurer would be able to buy 5.227 182-day T-bills ($F = \$1$ million):

$$\text{Number of 182-day T-bills} = \frac{\$5,000,000 + \$24,852}{\$961,243} = 5.227.$$

At maturity (182 days later), the treasurer would receive $5,227,000. For a $5,000,000 investment, this represents a 9.3% rate of return—the same rate we determined using Equation (14.6-1). That is:

$$\text{Rate} = \left[\frac{(5.227)(\$1,000,000)}{\$5,000,000}\right]^{365/182} - 1 = .093.$$

In contrast, if spot rates at the June expiration date were higher at 10% and 10.25% on 91-day and 182-day T-bills, respectively, then a $20,798 loss from closing both futures positions would result:

$$S(91) = f_T(\text{June}, 91) = \frac{\$1,000,000}{(1.10)^{91/365}} = \$976,518$$

$$\pi(\text{June}) = (\$976,518 - \$977,500)5.115 = -\$5023$$

$$S(182) = \frac{\$1,000,000}{(1.1025)^{182/365}} = \$952,508$$

$$f(\text{Sept}, 91) = S(182)(1 + R)^{91/365} = \$952,508(1.10)^{91/365} = \$975,413$$

$$\pi(\text{Sept}) = (\$975,413 - \$978,500)5.11 = -\$15,775$$

Total futures profit $= -\$5023 - \$15,775 = -\$20,798.$

With the $5,000,000 cash inflow, the treasurer now would have to spend $20,798 to close the futures positions, leaving him with only $4,979,202 to invest in 182-day T-bills. With the higher rates, though, 182-day T-bills would be selling at only $S(182) = \$952,508$. Thus, the treasurer would still be able to buy 5.227 182-day T-bills, realizing a 9.3% rate of return from the $5 million investment:

$$\text{Number of 182-day T-bills} = \frac{\$5,000,000 - \$20,798}{\$952,508} = 5.227$$

$$\text{Rate} = \left[\frac{(5.227)(\$1,000,000)}{\$5,000,000}\right]^{365/182} - 1 = .093.$$

In summary, to lock in the rate on 182-day T-bills to be purchased with cash inflows in September, the treasurer would need to take long positions in both June and September T-bill futures contracts, then at the September expiration date close the contracts and invest the cash inflows plus (or minus) the futures profit (costs) in 182-day T-bills. By doing this, the treasurer in effect would be creating a June futures contract on a T-bill with a maturity of 182-days.

14.6.3   Hedging a Variable-Rate Loan

As a third example of a naive hedge, consider the case of a bank that provides a corporation with a one-year, $1 million, variable-rate loan. In the loan agreement, suppose the loan rate is set every quarter equal to the spot LIBOR (annual) plus 150 basis points (.015, or 1.5%) divided by 4: (LIBOR % + 1.5%)/4, and the loan starts on date 9/20, with the rates reset on 12/20, 3/20, and 6/20.

To the bank this loan represents a variable-rate asset, which it can hedge against interest rate changes by issuing 90-day CDs each quarter that are tied to the LIBOR. To the corporation, though, the loan subjects them to interest rate risk (unless they are using the loan to finance a variable-rate asset). To hedge this variable-rate loan, though, the corporation could go short in a series of Eurodollar futures contracts expiring at 12/20, 3/20, and 6/20. The impact of this hedge on the variable-rate loan is illustrated in Table 14.6-1. The top part of the table shows assumed futures prices (IMM index) of 91.5, 91.75, and 92 on three Eurodollar futures contracts initiated at the loan's origination on 9/20 and expiring, respectively, on 12/20, 3/20, and 6/20. The middle part of the table shows LIBORs (column 2). These rates, along with their IMM settlement prices (column 3), are assumed to occur on the expiration dates shown in column 1. For example, on date 12/20, the assumed spot LIBOR is 9%, yielding a settlement IMM index price of 91 and a closing futures price of 97.75. At that rate, the corporation would realize a profit of $1250 from having one short position in the 12/20 futures contract:

$$f_0 = \frac{100 - (100 - 91.5)(.25)}{100}(\$1M) = \$978,750$$

$$f_T = \frac{100 - (100 - 91)(.25)}{100}(\$1M) = \$977,500$$

Profit on 12/20 contract = $978,750 − $977,500 = $1250.

At the 12/20 date, though, the new interest that the corporation would have to pay for the next quarter would be set at $26,250:

$$12/20 \text{ Interest} = \frac{(LIBOR/100) + .015}{4}(\$1M)$$

$$12/20 \text{ Interest} = \frac{.09 + .015}{4}(\$1M) = \$26,250.$$

Subtracting the futures profit from the $26,250 interest payment (and ignoring the time value factor), the corporation's effective interest payment for the next quarter is $25,000 (column 6).

On the other hand, if the 12/20 LIBOR is lower than 8.5%—for example, 8%—then the quarterly interest payment would be only [(.08 + .015)/4]($1M) =

TABLE 14.6-1

Hedging a Variable-Rate Loan with a Eurodollar Strip

Loan: 1. $1 million variable-rate loan starting at 9/20
   2. Rates set on 12/20, 3/20, and 9/20
   3. Rates equal to (LIBOR % + 1.5%)/4.

Hedge: Short contracts in Eurodollar futures contracts expiring on 12/20, 3/20, and 9/20, with the following IMM index prices and future prices based on $100 face value:
IMM index (12/20) = 91.5; $f_0 = 100 - (100 - 91.5)(.25) = 97.875$
IMM index (3/20) = 91.75; $f_0 = 100 - (100 - 91.75)(.25) = 97.9375$
IMM index (6/20) = 92; $f_0 = 100 - (100 - 92)(.25) = 98$

(1)	(2)	(3)	(4)	(5) QUARTERLY INTEREST ON VARIABLE-RATE LOAN $\frac{[(LIBOR) + 1.5]/100}{4}$($1M)	(6) QUARTERLY DEBT	(7) ANNUAL RATE
DATE	LIBOR	$f_T{}^*$	FUTURES PROFIT[†]		(5) − (4)	$\frac{COL\ (6) \times 4}{\$1,000,000}$(100)
9/20	9.75%	—	—	$28,125	$28,125	11.25%
12/20	9.00	97.75	$1250	26,250	25,000	10.00
3/20	8.75	97.8125	1250	25,625	24,375	9.75
6/20	9.25	97.6875	3125	26,875	23,750	9.50

(1) CONTRACT EXPIRATION DATE	(2) IMM INDEX	(3) ANNUAL LOCKED-IN RATE FOR NEXT QUARTER (100 − IMM INDEX) + 150/100
12/20	91.50	10.00%
3/20	91.75	9.75
6/20	92.00	9.50

Average locked-in annual rate = $[(1.1125)^{.25}(1.10)^{.25}(1.0975)^{.25}(1.095)^{.25}]^1 - 1 = .1012$

*Expiring futures price: $f_T = 100 - (LIBOR\ \%)(.25)$
[†]Futures profit = $[(f_0 - f_T)/100]($1M)$

$23,750. This gain to the corporation, though, would be offset by a $1250 loss on the futures contract (i.e., at 8%, $f_T = $980,000$; therefore, profit on the 12/20 contract is $978,750 − $980,000 = −$1250$). As a result, the total quarterly debt of the company again would be ($23,750 + $1250) = $25,000. Ignoring the time value factor, the annualized rate the company pays would be 10%:

$$\text{Rate} = \frac{(\$25,000)(4)}{\$1,000,000} = .10.$$

Thus, the corporation's short position in the 12/20 Eurodollar futures contract at 91.5 enables it to lock in a quarterly debt obligation of $25,000; this equates to a 10% annualized borrowing rate.

  In general, if the rate on a variable-rate loan is set at a future date by the prevailing LIBOR at that time plus basis points (BP) and the Eurodollar futures contract also expires at that date, then the annualized locked-in rate that can be attained using Eurodollar futures contract is:

$$\text{Locked-in rate} = [100 - (\text{IMM index value})] + \frac{BP}{100},$$

or in terms of the example:

$$\text{Locked-in rate} = (100 - 91.5) + 1.5 = 10\%.$$

Given the futures contract prices on the other settlement dates shown in Table 14.6-1, the other short futures position would enable the corporation to lock in rates of $(100 - 91.75) + 1.5 = 9.75\%$ and $(100 - 92) + 1.5 = 9.5\%$ for the last two quarters (see column 7 or column 3 in the lower part of Table 14.6-1). The spot LIBOR at the beginning of the loan, in turn, is assumed to be 9.75%, yielding an annualized rate for the first quarter of $.0975 + .015 = .1125$, or 11.25%. Thus, using the geometric mean, the one-year risk-free rate for the corporation on its variable-rate loan hedged with the Eurodollar futures contracts would be 10.12%:

$$\text{Rate} = [(1.1125)^{.25}(1.10)^{.25}(1.0975)^{.25}(1.095)^{.25}]^1 - 1 = .1012.$$

In this example, the corporation in hedging a variable-rate loan needed to go short in a series of futures contracts with different expirations dates. By definition, a series of futures contracts with different maturities is called a *strip*.[*]

14.6.4 Other Uses of Naive Hedging Models

Naive hedging models can be applied to a number of other cases in which the spot security to be hedged is identical or highly correlated with the security underlying the futures contract. For example, a fixed-income portfolio manager planning to purchase T-bonds at a future date could hedge against changes in long-term interest rates by going long in T-bond futures contracts. Similarly, a mutual fund offering rates on money market securities could offer investors a two-year fixed rate by investing the fund in current 91- or 182-day T-bills or Eurodollar CDs, then locking in the reinvestment rates by going long in a series of T-bill or Eurodollar futures contracts with different expiration dates. Finally, a government bond dealer who purchases T-bonds, notes, or bills, then sells them over a certain period of time, could minimize his exposure to interest rate changes by hedging the spot position with Treasury futures.

In these and the other cases examined in this section, the securities underlying the futures were identical to the spot securities to be hedged. In such cases, a naive hedging model that matches either the face value of the spot position with the market value of the futures or the current value of the spot position with the

---

[*]Instead of the corporation's being subject to interest rate risk, the bank could have assumed the risk by providing the corporation with a fixed-rate loan. If the bank assumed the risk, it could hedge its exposure to interest rate risk by financing the one-year loan to the corporation with short-term CDs hedged with a short Eurodollar strip.

futures value will be effective. We now turn to cross-hedging cases in which the K-C price-sensitivity model is usually more effective.

14.7 CROSS-HEDGING INTEREST RATE POSITIONS

14.7.1 Kolb-Chiang Price-Sensitivity Model

The *Kolb-Chiang* (K-C) *price-sensitivity model* for hedging interest rate positions determines the number of futures contracts that will make the value of a portfolio consisting of a fixed-income security and an interest rate futures contract invariant to small changes in interest rates. The derivation of this model is presented in Appendix 14A at the end of this chapter. The optimum number of futures contracts that achieves this objective is:

$$n_f = -\frac{\mathrm{DUR}_S}{\mathrm{DUR}_f}\left(\frac{S_0}{f_0}\right)\frac{1 + \mathrm{YTM}_f}{1 + \mathrm{YTM}_s}, \qquad (14.7\text{-}1)$$

where:

DUR_s = duration of bond being hedged

DUR_f = duration of bond underlying futures contract (for T-bond futures this would be the bond cheapest to deliver)

YTM_s = yield to maturity on bond being hedged

YTM_f = yield to maturity implied by futures contract.

Duration is the average date that cash is received on the bond. Several approaches for measuring the average date can be taken. The most widely used is the weighted average of the bond's time periods, with the weights being the present value of each year's cash flows expressed as a proportion of the bond's price (see Appendix E at the end of the book for a further discussion). That is:

$$\mathrm{DUR} = \sum_{t=1}^{M} t\,\frac{\mathrm{PV}_t}{P_0^b}, \qquad (14.7\text{-}2)$$

where:

PV_t = present value of bond's cash flow at time t

P_0^b = price of bond.

For example, the duration of a two-year 10% annual coupon bond selling at its par value of $1000 (or equivalently at a YTM of 10%) would be 1.9091 years:

$$\mathrm{DUR} = (1\ \mathrm{yr})\frac{\$100/1.10}{\$1000} + (2\ \mathrm{yr})\left[\frac{(\$100 + \$1000)/(1.10)^2}{\$1000}\right] = 1.9091\ \text{years}.$$

Note that the durations for pure discount bonds such as commercial paper or T-bills equal the bonds' maturity since all the cash flows are received at maturity.*

◆   14.7.2   **Example of Hedging a Commercial Paper Issue**

Suppose that in June the treasurer of ABC Autos makes plans for financing the purchase of the company's fall car inventory. The treasurer decides to raise funds by selling a commercial paper (CP) issue in September with a face value of $10 million and a maturity of 182 days. Fearing short-term interest rates could increase over the next three months, the treasurer also decides to hedge the price of the CP issue by taking a short position in September T-bill futures contracts. In June, a 182-day CP is trading at a YTM of 6%, making the current spot price of a 182-day CP issue [$S_0(182)$] with a face value of $10 million worth $9,713,634:

$$S_0(182) = \frac{\$10,000,000}{(1.06)^{182/365}} = \$9,713,634.$$

The IMM index on the September T-bill futures contract is 95, making the T-bill futures worth $987,500 and the implied yield on the futures contract (YTM_f) 5.175%:

$$f_0 = \left[\frac{100 - (100 - 95)(90/360)}{100}\right](\$1,000,000) = \$987,500$$

$$\text{YTM}_f = \left(\frac{\$1,000,000}{\$987,500}\right)^{365/91} - 1 = .05175.$$

By the K-C price-sensitivity model, the treasurer would need to go short in n_f = 20 T-bill futures contracts to hedge the $10 million CP issue against interest rate risk:

$$n_f = -\frac{\text{DUR}_s}{\text{DUR}_f}\left(\frac{S_0}{f_0}\right)\frac{1 + \text{YTM}_f}{1 + \text{YTM}_s}$$

$$n_f = -\frac{182 \text{ days}}{91 \text{ days}}\left(\frac{\$9,713,634}{\$987,500}\right)\frac{1.05175}{1.06} = -19.52 \cong -20.$$

To illustrate the impact of the hedge, suppose the 182-day CP issue is sold at the September futures' expiration at an annual discount yield (R_D) that is 0.25 higher than the spot T-bill discount yield. As shown in Table 14.7-1, with 20 September T-bill futures contracts, the treasurer would be able to lock in $9,737,500 cash proceeds from selling the CP issue and closing the futures contracts. With $9,737,500 cash locked in, ABC's effective rate on the 182-day hedged issue would be 5.48%:

$$\text{Hedged rate} = \left(\frac{\$10,000,000}{\$9,737,500}\right)^{365/182} - 1 = .0548. \quad ◆$$

---

*Also, the measure of duration here assumes a flat yield curve. Other duration measures have been developed that incorporate different assumptions about the yield curve.

TABLE 14.7-1

Hedging $10M CP Issue with 20 T-Bill Futures Contracts				
(1) SPOT T-BILL DISCOUNT YIELD R_D AT EXPIRATION	(2) CLOSING T-BILL FUTURES PRICE* $S_T = f_T$	(3) FUTURES PROFIT $n_f(f_0 - f_T) =$ $20(\$987,500 - f_T)$	(4) PRICE OF CP†	(5) FUTURES PROFIT PLUS PRICE OF CP (3) + (4)
4%	$990,000	$-\$50,000$	$9,787,500	$9,737,500
5	987,500	0	9,737,500	9,737,500
6	985,000	50,000	9,687,500	9,737,500

$*S_T = f_T = \left[\frac{100 - R_D(.25)}{100}\right](\$1,000,000)$

$\dagger$Price of CP $= \left[\frac{100 - (R_D(.25)(180/360)}{100}\right](\$10,000,000)$

◆ **14.7.3   Example of Hedging a Bond Portfolio**

T-bond futures contracts often are used by fixed-income-portfolio managers to protect the future values of their portfolios against interest rate changes. To see this, suppose in January a fixed-income-portfolio manager believes that she may be required to liquidate the fund's long-term bond holdings in mid-May. The bond portfolio has an aggregate face value of $1 million, an average coupon rate of 12%, and an average maturity of 15 years and currently is valued at 102 per $100 par value. The estimated YTM on the bond portfolio is 11.75%, and its duration is 7.36 years. The manager is considering hedging the portfolio against interest rate changes by going short in June T-bond futures contracts that currently are trading at $f_0 = 72^{16}/_{32}$. After tracking several bonds, a T-bond futures expert advises the manager that a T-bond trading at a YTM of 9% and with a duration of 7 years is the most likely bond to be delivered on the June futures contract. Using the K-C price-sensitivity model, the portfolio manager could hedge the bond portfolio by selling 14 futures contracts:

$$n_f = -\frac{DUR_s}{DUR_f}\left(\frac{S_0}{f_0}\right)\frac{1 + YTM_f}{1 + YTM_s}$$

$$n_f = -\frac{7.36}{7.00}\left(\frac{\$1,020,000}{\$72,500}\right)\frac{1.09}{1.1175} = -14.43.$$

If the manager hedges the bond portfolio with 14 June T-bond short contracts, she will be able to offset changes in the bond portfolio's value resulting from interest rate changes. For example, suppose interest rates increased from January to mid-May, causing the price of the bond portfolio to decrease from 102 to 95 and causing the futures price on the June T-bond contract to decrease from $72^{16}/_{32}$ to $68^{22}/_{32}$. In this case, the fixed-income portfolio would lose $70,000 in value (decrease in value from $1,020,000 to $950,000). This loss, though, would be partially offset by a profit of $53,375 on the T-bond futures position:

Futures profit $= 14(\$72,500 - \$68,687.50) = \$53,375.$

Thus, by using T-bond futures, the manager is able to reduce some of the potential losses in the value of her portfolio that would result if interest rates increase.* ◆

14.8   CONCLUSION

Introduced during the volatile interest rate period of the 1970s and 1980s, interest rate futures have become one of the most popular futures contracts. In this chapter we've examined the characteristics, pricing, and speculative and hedging uses of these contracts. As we've seen, they can be used by banks to manage the maturity gaps between loans and deposits, by corporations and financial institutions to fix the rates on variable-rate loans, and by fixed-income-portfolio managers, money managers, investment bankers, and security dealers in locking in the future purchase or selling price on their fixed-income securities.

KEY TERMS

Treasury-bill futures contract
London Interbank Offer Rate (LIBOR)
Eurodollar futures contract
Treasury-bond futures contract
Treasury-note futures contract
cheapest-to-deliver bond
wild-card option
implied repo rate

implied forward rate
NOB spread
TED spread
turtle spread
strip
Kolb-Chiang price-sensitivity model
duration

SELECTED REFERENCES

A number of empirical studies have examined interest rate futures relationships. Many of these works have focused on futures pricing and market efficiency. Most frequently cited are Rendleman and Carabini (1979); Elton, Gruber, and Rentzler (1984); Resnick and Hennigar (1983); Resnick (1984); and Gay and Manaster (1986).

In their 1979 study, Rendleman and Carabini tried to determine whether arbitrage opportunities existed by taking positions in spot T-bills and opposite positions in T-bill futures. Examining over 1600 transactions for the period from 1976 to 1978, they found futures prices on T-bills were mispriced, but not to the extent that the profit realized from executing cash-and-carry arbitrage strategies would be sufficient to cover the transaction costs.

---

*The manager could have hedged the portfolio by buying a T-bond put option. In such applications the exercise price is used instead of the futures price in Equation (14.7-1), and the YTM implied on the option is used instead of the implied futures rate.

In a similar study, Elton, Gruber, and Rentzler (1984) compared the returns from investing in actual and synthetic T-bills (long in a 182-day spot T-bill and short in a T-bill futures contract). In examining actual and synthetic T-bill rates for the period from 1976 to 1982, they found the differences between such rates to be significant, with the differences, on average, exceeding the transaction costs. Their study thus questions whether the T-bill futures market is efficient and/or whether the carrying-cost model is valid, and also contradicts the findings of Rendleman and Carabini (1979).

Studies by Resnick and Hennigar (1983) and by Resnick (1984) examined equilibrium pricing and market efficiency for T-bond futures. Resnick and Hennigar examined T-bond futures for the period from 1979 to May of 1981, and found the differences in the returns earned by taking T-bond spot and futures positions were not significantly large enough to conclude that arbitrage opportunities existed. The Resnick study found similar conclusions in examining the pricing relationships between T-bonds with different expirations.

Finally, Gay and Manaster (1986) examined the efficiency of the T-bond futures market by trying to determine if arbitrage opportunities were inherent in the contract's delivery procedure. In their study, they compared, ex post, the optimal delivery procedure (cheapest to deliver) with the actual procedure followed by the market. They found that substantial profit opportunities were lost by not following the optimal procedure.

Akemann, C. "Predicting Changes in T-Bond Futures Spreads Using Implied Yields from T-Bill Futures." *Journal of Futures Markets* 6 (Summer 1986): 223–230.

Arak, M., and Goodman, L. "Treasury Bond Futures: Valuing the Delivery Option." *Journal of Futures Markets* 7 (1987): 269–286.

Arak, M., Goodman, L., and Ross, S. "The Cheapest to Deliver Bond on the Treasury Bond Futures Contract." *Advances in Futures and Options Research* 1 (1986): 49–74.

Benninga, S., and Smirlock, M. "An Empirical Analysis of the Delivery Option, Marking to Market, and the Pricing of Treasury Bond Futures." *Journal of Futures Markets* 5 (Fall 1985): 361–374.

Bierwag, G. *Duration Analysis.* Cambridge, Mass.: Ballinger, 1987.

Block, S., and Gallagher, T. "The Use of Interest Rate Futures and Options by Corporate Financial Managers." *Financial Management* 15 (Aug. 1986): 73–78.

Capozza, D., and Cornell, B. "Treasury Bill Pricing in the Spot and Futures Markets." In *Interest Rate Futures: Concepts and Issues*, edited by G. Gay and R. Kolb. Richmond, Va.: Robert F. Dame, 1982.

Chance, D. *Options and Futures*, Chicago: Dryden Press, 1991, pp. 356–395.

Chiang, R., Gay, G., and Kolb, R. "Interest Rate Hedging: An Empirical Test of Alternative Strategies." *Journal of Financial Research* (Fall 1983): 187–197.

Ederington, L. "The Hedging Performance of the New Futures Market." *Journal of Finance* 34 (Mar. 1979): 157–170.

Elton, E., Gruber. M., and Rentzler, J. "Intra-Day Tests of the Efficiency of the Treasury Bill Futures Market." *Review of Economics and Statistics* (Feb. 1984): 129–137.

Gay, G., and Kolb, R. "Immunizing Bond Portfolios with Interest Rate Futures." *Financial Management* 11 (1982): 81–89.

Gay, G., Kolb, R., and Chiang, R. "Interest Rate Hedging: An Empirical Test of Alternative Strategies." *Journal of Financial Research* 6 (Fall 1983): 187–197.

Gay, G., and Manaster, S. "Implicit Delivery Options and Optional Delivery Strategies for Financial Futures Contracts." *Journal of Financial Economics* 15 (1986): 41–72.

Hegde, S., and Branch, B. "An Empirical Analysis of Arbitrage Opportunities in the Treasury Bill Futures Market." *Journal of Futures Markets* 5 (1985): 407–424.

Kane, A., and Marcus, A. "Valuation and Optimal Exercise of the Wild Card Option in the Treasury Bond Futures Market." *Journal of Finance* 41 (Mar. 1986): 195–207.

Kane, E. "Market Incompleteness and Divergence Between Forward and Futures Interest Rates." *Journal of Finance* (May 1980): 221–234.

Klemkosky, R., and Lasser, D. "An Efficiency Analysis of the T-Bond Futures Market." *Journal of Futures Markets* 5 (1985): 607–620.

Kolb, R., and Chiang, R. "Improving Hedging Performance Using Interest Rate Futures." *Financial Management* 10 (Autumn 1981): 72–29.

McCable, G., and Franckle, C. "The Effectiveness of Rolling the Hedge Forward in the Treasury Bill Futures Market." *Financial Management* 12 (Summer 1983): 21–29.

Rendleman, R., and Carabini, C. "The Efficiency of the Treasury Bill Futures Market." *Journal of Finance* 34 (Sept. 1979): 895–914.

Rentzler, J. "Trading Treasury Bond Spreads Against Treasury Bill Futures—A Model and Empirical Test of the Turtle Trade." *Journal of Futures Market* 6 (1986): 41–61.

Resnick, B. "The Relationship Between Futures Prices for U.S. Treasury Bonds." *Review of Research in Futures Markets* 3 (1984): 88–104.

Resnick, B., and Hennigar, E. "The Relation Between Futures and Cash Prices for U.S. Treasury Bonds." *Review of Research in Futures Markets* 2 (1983): 282–299.

Senchak, A., and Easterwood, J. "Cross Hedging CD's with Treasury Bill Futures." *Journal of Futures Markets* 3 (1983): 429–438.

Siegel, D., and Siegel, D. *Futures Markets* Chicago: Dryden Press, 1990, pp. 203–342, 493–504.

Tamarkin, R. *The New Gatsbys: Fortunes and Misfortunes of Commodity Traders.* New York: William Morrow, 1985.

Toevs, A., and Jacob, D. "Futures and Alternative Hedge Methodologies." *Journal of Portfolio Management* (Spring 1986): 60–70.

Tucker, A. *Financial Futures, Options and Swaps*, St. Paul: West, 1991, pp. 216–227.

Viet, T., and Reiff, W. "Commercial Banks and Interest Rate Futures: A Hedging Survey." *Journal of Futures Markets* 3 (1983): 283–293.

Virnola, A., and Dale, C. "The Efficiency of the Treasury Bill Futures Market: An Analysis of Alternative Specifications." *Journal of Financial Research* 3 (1980): 169–188.

PROBLEMS AND QUESTIONS

1. Table 14.P-1 shows the IMM index prices on three T-bill futures contracts with expirations of 91, 182, and 273 days, along with the YTM on a spot 182-day T-bill.

   a. Calculate the actual futures prices and the YTMs (annualized) on the futures.

   b. Given that the spot 182-day T-bill is trading at an annualized YTM of 6.25%, what is the implied 91-day repo rate?

   c. If the carrying-cost model holds, what would be the price of a 91-day spot T-bill?

   d. What would be the equilibrium price on the March contract if the actual 91-day repo rate was 4.75%? What strategy would an arbitrageur pursue if the IMM index price was 93.764?

2. Table 14.P-2 shows the YTMs for spot T-bills with maturities of 91, 182, and 273 days.

   a. Calculate the implied forward rates, and outline the locking-in strategy for the following:

      (1) 91-day investment made 91 days from the present

      (2) 91-day investment made 182 days from the present

   b. Assuming the carrying-cost model holds, determine the actual price and the IMM index price on futures contracts with expirations of 91 and 182 days.

   c. Given the futures prices, check to see if the implied YTM on each futures contract is equal to the implied forward rule.

TABLE 14.P-1

T-BILL CONTRACT	DAYS TO EXPIRATION	IMM INDEX
March	91	93.764
June	182	93.3092
September	273	91.8607
Spot 182-day T-bill: YTM = .0625		

TABLE 14.P-2

DAYS TO MATURITY ON SPOT T-BILLS	YTM
91	6.00%
182	6.25
273	6.50

3. Sun Bank is preparing to provide a $10M loan to Midwest Manufacturing. In the loan contract, Midwest agrees to pay the principal and an interest of 12% (annual) at the end of 182 days. Since Sun Bank sells more 91-day CDs than 182-day CDs, it is planning to finance the loan by selling a 91-day CD now at the prevailing LIBOR, then 91 days later (mid-September) selling another 91-day CD at the prevailing LIBOR. Sun Bank would like to minimize its exposure to interest rate risk on its future CD sale by taking a position in a September Eurodollar contract. The current YTM on Sun Bank's CDs are 9.25% (annual), and September Eurodollar futures are trading at 91 (IMM index).

   a. How many September Eurodollar futures contracts would Sun Bank need to hedge its September CD sale against interest rate changes effectively? Assume perfect divisibility.

   b. Determine the total amount of funds Sun Bank would need to raise on its CD sale 91 days from the present if the LIBOR is 8.5% and again if it is 10% (assume futures are closed at the LIBOR). What would the bank's debt obligations be at the end of 182 days? What is Sun Bank's effective rate for the entire 182-day period?

   c. What is the bank's profit from the construction loan financed by 90-day CDs hedged with the futures?

4. Suppose in Problem 3 that Sun Bank was considering financing its construction loan either with a 182-day CD or with a series of 91-day CDs hedged with futures. Determine the rate and the price on a 182-day spot CD that would make the bank indifferent. Explain in terms of implied futures rates and implied forward rates the criterion it could use in determining the appropriate financing.

5. Explain the types of spreads bond speculators could use given the following:

   a. The yield curve is expected to shift down, with rates for bonds with differing maturities decreasing by roughly the same percentage.

   b. While the economy is growing, leading economic indicators auger an economic recession.

   c. While the economy is in recession, leading economic indicators auger economic expansion.

6. Explain what an arbitrageur would do given all of the following conditions:

   • The futures price on a September T-bond contract is 96.
   • The futures price on a December T-bond contract is 98.
   • The time period between the September contract and the December contract is 90 days.
   • The implied forward rate for a 90-day loan or investment made at the September expiration date is 6% (annual).

7. Table 14.P-7 shows the prices for T-bill futures contracts with expiration of 91, 182, and 273 days, along with the price for the spot 91-day T-bill.

   a. Calculate the implied YTM on the futures contracts.

TABLE 14.P-7

T-Bill Contract	Days to Expiration	Price = f_0
March	91	$984,410
June	182	983,273
September	273	979,652

Price of spot 91-day T-bill = $985,578

b. Explain in general how a money market fund planning to purchase 91-day T-bills every 91 days could use the T-bill futures in the table to offer its fund investors a guaranteed one-year fixed-rate investment. What would be the average annual rate the fund could promise its investors?

c. How many March ($T = 91$ days), June ($T = 182$ days), and September ($T = 273$ days) futures contracts would the fund need if it had $10M that it planned to invest in a series of 91-day T-bills (assume perfect divisibility)?

d. Given the futures contracts needed for hedging in part (c), explain how the fund would be managed under the following scenario (assume perfect divisibility):

- At the March expiration, the spot 91-day T-bill is trading at a YTM of 6%.

- At the June expiration, the spot 91-day T-bill is trading at a YTM of 7.25%.

- At the September expiration, the spot 91-day T-bill is trading at a YTM of 8%.

e. Based on your answer to part (d), does the fund earn the average rate you determined in part (b)? Given the rates in this scenario, what would be the fund's rate without the hedge?

8. Using the information from Table 14.P-7 (Problem 7), answer the following.

a. How many March and June futures contracts would a bank need in order to hedge the sale 91 days later of its current holdings of ten 273-day T-bills currently trading at a YTM of 6.5% (assume perfect divisibility, and use the implied futures rates determined in Problem 7).

b. Determine the amount of cash the bank would have at the March expiration when it liquidates its spot and futures positions if spot 91-day T-bills were trading at a YTM of 7% and spot 182-day T-bills were trading at 7.25%. Assume the carrying-cost model holds and the 91-day repo rate is 7%. What is the rate of return the bank would earn on its T-bill holdings for the 91-day period?

9. Using the information from Table 14.P-7 (Problem 7), answer the following.

a. Determine the number of March and June futures contracts a money market manager would need if he was expecting a $10M cash inflow in 91 days (at the March expiration) and wanted to lock in a rate of return on

182-day investments in T-bills (assume perfect divisibility). What rate of return would the manager be able to lock in (use the implied futures rates determined in Problem 7)?

b. Based on your answer to part (a), how many T-bills would the manager be able to purchase at the March expiration with the $10M cash inflow and futures profits or losses if both spot 91-day and 182-day T-bills are trading at a YTM of 6% (assume perfect divisibility)? Assume the carrying-cost model holds and the 91-day repo rate is 6%. Calculate the T-bill rate of return from the $10M inflow for the next 182-day period.

10. Ms. James is an investment manager. In June, she forecast a September cash inflow of $3M that she plans to invest for 91 days in T-bills. Ms. James is uncertain about future short-term interest rates and would like to lock in the rate on her September investment with T-bill futures contracts. Currently, September T-bill contracts are trading at 92 (IMM index).

a. What is the implied YTM on the September T-bill futures contract?

b. How many September contracts does Ms. James need to lock in the implied futures YTM (assume perfect divisibility)?

c. Assuming Ms. James' $3M cash inflow comes at the same time as the September futures contracts expire, show that Ms. James futures-hedged T-bill purchase yields the same rate from a $3M investment as the implied YTM on the futures. Evaluate at spot T-bill rates at the futures' expiration of 8% and 9%.

11. Suppose Ms. James in Problem 10 wanted to invest her $3M September cash inflow in 182-day T-bills, instead of 91-day bills, and again wanted to lock in the rate. Assume September and December T-bill futures are available, with 91 days separating the expiration dates of the contracts, and assume the IMM prices of each are IMM(Sept) = 92 and IMM(Dec) = 93.

a. Calculate the rate of return on the 182-day investment implied by the September and December contracts.

b. Explain how Ms. James could lock in the implied futures rate on the 182-day investment using September and December contracts.

c. Show how Ms. James could attain the implied 182-day rate on her $3M cash flow in September by investing the $3M and the futures profit (or covering the futures loss). Assume at the September expiration date 91-day spot T-bills are trading at a YTM of 8% (annual) and 182-day spot T-bills are at 7.5%, the 91-day repo rate is 8%, the carrying-cost-model holds, and perfect divisibility.

d. Repeat part (c), except assume that at the September expiration date the YTM on the 91-day T-bill is 9%, the YTM on the 182-day T-bill is 8.6%, and the 91-day repo rate is 9%.

12. On December 20, the R. A. Jones Department Store obtained a $5M variable-rate loan from Boone Bank to finance its inventory. The loan has a maturity of 270 days (or .75/year), and the rate on the loan is set each quarter. The initial

quarterly rate is equal to 9.5%/4; the other rates, set on 3/20 and 6/20, equal one-fourth of the sum of the annual LIBOR on those dates and 100 basis points: (LIBOR % + 1%)/4. On December 20, the Eurodollar futures contract expiring on 3/20 is trading at 91 (IMM index), the contract expiring on 6/20 is trading at 92 (IMM index), and the time separating each contract is .25/year.

a. Calculate the rate R. A. Jones could lock in by hedging its variable-rate loan with five 3/20 Eurodollar futures contracts and five 6/20 contracts.

b. Calculate and show in a table R. A. Jones' quarterly interest payments, futures profit, and hedged interest payments (interest minus futures profit) for each period: 12/20, 3/20, and 6/20. Assume LIBOR is 10% (annual) on 3/20 and 9% on 6/20 and that the LIBOR is used both to determine the cash settlement on the Eurodollar futures contract and to set the loan rate.

c. Annualize R. A. Jones' quarterly hedged interest payments (multiply each by 4), and then calculate each annualized payment as a proportion of the company's $5M loan. Are these rates consistent with the rates you calculated in part (a)?

13. In January, the J. R. Development Company closed a deal with local officials to develop a new office building. The project is expected to begin in June and to take 272 days to complete. The cost of the development is expected to be $8M, with L. B. Insurance Company providing the permanent financing of the development once the construction is completed. J. R. Development has obtained a 272-day construction loan from Star Financing Company. Star Financing will disperse funds to J. R. at the beginning of the project in June, with the interest rate on the loan being set equal to the prevailing CP rate on that date plus 50 BP. The loan will have a maturity of 272 days, with the principal and interest on the loan to be paid at maturity.

Fearful that interest rates could increase between January and June, J. R. Development would like to lock in its rate on the $8M construction loan by taking a position in June T-Bill futures contracts. J. R. would use any profits from the futures to defray the $8M construction costs; any losses, it would add to its $8M loan. Currently, a 272-day CP is trading at a YTM of 10% (annual) and June T-Bill futures are trading at 91 (IMM index).

a. Using the K-C price-sensitivity model, show how J. R. Development could immunize its construction loan against interest rate changes.

b. How much would J. R. need to borrow at the June expiration if the CP rate was at 11% and the spot 91-day T-bill was trading at a discount yield of 10% (R_D)? What would be J. R.'s futures-hedge interest rate on the 272-day loan ($8M loan)?

14. Mr. Bush is a fixed-income-portfolio manager for WJM Investments. Mr. Bush forecast a cash inflow of $5M in June and plans to invest the funds in his baseline bond portfolio, which currently has an A quality rating, a duration of seven years, an annual coupon rate of 10.25%, and a YTM of 10.25% (or selling at a par of 100). Afraid that long-term interest rates could decline, Mr. Bush decides to hedge his June investment by taking a position in June T-bond

futures contracts when the June T-bond contract is trading at $80^{16}/_{32}$ and the T-bond most likely to be delivered on the contract has a YTM of 9.5% and a duration of nine years.

a. Using the K-C price-sensitivity model, show how Mr. Bush could hedge his June bond portfolio purchase against interest rate risk.

b. Suppose long-term interest rates decrease over the period such that at the June expiration, bonds matching Mr. Bush's baseline portfolio (A-rated, 10.25% coupon rate, and seven-year duration) are trading at 104 of par and the price on the expiring June T-bond contract(f_T) is 85. Determine Mr. Bush's costs of purchasing his baseline bond portfolio, his profit on the futures contracts, and his hedged-portfolio costs.

Derivation of Kolb-Chiang Price-Sensitivity Hedging Model

The Kolb-Chiang price-sensitivity model solves for the number of futures contracts (n_f) that makes the change in the value of a portfolio of a debt security and a debt futures contracts invariant to small changes in interest rates. The value of the portfolio is:

$$V = B_0 + n_f f_0, \qquad (14.A\text{-}1)$$

where:

B_0 = current value of debt security or portfolio.

To measure the change in the portfolio value with respect to changes in interest rates, let R be the rate of return representing general interest rates in the economy (e.g., T-bond rate), let YTM_s be the discount rate on the debt instrument or debt portfolio, and let YTM_f be the discount rate implied by the futures contract. The change in the price of the bond resulting from a small change in R can be defined in terms of the impact of the change in R on YTM_s and the impact of the change in YTM_s on B_0. This relation can be defined by the chain rule, in which:

$$\frac{dB_0}{dR} = \frac{\partial B_0}{\partial YTM_s}\frac{\partial YTM_s}{\partial R}. \qquad (14.A\text{-}2)$$

The change in f_0 resulting from a change in R can be defined similarly:

$$\frac{df_0}{dR} = \frac{\partial f_0}{\partial YTM_f}\frac{\partial YTM_f}{\partial R}. \qquad (14.A\text{-}3)$$

Given $\partial B_0/\partial R$ and $\partial f_0/\partial R$, the optimum n_f can be found by taking the derivative of Equation (14.A-1) with respect to R, setting the resulting equation equal to zero, and solving for n_f:

$$\frac{dV}{dR} = \frac{\partial B_0}{\partial YTM_s}\frac{\partial YTM_s}{\partial R} + n_f\left(\frac{\partial f_0}{\partial YTM_f}\right)\frac{\partial YTM_f}{\partial R} = 0. \quad (14.A-4)$$

If we assume $\partial YTM_s/\partial R$ is approximately equal to $\partial YTM_f/\partial R$, then the optimum n_f is:

$$n_f^* = \frac{-\partial B_0/\partial YTM_s}{\partial f_0/\partial YTM_f}. \quad (14.A-5)$$

As discussed in Appendix E at the end of the book, the duration of a security is equal to the percentage change in the security's price divided by the percentage change in 1 plus its YTM. The durations for the bond and the futures, therefore, can be expressed as:

$$DUR_s = \frac{\%\Delta B_0}{\%\Delta(1 + YTM_s)} = \frac{\partial B_0/B_0}{\partial(YTM_s)/(1 + YTM_s)} \quad (14.A-6)$$

$$DUR_f = \frac{\%\Delta f_0}{\%\Delta(1 + YTM_f)} = \frac{\partial f_0/f_0}{\partial(YTM_f)/(1 + YTM_f)}. \quad (14.A-7)$$

Thus:

$$\frac{\partial B_0}{\partial YTM_s} = DUR_s\frac{B_0}{1 + YTM_s} \quad (14.A-8)$$

$$\frac{\partial f_0}{\partial YTM_f} = DUR_f\frac{f_0}{1 + YTM_f}. \quad (14.A-9)$$

By substituting Equations (14.A-8) and (14.A-9) into Equation (14.A-5), n_f^* can be written as:

$$n_f^* = \frac{-DUR_s}{DUR_f}\left(\frac{B_0}{f_0}\right)\frac{1 + YTM_f}{1 + YTM_s}, \quad (14.A-10)$$

which is the same as Equation (14.7-1).

CHAPTER 15

Foreign Currency Futures and Forward Contracts

15.1 INTRODUCTION

Since the introduction of the flexible exchange rate system in the early 1970s, the use of foreign currency futures and forward contracts has increased dramatically. In this chapter, we conclude our analysis of futures by examining the markets, uses, and pricing of these contracts.

15.2 FOREIGN CURRENCY FUTURES AND FORWARD MARKETS

15.2.1 Foreign Currency Futures Market

Foreign currency futures were introduced in May of 1972 by the International Monetary Market (IMM) of the Chicago Mercantile Exchange. Today, the IMM is the largest foreign currency futures exchange. As shown in Table 15.2-1, the IMM provides trading on a number of foreign currency futures contracts. Each of the IMM's currency contracts calls for the delivery (or purchase) of a specified amount of foreign currency (FC) at the delivery date.

The contract prices of the currency futures are quoted in terms of dollars per unit of FC. For example, the September futures contract on the Swiss franc shown in Exhibit 15.2-1 calls for the delivery (or purchase) of 125,000 Swiss francs (SF) at a price of $0.7415/SF (total contract price of $92,687.50). The expiration day of an IMM's currency contract is the second business day preceding the third Wednesday of the expiration month.

The second-largest exchange for trading foreign currency futures is the London International Financial Futures Exchange (LIFFE). Foreign currency futures also

TABLE 15.2-1

Select Foreign Currency Futures Contracts			
CONTRACT	EXCHANGE*	DELIVERY MONTHS	CONTRACT SIZE
Deutsche mark	IMM	Jan/Apr/June/July/Sept/Oct/Nov; current spot month	125,000 DM
Canadian dollar	IMM	Jan/Apr/June/July/Sept/Oct/Nov; current spot month	100,000 CD
French franc	IMM	Jan/Apr/June/July/Sept/Oct/Nov; current spot month	250,000 FF
Swiss franc	IMM	Jan/Apr/June/July/Sept/Oct/Nov; current spot month	125,000 SF
British pound	IMM	Jan/Apr/June/July/Sept/Oct/Nov; current spot month	25,000 BP
Japanese yen	IMM	Jan/Apr/June/July/Sept/Oct/Nov; current spot month	12,500,000 JY
Australian dollar	IMM	Jan/Apr/June/July/Sept/Oct/Nov; current spot month	100,000 AD
British pound	MCE	Mar/June/Sept/Dec	12,500 BP
Canadian dollar	MCE	Mar/June/Sept/Dec	50,000 CD
British pound	PHLX	Mar/June/Sept/Dec and two nearest months	25,000 BP
Japanese yen	PHLX	Mar/June/Sept/Dec and two nearest months	12,500,000 JY
British pound	LIFFE	Mar/June/Sept/Dec	25,000 BP

*IMM = International Monetary Market; MCE = Mid-American Commodity Exchange; PHLX = Philadelphia Exchange; LIFFE = London International Financial Futures Exchange.

are traded on a number of other exchanges, including the Philadelphia Exchange, the Singapore International Monetary Market, and the Sydney Futures Exchange.*

15.2.2 Interbank Forward Market

As discussed in Chapter 10, forward contracts on foreign currencies are provided in the Interbank Foreign Exchange Market. This market is considerably larger than the currency futures market, consisting primarily of major banks that provide forward contracts to their clients, which often are large multinational corporations. In the interbank market, banks provide tailor-made contracts to their customers. Typically, the minimum size of an interbank forward contract is $1 million, with expirations ranging from 1 to 12 months, although longer-term maturities can be arranged.

Foreign currency forward contracts are governed by the same economic forces and have similar hedging and speculative uses as currency futures. However, because forward contracts are tailor-made, an active secondary market does not

*Many innovations in futures trading, such as cooperative linkage agreements, multiple futures listings, and 24-hour trading, were introduced by the exchanges offering currency futures.

EXHIBIT 15.2-1

CURRENCY

	Open	High	Low	Settle	Change	Lifetime High	Low	Open Interest
JAPAN YEN (CME)—12.5 million yen; $ per yen (.00)								
Sept	1.0193	1.0206	.9998	1.0023	− .0159	1.0408	.8942	70,300
Dec	1.0275	1.0280	1.0090	1.0100	− .0159	1.0490	.9525	10,230
Mr95	1.0250	1.0250	1.0200	1.0186	− .0159	1.0560	.9680	1,016
Jun	1.0450	1.0450	1.0350	1.0281	− .0159	1.0670	.9915	217
Est vol 35,027; vol Wed 27,374; open int 77,374, +1,626.								
DEUTSCHEMARK (CME)—125,000 marks; $ per mark								
Sept	.6343	.6382	.6268	.6279	− .0065	.6595	.5364	83,092
Dec	.6360	.6385	.6275	.6284	− .0066	.6606	.5351	4,218
Mr95	.6380	.6385	.6297	.6297	− .0067	.6595	.5798	1,094
Est vol 54,675; vol Wed 33,418; open int 88,450, +515.								
CANADIAN DOLLAR (CME)—100,000 dirs.; $ per Can $								
Sept	.7225	.7240	.7220	.7239	+ .0006	.7740	.7068	32,137
Dec	.7200	.7210	.7200	.7212	+ .0007	.7670	.7038	2,514
Mr95	....	....	....	.7181	+ .0007	.7618	.7020	611
June	.7136	.7142	.7136	.7141	+ .0007	.7600	.6990	434
Est vol 3,383; vol Wed 3,514; open int 35,768, +169.								
BRITISH POUND (CME)—62,500 pds.; $ per pound								
Sept	1.5304	1.5364	1.5230	1.5256	− .0046	1.5764	1.4440	31,164
Dec	1.5340	1.5350	1.5220	1.5246	− .0050	1.5760	1.4400	857
Mr95	1.5310	1.5340	1.5220	1.5236	− .0052	1.5750	1.4530	153
Est vol 12,907; vol Wed 8,819; open int 32,174, −47.								
SWISS FRANC (CME)—125,000 francs; $ per franc								
Sept	.7497	.7548	.7403	.7415	− .0082	.7817	.6590	38,005
Dec	.7550	.7561	.7421	.7432	− .0082	.7840	.6885	1,527
Est vol 25,353; vol Wed 17,037; open int 39,561, +1,116.								
AUSTRALIAN DOLLAR (CME)—100,000 dirs.; $ per A.$								
Sept	.7360	.7376	.7336	.7372	− .0018	.7467	.6645	7,864
Est vol 922; vol Wed 452; open int 7,891, +10.								
U.S. DOLLAR INDEX (FINEX)—1,000 times USDX								
Sept	89.54	90.50	89.16	90.40 +	.82	98.55	87.05	6,839
Dec	89.82	90.60	89.47	90.65 +	.82	99.00	87.38	3,092
Est vol 1,800; vol Wed 2,874; open int 9,940, −1,636.								
The index: High 90.27; Low 89.00; Close 90.20 + .80								

SOURCE: *Wall Street Journal*, April 8, 1994

exist for them as it does for foreign currency futures. As a result, most foreign currency forward contracts are held to maturity where they are delivered. This, of course, contrasts with standardized futures contracts, which usually are closed prior to expiration, with the holder taking an offsetting position. Also, since currency forward contracts often are written for the customers of a bank, margin requirements usually are not imposed by the bank as they are with futures.

15.3 FOREIGN CURRENCY FUTURES AND FOWARD PRICES

15.3.1 Interest Rate Parity Theorem

The equilibrium currency forward price or forward exchange rate can be determined by the carrying-cost model. In international finance, the carrying-cost model governing the relationship between spot and forward exchange rates is referred as the *interest rate parity theorem* (IRPT). In terms of the IRPT, the forward price of a currency or forward exchange rate (E_f) is equal to the costs of carrying the spot currency (priced at the spot exchange rate of E_0) for the contract's expiration period.

In terms of a U.S. dollar position, carrying a foreign currency for the period (T) would require borrowing $E_0[1/(1 + R_F)^T]$ dollars at the rate R_{US}, where R_F is the foreign risk-free rate, converting the dollars to $1/(1 + R_F)^T$ units of foreign currency at the spot exchange rate of E_0, and investing the currency in the foreign risk-free security yielding rate R_F. At the end of the period, you would have one unit of FC and a debt obligation of $[E_0/(1 + R_F)^T](1 + R_{US})^T$. Thus, the forward price of purchasing one unit of currency should not be different from the debt obligation or the net financing cost of carrying the currency.* If it did, then an arbitrage opportunity would exist. Thus, the equilibrium foreign currency forward price or exchange rate is[†]

$$E_f = E_0 \frac{(1 + R_{US})^T}{(1 + R_F)^T}. \qquad (15.3\text{-}1)$$

Equation (15.3-1) defines the IRPT. It shows that the relationship between the forward and spot exchange rates depends on the relative levels of domestic and foreign interest rates. Specifically, if $R_{US} > R_F$, then from Equation (15.3-1) $E_f > E_0$ and the forward rate is said to be trading at a premium above the spot. On the other hand, if $R_{US} < R_F$, then $E_f < E_0$ and the forward rate is said to be selling at a discount. In the interbank market, the forward premiums and discounts often are quoted as an annual percentage of the spot exchange rate:

$$\text{Annualized forward premium (discount)} = \left(\frac{E_f - E_0}{E_0}\right)\left(\frac{365}{n}\right), \qquad (15.3\text{-}2)$$

where:

n = number of days to expiration on the forward contract.

15.3.2 Covered Interest Arbitrage

If the interest rate parity condition does not hold, an arbitrage opportunity will exist. The arbitrage strategy to apply in such situations is known as *covered interest arbitrage* (CIA). Introduced by John Maynard Keynes, CIA involves taking long and short positions in the currency spot and forward markets, as well as positions in the domestic and foreign money markets.

To illustrate, suppose the annualized U.S. and foreign interest rates are $R_{US} = 4\%$ and $R_F = 6\%$, respectively, and the spot exchange rate is $0.40 per unit of foreign currency (FC). By the IRPT, a one-year forward contract would equal $E_f = $0.392/FC$ and the annualized forward discount would be 2%:

$$E_f = (\$0.40/\text{FC})\frac{1.04}{1.06} = \$0.392/\text{FC}$$

$$\begin{array}{l}\text{Annualized forward} \\ \text{premium (discount)}\end{array} = \left(\frac{\$0.392/\text{FC} - \$0.40/\text{FC}}{\$0.40/\text{FC}}\right)\left(\frac{365}{365}\right) = -.02.$$

---

*In contrast, you could borrow $(1 + R_F)^{-T}$ units of foreign currency at the foreign rate of R_F, buy $E_0(1 + R_F)^{-T}$ dollars, and invest the dollars in a U.S security at rate R_{US}. Doing this would result in a debt of one unit of currency at the end of the period and a dollar return of $E_0(1 + R_F)^{-T}(1 + R_{US})^T$.
[†]For continuous time, the carrying-cost model is $E_f = E_0e^{(R_{US} - R_F)T}$, where R_{US} and R_F are the continuously compounded risk-free rates.

If the actual forward rate in the market (E_f^m) exceeds \$0.392/FC, an arbitrage profit would exist by: (1) borrowing dollars at rate R_{US}, (2) converting the dollar to the foreign currency at E_0, (3) investing the funds in the foreign risk-free security at the rate R_F, and (4) entering a forward contract to sell the foreign currency at the end of the period at the forward rate of E_f^m. For example, if $E_f^m = \$0.40/FC$, an arbitrageur could:

1. Borrow \$40,000 at $R_{US} = 4\%$ [creating a loan obligation at the end of the year of \$41,600 = (\$40,000)(1.04)].

2. Convert the dollars at the spot exchange rate of $E_0 = \$0.40/FC$ to 100,000 FC.

3. Invest the 100,000 FC in the foreign risk-free security at $R_F = .06$ (creating a return of principal and interest of 106,000 FC at the end of the year).

4. Enter a forward contract to sell 106,000 FC at the end of the year at $E_f = \$0.40/FC$.

At the end of the year, the arbitrageur would receive \$42,400 when he sells the 106,000 FC on the forward contract and would owe \$41,600 on his debt obligation, for an arbitrage return of \$800. Such riskless profit opportunities, of course, would lead arbitrageurs to try to implement the CIA strategy. This would cause the contract price on the forward contract to fall (and perhaps the spot price to rise) until riskless profit opportunities disappear. The zero arbitrage profit would occur when the interest rate parity condition (15.3-1) is satisfied.

On the other hand, if the forward rate is below its equilibrium value, then this CIA strategy is reversed. In the example case, if $E_f^m = \$0.38/FC$, an arbitrageur could earn riskless profit by:

1. Borrowing 100,000 FC at $R_F = 6\%$ (creating a 106,000 FC debt).

2. Converting at the spot exchange rate the 100,000 FC to \$40,000.

3. Investing the \$40,000 in a U.S. risk-free security at $R_{US} = .04$.

4. Entering a forward contract to buy 106,000 FC at the end of the year at $E_f^m = \$0.38/FC$ in order to pay the foreign debt obligation.

At the end of the year, the arbitrageur's profit would be \$1320:

$$\$40,000(1.04) - (\$0.38/FC)(106,000 \text{ FC}) = \$1320.$$

As arbitrageurs attempt to implement this strategy, they will push up the price on the forward contract until the arbitrage profit is zero; this occurs when the interest rate parity condition is satisfied. Thus, like the carrying-cost models governing the prices of other commodity and financial forward contracts, the forward exchange rate also is determined by an arbitrage condition.

15.3.3   Hedging Interbank Forward Contracts

Banks often provide forward contracts to their customers, then hedge their forward contracts by taking a position in the spot market. For example, suppose the current dollar/mark exchange rate is \$0.40/DM, the one-year German risk-free rate is 6%, and the one-year U.S. rate is 4%. Using the interest rate parity model, a bank could offer its customers a one-year forward exchange rate of $0.39245283/DM, then hedge the contract by using a CIA strategy.

To see how a bank would hedge its forward position, suppose one of the bank's customers wanted to buy 10,000,000 DM one year from the present. To meet this request without exposing itself to exchange rate risk, the bank provides the customer with a forward contract in which it agrees to sell forward 10,000,000 DM to the customer at the end of one year at the $0.39245283/DM forward price (total cost of $3,924,528). To hedge this short forward position, the bank, in turn, could:

1. Borrow (10,000,000 DM/1.04)($0.39245283) = $3,773,585.
2. Convert the dollars to $3,773,585/($0.40/DM) = 9,433,962 DM.
3. Invest the 9,433,962 DM for one year at $R_F = 6\%$.

At the end of the year, the bank would have 9,433,962 DM(1.06) = 10,000,000 DM and would owe $3,773,585(1.04) = $3,924,528, which would offset the bank's short forward contract position.

On the other hand, suppose the bank's customer wanted to sell 10,000,000 DM at the end of the year. In this case the bank could provide the customer with a forward contract in which the bank agrees to buy 10,000,000 DM at $E_f = $0.39245283/DM. The bank then could hedge this position by reversing the previous strategy: Borrow 9,433,962 DM at $R_F = 6\%$, convert to $3,773,585 at $E_0 = $0.40/DM, and invest in the U.S. risk-free security at $R_{US} = 4\%$. At the end of the year, the bank would owe 10,000,000 DM and would have $3,924,528 in principal and interest, which would offset its long forward position.

In hedging their forward rate contracts, banks are in a position in which they can take advantage of any mispricing that occurs if the forward price does not satisfy the interest rate parity condition. By taking advantage of such opportunities, they will push the forward rate to its equilibrium level. Without the opportunity for arbitrage profits as compensation for providing forward contracts, banks will either charge a commission or request that the customer deposit some funds in a demand deposit account with the bank (i.e., a compensating balance).

15.3.4 Forward Exchange Rates and Expected Spot Exchange Rates

In addition to defining how banks can hedge their forward exchange rate positions, the IRPT also can be used by investors to define the cutoff spot exchange rate that helps determine whether they should invest domestically or internationally.

To illustrate, consider the preceding example in which $R_{US} = 4\%$, $R_F = 6\%$, $E_0 = $0.40/DM, $T = 1$ year, and $E_f = $0.39245283/DM. If an investor knew *with certainty* that exchanges rates one year from now would be $0.39245283/DM, then she would be indifferent to an investment in a one-year U.S. risk-free security yielding 4% and a one-year German risk-free security yielding 6%. If the U.S. investor, though, was certain that the spot exchange rate at the end of the year would exceed $0.39245283/DM, then she would prefer to invest her dollars in the German security rather than in the U.S. security. For example, if a U.S. investor knew with certainty that the expected spot exchange rate at the end of the year, $E(E_T)$, would be $0.41/DM, then she would prefer the German security, in which a rate of 8.65% could be earned, instead of the U.S. security, which pays only 4%.

To attain 8.65%, the investor would have to convert each of her investment dollars to $1/E_0 = 1/\$0.40/\text{DM} = 2.5$ DM and invest the 2.5 DM at $R_F = 6\%$. At the end of the year, the investor then would have $(1/E_0)(1 + R_F) = 2.5(1.06) = 2.65$ DM, which she would be able to convert to $1.0865 if the exchange rate was $0.41/FC. Thus, the dollar investment in the German security would yield a rate of return of 8.65%:

$$\text{Rate} = \frac{(1/E_0)(1 + R_F)E(E_T)}{\$1} - 1$$

$$\text{Rate} = \frac{(1/\$0.40/\text{DM})(1.06)(\$0.41/\text{DM})}{\$1} - 1 = .0865.$$

On the other hand, if a U.S. investor knew with certainty that the exchange rate at the end of the year would be less than $0.39245283/DM, then she would prefer the U.S. risk-free investment to the German one. For example, if $E(E_T) = \$0.39/\text{DM}$, then the investor would earn only 3.35% from the German investment, compared to 4% from the U.S. investment:

$$\text{Rate} = \frac{(1/\$0.40/\text{DM})(1.06)(\$0.39/\text{DM})}{\$1} - 1 = .0335.$$

The example suggests that in a world of certainty, the equilibrium forward rate as specified by the IRPT can be used to define the expected cutoff exchange rate, $E(E_T^c)$, needed to determine whether one should invest in a domestic or a foreign risk-free security. That is:

$$E(E_T^c) = E_f = E_0 \frac{(1 + R_{US})^T}{(1 + R_F)^T}. \tag{15.3-3}$$

In the world of uncertainty where future spot exchange rates are unknown, the required cutoff rate depends on investors' attitudes toward risk. For example, if investors are risk-neutral (requiring no risk premium), then the expected rate from a risky investment would equal the risk-free rate. In this case, the cutoff exchange rate for investors would be the equilibrium forward rate; the forward exchange rate, in turn, would be an unbiased estimate of the expected spot rate.

If investors, though, are risk-averse, as we would expect, then the expected rate from a risky investment would have to exceed the risk-free rate. This would require that the investor's cutoff exchange rate exceed the forward rate. For instance, if risk-averse U.S. investors required an annualized 2% risk premium (RP) in order to invest in a foreign security, then the expected cutoff exchange rate would be $0.40/FC (instead of $E_f = \$0.39245283/\text{DM}$):

$$E(E_T^c) = E_0 \frac{(1 + R_{US} + RP)^T}{(1 + R_F)^T}$$

$$E(E_T^c) = (\$0.40/\text{DM}) \frac{1 + .04 + .02}{1.06}$$

$$E(E_T^c) = \$0.40/\text{DM}.$$

Thus, if investors are risk-averse, then $E(E_T)$ would have to be greater than E_f for them to invest in the risky foreign investment instead of the risk-free domestic investment. In this case, E_f would not be an unbiased estimate of $E(E_T)$.

15.3.5 Currency Futures Prices

As discussed in Chapter 12, a sufficient condition for futures and forward prices to be equal is for short-term interest rates to be constant over time. In the case of currency futures and forward contracts, the requirement for equality is for both the foreign and domestic short-term rates to be constant. If this occurs, then the IRPT can be extended to determining the equilibrium futures exchange rate; if these rates are not stable, though, then the interest rate parity model would be only an estimate of the equilibrium futures price. Empirically, several studies comparing currency futures and forward exchange rates have found no significant differences between them.* Thus, even with market imperfections such as taxes and transaction costs, the IRPT appears to be a good description of what determines both the forward and futures exchange rates.

15.4 CURRENCY SPECULATION

In Chapter 10, we examined how a long position in a currency call (put) option could be used to speculate on an expected increase (decrease) in the exchange rate. Speculating on exchange rates also can be done by taking pure or outright positions in currency futures or forward contracts or by forming an intracommodity or intercommodity currency spread.

15.4.1 Pure Speculative Positions

A speculator anticipating an increase in the spot exchange rate could profit by going long in a currency forward contract or futures; speculators forecasting a decrease in the exchange rate would, in turn, take short futures or forward contract positions.

It should be noted that the profitability from pure speculative positions in currency futures and forward contracts depends not only on forecasting correctly the direction of the change in the spot exchange rate, but also on estimating to some extent the degree of the change. In terms of our illustrative example in which $R_{US} = 4\%$, $R_F = 6\%$, $T = 1$ year, $E_0 = \$0.40/FC$, and $E_f = \$0.392/FC$, if the actual and equilibrium forward rates are equal, then the spot exchange rate would have to decrease by at least 2% (the annualized forward discount) for a speculator to profit from a short position in the forward contract. That is, a 2% decrease in the spot over one year would yield a spot exchange rate equal to the forward exchange rate: $E(E_T) = (1 - .02)(\$0.40/FC) = \$0.392/FC$. On the other hand, a speculator could profit from a long forward position provided the exchange rate did not decrease by more than 2%.

Note that speculating on the spot exchange rate using futures or forward contracts represents an alternative to using the money market. In our example, if

---

*See Park and Chen (1985). A number of empirical studies investigating the validity of the IRPT also has been conducted; see Branson (1979) and Stokes and Neuburger (1979).

a speculator expected the exchange rate to rise over the next year (or at least not decrease past $0.392/FC), then instead of using the futures or forward market he could borrow $40,000, for example, convert the dollars to 100,000 units of FC, and invest FC in the foreign risk-free security at $R_F = 6\%$. If the spot exchange rate was greater than $0.392/FC at the end of the year, then the speculator would earn a profit when he converted the FC back to dollars. For example, if $E_T = \$0.40/FC$, the speculator would realize a profit of 106,000 FC($0.40/FC) − $40,000(1.04) = $800. In contrast, if the speculator expected the spot exchange rate to decrease by more than 2% (such that the spot rate was less than $0.392/FC), then instead of taking a short futures or forward position, he could borrow 100,000 FC, convert to $40,000, and invest in the U.S. security at 4%. If the spot exchange rate decreased to $E_T = \$0.38$ by the end of the year, then the speculator would need only to pay ($0.38/FC)(106,000 FC) = $40,280 to close his foreign loan obligation, leaving him with a profit of $41,600 − $40,380 = $1320.

15.4.2 Currency Futures Spreads

Instead of assuming the risk inherent in an outright futures position, speculators instead can hedge some of their exchange rate risk by forming intercommodity or intracommodity currency spreads. A speculator could form an intercommodity spread by going long and short in different currency futures. For example, if a speculator expects the dollar price of both the Swiss franc and the British pound to increase, she could form an intercommodity spread by going long in the currency with the greater exchange rate elasticity and short in the other currency. Similarly, a U.S. speculator who expects the $/DM exchange rate to change, for example, could form an intracommodity spread by taking a position in a nearby DM currency futures contract and an opposite position in more deferred DM currency futures.*

15.4.3 Cross-Exchange Rate Relations

Currency futures contracts on many exchanges are listed in terms of the U.S. dollar price of a currency. A speculator who trades on such an exchange and wants to speculate on an exchange rate not defined by the dollar could do so by taking two futures positions, with the positions defined by the *cross-exchange rate* relationship between the two currencies and the dollar.

The cross rate defines the relationship between different exchange rates. For example, if the spot DM/$ exchange rate is 2.50 DM/$1 and the FF/$ rate is 4 FF/$1, then the equilibrium DM/FF exchange rate would have to be 0.625 DM/FF:

---

*In forming foreign currency intracommodity spreads, you need to account for foreign and domestic interest rates. If the foreign interest rate exceeds the U.S. rate, then a U.S. spreader expecting an increase in the $/FC exchange rate would need to go long in the short-term contract and short in the longer-term one. On the other hand, if the U.S. rate exceeds the foreign rate, the spreader would need to do the opposite: Go long in the longer-term contract and short in the shorter-term one.

$$2.5 \text{ DM} = \$1 = 4 \text{ FF}$$

$$\frac{2.5 \text{ DM}}{4} = 1 \text{ FF}$$

$$0.625 \text{ DM} = 1 \text{ FF}.$$

If the actual DM/FF exchange rate is not 0.625, then an arbitrage strategy, known as *triangular arbitrage*, can be employed to earn riskless profit. For example, suppose the DM/FF exchange rate is 0.7 DM/FF instead of 0.625 DM/FF. An arbitrageur with a position in dollars could earn a riskless return of $0.12 for each dollar invested by:

1. Buying 4 FF with $1.
2. Converting the 4 FF to 2.8 DM [4 FF(0.7 DM/FF)].
3. Converting the 2.8 DM to $1.12 [2.8 DM($0.40/DM)].

By executing this triangular arbitrage strategy, the arbitrageur would be supplying the exchange market with FF and demanding DM, which would push the DM/FF exchange rate toward 0.625. On the other hand, if the DM/FF exchange rate is at 0.5 (or 2 FF/DM), an arbitrageur could earn $0.25 by:

1. Buying 2.5 DM for $1.
2. Converting the 2.5 DM to 5 FF [(2.5 DM)(2 FF/DM)].
3. Converting the 5 FF to $1.25 [(5 FF)($0.25/FF)].

These actions, in turn, would serve to push the DM/FF exchange rate up toward 0.625.

The triangular arbitrage strategy also can help explain how currency futures priced in terms of dollars can be used to speculate on different exchange rates. To illustrate, again assume that the spot exchange rates are 4 FF/$1 (or $0.25/FF) and 2.5 DM/$ (or $0.40/DM) and that the DM/FF exchange rate is in equilibrium at 0.625 DM/FF. Also assume for simplicity that U.S., German, and French interest rates are equal and, as a result, that the forward exchange rates for the FF and the DM in terms of the dollar equal the spot rates. If a speculator with a position in DM expected the spot DM/FF rate to decrease, then with no DM/FF futures contracts available, the speculator could profit alternatively from a DM/FF exchange rate decrease by:

1. Going long in 2.5-DM forward contracts at $E_f = \$0.40/\text{DM}$.
2. Going short in 4-FF forward contracts at $E_f = \$0.25/\text{FF}$.

If at expiration the DM/FF exchange rate decreases to 0.5, the speculator would earn a profit of 0.5 DM by:

1. Buying 4 FF for 2 DM on the spot (0.5 DM/FF).
2. Selling the 4 FF on the short forward contracts for $1 ($E_f = \$0.25/\text{FF}$).
3. Buying 2.5 DM for $1 on the long forward contracts.

If the spot DM/FF exchange rate increased to 0.7 DM/FF, however, the speculator would have to pay 2.8 DM to buy 4 FF, resulting in a loss of 0.3 DM.

In contrast, if an investor with a DM position expected DM/FF to increase, then he would need to go short in 2.5-DM forward contracts and long in 4-FF forward contracts. If the spot DM/FF exchange rate was 0.7 DM/FF at expiration, then the speculator would earn a profit of 0.3 DM by:

1. Selling 2.5 DM for $1 on the short forward contract (E_f = $0.40/DM).
2. Buying 4 FF for $1 on the long forward contracts (E_f = $0.25/FF).
3. Selling the 4 FF for 2.8 DM on the spot market (E_T = 0.7 DM/FF).

15.5 HEDGING WITH CURRENCY FUTURES AND FORWARD CONTRACTS

In Chapter 10, we examined how foreign currency positions could be hedged with currency options: By going long in a currency call option, you can lock in the maximum dollar costs of a future cash outflow or liability denominated in a foreign currency while still maintaining the chance for lower dollar outlays if the exchange rate decreases. In contrast, by going long in a currency put, you can lock in the minimum dollar value of a future inflow or asset denominated in foreign currency while still maintaining the possibility of a greater dollar inflows in case the exchange rate increases. With foreign currency futures and forward contracts, the domestic currency value of future cash flows or the future dollar value of assets and liabilities denominated in another currency can be locked in. Unlike option hedging, however, no exchange rate gains exist when futures or forward contracts are used.

15.5.1 Hedging Future Currency Cash Flows with a Naive Hedge

Large multinational corporations usually hedge their currency positions in the interbank forward market, whereas smaller companies, some portfolio managers, and individuals often use the futures markets. Either way, the currency position usually is hedged with a naive hedging model in which the number of futures or forward contracts is equal to the value of the foreign currency position to be hedged.

To illustrate currency hedging, consider the option hedging example presented in Chapter 10 (Section 10.4.3) in which a U.S. company expected a receipt of 625,000 DM at the end of three months. Instead of hedging with a DM put (as presented in Chapter 10), suppose the company decides to hedge its receipt with a DM futures contracts expiring at the end of three months, currently trading at E_f = $0.40/DM when the spot exchange rate is at E_0 = $.40/DM. Since the contract size on the DM futures contract is 125,000 DM, the company would need to go short in five DM contracts, if it uses a naive hedging approach:

$$\frac{(\$0.40/DM)(625,000 \text{ DM})}{(\$0.40/DM)(125,000 \text{ DM})} = 5.$$

Doing this, the company would, in turn, ensure itself of a $250,000 receipt at expiration when it converts its 625,000 DM to dollars at the spot $/DM exchange rate and closes its short futures position (see Table 15.5-1).

TABLE 15.5-1

Hedging a Future DM Receipt with DM Futures Contracts			
Revenue at expiration = 625,000 DM. *Hedge:* short in five DM futures contracts (contract size of 125,000 DM) at E_f = \$0.40/DM			
(1) SPOT EXCHANGE RATE AT EXPIRATION: E_T = \$/DM	(2) FUTURES CASH FLOW: $5[(\$0.40/\text{DM}) - E_T](125{,}000 \text{ DM})$	(3) DOLLAR VALUE OF 625,000 DM: $(E_T)(625{,}000 \text{ DM})$	(4) TOTAL REVENUE (2) + (3)
\$0.30/DM	\$62,500	\$187,500	\$250,000
0.35/DM	31,250	218,750	250,000
0.40/DM	0	250,000	250,000
0.45/DM	− 31,250	281,250	250,000
0.50/DM	− 62,500	312,500	250,000

TABLE 15.5-2

Hedging a Future DM Cost with DM Futures Contracts			
Debt at expiration = 625,000 DM. *Hedge:* long in five DM futures contracts (contract size of 125,000 DM) at E_f = \$0.40/DM			
(1) SPOT EXCHANGE RATE AT EXPIRATION: E_T = \$/DM	(2) FUTURES CASH FLOW: $5[E_T - (\$0.40/\text{DM})](125{,}000 \text{ DM})$	(3) DOLLAR COST OF 625,000 DM: $(E_T)(625{,}000 \text{ DM})$	(4) TOTAL COSTS (3) − (2)
\$0.30/DM	− \$62,500	\$187,500	\$250,000
0.35/DM	− 31,250	218,750	250,000
0.40/DM	0	250,000	250,000
0.45/DM	31,250	281,250	250,000
0.50/DM	62,500	312,500	250,000

If a multinational company has a future debt obligation that it is required to pay in foreign currency, then it could lock in the dollar cost of the obligation by taking a long futures or forward position. This hedging strategy can be seen in Table 15.5-2, where the dollar costs of purchasing 625,000 DM at the end of three months is hedged with five long DM contracts priced at E_f = \$0.40/DM. In this case, the net costs of purchasing the marks on the spot and closing the futures is \$250,000, regardless of the spot exchange rate.

Note, in the preceding examples, the hedge involves a foreign currency conversion to or from dollars. However, if the hedge does not involve the dollar and the only currency futures and forward contracts available are those defined in dollars, then the cross-exchange rate relationship discussed earlier needs to be used to set up the appropriate hedge. For example, suppose a German investor wanted to lock in the DM value of her future dividend receipt of 4 FF from Michelin stock using the futures contract available on the IMM. To do this, the investor would need to take positions in the $/DM and $/FF futures contracts, and use the cross-exchange rate relationship to define each futures position. If the futures rates are $0.25/FF and $0.40/DM, then the German investor would need to take a short position in four FF futures at $E_f = \$0.25/FF$, and a long position in 2.5 DM at $E_f = \$0.40/DM$. By doing this, the investor would be able to lock in a receipt of 2.5 DM when she converts the 4 FF to $1 on the short position, then converts the $1 to 2.5 DM on the long position.

15.5.2   Hedging International Portfolios

Currency futures, forward, and option contracts often are used by portfolio managers to immunize their international portfolios against exchange rate risk. For example, suppose a U.S. investor who owned 1000 shares of a French stock worth 2500 FF per share wanted to hedge the dollar value of his stock. Suppose the $/FF spot and three-month IMM futures exchange rates are both $0.15/FF (or 6.6667 FF/$), making the current dollar value of the stock worth:

$$(\$0.15/FF)(1000)(2500 \text{ FF}) = \$375,000.$$

If the investor wanted to hedge the dollar value of the stock at the end of three months against exchange rate risk, he would need to go short in ten FF futures contracts expiring in three months (contract size is 250,000 FF):

$$\frac{\$375,000}{(\$0.15/FF)(250,000 \text{ FF})} = 10.$$

If, at the end of three months, no change in the price of the French stock occurred, then the futures-hedged dollar value of the stock would be $375,000, irrespective of the spot $/FF exchange rate. If the $/FF rate decreased by 10% over the period, from $0.15/FF to $0.135/FF, then the dollar value of the stock also would decrease by 10%, from $375,000 to $337,500; this decrease, though, would be offset by a $37,500 profit:

$$10(250,000 \text{ FF})[(\$0.15/FF) - (\$0.135/FF)] = \$37,500.$$

Hedging with currency futures or forward contracts allows international investors to focus on selecting stocks or portfolios without having to worry about short-run changes in the exchange rate. For instance, in our example if the price of the French stock increased by 5% from 2500 FF to 2625 FF at the same time the $/FF exchange rate decreased by 10%, then an unhedged position would lose 5.5% in dollars:

$$\text{Rate} = \frac{[(\$0.135/FF)(1000)(2625 \text{ FF})] - [(\$0.150/FF)(1000)(2500 \text{ FF})]}{(\$0.150/FF)(1000)(2500 \text{ FF})}$$

$$\text{Rate} = \frac{\$354,375 - \$375,000}{\$375,000} = -.055.$$

If the position is hedged with 10-FF futures contracts, however, a $37,500 futures profit would exist, and the rate of return on the exchange-rate hedged investment would be 4.5%:

$$\text{Rate} = \frac{(\$354,375 - \$375,500) + \$37,500}{\$375,000} = .045.$$

Thus, the futures hedge allows the investor to profit from good stock selection.

The rate of return in dollars earned from the currency-hedged stock in this example is less than the 5% FF increase in the stock price. This is because a naive hedge protects only the initial value; dividends and stock appreciation are not hedged against exchange rate risk. To hedge stock price changes against exchange rate changes would require knowing the correlation between the exchange rate and the stock price.

15.6   CONCLUSION

The flexible exchange rate system that began in 1972 made it necessary for multinational corporations, international investors, and international organizations to deal with the problems of exchange rate risk. To this end, forward contracts on the interbank market, futures contracts on the exchanges, and currency options have provided these entities with a relatively effective tool for reducing exchange rate risk.

KEY TERMS

interest rate parity theorem   cross-exchange rate
covered interest arbitrage   triangular arbitrage

SELECTED REFERENCES

Aliber, R. "The Interest Rate Parity Theorem: A Reinterpretation." *Journal of Political Economy* (Dec. 1973): 1451–1459.

Branson, W. "The Minimum Covered Interest Differential Needed for International Arbitrage Activity." *Journal of Political Economy* (Dec. 1979): 1029–1034.

Chance, D. *Options and Futures*. Chicago: Dryden Press, 1991, pp. 439–465.

Cornell, B. "Spot Rates, Forward Rates, and Exchange Market Efficiency." *Journal of Financial Economics* (Aug. 1977): 55–65.

Cornell, B., and Reinganum, M. "Forward and Futures Prices: Evidence from the Foreign Exchange Markets." *Journal of Finance* 36 (Dec. 1981): 1035–1045.

Grammatikos, T., and Saunders, A. "Stability and the Hedging Performance of Foreign Currency Futures." *Journal of Futures Markets* (Fall 1983): 295–305.

Hill, J., and Schneewis, T. "The Hedging Effectiveness of Foreign Currency Futures." *Journal of Financial Research* (Spring 1982): 95–104.

Huang, R. "Some Alternative Tests of Forward Exchange Rates as Predictors of Future Spot Rates." *Journal of International Money and Finance* (Aug. 1984): 153–178.

Huang, R. "An Analysis of Intertemporal Pricing for Forward Foreign Exchange Contracts." *Journal of Finance* 44 (Mar. 1989): 183–194.

Johnson, R., Hultman, C., and Zuber, R. "Currency Cocktails and Exchange Rate Stability." *Columbia Journal of World Business* 14 (Winter 1979): 117–126.

Kidwell, D., Marr, W., and Thompson, R. "Eurodollar Bonds: Alternative Financing for U.S. Companies." *Financial Management* 14 (Winter 1985): 18–27.

Kohlhagen, S. "The Forward Rate as an Unbiased Predictor of the Future Spot Rate." *Columbia Journal of World Business* (Winter 1979): 77–85.

Kolers, T., and Simpson, W. "A Comparison of the Forecast Accuracy of the Futures and Forward Markets for Foreign Exchange." *Applied Economics* (July 1987): 961–967.

Madura, J., and Nosari, E. "Utilizing Currency Portfolios to Mitigate Exchange Rate Risk." *Columbia Journal of World Business* (Spring 1984): 96–99.

Panton, D., and Joy, M. "Empirical Evidence on International Monetary Market Currency Futures." *Journal of International Business Studies* (Fall 1978): 59–68.

Papdia, F. "Forward Exchange Rates as Predictors of Future Spot Rates and the Efficiency of the Foreign Exchange Market." *Journal of Banking and Finance* (June 1981): 217–240.

Park, H., and Chen, A. "Differences Between Futures and Forward Prices: A Further Examination of the Marking-to-the-Market Effects." *Journal of Futures Markets* (Spring 1985): 77–85.

Solnik, Bruno. *International Investments*. Reading, Mass.: Addison-Wesley, 1988.

Stokes, H., and Neuburger, H. "Interest Arbitrage, Forward Speculation and the Determination of the Forward Exchange Rate." *Columbia Journal of World Business* 4 (1979): 86–99.

Swanson, P., and Caples, S. "Hedging Foreign Exchange Risk Using Forward Exchange Markets: An Extension." *Journal of International Business Studies* (Spring 1987): 75–82.

PROBLEMS AND QUESTIONS

1. Explain the differences between the forward market and the futures market for foreign currency.

2. Suppose the spot dollar/Swiss franc exchange rate is $0.375/SF, the U.S. risk-free rate is 6% (annual), and the Swiss risk-free rate is 8%.

   a. Assuming the interest rate parity theorem holds, what should be the equilibrium 90-day $/SF forward rate?

b. What is the annualized forward discount, or premium?

c. Suppose a U.S. bank provides one of its business customers with a forward contract in which the customer agrees to sell the bank 15 million Swiss francs at the end of 90 days at $E_f = \$0.3732756/SF$. Assuming the bank can borrow and lend dollars and Swiss francs at the given risk-free rates, explain how the bank would hedge its forward position.

d. Explain the forward contract the bank would provide the business customer and how it would hedge the contract if its business customer wanted to buy 15M SF at the end of 90 days instead of selling SF.

3. Explain why a risk-neutral U.S. investor would be indifferent between a 90-day U.S. investment in a risk-free security at 7% (annual) and a 90-day German risk-free investment at 5% if the investor expected the spot exchange rate at the end of 90 days to equal the forward rate as determined by the IRPT. In your explanation assume the current spot exchange rate is $0.35/DM.

4. Suppose the U.S. investor in Problem 3 is risk-averse instead of risk-neutral, and wants a risk premium of 2% (annual) for assuming the exchange rate risk on the international investment.

a. Find the expected spot exchange rate that would make the risk-averse investor indifferent between the U.S. and German 90-day risk-free investments.

b. Demonstrate that the investor would earn that return if this expected exchange rate is realized.

5. Given the following spot exchange rates: 2.75 DM/$ and $0.375/SF:

a. What is the DM/SF exchange rate?

b. Describe the triangular arbitrage strategy a U.S. arbitrageur could pursue if the DM price of a SF was 1.1 DM/SF.

c. Describe the triangular arbitrage strategy a U.S. arbitrageur would pursue if the DM price of a SF was 1.01 DM/SF.

6. Given the following:

$$E_0 = \$1.80/FC$$

$$E_f = \$1.80 \text{ (one-year contract)}$$

$$R_{US} = 10\% \text{ (annual)}$$

$$R_F = 10\% \text{ (annual)}$$

a. Explain how you would speculate on the FC using the forward market if you expected the spot exchange rate to be $1.70/FC at the end of the year.

b. Explain how you would speculate on the FC using the money market if you expected the spot exchange rate to be $1.70/FC at the end of the year (assume you can borrow and lend at $R_{US} = R_F = 10\%$).

c. Explain how you would speculate on the FC using the forward market if you expected the spot exchange rate to be $1.90/FC at the end of the year.

d. Explain how you would speculate on the FC using the money market if you expected the spot exchange rate to be $1.90/FC at the end of the year (assume you can borrow and lend at $R_{US} = R_F = 10\%$).

7. Given the following:

$/CD exchange = $0.8333/CD or CD/$ = $1.20/CD/$

$/DM exchange = $0.666/DM or DM/$ = 1.5/DM/$

$R = 6\%$ (annual) in U.S., Canada, and Germany

a. Determine the equilibrium spot and one-year forward CD/DM exchange rates.

b. Explain how Canadian speculators could use a CD/DM forward contract to profit if they expected the spot CD/DM rate to decrease from 0.8 CD/DM to 0.75 CD/DM.

c. Explain how U.S. speculators would use the IMM futures market if they also expected the CD/DM spot exchange rate to decrease to 0.75 CD/DM and expected no change in the $/DM rate (assume the futures and forward rates are the same).

8. B. P. Larken just signed a contract to play professional basketball in France for the Paris Stars. The team owner has agreed to pay his living expenses for the year and an annual salary of 500,000 FF, with half of the payment to be paid in December and the other half in March. Mr. Larken plans to play one year, then return to the United States. He would like to hedge the dollar value of his contract. Currently, the spot $/FF exchange rate is $0.16666/FF, the French risk-free rate is 8% (annual), the U.S. risk-free rate is 6%, forward rates offered by U.S. and French banks are governed by the IRPT, and the December payment date is .25 of a year away and the March date is .5.

a. Explain how Mr. Larken could hedge the dollar value of his salary using forward contracts.

b. Suppose Mr. Larken could not find a bank to provide him with a forward contract. Explain how he could alternatively hedge his salary against exchange rate risk by using the money market. Assume Mr. Larken can borrow FF at 8% and can invest dollars at 6%.

c. Suppose the December FF futures contract is trading on the IMM exchange at $0.1662752 (contract size = 250,000 FF). Explain how Mr. Larken could hedge his December salary against exchange rate risk by using the December contract. In your explanation, assume that Mr. Larken will close his futures position at expiration, convert his 250,000 FF on the spot, and that the December futures expiration date and payment date coincide. Evaluate his position by assuming possible spot $/FF exchange rates at expiration of $0.14/FF, $0.15/FF, $0.16/FF, $0.17/FF, and $0.18/FF.

9. The Parson Company is a U.S. company with jewelry stores located across the United States. In April, the company signs a contract with Swiss Watch, Inc., to purchase 100,000 watches in June ($T = .25$ per year) and 100,000 in December ($T = .75$ per year) at the cost of 30 SF per watch, with the payments to be made at the times of the June and December deliveries. Currently, U.S. and Swiss risk-free interest rates are both 6% (annual), the $/SF spot exchange rate is $0.66667/SF, and the $/SF forward rates and the IMM futures rate are governed by the IRPT.

   a. Explain how the Parson Company could hedge its dollars costs of the watches against exchange rate risk using forward contracts.

   b. Explain how the Parson Company could hedge its June payment by using the money market. Assume it can borrow and lend dollars and Swiss francs at 6%.

   c. Explain how the Parson Company could hedge its December payment by taking a position in the IMM's SF futures contract (contract size is 125,000 SF). Evaluate the hedge at possible spot exchange rates at the December expiration of $0.60/SF and $0.70/SF.

10. A U.S. investor bought one share of Heinken stock (listed on the Amsterdam Exchange) for 200 guilders (g) when the dollar/guilder spot exchange rate was $0.5/g. The investor expects the stock to pay a dividend worth 5 guilders and to appreciate by 10% after one year.

   a. Calculate the one-year expected rate of return on the stock for an investment made in guilders.

   b. Calculate the possible one-year expected rates of return on the stock in terms of a dollar investment. Assume possible end-of-the-year exchange rates of $0.40/g, $0.45/g, $0.50/g, and $0.55/g.

   c. If the U.S. risk-free rate was 7% (annual) and the Netherlands risk-free rate was 5%, what would be the one-year forward rate a bank could provide the investor if it provides forward contracts based on the IRPT?

   d. What would be the investor's possible expected rates of return if he hedged the dollar price of the stock (200 g) by going short in a forward contract as determined by the IRPT? Evaluate at possible exchange rates of $0.40/g, $0.45/g, $0.50/g, and $0.55/g.

PART V

Futures Options, Swaps, and Other Derivative Securities

CHAPTER 16

Options and Futures Relations and Options on Futures Contracts

16.1 INTRODUCTION

Up to now, we have examined futures and option contracts separately. As we might expect, when an asset has both an option and a futures contract, the put, call, futures, and spot prices all are related to each other. In this chapter, we continue our analysis of derivative securities by examining the relationships among options, futures, and spot securities. We begin by examining the relation between options and futures as defined by the put-call-futures parity model and by constructing the BOPM with a futures contract instead of a spot position in the underlying asset. After delineating these models, we will examine the market for another derivative security—options on futures contracts.

16.2 OPTION PRICING RELATIONS IN TERMS OF FUTURES*

16.2.1 Put-Call-Futures Parity

The put-call parity model derived in Chapter 4 determined the equilibrium relationship between put and call prices from a conversion (or reversal) strategy consisting of long positions in the underlying asset and a European put and a short position in a European call. Recall that in the case of a non-dividend-paying stock, the value of the conversion at expiration equals the options' exercise price,

---

*In this chapter, we will treat futures and forward contracts as identical. Recall that for pricing purposes, the contracts can be treated as the same, provided short-term interest rates are constant.

regardless of the price on the underlying spot asset. As a result, in equilibrium the value of the conversion equals the present value of a riskless pure discount bond with a face value equal to the exercise price.

The **put-call-futures parity model** is similar to the put-call parity model. As the name implies, though, the put-call-futures parity model is derived using a futures position on the options' underlying asset instead of a position on the spot or cash asset. The model's conversion strategy consists of a long position in a futures contract at price f_0 and a synthetic short futures position formed by buying a European put and selling a European call on the futures' underlying spot security, with the options having the same expiration date as the futures contract. As shown in Table 16.2-1, with the price of the expiring futures contract (f_T) equal to the spot price on the underlying asset (S_T) at expiration, the value of the conversion formed with a long position in a futures contract is $X - f_0$ at expiration, regardless of the spot price. Thus, the equilibrium value of the conversion with a futures position is equal to the value of a riskless pure discount bond with a face value of $X - f_0$ and maturity of T. That is:

$$P_0^e - C_0^e = (X - f_0)(1 + R)^{-T}, \qquad (16.2\text{-}1)$$

where the initial value of the futures contract is zero. If the equilibrium condition (16.2-1) for put-call-futures parity does not hold, then an arbitrage opportunity will exist by taking a position in the put and the futures contract and an opposite position in the call and a riskless bond with face value equal to $X - f_0$.

16.2.2   Equivalence of Put-Call-Spot and Put-Call-Futures Models

The put-call-futures parity model defines the equilibrium relationship between call, put, and futures prices. If the carrying-cost model holds in which $f_0 = S_0(1 + R)^T$, then the put-call-futures parity model and the put-call parity model defined for the underlying spot will be equivalent. The equivalence of the models can be shown algebraically simply by substituting $S_0(1 + R)^T$ for f_0 in Equation (16.2-1) to obtain the put-call parity equation defined in terms of the spot asset:

$$P_0^e - C_0^e = [X - S_0(1 + R)^T](1 + R)^{-T} = X(1 + R)^{-T} - S_0.$$

TABLE 16.2-1

Put-Call-Futures Parity Conversion			
$\{+f_0, +P_0^e, -C_0^e\}$			
		EXPIRATION CASH FLOW	
POSITION	INVESTMENT	$S_T < X$	$S_T = X$	$S_T > X$
Long futures	0	$S_T - f_0$	$S_T - f_0$	$S_T - f_0$
Long put	P_0^e	$X - S_T$	0	0
Short call	$-C_0^e$	0	0	$-(S_T - X)$
Total	$P_0^e - C_0^e$	$X - f_0$	$X - f_0$	$X - f_0$

Note that for foreign currency positions, the put-call-spot parity and put-call-futures parity also include the foreign interest rate. That is, the foreign currency put-call-futures model is:

$$P_0^e - C_0^e = (X - E_{f0})(1 + R_{US})^{-T}, \qquad (16.2\text{-}2)$$

where:

$$E_{f0} = \text{forward exchange rate.}$$

Recall from Chapter 15 that the interest rate parity condition is $E_{f0} = E_0(1 + R_{US})^T(1 + R_F)^{-T}$. By substituting this expression for E_{f0} in Equation (16.2-2), we obtain the foreign currency put-call-parity condition derived earlier in Chapter 10:

$$P_0^e - C_0^e = [X - E_0(1 + R_{US})^T(1 + R_F)^{-T}](1 + R_{US})^{-T}$$

$$P_0^e - C_0^e + E_0(1 + R_F)^{-T} = X(1 + R_{US})^{-T}.$$

16.3 BINOMIAL OPTION PRICING MODEL IN TERMS OF FUTURES POSITIONS

If a European option's underlying asset also has a futures contract, then, like the preceding put-call parity relations, the OPM can be specified in terms of the futures position. Moreover, if the carrying-cost model holds and the futures contract and the option contract expire at the same time, then the OPM specified in terms of futures will equal the OPM defined in terms of the underlying spot asset.

To illustrate, consider the foreign currency pricing example presented in Chapter 10. In that example, we used a single-period BOPM to determine the equilibrium price of $C_0^* = \$0.066/FC$ on a $1.50 European call option on a foreign currency (FC). In that example, we assumed: the spot exchange rate was at $1.50/FC; the u and d parameter values on the spot exchange rate were 1.1 and .95, respectively; the foreign risk-free rate for the period was 3%; and the period U.S. rate was 5%. To price this same FC call option using a foreign currency futures (or a forward contract) position instead of a spot position, we first need to determine the value of a replicating portfolio consisting of the FC futures position and a debt of B_0 dollars.

In terms of the example, assume there is a futures contract on the FC that expires at the end of the period and that the price on the futures contract is determined by the interest rate parity model. As shown in Table 16.3-1, with $E_0 = \$1.50/FC$, $r_{US} = 1 + R_{US} = 1.05$, and $r_F = 1 + R_F = 1.03$, the current price on the futures contract (or the futures exchange rate) would be $E_{f0} = \$1.529/FC$, and the two possible values at expiration from a long position in the futures contract would be $0.121 and -0.104. The possible call values of

$$C_u = \text{Max}[\$1.65 - \$1.50, 0] = \$0.15/FC \qquad \text{and} \qquad C_d = \text{Max}[\$1.425 - \$1.50, 0] = 0$$

TABLE 16.3-1

Single-Period Foreign Currency Binomial Option Pricing Model with Currency Futures

$E_0 = \$1.50/FC$, $u = 1.1$, $d = .95$, $R_{US} = .05$, $R_F = .03$, $X = \$1.50$

Spot: $E_T = uE_0 = 1.1(\$1.50) = \$1.65/FC$
Long futures position $= uE_0 - E_{f0}$
$= (\$1.65/FC) - (\$1.529/FC) = \$0.121/FC$
Call position: $C_u = \text{Max}[uE_0 - X, 0]$
$C_u = \text{Max}[(\$1.65/FC) - (\$1.50/FC), 0] = \$0.15/FC$

Spot: $E_0 = \$1.50/FC$
Futures: $E_{f0} = E_0\left(\frac{r_{US}}{r_F}\right)$
$E_{f0} = (\$1.50/FC)\left(\frac{1.05}{1.03}\right) = \$1.529/FC$

Call: $C_0^* = \frac{pC_u + (1-p)(d)}{r_{US}}$

$C_0^* = \frac{.4622(\$0.15) + .5378(0)}{1.05} = \$0.066$

Spot: $E_T = dE_0 = .95(\$1.50) = \$1.425/FC$
Long futures position $= dE_0 - E_{f0}$
$= (\$1.425/FC) - (\$1.529/FC) = -\$0.104/FC$
Call position: $C_d = \text{Max}[dE_0 - X, 0]$
$C_d = \text{Max}[(\$1.425/FC) - (\$1.50/FC), 0] = 0$

can be replicated with a FC futures position and debt of B_0 dollars by forming a replicating portfolio consisting of $H_{f0}^* = .6667$ long futures contracts at $E_{f0} = \$1.529/FC$ and a debt of $B_0^* = -\$0.066$ (where the negative sign means an investment of $0.066). Formally, to construct this replicating portfolio with futures requires:

$$H_{f0}(uE_0 - E_{f0}) - B_0r_{US} = C_u \qquad (16.3-1)$$
$$H_{f0}(dE_0 - E_{f0}) - B_0r_{US} = C_d.$$

The H_{f0}^* and B_0^* that satisfy Equation set (16.3-1) are:

$$H_{f0}^* = \frac{C_u - C_d}{E_0(u - d)} \qquad (16.3-2)$$

$$B_0^* = \frac{C_u(dE_0 - E_{f0}) - C_d(uE_0 - E_{f0})}{r_{US}E_0(u - d)}. \qquad (16.3-3)$$

In terms of the example:

$$H_{f0}^* = \frac{\$0.15 - 0}{\$1.50(1.1 - .95)} = .6667$$

$$B_0^* = \frac{\$0.15(\$1.425 - \$1.529) - 0(\$1.65 - \$1.529)}{(1.05)(\$1.50)(1.1 - .95)} = -\$0.066.$$

Given the replicating portfolio, the equilibrium FC call price is found by setting the FC call price equal to the current value of the replicating portfolio. (In doing this, recall that the futures contract does not have an initial value.) Thus, the equilibrium price on the FC call is:

$$C_0^* = H_{f0}^*(0) - B_0^*, \tag{16.3-4}$$

or, upon substituting Equation (16.3-3) for B_0^*:

$$C_0^* = -\frac{C_u(dE_0 - E_{f0}) - C_d(uE_0 - E_{f0})}{r_{US}E_0(u - d)}$$

$$r_{US}C_0^* = C_u\left[\frac{E_{f0} - dE_0}{E_0(u - d)}\right] + C_d\left[\frac{uE_0 - E_{f0}}{E_0(u - d)}\right]$$

$$C_0^* = \frac{1}{r_{US}}[pC_u + (1 - p)C_u], \tag{16.3-5}$$

where:

$$p = \frac{E_{f0} - dE_0}{E_0(u - d)}.$$

In terms of the example:

$$C_0^* = -B_0^* = -(-\$0.066) = \$0.066,$$

or

$$C_0^* = \frac{.4622(\$0.15) + (.5378)(0)}{1.05} = \$0.066,$$

where:

$$p = \frac{E_{f0} - dE_0}{E_0(u - d)} = \frac{\$1.529 - .95(\$1.50)}{\$1.50(1.1 - .95)} = .4622.$$

Note that the equilibrium call price of $0.066 is the same price obtained earlier with the foreign currency BOPM specified in terms of a spot exchange rate position. Formally, the equality between this BOPM with futures and the spot BOPM derived in Chapter 10 can be seen by substituting $E_0(r_{US}/r_F)$ (interest rate parity) for E_{f0} in Equation (16.3-5):

$$p = \frac{E_0[(r_{US}/r_F) - (r_F/r_F)d]}{E_0(u - d)} = \frac{r_{US} - r_F d}{r_F(u - d)}.$$

Thus, Equation (16.3-5) is the same as the equation obtained earlier for the foreign currency BOPM using the spot exchange rate.

16.3.1   Binomial Option Pricing Model Arbitrage Strategy Using Futures

In the preceding case, if the market price of the call is not equal to $0.066, then riskless profit can be earned using an arbitrage strategy with a futures position

TABLE 16.3-2

Single-Period BOPM Arbitrage Strategy Using Futures	
$C_0^m > C_0^*$	
POSITION	STRATEGY
Short call	Sell call at $C_0^m = \$.075$.
Futures	Take a long position in $H_{f0}^* = .6667$ FC futures contracts at $E_{f0} = \$1.529/FC$.
Investment	Invest $B_0^* = \$0.066$ in riskless security.
Investment	Invest excess of $C_0^m - C_0^* = \$0.075 - \$0.066 = \$0.009$ in riskless security.

	END-OF-THE-PERIOD CASH FLOW	
POSITION	$C_u = \$0.15, E_T = f_T = \$1.65/FC$	$C_d = 0, E_T = f_T = \$1.425/FC$
Short call	$= -\$0.15$	$= 0$
Futures	$.6667(\$1.65 - \$1.529) = \$0.0807$	$.6667(\$1.425 - \$1.529) = -\$0.0693$
Investment	$\$.066(1.05) = \$0.0693$	$\$.066(1.05) = \$0.0693$
Investment	$(\$0.075 - \$0.066)1.05 = \$0.0094$	$(\$.075 - \$.066)1.05 = \$0.0094$
Cash Flow	$= \$0.0094$	$= \$0.0094$

instead of a spot. For example, if $C_0^m = \$0.075$, then as shown in Table 16.3-2, an arbitrageur could earn a riskless profit of $\$0.0094$ by:

1. Selling the call at $C_0^m = \$.075$.
2. Taking a long position in $H_{f0}^* = .6667$ currency futures contracts at $E_{f0} = \$1.529$.
3. Investing $\$0.066 \ (-B_0^*)$ plus $C_0^m - C_0^* = \$0.075 - \$0.066 = \$0.009$ in a riskless security.

The arbitrage cash flow of $\$0.0094/FC$ is the same arbitrage flow earned using the spot FC position (allow for some rounding errors; see Section 10.5.3). Using futures or forward contracts instead of a spot position, however, simplifies the arbitrage strategy. Recall that with mispriced foreign currency options, the arbitrage strategy using the spot foreign currency market entails combining the option position with positions in the spot currency market and the spot domestic and foreign money markets. Using futures, arbitrageurs avoid having to use both of these markets.

Similar pricing and arbitrage strategies with futures also apply for interest rate and stock index options. These relations are brought out in several problems at the end of this chapter.*

---

*In the case of stock index options, the program trading strategies described in Chapter 13 in terms of proxy portfolios can be constructed more easily using futures contracts. This point is highlighted in Problem 9 at the end of this chapter.

16.4 FUTURES OPTIONS

16.4.1   Characteristics of Futures Options

Options on futures contracts (also called *options on futures, futures options*, and *commodity options*) are option contracts that give the holder the right to take a position in a futures contract.

A call option on a futures contract gives the holder the right to take a long position in the underlying futures contract when he exercises, and requires the writer to take the short position in the futures if she is assigned. Upon exercise, the holder of a futures call option takes a long position in the futures contract at the *current* futures price, and the assigned writer takes the short position. The writer then pays the holder the difference between the current futures price and the exercise price.

A put option on a futures contract entitles the holder to take a short futures position and the assigned writer the long position. Thus, whenever the put holder exercises, he takes a short futures position at the *current* futures price, and the assigned writer takes the long position and pays the holder the difference between the exercise price and the current futures price.

Like all option positions, the futures option buyer pays an option premium in full (i.e., no margin purchases are allowed) for the right to exercise. The writer, in turn, receives a credit when she sells the option, and is subject to initial and maintenance margin requirements (similar to those described in Chapter 2). If the option is exercised, both the holder and the assigned writer are marked to market on the futures positions.

16.4.2   Market for Futures Options

Before 1936, the U.S. futures exchanges offered futures options for a number of years. In 1936, however, the instruments were banned when U.S. security regulations were tightened following the 1929 stock market crash.* The current U.S. market for futures options began in 1982 when the Commodity Futures Trading Commission (CFTC) initiated a pilot program in which it allowed each futures exchange to offer one option on one of its futures contracts. In 1987, the CFTC gave the exchanges permanent authority to offer futures options.

A number of futures options contracts are listed in Table 16.4-1, and the price quotes on several futures options as they appear in the WSJ are shown in Exhibit 16.4-1. Currently, the most popular futures options are the options on the financial futures: SP 500, T-bond, T-note, T-bill, Eurodollar deposit, and the major foreign currencies. Many of the these contracts have expiration months, position limits, and contract specifications similar to their underlying futures contracts. A number of futures options contracts, though, do not have the same expiration date as their underlying futures contract. For example, options on Treasury-bond futures expire before the futures contract. In addition to options on financial futures contracts,

---

*Futures options have been available on foreign exchanges for a number of years.

TABLE 16.4-1

Select Futures Options		
UNDERLYING FUTURES CONTRACT	EXCHANGE*	CONTRACT SIZE
Financials		
Treasury bonds	CBT	$100,000
Treasury notes	CBT	$100,000
Municipal bond index	CBT	$100,000
Mortgage-backed securities	CBT	$100,000
Eurodollars	IMM	$1,000,000
Treasury bills	IMM	$1,000,000
SP 500 index	CME	$500 (Index)
NYFE Composite Index	NYFE	$500 (Index)
Commodities		
Corn	CBT	5,000 bu
Soybeans	CBT	5,000 bu
Wheat	CBT	5,000 bu
Gasoline, unleaded	NYMEX	42,000 gal
Feeder cattle	CME	44,000 lb
Pork bellies	CME	40,000 lb
Copper	COMEX	25,000 lb
Gold	COMEX	100 troy oz
Silver	COMEX	5,000 troy oz
Silver	CBT	1,000 troy oz
Lumber	CME	150,000 bd ft
Currencies		
Australian dollar	IMM	$100,000 AD
British pound	IMM	62,500 BP
Canadian dollar	IMM	100,000 CD
German mark	IMM	125,000 DM
Japanese yen	IMM	12,500,000 JY
Swiss franc	IMM	125,000 SF

*CME = Chicago Mercantile Exchange; CBT = Chicago Board of Trade; NYFE = New York Futures Exchange; IMM = International Monetary Market; NYMEX = New York Mercantile Exchange; COMEX = Commodity Exchange.

futures options also are available on gold, precious metals, agriculture commodities, and energy products. As of 1990, options on financial futures accounted for approximately 40% of the total volume of futures options, with foreign currency futures and agriculture futures representing approximately 20% each, energy futures, one of the fastest growing contracts, accounting for 15%, and metals, approximately 5%.

16.4.3   Differences Between Spot Options and Futures Options

As we will see, the pricing models for spot options and futures options show that these two instruments are equivalent if the spot options and the futures contract expire at the same time, the carrying-cost model holds, and the options are

EXHIBIT 16.4-1

Futures Options Quotes
from the *Wall Street
Journal*

FUTURES OPTIONS PRICES

Thursday, July 28, 1994.

AGRICULTURAL

CORN (CBT)
5,000 bu.; cents per bu.

Strike	Calls – Settle			Puts – Settle		
Price	Sep	Dec	Mar	Sep	Dec	Mar
200	16	20	28	⅛	1	....
210	8	12½	19¼	1⅜	3⅜	1¾
220	3	6⅞	12	6¼	7⅞	5
230	1	3⅞	8	15	14½	10
240	⅜	2¼	5	24½	22⅞	17
250	¼	1¼	3	34¼	31¾	25

Est vol 8,000   Wed 5,427 calls 3,890 puts
Op int Wed   149,960 calls 56,413 puts

WHEAT (CBT)
5,000 bu.; cents per bu.

Strike	Calls – Settle			Puts – Settle		
Price	Sep	Dec	Mar	Sep	Dec	Mar
310	22¼	36¾	44	⅞	2¾	5½
320	13¾	29	36¾	2⅜	5	9
330	7¾	22¼	30	6¼	8	10⅞
340	4	16¾	25¼	12½	12¼	15
350	2	12¾	20	20¼	18	20½
360	1⅛	9½	18½	29¼	25	27

Est vol 3,000   Wed 1,894 calls 1,920 puts
Op int Wed   28,121 calls 19,415 puts

CURRENCY

JAPANESE YEN (CME)
12,500,000 yen; cents per 100 yen

Strike	Calls – Settle			Puts – Settle		
Price	Aug	Sep	Oct	Aug	Sep	Oct
9900	1.49	2.20	....	0.26	0.98	1.18
9950	1.13	1.91	....	0.40	1.18	1.37
10000	0.83	1.65	....	0.60	1.42	1.57
10050	0.58	1.41	....	0.85	1.68	....
10100	0.39	1.21	....	1.16	1.97	2.05
10150	0.26	1.01	....	1.53	2.27	2.32

Est vol 12,325   Wed 5,456 calls 5,395 puts
Op int Wed   63,550 calls 87,689 puts

SWISS FRANC (CME)
125,000 francs; cents per franc

Strike	Calls – Settle			Puts – Settle		
Price	Aug	Sep	Oct	Aug	Sep	Oct
7300	1.32	1.88	....	0.17	0.74	1.00
7350	0.95	1.59	....	0.30	0.94	1.20
7400	0.64	1.31	....	0.50	1.16	1.42
7450	0.41	1.07	....	0.76	1.42	1.67
7500	0.26	0.86	....	1.11	1.71	1.94
7550	0.15	0.69	....	1.50	2.03	....

Est vol 3,348   Wed 1,779 calls 1,584 puts
Op int Wed   21,602 calls 28,962 puts

LIVESTOCK

CATTLE-FEEDER (CME)
50,000 lbs.; cents per lb.

Strike	Calls – Settle			Puts – Settle		
Price	Aug	Sep	Oct	Aug	Sep	Oct
77	1.95	....	....	0.40	....	....
78	1.32	1.30	1.35	0.77	1.97	2.70
79	0.85	....	....	1.30	....	....
80	0.40	0.60	0.70	1.85	3.27	4.00
81	0.20	....	....	....	....	....
82	0.07	0.17	0.30	3.52	4.82	....

Est vol 223   Wed 120 calls 170 puts
Op int Wed   4,702 calls 7,249 puts

METALS

COPPER (CMX)
25,000 lbs.; cents per lb.

Strike	Calls – Settle			Puts – Settle		
Price	Sep	Dec	Mar	Sep	Dec	Mar
106	5.35	7.45	8.15	1.05	3.65	5.35
108	3.80	6.35	7.05	1.50	4.55	6.25
110	2.60	5.30	6.20	2.30	5.50	7.40
112	1.80	4.50	5.90	3.50	6.70	8.60
114	1.10	3.80	5.00	4.80	8.00	10.20
116	.65	3.15	4.20	6.30	9.35	11.30

Est vol 700   Wed 876 calls 335 puts
Op int Wed   8,254 calls 6,428 puts

GOLD (CMX)
100 troy ounces; $ per troy ounce

Strike	Calls – Settle			Puts – Settle		
Price	Sep	Oct	Dec	Sep	Oct	Dec
370	18.10	18.40	22.00	.10	.80	2.10
380	8.80	10.00	14.80	.70	2.20	4.40
390	2.00	4.90	9.80	4.00	6.90	8.60
400	.70	2.50	6.40	12.70	14.40	15.30
410	.30	1.10	4.40	22.30	23.00	23.30
420	.10	.60	2.90	32.10	32.40	30.90

Est vol 5,000   Wed 6,867 calls 1,355 puts
Op int Wed   88,439 calls 35,905 puts

INDEX

S&P 500 STOCK INDEX (CME)
$500 times premium

Strike	Calls – Settle			Puts – Settle		
Price	Aug	Sep	Oct	Aug	Sep	Oct
445	11.70	14.25	....	1.65	4.20	6.00
450	7.70	10.55	14.85	2.60	5.50	7.35
455	4.40	7.35	11.45	4.30	7.25	8.90
460	2.10	4.60	8.50	7.00	9.45	....
465	0.80	2.60	6.00	10.65	12.45	13.35
470	0.25	1.30	3.90	15.10	16.10	....

Est vol 5,120   Wed 3,050 calls 5,601 puts
Op int Wed   59,331 calls 100,094 puts

INTEREST RATE

T-BONDS (CBT)
$100,000; points and 64ths of 100%

Strike	Calls – Settle			Puts – Settle		
Price	Sep	Dec	Mar	Sep	Dec	Mar
101	2-27	....	....	0-27	....	....
102	1-46	2-40	3-00	0-46	2-24	3-30
103	1-08	....	1-08	....	....	....
104	0-43	1-45	2-12	1-43	3-28	4-38
105	0-23	....	....	2-23	....	....
106	0-11	1-02	1-32	3-10	4-47	5-56

Est. vol. 85,000;
Wed vol. 34,932 calls; 38,725 puts
Op. int. Wed 422,376 calls; 310,421 puts

T-NOTES (CBT)
$100,000; points and 64ths of 100%

Strike	Calls – Settle			Puts – Settle		
Price	Sep	Dec	Mar	Sep	Dec	Mar
101	....	....	....	0-07	1-07	....
102	2-07	2-23	....	0-16	1-29	....
103	1-23	1-49	....	0-31	1-55	....
104	0-49	1-18	....	0-57	2-23	....
105	0-23	0-56	....	1-31	2-60	....
106	0-10	0-37	....	2-18	3-41	....

Est vol 24,260   Wed 10,998 calls 10,-
761 puts
Op int Wed   108,805 calls 152,424 puts

MUNICIPAL BOND INDEX (CBT)
$100,000; pts. & 64ths of 100%

Strike	Calls – Settle			Puts – Settle		
Price	Aug	Sep	Oct	Aug	Sep	Oct
88	....	3-24	....	0-37	....	....
89	....	2-38	....	0-50	....	....
90	....	1-59	....	1-07	....	....
91	....	1-25	....	....	....	....
92	....	0-60	....	....	....	....
93	....	0-42	....	2-53	....	....

Est vol 0   Wed 0 calls 25 puts
Op int Wed   954 calls 671 puts

OIL

CRUDE OIL (NYM)
1,000 bbls.; $ per bbl.

Strike	Calls – Settle			Puts – Settle		
Price	Sep	Oct	Nov	Sep	Oct	Nov
1900	.97	.98	1.02	.20	.59	.86
1950	.65	.73	.80	.38	.84	....
2000	.44	.54	.62	.67	1.15	1.45
2050	.27	.39	.48	....	....	....
2100	.16	.29	.37	....	1.89	....
2150	.06	.15	.23	....	....	....

Est vol 16,754   Wed 19,020 calls 8,-
208 puts
Op int Wed   187,344 calls 121,579 puts

SOURCE: *Wall Street Journal*, April 8, 1994

European. (In contrast, spot options and futures options will differ to the extent that these conditions do not hold.)

There are, however, several factors that serve to differentiate the two contracts. First, since most futures contracts are relatively more liquid than their corresponding spot security, it is usually easier to form hedging or arbitrage strategies with futures options than with spot options. Second, futures options often are easier to exercise than their corresponding spot. For example, to exercise an option on a T-bond or foreign currency futures contract, you simply assume the futures position, whereas exercising a spot T-bond or a foreign currency option requires an actual purchase or delivery. Finally, most futures options are traded on the same exchange as their underlying futures contract, while most spot options are traded on exchanges different from their underlying securities. This, in turn, makes it easier for futures options traders to implement arbitrage and hedging strategies than it is for spot options traders.

16.5   FUNDAMENTAL FUTURES OPTIONS STRATEGIES

Some of the characteristics of futures options can be seen by examining the profit relationships for the fundamental strategies formed with these options. Figure 16.5-1 shows the profit and futures price relationship at expiration for the six fundamental option strategies using call and put options on the SP 500 futures contract. Both the call and the put have an exercise price of 250 times a $500 multiple and a premium of 10 times $500, and it is assumed that the futures options expire at the same time as the futures contract.

Figure 16.5-1(a) shows the profit and futures price relationship at expiration for the call purchase strategy. The numbers reflect a case in which the holder exercises the call at expiration, if profitable, when the spot price is equal to the price on the expiring futures contract. For example, at $S_T = f_T = 270$, the holder of the 250 futures calls would receive a cash flow of $10,000 and a profit of $5000. That is, upon exercising, the holder would assume a long position in the expiring SP 500 futures at 270, which she subsequently would close by taking an offsetting short futures position at 270, and the holder would receive $(f_T - X)\$500 = (270 - 250)\$500 = \$10,000$ from the assigned writer. The opposite profit and futures price relation is attained for a naked call write position [Figure 16.5-1(b)]. In this case, if the index is at 250 or less, the writer of a 250 SP 500 futures call would earn the premium of $5000, and if $f_T > 250$, she, upon assignment, would have to pay the difference between f_T and X and would have to assume a short position at f_T, which she would close with an offsetting long position.

Figures 16.5-1(c) and (d) show the long and short put positions. In the case of a put purchase, if the holder exercises when $f_T < X$, then she will receive $X - f_T$ and a short futures position, which she can offset. For example, if $S_T = f_T = 230$ at expiration, then the put holder upon exercising would receive $(250 - 230)(\$500) = \$10,000$ from the put writer for a net profit of $5000. Her short position then would be closed by taking a long position in the SP 500 futures contract. The put writer's position, of course, would be the opposite.

FIGURE 16.5-1

Fundamental Futures Options Strategies 250 Options on SP 500 Futures Contracts

Call and put exercise price = 250, call and put premiums = 10, multipler = $500, futures option and futures contract have same expiration date

(a) Call Purchase

$S_T = f_T$	PROFIT
230	− $ 5,000
240	− 5,000
250	− 5,000
260	0
270	5,000
280	10,000

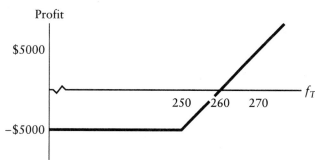

$S_T = f_T$	PROFIT
230	$ 5,000
240	5,000
250	5,000
260	0
270	− 5,000
280	− 10,000

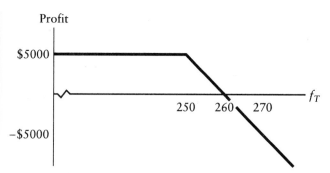

(c) Put Purchase

$S_T = f_T$	PROFIT
220	$10,000
230	5,000
240	0
250	− 5,000
260	− 5,000
270	− 5,000

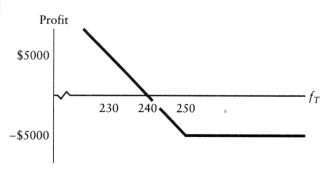

(d) Naked Put Write

$S_T = f_T$	PROFIT
220	− $10,000
230	− 5,000
240	0
250	5,000
260	5,000
270	5,000

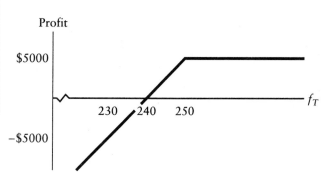

FIGURE 16.5-1

(continued)

(e) Covered Call Write:
Long in SP 500 futures at $f_0 = 250$

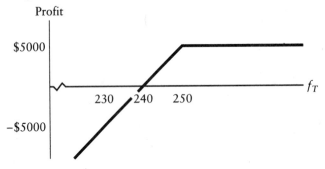

$S_T = f_T$	SHORT CALL PROFIT	FUTURES PROFIT	TOTAL
230	$ 5,000	− $10,000	− $5,000
240	5,000	− 5,000	0
250	5,000	0	5,000
260	0	5,000	5,000
270	− 5,000	10,000	5,000
280	− 10,000	15,000	5,000

(f) Covered Put Write:
Short in SP 500 futures at $f_0 = 250$

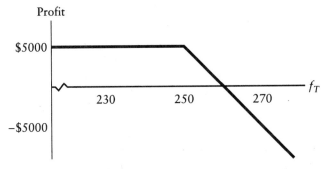

$S_T = f_T$	SHORT PUT PROFIT	FUTURES PROFIT	TOTAL
220	− $10,000	$15,000	$ 5,000
230	− 5,000	10,000	5,000
240	0	5,000	5,000
250	5,000	0	5,000
260	5,000	− 5,000	0
270	5,000	− 10,000	− 15,000
280	5,000	− 15,000	− 10,000

Figures 16.5-1(e) and (f) show the covered call and put positions. In Figure 16.5-1(e), the profit and futures price relation is shown for a position in which the writer sells the 250 call on the SP 500 futures contract and has a long position in the SP 500 futures contract with a 250 contract price. If $f_T > 250$ at expiration, the covered writer would earn a profit equal to the premium. For example, if a holder exercises at $f_T = 270$, the assigned covered writer in this case would be assigned a short position at the current price of 270, which she would use to close her initial long futures position established at 250. In this case, the covered writer would receive $(270 - 250)(\$500) = \$10,000$ from the clearinghouse, which she then would use to cover the $10,000 obligation to the exercising call holder $[(f_T - X)(\$500) = (270 - 250)(\$500) = \$10,000]$. On the other hand, if $f_T \leq X$, the holder would not exercise; however, the covered call writer loses on her futures position. In the case of a covered put write, the strategy consists of selling the put and having a short futures position. In this case, limited profit, equal to the premium, is earned if $f_T \leq X$, and losses on the short futures position are incurred if $f_T > 260$.

While the technicalities on exercising futures options are cumbersome, the profits from closing a futures option at expiration still equal the maximum of either zero or the difference in $f_T - X$ (for calls) or $X - f_T$ (for puts), minus the option premium. Moreover, if the futures option and the underlying futures contract expire at the same time, as we assumed, then $f_T = S_T$, and the futures option can be viewed simply as an option on the underlying spot security, with the option having a cash settlement clause.

16.6   FUTURES OPTIONS PRICING RELATIONS

16.6.1   Arbitrage Relations

Many of the option price relations and the arbitrage strategies governing option prices that were delineated in Chapter 4 also apply to futures options. For example, the price on an American futures call option at time t must be at least equal to the call's intrinsic value as defined by the price on the futures contract at time t (f_t):

$$C_t^a \geq \text{Max}[f_t - X, 0].$$

If this condition does not hold, an arbitrageur could buy the call, exercise, and close the futures position. For example, if the 250 call on the SP 500 futures contract in the earlier example was trading at 9 when the futures contract was trading at 260, an arbitrageur could (1) buy the call at 9, (2) exercise the call to obtain $f_t - X = 260 - 250 = 10$ from the assigned writer plus a long position in the SP 500 futures contract priced 260, and (3) close the long futures position by taking an offsetting short position at 260. Doing this, an arbitrageur would realize a riskless profit of $1 (or $500 per contract).

Some of the arbitrage strategies described in Chapter 4, such as the price relationships between spot options with different exercise prices and times to expirations, are similar for futures options. Differences between spot and futures options do exist, however. For example, the minimum price of a European futures call is obtained by comparing a long futures position with a long position in the futures option and an investment in a riskless bond with a face value of $f_0 - X$. This contrasts with a spot or cash option in which the comparison is with a long position in the spot security and a call and bond with face value equal to X.

16.6.2 Early Exercise

As noted previously in this book, options generally are more valuable alive than dead. Both call and put futures options can pose exceptions to this rule. Consider a case in which there is a 70 call option on a T-bond futures contract and a spot T-bond paying an 8% coupon and trading at par (100). With the T-bond at 100, the 70 option on the T-bond futures contract would be deep in the money. As a result, the option should be trading at close to its intrinsic value of 30, and the price of the deep-in-the-money futures option should be highly correlated with changes in the prices of the T-bond futures, as well as spot.

If this is the case, a long position in the option would have approximately the same risk as a long position in the spot T-bond. Given this, a holder of the T-bond futures option (which is American) would find it advantageous to sell his call at 30, then use the funds to buy the T-bond on the spot market at 100. By doing this, the option holder would be able to earn an $8 coupon return from a $70 investment, for a 11.4% rate of return ($8/$70). Thus, for the same risk as the option, the option holder would be able to obtain a higher return from the bond than from the call option. Moreover, if enough holders of the 70 T-bond futures call try to sell their options to take advantage of this situation, they would push the price of the call below its intrinsic value. If this occurred, arbitrage opportunities would then exist by exercising the futures options early.

16.6.3 Put-Call Parity Model for Futures Options

The put-call parity model for futures options can be derived from a conversion strategy consisting of a long position in a futures contract with a contract price of f_0 and a synthetic short futures position formed by purchasing a European put and selling a European call on the futures contract with an exercise price of X. As shown in Table 16.6-1, if the options and the futures contract expire at the same time, then the conversion would be worth $X - f_0$ at expiration, regardless of the price on the futures contract. Since the conversion yields a riskless return, in equilibrium its value would equal the present value of a riskless bond with a face value of $X - f_0$:

$$P_0^e - C_0^e = (X - f_0)(1 + R)^{-T}. \tag{16.6-1}$$

Equation (16.6-1) is the same as the put-call-futures parity equilibrium condition (Equation 16.2-1). Thus, the put-call parity defining the equilibrium relation for European futures options and the put-call-futures parity are the same, provided the European spot options, European futures options, and futures contract expire at the same time. This equivalence should not be too surprising, since the futures contract, spot options, and futures options all derive their values from the same

TABLE 16.6-1

Conversion Position with Futures Options				
$\{+f_0,\ +P_0^e,\ -C_0^e\}$				
		EXPIRATION CASH FLOW		
POSITION	INVESTMENT	$f_T < X$	$f_T = X$	$f_T > X$
Long futures	0	$f_T - f_0$	$f_T - f_0$	$f_T - f_0$
Long put	P_0^e	$X - f_T$	0	0
Short call	C_0^e	0	0	$-(f_T - X)$
Total	$P_0^e - C_0^e$	$X - f_0$	$X - f_0$	$X - f_0$

underlying security. It also should be noted that if the carrying-cost model holds and the futures and options expire at the same time, then Equation (16.6-1) equals the equation for the put-call parity model for the European spot option.

16.7   OPTION PRICING MODELS FOR FUTURES OPTIONS

Earlier we derived the BOPM in terms of futures contracts and showed that if the carrying-cost model holds and the option and futures contracts expire at the same time, then the BOPM defined by futures and the BOPM defined in terms of spot positions are the same. Similar price relations also apply to futures options. Specifically, if the carrying-cost and expiration conditions hold, then the price of a futures option also will be the same as the price of the spot option. However, a number of futures options do not have the same expirations as their corresponding futures contracts, and as a result their equilibrium values will differ from those on the spot option. In this section, we will examine the option pricing models for futures options.

16.7.1   Binomial Option Pricing Model for Futures Call Options

The equilibrium price of a European call option on a futures contract is equal to the value of a replicating portfolio consisting of futures and debt positions. Using the binomial framework, the replicating portfolio for a futures call is formed from the up and down parameters on the futures prices. These parameters can be derived from the u and d parameters on the futures' underlying spot asset and the carrying-cost model.

To see this, assume a single period to expiration in which the possible values on the underlying spot asset are either uS_0 or dS_0 and the relationship between the futures and spot price, as defined by the carrying-cost model, is:

$$f_0 = S_0 r^{n_f},$$

(16.7-1)

where:

$$r = 1 + \text{period risk-free rate}$$

$$n_f = \text{number of periods to expiration on the futures contract.}$$

Using the carrying-cost model, the two possible futures prices at the end of the period (f_u and f_d) are:

	Spot: $S_u = uS_0$ Futures: $f_u = uS_0 r^{n_f - 1}$
Spot: S_0 Futures: $f_0 = S_0 r^{n_f}$	
	Spot: $S_d = dS_0$ Futures: $f_d = dS_0 r^{n_f - 1}$

If the number of periods to expiration on the futures contract is the same as the option's (that is, if $n_f = 1$ in this single-period case), then the possible futures prices f_u and f_d will equal the possible spot prices S_u and S_d.

The possible futures prices can also be defined in terms of up and down parameters of the futures prices. Specifically, let u^* and d^* be the proportional increases and decreases in the futures prices, where $u^* = f_u/f_0$ and $d^* = f_d/f_0$, then substitute the carrying-cost equations for f_u, f_d, and f_0. By doing this, u^* simplifies to u/r and d^* to d/r:

$$u^* = \frac{f_u}{f_0} = \frac{uS_0 r^{n_f - 1}}{S_0 r^{n_f}} = \frac{u}{r}$$

$$d^* = \frac{f_d}{f_0} = \frac{dS_0 r^{n_f - 1}}{S_0 r^{n_f}} \frac{d}{r}.$$

Thus, if the period risk-free rate is $R = 2\%$ and the u and d parameters on the futures underlying spot security are 1.1 and .95, then the up and down parameters for the futures contract price would be $u^* = 1.1/1.02 = 1.078$ and $d^* = .95/1.02 = .931$. The possible futures prices at end of the period therefore can be expressed alternatively as:

	$f_u = u^* f_0 = \left(\dfrac{u}{r}\right) f_0$
f_0	
	$f_d = d^* f_0 = \left(\dfrac{d}{r}\right) f_0$

Given the possible prices on the futures contract, the equilibrium price on a European call option on the futures contract is found by constructing a replicating portfolio with cash flows that match the futures call option's possible values of C_u and C_d:

$$C_0 \quad \begin{array}{l} C_u = Max[f_u - X, 0] \\ \\ C_d = Max[f_d - X, 0] \end{array}$$

The replicating futures call portfolio is formed by taking a long position in the futures contract in which H_{f0} futures contracts are purchased at the contract price of f_0 and by borrowing B_0 dollars. The possible values of the portfolio are:

$$\text{Long } H_{f0} \text{ futures contracts at } f_0 \text{ and borrowing } B_0 \quad \begin{array}{l} H_{f0}(f_u - f_0) - rB_0 \\ \\ H_{f0}(f_d - f_0) - rB_0 \end{array}$$

Setting the replicating portfolio values equal the call's values,

$$H_{f0}(f_u - f_0) - rB_0 = C_u \qquad (16.7\text{-}2)$$

$$H_{f0}(f_d - f_0) - rB_0 = C_d,$$

and solving for the H_{f0} and B_0 that satisfy the two-equation system, we obtain:

$$H_{f0}^* = \frac{C_u - C_d}{f_u - f_d} \qquad (16.7\text{-}3)$$

$$B_0^* = \frac{C_u(f_d - f_0) - C_d(f_u - f_0)}{r(f_u - f_d)}. \qquad (16.7\text{-}4)$$

The equilibrium price of the call option on the futures contract is therefore:

$$C_0^* = H_{f0}^*(\text{value of futures contract}) - B_0^* \qquad (16.7\text{-}5)$$

$$C_0^* = H_{f0}^*(0) - B_0^*$$

$$C_0^* = -B_0^*$$

$$C_0^* = -\frac{C_u(f_d - f_0) - C_d(f_u - f_0)}{r(f_u - f_d)}. \qquad (16.7\text{-}6)$$

Note that the futures contract has no initial value, and also, since $f_d < f_0$, C_0^* is positive.

Equation (16.7-6) also can be rewritten in the familiar binomial form:*

$$C_0^* = \frac{pC_u + (1 - p)C_d}{r},$$ (16.7-7)

where:

$$C_u = \text{Max}[f_u - X, 0]$$
$$C_d = \text{Max}[f_d - X, 0]$$
$$p = \frac{r - d}{u - d}.$$

Equation (16.7-7) defines the equilibrium price of a European call option on a futures contract for a single period. The model is similar in form to the BOPM for the spot security, except for the C_u and C_d values, which are defined in terms of the contract prices on the futures instead of the spot prices. If the futures contract and the futures option expire at the same time, then the possible prices on the futures contract at expiration will equal the possible spot prices ($f_u = S_u$ and $f_d = S_d$); in this case, C_u and C_d will be the same for the spot option and the futures option. Thus, if the futures contract and the option have the same expiration, the carrying-cost model holds, and the futures and spot options are both European, then futures and spot options will be equivalent.

---

*Equation (16.7-7) is derived from Equation (16.7-6) as follows:

$$C_0^* = -\frac{C_u(f_d - f_0) - C_d(f_u - f_0)}{r(f_u - f_d)}$$

$$C_0^* r = -\left[C_u\left(\frac{f_d - f_0}{f_u - f_d}\right) - C_d\left(\frac{f_u - f_0}{f_u - f_d}\right)\right]$$

$$C_0^* r = -\left\{C_u\left[\frac{f_0(d^* - 1)}{f_0(u^* - d^*)}\right] - C_d\left[\frac{f_0(u^* - 1)}{f_0(u^* - d^*)}\right]\right\}$$

$$C_0^* r = C_u\left(\frac{1 - d^*}{u^* - d^*}\right) + C_d\left(\frac{u^* - 1}{u^* - d^*}\right)$$

$$C_0^* = \frac{1}{r}[p^*C_u + (1 - p^*)C_d],$$

where:

$$p^* = \frac{1 - d^*}{u^* - d^*}$$

$$1 - p^* = \frac{u^* - d^*}{u^* - d^*} - \frac{1 - d^*}{u^* - d^*} = \frac{u^* - 1}{u^* - d^*}.$$

By substituting u/r and d/r for u^* and d^*, the equation for p^* becomes the same as the equation for p in the spot BOPM. That is:

$$p^* = \frac{1 - d^*}{u^* - d^*} = \frac{(r/r) - (d/r)}{(u/r) - (d/r)} = \frac{r - d}{u - d} = p.$$

Thus:

$$C_0^* = \frac{pC_u + (1 - p)C_d}{r}.$$ (16.6-7)

◆   **16.7.2**   **Example of Binomial Option Pricing Model**

As an example, consider a 250 European call option on a stock index futures contract. Assume the futures option expires at the end of the first period, whereas the index futures contract expires at the end of two periods ($n_f = 2$). Also, the spot index is currently at 240.29 and has up and down parameters of $u = 1.122$ and $d = .969$, the period risk-free rate is 2%, no dividends are to be paid on the index (or the stocks comprising it), and the futures prices are determined by the carrying-cost model.

Given these assumptions, the current futures price on the index futures contract would be 250 (for simplicity we will assume no multiplier), and the possible prices on the contract next period would be $f_u = 275$ and $f_d = 237.5$. That is:

$$f_u = \left(\frac{u}{r}\right)f_0 = u^*f_0$$
$$f_u = \left(\frac{1.122}{1.02}\right)(250) = 275$$

$$f_0 = S_0 r^{n_f}$$
$$f_0 = (240.29)(1.02)^2 = 250$$

$$f_d = \left(\frac{d}{r}\right)f_0 = d^*f_0$$
$$f_d = \left(\frac{.969}{(1.02)}\right)(250) = 237.5$$

The possible values of the futures call option expiring at the end of the period would be 25 or 0:

$$C_u = \text{Max}[f_u - X, 0]$$
$$C_u = \text{Max}[275 - 250, 0] = 25$$

$$C_0$$

$$C_d = \text{Max}[f_d - X, 0]$$
$$C_d = \text{Max}[237.5 - 250, 0] = 0$$

Using the single-period BOPM, the equilibrium price of the 250 call option on the index futures contract would be 8.17:

$$C_0^* = -B_0^* = -\left[\frac{25(237.5 - 250) - 0(275 - 250)}{1.02(275 - 237.5)}\right] = 8.17$$

or

$$C_0^* = \frac{pC_u + (1 - p)C_d}{r}$$
$$C_0^* = \frac{.3333(25) + .6667(0)}{1.02} = 8.17,$$

where:

$$p = \frac{r - d}{u - d} = \frac{1.02 - .969}{1.122 - .969} = .3333.$$

Note that since the futures and the futures option do not expire at the same time, the price of the futures option differs from the price on an option on the spot index. For example, the equilibrium price of a European call option on the spot index with an exercise price of 250 and expiring at the end of one period is 9.966:

$$C_0^* = \frac{pC_u + (1 - p)C_d}{r}$$

$$C_0^* = \frac{.3333(30.5) + .6667(0)}{1.02} = 9.966,$$

where:

$$C_u = Max[S_u - X, 0] = Max[1.122(250) - 250, 0] = 30.5$$
$$C_d = Max[S_d - X, 0] = Max[.969(250) - 250, 0] = 0.$$

The 250 futures option also would equal 9.966 if the futures contract expired at the end of the first period instead of the second (this would make C_u on the futures option 30.5 and therefore $C_0^* = 9.966$). ◆

16.7.3   Single-Period Arbitrage Strategy

If the market price on a futures call option does not equal the equilibrium value, then an arbitrage opportunity will exist by taking a position in the call and an opposite position in the replicating portfolio. For example, in the preceding case, if the market price of the 250 index futures call is $C_0^m = \$8.50$ instead of $C_0^* = \$8.17$, then as shown in Table 16.7-1, a riskless return of $0.3366 could be earned by selling the call for $8.50, taking a long position in a replicating portfolio in which $H_{f0}^* = (C_u - C_d)/(f_u - f_d) = (25 - 0)/(275 - 237.5) = .6667$ index futures contracts are purchased at $f_0 = 250$, and $8.50 is invested in a risk-free security: $B_0^* + (C_0^m - C_0^*)$.

On the other hand, if the market price of the futures call is below 8.17, then an underpriced BOPM arbitrage strategy is employed in which C_0^m dollars are borrowed at the risk-free rate and used to finance the purchase of the call and H_{f0}^* futures contracts are sold at f_0.

16.7.4   Multiple-Period Binomial Option Pricing Model for Futures Options

In Table 16.7-2, the 250 call option on an index futures contract is priced using the two-period BOPM in which $u^* = 1.1$, $d^* = .95$, and $r = 1.02$ for each period. As shown in the table, with two periods to expiration, the equilibrium call price is 10.40. If the futures call is not equal to its equilibrium value, then an arbitrage profit can be realized by initiating the multiple-period arbitrage strategy.

For example, if the call is priced initially at $10.75 in the market, then an arbitrageur could earn riskless profit by purchasing $H_{f0}^* = .5554$ futures contracts

TABLE 16.7-1

Single-Period Arbitrage Strategy for Overpriced Futures Option

$f_0 = 250, n_f = 2, C_0^m = \$8.50, C_0^* = \$8.17, u^* = 1.1, d^* = .95, r = 1.02$

Strategy:
Sell call at $8.50.
Long in $H_{f0} = .6667$ futures contract at 250.
Invest $B_0^* = \$8.17$ in risk-free security.
Invest excess of $C_0^m - C_0^* = (\$8.50 - \$8.17) = \$0.33$ in risk-free security.

	CASH FLOW AT EXPIRATION	
CLOSING POSITION	$f_u = 275, C_u = 25$	$f_d = 237.5, C_d = 0$
Call purchase: $-C_T$	$-\$25.000$	0
Closing futures: $.6667(f_T - 250)$	16.667	$-\$8.333$
Investment: $B_0^* r = 8.17(1.02)$	8.333	8.333
Investment: $(C^m - C_0^*)r = 0.33(1.02)$	0.3366	0.3366
Total	$ 0.3366	$0.3366

at $f_0 = 250$, selling the call for $10.75, and investing $B_0 + (C_0^m - C_0^*) = \$10.40$ + $0.35 = $10.75 in a risk-free security.

This position would be either closed or readjusted next period, depending on whether the call is over- or underpriced. For example, if the futures contract is at $f_u = 275$ and the call is trading at $C_1^m = 25$ instead of $C_u = 24.50$, then the initially overpriced call again would be overpriced. Following the adjustment strategy delineated in Chapter 5, the arbitrageur in this case would lose $0.14 if she closed:

CLOSING POSITION	CASH FLOW
Closing futures: $.5554(275 - 250)$	$13.89
Call purchase: -25.00	$- 25.00$
$(-B_0)$ Investment: $10.40(1.02)$	10.61
$(C_0^m - C_0^*)$ Investment: $0.35(1.02)$	0.36
	$-\$ 0.14$

To avert this loss, the arbitrageur would need to move from $H_{f0}^* = .5554$ futures contract to $H_{fu} = 1$. She could do this by closing the .5554 futures contract and investing the profit, then entering a new contract to buy $H_{fu} = 1$ index futures contract at $f_u = 275$. In closing the initial contract, the arbitrageur would receive $.5554(275 - 250) = \$13.89$, which she could invest in the risk-free security for the final period. The $13.89 investment would augment her required investment in the replicating portfolio to $B_u = \$13.89 + \$10.40(1.02) = \$24.50$.

After readjusting, the arbitrageur then would be assured of a cash flow of $0.36 at the end of the next period at either futures price: $f_{uu} = 302.5$ or $f_{ud} = 261.25$:

	CASH FLOW	
CLOSING POSITION	$f_{uu} = 302.5$ $C_{uu} = 52.5$	$f_{ud} = 261.25$ $C_{ud} = 11.25$
Closing futures: $1(f_T - 275)$ Call purchase: $-C_T$ $(-B_u)$ Investment: $24.50(1.02)$	$\$27.5$ $-\ 52.5$ $\underline{25.0}$ 0	$-\$13.75$ $-\ 11.25$ $\underline{25.00}$ 0
$(C_0^m - C_0^*)$ Investment: $\$0.35(1.02)^2 = \$0.36$		

The opposite strategy and readjustment rules apply to cases in which futures options are initially underpriced.

TABLE 16.7-2

Two-Period BOPM for Futures Options

$f_0 = 250, X = 250, u^* = 1.1, d^* = .95, r = 1.02, u = 1.122, d = .969, p = (r - d)/(u - d) = .333$

$$\begin{aligned}
&f_{uu} = u^{*2}f_0 = 302.5 \\
&C_{uu} = \text{Max}[f_{uu} - X, 0] = 52.5
\end{aligned}$$

$$\begin{aligned}
&f_u = u^*f_0 = 1.1(250) = 275 \\
&C_u = \frac{pC_{uu} + (1 - p)C_{ud}}{r} = -B_u \\
&C_u = \frac{.333(52.5) + .667(11.25)}{1.02} \\
&C_u = 24.50 \\
&H_{fu} = \frac{C_{uu} - C_{ud}}{f_{uu} - f_{ud}} = 1
\end{aligned}$$

$$\begin{aligned}
&f_0 = 250 \\
&C_0^* = \frac{pC_u + (1 - p)C_d}{r} = -B_0^* \\
&C_0^* = \frac{.333(24.50) + .667(3.673)}{1.02} \\
&C_0^* = 10.40 \\
&H_{f0}^* = \frac{C_u - C_d}{f_u - f_d} = .5554
\end{aligned}$$

$$\begin{aligned}
&f_{ud} = u^*d^*f_0 = 261.25 \\
&C_{ud} = \text{Max}[f_{ud} - X, 0] = 11.25
\end{aligned}$$

$$\begin{aligned}
&f_d = d^*f_0 = (.95)(250) = 237.5 \\
&C_d = \frac{[pC_{ud} + (1 - p)C_{dd}]}{r} = -B_d \\
&C_d = \frac{.333(11.25) + .667(0)}{1.02} \\
&C_d = 3.673 \\
&H_{fd} = \frac{C_{ud} - C_{dd}}{f_{ud} - f_{dd}} = .3158
\end{aligned}$$

$$\begin{aligned}
&f_{dd} = d^{*2}f_0 = 225.625 \\
&C_{dd} = \text{Max}[f_{dd} - X, 0] = 0
\end{aligned}$$

16.7.5 American Futures Options

In Table 16.7-2, the in-the-money futures call at the end of period 1 is priced at 24.50; thus, it is trading below its intrinsic value: IV = Max$[f_u - X, 0]$ = Max$[275 - 250, 0]$ = 25. If the futures option is American and is trading at 24.50, then arbitrageurs would be able to earn riskless profit by buying the futures option, then exercising it. Their actions, in turn, would push the price of the American futures call up to 25. As noted earlier, it is possible for such a situation to exist for in-the-money futures call options. For American call options on futures contracts, the BOPM therefore needs to be adjusted by constraining each possible price to be the maximum of either its European value, as determined by the BOPM, or its IV: C^a = Max$[C^e, IV]$.

16.7.6 Binomial Option Pricing Model for Put Futures Options

For European puts on futures contracts, the put-call parity model can be used to determine the price of the put. The equilibrium put price also can be determined by the BOPM for puts. The latter model is derived by forming a replicating put portfolio consisting of a short position in the futures contract in which H^{p*}_{f0} futures are sold at f_0 and an investment of I^*_0 dollars in a risk-free security. For one period, the BOPM for put options on futures contracts is:

$$P^*_0 = \frac{pP_u + (1 - p)P_d}{r}, \qquad (16.7\text{-}8)$$

where:

$$P_d = \text{Max}[X - f_d, 0]$$
$$P_u = \text{Max}[X - f_u, 0].$$

For American futures puts, this model can be adjusted, as with American calls, by constraining the possible values at each node to be the maximum of either the European put value or its IV.

16.7.7 Black Model for Pricing Futures Options

In 1976, Myron Black extended the B-S OPM for spot options to the pricing of futures options. For calls, the **Black futures option pricing model** is defined as follows:

$$C^*_0 = [f_0 N(d_1) - XN(d_2)]e^{-RT} \qquad (16.7\text{-}9)$$

$$d_1 = \frac{\log_e(f_0/X) + (\sigma^2_f/2)T}{\sigma_f\sqrt{T}}$$

$$d_2 = d_1 - \sigma_f\sqrt{T},$$

where:

$$\sigma^2_f = \text{variance of the logarithmic return of futures prices} = V\log_e\left(\frac{f_n}{f_0}\right).$$

The Black futures model differs from the B-S OPM for spot securities by the exclusion of the risk-free rate in the equations for d_1 and d_2. Like the BOPM for futures options, if the carrying-cost model holds and the underlying futures contract and the futures option expire at the same time, then the B-S OPM for European spot options and the Black model for European futures options will be the same. This can be proved by substituting $S_0 e^{-RT}$ for f_0 in the Black futures OPM to obtain the B-S OPM for the spot asset.

To illustrate the application of the Black model, consider a June 250 call on a European index futures contract in which $f_0 = 248$, $T = .25$ (per year), $R = .0488$ (continuously compounded rate), and the annualized $\sigma_f = .165$.* The equilibrium call price using the Black model is 7.14:

$$C_0^* = [248(.47782) - 250(.44509)]e^{-(.0488)(.25)} = 7.14,$$

where:

$$d_1 = \frac{\log_e(248/250) + [(.165)^2/2](.25)}{.165\sqrt{.25}} = -.05611$$

$$d_2 = -.05611 - .165\sqrt{.25} = -.13861$$

$$N(d_1) = N(-.05611) = .47782$$

$$N(d_2) = N(-.13861) = .44509.$$

If the futures call does not equal 7.14, you could earn riskless profit by forming an arbitrage portfolio. In the Black model, the number of futures contracts for the arbitrage strategy is equal to the hedge ratio of $H_{f0}^* = N(d_1)e^{-RT}$, and the risk-free investment is $-B_0 = XN(d_2)e^{-RT}$.†

The Black model, like the B-S OPM, prices only European futures options. If the futures option is American, then as noted in Section 16.6.2, an early-exercise advantage may exist for both calls and puts. In such cases, either the BOPM adjusted for American options or the Barone-Adesi and Whaley (BAW) model presented in Appendix 7C can be employed to estimate the call price. When the BAW model is applied to futures options, the futures price is used instead of the stock price, and the risk-free rate is used instead of the dividend yield.

16.8   CONCLUSION

In this chapter, we've examined the relationship between options and futures, and explored the markets, fundamental strategies, and pricing of futures options. In today's security world, many securities can be traded on four different markets—spot, spot options, futures, and futures option. The pricing relationships examined in this chapter suggest that under certain conditions some of these markets may

---

*It can be shown that the variance in the logarithmic returns in futures prices is equal to the logarithmic return in spot prices if interest rates are constant.

†The Black put model for pricing futures options can be found by substituting the equilibrium call price into the put-call parity model, then solving for the price of the put.

indeed be redundant. Each market, though, often provides different liquidity, delivery procedures, or comparative locational advantages to particular investors, and as such may be justified, at least for the foreseeable future.

KEY TERMS

put-call-futures parity model
options on futures contracts
Black futures option pricing model

SELECTED REFERENCES

Blomeyer, E., and Boyd, J. "Empirical Tests of Boundary Conditions for Options on Treasury Bond Futures." *Journal of Futures Markets* 4 (1988): 185–198.

Brenner, M., Courtadon, G., and Subrahmanyam, M. "Options on the Spot and Options on Futures." *Journal of Finance* 40 (Dec. 1985): 1303–1317.

Chance, D. *Options and Futures*. Chicago: Dryden Press, 1991, pp. 473–504.

Followill, R. "Relative Call Futures Option Pricing: An Examination of Market Efficiency." *Review of Futures Markets* 6 (1987): 354–381.

Kolb, R. *Understanding Futures Markets*. Glenview, Ill.: Scott, Foresman, 1988, pp. 383–412.

Ramaswany, K., and Sundaresan, S. "The Valuation of Options on Futures Contracts." *Journal of Finance* 60 (Dec. 1985): 1319–1340.

Shastri, K., and Tandon, K. "Options on Futures Contracts: A Comparison of European and American Pricing Models." *Journal of Futures Markets* 6 (Winter 1986): 593–618.

Siegel, D., and Siegel, D. *Futures Markets*. Chicago: Dryden Press, 1990, pp. 448–488.

Thorp, E. "Options on Commodity Forward Contracts." *Management Science* 29 (Oct. 1985): 1232–1242.

Whaley, R. "Valuation of American Futures Options: Theory and Tests." *Journal of Finance* 41 (Mar. 1986): 127–150.

Wolf, A. "Fundamentals of Commodity Options on Futures." *Journal of Futures Markets* 2 (1982): 391–408.

Wolf, A., and Pohlman, L. "Tests of the Black and Whaley Models for Gold and Silver Futures Options." *Review of Futures Markets* 6 (1987): 328–347.

PROBLEMS AND QUESTIONS

1. Determine the equilibrium price of a 300 index European put expiring in six months ($T = .5$ year) when a 300 index European call expiring in six months is trading at 12.74, a futures contract on the index expiring in six months is trading at 309, and the annual risk-free rate is 6%. Assume no dividends and no multipliers for the options and futures contract.

2. Explain what an arbitrageur would do if the index put in Problem 1 was trading at 5. Show that the arbitrageur's strategy incurs no liabilities at expiration.

3. Determine the equilibrium price of a stock index futures contract expiring in three months ($T = .25$ per year) when a 250 stock index European call is trading at 8, a 250 stock index European put is trading at 4, and the annual risk-free rate is 5%. Assume no dividends and multipliers.

4. Explain what an arbitrageur would do if the futures contract in Problem 3 is trading at 240. Show that the arbitrageur's strategy incurs no liabilities at expiration.

5. Determine the equilibrium price of a 40-DM European call option ($X = \$0.40/DM$) expiring in three months ($T = .25$ per year) when the price of a three-month 40-DM European put is trading at $0.05/DM, the three-month $/DM forward exchange rate is trading at $0.38/DM, and the annual risk-free rate is 6%.

6. Explain what arbitrageurs would do if the call in Problem 5 was trading at $0.04/DM. Show that the strategy is riskless.

7. Given:

   - Spot exchange rate = $E_0 = \$0.40/DM$
   - Period U.S. risk-free rate = $R_{US} = .02$
   - Period German risk-free rate = $R_F = .025$
   - Proportional increase in spot exchange rate = $u = 1.05$
   - Proportional decrease in spot exchange rate = $d = 1/1.05$
   - Number of periods to expiration on European DM options contract = $n = 2$
   - Number of periods to expiration on a DM forward contract = $n_f = 2$.

   a. Assuming a two-period binomial framework, show with an event tree the equilibrium $/DM forward exchange rate at each node using the interest rate parity theorem.

   b. Using the forward exchange rate, show the BOPM's equilibrium price at each node for a DM European call with an exercise price of $0.40/DM.

8. Describe the replicating portfolio that includes DM forward contracts that an arbitrageur would use if the 40-DM call in Problem 7 was trading at $0.01/DM. What would be the arbitrageur's cash flow in period 1 if the spot $/DM exchange rate was $0.42/DM and the 40-DM call was trading at $0.03/DM (assume IRPT holds)? Show the adjustments an arbitrageur would need to make to avoid a loss, and the cash flow at expiration that would result after making the adjustments.

9. P. T. Investment Company has contructed a proxy portfolio for identifying arbitrage opportunities. The portfolio is currently worth $4.3M, is highly correlated with the SP 500, currently priced at 212.03156, has a $\beta = 1$, and is expected to generate dividends worth $52,000 at the end of 90 days.

a. If the spot SP 500 is at 212.03156 and the annual risk-free rate is at 6%, what would be the equilibrium price on a SP 500 futures contract expiring in 90 days using P. T. Investment Company's proxy portfolio?

b. Describe the program trading arbitrage strategy the P. T. Investment Company could employ using its proxy portfolio if the SP 500 futures contract is trading at 213. Show the cash flow that would result when the P. T. Investment Company closes its position at expiration after the spot SP 500 increases 10% and after it decreases 10% (assume perfect divisibility).

c. Using the put-call parity model with dividends and P. T. Investment Company's proxy portfolio, determine the equilibrium price of an SP 500 European put with an exercise price of 210 and expiration of 90 days when a comparable SP 500 call ($X = 210$, expiration = 90 days) is trading at 5 and the annual risk-free rate is 6%.

d. Describe the arbitrage strategy the P. T. Investment Company could employ using its proxy portfolio if the price of the 210 SP 500 put described in part (c) was trading at 2 (assume perfect divisibility). Determine the initial cash flow, and show that there are no liabilities at expiration given a 10% increase in the spot index and a 10% decrease.

e. Show that if the carrying-cost model holds, the equilibriuim price of the 210 put is the same using either the put-call parity model or the put-call futures parity model.

f. Describe the arbitrage strategy the P. T. Investment Company could employ using futures contracts instead of its proxy portfolio if the price of the 210 SP 500 put was trading at 2.

10. Explain the arbitrage strategy underlying each of the following boundary conditions for American futures options.

a. $C_0^a \geq \text{Max}[f_0 - X, 0]$

b. $P_0^a \geq \text{Max}[X - f_0, 0]$

11. Given:

- $E_0 = \$1.15/\text{BP}$
- $u = 1.042$
- $d = .96$
- U.S. period risk-free rate = $R_{US} = 2\%$
- British period risk-free rate = $R_F = 3\%$

a. Assuming a two-period binomial case, show the spot \$/BP exchange rate at each node.

b. Assuming a two-period binomial case, show the futures \$/BP exchange rate at each node for a contract that expires at the end of three periods.

c. Using the BOPM, determine the equilibrium price and replicating portfolio at each node for a 115 call on the BP futures contracts. Assume that the call expires at the end of the second period and the futures expires at the end of the third period.

d. Describe the arbitrage strategy you would employ if the BP futures call was overpriced and again if it was underpriced.

e. Would the price on a 115 call on the spot BP expiring at the end of the second period be greater or less than the 115 call on the BP futures? Explain your answer.

f. Under what conditions would the price of the call on the spot BP and the price on BP futures call be equal?

12. Given:

- $E_0 = \$1.15/BP$
- R_{US} = annual continuously compounded U.S. risk-free rate = .06
- R_F = annual continuously compounded British risk-free rate = .07
- σ^2 = annualized variance on SP 500 spot and futures returns = .030625

Determine the following.

a. The equilibrium price of a BP futures contract expiring in 90 days

b. The equilibrium price and replicating portfolio of a 115 spot BP European call expiring in 90 days using the B-S OPM for foreign currency (see Chapter 10)

c. The equilibrium price of a 115 BP futures call expiring in 90 days using the Black model

d. The equilibrium price on a 115 spot BP European put expiring in 90 days

e. The equilibrium price on a 115 BP European futures put expiring in 90 days

CHAPTER 17

Swaps and Other Derivative Securities

17.1 INTRODUCTION

Just as striking as the growth in option and futures markets over the last two decades is the growth in derivative products. Often referred to as **hybrids**, these products have option or futures characteristics, and as such they are used primarily for hedging. Different from exchange-traded options and futures, *hybrids* customarily are written by financial institutions or corporations. As a result, they are usually more tailor-made, but also less liquid, than exchange-traded options and futures. In this chapter, we examine these other derivative products. In the next two sections, we will describe the construction, use, and markets for interest rate and currency swaps, and in subsequent sections, we will examine several other derivative products: interest rate options, caps, floors, collars, PRIMEs and SCOREs.

17.2 INTEREST RATE SWAPS

Since the introduction of currency swaps in the late 1970s and interest rate swaps in the early 1980s, the swap market has grown from $5 billion a year (as measured by contract value) in the early 1980s to $700 billion by the end of that decade. By definition, a **financial swap** is an exchange of periodic cash flows between two parties. Two general types of swaps exist: interest rate swaps and foreign currency swaps. In this section, we examine the features and market for interest rate swaps; in Section 17.3, we examine currency swaps.

17.2.1   Terms

The simplest type of *interest rate swap* is called the generic, or "plain vanilla," swap. In this agreement, one party provides fixed-rate interest payments to another party, who provides variable-rate payments. The parties to the agreement are referred to as *counterparties*. The party who pays fixed interest and receives variable-rate payments is called the *fixed-rate payer*; the other party (who pays at a variable rate and receives at a fixed rate) is the *floating-rate payer*.

On a generic swap, principal payments are not exchanged. As a result, the interest payments are based on a notional (or hypothetical) principal. The interest rate paid by the fixed-rate payer often is specified in terms of the yield to maturity on a T-note, plus basis points; the rate paid by the floating-rate payer usually is the LIBOR plus basis points. Swap payments are usually made semiannually, and the maturities on generic swaps range from three to five years. The swap contract specifies a trade date, an effective date, a settlement date, and a maturity date. The *trade date* is the day the parties agree to commit to the swap; the *effective date* is the date when interest begins to accrue; the *settlement date* (*payment date*) is when interest payments are made (six months after the effective date); and the *maturity date* is the last payment date. On the payment date, only the interest differential between the counterparties is paid. If a fixed-rate payer owes $100 and a floating-rate payer owes $90, then only a $10 payment by the fixed-rate payer to the floating-rate payer is made.

◆   17.2.2   Example of Interest Rate Swap

Consider an interest rate swap with a maturity of three years, first effective date of 3/23/95, and a maturity date of 3/23/98. In this swap agreement, assume the fixed-rate payer agrees to pay the current YTM on a three-year T-note of 9%, plus 50 basis points, and the floating-rate payer agrees to pay the six-month LIBOR as determined on the effective date and each date six months later, with no basis points. Also, assume the semiannual interest rate is determined by dividing the annual rate (LIBOR and 9.5%) by 2. Finally, assume the notional principal on the swap is $10 million.

Table 17.2-1 shows the interest payments on each payment date based on assumed LIBORs on the effective dates. In examining the table, several points should be noted. First, the payments are determined by the LIBOR prevailing six months prior to the payment date; thus, each payer on the swap would know his obligation in advance of the payment date. Second, when the LIBOR is below the fixed 9.5% rate, the fixed-rate payer pays interest to the floating-rate payer; when it is above 9.5%, the fixed-rate payer receives the interest differential from the floating-rate payer. The net interest received by the fixed-rate payer is shown in column 5 of the table. The fixed-rate payer's position is very similar to a short position in a series of Eurodollar futures contracts, with the futures price determined by the fixed rate, that is, a Eurodollar strip. The floating-rate payer's position, on the other hand, is similar to a long position in a Eurodollar strip.   ◆

TABLE 17.2-1	Interest Rate Swap				
	(1)	(2)	(3)	(4)	(5)
	EFFECTIVE DATE	LIBOR	FLOATING-RATE PAYER'S PAYMENTS*	FIXED-RATE PAYER'S PAYMENTS†	NET INTEREST RECEIVED BY FIXED-RATE PAYER (3) − (5)
	March 23, 1995	.085	—	—	—
	Sept. 23, 1995	.09	$.425M	$.475M	− $.050M
	March 23, 1996	.095	.450	.475	− .025
	Sept. 23, 1996	.10	.475	.475	0
	March 23, 1997	.105	.500	.475	.025
	Sept. 23, 1997	.11	.525	.475	.050
	March 23, 1998		.550	.475	.075

$*\left(\frac{\text{LIBOR}}{2}\right)(\$10,000,000)$

$†\left(\frac{.095}{2}\right)(\$10,000,000)$

17.2.3 Similarities Between Swaps and Eurodollar Strips

To see the similarities between an interest rate swap and a Eurodollar strip, consider a short position in a Eurodollar strip in which the short holder agrees to sell 10 Eurodollar deposits, each with a face value of $1 million and maturity of six months, at the IMM-index price of 90.5 (or discount yield of $R_D = 9.5\%$), with the expirations on the strip being March 23 and September 23 for a period of 2½ years.

With the index at 90.5, the contract price on one Eurodollar futures contract is $952,500:

$$f_0 = \left[\frac{100 - (9.5)(180/360)}{100}\right](\$1,000,000) = \$952,500.$$

Table 17.2-2 shows the cash flows at the expiration dates from closing the 10 Eurodollar contracts at the same assumed LIBOR used in the swap example, with the Eurodollar settlement index being $100 - \text{LIBOR}$. For example, with the LIBOR at 9% on 9/23/95, a $25,000 loss results from settling the 10 futures contracts:

$$f_T = \left[\frac{100 - 9(180/360)}{100}\right](\$1,000,000) = \$955,000$$

Futures cash flow $= 10(f_0 - f_T) = 10(\$952,500 - \$955,000) = -\$25,000.$

Comparing the fixed-rate payer's net receipts, shown in column 5 of Table 17.2-1, with the cash flows from the short positions on the Eurodollar strip, shown in Table 17.2-2, we can see that the two positions yield the same numbers. There are, however, some differences between the Eurodollar strip and the swap. First, a six-month differential occurs between the swap payment and the futures payments. This time differential is a result of the interest payments on the swap being determined by the LIBOR at the beginning of the period, while the futures

TABLE 17.2-2

		Short Positions in Eurodollar Futures			
(1)	(2)	(3)	(4) CASH FLOW* $10(f_0 - f_T)$
DATES	LIBOR	f_T	
Sept. 23, 1995	.09	$955,000	− $25,000
March 23, 1996	.095	952,500	0
Sept. 23, 1996	.10	950,000	25,000
March 23, 1997	.105	947,500	50,000
Sept. 23, 1997	.11	945,000	75,000

*$f_0 = \$952,500$

$$f_T = \frac{100 - \frac{(LIBOR\%)(180/360)}{100}}{100}(\$1,000,000)$$

position's profit is based on the LIBOR at the end of its period. Second, we've assumed the futures contract is on a Eurodollar deposit with a maturity of six months instead of the standard three months. (For the Eurodollar strip and swap to be more similar, we would need to compare the swap to a synthetic contract on a six-month Eurodollar deposit formed with two short positions on three-month Eurodollar deposits: one expiring at T and one at $T + 90$ days.) In addition to these technical differences, other differences exist: The maturity of some strips can be extended out three years, while some swaps have a maturity as long as 10 years; strips are guaranteed by a clearinghouse, whereas banks often act as guarantors for swaps; and strip contracts are standardized, while swap agreements often are tailor-made.

17.2.4   Uses of Interest Rate Swaps

Since interest rate swaps are like interest rate futures, they can be used in many of the same ways as futures. One important use of a swap is in creating a synthetic fixed-rate or variable-rate loan.

To illustrate, suppose a corporation needs to borrow $10 million on March 23, 1995, and wants a fixed-rate loan with the principal to be paid back at the end of three years. Suppose one possibility available to the company is to borrow $10 million from a bank at a fixed rate of 10% (assume semiannual payments) with a three-year maturity on the loan. Suppose, though, that the bank also is willing to provide the company with a three-year variable-rate loan, with the rates set equal to the LIBOR on March 23 and September 23 each year for three years.

If a swap agreement identical to the one previously described were available, then instead of the fixed-rate loan, the company alternatively could attain a fixed rate by borrowing $10 million on the variable-rate loan, then fixing the interest rate by taking a fixed-rate payer's position on the swap. As shown in Table 17.2-3, if the variable-rate loan is hedged with a swap, any change in the LIBOR would be offset by an opposite change in the net receipts on the swap position. In this example, the company (as shown in the table) would end up paying a constant $0.475 million every sixth month, which equates to an annualized borrowing rate of 9.5%:

$$R = \frac{2(\$0.475 \text{ million})}{\$10 \text{ million}} = .095.$$

TABLE 17.2-3

			Synthetic Fixed-Rate Loan		
(1)	(2)	(3)	(4)	(5)	
		SEMIANNUAL INTEREST ON	NET INTEREST RECEIVED BY	EFFECTIVE INTEREST COST	
DATES	LIBOR	VARIABLE LOAN*	FIXED-RATE PAYER†	(3) − (4)	
March 23, 1995	.085	—	—	—
Sept. 23, 1995	.09	$.425M	− $.050M	$.475M
March 23, 1996	.095	.450	− .025	.475
Sept. 23, 1996	.10	.475	0	.475
March 23, 1997	.105	.500	.025	.475
Sept. 23, 1997	.11	.525	.050	.475
March 23, 1998	—	.550	.075	.475

*Interest $= \left(\frac{LIBOR}{2}\right)(\$10,000,000)$
†See Table 17.2-1, column 5.

TABLE 17.2-4

			Synthetic Variable-Rate Loan		
(1)	(2)	(3)	(4)	(5)	(6)
			NET INTEREST RECEIPT BY	EFFECTIVE	
		SEMIANNUAL INTEREST ON 9%	FLOATING-RATE	INTEREST COST	EFFECTIVE
DATES	LIBOR	FIXED-RATE LOAN	PAYER*	(3) − (4)	INTEREST RATE†
March 23, 1995	.085	—	—	—	—
Sept. 23, 1995	.09	$.450M	$.050M	$.400M	.080
March 23, 1996	.095	.450	.025	.425	.085
Sept. 23, 1996	.10	.450	0	.450	.090
March 23, 1997	.105	.450	− .025	.475	.095
Sept. 23, 1997	.11	.450	− .050	.500	.100
March 23, 1998	—	.450	− .075	.525	.105

*See Table 17.2-1, column 5.
†Rate $= \frac{2(\text{Effective interest costs})}{\$10M}$

Thus, the corporation would be better off combining the swap position as a fixed-rate payer and the variable-rate loan to create a synthetic fixed-rate loan than simply taking the straight fixed-rate loan.

In contrast, a synthetic variable-rate loan can be formed by combining a floating-rate payer's position with a fixed-rate loan. This loan then can be used as an alternative to a variable-rate loan. An example of a synthetic variable-rate loan is shown in Table 17.2-4. The synthetic loan is formed with a 9% fixed-rate loan (semiannual payments) and the floating-rate payer's position in our swap example. As shown in the table, the synthetic variable-rate loan yields an interest rate that is 0.5% lower each period (annualized rate) than would a variable-rate loan with rates set equal to LIBOR.

Note that in both of the preceding examples, the borrower was able to attain a better borrowing rate with a synthetic loan using swaps than with a straight debt position. If significant differences between the rates on actual and synthetic loans do exist, then arbitrage or quasi-arbitrage opportunity would be possible.

17.2.5   Swap Banks

Corporations, financial institutions, and others who use swaps are linked by a group of brokers and dealers collectively referred to as *swap banks*. These swap banks consist primarily of commercial banks and investment bankers.

As brokers, swap banks try to match parties with opposite needs. To this end, they often maintain lists of companies and financial institutions who are potential parties to a swap. Also, to facilitate the swap agreement, swap banks often will guarantee both sides of the transaction. As dealers, swap banks take positions as counterparties. When a swap bank acts as a dealer, it will post a bid-and-ask quote, similar to the one shown in Table 17.2-5. The quotes are often stated in terms of the rate they will pay as a fixed-rate payer in return for the LIBOR and the fixed rate they will receive as a floating-rate payer in return for paying the LIBOR.

In acting as dealers, swap banks try to maintain a perfect hedge. Ideally, this is done by matching the fixed-rate payer's position with a floating-rate payer's position. If the swap bank can do this, it will be able to earn the spread between the quoted fixed rates. For example, if the swap bank is able to take both positions shown in Table 17.2-5, it would be able to earn a profit of 20 basis points.

Frequently, though, swap banks have difficulty in matching counterparties. As a result, they will try to hedge their swap positions with positions either in the spot or the futures markets. For example, a swap bank might hedge a $10 million, three-year floating-rate position by borrowing $10 million, then use the proceeds to buy a 180-day spot Eurodollar CD, with the investment rolled over each period into a new Eurodollar CD. Given the high correlation between the LIBOR and Eurodollar CD rates, the return earned from the Eurodollar position should be close to the LIBOR the swap bank has to pay on its swap position. Usually this hedge is temporary, with the swap bank closing the position once an opposite counterparty is found.

17.2.6   Closing Swap Positions with Offsetting Positions

Unlike futures, swap contracts are more difficult to close. Prior to maturity, a swap position can be closed either by taking an offsetting position, by hedging the

TABLE 17.2-5

Swap Bank Quote	
Pay: LIBOR	*Receive*: LIBOR
Receive: Current yield on five-year T-note rate plus 80 basis points	*Pay*: Current yield on five-year T-note rate plus 60 basis points

TABLE 17.2-6

Closing a Fixed-Rate Payer's Position	
First swap	*Pay*: 9.5%
	Receive: LIBOR
Offset swap	*Receive*: 9%
	Pay: LIBOR
Net	*Pay*: .5%
Semiannual payment	(.5)(.005)($10,000,000) = $25,000

position for the remainder of the maturity period with a futures position, or by selling the swap to another party. Usually a counterparty closes her swap by taking an offsetting position. For example, a fixed-rate payer who sees interest rates decreasing unexpectedly and, as a result, wants to close her position could do so by either selling the swap to another party (at a discount), going long in an appropriate futures contract, or taking a floating-rate payer's position in a new swap contract.

If the swap holder closes by taking the opposite position on a new swap, the new swap position would require a payment of the LIBOR and BP, which would cancel out the receipt of the LIBOR plus BP on the first swap. The difference in the positions would equal the difference in the higher fixed interest rate paid on the first swap and the lower fixed interest rate received on the offsetting swap. For example, suppose in our illustrative swap example, a decline in interest rates occurs one year after the initiation of the swap, causing the fixed-rate payer to want to close her position. To this end, suppose the fixed-rate payer offsets her position by entering a new two-year swap as a floating-rate payer in which she agrees to pay the LIBOR for a 9% fixed rate. As shown in Table 17.2-6, the two positions would result in a fixed payment of $25,000 semiannually for two years. If interest rates decline over the next two years, this offsetting position would turn out to be the correct strategy.

17.2.7 Swaptions

Interest rate swaps have the characteristics of futures contracts. As such, they are used to lock in future interest rate positions, usually for longer periods than can be obtained with exchange-traded futures. However, financial managers who want downside protection for their position, with the potential for gains if conditions become favorable, can also take a position in *swaptions*, or *options on swaps*. Swaptions are options that give the holders the right to take a specific interest rate swap at certain times in the future, for example, a fixed-rate payer's position (or a floating-rate payer's position), with the exercise price set by the fixed rate on the swap.

17.3 CURRENCY SWAPS

In a *currency swap*, one party exchanges with another party a liability denominated in one currency in return for that party's liability denominated in a different currency. The market for currency swaps comes primarily from corporations who borrow in one currency but need to borrow in another. For example, a U.S. multinational corporation that can obtain favorable borrowing terms for a dollar loan made in the United States but that really needs a loan in French francs to finance its operations in France might use a currency swap. To meet such a need, the company could go to a swap dealer, who would try to match its needs with another party wanting the opposite position. The dealer might match the U.S. company with a French multinational corporation with operations in the United States that it is financing with a French franc loan but would prefer instead a dollar-denominated loan. If the loans are approximately equivalent, then the dealer could arrange a swap agreement in which the companies simply exchange their principal and interest payments. If the loans are not equivalent, the swap dealer may have to bring in other parties who are looking to swap, or the dealer could take the opposite position, possibly hedging it with a position in an exchange-traded currency futures contract.*

♦ **17.3.1   Example of Currency Swap**

There is a German auto company that can issue a five-year, DM 62.5M bond paying 7.5% interest to finance the construction of its U.S. manufacturing plant but that really needs an equivalent dollar loan, which at the current spot exchange rate of $0.40/DM would be $25M. There is also an American development company that can issue a five-year, $25M bond at 10% to finance the development of a hotel complex in Munich but that really needs a five-year, DM 62.5M loan. To meet each other's needs, both companies go to a swap bank, which sets up the following agreement:

1. The German company will issue a five-year, DM 62.5M bond paying 7.5% interest, then will pay the DM 62.5M to the swap bank, which will pass it on to the American company to finance its German investment project.

2. The American company will issue a five-year, $25M bond paying 10% interest, then will pay the $25M to the swap bank, which will pass it on to the German company to finance its U.S. investment project.

The initial cash flows of the agreement are shown in Figure 17.3-1(a).

For the next five years, each company will make annual interest payments. To this end, the swap dealer would make the following arrangements:

1. The German company, with its U.S. asset (manufacturing plant), will pay the 10% interest on $25M ($2.5M) to the swap bank, which will pass it on to the American company so it can pay its U.S. bondholders.

2. The American company, with its German asset (hotel), will pay the 7.5% interest on DM 62.5M (DM 4.6875M) to the swap bank, which will pass it on to the German company so it can pay its German bondholders.

*Currency swaps evolved from two similar types of arrangements—back-to-back loans and parallel loans. In a back-to-back loan, companies exchange loans denominated in different currencies; in a parallel loan, one multinational corporation lends to the subsidiary of a foreign multinational, and vice versa. These loan arrangements were set up to circumvent foreign exchange controls.

FIGURE 17.3-1

Currency Swap

American company issues a five-year, $25M bond at 10% interest that it swaps with a German company that issues a five-year, DM 62.5M bond at 7.5% interest

(a) Initial Cash Flow

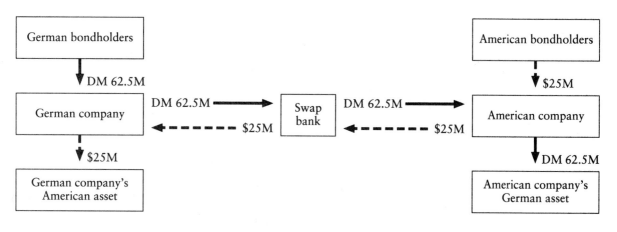

(b) Annual Interest Cash Flow

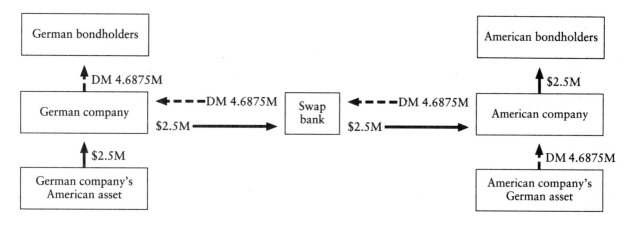

(c) Principal Payment at Maturity

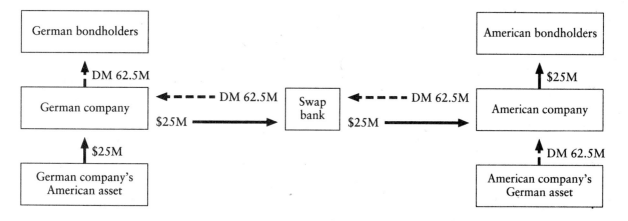

The yearly cash flows of interest are summarized in Figure 17.3-1(b).

Finally, to cover the principal payments at maturity, the swap dealer would set up the following agreement:

1. At maturity, the German company will pay $25M to the swap bank, which will pass it on to the American company so it can pay its U.S. bondholders.

2. At maturity, the American company will pay DM 62.5M to the swap bank, which will pass it on to the German company so it can pay its German bondholders.

The cash flow of principals are shown in Figure 17.3-1(c). ◆

17.3.2 Similarities Between Currency Swaps and Currency Forward Contracts

In the preceding swap agreement, the German company agreed to pay $2.5M each year for DM 4.6875M and $25M at maturity for DM 62.5M. To the German company, the interest agreement represents a series of long currency forward contracts with an implied forward exchange rate of $0.53/DM:

$$E_f = \frac{\$2.5M}{DM\ 4.6875M} = \frac{\$0.53}{DM}.$$

The principal swap, in turn, represents a long contract with an implied forward exchange rate of $0.40/DM:

$$E_f = \frac{\$25M}{DM\ 62.5M} = \frac{\$0.40}{DM}.$$

In contrast, the American company has agreed to sell DM 4.6875M each year for $2.5M and DM 62.5M at maturity for $25M. To the American company, the swap agreement represents a series of short currency forward contracts at implied forward rates of $0.53/DM on the interest swaps and $0.40/DM on the principal swap.

17.3.3 Comparative Advantage

The currency swap in the preceding example represents an exchange of equivalent loans. Most currency swaps, however, result when borrowers and swap banks take comparative advantage of different rates in different countries. To see this, suppose the American and German companies in the preceding example both have access to each country's lending markets and that the American company is more creditworthy and, as such, can obtain lower rates than the German company in both the U.S. and German markets.

Say the American company can obtain 10% in the U.S. market and 7.25% in the German market, while the best the German company can obtain is 11% in the U.S. market and 7.5% in the German market (see Table 17.3-1). With these rates, the American company has a comparative advantage in the U.S. market: It pays 1% less than the German company in the U.S. market, compared to only .25% less in

TABLE 17.3-1

Loan Rates for American and German Companies in the United States and Germany		
	U.S. MARKET	GERMAN MARKET
American company	10%	7.25%
German company	11%	7.5%

FIGURE 17.3-2

Currency Swap

American company issues a five-year, $25M loan at 10% interest that it swaps for a five-year, DM 62.5M loan at 7%. German company issues a five-year, DM 62.5M loan at 7.5% that it swaps for a five-year, $25M loan at 10.5%.

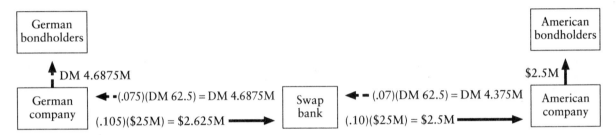

the German market. On the other hand, the German company has a comparative advantage in the German market: It pays .25% more than the U.S. company in Germany, compared to 1% more in the United States.

When such a comparative advantage exists, a swap bank is in a position to arrange a swap to benefit one or both companies. Suppose in this case that a swap bank sets up the following swap arrangement:

1. The American company borrows $25M at 10%, then agrees to swap it for a DM 62.5M loan at 7%.

2. The German company borrows DM 62.5M at 7.5%, then agrees to swap it for a $25M loan at 10.5%.

Figure 17.3-2 shows the annual cash flows of interest for the agreement (the cash flow at the outset and at maturity are the same as in the previous example shown in Figure 17.3-1).

In this swap arrangement, the American company benefits by paying .25% less than it could obtain by borrowing directly in the German market, and the German company gains by paying .5% less than it could obtain in the U.S. market. The swap bank, as shown in Figure 17.3-2, will receive $2.652M each year from the German company while only having to pay $2.5M to the American company, for a net dollar inflow of $0.125M. On the other hand, the swap bank receives only DM 4.375M from the American company while paying DM 4.6875M to the German company, for a net DM outflow of DM 0.3125M. Thus, the swap bank has the equivalent of a series of currency forward contracts in which it agrees to exchange DM 0.3125M for $0.125M. The swap bank's implied forward rate on each of these contracts is $0.40/DM:

$$E_f = \frac{\$0.125M}{DM\ .3125M} = \frac{\$0.40}{DM}.$$

The swap bank, in turn, could hedge its position by going long in a currency forward contract. If the exchange-traded or dealer's actual forward rate is $0.40/DM, the bank could agree to buy DM 0.3125 at $0.40/DM (using its swap revenue of $0.125M). If the rate is less than $0.40/DM, the bank could gain from hedging the swap agreement. For example, if the forward rate is $0.39/DM, then the bank could buy DM 0.3125M for $0.122M on the forward contract, then deliver the DM 0.3125M on the swap, leaving the swap bank with a profit from the swap and forward contract of $0.125M − $0.122M = $0.003M. Moreover, since the swap bank is arranging the swap, and since it is also exposed to the credit risk from the swap agreement, it would more than likely take into account the forward rate, so it could obtain some compensation for arranging the swap.

17.4 OTHER SWAPS

The plain vanilla interest rate swap described earlier represents the most general type of interest rate swap. There are a number of other types of swaps offered by swap banks. These swaps usually differ in terms of their rates, principal, and/or effective dates. For example, instead of defining swaps in terms of the three-month LIBOR, some swaps use T-bill or commercial paper rates with different maturities. Similarly, the principals defining a swap can vary. An *amortizing swap*, for example, is a swap in which the principals are reduced based on a specified loan amortization schedule. Finally, there are deferred, or forward, swaps. These swaps, in turn, extend the payment dates to start at dates in the future.

Like interest rate swaps, currency swaps can vary, and they also can be combined with interest rate swaps. For example, a swap bank could set up an agreement in which one party could exchange a fixed interest in one currency for a floating interest in another currency.*

17.5 INTEREST RATE OPTIONS

In Chapter 9, we examined the markets and uses of options on T-bills, T-notes, and T-bonds, and in the last chapter we described futures options on these securities. These exchange-traded options represent contracts on specific spot and futures

---

*Swap agreements also are expanding beyond interest rates and currency to commodities such as oil.

securities and, as we have seen, can be used to hedge interest rate positions. In addition to these options, another instrument that corporate treasurers, money managers, and others increasingly are using is the ***interest rate option.***

Like exchange-traded debt options, interest rate options are utilized primarily to hedge positions against interest rate risk. However, instead of providing holders with the right to purchase (or sell) a specific debt security at a specific price, interest rate options give holders the right to a payoff if a specific interest rate level is greater (call) or less (put) than the option's exercise rate.

17.5.1   Characteristics of Interest Rate Options

Interest rate options usually are written by commercial banks in conjunction with a loan they plan to provide their clients. Unlike the standardized exchange-traded options, interest rate options usually are tailored to meet the needs of the holder. Thus, the expiration on the option and the principal on which the interest applies are often determined by the option buyer, frequently in conjunction with a loan being provided by the bank. The exercise price (or rate) on the option ordinarily is set near the current spot rate, with that rate often being tied to the LIBOR. In addition, the options are usually European. At expiration, if the option is in the money, the holder upon exercising will be entitled to a payment from the writer equal to the loan principal times the difference between the current rate and the exercise rate. The payment, however, is customarily not received until the maturity date on the corresponding loan.

◆   17.5.2   Example of Interest Rate Options

Interest Rate Call

Suppose the N.C. Company, a large furniture manufacturer, plans to finance its future lumber purchases 60 days from the present time by borrowing $10M from the Sun Bank. The loan will have a maturity of 90 days, and the loan rate will be set equal to the LIBOR + 100 BP, with the rate based on a 360-day year. Furthermore, the N.C. Company is concerned that interest rates could increase during the next 60 days and, as a result, pays Sun Bank $20,000 for an interest rate call option with an exercise rate equal to the current LIBOR (for such loans) of 8% (based on a 360-day year) and an expiration of 60 days. The N.C. Company agrees that if it exercises at expiration, it will wait until the loan matures before collecting on the option.

Table 17.5-1 shows the N.C. Company's cash flows from the call, interest paid on the loan, and effective interest costs that would result, given different LIBORs at the option's expiration date. As shown in column 6 of the table, the company is able to lock in a maximum interest cost of 9.26% if the LIBORs are 7% or greater at expiration while still benefiting with lower rates if the LIBORs are less than 7%.

Interest Rate Put

A corporation, financial institution, or other economic entity that is planning to make an investment at some future date could hedge that investment against interest rate decreases by purchasing an interest rate put. For example, suppose that

TABLE 17.5-1

Hedging a Loan with Interest Rate Call Option

N.C. Company's loan at T: $10,000,000 at LIBOR + 100 BP for 90 days
Call option: $X = 7\%$, $T = 60$ days

(1) LIBOR$_T$	(2) INTRINSIC VALUE* OF CALL AT T	(3) COSTS OF OPTION AT $T^\dagger$	(4) INTEREST PAID ON LOAN AT MATURITY‡	(5) TOTAL COSTS AT MATURITY (4) − (2)	(6) ANNUALIZED HEDGED LOAN RATE§
5%	0	$20,233	$150,000	$150,000	7.10%
6	0	20,233	175,000	175,000	8.17
7	0	20,233	200,000	200,000	9.26
8	$25,000	20,233	225,000	200,000	9.26
9	50,000	20,233	250,000	200,000	9.26

*Intrinsic value $= \$10,000,000\left(\frac{90}{360}\right)\frac{\text{Max}[\text{LIBOR}_T - 7\%, 0]}{100}$.

†Costs of option at $T = \$20,000[1 + .07\left(\frac{60}{360}\right)] = \$20,233$.

‡Interest paid on loan at maturity $= \$10,000,000\left(\frac{\text{LIBOR}_T}{100} + .01\right)\left(\frac{90}{360}\right)$.

§Annualized hedged loan rate $= \left(\frac{\$10,000,000 + \text{Column 5}}{\$10,000,000 - \text{Column 3}}\right)^{365/90} - 1$.

TABLE 17.5-2

Hedging a CD Investment with Interest Rate Put Option

N.C. Company's investment at T: $10,000,000 at LIBOR for 90 days
Put option: $X = 7\%$, $T = 60$ days

(1) LIBOR$_T$	(2) INTRINSIC VALUE* OF PUT AT T	(3) COSTS OF OPTION AT $T^\dagger$	(4) INTEREST RECEIVED ON CD AT MATURITY‡	(5) REVENUES AT MATURITY (2) + (4)	(6) ANNUALIZED HEDGED RATE§
5%	$50,000	$15,175	$125,000	$175,000	6.63%
6	25,000	15,175	150,000	175,000	6.63
7	0	15,175	175,000	175,000	6.63
8	0	15,175	200,000	200,000	7.70
9	0	15,175	225,000	225,000	8.77

*Intrinsic value $= \$10,000,000\left(\frac{90}{360}\right)\left[\frac{\text{Max}[7\% - \text{LIBOR}, 0]}{100}\right]$.

†Costs of option at $T = \$15,000[1 + .07\left(\frac{60}{360}\right)] = \$15,175$.

‡Interest received on CD at maturity $= \$10,000,000\left(\frac{\text{LIBOR}_T}{100}\right)\left(\frac{90}{360}\right)$.

§Annualized hedged rate $= \left(\frac{\$10,000,000 + \text{Column 5}}{\$10,000,000 + \text{Column 3}}\right)^{365/90} - 1$.

instead of needing to borrow $10M, the N.C. Company was expecting a net cash inflow of $10M in 60 days from its operations and was planning to invest the funds in a 90-day Sun Bank CD paying the LIBOR. To hedge against any interest rate decreases, the N.C. Company purchases an interest rate put (corresponding to the bank's CD it plans to buy) from the Sun Bank for $15,000, with the put having an exercise rate of 7%, expiration of 60 days, and payment made at the maturity date on the CD. As shown in Table 17.5-2, the put would make it possible for the N.C. Company to earn higher rates if the LIBOR is greater than 7% and to lock in a minimum rate of 6.63% if the LIBOR is 7% or less. ◆

17.6 CAPS, FLOORS, AND COLLARS

17.6.1 Caps

A *cap* is a series of European interest rate calls that expire at or near the interest payment dates on a loan. They are often written by financial institutions in conjunction with a variable-rate loan and are used by buyers as a hedge against interest rate risk.

As an example, suppose the Diamond Development company borrows $50M from Commerce Bank to finance its yearly construction projects. The loan starts on March 1 at a rate of 8% for the next quarter, then resets every three months at the prevailing LIBOR. In entering this loan agreement, the Diamond Company is uncertain of future interest rates and therefore would like to lock in a maximum rate while still benefiting from lower rates if LIBORs decrease. To achieve this, the company buys a cap, corresponding to its loan, for $100,000, with an exercise, or cap, rate of 8%. At each effective date, the intrinsic value of the cap would be:

$$IV = \$50,000,000 \left(\frac{\text{Days in period}}{360} \right) \left(\frac{\text{Max}[\text{LIBOR} - 8, 0]}{100} \right),$$

and, as with interest rate options, if the cap is exercised, the payoff would be received at the end of the interest period.

Since the Diamond Company would exercise the cap when the LIBOR is greater than 8%, it would be able to lock in a maximum rate each quarter while still benefiting with lower interest costs if rates decrease. This can be seen in Table 17.6-1, where the net cash flows of the loan and cap are shown for different LIBORs at each effective date on the loan and cap.

17.6.2 Floors

A *floor* is a series of European interest rate puts that, like caps, expire at or near the effective dates on a loan. Floors are often purchased by institutional lenders as a tool to hedge their variable-rate loans against interest rate declines.

As an example, suppose the Commerce Bank purchased an interest rate floor with an exercise rate of 8% for $70,000 from another institution to protect its variable-rate loan to the Diamond Company. At each effective date, the intrinsic value of the floor would be:

$$IV = \$50,000,000 \left(\frac{\text{Days in period}}{360} \right) \left(\frac{\text{Max}[8\% - \text{LIBOR}, 0]}{100} \right),$$

TABLE 17.6-1

Hedging Variable-Rate Loan with Cap						
Loan: $50,000,000 variable rate; *cap*: exercise rate = 8%, premium = $100,000						
(1) EFFECTIVE DATE	(2) DAYS IN QUARTER	(3) LIBOR	(4) LOAN INTEREST PAYMENT*	(5) CAP CASH FLOW†	(6) CASH FLOW WITH CAP	(7) RATE PAID WITH CAP‡
3/1	92	8.0%	—	− $100,000	$49,900,000	—
6/1	92	8.5	1,022,222	0	− 1,022,222	8%
9/1	91	9.0	1,086,111	63,889	− 1,022,222	8%
12/1	90	7.0	1,137,500	126,389	− 1,011,111	8%
3/1	90		875,000	0	− 50,875,000	7%

*Loan interest payment $= \$50,000,000\left(\frac{\text{Days in period}}{360}\right)\frac{\text{LIBOR}}{100}$

†Cap cash flow $= \$50,000,000\left(\frac{\text{Days in period}}{360}\right)\left(\frac{\text{Max[LIBOR} - 8\%, 0]}{100}\right)$
Initial cash flow $= -\$100,000$

‡Rate $= \left(\frac{\text{Column 4} - \text{Column 5}}{\$50,000,000}\right)\left(\frac{360}{\text{Days in period}}\right)$

TABLE 17.6-2

Bank Hedging Loan with a Floor						
Loan: $50,000,000						
Floor: premium = $70,000, exercise rate = 8%						
(1) EFFECTIVE DATE	(2) DAYS IN QUARTER	(3) LIBOR	(4) LOAN INTEREST RECEIPT*	(5) FLOOR CASH FLOW†	(6) CASH FLOW WITH FLOOR	(7) RATE RECEIVED WITH FLOOR‡
3/1	92	8.0%	—	− $ 70,000	− $50,070,000	—
6/1	92	8.5	$1,022,222	0	1,022,222	8%
9/1	91	7.0	1,086,111	0	1,086,111	8.6
12/1	90	6.0	884,722	126,389	1,011,111	8
3/1	90		750,000	250,000	51,000,000	8

*Loan interest receipt $= \$50,000,000\left(\frac{\text{Days in period}}{360}\right)\left(\frac{\text{LIBOR}}{100}\right)$

†Floor cash flow $= \$50,000,000\left(\frac{\text{Days in period}}{360}\right)\left(\frac{\text{Max[8\%} - \text{LIBOR, 0]}}{100}\right)$
Initial cash flow $= -\$70,000$

‡Rate $= \left(\frac{\text{Column 4} + \text{Column 5}}{\$50,000,000}\right)\left(\frac{360}{\text{Days in period}}\right)$

which would be received at the end of the period. Table 17.6-2 shows the cash flows from the floor and the loan given different LIBORs at the four effective dates. The floor is in the money on dates 9/1 and 12/1, enabling the Commerce Bank to offset the lower interest received from its loan to the Diamond Company.

17.6.3 Collars

A **collar** consists of one position in a cap and an opposite position in a floor with different exercise rates. For instance, a company with a variable-rate loan could

TABLE 17.6-3

Hedging a Variable-Rate Loan with a Collar							
Loan: One-year variable-rate for $50,000,000 *Cap purchase:* 8% exercise rate, premium = $100,000 *Floor sale:* 7% exercise rate, premium = $70,000							
(1) EFFECTIVE DATE	(2) DAYS IN QUARTER	(3) LIBOR	(4) LOAN INTEREST PAYMENT*	(5) CASH FLOW FROM CAP†	(6) CASH FLOW FROM SHORT FLOOR‡	(7) CASH FLOW WITH CAP AND FLOOR	(8) RATE PAID WITH CAP AND FLOOR§
3/1	92	10%	—	—		$50,030,000	—
6/1	92	9	$1,277,778	$255,556	0	− 1,022,222	8%
9/1	91	7	1,150,000	127,778	0	− 1,022,222	8%
12/1	90	6	884,722	0	0	− 884,722	7%
3/1	90		750,000	0	− $125,000	− 50,875,000	7%

*Loan interest payment $= \$50,000,000 \left(\frac{\text{Days in period}}{360}\right)\left(\frac{\text{LIBOR}}{100}\right)$

†Cap receipt $= \$50,000,000 \left(\frac{\text{Days in period}}{360}\right)\left(\frac{\text{Max}[\text{LIBOR} - 8\%, 0]}{100}\right)$

‡Floor payment $= \$50,000,000 \left(\frac{\text{Days in period}}{360}\right)\left(\frac{\text{Max}[7\% - \text{LIBOR}, 0]}{100}\right)$

§Rate paid $= \left(\frac{\text{Column 4} - \text{Column 5} - \text{Column 6}}{\$50,000,000}\right)\left(\frac{360}{\text{Days in period}}\right)$

purchase a cap to lock in a maximum rate and then sell a floor to defray the cost of the cap, in return giving up potential lower rates.

As an example, consider again the Diamond Company with the one-year, $50M variable-rate loan. Suppose this time the company decides to finance the $100,000 cost of its 8% cap by selling a 7% floor for $70,000. By using the collar instead of the cap, the company reduces its hedging cost from $100,000 to $30,000, and, as shown in Table 17.6-3, it can lock in a maximum rate of 8%. However, when the LIBORs are less than 7%, the company does not benefit from lower rates, but rather must pay a rate of 7%.

17.7 HYBRID EQUITY SECURITIES

17.7.1 Prescribed Right to Income and Maximum Equity (PRIME) and Special Claim on Residual Equity (SCORE)

In 1986, Americas Trust introduced the **PRIME** (prescribed right to income and maximum equity) and the **SCORE** (special claim on residual equity). These securities traded for five years on the American Stock Exchange. Both securities entitled the holder to a claim on parts of the returns on an equity security.* To create these

---

*PRIMEs and SCOREs are similar to dual-purpose funds that break up the returns of a mutual fund.

TABLE 17.7-1

	Value of PRIME, SCORE, and Stock at Expiration		
	CASH FLOW AT EXPIRATION		
	$S_T < X$	$S_T = X$	$S_T > X$
PRIME	$S_T + D_T$	$S_T + D_T$	$X + D_T$
SCORE	0	0	$S_T - X$
PRIME + SCORE	$S_T + D_T$	$S_T + D_T$	$S_T + D_T$
Stock	$S_T + D_T$	$S_T + D_T$	$S_T + D_T$

securities, a trust unit was formed that was equal in value to a share of stock. Each trust unit was then divided into two units, a PRIME and a SCORE, and sold to investors. The holder of the PRIME would be entitled to any dividends paid on the stock, and at the expiration date on the PRIME would be entitled to the value of the stock (S_T) up to a specified value (X). That is:

$$\text{Value of PRIME at } T = \text{Min}[S_T, X] + D_T.$$

Thus, the PRIME was equivalent to a covered call position.

The holder of the SCORE, on the other hand, would receive at expiration $S_T - X$ if $S_T > X$, and zero otherwise:

$$\text{Cash flow on SCORE at } T = \text{Max}[S_T - X, 0].$$

Thus, the SCORE represented a European call option on the stock underlying the trust unit.

At expiration the sum of the PRIME (PR) and the SCORE (SC) should equal the value of the stock. This can be seen in Table 17.7-1, which shows the values of each at $S_T < X$, $S_T = X$, and $S_T > X$. Thus, a priori, we should expect the value of the PRIME and the SCORE to equal the value of the trust unit or its underlying stock: $PR_t + SC_t = S_t$. If not, arbitrage opportunities would exist.

The American Stock Exchange provided trading for 24 trust units. They were replaced, though, by two similar securities: PERCS and LEAPS.

17.7.2   Preferred Equity-Redemption Cumulative Stocks (PERCS)

Preferred equity-redemption cumulative stocks, or simply *PERCS*, are similar to PRIMEs, except they are issued by a corporation instead of a trust, pay larger dividends, have a longer life (three years), and are callable, with the premium declining over the period. When PERCS are called, they are exchanged for common shares at a call price. If they are not called, the holder is required to convert to common stock at expiration. If the stock price (S_t) is greater than the call price, the holder of the PERCS receives less than S_t for a share (like a PRIME). PERCS are similar to covered call writes.

17.7.3 Long-Term Equity-Anticipation Securities (LEAPS)

In 1990, the CBOE began trading in long-term equity-anticipation securities, or ***LEAPS.*** LEAPS are similar to SCOREs, except they are offered by the option exchange, instead of a trust, and are American. The exchange offers both call and put LEAPS, with expirations of one, two, and three years, and with different exercise prices. Currently, LEAPS are available on over 100 securities and on several stock indices. Exhibit 17.7-1 shows the price quotes on several LEAPS as they appear in the *Wall Street Journal.*

EXHIBIT 17.7-1

Quotes on LEAPS from the *Wall Street Journal*

LEAPS — LONG TERM OPTIONS

			–Call–		–Put–	
Option/Strike		Exp.	Vol.	Last	Vol.	Last
3Com	65	Jan 97	20	11½	...	...
ABarck	25	Jan 96	12	4	...	...
23	25	Jan 97	20	6	...	...
ASA	35	Jan 96	11	13⅛	...	...
46⅞	45	Jan 96	13	7	...	...
46⅞	55	Jan 97	30	6	...	...
AT&T	60	Jan 96	20	4	...	...
54⅝	65	Jan 96	12	2¼	...	...
Amgen	40	Jan 96	...	...	16	3⅛
49⅛	60	Jan 96	7	5	20	13
AppleC	30	Jan 96	33	7⅞	12	4¾
31⅞	40	Jan 96	11	4¼	...	...
Boeing	55	Jan 96	50	2⅜	...	...
BorInf	10	Jan 96	20	4⅝	...	...
11⅝	15	Jan 96	20	2¾	...	...
11⅝	15	Jan 97	20	3¼	...	...
BrMySq	60	Jan 96	616	2⅛	5	9¼
Centcr	10	Jan 97	30	5¾	...	...
12	20	Jan 97	36	3	...	...
Chase	35	Jan 96	...	...	105	2⅞
Chiron	35	Jan 97	...	...	60	3⅝
52¾	50	Jan 97	...	...	12	9⅛
52¾	75	Jan 97	15	9¾	7	24¼
52¾	100	Jan 96	68	2	...	...
52¾	100	Jan 97	49	5⅛	...	...
Chrysl	60	Jan 96	35	3⅞	...	...
Chubb	110	Jan 96	50	¾	...	...
Cisco	15	Jan 96	8	8¼	30	1⅞
19⅞	20	Jan 96	52	5⅜	34	4¼
19⅞	30	Jan 97	19	4⅜	...	...
19⅞	35	Jan 96	24	2	...	...
Citicp	50	Jan 96	10	3⅛	...	...
CocaCl	30	Jan 96	31	15	...	...
44⅛	40	Jan 96	24	7⅝	35	2⅛
44⅛	40	Jan 97	11	10	...	...
Compaq	23⅜	Jan 96	...	...	10	2¼
30⅞	31⅝	Jan 96	10	6¾	...	...
ConrPr	15	Jan 96	20	1¾	...	...
Conseco	40	Jan 97	50	18⅞	...	...
DeltaA	40	Jan 97	...	...	25	3⅛
Digital	15	Jan 97	27	8½	12	2 1/16
19⅜	20	Jan 96	...	...	10	3¾
19⅜	20	Jan 97	50	6¼	...	...
19⅜	30	Jan 96	...	...	28	11⅜
Disney	30	Jan 96	11	14½	...	...
42⅛	40	Jan 96	...	...	10	3
42⅛	50	Jan 96	134	3¼	60	8¾
42⅛	50	Jan 97	30	6⅛	60	9⅜
FedNMt	80	Jan 97	50	16¼	50	6¼
Ford	25	Jan 97	55	9⅜	...	...
35	35	Jan 97	43	4⅝	...	...
FordM	32½	Jan 96	41	4⅛	...	...
GTE	35	Jan 96	53	1 9/16	...	...
31½	45	Jan 96	20	¼	...	...
Glaxo	20	Jan 96	59	1 11/16	10	4⅜
17½	20	Jan 97	15	2½	...	...
GnMotr	40	Jan 96	32	14⅜	...	...
50¼	50	Jan 96	15	8½	...	...
50¼	60	Jan 96	25	4⅜	...	...
50¼	70	Jan 96	10	2 5/16	...	...

			–Call–		–Put–	
Option/Strike		Exp.	Vol.	Last	Vol.	Last
Heinz	35	Jan 97	...	...	20	4⅛
HmeDep	45	Jan 96	...	...	50	6¾
40⅛	45	Jan 97	6	6¾	50	7⅞
40⅛	55	Jan 96	11	2⅛	...	...
Homstk	17½	Jan 96	12	5⅜	...	...
IBM	50	Jan 96	33	16	...	...
62¼	60	Jan 96	81	10½	102	5½
62¼	60	Jan 97	19	15	2	6⅝
62¼	70	Jan 96	21	6½	...	...
62¼	70	Jan 97	38	9¾	...	...
IGame	20	Jan 96	10	4½	5	4
18⅞	30	Jan 96	15	1½	...	...
IntGame	20	Jan 97	17	5½	...	...
Intel	50	Jan 96	30	14¾	...	...
57⅞	65	Jan 96	1412	7¾	...	...
57⅞	80	Jan 97	14	7½	...	...
JohnJn	40	Jan 96	22	9⅞	8	1 3/16
47	40	Jan 97	20	12	7	2⅜
47	45	Jan 96	...	...	221	3⅛
47	50	Jan 96	97	4	26	5⅝
Limitd	17½	Jan 96	57	4¾	...	...
Lotus	30	Jan 97	11	11⅛	15	7¼
MCI	30	Jan 96	52	1⅝	...	...
MMM	55	Jan 96	15	4½	...	...
52½	65	Jan 96	39	1 13/16	...	...
McDnld	25	Jan 97	...	...	50	2
MerLyn	40	Jan 96	15	4⅛	...	...
35⅛	50	Jan 96	10	1⅝	...	...
Merck	30	Jan 96	71	3¾	30	3⅛
29¾	30	Jan 97	54	5¼	...	...
29¾	35	Jan 96	25	1⅞	1	6¼
29¾	40	Jan 96	4	13/16	10	10½
29¾	40	Jan 97	227	2¼	...	...
29¾	50	Jan 96	112	5/16	...	...
MicrTc	40	Jan 96	...	...	16	9½
Micsft	55	Jan 96	...	...	50	7⅞
97¾	55	Jan 97	10	9⅞	50	9⅛
49½	57½	Jan 96	29	5¼	...	...
Morgan	60	Jan 96	...	...	10	4¾
Motorla	40	Jan 96	34	17	18	1⅞
52	50	Jan 96	34	10⅜	2	5¼
52	50	Jan 97	42	14	10	6
52	60	Jan 97	31	9¾	...	...
NatnsBk	55	Jan 96	50	6½	75	5
55	65	Jan 96	50	2½	...	...
NewbNk	40	Jan 97	14	14	...	...
OcciPt	25	Jan 97	20	1 1/16	...	...
Oracle	25	Jan 96	10	16¼	...	...
36 13/16	30	Jan 96	...	...	52	4
PepsiC	30	Jan 96	71	3¾	65	3
29¾	35	Jan 96	59	2⅛	8	6
PhilMr	40	Jan 96	27	15¼	...	...
54¾	40	Jan 97	50	16⅝	...	...
54¾	45	Jan 96	...	...	50	2¼
54¾	50	Jan 96	40	8⅝	135	4
54¾	60	Jan 96	100	4½	82	9¼
54¾	70	Jan 96	10	2	...	...
54¾	80	Jan 96	11	1	...	...
PlacrD	25	Jan 96	10	3⅛	...	...
21⅛	30	Jan 96	30	2	10	9

SOURCE: *Wall Street Journal*, July 29, 1994

17.8   CONCLUSION

In this final chapter, we have examined some of the newer derivative securities that have been introduced over the last decade. Like exchange-traded options and futures, swaps, interest rate options, caps, floors, PRIMEs, SCOREs, PERCS, and LEAPS provide investors with a tool for speculating on positions.

We have not exhausted all derivative securities, just as we have not covered all the strategies, uses, markets, and pricing models on options and futures. What we hope we have done here, and in this book, is to develop a foundation for understanding derivative securities. To the extent that most securities and assets derive their values from another asset, we hope we also have established a foundation and methodology for understanding finance through derivative assets.

KEY TERMS

hybrid	effective date	floor
financial swap	settlement date (payment date)	collar
interest rate swap	swap bank	PRIME
counterparties	swaption	SCORE
fixed-rate payer	currency swap	PERCS
floating-rate payer	interest rate option	LEAPS
trade date	cap	

SELECTED REFERENCES

Arak, M., Estrella, A., Goodman, L., and Silver, A. "Interest Rate Swaps: An Alternative Explanation." *Financial Management* 17 (Summer 1988): 12–18.

Arnold, T. "How to Do Interest Rate Swaps." *Harvard Business Review* 62 (Sept.–Oct. 1984): 96–101.

Beidleman, C. *Financial Swaps.* Homewood, Ill.: Dow-Jones-Irwin, 1985.

Bicksler, J., and Chen, A. "An Economic Analysis of Interest Rate Swaps." *Journal of Finance* (July 1986): 645–655.

Chance, D. *Options and Futures.* Chicago: Dryden Press, 1991, pp. 500–503, 534–549.

Felgran, S. "Interest Rate Swaps: Use, Risk, and Prices." *New England Economic Review* (Nov. 1987): 22–32.

Goodman, L. "The Use of Interest Rate Swaps in Managing Corporate Liabilities." *Journal of Applied Corporate Finance* 2 (1990): 35–47.

Marshall, J., and Kapner, K. *Understanding Swap Finance.* Cincinnati, Ohio: South-Western, 1990.

Park, Y. "Currency Swaps as a Long-Term International Financing Technique." *Journal of International Business Studies* 15 (Winter 1984): 47–54.

Price, J., Keller, J., and Nelson, M. "The Delicate Art of Swaps." *Euromoney* (Apr. 1983): 118–125.

Shirreff, D. "The Fearsome Growth of Swaps." *Euromoney* (Oct. 1985): 247–261.

Smith, C., Smithson, C., and Wakeman, L. "The Evolving Market for Swaps." *Midland Corporate Finance Journal* 41 (Winter 1986): 20–32.

———. "The Market for Interest Rate Swaps." *Financial Management* 17 (Winter 1988): 34–44.

Turnball, S. "Swaps: A Zero Sum Game." *Financial Management* 16 (Spring 1987): 15–22.

Wall, L., and Pringle, J. "Alternative Explanations of Interest Rate Swaps." *Financial Management* 18 (Summer 1989): 59–73.

PROBLEMS AND QUESTIONS

1. Given the following interest-rate swap:

   - Fixed-rate payer pays half of the YTM on a T-note of 9% (annual) plus 50 BP on each delivery date.
   - Floating-rate payer pays half of the LIBOR (annual).
   - Notional principal is $10M.
   - Effective dates are 3/23 and 9/23 for the next four years.

   a. Determine the net receipts of the fixed-rate payer given the following annual LIBOR:

3/23/94:	.09	6/23/94:	.095
3/23/95:	.10	6/23/95:	.105
3/23/96:	.11	6/23/96:	.115
3/23/97:	.12	6/23/97:	.125

   b. Show in a table how a company with a $10M variable-rate loan, with the rate set by the LIBOR on the dates coinciding with the swap, could make the loan a fixed-rate one by taking a position in the swap. What would be its fixed rate?

2. Given the LIBORs shown in Table 17.P-2, determine the schedule of payments for a floating-for-fixed-rate interest swap in which the notional principal is $30M, the floating-rate payer pays half of the annual LIBOR + 100 BP, and the fixed-rate payer pays half of a 10% (annual) rate on each effective date.

TABLE 17.P-2

EFFECTIVE DATE	LIBOR
3/1/95	12%
9/1/95	11
3/1/96	10
9/1/96	9
3/1/97	8
9/1/97	7
3/1/98	6

3. Given the LIBOR in Table 17.P-2, determine the schedule of payments for a synthetic variable-rate loan formed by borrowing $30M at an annual fixed rate of 9% (with the semiannual payments beginning 9/1/95 and ending 3/1/98) and taking the floating-rate payer's position described in Problem 2. Which would be better, a variable-rate loan paying the LIBOR or the synthetic variable-rate loan?

4. Describe some of the similarities and differences between interest rate swaps and Eurodollar strips.

5. Explain how a counterparty can close or offset his position prior to the swap's expiration.

6. Suppose the Paris Coat Company, a well-known company in France, plans to issue a five-year bond worth 10M FF at 8% interest but actually needs an equivalent amount in dollars, $1.75M (current $/FF rate is $0.175/FF), to finance its new manufacturing facility in the United States. Also, the Barkley Shoe Company, a well-known U.S. company, plans to issue $1.75M in bonds at 10%, with a maturity of five years, but it really needs 10M FF to set up its distribution center in France.

   a. Explain how a swap bank could arrange a currency swap after the Paris and Barkley companies issue their bonds.

   b. Explain how the swap bank would arrange for the annual interest payments. Assume the swap bank determines the interest swap based on the rates each company can attain.

   c. Explain how the swap bank would arrange for the principal payments at maturity.

   d. How could the swap bank profit from setting up the swap?

   e. Explain how the swap arrangement of principal at maturity is similar to a foreign currency forward contract.

7. Table 17.P-7 shows the annual loan rates that an American company and a French company can each obtain on a five-year, $20M loan in the United States, and on a five-year, FF 3.5M loan in the French market.

   a. Discuss the comparative advantages that exist for the American and French companies.

TABLE 17.P-7

Loan Rates for American and French Companies in the United States and France		
Spot: E_0 = $/FF = $0.175/FF		
	AMERICAN MARKET	FRENCH MARKET
Risk-free rate	8%	6%
American company	11%	8.5%
French company	12%	9.0%

b. Suppose the U.S. multinational wants to borrow FF 114.2857M for five years to finance its French operation, while the French company wants to borrow $20M for five years to finance its U.S. operations. Explain how a swap bank could arrange a currency swap that would benefit the American company by lowering its FF loan by .25% and would benefit the French company by lowering its dollar loan by .1%. Show the interest rate and principal swap arrangements in a diagram.

c. Describe how the swap bank's position on the currency interest exchange is similar to a series of FF forward contracts.

d. What would be the bank's dollar position if it hedged the swap position using the forward market at a forward rate determined by IRPT?

e. Describe how the American company's interest swap position is similar to forward contract position, and how the French company's swap position is similar to a forward contract.

8. Thirty days from now, A.C. Auto is planning to borrow $5M from Northside Bank to finance its fall inventory. The loan will have maturity of 90 days and a rate equal to the LIBOR + 100 BP. The current LIBOR is 7%. Concerned that interest rates could rise during the interim, the company pays Northside Bank $10,000 for an interest rate call corresponding to its planned loan with an exercise rate of 7%, expiration of 30 days, and payments received at the loan's maturity if the call is exercised.

Construct a table showing at expiration the call's intrinsic value, the option's costs at expiration, the interest on the loan, and the hedged borrowing rate given possible LIBORs at expiration of 6%, 6.5%, 7%, 7.5%, and 8%.

9. In thirty days the Webb Company is anticipating a cash inflow of $5M that it plans to invest in a 90-day CD offered by the Commerce Bank at the LIBOR. To minimize its exposure to interest rate risk, the Webb Company buys an interest rate put corresponding to the planned CD investment from the Commerce Bank for $10,000. The exercise rate on the put is equal to the current LIBOR of 7%, and the receipts from exercising the put are to be received at the CD's maturity.

Construct a table showing the put's intrinsic values, the option's costs at expiration, the interests earned on the CD, and the total returns and rates earned from the hedge investment for possible LIBORs at expiration of 6%, 6.5%, 7%, 7.5%, and 8%.

10. Given the LIBORs in Table 17.P-10, determine the cash flows and hedged rate with a cap on a one-year, $20M variable-rate loan that starts on March 1 and has its rate set each quarter at LIBOR, and a cap purchased for $50,000 with effective dates of 6/1, 9/1, and 12/1. Assume the cap corresponds to the loan and has an exercise rate of 9%, with the payoffs received at the end of the interest period.

11. On March 1, the Farmer's Bank provides a one-year, $10M variable-rate loan to ABC Enterprises. The initial rate on the loan is 8%, with subsequent rates set every quarter to equal the LIBOR. Farmer's Bank, though, is concerned that short-term interest rates will decline over the next year. Construct a floor corresponding to the loan that Farmer's Bank could purchase that would

TABLE 17.P-10

EFFECTIVE DATE	DAYS IN QUARTER	LIBOR
3/1	92	8%
6/1	92	9%
9/1	91	9.5%
12/1	90	7%
3/1		

TABLE 17.P-11

EFFECTIVE DATE	DAYS IN QUARTER	LIBOR
3/1	92	8%
6/1	92	7%
9/1	91	6.5%
12/1	90	9%
3/1		

TABLE 17.P-12

EFFECTIVE DATE	DAYS IN QUARTER	LIBOR
3/1	92	10%
6/1	92	9%
9/1	91	7%
12/1	90	6%
3/1		

ensure a minimum rate. Show in a table the quarterly cash flows, loan receipts, and rates with the floor given the LIBORs shown in Table 17.P-11.

12. On March 1, Cagle Inc. borrowed $30M on a one-year variable-rate loan from UCON Bank. The initial rate was 8%, and subsequent rates were to be set on effective dates of 6/1, 9/1, and 12/1 at the LIBOR, with payment made at the next effective date. Cagle Inc. would like to hedge against interest rate increases by buying a cap with an exercise rate of 8% for $100,000, but does not want to spend $100,000.

   a. If the UCON Bank offered positions in a floor with a rate of 7% for $85,000, explain how Cagle Inc. could finance part of the cost of the cap by forming a collar. What would be the cost of the collar?

   b. Given the LIBORs shown in Table 17.P-12, show the cash flows, interest payments, and rates hedged with the collar.

13. Construct a table of cash flow at expiration for a PRIME and a SCORE on a unit of ABC stock with a termination price of $50. Assume ABC stock pays dividends worth $1.00 at expiration, and evaluate at possible stock/unit prices at expiration of $40, $45, $50, $55, and $60. To what are the PRIME and SCORE positions equivalent?

APPENDIX A

Short Sales

In contrast to the typical investment strategy in which you buy a security now and sell it later, short sales involve selling a security now and buying it later. To implement this strategy, the investor borrows the security, sells it in the market, then repays his debt obligation by buying the security later. To profit from a short sale (also known as *selling short* or *selling under*), the security's price must decrease. For example, suppose an investor sells ABC stock short by borrowing one share and selling it in the market for $100. If the stock price declines to $50, the short seller could repay his obligation (also known as *covering the position*) by buying back the stock in the market at $50 and returning the borrowed share, netting a profit of $50. However, if the stock price increased to $150 and the short seller had to cover, he would lose $50.

The process involved in executing a short sale involves several steps. First, the investor informs his broker that he wants the broker to execute a short sale. For example, suppose a short seller wants 100 shares of ABC stock sold short when the market price is $50. The broker then will find a buyer of the stock and sell 100 shares at $50. To find a lender of 100 shares of ABC stock, the broker may use one of the brokerage firm's customers who has the stock held in street name (possibly one who has a margin account), or she may have to contact another brokerage firm. In either case, the share lender (also known as the *lender of shares*) is often unaware of the loan (and should not worry). With the borrowed shares, the broker then will settle the stock purchase by delivering the 100 shares and receiving $5000. Once settled, the broker then will hold the short seller's $5000 as security with no interest paid (known as a *flat hold*). The short seller also must post collateral in cash or equity (see Appendix B for a discussion of the margin requirements for a short sale).

Both the short seller and the share lender have the right to close their positions at any time. Technically, no time limits exist on a short sale. It is, by definition, a "call" loan that is cancelable at any time by either party. Thus, if the stock price increases or the share lender needs cash, he could ask his broker to sell the shares. In this case, the broker either will find another share lender or will ask the short seller to cover by buying the shares in the market. If the short seller wants to close because the stock price decreases, he is instructed to do so by the share lender's broker; or if he wants to close because he fears a call, then he simply instructs the broker to buy the 100 shares. If the market price of the stock in our example goes to $30, then the broker would use $3000 of the $5000 she is holding to buy the 100 shares, then return the 100 shares and give the short seller both his $2000 profit and collateral. Of course, if the stock price increases, the broker would have to use $5000 plus part of the collateral to cover the short sale.

In addition to the mechanics of a short sale, the reader also should be aware of two other aspects of selling short. First, the Securities Exchange Commission requires that short sales be executed only on an *up-tick* (when the price at which the borrowed shares are sold exceeds the previous trading day's close) or a *zero-plus-tick* (when the price is equal to the previous trade but higher than the last trade at a different price). Underlying this rule is the desire to slow down or stop a possible "bear run" on a security. Second, a short seller is expected to cover any dividends that are paid. After the execution of a short sale, the new security buyer is the shareholder of record and thus will receive all dividends. The share lender also is entitled to dividends. Accordingly, he will be paid by the short seller.

SELECTED REFERENCE

Alexander, G. J., and Sharpe, W. F. *Fundamentals of Investments.* Englewood Cliffs, N.J.: Prentice Hall, 1989, pp. 23–28.

Margins on Stock Positions

Purchasing stock on margin (also known as a *margin purchase*) means that part of the purchase is financed by borrowing. When a margin purchase is set up through a brokerage firm, the investor establishes a margin account with the firm. In contrast to a cash account, in which the investor deposits cash with the brokerage firm in an amount equal to the full value of the security, a margin account requires only a portion of cash to be deposited in order to cover the acquisition, with the remaining portion borrowed from the brokerage firm. When such accounts are set up, the investor usually signs a contract known as a *hypothecation agreement*, in which the investor gives the broker the right to use the securities to be acquired as its collateral for a bank (or other financial institution) loan to the broker, which is the source of the loan money. The broker, in turn, usually charges as its service fee a higher rate than the bank's.

Given the risk involved in margin purchases, as well as some past abuses, the maximum loan amounts a broker can advance toward the purchase of a security is governed by the Federal Reserve Board (Fed). In accordance with Regulation T, the Fed has the right to limit the initial amount of loans brokers can provide. The security exchanges can, however, set lower loan limits than the Fed's, and the brokerage firm is allowed to set loan limits even lower than the exchange's. The Fed regulations are stated in terms of initial margin requirements. A *margin* is defined as the percentage of investor's equity (cash) to the value of the security. That is, the initial margin, M_i, is:

$$M_i = \frac{\text{Investor's cash}}{\text{Market value of securities}}$$

$$M_i = \frac{\text{Market value of securities} - \text{Loan}}{\text{Market value of securities}}.$$

In addition to initial margin requirements, most brokerage firms also require that the investor adhere to a maintenance margin requirement and to rules governing restrictive accounts if the security's price decreases. To determine the status of an investor's margin, the brokerage firm will calculate each day the customer's actual margin, with the market value of the security being determined from the previous day's closing prices; this daily calculation of the actual margin is known as having the account *marked to the market*.

If a decline in the security's price leads to an actual margin that is lower than the initial margin requirement but higher than the broker-stipulated maintenance margin, then the investor is said to have a *restricted* account. With a restricted account, the investor would be prohibited from acquiring any more shares on margin, but would not have to put up any more cash.

However, if the security's price decreases to a level such that the actual margin is below the maintenance margin requirement, then the account is said to be *undermargined* and the investor will receive a "margin call" from the brokerage firm instructing her to adjust the margin position to meet the maintenance requirement. The investor could meet the deficiency either by depositing more cash in her account or by selling some of the security shares held.

If the security price increases so that the actual margin exceeds the initial margin, then the account is said to be *unrestricted* or *overmargined*. In this case, the investor is free to withdraw cash until the actual margin equals the initial margin.

Similar margin requirements apply to short sales. Specifically, to secure a short sale, most brokerage firms hold the cash proceeds generated from the sale of the borrowed securities and also require the short seller to post additional collateral in cash (or some security). The investor's margin is defined as the total amount of cash or "investor's assets" that is required initially and the amount that must be maintained if the price of the security increases. For a short sale, the margin (M_i^{ss}) is:

$$M_i^{ss} = \frac{\text{Investor's assets} - \text{Loan}}{\text{Loan}}$$

where:

Investor's assets = cash from short sale and cash deposited with the broker

Loan = market value of the securities that were borrowed.

If the brokerage firm had an initial margin requirement of 0.6, then an investor who sold 100 shares of ABC stock short at $50 would need to add $3000 to the $5000 cash obtained from the sale of the borrowed shares to make his margin account equal 0.60. That is:

$$M_i^{ss} = \frac{(\$5000 + \text{Cash}) - \$5000}{\$5000} = 0.60$$

Cash = .60($5000) = $3000.

As with margin purchases, the brokerage house also will require a maintenance margin to protect itself in case the security price increases.

SELECTED REFERENCES

Alexander, G. J., and Sharpe, W. F. *Fundamentals of Investments*. Englewood Cliffs, N.J.: Prentice Hall, 1989, pp. 17–23.

Francis, J. C. *Investments: Analysis and Management*. New York: McGraw-Hill, 1986, pp. 65–68.

Mathematical Statistical Concepts

In this appendix we define some of the important statistical concepts for analyzing investment strategies.

Random Variable

A random variable is a variable whose value is uncertain. Signified with a tilde (˜) over the symbol of the variable, a random variable is sometimes referred to as a *stochastic variable*. The opposite of a random variable is a *deterministic* or *controlled variable*, referred to as a *nonstochastic variable*.

Probability Distribution

A probability distribution is a function that assigns probabilities to the possible values of a random variable. The function can be *objective* (as when using past frequencies or assuming the distribution takes a certain form) or *subjective*. Also, the distribution can be either *continuous*, where it takes on all possible values over the range of the distribution and the probabilities are defined for a particular range, or *discrete*, where the distribution takes on only a few possible values and the probabilities are assigned to each possible value. Table C-1 shows a probability distribution for next period's interest rates (random variable $\tilde{r}$). This discrete distribution is defined by five possible interest rate values (column 1) and their respective probabilities (column 2) and is shown graphically in Figure C-1.

The most common way to describe the probability distribution is in terms of its parameters: expected value (mean), variance, and skewness.

Expected Value

The expected value of a random variable is the weighted average of the possible values of the random variable, with the weights being the probabilities assigned each possible value (P_i). The expected value, or mean, is the first moment of the distribution and, along with the median and the mode, is a measure of the central

TABLE C-1

Probability Distribution							
(1) $\tilde{r}_i$	(2) P_i	(3) $P_i\tilde{r}_i$	(4) $\tilde{r}_i - E(\tilde{r})$	(5) $[r_i - E(\tilde{r})]^2$	(6) $P_i[r_i - E(\tilde{r})]^2$	(7) $[r_i - E(\tilde{r})]^3$	(8) $P_i[\tilde{r}_i - E(\tilde{r})]^3$
4%	0.1	0.4%	−2%	4	0.4	−8	−0.8
5	0.2	1.0	−1	1	0.2	−1	−0.2
6	0.4	2.4	0	0	0.0	0	0.0
7	0.2	1.4	1	1	0.2	1	0.2
8	0.1	0.8	2	4	0.4	8	0.8
	1.0	$E(\tilde{r}) = 6\%$			$V(\tilde{r}) = 1.2$		$S_k(\tilde{r}) = 0$

FIGURE C-1

Probability Distribution

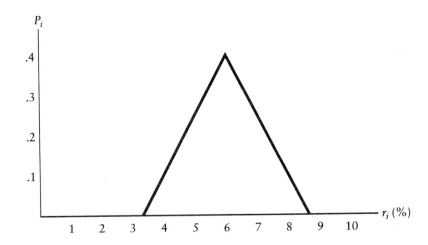

tendency of the distribution. The expected value for random variable $\tilde{r}$, $[E(\tilde{r})]$, shown in Table C-1 and Figure C-1, is 6%:

$$E(\tilde{r}) = \sum_{i=1}^{T} P_i r_i = P_1 r_1 + P_2 r_2 + \cdots + P_T r_T$$

$$E(\tilde{r}) = (.1)(4\%) + (.2)(5\%) + (.4)(6\%) + (.2)(7\%) + (.1)(8\%) = 6\%.$$

A random variable may be described algebraically, for example:

$$\tilde{r} = a + b\tilde{Y},$$

where a and b are coefficients and Y is the independent variable. To describe the expected value of $\tilde{r}$ as $E(a + b\tilde{Y})$, we can make use of the following *expected value operator rules*:

1. Expected value of a constant (a) is equal to the constant:

   EV Rule 1: $E(a) = a$.

2. Expected value of a constant times a random variable is equal to the constant times the expected value of the random variable:

   EV Rule 2: $E(b\tilde{Y}) = bE(\tilde{Y})$.

3. Expected value of a sum is equal to the sum of the expected values:

   EV Rule 3: $E(\tilde{X} + \tilde{Y}) = E(\tilde{X}) + E(\tilde{Y})$.

By applying the three rules to the equation $\tilde{r} = a + b\tilde{Y}$, $E(\tilde{r})$ can be expressed as:

$$E(\tilde{r}) = E(a + b\tilde{Y})$$

$$E(\tilde{r}) = E(a) + E(b\tilde{Y}) \qquad \text{EV Rule 3}$$

$$E(\tilde{r}) = a + bE(\tilde{Y}). \qquad \text{EV Rules 1 and 2}$$

Variance

The variance of a random variable $[V(\tilde{r})]$ is the expected value of the squared deviation from the mean:

$$V(\tilde{r}) = E[\tilde{r} - E(\tilde{r})]^2.$$

The variance is defined as the second moment of the distribution. It is a measure of the distribution's dispersion, indicating the squared deviation most likely to occur. As an expected value, the variance is obtained by calculating the weighted average of each squared deviation, with the weights being the relative probabilities:

$$V(\tilde{r}) = \sum_{i=1}^{T} P_i[\tilde{r}_i - E(\tilde{r})]^2$$

$$V(\tilde{r}) = P_i[r_1 - E(\tilde{r})]^2 + P_2[\tilde{r}_2 - E(r)]^2 + \cdots + P_T[\tilde{r}_T - E(r)]^2.$$

The random variable described in Table C-1 has a variance of $V(\tilde{r}) = 1.2$:

$$V(\tilde{r}) = .1(4\% - 6\%)^2 + .2(5\% - 6\%)^2 + .4(6\% - 6\%)^2$$
$$+ .2(7\% - 6\%)^2 + .1(8\% - 6\%)^2 = 1.2.$$

Standard Deviation

The standard deviation, $\sigma(\tilde{r})$, is the square root of the variance. Therefore, $\sigma(r)^2$ can be used to define the variance:

$$\sigma(\tilde{r}) = \sqrt{V(\tilde{r})}.$$

The standard deviation provides a measure of dispersion that is on the same scale as the distribution's deviations. The standard deviation of the random variable $\tilde{r}$ in Table C-1 is 1.0954451; this indicates the distribution has an average deviation of ± 1.0954451.

Note that the risk of a security can be defined as the uncertainty that the actual return earned from investing in a security will deviate from the expected. By definition, the variance and standard deviation of a security's rate of return define the security's relative risk. That is, the greater a security's variance relative to another security, the greater that security's actual return can deviate from its expected return and thus the greater the security's risk relative to the other security.

Skewness

Skewness measures the degree of symmetry of the distribution. A distribution that is symmetric about its mean is one in which the probability of $r = E(r) + x$ is equal to the probability of $r = E(r) - x$, for all values of x. Skewness is defined as the third moment of the distribution $[S_k(\tilde{r})]$ and can be measured by calculating the expected value of the cubic deviation:

$$S_k(\tilde{r}) = E[\tilde{r} - E(\tilde{r})]^3$$

$$S_k(\tilde{r}) = \sum_{i=1}^{T} P_i [\tilde{r}_i - E(\tilde{r})]^3.$$

The skewness of the distribution in Table C-1 is zero.

Covariance

The covariance is a measure of the extent to which one random variable is above or below its mean at the same time or state that another random variable is above or below its mean. The covariance measures how two random variables move with each other. If two random variables, on average, are above their means at the same time and, on average, are below at the same time, then the random variables would be positively correlated with each other and would have a positive covariance. In contrast, if one random variable, on average, is above its mean when another is below, and vice versa, then the random variables would move inversely, or negatively, to each other and would have a negative covariance.

The covariance between two random variables, $\tilde{r}_1$ and $\tilde{r}_2$, is equal to the expected value of the product of the variables' deviations:

$$\text{Cov}(\tilde{r}_1, \tilde{r}_2) = E[\tilde{r}_1 - E(\tilde{r}_1)][\tilde{r}_2 - E(\tilde{r}_2)]$$

$$\text{Cov}(\tilde{r}_1, \tilde{r}_2) = \sum_{i=1}^{T} P_i [\tilde{r}_{1i} - E(\tilde{r}_1)][\tilde{r}_{2i} - E(\tilde{r}_2)].$$

In Table C-2, the possible rates of return for securities 1 and 2 are shown for three possible states (A, B, and C), along with the probabilities of occurrence of each state. As shown in the table, $E(\tilde{r}_1) = 18\%$, $V(\tilde{r}_1) = 36$, $E(\tilde{r}_2) = 16\%$, and $V(\tilde{r}_2) = 16$. In addition, the table shows that in State A security 1 yields a return below its mean, while security 2 yields a return above its mean; in State B both yield rates of return equal to their mean; in State C security 1 yields a return above its mean, while security 2 yields a return below. Securities 1 and 2 therefore are negatively correlated and, as shown in Table C-2, have a negative covariance $[\text{Cov}(\tilde{r}_1, \tilde{r}_2) = -24]$.

Correlation Coefficient

The correlation coefficient between two random variables r_1 and r_1 (ρ_{12}) is equal to the covariance between the variables divided by the product of each random variable's standard deviation:

TABLE C-2

Correlation Between Random Variables

STATE	P_i	$\tilde{r}_{1i}$	$\tilde{r}_{2i}$	$P_i(\tilde{r}_{1i})$	$P_i(\tilde{r}_{2i})$	$P_i[\tilde{r}_{1i} - E(\tilde{r}_1)]^2$	$P_i[\tilde{r}_{2i} - E(\tilde{r}_2)]^2$	$\tilde{r}_{1i} - E(\tilde{r}_1)$	$\tilde{r}_{2i} - E(\tilde{r}_2)$	$P_i[\tilde{r}_{1i} - E(\tilde{r}_1)][\tilde{r}_{2i} - E(\tilde{r}_2)]$
A	1/8	6%	24%	0.75%	3.0%	(1/8)(144)	(1/8)(64)	−12	+8	(1/8)(−12)(8) = −12
B	6/8	18	16	13.50	12.0	(6/8)(0)	(6/8)(0)	0	0	(6/8)(0)(0) = 0
C	1/8	30	8	3.75	1.0	(1/8)(144)	(1/8)(64)	+12	−8	(1/8)(12)(−8) = −12
				$E(\tilde{r}_i)$ = 18.00%	$E(\tilde{r}_2)$ = 16.0%	$V(\tilde{r}_1) = 36$ $\sigma(\tilde{r}_1) = 6$	$V(\tilde{r}_2) = 16$ $\sigma(\tilde{r}_2) = 4$			$Cov(\tilde{r}_1, \tilde{r}_2) = -24$ $\rho_{12} = \dfrac{-24}{(6)(4)} = -1$

$$\rho_{12} = \frac{\text{Cov}(\tilde{r}_1, \tilde{r}_2)}{\sigma(\tilde{r}_1)\sigma(\tilde{r}_2)}.$$

The correlation coefficient has the mathematical property that its value must fall within the range from -1 to $+1$:

$$-1 \leq \rho_{12} \leq +1.$$

If two random variables have a correlation coefficient equal to 1, they are said to be perfectly positively correlated; if their coefficient is equal to -1, they are said to be perfectly negatively correlated; if their correlation coefficient is equal to 0, they are said to be zero correlated and statistically independent. That is:

$$\rho_{12} = \quad 1 \qquad \text{perfectly positively correlated}$$

$$\rho_{12} = -1 \qquad \text{perfectly negatively correlated}$$

$$\rho_{12} = \quad 0 \qquad \text{zero correlated.}$$

Parameter Estimates Using Historical Averages

In most cases we do not know the probabilities associated with the possible values of the random variable and must therefore estimate the parameter characteristics. The simplest way to estimate a parameter is to calculate the parameter's historical average value from a sample. For the rate of return on a security $(\tilde{r})$, this can be done by calculating the average rate of return per period, or the holding period yield, HPY_t {Stock HPY $= [(S_t - S_{t-1}) + \text{Dividend}]/S_{t-1}$} over n historical periods:

$$\bar{r} = \frac{1}{n}\sum_{t=1}^{n}\text{HPY}_t.$$

Similarly, the variance of a security can be estimated by averaging the security's squared deviations $[\hat{V}(r)]$, and the covariance between two securities can be estimated by averaging the product of the securities' deviations $[\widehat{\text{Cov}}(r_1, r_2)]$. Note that in estimating variances and covariances, averages usually are found by dividing by $n - 1$ instead of n. This yields better unbiased estimates:

$$\hat{V}(r) = \frac{1}{n-1}\sum_{t=1}^{n}(\text{HPY}_t - \bar{r})^2$$

$$\widehat{\text{Cov}}(r_1, r_2) = \frac{1}{n-1}\sum_{t=1}^{n}(\text{HPY}_{1t} - \bar{r}_1)(\text{HPY}_{2t} - \bar{r}_2).$$

An example of estimating parameters is shown in Table C-3, in which the average HPY, variances, and covariance are computed for a stock and a stock index (S_m).

Linear Regression

Regression involves estimating the coefficients of an assumed algebraic equation. A linear regression model has only one explanatory variable; a multiple regression model has more than one independent variable.

TABLE C-3

			Historical Averages		
(1) TIME PERIOD (QUARTER)	(2) PRICE (S_t)	(3) DIV$_t$	(4) HPY$_t$ = $\frac{(S_t - S_{t-1}) + \text{DIV}_t}{S_{t-1}}$	(5) HPY$_t$ − $\bar{r}$	(6) [HPY$_t$ − $\bar{r}$]^2
1993.4	$100	$0.00	—	—	—
1994.1	105	0.00	.0500	0.032338	.0010457
1994.2	110	1.00	.0571	0.039438	.0015553
1994.3	115	0.00	.0454	0.027738	.0007694
1994.4	110	1.00	−.0348	−0.052463	.0027524
1995.1	105	0.00	−.0454	−0.063063	.0039769
1995.2	100	1.00	−.0381	−0.055763	.0031095
1995.3	105	0.00	.0500	0.032338	.0010457
1995.4	110	1.00	.0571	0.039438	.0015553
			.1413		.01581

$\bar{r} = \frac{.1413}{8} = .0176625$ $\hat{V}(r) = .01581/7$
$\hat{V}(r) = .0022586$
$\hat{\sigma}(r) = .0475247$

(7) TIME PERIOD (QUARTER)	(8) INDEX (S_{mt})	(9) HPY$_m$	(10) HPY$_{mt}$ − $\bar{R}_m$	(11) [HPY$_{mt}$ − $\bar{R}_m$]^2	(12) (HPY$_{mt}$ − $\bar{R}_m$)(HPY$_t$ − $\bar{r}$) 5 × 10
1993.4	300	—	—	—	—
1994.1	315	.0500	0.033638	.0011315	.0010878
1994.2	333	.0571	0.040738	.0016596	.0016066
1994.3	346	.0390	0.022638	.0005125	.0006279
1994.4	334	−.0347	−0.051063	.0026074	.0026789
1995.1	319	−.0449	−0.061263	.0037531	.0038634
1995.2	306	−.0407	−0.057063	.0032562	.0031820
1995.3	320	.0457	0.029338	.0008607	.0009487
1995.4	339	.0594	0.043038	.0018523	.0016973
		.1309		.01563	.0156926

$\bar{R}_m = \frac{1309}{8} = .0163625$ $\hat{V}(R_m) = .01563/7$ $\widehat{\text{Cov}}(r, R_m) = .0156926/7$
$\hat{V}(R_m) = .002233$ $\widehat{\text{Cov}}(r, R_m) = .0022418$
$\hat{\sigma}(R_m) = .047255$ $\rho_{1m} = \frac{.0022418}{(.0475247)(.047255)} = .998$

Regression:

$\bar{r} = \alpha + \beta\bar{R}_m + \bar{\epsilon}$

$\hat{\beta} = \frac{\widehat{\text{Cov}}(r, R_m)}{V(\bar{R}_m)} = \frac{.0022418}{.002233} = 1.0039$

$\hat{\alpha} = \bar{r} - \hat{\beta}\bar{R}_m = .0176625 - 1.0039(.0163625) = .001236$

$V(\epsilon) = \hat{V}(r) - \beta^2\hat{V}(R_m) = .0022586 - (1.0039)^2(.002233) = .000008148$

$E(\bar{r}) = \hat{\alpha} + \hat{\beta}E(\bar{R}_m) = .001236 + 1.0039E(\bar{R}_m)$

$V(\bar{r}) = \beta^2V(\bar{R}_m) + V(\bar{\epsilon}) = 1.0078V(\bar{R}_m) + .000008148$

As an example, consider a linear regression model relating the rate of return on a security (dependent variable) to the market rate of return (R_m) (independent variable), where R_m is measured by the proportional change in a stock index:

$$\tilde{r}_j = \alpha + \beta \tilde{R}_{mj} + \tilde{\epsilon}_j,$$

where:

α = intercept

β = slope = $\dfrac{\Delta r}{\Delta R_m}$

j = observation

ϵ = error.

In the equation, ϵ_j is referred to as the *error term* or the *stochastic disturbance term*. Thus, the model assumes that for each observation j, errors in the relationship between r and R_m can exist, causing r to deviate from the algebraic relation defined by α and β. Since, a priori, the errors are not known, the regression model needs to provide assumptions concerning $\tilde{\epsilon}_j$. The standard assumptions are:

$$E(\tilde{\epsilon}_j) = 0$$

$$V(\tilde{\epsilon}) \text{ is constant over j observations}$$

$$\text{Cov}(\tilde{\epsilon}, \tilde{R}_m) = 0.$$

This regression model is shown graphically in Figure C-2. As shown, for each observation (R_{m1}, R_{m2}, and R_{m3}), there are respective values for r, given α and β (r_1, r_2, and r_3), and there are possible errors that can cause r to be greater or less than the values determined by the intercept and slope. The assumption $E(\tilde{\epsilon}_j) = 0$, though, indicates that, on average, the errors cancel each other out, causing $E(\tilde{r})$ to equal $E(\alpha + \beta \tilde{R}_m)$. The second assumption of a constant $V(\epsilon)$, in turn, implies that the distribution of error terms is the same at each observation; the third assumption indicates that ϵ and R_m are independent.

FIGURE C-2

Regression Line

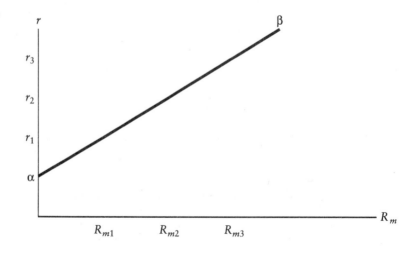

With these assumptions and the expected value operator rules, the expected value and variance of $\tilde{r}$ can be defined in terms of the regression model as follows:

$$E(\tilde{r}) = E(\alpha + \beta\tilde{R}_m + \tilde{\epsilon}_j)$$

$$E(\tilde{r}) = \alpha + \beta E(R_m)$$

$$V(\tilde{r}) = E[\tilde{r} - E(\tilde{r})]^2$$

$$V(\tilde{r}) = \beta^2 V(\tilde{R}_m) + V(\tilde{\epsilon}).$$

The first term on the right of the equation for $V(\tilde{r})$ defines systematic risk: the amount of variation in r that can be attributed to the market (factors that affect all securities). The second term defines unsystematic risk: the amount of variation in r that can be attributed to factors unique to that security (industry and firm factors).

If two securities (1 and 2) both are related to R_m, such as

$$\tilde{r}_1 = \alpha_1 + \beta_1\tilde{R}_m + \tilde{\epsilon}_1$$

$$\tilde{r}_2 = \alpha_2 + \beta_2\tilde{R}_m + \tilde{\epsilon}_2,$$

(where the j subscript is deleted) and $\tilde{\epsilon}_1$ and $\tilde{\epsilon}_2$ are independent $[\text{Cov}(\tilde{\epsilon}_1, \tilde{\epsilon}_2) = 0]$, then $\text{Cov}(\tilde{r}_1, \tilde{r}_2)$ simplifies to:

$$\text{Cov}(r_1, r_2) = \beta_1\beta_2 V(R_m).$$

The intercept and slope of the regression model can be estimated by the *ordinary least squares estimation* procedure. This techniques uses sample data for the dependent and independent variables (time series data or cross-sectional data) to find the estimates of α and β that minimize the sum of the squared errors. The estimates for α and β, $\hat{\alpha}$ and $\hat{\beta}$, in which the errors are minimized are:

$$\hat{\beta} = \frac{\widehat{\text{Cov}}(r, R_m)}{\hat{V}(R_m)}$$

$$\hat{\alpha} = \bar{r} - \hat{\beta}\bar{R}_m,$$

where $\widehat{\text{Cov}}(r, R_m)/\hat{V}(R_m)$, $\bar{r}$, and $\bar{R}_m$ are estimates (averages). An estimate of unsystematic risk, $V(\tilde{\epsilon})$, can be found using the equation for $V(\tilde{r})$:

$$V(\tilde{\epsilon}) = V(\tilde{r}) - \beta^2 V(R_m),$$

where $V(r)$ and $V(R_m)$ can be estimated by using the sample averages and β can be estimated by using the ordinary least squares estimating equation. Table C-3 shows a regression model relating the rate of return on the security to the market rate as measured by the rate of change in the index.

It should be noted that the coefficients between any variables can be estimated with a regression model. Whether the relationship is good or not depends on the quality of the regression model. All regression models therefore need to be accompanied by information about the quality of the regression results. Regression qualifiers include the coefficient of determination (R^2), t-tests, and F-tests.

APPENDIX D

Uses of Exponents and Logarithms

D.1 EXPONENTIAL FUNCTIONS

An exponential function is one whose independent variable is an exponent. For example:

$$y = b^t,$$

where:

y = dependent variable
t = independent variable
b = base ($b > 1$).

In calculus, many exponential functions use as their base the irrational number 2.71828, denoted by the symbol e:

$$e = 2.71828.$$

An exponential function that uses e as its base is referred to as a *natural exponential function*. For example:

$$y = e^t$$

$$y = Ae^{Rt}.$$

These functions also can be expressed as:

$$y = \exp(t)$$

$$y = A \exp(Rt).$$

In calculus, natural exponential functions have the useful property of being their own derivative. In addition to this mathematical property, e also has a finance meaning. Specifically, e is equal to the future value (FV) of $1 compounded continuously for one period at a nominal interest rate (R) of 100%.

To see e as a future value, consider the future value of an investment of A dollars invested at an annual nominal rate of R for t years, and compounded m times per year:

$$FV = A\left(1 + \frac{R}{m}\right)^{mt}. \qquad (D.1\text{-}1)$$

If we let $A = \$1$, $t = 1$ year, and $R = 100\%$, then the FV would be:

$$FV = \$1\left(1 + \frac{1}{m}\right)^{m}. \qquad (D.1\text{-}2)$$

If the investment is compounded one time ($m = 1$), then the value of the $1 at end of the year will be $2; if it is compounded twice ($m = 2$), the end-of-year value will be $2.25; if it is compounded 100 times ($m = 100$), then the value will be $2.7048138:

$$m = 1: \qquad FV = \$1\left(1 + \frac{1}{1}\right)^{1} = \$2.00$$

$$m = 2: \qquad FV = \$1\left(1 + \frac{1}{2}\right)^{2} = \$2.25$$

$$m = 100: \qquad FV = \$1\left(1 + \frac{1}{100}\right)^{100} = \$2.7048138$$

$$m = 1000: \qquad FV = \$1\left(1 + \frac{1}{1000}\right)^{1000} = \$2.716924.$$

As m becomes large, FV approaches the value of $2.71828. Thus, in the limit:

$$FV = \lim_{m \to \infty}\left(1 + \frac{1}{m}\right)^{m} = 2.71828. \qquad (D.1\text{-}3)$$

If A dollars are invested instead of $1, and the investment is made for t years instead of 1 year, then given a 100% interest rate the future value after t years would be:

$$FV = Ae^{t}. \qquad (D.1\text{-}4)$$

Finally, if the nominal interest rate is other than 100%, then FV is:

$$FV = Ae^{Rt}. \qquad (D.1\text{-}5)$$

To prove Equation (D.1-5), rewrite Equation (D.1-1) as follows:

$$FV = A\left(1 + \frac{R}{m}\right)^{mt}$$

$$FV = A\left[\left(1 + \frac{R}{m}\right)^{m/R}\right]^{Rt}.$$ (D.1-6)

If we invert R/m in the inner term, we get:

$$FV = A\left[\left(1 + \frac{1}{m/R}\right)^{m/R}\right]^{Rt}.$$ (D.1-7)

The inner term takes the same form as in Equation (D.1-2). As shown earlier, this term, in turn, approaches e as m approaches infinity. Thus, for continuous compounding, FV is:

$$FV = Ae^{Rt}.$$ (D.1-8)

So, a two-year investment of $100 at a 10% annual nominal rate with continuous compounding would be worth $122.14 at the end of year 2:

$$FV = \$100e^{(.10)(2)} = \$122.14.$$

D.2   LOGARITHMS

A logarithm (or log) is the power to which a base must be raised to equal a particular number. For example, given:

$$5^2 = 25,$$

the power (or log) to which the base 5 must be raised to equal 25 is 2. Thus, the log of 25 to the base 5 is 2:

$$\log_5 25 = 2.$$

In general:

$$y = b^t \Leftrightarrow \log_b y = t.$$

Two numbers frequently used as the base are 10 and the number e. If 10 is used as the base, the logarithm is known as the *common log*. Some familiar common logs are:

$$
\begin{aligned}
\log_{10} 1000 &= \quad 3 \quad & (10^3 = 1000) \\
\log_{10} 100 &= \quad 2 \quad & (10^2 = 100) \\
\log_{10} 10 &= \quad 1 \quad & (10^1 = 10) \\
\log_{10} 1 &= \quad 0 \quad & (10^0 = 1) \\
\log_{10} .1 &= -1 \quad & \left(10^{-1} = \frac{1}{10^1} = .10\right) \\
\log_{10} .01 &= -2 \quad & \left(10^{-2} = \frac{1}{10^2} = \frac{1}{100} = .01\right)
\end{aligned}
$$

When e is the base, the log is known as the *natural logarithm* (denoted $\log_e$ or ln). For the natural log, we have:

$$y = e^t \Leftrightarrow \log_e y = t$$

$$\log_e e^t = t.$$

Thus, given an expression such as $y = e^t$, the exponent t is automatically the natural log.

D.3   RULES OF LOGARITHMS

Like exponents, logarithms have a number of useful algebraic properties. Though the following properties are stated in terms of natural log, they apply to any log regardless of its base.

Equality: $\log_e X = \log_e Y$ if $X = Y$

Product Rule: $\log_e (XY) = \log_e X + \log_e Y$

Quotient Rule: $\log_e \left(\dfrac{X}{Y}\right) = \log_e X - \log_e Y$

Power Rule: $\log_e (X^a) = a \log_e X$

D.4   USES OF LOGARITHM

The preceding properties of logarithms make logarithms useful in solving a number of algebraic problems.

Solving for R

In finance, logs can be used to solve for R when there is continuous compounding. That is, from Equation (D.1-5):

$$FV = Ae^{Rt}.$$

Via the log properties, R can be found as follows:

$$Ae^{Rt} = FV$$

$$e^{Rt} = \frac{FV}{A}$$

$$\log_e (e^{Rt}) = \log_e \left(\frac{FV}{A}\right)$$

$$Rt = \log_e \left(\frac{FV}{A}\right)$$

$$R = \frac{\log_e(FV/A)}{t}. \qquad (D.4\text{-}1)$$

Thus, a $100 investment that pays $120 at the end of two years would yield a nominal annual rate of 9.12% given continuous compounding:

$$R = \frac{\log_e(\$120/\$100)}{2} = .0912.$$

Similarly, a pure discount bond selling for $980 and paying $1000 at the end of 91 days would yield a nominal annual rate of 8.10% given continuous compounding:

$$R = \frac{\log_e(\$1000/\$980)}{91/365} = .0810.$$

Logarithmic Return

The expression for the rate of return on a security currently priced at S_0 and expected to be priced at S_T at the end of one period ($t = 1$) can be found via Equation (D.1-8):

$$S_T = S_0 e^{Rt}$$

$$R = \log_e\left(\frac{S_T}{S_0}\right). \tag{D.4-2}$$

When the rate of return on a security is expressed as the natural log of S_T/S_0, it is referred to as the security's *logarithmic return*. Thus, a security currently priced at $100 and expected to be $110 at the end of the period would have an expected logarithmic return of

$$R = \log_e\left(\frac{\$110}{100}\right) = .0953 = 9.53\%.$$

Time

With logarithms, we can solve for t in either the discrete or the continuously compounding cases. That is:

$$FV = A(1 + R)^t$$

$$(1 + R)^t = \frac{FV}{A}$$

$$\log_e[(1 + R)^t] = \log_e\left(\frac{FV}{A}\right)$$

$$t \log_e(1 + R) = \log_e\left(\frac{FV}{A}\right)$$

$$t = \frac{\log_e(FV/A)}{\log_e(1 + R)}. \tag{D.4-3}$$

$$FV = Ae^{Rt}$$

$$e^{Rt} = \frac{FV}{A}$$

$$\log_e(e^{Rt}) = \log_e\left(\frac{FV}{A}\right)$$

$$Rt = \log_e\left(\frac{FV}{A}\right)$$

$$t = \frac{\log_e(FV/A)}{R}. \tag{D.4-4}$$

Equations (D.4-3) and (D.4-4) can be applied in problems in which we know the interest or growth rate and want to know how long it will take for an investment to grow to equal a certain terminal value. For example, given an annual interest rate of 10% (no annual compounding), an investment of $800 would take 2.34 years to grow to $1000:

$$t = \frac{\log_e(\$1000/\$800)}{\log_e 1.10} = 2.34 \text{ years.}$$

SELECTED REFERENCE

Chiang, A. C. *Fundamental Methods of Mathematical Economics*. New York: McGraw-Hill, 1976, pp. 267–302.

Bond Fundamentals

In this appendix, we examine a number of features of bonds that are fundamental to an understanding of fixed-income securities. These features include bond value, rate of return, term structure, and bond risk.

E.1 BOND VALUATION

E.1.1 Bond Value

The value of an asset can be defined as the dollar value today of all the asset's expected future payments. Accordingly, the value of a bond is equal to the sum of the present values of its cash flows. For example, the value of a bond (V^b) paying a fixed annual coupon interest (C) at the end of each year and a par value or principal (F) at maturity (M) would be:

$$V^b = \sum_{t=1}^{M} \frac{C}{(1 + R)^t} + \frac{F}{(1 + R)^M} \tag{E.1-1}$$

$$V^b = \frac{C}{(1 + R)^1} + \frac{C}{(1 + R^2)} + \cdots + \frac{C}{(1 + R)^M} + \frac{F}{(1 + R)^M}$$

$$V^b = C\sum_{t=1}^{M} \frac{1}{(1 + R)^t} + \frac{F}{(1 + R)^M},$$

where:

$R =$ discount (required) rate

$\sum_{t=1}^{M} \frac{1}{(1 + R)^t} =$ present value interest factor of an annuity $(PVIF)_a$.

The present value interest factor of an annuity ($PVIF_a$) is the present value of $1 received each period for M periods given a rate of R. The $PVIF_a$ for different periods and discount rates can be calculated via the following formula:

$$PVIF_a(R, M) = \frac{1 - [1/(1 + R)^M]}{R}.$$

Thus, if investors required a 10% annual rate of return, the value of a 10-year bond paying an annual coupon equal to 9% of par and with a par value of $1000 would be $938.55:

$$V^b = \sum_{t=1}^{M} \frac{C}{(1 + R)^t} + \frac{F}{(1 + R)^M}$$

$$V^b = \sum_{t=1}^{10} \frac{\$90}{(1.10)^t} + \frac{\$1000}{(1.10)^{10}} = \$90 \sum_{t=1}^{10} \frac{1}{(1.10)^t} + \frac{\$1000}{(1.10)^{10}}$$

$$V^b = \$90 PVIF_a(10\%, \ 10 \text{ years}) + \frac{\$1000}{(1.10)^{10}}$$

$$V^b = \$90 \left[\frac{1 - (1/1.10)^{10}}{.10} \right] + \frac{\$1000}{(1.10)^{10}}$$

$$V^b = \$90(6.144567) + \$385.54 = \$938.55.$$

E.1.2   Bond-Price Relations

From the preceding example, several relationships should be noted. First, the value of the bond in the example is not equal to the par value. This can be explained by the fact that the discount rate and coupon rate (R^c) are different. Specifically, for an investor to obtain an effective annual rate of 10% from a bond promising to pay an annual rate of $R^c = 9\%$ of par, he would have to buy the bond at a price below par; that is, the bond would have to sell at a discount from its par, $V^b < F$. In contrast, if the coupon rate is equal to the discount rate (e.g., $R = 9\%$), then the bond's value would equal its par value, $V^b = F$. Finally, if the required rate is lower than the coupon rate, then investors would be willing to pay a premium over par for the bond, $V^b > F$. Thus, the first relationship to note is that a bond's price will be equal to, greater than, or less than its face value depending on whether the coupon rate is equal to, less than, or greater than the required discount rate:

> RELATION: Bond-Price Relation 1:
>
> If $R^c = R$, then $V^b = F$.
>
> If $R^c < R$, then $V^b < F$.
>
> If $R^c > R$, then $V^b > F$.

The second bond relationship to note follows from the first. Specifically, given known coupon and principal payments, the only way an investor can obtain a higher rate of return on a bond is for its price (value) to be lower. In contrast, the only way for a bond to yield a lower rate is for its price to be higher. Thus, an inverse relationship exists between the price of a bond and its rate of return. This, of course, is consistent with Equation (E.1-1) in which an increase in R increases the denominator and lowers V^b. Thus, the second bond relationship is that the price and the rate of return on a bond are inversely related:

RELATION: Bond-Price Relation 2:

If $R \uparrow$, then $V^b \downarrow$.

If $R \downarrow$, then $V^b \uparrow$.

The third bond relationship relates to a bond's price sensitivity to interest rate changes and its maturity. Specifically:

RELATION: Bond-Price Relation 3: The greater the bond's maturity, all other things being equal, the greater its price sensitivity to a given change in interest rates.

This relationship can be seen by comparing the price sensitivity to interest rate changes of the 10-year, 9% coupon bond in our earlier example with a 1-year, 9% coupon bond. If the required rate is 10%, then the 10-year bond will trade at $938.55, while the 1-year bond will trade at $1090/1.10 = $990.91. If interest rates decrease to 9% on each bond (10% change in rates), both bonds would increase in price to $1000. For the 10-year bond, the percentage increase in price would be ($1000 − $938.55)/$938.55 = 6.55%, while the percentage increase for the 1-year bond would be only 0.92%. Thus, the 10-year bond is more price-sensitive to the interest rate change than is the 1-year bond.

Finally, consider the case of two 10-year bonds, each priced at a discount rate of 10% and each having a principal of $1000, but with one bond having a coupon rate of 10% and therefore priced at $1000, while the other having a coupon rate of 2% and priced at $508.43:

$$V^b = \$100 \text{PVIF}_a(10\%, \ 10 \text{ years}) + \frac{\$1000}{(1.10)^{10}} = \$1000$$

$$V^b = \$20 \text{PVIF}_a(10\%, \ 10 \text{ years}) + \frac{\$1000}{(1.10)^{10}} = \$508.43.$$

Now suppose that the rate required on each bond decreases to a new level of 9%. The price on the 10% coupon bond, in turn, would increase by 6.4% to equal $1064.18, while the price on the 2% coupon bond would increase by 8.3% to $550.76:

$$V^b = \$100 \text{PVIF}_a(9\%, \ 10 \text{ years}) + \frac{\$1000}{(1.09)^{10}} = \$1064.18$$

$$\text{Proportional change} = \frac{\$1064.18 - \$1000}{\$1000} = .064.$$

$$V^b = \$20\text{PVIF}_a(9\%, 10 \text{ years}) + \frac{\$1000}{(1.09)^{10}} = \$550.76$$

$$\text{Proportional change} = \frac{\$550.76 - \$508.43}{\$508.43} = .083.$$

Thus, in this case the lower-coupon-rate bond's price is more responsive to given interest rate changes than is the price of the higher-coupon-rate bond. Thus, the fourth bond-price relationship is:

> RELATION: Bond-Price Relation 4: Lower-coupon-rate bonds have greater price sensitivities to a given change in rates than do higher-coupon-rate bonds, all other factors being constant.

E.1.3   Semiannual Coupon Payments

Equation (E.1-1) values a bond that provides annual coupon payments. Many bonds pay coupon interest semiannually. When bonds make semiannual payments, three adjustments to Equation (E.1-1) are necessary: (1) the number of periods is doubled; (2) the coupon rate is halved; (3) the annual discount rate is halved. Thus, if our 10-year, 9% coupon bond, trading at a quoted annual rate of 10%, paid interest semiannually instead of annually, it would be worth $937.69:

$$V^b = \$45 \sum_{t=1}^{20} \frac{1}{(1.05)^t} + \frac{\$1000}{(1.05)^{20}}$$

$$V^b = \$45\text{PVIF}_a(5\%, 20 \text{ periods}) + \$376.89 = \$937.69.$$

The rule for valuing semiannual bonds is extended easily to bonds paying interest even more frequently. For example, to determine the value of a bond paying interest four times a year, we would quadruple the periods and quarter the coupon and discount rates. In general, if we let n represent the number of payments per year (or compounding per year), M the maturity in years, and, as before, R the discount rate quoted on an annual basis, then we can express the general formula for valuing a bond as follows:

$$V^b = \sum_{t=1}^{Mn} \frac{C/n}{[1 + (R/n)]^t} + \frac{F}{[1 + (R/n)]^{Mn}}. \qquad (E.1\text{-}2)$$

Finally, for a bond with a maturity less than one year, with the discount rate quoted on an annual basis, the time period is expressed as a proportion of the year, with the year being 365 days. Thus, a bond paying $100 70 days from the present and trading at an annual discount rate of 8% would be worth $98.53:

$$V^b = \frac{\$100}{(1.08)^{70/365}} = \$98.53.$$

E.1.4   Bond Values at Noncoupon Dates

Equation (E.1-1) can be used to value bonds at dates for which the coupons are to be paid in exactly one period. However, most bonds purchased in the secondary market are bought not on a coupon date, but rather at dates in between coupon dates. When bonds are priced in between dates, the *ask price* on the bond is calculated as follows:

1. The value of the bond is determined at the next coupon date, including the coupon payment at that date.

2. The current value of the bond is determined by discounting the value of the bond at the next coupon date back to the current period.

3. The accrued interest is subtracted from the current value to obtain the ask price, where:

$$\text{Accrued interest} = \frac{\text{Days since last coupon}}{\text{Days between last coupon and next coupon}} \text{(Coupon interest)}.$$

Since the buyer of the bond receives the next coupon, she is required to pay the bond seller the interest that has accrued since the last date. Thus, the actual costs of the bond to the buyer is the ask price plus the accrued interest.

E.2   RATE OF RETURN

E.2.1   Yield to Maturity

The acceptable definition for the rate of return on a bond is the rate that equates the price of the bond with the present value of its future benefits. This definition provides a measure of the rate of return in terms of the annual rate at which the bond investment grows. Referred to as the yield to maturity (YTM), this rate is R in Equation (E.1-1). Thus, from Equation (E.1-1) we set the market price of the bond (P^b) equal to V^b and solve for R. From our first example, if the 10-year, 9% annual coupon bond actually was trading in the market for $938.55, then by solving for R we would obtain a rate of return, or YTM, on the bond of 10%.

It should be noted that if the period cash flows on the bond (coupons and principal) are not equal, then R in Equation (E.1-1) cannot be solved algebraically. In turn, we must employ trial and error, substituting different R values into Equation (E.1-1) until the R that yields a price equal to the given value is obtained. However, an estimate of the YTM can be found on a coupon bond with a principal paid at maturity by computing the average rate to maturity (ARTM). This measure determines the rate as the average return per year, as a proportion of the average price of the bond per year. The average return per year on a bond is its annual coupon plus its average capital gain, which for a bond with an M-year maturity is estimated as $(F - P^b)/M$. The average price of the bond is computed as the average of two known prices, the current price, P^b, and the price at maturity, F: $(F + P^b)/2$. Thus, the ARTM is given as:

$$\text{ARTM} = \frac{C + (F - P^b)/M}{(F + P^b)/2}. \tag{E.2-1}$$

The ARTM for the 9%, 10-year bond trading at $938.55 is .0992:

$$\text{ARTM} = \frac{\$90 + (\$1000 - \$938.55)/10}{(\$1000 + \$938.55)/2} = .0992.$$

E.2.2   Rates on Pure Discount Bonds

While no algebraic solution for R exists when a bond pays coupons and principal that are not equal, an algebraic solution does exist in the case of pure discount bonds:

$$P^b = \frac{F}{(1 + YTM_M)^M}$$

$$(1 + YTM_M)^M = \frac{F}{P^b}$$

$$YTM_M = \left(\frac{F}{P^b}\right)^{1/M} - 1. \qquad (E.2\text{-}2)$$

Thus, a pure discount bond with a par value of $1000 and a maturity of three years and trading for $800 ($P^b$) would have a YTM of 7.72%:

$$YTM_3 = \left(\frac{\$1000}{\$800}\right)^{1/3} - 1 = .0772.$$

Similarly, a pure discount bond paying $100 at the end of 182 days and trading at $96 would yield an annual rate of 8.53%:

$$YTM = \left(\frac{\$100}{\$96}\right)^{365/182} - 1 = .0853.$$

E.2.4   Annual Realized Return

Equation (E.2-2) provides the formula for finding the YTM for pure discount bonds. A useful extension of Equation (E.2-2) is the annual realized return (ARR). The ARR is the annual rate earned on a bond for the period from when the bond is bought to when it is converted to cash (which could be either maturity or a date prior to maturity if the bond is sold), with the assumption that the coupons are reinvested to that date. The ARR is computed by first determining the investor's *horizon date*, HD (defined as the date the investor needs cash), finding the HD value (defined as the total funds the investor would have at his HD), then solving for the ARR via an equation similar to Equation (E.2-2).

To illustrate, suppose an investor buys a three-year, 10% coupon bond selling at its par value of $1000. Assume the investor needs cash at the end of year 3 (HD = 3), is certain he can reinvest the coupons during the period in securities yielding 10%, and expects to sell the bond at his HD at a rate of 10%. To determine the investor's ARR, we first need to find the HD value. This is equal to the price the investor obtains from selling the bond and the value of the coupons at the HD. In this case, at his HD, the investor will be able to sell a one-year bond paying a $100 coupon and a $1000 par to the holder in one year for $1000, given the assumed discount rate of 10%. That is:

$$P^b = \frac{\$100 + \$1000}{(1.10)^1} = \$1000.$$

Also at the HD, the $100 coupon paid at the end of the first year will be worth, given the assumption it is reinvested at 10% for two years, $100(1.10)^2 = \$121$, and the $100 received at the end of year 2 will, in turn, be worth $100(1 + .10) = \$110$ at the HD. Finally, at the HD the investor would receive his third coupon of $100. Combined, the investor would have $1331 in cash at the HD (HD value = $1331), as is summarized in Table E.2-1.

Given the HD value of $1331, the ARR is found in the same way as the YTM for a pure discount bond. In this case, the $1000 investment in the bond yielding $1331 at the end of year 3 will provide an ARR of 10%:

$$P^b = \frac{\text{HD value}}{(1 + \text{ARR})^{\text{HD}}}$$

$$(1 + \text{ARR})^{\text{HD}} = \frac{\text{HD value}}{P^B}$$

$$\text{ARR} = \left(\frac{\text{HD value}}{P^B}\right)^{1/\text{HD}} - 1 \qquad \text{(E.2-3)}$$

$$\text{ARR} = \left(\frac{\$1331}{\$1000}\right)^{1/3} - 1 = 0.10.$$

Equation (E.2-3) provides the general formula for computing the ARR. In the preceding example, the ARR is 10%, which is the same rate at which the bond was purchased (i.e., 10% coupon bond, selling at par, yields a YTM of 10%). Moreover, given the fundamentals related to the time value of money, an ARR equal to the initial YTM should not be too surprising, since the coupons were assumed to be reinvested at the same rate as the YTM (10%) and the bond was assumed to be sold at the same rate. If the coupons were expected to be reinvested at a different rate and/or the bond sold at a different YTM, then an ARR equal to the initial YTM would not have been realized. Such differences, in turn, can be described as market risk, which is discussed later in this appendix.

E.2.3 Geometric Mean

Another useful way of measuring the interest rate is to calculate the geometric mean. Conceptually, the geometric mean can be viewed as an average of current and future rates. To see this, consider our previous example, in which we computed a YTM of 7.72% for a pure discount bond selling for $800 and paying $1000 at the end of year 3. The rate of 7.72% represents the annual rate at which $800 must grow to be worth $1000 at the end of three years. If we do not restrict ourselves to the same rate in each year, there are obviously other ways in which $800 can grow to equal $1000 at the end of three years.

For example, suppose one-year bonds are trading at a 10% rate, a one-year bond to be purchased one year from the present is expected to yield 8%, and a one-year bond to be purchased two years from the present is expected to yield 5.22%. With these rates, $800 could grow to $1000 at the end of year 3. Specifically, $800 after the first year would yield $800(1.10) = $880; after the

TABLE E.2-1

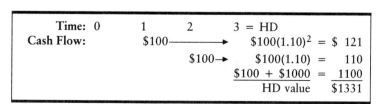

second, $800(1.10)(1.08) = 950.40; and after the third, $800(1.10)(1.08)$ $(1.0522) = 1000. Thus, an investment of $800 that yielded $1000 at the end of three years could be thought of as an investment that yielded 10% the first year, 8% the second, and 5.22% the third. Moreover, 7.72% can be viewed not only as the annual rate at which $800 can grow to yield $1000, but also as the average of three rates: one-year bonds today; one-year bonds available one year from the present, R_{11}, and one-year bonds available two years from the present, R_{12}:

$$P^b(1 + YTM_M)^M = F = P^b(1 + YTM_1)(1 + R_{11}) \cdots (1 + R_{1,M-1})$$

$$(1 + YTM_M)^M = \frac{F}{P^B} = (1 + YTM_1)(1 + R_{11}) \cdots (1 + R_{1,M-1}) \qquad \text{(E.2-4)}$$

$$(1.0772)^3 = \frac{\$1000}{\$800} = (1.10)(1.08)(1.0522).$$

Mathematically, the expression for the average rate on an M-year bond in terms of today's and future one-year rates can be found by solving Equation (E.2-4) for YTM_M. This yields:

$$YTM_M = [(1 + YTM_1)(1 + R_{11})(1 + R_{12}) \cdots (1 + R_{1,M-1})]^{1/M} - 1 \qquad \text{(E.2-5)}$$

$$YTM_3 = [(1.10)(1.08)(1.0522)]^{1/3} - 1 = .0772.$$

Equation (E.2-5) defines the rate of return on an M-year bond in terms of rates that are expected in the future. A more useful concept than an expected rate, though, is the *implied forward rate*. An implied forward rate (RI) is a future rate of return, implied by the present interest rate structure, that actually can be attained by going long and short in current bonds.

To see this, suppose the rate on a one-year, pure discount bond is 10% (YTM_1) and the rate on a similar two-year bond is 9% (YTM_2). Knowing today's rates we could solve for R_{11} in Equation (E.2-5) to determine the implied forward rate:

$$YTM_2 = [(1 + YTM_1)(1 + R_{11})]^{1/2} - 1$$

$$R_{11} = \frac{(1 + YTM_2)^2}{1 + YTM_1} - 1$$

$$R_{11} = \frac{(1.09)^2}{1.10} - 1 = .08.$$

Thus, with one-year and two-year bonds presently trading at 10% and 9%, respectively, the rate implied on one-year bonds to be bought one year from the present is 8%. This 8% rate, though, is simply an algebraic result. The rate actually can be attained by implementing the following locking-in strategy:

1. Sell the one-year discount bond short (or borrow an equivalent amount of funds at the one-year bond rate).
2. Use the cash funds from the short sale (or loan) to buy a multiple of the two-year bond.

3. Cover the short sale (or pay the loan principal) at the end of the first year.

4. Collect on the maturing two-year bond at the end of the second year.

In terms of the earlier example, the 8% implied forward rate could be obtained via the following strategy:

1. Execute a short sale by borrowing the one-year bond and selling it at its market price of $1000/1.10 = $909.09 (or borrowing $909.09 at 10%).

2. With two-year bonds trading at $1000/(1.09)^2 = $841.68, buy $909.09/ $841.68 = 1.08 issues of the two-year bond.

3. At the end of the first year, cover the short sale by paying the holder of the one-year bond her principal of $1000 (or repay the loan).

4. At the end of the second year, receive the principal on the maturing two-year bond issues of (1.08)($1000) = $1080.

With this locking-in strategy, an investor does not make a cash investment until the end of the first year when she covers the short sale; in the present, the investor simply initiates the strategy. Thus, the investment of $1000 is made at the end of the first year. In turn, the return on the investment is the principal payment on the 1.08 two-year bonds of $1080 that comes one year after the investment is made. Moreover, the rate of return on this one-year investment is ($1080 − $1000)/ $1000 = 8%. Hence, by using a locking-in strategy, an 8% rate of return on a one-year investment to be made one year in the future is attained, with the rate being the same as when we solved for R_{11} in Equation (E.2-5).

Given the concept of implied forward rates, the geometric mean now can be formally defined as the geometric average of the current one-year rate and implied forward rates. That is:

$$YTM_M = [(1 + YTM_1)(1 + RI_{11})(1 + RI_{12}) \cdots (1 + RI_{1,M-1})]^{1/M} - 1, \quad (E.2\text{-}6)$$

where:

RI_{ij} = implied forward rate on an i-year bond purchased j-years from the present.

Two points regarding the geometric mean should be noted. First, the geometric mean is not limited to one-year rates. That is, just as 7.72% can be thought of as an average of three one-year rates of 10%, 8%, and 5.22%, an implied rate on a two-year bond purchased at the end of one year, RI_{21}, can be thought of as the average of one-year implied rates purchased one and two years, respectively, from now. Accordingly, the geometric mean could incorporate an implied two-year bond by substituting $(1 + RI_{21})^2$ for $(1 + RI_{11})(1 + RI_{12})$ in Equation (E.2-6). Similarly, to incorporate a two-year bond purchased in the present period and yielding YTM_2, we would substitute $(1 + YTM_2)^2$ for $(1 + YTM_1)$ and $(1 + RI_{11})$.

Secondly, for bonds with maturities of less than one year, the same general formula for the geometric mean applies. For example, the annualized YTM on a pure discount bond maturing in 182 days [YTM(182)] is equal to the geometric average of a current 91-day bond's annualized rate [YTM(91)] and the annualized implied forward rate on a 91-day investment made 91 days from the present, RI(91, 91):

$$YTM(182) = \{[1 + YTM(91)^{91/365}][(1 + RI(91, 91)]^{91/365}\}^{365/182} - 1.$$

Thus, if a 182-day pure discount bond is trading at $S(182) = \$97$ (assume F of $\$100$) and a comparable 91-day bond is at $S(91) = \$98.35$, then the implied forward rate on a 91-day bond purchased 91 days later would be 5.7%. That is:

$$YTM(182) = \left(\frac{\$100}{\$97}\right)^{365/182} - 1 = .063$$

$$YTM(91) = \left(\frac{\$100}{\$98.35}\right)^{365/91} - 1 = .069$$

$$RI(91, 91) = \left[\frac{1 + YTM(182)^{182/365}}{1 + YTM(91)^{91/365}}\right]^{365/91} - 1$$

$$RI(91, 91) = \left[\frac{S(91)}{S(182)}\right]^{365/91} - 1$$

$$RI(91, 91) = \left(\frac{\$98.35}{\$97}\right)^{365/91} - 1 = .057.$$

E.3   TERM STRUCTURE OF INTEREST RATES

In the financial literature, the relationship between interest rates and maturity is referred to as the *term structure of interest rates*. Graphically, the relationship is explained in terms of a yield curve. By definition, a *yield curve* is a plot of the YTM against maturity for bonds that are otherwise alike. Ex ante, the slope of a yield curve is not known. As shown in Figure E.3-1, the yield curve could be positively sloped, with long-term bond rates being greater than short-term; negatively sloped, with short-term rates greater than long-term; or relatively flat. Three theories often offered to explain yield curves are the market segmentation theory, the liquidity preference theory, and the unbiased expectation theory.

E.3.1   Market Segmentation Theory

According to *market segmentation theory* (MST), the major factors that determine the interest rates within a maturity segment (sometimes referred to as *preferred habitats*) are the supply-and-demand conditions unique to each maturity segment. Specifically, MST says that interest rates for each maturity segment are determined by supply-and-demand conditions unique to that segment.

Important to MST is the idea of unique, or independent, markets. That is, in the context of MST, the short-term bond market would be unaffected by developments in the long-term market, and vice versa. This independence assumption

FIGURE E.3-1

Yield Curves

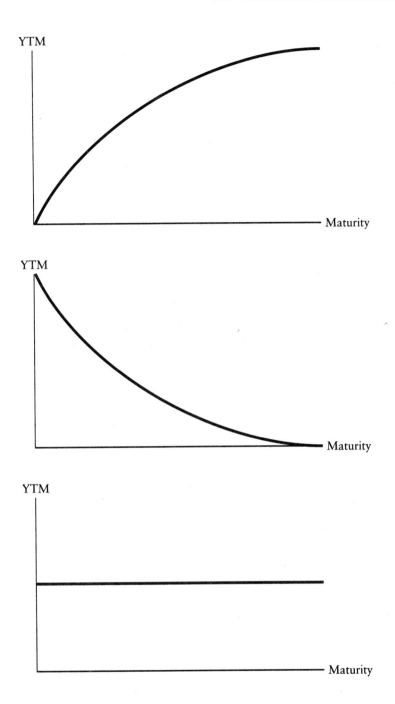

is, in turn, based on the premise that investors and borrowers match the maturities of their assets and liabilities.

For example, a steel company in building a plant with an estimated life of 20 years would prefer to finance that asset by selling a 20-year bond. Similarly, a life insurance company with an anticipated liability in 15 years would prefer to invest its premiums in 15-year bonds. In contrast, a money market manager with excess funds for 90 days would prefer to invest in a money market security, while a corporation financing its accounts receivable would prefer to finance the receivables by selling short-term securities or borrowing short-term. Moreover, the desire by investors and borrowers to avoid risk leads to hedging practices, which tends to segment the markets for bonds of different maturities.

E.3.2   Liquidity Preference Theory

The *liquidity preference theory* (LPT), also referred to as the *risk premium theory*, is based on the hypothesis that an interest rate premium exists for long-term bonds over short-term bonds ($YTM_{L-T} - YTM_{S-T} > 0$), causing the yield curve to be positively sloped. LPT can be thought of as an extension of MST. That is, according to the LPT, investors and bond issuers desiring particular segments because of their desire to hedge could be induced to forgo the hedge and move to another maturity segment if rates were high enough (investors) or low enough (issuers) to compensate them for the risk they would be assuming.

For example, consider a market for corporate debt in which investors, on average, prefer short-term to long-term instruments, while, on the supply side, corporations need to issue more long-term bonds than short-term. Combined, these relative preferences would cause an excess demand for short-term bonds and an excess supply for long-term claims. Given these conditions, an equilibrium adjustment would have to occur. Specifically, the excess supply in the long-term market would force issuers to lower their bond prices and increase their yields, inducing some investors to change their short-term investment demands; in the short-term market, the excess demand would cause bond prices to increase and rates to fall, inducing some corporations to finance their long-term assets by selling short-term claims. Ultimately, an equilibrium in both markets would be reached, with long-term rates higher than short-term rates, a premium necessary to compensate investors and issuers for the risk they've assumed.

E.4.3   Unbiased Expectations Theory

Expectations theories try to explain the impact of investors' expectations on the term structure of interest rates. A popular expectation model is the *unbiased expectations theory* (UET). Developed by Fredrick Lutz (1940), UET is based on the hypothesis that the interest rates on bonds of different maturities can be determined, in equilibrium, where the implied forward rates are equal to the expected spot rates.

To understand the UET, consider a market consisting of only two corporate bonds: a one-year pure discount bond and a two-year pure discount bond. Suppose that supply-and-demand conditions are such that both the one-year and the two-year bonds are trading at an 8% YTM. Also suppose that the market expects, with certainty, for the yield curve to shift up to 10% next year, but, as yet, has not factored that expectation into its current investment decisions (see Figure E.3-2). Investors with horizon dates of two years can buy either the two-year bond with an annual rate of 8% or the one-year bond yielding 8%, then reinvest the principal one year later in another one-year bond expected to yield 10%. In a world with

FIGURE E.3-2

Unbiased Expectations Theory

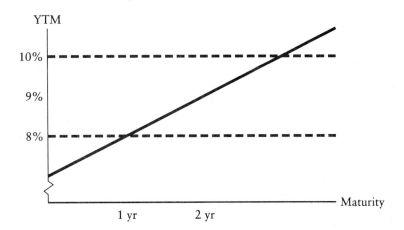

perfect certainty, such investors would prefer the latter investment, since it yields a higher average annual rate for the two years of 9%:

$$\text{YTM} = [(1.08)(1.10)]^{1/2} - 1 = .09.$$

Similarly, investors with one-year horizon dates would find it advantageous to buy a one-year bond yielding 8% than a two-year bond [priced at $1000/(1.08^2) = $857.34] that they would sell one year later to earn an expected rate of only 6%. That is:

$$P_2^b = \frac{\$1000}{(1.08)^2} = \$857.34$$

$$E(P_{11}^b) = \frac{\$1000}{(1.10)^1} = \$909.09$$

$$E[\text{Rate (1 yr)}] = \frac{\$909.09 - \$857.34}{\$857.34} = .06.$$

Thus, with perfect expectations of higher rates next year, investors with both one-year and two-year horizon dates would purchase one-year bonds instead of two-year bonds.

If enough investors do this, an increase in the demand for one-year bonds and a decrease in the demand for two-year bonds would occur until the average annual rate on the two-year bond is equal to the equivalent annual rate from the series of one-year investments (or the one-year bond's rate is equal to the rate expected on the two-year bond held one year). Moreover, these conditions will be met when the present structure of rates is such that the implied forward rates equal the expected spot rates.

In terms of the example, if the price on two-year bonds fell such that they traded at a YTM of 9%, then with the rate on one-year bonds at 8%, investors with two-year horizon dates would, in a world of certainty, be indifferent between two-year bonds yielding 9% and a series of one-year bonds yielding 10% and 8% (geometric mean of 9%). Investors with one-year horizon dates would likewise be indifferent between one-year bonds yielding 8% and a two-year bond purchased at 9% and sold one year later at 10% (rate of 8%). Thus, in this case, the impact of the market's expectation of higher rates would be to push the longer-term rates up and the short-term rates down. (If $YTM_2 = 9\%$ and $YTM_1 = 8\%$, then $RI_{11} = 10\%$; thus, the implied forward rate equals the expected spot rate.)

E.4   BOND RISK

In investment analysis, *risk* can be defined as the uncertainty that the actual rate of return obtained from holding a security will differ from the expected rate. In the case of bonds and fixed-income securities, three types of risk can be identified: default risk, call risk, and market risk.

E.4.1   Default Risk

Default risk is the uncertainty that the bond's contractual payments and obligations will not be met. Many investors, though, do not assess the chance of default on a bond directly, but rather evaluate default risk indirectly through quality ratings assigned to the bonds by such investment agencies as Moody's Investment Services, Standard and Poor, and Fetch. These agencies, in turn, evaluate the quality of bonds by providing a letter-grade opinion. The grades vary from triple A, the highest quality, with virtually no chance of default, to C, considered to be speculative, to D, which are bonds in default, whose price reflects the salvage value.

E.4.2   Call Risk

Call risk relates to the uncertainty that the issuer will call the bond. A call feature on a bond gives the issuer the right to buy back the issue before maturity at a stated price known as the *call premium*. The call premium usually is set initially at a certain percentage above the bond's par value, say, 110 ($1100 for par of $1000); for some bonds, the premium may decrease over time (e.g., a 20-year bond may decrease each year by 5%). Also, some callable bonds can be called at any time, while for others the call is deferred for a certain period, giving the investor protection during the deferment period.

A call provision becomes advantageous to the issuer if interest rates in the market decline. With a call provision, an issuer can lower his interest costs by selling a new issue at a lower interest rate, then using the proceeds to call the outstanding issue. What is to the advantage of the issuer, though, is to the disadvantage of the investor. When a bond is called, two effects on the investor's actual rate of return occur. First, since the call premium is above the face value, the actual rate of return the investor receives for the period from the purchase of the bond to its call generally is greater than the YTM on the bond at the time it was purchased. However, if the investor originally bought the bond because its maturity matched his horizon date, then he will be faced with the disadvantage of reinvesting the call premium at lower market rates. Moreover, this second effect often dominates the first, resulting in a lower actual rate of return for the investor's horizon period than the promised YTM when the bond was bought.

E.4.3   Market Risk

Market risk is the uncertainty that interest rates in the market will change, causing the actual rate of return earned on the bond to differ from the promised YTM. Such risk arises any time there is a chance that interest rates will change in the market. As noted in our discussion of the ARR, a change in interest rates will have two effects on a bond's return. First, interest rate changes affect the price of a bond. If the investor's horizon date is different from the bond's maturity date, then the investor will be uncertain about the price she will receive from selling the bond (HD < M) or will have to pay for a new bond (HD > M). Secondly, interest rate changes affect the rates of return the investor expects from reinvesting the coupons. Thus, if an investor buys a coupon bond, she automatically is subject to market risk.

One obvious way an investor can eliminate market risk is to purchase a pure discount bond with a maturity equal to the investor's horizon date. If such a bond does not exist (or exists but does not yield an adequate rate), an investor at least can minimize market risk by purchasing a bond with a duration equal to her horizon date. A bond's *duration* (D) can be defined as the weighted average of the time periods of the bond, with the weights being each time period's relative present value. That is:

$$D = \sum_{t=1}^{M} t\left(\frac{PV_t}{P^b}\right).$$ (E.4-1)

For example, if the yield curve is flat at 10%, an investor with an horizon date of 3.52 years could minimize her market risk by buying a four-year, 9% annual coupon bond (see Table E.4-1).

Duration also can be measured for a portfolio of bonds. The duration of a bond portfolio, D_p, is simply the weighted average of each of the bond's durations (D_i), with the weights being the proportion of investment funds allocated to each bond (w_i):

$$D_p = \sum_{i=1}^{n} w_i D_i.$$ (E.4-2)

Also, the duration of a bond can be defined as a measure of the bond's price sensitivity to interest rate changes:

TABLE E.4-1

(1) TIME PERIOD	(2) CASH FLOW	(3) PRESENT VALUE AT YTM = 10%	(4) WEIGHT PV_t/P^b	(5) TIME × WEIGHT (1) × (4)
1	$ 90	$ 81.818	.084496	0.084496
2	90	74.380	.076815	0.153630
3	90	67.618	.069832	0.209496
4	1090	744.485	.768857	3.075428
		P^b = $968.301		D = 3.52 yr*

$*D = \sum_{t=1}^{M} t\left(\frac{PV_t}{P^b}\right)$

$$D = -\frac{\% \ \Delta P^b}{\% \ \Delta (1 + YTM)}. \tag{E.4-3}$$

Equation (E.4-3) can be used to estimate the approximate percentage change in the price of a bond for a given percentage change in its YTM. For example, if the YTM on a bond with a duration of five years decreased from 12% to 10%, then its price would increase by approximately 8.93%:

$$\% \ \Delta P^b = -D[\% \ \Delta (1 + YTM)]$$

$$\% \ \Delta P^b = -5\left(\frac{1.10 - 1.12}{1.12}\right)$$

$$\% \ \Delta P^b = .0893.$$

SELECTED REFERENCES

Francis, J. C. *Investments: Analysis and Management*. New York: McGraw-Hill, 1986, pp. 327–440.

Lutz, F. A. "The Structure of Interest Rates." *Quarterly Journal of Economics* (Nov. 1940): 36–63.

Radcliff, R. C. *Investment: Concepts, Analysis, and Strategy*. Glenview, Ill.: Scott, Foresman, 1987, pp. 155–177, 361–426.

Market Indices

Security market indices and market averages are constructed so as to provide an indication of how the market is performing. A market average, such as the Dow Jones Industrial Average (DJIA), is a weighted average of security prices. Security indices, such as the SP 500, on the other hand, are pure numbers, often calculated as a ratio of averages of different security market values: for example, the ratio of current average security values to the average security values in a given period (base period). Security market indices and averages provide a summary measure of price movement in a specific market. For example, the rate of change in the SP 500 index gives an investor an indication of the rate of change of the average stock in the market.

The four broad-based indices in which options and futures are traded extensively are the SP 500, NYSE Composite Index, Value Line Composite Index (VLCI), and the Major Market Index (MMI). Each of the indices is constructed differently.

F.1 SP 500 INDEX

The SP 500 Index consists of 500 common stocks, most of them listed on the NYSE. Though this index includes approximately one-third of the total number of NYSE-listed stocks, the aggregate value of the stocks equals approximately 75% of the total value of the NYSE.

The SP 500 index is calculated as follows:

$$SP\ 500 = \left(\frac{\sum_{i=1}^{500} P_{it} n_{it}}{\sum_{i=1}^{500} P_{ib} n_{ib}} \right) 10,$$

where:

P_{it} = market price per share at time t

n_{it} = number of shares outstanding at time t

P_{bi}, n_{bi} = market price per share and number of shares of the ith stock during a base (b) period (base-period computation made during 1941–1943 period). The base value during the period was 10.

The SP 500 is a value-weighted index in which each stock's weight is proportional to the stock's total market value ($n_{it}P_{it}$). Like most indices, the SP 500 ignores dividends.

F.2   NYSE COMPOSITE INDEX

The NYSE Composite Index is constructed similarly to the SP 500. It is made up of every stock listed on the NYSE (approximately 2000), and is calculated from a base value of all shares on December 31, 1965, equal to 50. That is:

$$\text{NYSE Composite Index} = \left(\frac{\sum_{i=1}^{n} P_{it} n_{it}}{\sum_{i=1}^{n} P_{bt} n_{bt}} \right) 50.$$

F.3   MAJOR MARKET INDEX (MMI)

The MMI is constructed to be highly correlated with the DJIA. It consists of 20 stocks (many of which are included in the DJIA), and, like the DJIA, is a price-weighted index, calculated as follows:

$$\text{MMI}_t = \frac{\sum_{i=1}^{20} P_{it}}{\text{Divisor}}.$$

A price-weighted index is constructed initially with a divisor equal to the number of stocks comprising the index. As stock splits and stock dividends occur, the divisor needs to be adjusted. For example, if the index consists of just two stocks, one priced at $30 and the other at $20, then the index would be (30 + 20)/2 = 25, and the divisor would be 2. If the first stock had a 2-for-1 stock split, changing the price from $30 to $15, then the divisor would need to be changed to reflect an index value of 25. In this case the divisor would need to be changed from 2 to 1.4 [i.e., (15 + 20)/divisor = 25; divisor = 1.4].

Since the SP 500 and NYSE indices are calculated with market values, stock splits are adjusted for automatically in these indices.

F.4   VALUE LINE COMPOSITE INDEX (VLCI)

VLCI is a geometric average of all NYSE-listed stocks and some OTC and AMEX stocks. It is calculated as follows:

$$\text{VLCI}_t = \left[\left(\frac{P_{it}}{P_{it-1}} \right) \left(\frac{P_{2t}}{P_{2t-1}} \right) \cdots \left(\frac{P_{nt}}{P_{nt-1}} \right) \right]^{1/n} \text{VLCI}_{t-1}.$$

SELECTED REFERENCES

Francis, J. C. *Investments: Analysis and Management.* New York: McGraw-Hill, 1986, pp. 183–198.

Tucker, A. L. *Financial Futures, Options, and Swap.* St. Paul: West, 1991, pp. 181–186.

APPENDIX G

Portfolio Analysis

G.1 INTRODUCTION

In investments, the study of portfolios consists of the evaluation and selection of financial assets. Portfolio evaluation entails determining the expected rate of return and risk of a portfolio; portfolio selection involves finding the percentage of investment funds to allocate to each security in a portfolio that will yield a portfolio with either the maximum expected return given a specified risk or the minimum risk given a specified return.

G.2 PORTFOLIO EVALUATION

Evaluation usually involves describing a portfolio in terms of two parameters—the expected portfolio rate of return and the portfolio risk. The expected portfolio rate of return is the sum of the weighted expected rates of return of the securities comprising the portfolio, with the weights being the proportion of investment funds allocated to each security. That is:

$$E(R_p) = \sum_{i=1}^{n} w_i E(r_i), \qquad (G.2\text{-}1)$$

where:

$E(R_p)$ = expected portfolio rate of return

$E(r_i)$ = expected rate of return on the ith security for the period (expected holding period yield)

w_i = proportion of investment funds allocated to the ith security

n = number of securities in portfolio

$$\sum_{i=1}^{n} w_i = 1.$$

The risk of a portfolio can be measured by the variance in the portfolio's rate of return $[V(R_p)]$. In measuring the risk of a portfolio by its variance, two factors must be taken into account—the variances of the individual securities' rates of return $[V(r_i)]$ and the correlations that exist among the securities comprising the portfolio.

In Appendix C we measured the correlation between the rates of return of two securities by the covariance between their rates $\{\text{Cov}(r_i, r_j) = E[r_i - E(r_i)][r_j - E(r_j)]\}$ and their correlation coefficient $\{\rho_{ij} = \text{Cov}(r_i, r_j)/[\sigma(r_i)\sigma(r_j)]\}$. Both parameters provide a measure of the extent to which a security's rates of return are above or below its expected rate of return at the same time, or state, that another security's rates of return are above or below its expected return.

The importance of including the correlation between securities' rates of return can be seen by reference to Figure G.2-1, which is derived from the observations in Table G.2-1. The estimated parameters at the bottom of the table are based on

FIGURE G.2-1

Security Correlation

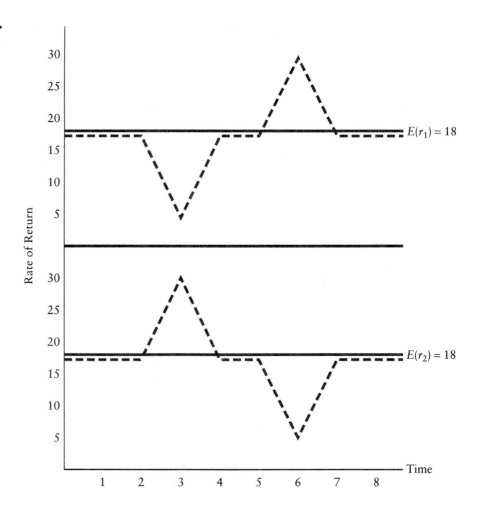

TABLE G.2-1

Correlation Between Stock X_1 and Stock X_2		
	STOCK X_1	STOCK X_2
PERIOD	RATE OF RETURN, r_1	RATE OF RETURN, r_2
1	18%	18%
2	18	18
3	6	30
4	18	18
5	18	18
6	30	6
7	18	18
8	18	18

$$E(r_1) = 18\% \qquad E(r_2) = 18\%$$
$$V(r_1) = 36 \qquad V(r_2) = 36$$
$$\sigma(r_1) = 6 \qquad \sigma(r_2) = 6$$
$$Cov(r_1, r_2) = -36$$
$$\rho_{12} = -1$$

the assumption that the next period's returns can be obtained from past observations (i.e., on averages). Both Figure G.2-1 and Table G.2-1 show the rates of return of two securities, X_1 and X_2, over time. Both securities have an expected rate of return of 18%, a risk factor as measured by their variances of 36%, a covariance of -36, and a correlation coefficient of -1.

Given the information on the securities, if a portfolio is formed with an equal allocation strategy (i.e., $w_1 = w_2 = .5$), then the risk of the portfolio would be zero, even though the individual securities have variances. The zero portfolio risk is due to the perfect negative correlation between the rates of return on X_1 and X_2. An examination of Figure G.2-1 shows that when X_1's return (r_1) is above its mean [$E(r_1)$], X_2's return (r_2) is below its mean [$E(r_2)$]; and when r_2 is above $E(r_2)$, r_1 is below $E(r_2)$. Specifically, r_1 and r_2 in this example are perfectly negatively correlated ($\rho_{12} = -1$). If an investor holding these securities in equal proportion computed her portfolio rate of return (R_p) in time period 1, she would obtain a rate of return of 18%. Similarly, if the investor computed the return for time period 3, she would likewise find an 18% rate of return; in fact, with exact variances, expected returns, and equal weights, the investor would find for any time period that her portfolio rate of return always would be 18%. Thus, since the investor can always attain an 18% rate of return, there is no portfolio risk. Figure G.2-1 therefore illustrates that the measurement of portfolio risk must take into account not only the risk germane to each security in the portfolio, but also the correlations that exist between the securities in the portfolio. Moreover, if we measure the risk of a portfolio by the variance, then both of these factors explicitly are taken into account.

To derive the equation for the variance of portfolio, $V(R_p)$, we start with the definition of $V(R_p)$:

$$V(R_p) = E[\tilde{R}_p - E(R_p)]^2. \tag{G.2-2}$$

If, for simplicity, we assume a two-security portfolio—that is,

$$R_p = w_1\tilde{r}_1 + w_2\tilde{r}_2,$$

then the portfolio variance expression (G.2-2) can be defined as:

$$V(R_p) = E[w_1\tilde{r}_1 + w_2\tilde{r}_2 - w_1E(r_1) - w_2E(r_2)]^2. \tag{G.2-3}$$

Second, we collect the variables in terms of w_1 and w_2; this yields:

$$V(R_p) = E\{w_1[\tilde{r}_1 - E(r_1)] + w_2[\tilde{r}_2 - E(r_2)]\}^2. \tag{G.2-4}$$

Equation (G.2-4) is similar to $(ab + cd)^2$, which is equal to $a^2b^2 + c^2d^2 + 2abcd$. As a third step, we can therefore take the square of Equation (G.2-4). Similar to $(ab + cd)^2$, this yields:

$$V(R_p) = E\{w_1^2[\tilde{r}_1 - E(r_1)]^2 + w_2^2[\tilde{r}_2 - E(r_2)]^2 \tag{G.2-5}$$
$$+ 2w_1w_2[\tilde{r}_1 - E(r_1)][\tilde{r}_2 - E(r_2)]\}.$$

The fourth step in the derivation is to apply the expected value operator rules (see Appendix C). Applying these rules to Equation (G.2-5) yields:

$$V(R_p) = w_1^2E[r_1 - E(\tilde{r}_1)]^2 + w_2^2E[\tilde{r}_2 - E(r_2)]^2 \tag{G.2-6}$$
$$+ 2w_1w_2E[\tilde{r}_1 - E(r_1)][r_2 - E(\tilde{r}_2)].$$

Finally, by definition we know:

$$V(r_1) = E[(\tilde{r}_1) - E(r_1)]^2 \tag{G.2-7}$$

$$V(r_2) = E[\tilde{r}_2 - E(r_2)]^2$$

$$\text{Cov}(r_1, r_2) = E[\tilde{r}_1 - E(r_1)][\tilde{r}_2 - E(r_2)].$$

Substituting then the expressions in Equation (G.2-7) into Equation (G.2-6) yields the desired two-security portfolio variance equation:

$$V(R_p) = w_1^2V(r_1) + w_2^2V(r_2) + 2w_1w_2\text{Cov}(r_1, r_2). \tag{G.2-8}$$

The portfolio standard deviation, denoted as $\sigma(R_p)$, which also can be used as the measure of risk, is obtained simply by taking the square root of Equation (G.2-8):

$$\sigma(R_p) = \sqrt{V(R_p)} = \sqrt{w_1^2V(r_1) + w_2^2V(r_2) + 2w_1w_2\text{Cov}(r_1, r_2)}. \tag{G.2-9}$$

Equations (G.2-8) and (G.2-9) are appropriate expressions for measuring the risk of a two-security portfolio. Note that the portfolio variance includes both the weighted variances of the individual securities' rates of return and the covariance between the securities' returns; hence, the correlation among securities explicitly is taken into account in the equations for the portfolio variance and standard deviation. Moreover, if we substitute into Equation (G.2-8) the parameter values from Table G.2-1, we can confirm our graphical interpretation that the risk of that portfolio is indeed zero:

$$V(R_p) = w_1^2 V(r_1) + w_2^2 V(r_2) + 2w_1 w_2 \text{Cov}(r_1, r_2)$$

$$V(R_p) = (.5)^2(36) + (.5)^2(36) + 2(.5)(.5)(-36) = 0.$$

If the securities in the preceding example had not been perfectly negatively correlated, then the portfolio risk obviously would not have been zero. For example, if X_2 had a 6% return in time period 3 and a 30% return in period 6, its expected return and variance would still be 18% and 36%, respectively. The covariance between X_1 and X_2, though, would be $+36$ instead of -36, and so $\rho_{12} = +1$ instead of -1; the two securities therefore would be perfectly positively correlated in this case. Calculating $V(R_p)$ with the $\text{Cov}(r_1, r_2) = 36$, we obtain a portfolio variance of 36:

$$V(R_p) = w_1^2 V(r_1) + w_2^2 V(r_2) + 2w_1 w_2 \text{Cov}(r_1, r_2)$$

$$V(R_p) = (.5)^2(36) + (.5)^2(36) + 2(.5)(.5)(36) = 36.$$

While Equation (G.2-8) is only for a two-security portfolio, the variance for a larger portfolio necessarily takes the same form, the only difference being the number of inputs (variances and covariances) included. For example, if we have a three-security portfolio, then our variance expression would consist of three security variances and three covariances, that is, the covariances for all combinations between security returns; if we had a four-security portfolio, there would be four variances and six covariances; and so on. Equation (G.2-10) gives the general portfolio variance formula for an n-security portfolio:*

$$
\begin{aligned}
V(R_p) = {} & w_1^2 V(r_1) + w_2^2 V(r_2) + \cdots + w_n^2 V(r_n) \qquad\qquad \text{(G.2-10)}\\
& + 2w_1 w_2 \text{Cov}(r_1, r_2) + \cdots + 2w_1 w_n \text{Cov}(r_1, r_n)\\
& + 2w_2 w_3 \text{Cov}(r_2, r_3) \cdots + 2w_2 w_n \text{Cov}(r_2, r_n + \cdots.
\end{aligned}
$$

In summary, the portfolio expected return Equation (G.2-1) and the portfolio variance Equation (G.2-10) are the important formulas needed to evaluate portfolios in terms of their return and risk. The expressions show that an investor, in constructing a portfolio by the criteria of return and risk, must search not only for securities with high expected returns and low risks, but also for ones that are highly uncorrelated and, ideally, negatively correlated with each other.

---

*For large portfolios the number of inputs $V(r_i)$ and $\text{Cov}(r_i, r_j)$ and thus the size of the portfolio expression can be quite substantial. For example, if we were to compute the variance of a 100-security portfolio, as inputs we would need to compute 100 variances and 4950 covariances. In general, the number of inputs for any n-security portfolio variances is: (1) n variances (for each security's return), and (2) $(n^2 - n)/2$ covariances.

G.3   PORTFOLIO SELECTION

In his seminal 1952 article, Markowitz predicated that the objective of portfolio selection is to determine the allocation of securities in a portfolio such that it yields the maximum expected return given a specified risk or, alternatively, the minimum portfolio risk given a specified portfolio expected return. In terms of Equations (G.2-1) and (G.2-10), Markowitz portfolio selection involves determining the weights (w_i) that yield either the maximum $E(R_p)$ given $V(R_p)$ or the minimum $V(R_p)$ given $E(R_p)$. There are a number of mathematical algorithms for determining the security allocation that satisfies the Markowitz portfolio selection objective.

G.4   ASSET THEORY

One of the important implications of portfolio analysis is that rational investors would prefer portfolio investment to individual security investment since unsystematic risk can be diversified away with a portfolio. In the 1960s, Sharpe (1964), Lintner (1965), Mossin (1966), and others showed that if investors make their investment decisions in a portfolio context, then the selection of individual securities would be based solely on that security's contribution to the overall portfolio's expected return and risk. As a result, the security's undiversified or unsystematic risk would not have an impact on the security's equilibrium price and rate of return.

The idea that a security was important only in a portfolio context was the foundation for the development of the capital asset pricing model (CAPM), which can be stated as follows: The equilibrium price of a security is determined by its systematic risk as measured by its β and not by unsystematic factors that investors can diversify away.

In CAPM, systematic risk is measured by the security's β. β, in turn, is the slope of the regression equation: $\tilde{r} = \alpha + \beta \tilde{R}_m + \tilde{\epsilon}$ (see Appendix C). Mathematically, β measures the change in the security's rate of return to a change in the market rate of return: $\beta = \Delta r / \Delta R_m$. Moreover, if r and R_m are linearly related, β measures the proportional relation between r and R_m. Thus, a security with $\beta = 1.5$ would change by 15% for a 10% change in the market. Statistically, β is equal to $\text{Cov}(r, R_m)/V(R_m)$ and, as such, measures the security's variability relative to the market. Thus, a security with $\beta = 1$ has the same variability as the market; one with $\beta > 1$ has greater variability than the market, and one with $\beta < 1$ has less variability.

In terms of the CAPM, a security with $\beta > 1$ has more risk than the market and therefore, in equilibrium, should be priced so its equilibrium expected rate $[E(r)^*]$ is greater than the expected market rate: $E(r)^* > E(R_m)$. In contrast, a security with a $\beta < 1$ in equilibrium should be priced such that its expected rate is less than the expected market rate: $E(r)^* < E(R_m)$. By the same reasoning, a security with $\beta = 1$ would, by definition, have the same risk as the market and therefore should be priced such that its expected rate is equal to the expected market rate: $E(r)^* = E(R_m)$. Finally, if systematic risk is the only determining

		IN EQUILIBRIUM, THE SECURITY
β	RISK	IS PRICED SUCH THAT:
β > 1	Security has more risk than the market	$E(r)^* > E(R_m)$
β = 1	Security has the same risk as the market	$E(r)^* = E(R_m)$
β < 1	Security has less risk than the market	$E(r)^* < E(R_m)$
β = 0	Security has no systematic risk	$E(r)^* = R_f$

TABLE G.4-1

FIGURE G.4-1

Security Market Line

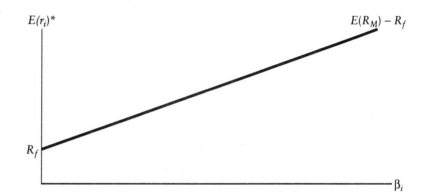

factor, then a security with $\beta = 0$ should be priced in equilibrium such that its rate is equal to the rate on a risk-free security (R_f): $E(r)^* = R_f$. These relations are summarized in Table G.4-1.

The direct relationship between any security's equilibrium rate of return and its β is shown in Figure G.4-1. The line is known as the *security market line* (SML). The equation of the line is:

$$E(r_i)^* = R_f + [E(R_m) - R_f]\beta_i \qquad (G.4-1)$$

where:

$i =$ the ith security.

SELECTED REFERENCES

Francis, J. C. and Archer, S. H. *Portfolio Analysis.* Englewood Cliffs, N.J.: Prentice Hall, 1979.

Lintner, J. "The Valuation of Risk Assets and the Selection of Risky Investments in Stock Portfolios and Capital Budgets." *Review of Economics and Statistics* 47 (Feb. 1965): 587–616.

Markowitz, H. "Portfolio Selection." *Journal of Finance* 7 (Dec. 1952): 77–91.

Mossin, J. "Equilibrium in a Capital Market." *Econometrica* 34 (Oct. 1966): 768–783.

Ross, S. "The Arbitrage Pricing Theory of Capital Asset Pricing." *Journal of Economic Theory* 13 (Dec. 1976): 342–362.

Sharpe, W. F. "Capital Asset Prices: A Theory of Market Equilibrium Under Conditions of Risk." *Journal of Finance* 19 (Sept. 1964): 425–442.

Answers to Select End-of-Chapter Problems and Questions and Exercises

---

CHAPTER 1

Problems and Questions

3. b. $S_T^* = \$41$.

 c. $S_T^* = \$51$.

 d. $S_T^* = \$52$.

4. *Break-even price*: $S_T^* = \$11.50$; *price yielding 10% rate of return*: $S_T = \$11.65$.

5. *Break-even price*: $S_T^* = \$27$; *price yielding 10% rate of return*: $S_T = \$26.70$.

CHAPTER 2

Problems and Questions

5. a. Contract is changed to 150 shares at $33.33 per share.

 b. Contract is changed to 105 shares at $47.62 per share.

 c. No adjustments.

7. *Initial margin*: $M_0 = \$1460$, and cash deposit of $960. At $S_t = \$62$ and $C_t = \$6$, the margin is $1840, which requires an additional $380 deposit.

8. *Initial margin*: $M_0 = \$1160$, and cash deposit of $760. At $S_t = \$36$ and $C_t = \$6.50$, the margin is $1370, which requires an additional $210 deposit.

9. Net deposits of $2680 and $2050.

10. Net deposits of $5500 and $5800.

11. a. $30.
    b. $86.
    c. $121.50.

12. c. $100, $28.
    d. $300, $84.
    e. $-\$200, -\$56$.
    f. $300, $84.

CHAPTER 3

Exercises

a. 1400, 900, 400, 0, -600, 0, 400, 1400.

b. -700, -200, 0, 300, 300, 300, 300, 300, 300.

c. -700, 0, 800, 1300, 800, 0, -700.

d. -600, -600, -600, -100, 0, 400, 400, 400.

e. -300, -300, 0, 300, 700, 300, 0, -300, -300.

f. -200, -200, -200, 0, 300, 800, 300, 0, -200, -700.

g. -300, -300, -300, -300, 0, 200, 700, 1200.

h. 1500, 500, 0, -500, 0, 500, 1500.

i. -800, -300, 0, 200, 700, 200, 0, -300, -800.

j. 2300, 1300, 300, 0, -700, -200, 0, 300, 800.

k. -1200, -700, -200, 0, 300, 800, 0, -200, -1200.

l. 900, 400, 0, -100, -600, -600, -100, 0, 400, 900.

m. -1300, -300, 0, 400, 700, 700, 700, 400, 0, -300, -1300.

n. 500, 500, 500, 0, -500, -500, -500.

o. -1000, -500, 0, 500, 1000.

p. 900, 400, 0, -100, -100, -100, -600, -1100.

Problems and Questions

1. *Liquidate*: $600. *Do nothing*: $-300, -300, -300, 0, 200, 700, 800,$ 1200, 1700. *Spread*: 0, 0, 0, 300, 500, 1000, 1000, 1000, 1000. *Roll up*: 0, 0, 0, 0, 0, 0, 200, 1000, 2000.

2. Spread by selling an ABC September 40 call. $500, 500, 0, -500, -500, -500.$

3. Sell three 55 calls at $2.50 per call; then use proceeds of $750 to close your 50 call contract. Your margin would go from $1300 to $3300.

5. *Liquidate*: $400. *Do nothing*: $1800, 1300, 800, 300, 0, $-200, -200, -200$. *Spread*: $500, 500, 500, 500, 200, 0, 0, 0. *Roll down*: $3000, 2000, 1000, 0, 0, 0, 0, 0.

9. For S_T values of 35, 40, 45, 50, 55, 60, and 65, the values of the simulated straddle are, respectively, $-35, -40, -45, -50, -45, -40,$ and -35.

10. Long in 80 call, short in two 90 calls, and long in 100 call.

11. Form butterfly spread: long 40 call, short two 50 calls, and long 60 call.

CHAPTER 4

Problems and Questions

6. $P_0^e = \$1.30$.

8. $C_0^e = \$4.38$.

11. For a dividend of 0, $4, and $10, the Min C_0^e is $11.82, $7.91, and $2.05, respectively; the Min C_0^a is $11.82, $7.91, and $6.77, respectively.

12. $D^* = \$5.17$.

13. For a dividend of 0, $4, and $10, the Min P_0^e is $4.55, $8.45, and $14.31, respectively; the Min P_0^a is $10, $12.49, and $18.32, respectively.

15. $R = 12\%$ and $D_T = \$1.12$.

CHAPTER 5

Problems and Questions

1. a. $1.19.

   b. Short in call, long .51219 share of stock, and borrow $16.738.

   c. Long in call, short .51219 share of stock, and invest $16.738 in risk-free security.

2. a. $C_{uu} = 5.125$, $C_{ud} = 0$, $C_{dd} = 0$, $C_u = \$3.48$, $C_d = 0$, $C_0^* = \$2.36$.

3. \$4.15.

6. a. $\mu_e = .00895$; $V_e = .002016$.

    b. $\mu_e^A = .02685$; $V_e^A = .006048$.

    c. $n = 4$: $u = 1.02499$ and $d = .97999$; $n = 16$: $u = 1.01185$ and $d = .98939$; $n = 120$: $u = 1.00418$ and $d = .99598$.

    d. $n = 4$: $u = 1.02270$ and $d = .97780$; $n = 16$: $u = 1.01129$ and $d = .98884$; $n = 120$: $u = 1.00411$ and $d = .99591$.

7. a. $\mu_e = 0$, $V_e = .0057027$.

    b. $\mu_e^A = 0$, $V_e^A = .0228108$.

    c. *Quarter*: $u = 1.0784407$ and $d = .9272647$; *month*: $u = 1.0445637$ and $d = .9573375$; *week*: $u = 1.0220390$ and $d = .9784362$; *day*: $u = 1.0079919$ and $d = .9920715$; *½ day*: $u = 1.0056445$ and $d = .9943872$; *⅛ day*: $u = 1.0028183$ and $d = .9971896$.

APPENDIX 5A

Exercises

2. $n = 1$: $E(r_1) = 0$, $V(r_1) = .000392$, $S_k(r_1) = 0$; $n = 2$: $E(r_2) = 0$, $V(r_2) = .000784$, $S_k(r_2) = 0$; $n = 3$: $E(r_3) = 0$, $V(r_3) = .001176$, $S_k(r_3) = 0$.

3. $n = 1$: $E(r_1) = .00396$, $V(r_1) = .000376$, $S_k(r_1) = .00000298$; $n = 2$: $E(r_2) = .00792$, $V(r_2) = .000752$, $S_k(r_2) = .00000596$; $n = 3$: $E(r_3) = .01188$, $V(r_3) = .001128$, $S_k(r_3) = .00000894$.

CHAPTER 6

Problems and Questions

1. a. \$0.50.

    b. Short in put, short .487767 share of stock, and invest \$17.57 in risk-free security.

    c. Long put, long in .487767 share, and borrow \$17.57.

2. a. \$0.85.

    b. \$0.65.

3. a. $P_{uu} = 0$, $P_{ud} = 0$, $P_{dd} = \$4.65$, $P_u = 0$, $P_d = \$1.40$, $P_0^* = \$0.42$.

4. $2.36.

5. $0.72.

6. a. $1.68.

   b. $1.70.

   c. $0.72.

   d. $0.72.

9. $0.22.

APPENDIX 6A

Problems and Questions

1. a. .6 and .4.

   b. $1.47.

   c. $0.49.

APPENDIX 6B

Problems and Questions

1. a. The *stock* is a portfolio of 52.5 state *u* contracts and 48.75 state *d* contracts. The *bond* is a portfolio of 1 state *u* contract and 1 state *d* contract. The *call* is a portfolio of 2.5 state *u* contracts and 0 state *d* contracts. The *put* is a portfolio of 0 state *u* contracts and 1.25 state *d* contracts.

   b. $0.58824 and $0.392155.

   c. $C_0^* = \$1.47$ and $P_0^* = \$0.49$.

2. *State preference prices* for each of the four states: $0.409477, $0.409304, $0.136377, and $0.0151466. *Option prices*: $C_0^* = \$4.176$ and $P_0^* = \$0.21$.

CHAPTER 7

Problems and Questions

1. a. $C_0^* = \$4.60$.

   b. $P_0^* = \$3.71$.

   d. If the ABC 60 call is overpriced, the arbitrage strategy would be formed by selling one call, purchasing $H_0^* = .56859$ share of ABC stock at $60 per share, and borrowing $B_0^* = \$29.512$.

   If the ABC 60 call is underpriced, the arbitrage strategy would be formed by buying one call, selling $H_0^* = .56859$ share of ABC stock short at $60 per share, and investing $B_0^* = \$29.512$ in a risk-free security.

   e. If the ABC 60 put is overpriced, the arbitrage strategy would be formed by selling one put, selling $H_0^{P*} = .43141$ share of ABC stock short at $60 per share, and investing $I_0^* = \$29.5947$ in a risk-free security.

   If the ABC 60 put is underpriced, the arbitrage strategy would be formed by buying one put, buying $H_0^{P*} = .43141$ share of ABC stock at $60 per share, and borrowing $I_0^* = \$29.5947$.

   f. Using the B-S model, the price of the ABC call would be $4.91 when $S_0 = \$60.50$. Using the put-call parity model, the price of the ABC put would be $3.5167.

2. a. At $S_0 = \$60$, the equilibrium price of the call is $4.60. If the market price of the call is at $4.91, the call would be overpriced. To exploit this you would go short in the call at $4.91 and long in the replicating portfolio: Buy $H_0^* = .56859$ share at $60 per share and borrow $B_0^* = \$29.512$. This strategy would generate a cash flow of $0.31.

   b. At $S_t = \$60.50$, the equilibrium price of the call is $4.91. If the market prices the call at $4.91, then closing the position would result in a loss of $0.02 (some rounding errors exist), leaving you with a net cash flow of $0.29.

3. a. If the market price of the put is at $3.91, the put would be overpriced. To exploit this you would go short in the put at $3.91 and long in the replicating portfolio: Sell $H_0^{P*} = .43141$ share of ABC short at $60 per share and invest $I_0^* = \$29.5947$ in risk-free security. This strategy would generate a cash flow of $0.20.

   b. At $S_t = \$60.50$, the equilibrium price of the put is $3.5167. Closing your position at $3.52 would result in a loss of $0.03, leaving you with a net cash flow of $0.17.

4. $C_0^* = Max[C_0, C_0^{ex}] = Max[\$3.79, \$2.49] = \$3.79; P_0^* = Max[P_0, P_0^{ex}]$
   $= Max[\$4.39, \$3.03] = \$4.39.$

5. With the continuous dividend-adjusted model, the dividend-adjusted stock price is $58.52, the call price is $3.79, and the put price is $4.38.

6. a. $C_0^* = \$3.82.$
   b. $P_0^* = \$1.45.$

10. a. The continuously compounded rate is .07566.
    b. The simple annual rate is .0786.

CHAPTER 8

Exercises

1. *Market's price*: $C_0^m = \$5.70$; *your price*: $C_0^* = \$5.31.$

2. *Strategy*: Go short in call, buy $H_0^* = .7881$ share at $100 per share, and borrow $B_0^* = \$73.50$. Value of initial cash flow is $0.39(1.025) = $0.40.

3. $C_t^m = \$7.58.$

4. Adjust by borrowing $22.22 to finance the purchase of .2119 share at $104.88 per share. There would be zero cash flows from closing at expiration.

Problems and Questions

3. Profit = $0.82.

4. Profit = $1.87.

5. a. $C^*(50, .25) = \$2.135; C^*(48, .25) = \$3.384.$
   b. Sell a 48 call and buy 1.2859 50 calls; initial cash flow = $0.64.
   c. In both cases the closing cash flow would be $-\$0.64$, offsetting the initial cash flow.

6. Go long in 1.2859 50 calls and short in one 48 call. This would result in an initial cash inflow of $0.75 and an outflow of $0.64 when the position is closed.

7. Go short in 1.2859 50 calls and long in one 48 call. This would result in an initial cash outflow of $0.49 and a cash inflow of $0.64 when the position is closed.

8. $\beta_c = 4.81$.

9. $E(R_c) = .61; \sigma(R_c) = 2.40$.

11. 27.46%.

12. a. $P_0^* = \$1.39$.

    b. $E(R_p) = 2.45; \sigma(R_p) = 2.61$.

    c. $\beta_p = -5.22$.

13. a. $C(100) = \$5.73; C(105) = \$3.56$.

    b. *100 call*: $\Delta = .57225, \Theta = -12.898, \Gamma = .031388$; *105 call*:
       $\Delta = .41780, \Theta = -12.0538, \Gamma = .031234$.

    c. Long in a 105 call and short in .73 100 call. Value (or cost) of the
       portfolio is $0.62. $\Theta_p = -2.638$ and $\Gamma_p = .00832$.

    d. The portfolio will decline in value if there is no change in the stock
       price, and will increase if the stock price changes.

    e. At $S_t = 105$, profit $= \$0.10$; and at $S_t = \$95$, the profit would be
       $0.03.

CHAPTER 9

Problems and Questions

1. a. $1500, 1000, 500, 0, -500, -100, -1500, -2000, -1500, -1000,
    -500, 0, 500, 1000, 1500$.

    b. $-\$2900, -2400, -1900, -1400, -900, -400, 0, 100, 600, 1300,
    1600, 2100$.

2. Purchase 400 SP 500 put contracts. *Hedged portfolio values*: $9.6M, 9.6M,
   9.6M, 9.6M, 9.6M, 9.8M, 10M, 10.2M, 10.4M.

3. Price of call $= 17.081604$. *Fiduciary call*: Liquidate $10M portfolio, invest
   proceeds in risk-free security, and buy 400 SP 500 calls.

4. $3.5M portfolio would be equivalent to owning 10,000 hypothetical shares
   at $350 per share.

5. a. $C_0^* = 18.71; P_0^* = 12.98$.

    b. *Call*: Invest $184.53 in highly correlated portfolio and borrow
    $165.8218. *Put*: Short a $132.2833 of a highly correlated portfolio and
    invest $145.265 in risk-free security.

11. a. $-\$1250, -1250, -1250, -1250, -1250, 0, 1250, 2500, 3750$.

    b. $4500, 3250, 2000, 750, 0, -500, -500, -500, -500, -500$.

12. To hedge, the manager should buy a September 90 T-bill put. At expiration the put-hedged T-bill sale at the various R_D values would be $974,500, 974,500, 974,500, 974,500, 974,500, 975,750, 977,000, 978,250, 979,500.

13. To hedge, the manager should buy a September 90 T-bill contract. Hedged expiration costs at various R_D values: $971,250, 972,500, 973,750, 975,000, 976,250, 976,250, 976,250, 976,250, 976,250.

14. *Profit*: $-\$1187.50, -1187.50, 1187.50, -187.50, 812.50, 1812.50, 2812.50. Break-even index price* $= 98.1875$.

15. *Profit*: $\$2218.75, 1218.75, 218.75, -781.25, -781.25, -781.25, -781.25. Break-even index price* $= 96.21875$.

16. $P_0 = PV(X) + C_0 - S_0; P_0 = 97/(1.060154)^{.25} + 1.1875 - 96 = .78125$.

17. *Put-hedged T-bond sale*: $\$96,218.75, 96,218.75, 96,218.75, 96,218.75, 97,281.75, 98,281.75, 99,281.75$.

CHAPTER 10

Problems and Questions

1. a. *Profit on DM spread*: $-\$625, -625, 0, 625, 625, 625, 625$.

   b. *Profit on BP long straddle*: $\$3750, 2187.50, 625, 0, -937.50, 0, 625, 2187.50, 3750$.

   c. *Profit on simulated long DM position*: $-\$2656.25, -1406.25, -171.25, 468.75, 1093.75, 1718.75, 2343.75$.

2. Purchase 20 March 115 BP put contracts. *Hedged receipts at different E_T values*: $\$687,500, 687,500, 687,500, 687,500, 718,750, 750,000$.

3. Purchase 30 June 110 BP call contracts. *Net costs at different E_T values*: $\$928,125, 975,000, 1,021,875, 1,068,750, 1,068,750, 1,068,750, 1,068,750$.

7. a. Long in call, borrow .99024 DM, and convert to dollars, and buy U.S. pure discount bond with face value of $0.50. This would yield an initial cash flow of $0.00225.

   b. Long in put, borrow $0.4928, and buy .99024 DM. This would yield an initial cash flow of $0.00745.

   c. Long in put, buy .99024 DM, short in call, and borrow $0.4928. This would yield an initial cash flow of $0.01034.

8. a. $C_0^* = \$0.0062$.

   b. Short call, buy .2848 DM, and borrow \$0.0849. This would yield a cash flow of \$0.0013, with no liabilities at expiration.

   c. Long in call, borrow .2848 DM, and convert to \$0.0911, and invest \$0.0849 in U.S. risk-free security. This would yield an initial cash flow of \$0.0017, with no liabilities at expiration.

9. a. $C_0^* = \$0.0055$.

   b. Short the call and go long in the replicating portfolio. This would provide an initial cash flow of \$0.002. There would be a loss of \$0.002 at the end of period 1.

   c. Borrow \$0.10956 and purchase .3263 DM at \$0.33577/DM.

11. $P_0^* = \$0.015$; $P_0^* = X(1 + R_{US}^{period})^{-n} + C_0^* - E_0(1 + R_F^{period})^{-n}$; $P_0^* = \$.33(1.0121266)^{-1} + \$.0062 - \$.32(1.00944)^{-1} = \$.015$.

12. Short in put and long in replicating portfolio. This would yield an initial cash flow of \$.0023, with no liabilities at expiration.

13. $C_0^* = \$0.053$.

CHAPTER 11

Problems and Questions

1. a. \$4.85M.

   b. \$15.15.

   d. $V_0^E = \$7.77M$ and $V_0^B = \$12.23M$.

3. a. \$1000.

   b. \$208.19.

   c. \$791.81.

4. a. \$1000.

   b. \$28.56.

   c. \$1028.56.

5. a. \$636.36.

   b. \$700.

7. a. 5.

   b. \$4.17.

8. a. \$100.

   b. \$900.

   c. \$887.

   d. \$900.

APPENDIX 11A

Problems and Questions

1. Value of put = $4.514M; V_0^E = $4.85.
2. V_0^B = $15.15M.

CHAPTER 12

Problems and Questions

7. a. Long in six September contracts.
   b. Net costs at expiration is $6000 regardless of the spot price.
   d. $300.

8. a. Short in two September contracts.
   b. Revenue at expiration is $42,000 regardless of the spot price.
   d. $2100.

9. a. Short in four May contracts.
   b. Net costs at expiration is $57,000 regardless of the spot price.
   c. $2850.

10. a. Short in ten September contracts.
    b. Revenue at expiration is $9,750,000 regardless of the spot price.

14. a. $1000.
    b. $1500, $1750, $1250, $500, 0, $1000.
    c. $0, 0, 0, $500, $1000, 0.

16. $4.95.

18. $1.92.

19. a. $982,309.
    b. $100.95.
    c. $23.01.
    d. $97.39.

CHAPTER 13

Problems and Questions

1. a. 500 short SP 500 futures contracts.

   b. Portfolio values, futures profit and hedged portfolio values, respectively, at 270, 280, 290, 300, 310, 320, 330: $42.5M, $7.5M, $50M; 45M, 5M, 50M; 47.5M, 2.5M, 50M; 50M, 0, 50M; 52.5M, −2.5M, 50M; 55M, −5M, 50M; 57.5M, −7.5M, 50M.

   c. 2500 SP 500 puts.

   d. Portfolio values, put profit, and hedged portfolio values, respectively, at 270, 280, 290, 300, 310, 320, 330: $42.5M, $3.75M, $46.25M; 45M, 1.25M, 46.25M; 47.5M, −1.25M, 46.25M; 50M, −3.75M, 46.25M; 52.5M, −3.75M, 48.75M; 55M, −3.75M, 51.25M; 57.5M, −3.75M, 53.75M.

2. a. Purchase of 62,500 index shares at $320 per share.

   b. *Cost*: $19,062,500, 19,375,000, 19,687,500, 20,000,000, 20,312,500, 20,625,000, 20,937,500.

   c. 125 long contracts. Hedged portfolio cost is $20M regardless of the spot index.

3. a. 18 short contracts.

   b. Unhedged portfolio value = $2.3105M; hedged portfolio value = $2.6345M.

4. Go long in six SP 500 futures contracts. Portfolio values with and without futures are $2.16554M, $2.01104M; 2.31036M, 2.20236M; 2.45518M, 2.39368M; 2.6M, 2.585M; 2.74482M, 2.77632M; 2.8896M, 2.9676M; 3.03446M, 3.15896M.

5. a. Go short in four SP 500 futures contracts.

   b. Stock value and futures profit—*scenario 1*: $550,000; *scenario 2*: $590,000.

   c. Rates for scenarios 1 and 2 without futures: 20% and 8%; with futures: 10% and 18%.

6. 212.70.

7. a. 20,280 shares at 212.03156 per share. Dividend per share is worth $2.564 at the end of the quarter.

   b. 212.53595.

   c. Borrow $4.3M, buy portfolio for $4.3M, and go short in 40.56 futures contracts.

   d. PI earns an arbitrage cash flow of $0.05M.

   e. Short the $4.3M portfolio, invest $4.3M in risk-free security, and go long in 40.56 futures contracts.

   f. PI earns an arbitrage cash flow of $0.05M.

CHAPTER 14

Problems and Questions

1. a. *March*: f_0 = \$984,410, YTM = .065; *June*: f_0 = \$983,273, YTM = .07; *September*: f_0 = \$979,652, YTM = .086.

   b. .06.

   c. \$985,578.

   d. f_0 = \$981,513. Short March futures contract and borrow \$970,223 at 4.75% for 91 days to finance the purchase of a 182-day T-bill.

2. a. (1) $R_I(91, 91)$ = .065. Short 91-day T-bill and buy $S_0(182)/S_0(90)$ 182-day T-bills.

      (2) $R_I(91, 182)$ = .07. Short 182-day T-bill and buy $S_0(182)/S_0(273)$ 273-day T-bills.

   b. $f_0(91)$ = \$984,422 and IMM Index(91) = 93.769; $f_0(182)$ = \$983,273 and IMM Index(182) = 93.309.

3. a. 10.4583285 contracts.

   b. After 91 days Sun Bank would need to raise \$10,247,763.86 if the LIBOR is 8.5%, and \$10,212,744.36 if the LIBOR is 10%. After 182 days the bank would owe \$10,458,328. Their effective rate is 9.4%.

   c. \$123,204.

4. Rate = 9.4% and $S_0(182)$ = \$956,176.

5. a. Long in T-bond contract and short in T-bill or T-note contract.

   b. Long in T-bond contract and short in Municipal Bond Index contract.

   c. Long in Municipal Bond Index contract and short in T-bond contract.

6. Short December contract, short T-bill or Eurodollar contract, and long September T-bond contract.

7. a. *March*: 6.5%; *June:* 7%; *September:* 8.6%.

   b. Go long in March, June, and September futures contracts. Average rate for the year would be 7%.

   c. *March*: n_f = 10.307; *June:* n_f = 10.48223; *September:* n_f = 10.7.

   d. (1) At the March expiration, the fund would close the futures for a profit of \$12,039 and would buy 10.307 T-bills; (2) at the June expiration, the fund would lose \$5996 and would buy 10.4823 T-bills; (3) at the September expiration, the fund would close the futures for a profit of \$14,370 and would buy 10.7 T-bills.

   e. With the hedge, the fund earns 7%; without the hedge, the fund earns 6.79%.

8. a. Short in 9.8328 March contracts and 10 June contracts.

    b. $9,679,630; 6%.

9. a. Long in 10.1584 March contracts and 10.1701 June contracts; rate of return = 6.75%.

    b. n_{TB} = 10.3312; rate = 6.75%.

10. a. 8.44%.

    b. n_f = 3.0612.

11. a. 7.89%.

    b. Go long in 3.0612 September contracts and short in 3.0534 December contracts.

    c. Closing the September and December contracts would result in a profit of $5391. This profit plus the $3M inflow would enable Ms. James to buy 3.11575 T-bills at a price of $964,581.

    d. Closing the September and December contracts would result in a loss of $9830. At a spot T-bill price of only $959,697, Ms. James would be able to buy 3.11574 contracts, after covering the futures loss with the $3M inflow.

12. a. 9.5%.

    b. Quarterly interest payments, futures profit, and hedged interest payment for quarterly periods starting on 12/20, 3/20, and 6/20, respectively, are: $118,750, 0, $118,750; $137,500, $12,500, $125,000; $125,000, $12,500, $112,500.

    c. Annualized rates for periods starting on 12/20, 3/20, and 6/20, respectively, are: 9.5%, 10%, and 9%. The average rate for the period is 9.5%, the same rate found in part (a).

13. a. Short 24 June T-bill contracts.

    b. Borrow $7.94M; rate = 10.379%.

14. a. Long 48 June T-bond contracts.

    b. Portfolio cost = $5,200,000; futures profit = $216,000; net cost = $4,984,000.

CHAPTER 15

Problems and Questions

2. a. $0.3732756/SF.

 b. $-.01865$

 c. Borrow 14.71803M SF, convert to $5.51926M, and invest at 6%.

 d. Borrow $5.51926, convert to 14.7180 SF, and invest at 8%.

4. a. $E(E_T^C)$ = $0.3532415/DM.

 b. Buy 2.8571429 DM with $1, invest the marks for 90 days at 5%, convert the marks at the end of 90 days at $E(E_T^C)$ = $0.3532415/DM.

5. a. 1.03125 DM/SF.

 b. Convert $ to SF, convert SF to DM, convert DM to $.

 c. Convert $ to DM, convert DM to SF, convert SF to $.

6. a. Short in forward contract.

 b. Borrow FC and convert to dollars and invest; at the end of year convert dollars to pay FC debt at lower expected exchange rate.

 c. Long in forward contract.

 d. Borrow dollars and convert to FC and invest; at end of the year convert FC to dollars at higher expected exchange rate.

7. a. 0.8 CD/DM. Spot and forward rates are the same.

 b. Enter forward contract to sell 1 DM for 0.8 CD.

 c. Go long in $/CD futures contract with the expectation that the exchange rate would be $0.888/CD at the end of a year.

8. a. Enter forward contract to sell 250,000 FF at $0.165883/FF in December, and enter forward contract to sell 250,000 FF at $0.1651096/FF in March.

 b. Borrow $250,000/(1.08)^{.25}$ FF, convert to $40,871, and invest dollars at 6% for three months. Borrow $250,000/(1.08)^{.5}$ FF, convert to $40,092, and invest dollars at 6% for six months.

 c. Go short in one December FF contract.

9. a. To hedge June payment, Parson should enter a June forward contract to buy 3M SF for $2M ($E_f$ = 0.66667/SF). Similarly, to hedge the December payment, it should enter a December forward contract to buy 3M SF for $2M.

 b. Borrow $1.9710767M, convert to 2.9566M SF, and invest SF at 6% for three months.

 c. Go long in 24 SF futures contracts.

10. a. 12.5%.

   b. For E_T = $0.40/g, $0.45/g, $0.50/g, and $0.55/g, rates of return are −10%, 1.25%, 12.5%, and 23.75%.

   c. $0.5095238/g.

   d. For E_T = $0.40/g, $0.45/g, $0.50/g, and $0.55/g, the rates of return are 11.905%, 13.155%, 14.405%, and 15.655%.

CHAPTER 16

Problems and Questions

1. 4.

2. Go short in 300 put, short in index futures contract, short in riskless pure discount bond with face value of 9, and long in 300 call.

3. 254.05.

4. Go long in put, short in call, long in futures, and short in riskless discount bond with face value of 10.

5. $0.03.

6. Go short in DM call, long in DM put, long in DM futures contract, and short in riskless discount bond with face value of $0.02.

7. a. E_{fuu} = $0.441, E_{fud} = $0.40, E_{fdd} = $0.362812, E_{fu} = $0.41795, E_{fd} ≐ $0.37909, E_{f0} = $0.396107.

   b. C_{uu} = $.041, C_{ud} = 0, C_{dd} = 0, C_u = .0176, C_d = 0, C_0^* = .0075.

8. Short call, long in .45073 DM forward contract, and invest $0.0075 in U.S. risk-free security. Loss of $0.01.

   To avoid loss, the arbitrageurs could close the DM futures with the cash flow invested in risk-free security and go long in 1 DM futures contract. At expiration the arbitrageur would realize a cash flow of $0.002494.

9. a. 212.5358.

   b. Short 40.56 SP 500 futures, borrow $4.3M, and buy portfolio. Cash flow at expiration would be $9413.

   c. 2.50.

   d. Buy $4.3M portfolio, buy 202.8 put contracts, sell 202.8 call contracts, and borrow $4,249,309. Initial cash flow would be $10,149.

   e. Put price is $2.50 using put-call-futures parity model.

   f. Long in put, short in call, long in futures, and long in bond with face value of $2.5358.

10. a. Buy call and exercise.

   b. Buy put and exercise.

11. a. $E_{uu} = \$1.2486$, $E_{ud} = \$1.15$, $E_{dd} = \$1.05984$, $E_u = \$1.1983$, $E_d = \$1.104$, $E_0 = \$1.15$.

   b. $E_{fuu} = \$1.23648$, $E_{fud} = \$1.1388$, $E_{fdd} = \$1.04955$, $E_{fu} = \$1.175145$, $E_{fd} = \$1.082667$, $E_{f0} = \$1.11683$.

   c. $C_{uu} = \$0.08648$, $C_{ud} = 0$, $C_{dd} = 0$, $C_u = \$0.0315467$, $C_d = 0$, $C_0^* = \$0.0114$.

   d. *Overpriced*: Short call, long H_0^* futures, invest B_0^* dollars. *Underpriced*: Long call, short H_0^* futures, borrow B_0^*.

   e. Call on the spot is greater than call on the futures.

12. a. $\$1.14717/BP$.

   b. $C_0^* = \$0.0375$. Replicating portfolio consists of purchasing .50595 BP and borrowing $\$0.53437$.

   c. $\$0.0375$.

   d. $\$0.0403$.

   e. $\$0.0403$.

CHAPTER 17

Problems and Questions

1. a. $-\$0.075M$, $-0.05M$, $-0.025M$, 0, 0.025M, 0.05M, 0.075M, and 0.1M.

   b. Fixed rate = 10.5%.

2. Net interest received by fixed-rate payer on effective dates are: $450,000, 300,000, 150,000, 0, -150,000, -300,000, and -450,000.

3. Semiannual interests on the fixed-rate loan minus net interest receipts of the floating-rate payer are: $1,800,000, 1,650,000, 1,500,000, 1,350,000, 1,200,000, 1,050,000, and 900,000.
   Both yield the same rates.

7. b. *Agreement:* (1) American company will obtain a $20M, five–year loan at 11%, then swap it for FF 114.2857M loan at 8.25%. (2) French company will obtain a FF 114.2857M, five-year loan at 9%, then swap it for $20M loan at 11.9%.

   c. The swap bank has the series of long FF forward contracts in which it agrees to buy FF 0.85713M for $0.18M each year.

8. Hedged borrowing rates at the different LIBORs are: 8.17%, 8.71%, 9.25%, 9.25%, and 9.25%.

9. Hedged rate at the different LIBORs are: 6.42%, 6.42%, 6.42%, 6.95%, and 7.48%.

10. Cash flows with the cap at the different effective dates are: $19,950,000, −408,889, −408,889, −404,445, and −20,350,000.

11. The rates with the floor, given the LIBORs at the effective dates, are: 8%, 8%, 8%, and 9%.

12. a. Buy the cap for $100,000 and sell the floor for $85,000.

    b. The collar-hedged rates are: 10%, 8%, 7%, and 7%.

13. *PRIMEs cash flows*: $41, 46, 51, 51, and 51. *SCOREs cash flows*: $0, 0, 0, 5, and 10.

Glossary of Terms

accrued interest The interest on a bond or fixed-income security that has accumulated since the last coupon date.

all-or-none order A buy or sell order instructing a broker to execute the transaction in its entirety or not at all.

American option An option that can be exercised at any time on or before the exercise date.

annualized forward premium or discount The difference between the forward and spot exchange rates expressed as an annual percentage of the spot exchange rate.

annualized mean The mean obtained by multiplying a mean for a given period (e.g., one week) by the number of periods of that length in a year (e.g., 52).

annualized variance The variance obtained by multiplying a variance for a given period (e.g., one week) by the number of periods of that length in a year (e.g., 52).

anticipatory hedge A hedging strategy of going long in a futures contract in order to lock in the future cost of a spot transaction.

arbitrage A transaction that provides a positive cash flow with no liabilities—a "free lunch." An arbitrage opportunity exists when positions generating identical cash flows are not equally priced. In such cases the arbitrage is formed by buying the lower-priced position and selling the higher-priced one.

arbitrageur An individual who engages in arbitrage.

ask price The price at which a dealer offers to sell a security.

assignment A procedure in which a brokerage firm or clearinghouse selects one of its customers who is short in an optioned stock to fulfill the terms of the option after a holder has exercised.

backwardation Describes a market where the futures price is less than the spot price.

Barone-Adesi and Whaley (BAW) model A model used for pricing options on continuous-leakage assets.

basis The difference between the futures price and the spot price.

basis point A measure equal to .01%.

basis risk *See* **timing risk.**

bear call money spread A vertical spread formed by purchasing a call at a certain exercise price and selling another call on the same security at a lower exercise price.

bear put money spread A vertical spread formed by purchasing a put at a certain exercise price and selling another put on the same security at a lower exercise price.

beta A measure of the responsiveness of a change in a security's rate of return to a change in the rate of return of the market.

bid-ask spread The difference between the bid price and the ask price.

bid price The price at which a dealer offers to buy a security.

binomial option pricing model (BOPM) A model for determining the equilibrium value of an option by finding the option price that equals the value of a replicating portfolio; assumes a binomial world in which the option's underlying security price can either increase or decrease in a given period.

Black model A model for pricing a futures option contract.

Black-Scholes model A model for valuing European options.

box spread A combination of a call money spread and a put money spread. A *long* box spread consists of a call bull money spread and a put bear money spread; it yields a certain return at expiration equal to the difference in the exercise prices. A *short* box spread (or reverse box spread) is a combination of a call bear money spread and a put bull money spread; it generates a credit for the investor at the initiation of the strategy and requires a fixed payment at expiration equal to the difference in the exercise prices.

break-even price   The price of the underlying security at the exercise date in which the profit from the option position is zero.

bucket trading   A price-manipulation scheme in which a commission broker with an order to execute tips off another broker (referred to as the *bagman*), who proceeds to take a position in the security. When conditions are favorable, the commission broker executes the order with the bagman.

bull call money spread   A vertical spread formed by purchasing a call at a certain exercise price and selling another call on the same security at a higher exercise price.

bull put money spread   A vertical spread formed by purchasing a put at a certain exercise price and selling another put on the same security at a higher exercise price.

butterfly money call spread   A spread formed with three call options, each with different exercise prices. A *long butterfly money spread* is formed by buying one call at a low exercise price, selling two calls at a middle exercise price, and buying one call at a high exercise price. A *short* butterfly money spread is formed by selling one call at a low exercise price, buying two calls at a middle exercise price, and selling one call at a high exercise price.

butterfly money put spread   A spread formed with three put options, each with different exercise prices. A *long* butterfly money spread is formed by buying one put at a low exercise price, selling two puts at a middle exercise price, and buying one put at a high exercise price. A *short* butterfly money spread is formed by selling one put at a low exercise price, buying two puts at a middle exercise price, and selling one put at a high exercise price.

calendar spread   *See* horizontal spread.

call   An option that gives the holder the right to buy an asset or a security at a specified price on or possibly before a specific date.

callable bond   A bond that gives the issuer the right to buy back the bond from the bondholders at a specified price before maturity.

call market   A market set up so that those wishing to trade in a particular security can do so only at that time when the exchange "calls" the security for trading.

call spread   A strategy in which you buy a call and simultaneously sell another call on the same stock but with different terms.

cap   A series of European interest rate calls that expire at or near the interest payment dates on a loan; often written by financial institutions in conjunction with a variable-rate loan.

carrying-cost model (or cost-of-carry model)   A model for determining the equilibrium price on a forward or futures contract. In this model the forward price equals the net cost of carrying the underlying asset to expiration.

cash-and-carry arbitrage   A riskless strategy formed by taking opposite positions in spot and forward contracts on a security. This strategy underlies the carrying-cost model.

cash market   *See* spot market.

cash settlement   A feature on some futures and option contracts whereby the contract is settled in cash at delivery instead of as an exchange of cash for the underlying asset.

cheapest-to-deliver bond   The least expensive bond (or note) among the Chicago Board of Trade's eligible bonds (or notes) that a short holder of a Treasury-bond (or note) futures contact can deliver.

clearinghouse   A corporation associated with a futures or options exchange that guarantees the performance of each contract and acts as intermediary by breaking up each contract after the trade has taken place.

closing order   Describes closing an option or futures position; requires taking an opposite position: selling an option or futures contract to close an initial long position, buying an option or futures contract to close an initial short position.

collar   A position in a cap and an opposite position in a floor, with the cap and floor having different exercise prices.

combination purchase   A strategy formed by purchasing a call and a put on the same underlying security but with different terms: different exercise prices (money or vertical combination), dates (time, calendar, or horizontal combination), or both (diagonal combination).

combination write A strategy formed by selling a call and a put on the same underlying security but with different terms: different exercise prices (money or vertical combination), exercise dates (time, calendar, or horizontal combination), or both (diagonal combination).

Commodity Futures Trading Commission (CFTC) The federal agency that oversees and regulates futures trading.

complete market A market in which all the possible state-contingent payouts are available to investors from the existing set of assets.

compound option An option on an option.

condor A strategy consisting of four call and/or put options on the same security but with different terms.

contango Describes a market where the futures price exceeds the spot price.

contingent claims analysis The analysis of the option characteristics embedded in corporate securities.

continuous dividend adjustment model The Black-Scholes option pricing model employed when the underlying stock pays a dividend; uses a continuous dividend-adjusted stock price instead of the current stock price.

continuous-leakage option An option on an asset that generates a continuous flow of benefits (e.g., interests or dividends).

continuously compounded return The rate of return in which the value of the asset grows continuously; equal to the natural logarithm of 1 plus the simple (noncompounded) rate.

continuous market A market that provides constant trading in a security. Such markets operate through specialists or market makers who are required by the exchange to take temporary positions in a security whenever there is a demand.

convenience yield Describes the situation in which the benefits from holding an asset exceed the costs of holding the asset.

conversion An arbitrage portfolio formed by going long in an underlying security, short in a European call, and long in a European put. The portfolio yields a cash flow equal to the exercise price at expiration regardless of the price of the underlying security.

conversion price A convertible bond's par value divided by its conversion ratio.

conversion ratio The number of shares of stock that can be acquired when a convertible bond is tendered for conversion.

conversion value A convertible bond's value as a stock; equal to the convertible bond's conversion ratio times the market price of the stock.

convertible bond A bond in which the holder can covert the bond to a specified number of shares of stock.

cooperative linkage agreement An agreement between exchanges in which a futures trader is allowed to open a position in one market and close it in another.

counterparties The parties to a swap agreement.

covered call write A position in which the writer of a call owns the underlying security.

covered interest arbitrage An arbitrage strategy consisting of long and short positions in currency spot and futures contracts, and positions in domestic and foreign risk-free securities; used by arbitrageurs when the interest-rate-parity condition does not hold.

covered put write A position in which a seller of a put is short in the underlying security.

cross-exchange rate The exchange rate between two currencies that is implied by the relationship between three exchange rates.

cross-hedge A futures hedge in which the futures' underlying asset is not the same as the asset being hedged.

currency swap A contract in which one party agrees to exchange a liability denominated in one currency to another party, who agrees to exchange a liability denominated in a different currency.

day order An investor's buy or sell order to a broker that is only in effect for the duration of the day.

day trader A trader who holds a position for a day.

dealer A trader who provides a market for investors to buy and sell a security by taking a temporary position in the security.

debt option An option on a debt security.

deep in-the-money call A call in which the price of the underlying security is substantially above the call's exercise price.

deep in-the-money put A put in which the price of the underlying security is substantially below the put's exercise price.

deep out-of-the-money call A call in which the price of the underlying security is substantially below the call's exercise price.

deep out-of-the-money put A put in which the price of the underlying security is substantially above the put's exercise price.

delta The change in an option price for a small change in the price of the underlying security.

derivative security A security whose value depends on another security or asset.

designated order turnaround (DOT) The New York Stock Exchange system that expedites security trades.

diagonal spread A spread formed with options that have both different exercise prices and different expiration dates.

direct hedge A futures hedge in which the futures' underlying asset is the same as the asset being hedged.

discrete-leakage option An option on an asset that generates a discrete flow of benefits (e.g., interests or dividends).

dual trading A security trading practice in which an exchange member trades for both her client and herself.

duration The average date that cash is received on a bond. It can be measured by calculating the weighted average of the bond's time periods, with the weights being the present value of each year's cash flows expressed as a proportion of the bond's price.

dynamic hedge ratio The ratio that determines the number of stock index futures contracts that will replicate a put-insured stock portfolio.

dynamic portfolio insurance A strategy in which a stock portfolio is combined with bonds or futures and adjusted over time such that its possible future values replicate the values of a put-insured portfolio.

early exercise The exercise of an American option before its expiration.

effective date The date when interest begins to accrue on a swap agreement.

efficient market A market in which the actual price of a security is equal to its intrinsic (true economic) value.

elasticity A measure of the percentage change in a dependent variable relative to the percentage change in an independent variable.

embedded option An option characteristic that is part of the features of an equity or debt security. Features include call and put features on corporate debt securities, the conversion clauses on convertible bonds, and the preemptive rights of existing stockholders.

end-of-the-day exercise feature A feature of index options in which the closing value of the spot index on the exercising day is used to determine the cash settlement when the index option is exercised.

equivalent strategies Strategies that have the same profit and security price relationships.

Eurodollar deposit A deposit in dollars in a bank located or incorporated outside the United States.

Eurodollar futures contract A futures contract on a Eurodollar deposit. The contract has a cash-settlement feature.

European currency unit (ECU) A weighted-average index of the exchange rates of countries comprising the European Economic Community.

European option An option that can be exercised only on the exercise date.

ex ante Before the fact.

exchange rate The number of units of one currency that can be exchanged for one unit of another; the price of foreign currency.

ex-dividend date The date on which the ownership of stock is declared for purposes of determining who is entitled to dividends. Stock owners who purchase shares before this date are entitled to the dividend; investors who purchase shares of the stock on or after that date are not entitled to receive the dividend.

exercise limit The maximum number of option contracts that can be exercised on a specified number of consecutive business days by any investor or investor group. An exercise limit is determined by the exchange for each stock and nonstock option.

exercise price The price specified in the option contract at which the underlying asset or security can be purchased (call) or sold (put).

expiration cycle The standard expiration dates on an exchange-traded option or futures that are set by the exchanges.

expiring transaction Describes doing nothing when an expiration date arrives.

fiduciary call An investment in a risk-free bond and call option that yields a position equivalent to a portfolio insurance position.

fill-or-kill order An investor's buy or sell order to a broker that is an all-or-none order with a stipulation that the order is to be canceled if the entire order cannot be executed when it is initially introduced to the market.

financial engineering Describes strategies of buying and selling derivatives and their underlying securities in order to create portfolios with certain desired features.

financial swap An agreement between two parties to exchange the cash flows from each party's liabilities.

fixed-rate payer The party in a financial swap that agrees to pay fixed interest and receive variable interest.

floating-rate payer The party in a financial swap that agrees to pay variable interest in return for fixed interest.

floor A series of interest rate puts that expire at or near the effective dates on a loan; often used as a hedging tool by financial institutions.

floor broker A member of an exchange who executes buy and sell orders on behalf of his client.

follow-up strategy A strategy used after setting up an initial option position; can be classified as either an *aggressive* follow-up strategy (used when the price of the underlying security moves to a profitable position) or a *defensive* follow-up strategy (employed when the security price moves to a potentially unprofitable position).

foreign currency futures A futures contract on a foreign currency.

foreign currency option An option on a foreign currency.

forward contract An agreement between two parties to trade a specific asset or security at a future date, with the terms and price agreed upon today.

futures contract A marketable forward contract.

futures fund A mutual fund that pools investors' monies and uses them to set up futures positions.

futures hedge ratio The optimal number of futures contracts needed to hedge a position.

futures options (or options on futures, or commodity options) An option contract that gives the holder the right to take a position in a futures contract on or before a specific date. A call option on a futures contract gives the holder the right to take a long position in the underlying futures contract when she exercises, and requires the writer to take the short position in the futures if he is assigned. A put option on a futures option entitles the holder to take a short futures position and the assigned writer the long position.

futures purchase See **long futures position.**

futures sale See **short futures position.**

futures spread Futures position formed by taking simultaneous long and short positions in different futures contracts.

gamma The change in an option's delta with respect to a small change in the underlying security's price.

Garman and Kohlhagen model A model for pricing foreign currency options.

generic swap An interest rate swap in which fixed-interest payments are exchanged for floating-interest payments.

GLOBEX A computer trading system in which bids and asks are entered into a computer that then matches them.

good-till-canceled order An investor's buy or sell limit order to a broker that stipulates that the order will stay in effect until the investor cancels it.

hedge A strategy in which an investor protects the future value of a position by taking a position in a futures contract, option, or other derivative security.

hedge purchase See **long futures hedge.**

hedge sale See **short futures hedge.**

horizontal spread A spread formed with options that have the same exercise prices but different expiration dates.

IMM Index The quoted index price for futures on Treasury-bill contracts and Eurodollar contracts traded on the International Monetary Market. The index is equal to 100 minus the annual percentage discount yield.

implied forward rate The rate in the future that is implied by current rates; can be attained via a locking-in strategy consisting of a position in a short-term bond and an opposite position in a long-term one.

implied futures rate The rate implied on an interest rate futures contract.

implied repo rate The rate at which the arbitrage profit from implementing a cash-and-carry arbitrage strategy with futures contracts is zero; also the rate earned from an investment in a synthetic Treasury bill.

implied variance The variance that equates the option pricing model's price to the market price. Conceptually, it can be thought of as the market's consensus on the stock's volatility.

implied volatility *See* **implied variance.**

independent A member of an exchange who trades from her own accounts.

index arbitrage An arbitrage strategy formed by taking a position in a spot index portfolio (or proxy portfolio) and an opposite one in a stock index futures contract. The strategy is implemented when the market price on the futures contract does not equal its equilibrium price as determined by the carrying-cost model.

initial margin The amount of cash or cash equivalents that must be deposited by the investor on the day a futures or option position is established.

interbank currency option market A market in which tailor-made foreign currency option contracts are provided by banks; part of the interbank market.

interbank market A spot and forward currency exchange market consisting primarily of major banks who act as currency dealers.

intercommodity spread A spread formed with futures contracts with the same expiration dates but on different underlying assets.

interest rate option An option that gives the holder the right to a payoff if a specific interest rate is greater (call) or less (put) than the option's exercise rate.

interest rate parity theorem (IRPT) The carrying-cost model that governs the relationship between spot and forward exchange rates.

interest rate swap An agreement between two parties to exchange interest payments on loans.

in-the-money option A call (put) option in which the price of the underlying asset is above (below) the exercise price.

intracommodity spread A spread formed with futures contracts on the same underlying asset but with different expiration dates.

intrinsic value of a call The maximum of zero or the difference between a call's underlying security price and its exercise price.

intrinsic value of a put The maximum of zero or the difference between a put's exercise price and its underlying security's price.

inverted market A market where the futures price is less then the spot price.

kappa *See* **vega.**

Kolb-Chiang price-sensitivity model A price-sensitivity model for hedging interest rate positions; determines the number of futures contracts that will make the value of a portfolio consisting of a fixed-income security and an interest rate futures contract invariant to small changes in interest rates.

Law of One Price An economic principle that two assets with the same future payouts will be priced the same.

LEAPS An acronym for "long-term equity-anticipation securities." LEAPS are stock options with long-term expirations.

limit down Describes when a futures contract price hits its minimum price limit.

limit order An investor's buy or sell order to a broker that specifies the maximum price the broker can pay when buying a security or the minimum he can accept when selling a security.

limit-order book A book maintained by a specialist (order-book official) that records limit orders.

limit up Describes when a futures contract price hits its maximum price limit.

listing The offering of a security for trading on an exchange.

logarithmic return The continuously compounded return; equal to the natural logarithm of the security price relatives.

London Interbank Offer Rate (LIBOR) The average rate paid by a sample of London Eurobanks on

Eurodollar deposits. The interest rates paid on Eurodollar deposits, Eurodollar loans, certificates of deposit, and bank loans are often quoted relative to this rate.

long futures hedge   A long position in a futures contract taken in order to protect against an increase in the price of the underlying asset or commodity.

long futures position   A position in which one agrees to buy the futures' underlying asset at a specified price, with payment and delivery to occur on the expiration date.

maintenance margin   The minimum amount of cash or cash equivalents that must be kept in a margin account after a security transaction is initiated.

marketability   An asset characteristic that defines the ease or speed with which the asset can be traded.

market maker   A dealer on an exchange who specializes in the trading of a specific security.

market nonheld order   An investor's buy or sell order to a broker giving the broker the right to use his own discretion in executing the order.

market-on close order   An investor's buy or sell order to a broker that requires that the trade be executed at or near the close of trading for the day.

market order   An investor's order to a broker to buy or sell a security at the best price as soon as the order reaches the market.

market timing   Describes the changing of a stock portfolio's exposure to the market by changing its beta. This can be done by changing the allocations of the stocks in the portfolio or by taking positions in index futures or option contracts.

mark (or marking) to the market   The process of adjusting the equity in a commodity or margin account to reflect the daily changes in the market value of the account.

mark-to-market tax rule   The tax requirement in which the profit on a futures position is taxed in the year the contract is established; requires that at the end of the year, all futures contracts be marked to the market to determine any unrealized gain or loss for tax purposes.

maximum call price   The market price of the underlying security.

maximum put price   For an American put, the exercise price; for a European put, the present value of the exercise price.

minimum American put price   On a stock not paying a dividend, the put's intrinsic value.

minimum call price   For an American or European call on a stock not paying a dividend, the maximum of either zero or the difference between the call's stock price and the present value of its exercise price.

minimum European put price   On a stock not paying a dividend, the maximum of either zero or the difference between the present value of the put's exercise price and the stock price.

money spread   *See* vertical spread.

multiple listing   The listing of a security on more than one exchange.

municipal bond index futures contract   A futures contract on the municipal bond index; an index based on the average value of 40 municipal bonds.

naive hedging ratio   A hedge ratio in which one unit of a futures position hedges one unit of a spot position; found by dividing the value of the spot position to be hedged by the price of the futures contract.

naked call write   An option position in which an option trader sells a call but does not own the underlying stock.

naked position   Describes a long or short speculative futures position.

naked put write   An option position in which an option trader sells a put but does not cover the put obligation by selling short the underlying stock.

National Futures Association (NFA)   An organization of firms that oversees futures trading.

neutral ratio spread (or neutral delta strategy)   A spread position constructed such that its value is invariant to price changes in the options' underlying security; a spread with a position delta of zero.

NOB spread   A futures spread formed with Treasury-note and Treasury-bond futures contracts.

normal market   A market where the futures price exceeds the spot price.

notional principal   The principal used to determined the amount of interest paid on a swap agreement. This principal is not exchanged.

offsetting order   *See* **closing order.**

opening transaction   The transaction in which an investor initially buys or sells an option or futures contract.

open interest   The number of option or futures contracts that are outstanding at a given point in time.

open outcry   Describes the process of shouting bids and offers in an exchange trading area.

option   A security that gives the holder the right to buy (call) or sell (put) an asset at a specified price on or possibly before a specific date.

option class   Describes all options on a given stock or security that are of a particular type, either call or put.

Option Clearing Corporation (OCC)   A firm whose primary function is to facilitate the marketability of option contracts, by intermediating each option transaction that takes place on the exchange and by guaranteeing that all option writers fulfill the terms of their option contracts.

option exchange   The place where brokers and dealers go to buy and sell options on behalf of their clients and themselves; also, a corporate association consisting of member brokers.

option holder   The buyer of an option. The holder buys the right to exercise or evoke the terms of the option claim. An option buyer is said to have a long position in the option.

option premium   The price of the option (call premium and put premium).

option series   Describes all of the options of a given class with the same exercise price and expiration.

option writer   The seller of an option. The writer is responsible for fulfilling the obligations of the option if the holder exercises. The option writer is said to have a short position in the option.

order-book official   An employee of an exchange who keeps the limit-order book.

out of the money   A call (put) option in which the price of the underlying security is below (above) the exercise price.

outright position   *See* **naked position.**

performance margin   *See* **initial margin.**

pin-stripe pork bellies   Describes stock index futures contracts.

plain vanilla swap   *See* **generic swap.**

position limit   The maximum number of option or futures contacts an investor can buy and sell on one side of the market. (A *side* of the market is either a bullish or a bearish position.)

position trader   A futures dealer who holds a position for a period longer than a day.

preemptive right   The right of the stockholders of a corporation to maintain their shares of ownership in the corporation when new stock is issued.

price limits   The maximum and minimum prices at which a futures contract can trade.

price-sensitivity model   A model that determines the optimum number of stock index futures contracts needed to hedge a stock portfolio.

PRIME   An acronym for "prescribed right to income and maximum equity"; a security that pays the holder the dividend from a stock and cash equal to the value of the stock up to a specified value.

program trading   Describes the use of computers in constructing and executing security portfolio positions; often involves using computer programs to monitor real-time data of stocks, futures, and option prices, to identify any mispricing of values of a stock portfolio relative to the values of index futures or option positions, and to define and execute appropriate arbitrage strategies when portfolios, futures, and option positions are mispriced.

protective put   The purchase of a put in order to obtain protection against possible decreases in the value of a long position in the put's underlying security

proxy portfolio   A portfolio constructed such that there is a high correlation between its returns and the returns of another portfolio or index.

pseudo-American option model   The Black-Scholes option pricing model used when the underlying stock pays a dividend. In the model, an option value computed with a dividend-adjusted stock price is compared to the estimated call value obtained by assuming the option is exercised just prior to the stock's ex-dividend date. The larger of the two values is used to price the option.

pure discount bond   A bond that pays no coupon interest and sells at a price below its face value.

pure position   *See* **naked position.**

put An option that gives the holder the right to sell an asset or a security at a specified price on or possibly before a specific date.

putable bond A bond that gives the bondholder the right to sell the bond back to the issuer at a specified price.

Put and Call Brokers and Dealers Association An early association of investment firms that acted as brokers and dealers on option contracts. An investor who wanted to buy an option could do so through a member of the association, who either would find a seller through other members or would sell (write) the option himself.

put-call-futures parity The equilibrium relationship between the prices on put, call, and futures contracts on the same asset. If the equilibrium condition for put-call-futures parity does not hold, then an arbitrage opportunity will exist by taking a position in the put and the futures contract and an opposite position in the call and a riskless bond with a face value equal to the difference between the exercise price and the futures price.

put-call parity The equilibrium relationship governing the prices on put and call contracts. If the equilibrium condition for put-call parity does not hold, then an arbitrage opportunity will exist by taking a position in the put and the underlying security and an opposite position in the call and a riskless bond with a face value equal to the exercise price.

put spread A strategy in which you buy a put and simultaneously sell another put on the same stock but with different terms.

quality risk A hedging risk that precludes your obtaining zero risk because the commodity or asset being hedged is not identical to the one underlying the futures contract.

quantity risk A hedging risk that precludes your obtaining zero risk because the size of the standard futures contract differs from the number of units of the underlying asset to be hedged.

range-forward contract A combination of a long position in a currency put and a short position in a currency call; equivalent to a short position in a currency forward contract.

ratio call write An option strategy formed by selling calls against more shares of stock than you own.

ratio money spread A vertical spread formed by taking long and short positions in options that have different exercise prices, with the option positions being combined in a ratio different than 1-to-1.

ratio put write A strategy formed by selling puts against shares of stock shorted at a ratio different than 1-to-1.

redundant security A security whose possible cash flows can be replicated by another security or portfolio.

registered option trader A member of an exchange who can both buy and sell securities for herself and act as a broker.

regression hedging model A hedging model where the estimated slope coefficient from a regression equation is used to determine the hedge ratio. The coefficient, in turn, is found by regressing the spot price on the security to be hedged against its futures price.

replicating call portfolio A portfolio consisting of the purchase of H units of a security and the borrowing of B dollars, where H and B are set so the cash flows of the portfolio equal the cash flows of a call on the underlying security.

replicating put portfolio A portfolio consisting of the shorting of H units of a security and the investing of I dollars in a risk-free security, where H and I are set so the cash flows of the portfolio equal the cash flows of a put on the underlying security.

repo rate The rate on a repurchase agreement.

repurchase agreement A transaction in which one party sells a security to another party, with the obligation of repurchasing it at a later date. To the seller, the repurchase agreement represents a secured loan in which he receives funds from the sale of the security, with the responsibility of purchasing the security later at a higher price that reflects the shorter time remaining to maturity.

Retail Automatic Execution System (RAES) A computerized system designed to fill public orders by matching them with the highest bids or lowest offers.

reversal An arbitrage portfolio formed by going short in an underlying security, long in a European call, and short in a European put; generates a credit for the investor at the initiation of the strategy and requires a fixed payment equal to the exercise price at expiration; is the negative of a conversion.

reverse hedge A strategy formed by purchasing puts and shares of stock in a ratio different than 1-to-1.

rho The change in an option's price with respect to a small change in interest rates.

right A security issued by a corporation to an existing shareholder giving him the right to buy new issues of stock at a specified price, known as the *subscription price*. Rights are issued as part of a new stock issue and are used to ensure that the preemptive rights of existing shareholders are maintained.

risk neutrality A state in which an investor is indifferent to risk.

risk-neutral market A market in which investors accept the same expected rate of return from a risky investment as from a risk-free one.

risk-neutral pricing An approach for pricing securities in which it is assumed that the value of a security is determined as though it and other securities are trading in a risk-neutral market; can be used to price options and other derivative securities.

roll-down strategy A follow-up strategy in which you move your position to a lower exercise price.

rolling-credit strategy A defensive follow-up strategy for a naked call (put) write position in which the naked writer sells calls (puts) with a higher (lower) exercise price if the price of the underlying security increases (decreases), then uses the proceeds to close his initial short position by buying the calls (put) back.

roll-up strategy A follow-up strategy in which you move your option position to a higher exercise price.

scalper A floor trader who buys and sells securities on her own account, holding them for a short period.

SCORE An acronym for "special claim on residual equity"; a security that pays the difference between a stock price and an exercise price if the stock price exceeds the exercise price; sold in conjunction with a PRIME.

seat Describes membership on an exchange.

self-financing requirement A requirement governing a multiple-period arbitrage strategy that prohibits any outside funds from being added to or removed from an arbitrage position when it is being readjusted.

short futures hedge A short position in a futures contract that is taken in order to protect against a decrease in the price of the underlying asset.

short futures position A position in which an investor agrees to sell the underlying asset on a futures contract.

short sale The sale of a security now, then purchasing it later. To implement this strategy, the investor must borrow the security, sell it in the market, then repay his debt obligation by later buying the security and returning it to the share lender.

side-by-side trading Describes the listing of both American and European options available on the same security.

simulated long position A strategy formed by buying a call and selling a put with the same terms.

simulated put A position formed by purchasing a call and selling the underlying security short on a 1-to-1 basis; yields a profit and security price relationship similar to a put purchase.

simulated short position A strategy formed by selling a call and buying a put with the same terms.

simulated straddle A position formed by purchasing two calls and shorting one unit of the underlying security (or a multiple of this); yields a strategy equivalent to a straddle.

specialist A dealer on an exchange who specializes in the trading of a specific security and who is responsible for maintaining the order book.

speculation An investment characterized by risk.

speculator One who engages in speculation.

splitting the strike A strategy formed by purchasing a call with a high exercise price and selling a put on the same security with a lower exercise price but with the same expiration date.

spot market A market in which there is an immediate sale and delivery of the asset or commodity.

spot price The price an asset or commodity trades for in the spot market.

spread An option or futures position consisting of a long position in one contract and a short position in a similar, but not identical, contract.

stochastic error The estimating error that results from the exclusion of an important explanatory variable and/or an incorrect mathematical specification of the model being tested.

stock index call option An option on a stock index that gives the holder the right to purchase an amount of cash equal to the closing spot index on the exercising day at the call's exercise price. To settle, the exercising holder receives from the assigned writer a cash settlement equal to the difference between the spot index and the exercise price.

stock index put option An option on a stock index that gives the holder the right to sell cash equal to the closing spot index on the exercising date at the put's exercise price. To settle, the exercising holder receives from the assigned writer a cash settlement equal to the difference between the exercise price and the spot index.

stock price relative A ratio of the stock price in one period to its price in the preceding period.

stop-limit order An investor's buy or sell order to a broker that instructs her to execute a limit order when the option hits a specific price.

stop-loss order An investor's buy or sell order to a broker that requires him to execute a market order once the security hits a specific price.

straddle purchase A strategy formed by buying a put and a call with the same underlying security, exercise price, and expiration date.

straddle write A strategy formed by selling a put and a call with the same underlying security, exercise price, and expiration date.

straight debt value A convertible bond's value as a nonconvertible bond; found by discounting the convertible bond's cash flows by the yield to maturity on an identical, but nonconvertible, bond.

strangle A combination of a long put and a long call with different exercise prices.

strap purchase A strategy formed by purchasing more calls than puts, with the calls and puts having the same terms.

strap write A strategy formed by selling more calls than puts, with the calls and puts having the same terms.

strike price See **exercise** price.

strip A series of futures contracts with different maturities; also, a combination of long or short call and put positions in which the number of puts exceeds the number of calls.

strip purchase A strategy formed by purchasing more puts than calls, with the calls and puts having the same terms.

strip write A strategy formed by selling more puts than calls, with the calls and puts having the same terms.

subscription warrant See **rights**.

swap See **financial swap**.

swap banks A group of brokers and dealers who intermediate swap agreements between swap users. As brokers, swap banks try to match parties with opposite needs; as dealers, swap banks take positions as counterparties.

swaption An option that gives the holder the right to take a certain interest rate swap position.

synthetic call A portfolio consisting of long positions in the put and the underlying security and a short position in the bond; yields the same profit and security price relation as a comparable call.

synthetic put A portfolio consisting of long positions in the call and the bond and a short position in the underlying security; yields the same profit and security price relation as a comparable put.

synthetic Treasury bill The purchase of a Treasury bill with its selling price locked in by going short in a Treasury-bill futures contract.

systematic risk The risk of a security that is attributable to market factors (i.e., factors that affect all securities).

TED spread A spread formed with Treasury-bill and Eurodollar contracts.

theta The change in an option's price with respect to a small change in the time to expiration.

time spread See **horizontal spread**.

time value decay Describes the decrease in an option's time value as the time to expiration decreases.

time value premium (TVP) The difference between the price of an option and its intrinsic value.

timing risk A hedging risk that precludes your obtaining zero risk because the delivery date on the futures contract does not coincide with the date the hedged assets or liabilities need to be purchased or sold.

Treasury-bill futures A futures contract that calls for the delivery or purchase of a Treasury bill with a maturity of 90, 91, or 92 days and a face value of $1 million.

Treasury-bill option   An option that gives the holder the right to buy (call) or sell (put) a Treasury bill with a face value of $1 million and maturity of 91 days at a specified price.

Treasury-bond futures contract   A futures contract that calls for the delivery or purchase of a Treasury bond.

Treasury-bond option   An option on a Treasury bond.

Treasury-note futures contract   A futures contract that calls for the delivery or purchase of a Treasury note.

triangular arbitrage   An arbitrage strategy formed by taking positions in several currencies; used when the cross-exchange rate relation does not hold.

triple witching hour   The last hour of trading on the day when index futures, stock index options, and options on stock index futures all expire. Often during such a period, an abnormally large volume of trading occurs on the exchanges as program traders, arbitrageurs, and hedgers close their futures and option positions and liquidate or purchase large blocks of stock.

TURTLE spread   A spread formed with a combination of two positions on Treasury-bond futures with different expirations and one position in a Treasury-bill futures contract.

uncovered call write   *See* naked call write.

uncovered put write   *See* naked put write.

unsystematic risk   The risk of a security that is attributable to factors other than market factors.

variation margin   *See* maintenance margin.

vega   The change in an option's price with respect to a small change in the underlying security's variability.

vertical spread   A spread formed with options that have the same expiration dates but different exercise prices.

warrant   A call option issued by a corporation giving the holder the right to buy a specified number of shares of the company's stock.

wash sale   The sale of a security at a loss and its subsequent repurchase. Tax laws disallow claiming such losses for tax purposes.

Weiner stock process   A process in which the proportional change in stock prices grows along the path of its logarithmic return, known as a *drift component*, with the actual price being above or below the path at any time and with the extent of the deviation determined by the stock's variability.

wild-card option   The right on a Chicago Board of Trade's Treasury-bond futures contract to deliver the bond after the close of trading on the exchange.

yield curve   A graph showing the relationship between the yields to maturity on comparable bonds and their maturities.

yield to maturity (YTM)   The discount rate on a bond; the rate that equates the price of the bond to the present value of its coupons and principal.

zero-leakage option   An option on an asset that generates no benefits during the option period.

Glossary of Symbols

Acc Int = accrued interest
b = basis
B_0 = price of bond; debt level of replicating call portfolio
β = beta
β_{TR} = target beta
BP = basis points
C = price of call
C^a = price of American call
C^e = price of European call
C^x, C_{ex} = call price on ex-dividend date
CF = conversion factor; cash flow
CP = conversion price
CR = conversion ratio
CV = conversion value
Cov( ) = covariance of
d = downward parameter in BOPM
d_1, d_2 = variables in Black-Scholes OPM
D = dividend; value of benefit from security
D^* = threshold dividend
DUR = duration
Δ = delta
E_0 = spot exchange rate
E_d = foreign-interest-rate-adjusted exchange rate
E_f = forward exchange rate
E^c = cutoff exchange rate
$E( )$ = expected value of
ex = ex-dividend date
f = futures price
F = forward price; face value on bond
F^j = face value of bond with junior claim
F^s = face value of bond with senior claim
FC = foreign currency
g = growth rate

Γ = gamma
H^{P*} = BOPM hedge ratio for a put
H^* = BOPM hedge ratio
I^* = replicating put portfolio's risk-free investment
IV = intrinsic value
IV_r = intrinsic value of right
IV_w = intrinsic value of warrant
IV^x = ex-dividend intrinsic value
IN = index value
j = number of upward moves in n periods
k = discount rate
K = storage cost per period
λ = state-preference price
m = market; margin requirement
M = maturity
M_0 = initial margin
μ_e = estimated mean
μ_e^A = annualized mean
NPV = net present value
N = number of options, securities, or futures
n = number of periods; number of securities
n_f = number of futures contracts
$N(d)$ = cumulative normal probability of
π = profit; 3.14159
p = term in BOPM equation
p_{nj} = probability of security's increasing j times in n periods
P = price of put
P^a = price of American put
P^b = bond price
P^{cb} = price of convertible bond
P^e = price of European put
P^x = ex-dividend put price
P_{tb} = price of Treasury bill

PV = present value

q = probability of security's increasing in one period

q_0, q_1 = variables in BAW model

Q_0, Q_1, Q_2 = parameters in BAW model

r_f = 1 plus risk-free rate

r_n = logarithmic return for total period

r_t = logarithmic return

R = risk-free rate; continuously compounded risk-free rate; repo rate

R_c = rate of return on call

R_D = annual discount yield

R_f = risk-free rate

R_F = foreign risk-free rate; rate on futures contract

R_I = implied forward rate

R_P = rate of return on put

R_{US} = U.S. interest rate; domestic interest rate

R^A = annual rate

R^P = period rate

R^S = simple annual rate

S = stock price; spot price; spot index price

S^c = critical stock price

S_d = dividend-adjusted stock price

S_x = ex-dividend stock price

$S_k(\ )$ = skewness of

σ = standard deviation; annualized standard deviation in B-S OPM

σ^A = annualized standard deviation

σ^2 = variance

SDV = straight debt value

θ = option theta

T = time to expiration; expiration; exercise time

t^* = time to dividend-payment date; time to ex-dividend date

t = point in time

TRC = transportation cost

TVP = time value premium

u = upward parameter in BOPM

V = value

$V(\ )$ = variance of

V^A = value of asset; value of firm

V_e^A = annualized variance

V^B = value of bond

V^{Bs} = value of bond with senior claim

V^{Bj} = value of bond with junior claim

V^E = equity value of the firm

V^F = value of futures contract

V^{SP} = value of stock portfolio and the puts ensuring it

V_{co}, V_{cu}, V_{cd} = value of replicating portfolio

V_e = estimated variance

V_h = value of stock and call portfolio

Λ = option vega

W_{ex} = cash flow on ex-dividend date

Ψ = annual dividend yield

X = exercise price

X_B = exercise price at which an issuer can redeem convertible bond

YTM = yield to maturity

YTM_f = yield to maturity implied on interest rate futures contract

Z = stock price relative; standard normal-distribution random variable

Z_c = rate of return on replicating call portfolio

Index